THE APOSTLE OF PEACE

Volume One

The Christian Commonwealth, September 20th, 1911.

NATIONAL BROTHERHOOD CONFERENCE.

The Christian Commonwealth

The Organ of the Progressive Movement in Religion and Social Ethics.

No. 1,562. VOL. XXXI. WEDNESDAY, SEPT. 20, 1911. PRICE ONE PENNY. with Supplement 1½d.

The Vanishing of the Veil.

Abdul Baha at St. John's, Westminster.

Archdeacon Wilberforce's Welcome.

Eighteen months ago Archdeacon Wilberforce, who had been watching the Bahai movement for some time with interest, sent a message to Abdul Baha. "We are all one," he said, "there, behind the veil." And Abdul Baha replied from

ABDUL BAHA (Abbas Effendi).

his home in Akka, "Tell him the veil is very thin, and it will vanish quite."

All who were present in St. John's, Westminster, last Sunday evening, could not fail to realise that the veil was vanishing. Archdeacon Wilberforce's beautiful intercessory service was a means to that end. He asked that each one in the vast congregation should at that time put away all selfish thought and

ness of the sick woman and the keen anxiety of the daughter hastening to her side. So the spirit of unity was spread abroad.

Then Dr. Wilberforce told of the teacher—"Master" he called him—who had come to London to emphasise unity, and who was present that evening at St. John's to proclaim the meaning of it. "Whatever our views," the Archdeacon said, "we shall, I am sure, unite in welcoming a man who has been for forty years a prisoner for the cause of brotherhood and love."

Abdul Baha is not an orator or even a preacher, but, in view of all he stands for, we are keenly interested in every-

Baha. All eyes were fixed on the leader of the Bahai movement. In his customary Eastern robe and head-dress, walking hand in hand with a leader of the West, it did indeed seem that the veil was vanishing.

Down the aisle they passed to the bishop's chair, which had been placed in front of the altar for Abdul Baha. Standing at the lectern, Archdeacon Wilberforce introduced the "wonderful" visitor. He told of his life in prison, of his sufferings and bravery, of his self-sacrifice, of his clear and shining faith. He voiced his own belief that religion is one, as God is love.

Then Abdul Baha rose. Speaking very clearly, with wonderful intonations in his voice and using his hands freely, it seemed to those who listened almost as if they grasped his meaning, though he spoke in Persian. When he had finished, Archdeacon Wilberforce read the translation of his address.

His theme was the Character of the Manifestations of God. He said that God the Infinite could not be comprehended of man; that whatever man understands of God is born of his imagination. For illustration he pointed to the mineral, which does not comprehend the vegetable, as the vegetable cannot understand the animal, or the animal cannot reach the intelligence of humanity. Neither, he said, is it possible for man, a created being, to understand the Almighty Creator. Nevertheless, the perfection and qualifications of God are seen in every created being and in the most perfect beings in the most perfect manner. In the manifestations of God, Abdul Baha likened these qualities to the rays of the sun focussed in a mirror. If we claim that the sun is seen in the mirror, we do not mean that the whole sun has descended from the holy heights of heaven and entered into the mirror, that is impossible. The Eternal Nature is seen in the manifestations, and its light and splendour are visible in extreme glory. Therefore men have always been taught and led by the prophets of God. The prophets of God are the mediators of God. All the prophets and messengers have come from one Holy Spirit and bear the message of God, suited to the age in which they appear.

It is the *One* Light in them, and they are one with each other. But the eternal does not become phenomenal, neither can the phenomenal become eternal. St. Paul, the great apostle, said, "We all, with open face, beholding as in a mirror the glory of God, are changed into the same image, from glory to glory."

Then, raising his hands, Abdul Baha prayed: "O God, the Forgiver! O Heavenly Educator! This assembly is adorned with the mention of thy holy name. Thy children turn their face towards thy kingdom. Hearts are made happy and souls are comforted. Merciful God! Cause us to repent of our shortcomings! Accept us in thy heavenly kingdom and give unto us an abode where there shall be no error. Give us peace. Give us knowledge, and open unto us the gates of thy heaven.

"Thou art the Giver of all! Thou art the Forgiver! Thou art the Merciful!"

The final note of a real chord of harmony was struck when Archdeacon Wilberforce asked that Abdul Baha would pro-

THE APOSTLE OF PEACE

A Survey of References to 'Abdu'l-Bahá in the Western Press 1871–1921

Volume One: 1871–1912

by

Amín Egea

GEORGE RONALD
OXFORD

George Ronald, Publisher
Oxford
www.grbooks.com

A catalogue record for this book is available from the British Library

ISBN 978–0–85398–600–3

Cover design: Steiner Graphics
Printed and bound in Great Britain by TJ International Ltd, Padstow

CONTENTS

'ABDU'L-BAHÁ

'Abdu'l-Bahá (1844–1921) was the eldest surviving son of Bahá'u'lláh, the founder of the Bahá'í Faith. Named 'Abbás after his grandfather, 'Abdu'l-Bahá was known as 'Abbás Effendi outside the Bahá'í community. Bahá'u'lláh gave Him the titles the Most Great Branch, the Mystery of God and the Master. He chose the name 'Abdu'l-Bahá (Servant of Bahá) after the passing of Bahá'u'lláh.

Born in Tehran on 23 May 1844, 'Abdu'l-Bahá recognized His father's station even before it had been openly revealed. Later, He often served as His father's deputy when dealing with officials and the public. He shared Bahá'u'lláh's banishment and exile and was, like Bahá'u'lláh, eventually imprisoned in 'Akká, a remote outpost of the Ottoman Empire, in 1868.

Bahá'u'lláh described the station of 'Abdu'l-Bahá in the Tablet of the Branch (Súriy-i-Ghuṣn):

> There hath branched from the Sadratu'l-Muntahá this sacred and glorious Being, this Branch of Holiness; well is it with him that hath sought His shelter and abideth beneath His shadow. Verily the Limb of the Law of God hath sprung forth from this Root which God hath firmly implanted in the Ground of His Will, and Whose Branch hath been so uplifted as to encompass the whole of creation. Magnified be He, therefore, for this sublime, this blessed, this mighty, this exalted Handiwork! . . . Render thanks unto God, O people, for His appearance; for verily He is the most great Favor unto you, the most perfect bounty upon you; and through Him every moldering bone is quickened. Whoso turneth towards Him hath turned towards God, and whoso turneth away from Him hath turned away from My beauty, hath repudiated My Proof, and transgressed against Me. He is the Trust of God amongst you, His charge

> within you, His manifestation unto you and His appearance among His favored servants . . .

In the Book of the Covenant Bahá'u'lláh named 'Abdu'l-Bahá His successor and the authorized interpreter of His writings. He is the Center of the Covenant to whom all Bahá'ís were to turn after the passing of Bahá'u'lláh.

'. . . though essentially human and holding a station radically and fundamentally different from that occupied by Bahá'u'lláh and His Forerunner,' Shoghi Effendi, the Guardian of the Bahá'í Faith, explained, 'Abdu'l-Bahá was 'the perfect Exemplar of His Faith . . . endowed with superhuman knowledge, and to be regarded as the stainless mirror reflecting His light'. (*God Passes By* p. 242)

Bahá'u'lláh passed away in 1892 and 'Abdu'l-Bahá became the head of the Bahá'í Faith. Largely confined to 'Akká by the Ottoman authorities, 'Abdu'l-Bahá began to receive a few western pilgrims from 1898.

In1908 'Abdu'l-Bahá was set free after the Young Turks' revolution and in 1911 He began His historic journeys to Europe and North America to proclaim His father's message. The two volumes of *The Apostle of Peace* document those journeys through the eyes of journalists and commentators who encountered 'Abdu'l-Bahá.

PREFACE

This book was originally intended as a general survey of press references to the Bábí and Bahá'í religions during the period 1844 to 1921, known in Bahá'í history as the Heroic Age, and was to be based on research that began in 1996 and which, over the years, has resulted in more than five thousand documents that record many episodes of the early history of the religions of the Báb and Bahá'u'lláh.

While often inaccurate, inexact or even biased, these press articles stand as an important primary source for the study of the early history of the Bábí-Bahá'í Faith. They shed light on historical episodes, complement available sources and give an exact picture of how westerners received and perceived the new religion.

When in 2006 I started the process of writing this book, it soon became evident that one particular episode – the travels of 'Abdu'l-Bahá in the West (1911 to 1913) – had received so much attention in the press that it would have been impossible to give it a fair treatment if it were to share a volume with other periods in Bahá'í history. Thus, after consulting with the editors, it was decided to limit the scope of the book to press references about 'Abdu'l-Bahá published during His lifetime.

This book, therefore, attempts to present and contextualize over 2,200 press articles about 'Abdu'l-Bahá published between 1871 and 1921, most of them during the period of His travels. This has required two volumes, rather than the intended one.

The documents from the United Kingdom here included have been researched for the most part in the British Library (London). Research has also been conducted in the Bodleian Library (Oxford), the Library of the Religious Society of Friends (London), the Dr Williams and Congregationalist Library (London) and the library of the Theosophical Society of England (London).

Articles in English published in Egypt have also been researched at the British Library. Copies of articles from the Egyptian Arabic press were kindly supplied by the International Bahá'í Library (Haifa).

Many of the French articles were shared with me during my visit to the National Bahá'í Archives of France in Paris. Other documents were found at the National Library of France (Paris) or in its digital platform Gallica.

Some three hundred American newspaper clippings were acquired from the US National Bahá'í Archives. An equally large number of articles were found in different online databases and archives. Other documents were acquired from the Boston Public Library, the Bureau of State Library (Harrisburg, PA), the California State Library, the Carnegie Library of Pittsburgh, the Cleveland Public Library, the Minneapolis Historical Society Library, the New York Public Library, the Public Library of Cincinnati and Hamilton County, the Swarthmore College Peace Collection, the Toronto Public Library and the Wilmington (Delaware) Public Library, among others. Despite the large number of articles published in the American press that are presented in this volume, much more research is yet to be conducted in American journals and magazines, especially in the organs of various organizations and religious centers and in the many newspapers published by different ethnic and cultural communities in the United States.

For the most part, articles from Canadian newspapers were acquired from the Library and Archives of Canada or kindly shared by the National Bahá'í Archives of Canada.

Documents from Germany were generously sent to me by the National Spiritual Assembly of the Bahá'ís of Germany.

I had access to the bulk of newspaper articles published in Budapest when I visited the Hungarian National Bahá'í Archives. Other documents were acquired at the National Library of Hungary (Budapest).

Most articles in Esperanto journals presented in this book were found in the National Library of Austria (Vienna) and in two large private libraries in Spain: the Esperanto Biblioteko 'Ramon Molera Pedrals' (Moià, Barcelona) and the Esperanto-Muzeo de Subirats (Sant Pau d'Ordal, Barcelona).

The two volumes of this book are divided into sections. The first part of volume I includes references made to 'Abdu'l-Bahá before His travels in the West. In the first chapter, the reader will find various articles written by authors who were not Bahá'ís who visited Him during His imprisonment in 'Akká. The second chapter presents accounts about 'Abdu'l-Bahá written by western Bahá'í pilgrims. From the early days of the Bahá'í Faith in America, most of the articles mentioning the Bahá'ís also mention 'Abdu'l-Bahá, therefore it was necessary to limit this chapter to only those references which provided information about Him. The third chapter presents accounts about 'Abdu'l-Bahá produced by non-Bahá'ís who visited Him in the Holy Land in the short period between His liberation and His first sojourn in Egypt.

The second part of this volume focuses on 'Abdu'l-Bahá's first two visits to Egypt, His early visits to Europe and His travels in North America. In addition to interviews, accounts of His public talks and texts written by 'Abdu'l-Bahá Himself, the reader will find a significant amount of contextual information which in many instances is not available from other sources. Some articles, for instance, will help to fix the exact time and place of some of His talks. Others give the names of people who visited Him, record the reactions of the audiences who listened to Him, or summarize the contents of talks of which no transcription has survived.

The chapters have been arranged chronologically and geographically. However, at the end of this section I have added one chapter of general articles about 'Abdu'l-Bahá in America.

The second volume opens with chapters concerning 'Abdu'l-Bahá's second tour of Europe and His third visit to Egypt. Its second section comprises chapters detailing His contact in Europe and North America with suffragist organizations, the civil rights movement, Esperantists, the Theosophical Society and with various figures and organizations linked with spiritualist and esoteric movements. The second section closes with a chapter summarizing different instances of opposition to 'Abdu'l-Bahá.

The third part of volume 2 comprises articles about 'Abdu'l-Bahá published after His return to the Holy Land, including the many articles published about His passing.

As a general rule, the articles in both volumes are reproduced in their entirety. However, to avoid an excessive redundancy and for the sake of brevity, I have not reproduced summaries or introductions to the Bahá'í Faith found in the articles and have quoted only those texts that are devoted to 'Abdu'l-Bahá.

Where possible, the political or ideological tendency of each publication is indicated. Biographical notes of some of the authors who wrote about 'Abdu'l-Bahá or met Him have also been included. Where available, I have included the number of copies produced by each newspaper in the year a specific article was published or in the closest year for which statistics exist.

In my commentary, I have used the transliteration system standardized for Bahá'í literature for Persian and Arabic names and words. Similarly, I have chosen to capitalize the pronouns that refer to the central figures of the Bahá'í Faith, including 'Abdu'l-Bahá. The articles reproduced in this volume have not been edited and are reproduced as they appeared in the original periodicals.

ACKNOWLEDGMENTS

I am indebted to many people for their valuable assistance and help during my research. First, I would like to mention my parents Emilio and Talieh, my sister Leili, and the rest of my family for their constant support and encouragement.

Since October 2011, and for a period of six months, I received the generous financial help of a friend, who does not wish his name to be mentioned, without which it would have been impossible for me to complete the research and dedicate the necessary time needed to finish the last stages of this book.

Dr Wendi Momen has patiently edited the manuscript and made many valuable suggestions for its improvement. Any mistakes are my sole responsibility.

Many friends have shared documents and information which has been used in this volume. I would like to thank Pedro Armindo, Frederic Autret, Jan Jasion, Chad Jones, Mona Khademi, Günter Maltz, Judit Manno, Eugenio Marcano, David Merrick, Tom Moritz, Ana María Molera, Zoltan Seress, Adam Thorne, Duane Troxel, and Robert Weinberg. I am specially indebted to Parivash Ardei of the National Bahá'í Archives of France, to Joseph Keith of the Quaker library in London, and to Lewis Walker of the US National Bahá'í Archives. I also would like to mention Richard Arpi, Eric Biddy, Bob Brodbeck, Dr. Wendy Chmielewski, Stephanie Hoover, Suzanne Johnston, Alice Kane, Rhonda Konig and Alice Morrow for their help in obtaining for me documents in different American libraries. I am also grateful to Heather Eason, Anneliese Garvie, Rodha Lane, Elham Simmons and Tina Vonhof for their translations.

Sant Cugat del Vallés, March 2016.

A mi hijo Naim

INTRODUCTION

With the message 'What Hath God Wrought',[1] sent from Washington to Baltimore on 24 May 1844, Samuel Morse officially opened the first telegraphic line in the world. That historic occasion, which signaled a turning point in the history of human communications, was followed by the rapid development of a network of telegraphs across the world that in a few years transformed many areas of human endeavor including that of journalism.

Only a few years earlier, in 1835, Charles Louis Havas (1783–1858) had founded the first international news agency. His Bureau in Paris, today known as Agence France-Press, compiled for its subscribers a bulletin with news published in European newspapers or received from correspondents, and would also send French news abroad. In its early stages the Bureau's news would be sent by pigeons or by messengers on horseback. But as telegraph lines were opened in Europe, Havas made extensive use of them, thus gaining immediacy and, with it, more subscribers to his news.

Soon after the establishment of the first telegraphic line to Berlin, one of Havas's employees, Bernhard Wolff (1811–1879), opened in 1849 his own firm in Germany The Wolffs Telegraphisches Bureau operated until the Second World War. In 1851, when a telegraphic line connecting England with the European continent was opened, Paul J. Reuter (1816–1899), also one of Havas's workers, founded in London the agency bearing his name. Meanwhile, in America, five New York newspapers wanting to share the expenses of covering the news of the war between the United States and Mexico established in 1846 the Associated Press, the first news agency in the American continent.

All these developments in the genesis of modern communications run in parallel with the birth of the Bábí-Bahá'í movement. Morse's first official telegram, for instance, was sent the day after of the declaration of the Báb in Shiraz and the birth of 'Abdu'l-Bahá in Tehran.

From its inception the young religion was mentioned in the pages of hundreds of western newspapers. As early as 12 April 1845, *The Bombay Times* published a brief note about the sentence to death of Mullá 'Alíy-i-Bastámí, which was later reproduced in a London weekly.[2] Just five months later *The Bombay Courier* reported the torture inflicted on Quddús and other Bábís in Shiraz. Soon afterwards, this news was reproduced in several journals in England, France, Germany, the United States, Australia and New Zealand.[3] In 1848 at least one newspaper reported the trial of the Báb in Tabriz[4] and some months later news of the Shaykh Ṭabarsí upheaval was reported in various publications.[5] In 1850 news of the execution of the Báb was also published in no less than 30 newspapers in different countries. In that same year the press also reported the Zanján upheaval and the martyrdom of a group of Bábís in Tehran.[6]

When in 1852 Náṣiri'd-Dín Sháh suffered an attempt on his life, the Bábís and the persecutions they suffered were mentioned across the world in hundreds of articles. Later, news of other episodes in the history of the Bahá'í religion such as the banishment of Bahá'u'lláh to 'Akká, the martyrdom of Badí', the execution of the King and Prince of the Martyrs, and the martyrdom of seven Bahá'ís in Yazd in 1891, amongst others, were also published in both Europe and North America. In the weeks following the death of Náṣiri'd-Dín Sháh in 1896, over six hundred news items mentioned the Bahá'ís.

As well as these references in popular newspapers, during this period many scholars and missionaries also wrote profusely about the new religion in specialized and scientific periodicals. Thus, thanks to the press, and also to the work of authors like Comte de Gobineau and Edward G. Browne, many westerners became acquainted with the existence of the new religion born in Persia. The familiarity with the terms 'Bab' and 'Babism' was such that, except for a few cases, the general public referred to the Bahá'ís as Bábís until well entered the 20th century. Even the early Bahá'ís in the United States were called Bábís in the press for several years. That was more or less the situation when 'Abdu'l-Bahá visited the West. Through the publicity generated during His visit, one of the immediate results of His travels was the normalization of the term 'Bahá'í' and the clarification in the public mind of the differences – and at the same time continuity – between the religions of the Báb and Bahá'u'lláh.

By the time 'Abdu'l-Bahá visited the West, the press had reached a level of industrialization such as to allow some newspapers to produce more than one million copies per day. The first illustrated dailies were born only a few years before the arrival of 'Abdu'l-Bahá to England. Until then, the technique used to include pictures in a periodical was so slow that it was only viable in weekly publications.

The British daily press was divided between broadsheet newspapers and tabloids. The latter, with smaller dimensions, were born with the *Daily Mail* in 1896 and cost a halfpenny, while broadsheet journals cost one penny. Owing to their cheaper price, tabloids quickly became popular. Their contents focused more on sensationalistic information while broadsheets targeted a readership more interested in the editorial and political orientation of the newspaper. When in 1911 'Abdu'l-Bahá visited London, some 20 dailies were published simultaneously in the city.

In France, the press had developed along similar lines but was much more fragmented. In 1911, for instance, in the city of Paris alone, more than 70 daily journals were published simultaneously, not including financial and sports papers and newspapers in foreign languages.

In the United States the competition between the Hearst newspapers owned by William R. Hearst, son of the early American Bahá'í Phoebe Hearst, and Joseph Pulitzer at the end of the 1890's degenerated in the birth of yellow journalism, characterized by its sensationalism and the lack of informative rigor. The two-party system also resulted in fragmentation of the media and, therefore, a lower number of newspapers in big cities compared to European capitals. Newspapers were simply categorized as Republican, Democratic or independent. In some cities, ethnic and national minorities and religious denominations also had their own daily or weekly publications.

'Abdu'l-Bahá gave much importance to the press. As will be shown, on several occasions He made interesting comments on the social role of journalism and gave recommendations to journalists about the ethical and moral values that they had to take into account in carrying out their profession. He also conceded interviews in almost every city He visited, granted press conferences and even agreed to have pictures of Him taken, something that previously not even Bahá'ís visiting Him in the Holy Land were allowed to do. At the request of the editors of various periodicals 'Abdu'l-Bahá also wrote 'articles' for them. Some of these were published along with a facsimile of the original. He also authorized that notes of some of His talks be sent to the press for publication and on many occasions He requested that several copies of a newspaper with Bahá'í content be bought and sent with their translations to the afflicted Bahá'ís in Persia.

In some European cities, 'Abdu'l-Bahá asked a few Bahá'ís, such as Isabel Fraser, to contact the media and inform them about the Bahá'í Faith. In the United States a 'Publicity Bureau' acting under the auspices of the Persian–American Educational Society was established in early 1912 to inform the media as well as different personalities, churches and organizations about the visit of 'Abdu'l-Bahá to America. A compilation of Bahá'í writings under the title *Universal Principles of the Bahai Movement* was sent to the major journals in the country as well as to many individuals.[7] It would be wrong, however, to conclude that the publicity given in the press to 'Abdu'l-Bahá was gained solely by the efforts made by the Bahá'ís. On the contrary, and as the reader will rapidly acknowledge, the media had a genuine interest for the Master both as a religious figure and as a promulgator of progressive ideals.

In a Tablet written soon after the beginning of World War I, 'Abdu'l-Bahá mentioned as one of the outcomes of His travels the publicity gained for the Bahá'í Faith in the media:

> Undoubtedly you have read the contents of the American and European newspapers which are mirrors reflecting the public opinion of other nations. Verily, truth is that which is concurrently testified to by all wise men! The contents of these magazines and newspapers are the traces of the pen of the followers of Christ, the people of Moses, philosophers, professors and thinkers of the West. For example, amongst them might be mentioned the Palo Altan, published in the town wherein the Leland Stanford University is founded, the newspapers of Oxford, Christian Commonwealth, Century, Herald, Standard, Review of Reviews, the Arabic newspapers of New York, etc. etc. The philosophers, professors and literary men have expressed their opinions concerning this Cause in these periodicals. This was again through the mercy and providence of the Blessed Perfection whose Absolute Will had ordained the promotion of the Cause of God in all parts of the world and who confirmed this servant of the Threshold in this service.[8]

It is impossible to estimate the actual number of people who read about 'Abdu'l-Bahá in the press. This volume includes the circulation figures of only some of the newspapers which mentioned Him between 1910 and 1913. Their total circulation number rises to over 22.2 million copies. At a time when the press was the only means of communication of news available to the masses this figure is very significant.

The large number of articles about 'Abdu'l-Bahá that are presented in this volume is in itself an evidence of His enormous fame and demonstrates that He was far better known by the public than previously thought. Further research will undoubtedly bring to light more evidence of this.

A NOTE FROM THE PUBLISHER

The first mention in the western press of the religion of the Báb and Bahá'u'lláh came as early as 1845 when on 19 April the *Illustrated London News* published a brief note regarding the death sentence passed on Mullá 'Alíy-i-Bastámí[9] and *The Times* of London on 1 November an article about the arrest of the Báb.[10] Thereafter, the religion was mentioned more frequently in the print media. However, it was the travels of 'Abdu'l-Bahá, son of Bahá'u'lláh, in the West that attracted by far the most media interest, with literally thousands of articles appearing in the years 1911 to 1913.

However, at the time, the Bahá'í Faith was largely unknown in the West and most people knew nothing at all about it. Even those who were Bahá'ís had a very imperfect understanding of the religion and its teachings, and newspaper reporters had virtually no knowledge of it. Few understood the station of 'Abdu'l-Bahá as the Center of the Covenant, as the Perfect Exemplar of Bahá'u'lláh's teachings, as the Servant of the Glory of God. Therefore He was considered a prophet, a prince, the return of Christ. Thus the articles that were published were often inaccurate. Reporters sometimes framed their questions to 'Abdu'l-Bahá inappropriately and then cast His answers in ways that distorted His message. In addition, the interviews with 'Abdu'l-Bahá and His talks were translated from the Persian into English, which added another dimension of difficulty. The articles reproduced in this book reflect these challenges.

The spelling of names and terms relating to the Bahá'í Faith in the articles reproduced here reflects the uncertainty about the transliteration of these words in the early years of the religion. The spelling of words such as Bahá'í, Bahá'u'lláh and 'Abdu'l-Bahá did not become standardized until Shoghi Effendi provided a list of the transliteration of Bahá'í-related names, places and terms in 1923. The adoption of this system by the Bahá'ís took many years and even today newspapers, journals and books written by those who are not Bahá'ís adopt their own spellings of these words. Similarly, the articles appeared in publications from a number of countries and the spelling of common words varies, as, for example, with the American and British spellings of words such as center/centre and honor/honour. The publisher has not changed the spelling, punctuation or grammar of the articles reproduced or quoted in this book and therefore there are inconsistencies throughout the text.

The words, talks and letters of 'Abdu'l-Bahá published in newspaper articles and in publications such as *Star of the West* are reproduced here as they appeared. They are not authorized translations of His words, which can be found in such books as *Selections from the Writings of 'Abdu'l-Bahá*.

ABBREVIATIONS

American States

AL	Alabama	MT	Montana
AR	Arkansas	NC	North Carolina
AZ	Arizona	ND	North Dakota
CA	California	NE	Nebraska
CO	Colorado	NJ	New Jersey
CT	Connecticut	NM	New Mexico
DC	District of Columbia	NV	Nevada
DE	Delaware	NY	New York
FL	Florida	OH	Ohio
GA	Georgia	OK	Oklahoma
HI	Hawaii	OR	Oregon
IA	Iowa	PA	Pennsylvania
ID	Idaho	RI	Rhode Island
IL	Illinois	SC	South Carolina
IN	Indiana	SD	South Dakota
KS	Kansas	TN	Tennessee
KY	Kentucky	TX	Texas
LA	Louisiana	UT	Utah
MA	Massachusetts	VT	Vermont
MD	Maryland	WA	Washington
ME	Maine	WI	Wisconsin
MI	Michigan	WY	Wyoming
MN	Minnesota		

Months

Jan.	January	Sept.	September
Feb.	February	Oct.	October
Mar.	March	Nov.	November
Apr.	April	Dec.	December
Aug.	August		

PART I

I

EXILE AND IMPRISONMENT

References during the Lifetime of Bahá'u'lláh

The news that 'a second Báb' or 'the present leader of the Bábís', as some westerners would call and consider Bahá'u'lláh, was imprisoned in 'Akká started to circulate in Europe and America, especially in missionary circles, as early as 1868, and in the following years some westerners tried to meet Him personally. One of them was the young orientalist Edward G. Browne (1862–1926), who visited 'Akká in 1891 and who left for posterity his well-known pen portrait of Him.[1] Years before, a German Templer residing in Haifa was also able to meet Bahá'u'lláh and afterwards wrote his impressions in an article which appeared on 20 July 1871 in the *Süddeutsche Warte* (Stuttgart) and which briefly mentioned 'Abdu'l-Bahá.[2]

Most of the time, however, visitors calling on Bahá'u'lláh would be referred to 'Abdu'l-Bahá. One of them was Dr Thomas Chaplin (1853–1904), a missionary in Syria, who in 1871 wrote a lengthy letter to *The London Times* about his visit to the 'Babis' and which contains what is perhaps the earliest account of 'Abdu'l-Bahá in the western press.

> In the spring of the present year I had an opportunity of visiting the Babs in their place of confinement. Beheyah Allah himself does not readily concede an interview to strangers, and receives only such as are desirous of obtaining from him instruction in religious truth. We were received by his son, who is apparently about 30 years of age, and has a fine intellectual countenance, with black hair and beard, and that sallow, melancholic look which distinguishes nearly all Persians of the intelligent and religious class. He was dressed in a robe of white flannel, with cap of the same material, and a small white turban. Over his shoulders was thrown a brown cloth abbái. He appeared pleased to see us but objected to answer questions

> respecting the origin and history of the sect. 'Let us speak of things spiritual,' he said, 'what you are now asking me is of no importance.' But on our telling him that people in England would naturally be curious to know in what way so remarkable a religious movement had arisen, and who were the originators of it, he gave us the information here detailed. He had a remarkably earnest, almost solemn manner, spoke excellent Arabic, fluently, and showed a minute and accurate knowledge of the Old and New Testaments, as well as an acquaintance with the history of religious thought in Europe. Our interview lasted two hours, during the whole of which time an animated conversation was maintained. Like a true Oriental, he seldom gave direct answer to a question upon any point of doctrine, but replied by another question, or by an illustration, his object throughout apparently being to convince his questioners of what he considered to be truth. He seemed to speak as one conscious of possessing superior light – as a great teacher might speak to his disciples. 'Why,' he inquired, 'did not the Jews, who at the time of our Lord's advent were in expectation of their Messiah, believe in him?' And, assenting to our reply that it was because they misunderstood the Scriptures, he asked whether it might not be the case that Christians in like manner now misunderstood the Scriptures – the inference (not expressed) being that his father was sent by God to teach the true doctrine.[3]

Chaplin's letter was the basis of other articles – not always including the section about 'Abdu'l-Bahá – published in, at least, the United Kingdom,[4] the United States,[5] Spain[6] and Germany.[7]

In 1874 another missionary, probably Edwin E. Bliss (1817–92), also visited 'Akká and afterwards briefly mentioned 'Abdu'l-Bahá in an account for the *Bible Society Record* (New York):

> 'Then I went to Acre and spent that night there, and found that the Moslems now are beginning to have some religious thoughts, especially concerning the divinity of Christ. This was from the new religion of the Babites, which rose in these days. For Abbas Effendi, the son of Beha Allah, has opened a place in Acre, to receive all his people who come for conversation upon their new religion. I learned, too, that they had bought Bibles for reading. We ask God

> to bring forth, out to this schism, means for the extension of his kingdom.[8]

Lawrence Oliphant (1829–88), a British citizen residing in Haifa, wrote a series of articles about his experiences in the Holy Land for *The Sun* (New York). In one of these letters, dated 7 November 1883, he describeed his attempts to see Bahá'u'lláh and briefly mentioned 'Abdu'l-Bahá.[9] Some years later, in an article about his visit to the Sea of Galilee for the *English Illustrated Magazine* (London), Oliphant stated that 'I lunched at the bottom of the mountains at the tents of some Erkebat Arabs. They are a small amiable tribe, inhabiting this shore of the lake, numbering about 100 tents, of whom half are tenants of Abbas Effendi, the son of the Persian Holy-man, who lives at Acre, and is chief of the Persian sect of Babs. He has a granary, which we shortly after passed, at the south end of the lake, and owns a good deal of land in this neighbourhood.'[10] This article was later published in other journals.[11]

The politician Sir Mountstuart E. Grant Duff (1829–1906), former governor of Madras and an acquaintance of Oliphant, mentioned in an article for *The Contemporary Review* (London) that in the course of his travels he visited 'Akká in early December 1887 and as well as gathering some information about the Bahá'ís, sent a messenger 'to call on the son of a man who claims, or is said to claim, to be the head of the Persian sect known as the Bâbis'.[12] Apparently 'Abdu'l-Bahá did not provide Duff with the kind of information he wanted and the latter concluded that 'I learnt nothing from the person to whom I have alluded, and his position in the midst of Turkish territory and under the observation of the Turkish authorities is such that he is not likely to know much of what is going on in Persia'. As noted above, 'Abdu'l-Bahá had also been reluctant to speak about the history of the Bábí-Bahá'í movement with Chaplin. Meeting with westerners and speaking with them openly on religion certainly posed a great danger to the already harshly oppressed group of Bahá'í prisoners in 'Akká. Even in later years, when the conditions of the Bahá'ís in 'Akká were more relaxed, the chronicle known as *A Traveller's Narrative*, written by 'Abdu'l-Bahá, was submitted to Browne in Bahjí as an anonymous work.

The Druze Amír Amín Arslan (1866–1943), governor of Tiberias and later diplomat in several European cities and in Argentina, was able to see Bahá'u'lláh in 1891 and wrote a sympathetic account, not devoid of inaccuracies, for *Revue Bleue* (Paris), which was published in September 1896. In the course of his article Arslan mentioned that 'Upon my arrival I hastened to visit Abbas Effendi, the eldest son of the "Word" and responsible for the external relations of the community. I had known him in Beirut, Syria, and bonds of true friendship had quickly developed between us.' Describing Bahá'u'lláh, Arslan stated that 'Seeing him struck my imagination in such a way that I cannot better represent him than evoking the image of God the Father surrounded by clouds while commanding in his majesty the elements of nature,' and further added that 'my friend Abbas Effendi continues to direct the temporal affairs of the cult; he is of a rare intelligence, and although Persian, he knows in deep our Arabic language. I got from him some letters in Arabic which are masterpieces in their style, thought, and especially in their oriental calligraphy.'[13]

Visiting the Center of the Covenant

After the passing of Bahá'u'lláh, 'Abdu'l-Bahá continued to receive visitors who wanted to know about Him and about the religion of which He was now the appointed head. In the spring of 1901 William Elroy Curtis (1850–1911) and William H. Baldwin (1851–1923) and their families visited the Holy Land.

Curtis was a journalist on the *Chicago Record-Herald*, the secretary of the Bureau of American Republics and the author of several travel books. During his travels in Syria and Palestine he sent to his journal a series of letters describing his experiences. While visiting 'Akká, the party of American travelers met 'Abdu'l-Bahá. Curtis afterwards wrote a letter summarizing the history of the Bahá'í Faith, which included comments about the Master and the construction of the Shrine of the Báb:

> The most interesting prisoner at Acre at present is Abbas Effendi, a learned Persian prophet, who proclaims a new religion, and is the head of the sect known as Babies, or Babites, so called from the word Bab, which means a gate . . .
>
> Abbas Effendi is a fascinating mystic, a man of most impressive presence and conversation, and his voice is musical and hypnotizing.
>
> He claims to have a church of 300 followers in Chicago, all of the

> highest social standing, and twelve of whom lived with him here for some time, studying the doctrines, like Paul at the feet of Gamaliel. Dr. Getzinger of Ithaca, NY, left his card upon the table of the great Babite's reception room, and it still lies there. Down in the corner is the word cosmologist, which, I presume, was intended to describe his profession. I do not know what it means, and Abbas Effendi could not explain. Mrs. Thornburgh, Mrs. Jackson and Miss Josephine Locke of Chicago are devoted disciples and liberal contributors; Miss Helen Ella Cole of Boston and Mrs. Alice Barney and Charles B. Burdettee are among his regular supporters and correspondents, while Mrs. Phoebe A. Hearst has been here, and, as usual, left a liberal donation – $30,000 I was told – the most of which was used in the construction of a shrine and temple upon Mount Carmel, above the town of Haifa, where Abbas Effendi intended to bury the remains of his father and establish the center of the church.
>
> As the movement is supposed to be secret the Turkish authorities became alarmed at the number of American visitors and their liberal contributions, so Abbas Effendi was prohibited from leaving Acre, and has not been able to complete the shrine. The walls are up, the roof is laid, and part of the interior is finished. For the time being the Babite movement is in a position of arrested development, but Abbas Effendi is full of faith and confidence, and says that if his American supporters are loyal he expects soon to persuade the Turkish authorities to set him free to carry salvation to all the earth.[14]

Some Christian missionaries and religious scholars also visited 'Abdu'l-Bahá. Two of them were the Chicago theologian Samuel Ives Curtiss (1844–1904)[15] and the Presbyterian missionary in Syria Henry Harris Jessup (1832–1910), who in their chronicles did not conceal their irritation at the rapid growth of the Bahá'í Faith in Christian countries. 'It is difficult to regard without indignation the Babite proselytism now being carried on in the United States,'[16] stated Jessup, who paradoxically in 1893 had written a paper for the Parliament of World's Religions in which he mentioned Bahá'u'lláh with sympathy and which had a great influence on the beginnings of the Bahá'í Faith in America. In later years, Jessup published various articles against the Bahá'í Faith, which were reprinted as free pamphlets to coincide with 'Abdu'l-Bahá's travels in the West.[17]

The Swede Gustaf Henrik Lundquist (1865–1930) also visited 'Abdu'l-Bahá in 'Akká. He was a mystic, Esperantist and littérateur who took the name of Sébastien Voirol after establishing himself in France. As a vanguard writer and founder of the 'Cercle de Artistes de Passy', he was in contact with many artists of the time, including the architect Le Corbusier – whom he knew through his brother-in-law, the famed architect Auguste Perre (1874–1954) – Matisse, Picasso, etc. As well as being the author of several works and translator of various Swedish titles, Voirol was also a regular contributor to several literary magazines, including *Akademos* and *Mercure de France*.

While travelling in Egypt in 1902 he came into contact with the Bahá'ís of Port Said and through them obtained permission to visit 'Abdu'l-Bahá in Haifa, arriving there on 14 February and staying for a few days. Three years later he wrote a lengthy article on the Bahá'í Faith which included an account of his meetings with 'Abdu'l-Bahá. Interestingly, Voirol's intention in writing the article was, as he himself stated, to furnish the readers with good information about a movement of which much was written in the press but sometimes 'with the obvious aim to convince Europe that the Babis are very terrible criminals' whereas 'Those who have had a close acquaintance with members of the sect are well aware that they are not concerned with politics and their religious belief is based in a gentleness even greater than the one taught by Jesus Christ.'[18]

Voirol's impressions of 'Abdu'l-Bahá were later briefly mentioned in an article in *A Travers le Monde* (Paris) in 1907[19] and he wrote again on the Bahá'í Faith on at least one more occasion.[20]

The prominent American politician William Jennings Bryan (1860–1925) also visited 'Abdu'l-Bahá. He had run for president for the Democratic party in 1896 and 1900, and would try again in 1908. In 1913 he was appointed by Woodrow Wilson as Secretary of State and held the office until 1915. As an internationalist and pacifist, he had a deep interest in the doctrine of non-resistance and in meeting with prominent pacifists of his time. After his second defeat in the presidential elections he started a series of travels around the world in which he lectured about his ideas and visited figures such as Leo Tolstoy. In his 1906 tour Bryan included 'Akká as one of his destinations and tried to see 'Abdu'l-Bahá on two occasions but owing to restrictions was only able to see Him once. Bryan wrote about this meeting in one of the articles he submitted regularly to *The Minneapolis Journal* describing his travel experiences:

> Abbas Effendi, now a political prisoner at Akka, in Palestine, is the head of the reform movement. He was born in Persia, and is carrying on the work to which his father and grandfather devoted their lives. He discards force as a means of propagating truth, and while he does not command monogamy, has set the example by having but one wife. While Abbas Effendi's father preached moral suasion, his followers were charged with revolutionary designs and the family was exiled. After remaining a time at Constantinople under the surveillance of the sultan, the reform leaders were removed to Akka, a seaport not far from Haifa. Here, surrounded by a few followers, the son holds such communication as he can with the rest of the church in Persia, his doctrines having as yet taken but little root among the Turks and Arabs. It is believed in Akka that he receives financial aid from a number of wealthy Americans who have become interested in his work.
>
> We called upon Abbas Effendi as we were leaving Palestine and found him an earnest old man with a careworn but kindly face. His hair and beard are gray, and he speaks with animation when his favorite topic is under discussion. His doctrines are something like those of Tolstoy, but he does not carry the doctrine of non-resistance so far as does the Russian philosopher. How much he may be able to do in the way of eliminating the objectionable features of Mohammedanism no one can say, but it is a hopeful sign that there is among the followers of Mohammed an organized effort to raise the plane of discussion from brute force to an appeal to intelligence.[21]

At the end of the same article Bryan further added that 'At Beyrout, one of the Turkish ports, a copy of the Koran and a copy of the life of Abbas Effendi were taken from me by the censor.'[22] Bryan's article was syndicated and thus appeared in many journals across America.[23] It was also included in his book *The Old World and Its Ways* (1907).

When in 1912 'Abdu'l-Bahá visited Minneapolis He visited Bryan's home but the latter was away campaigning for Woodrow Wilson. 'Abdu'l-Bahá met with his family and signed their guest book (see chapter 21).

Around 1906 the Californian writer Ada Cunnick Inchbold and her husband, the British artist and photographer Edward Stanley Inchbold (1855–1921), travelled trough Lebanon and Syria. They expected to meet 'Abdu'l-Bahá in 'Akká but were unable to do so. Nevertheless, Ada's comments in the account of her travels are worth reproducing here, for they are a good indicator of the fame that 'Abdu'l-Bahá had already achieved in the West:

> There is a personality in Akka whose name always stirs up interest in the minds of travelers who desire to do more than skim the surface of things. The name of Abbas Effendi is known not only in Akka but in all Syria, in Persia, India, Turkey, the United States; and even in Paris he has not one but many supporters of his creed.
>
> He is the present head of a remarkable religious sect which, developing in Persia some fifty years ago, soon attained such hold on the minds of the people that its influence was considered pernicious by the ruling powers, and persecution promptly followed . . .
>
> Abbas Effendi lives in a house situated at the extreme end of Akka, as remote from the gate of entrance as he could well be placed. A villa was built for him by his adherents on the slope of Carmel above the German colony. At one time he was allowed to resort to it freely for a change of residence, but owing to injudicious efforts made on his behalf by numbers of his admirers, the authorities took alarm, and he is now kept a close prisoner in Akka.
>
> He was invisible on the day of our visit to Akka, and we had no later opportunity of going there, as our long stay in Galilee had drawn to an end.[24]

Myron H. Phelps

Among the westerners who visited 'Abdu'l-Bahá in Palestine the American Myron H. Phelps (1856–1916) deserves special attention. A lawyer by profession, Phelps was highly interested in Indian religions, particularly Vedantism. This put him in contact with many westerners looking to the East for new religious paths. One of these was Countess Canavarro, known as Sister Sanghamita, a lady of peculiar character who adhered to Buddhism. It was through her that Phelps, in the course of a visit to London, heard of the Bahá'í Faith in the summer of 1902 and became acquainted with some of the early British Bahá'ís, such as Ethel Rosenberg.[25]

Phelps became very interested in the Bábí and Bahá'í religions and started to study some of Browne's works on the subject. His desire to further research on the Bahá'í Faith led him to write to the Holy Land and request permission to visit 'Akká. Permission was granted and in late 1902 he, together with Countess Canavarro, visited 'Abdu'l-Bahá. They remained in 'Akká for a period of one month, which Phelps describes as 'one of the most memorable in my life for not only was I able to gain a satisfactory general view of this religion, but I made the acquaintance of Abbas Effendi, who is easily the most remarkable man whom it has ever been my fortune to meet'.[26]

In the course of that month both Phelps and Canavarro asked several questions of 'Abdu'l-Bahá and Canavarro also interviewed some members of His family.[27] From his notes of these interviews Phelps prepared, probably in Egypt, his book *The Life and Teachings of Abbas Effendi*, which was published in late 1903 by Pitman & Sons (New York and London) and which included an introduction by Edward G. Browne.

Despite its historical interest and the sympathy with which the author wrote about the Bahá'í Faith and 'Abdu'l-Bahá, the book had a number of inaccuracies and attributed to the Master ideas and concepts which were actually Canavarro's opinions. Aware of this fact, in 1909 Phelps again visited the Holy Land and received from 'Abdu'l-Bahá corrections to his book. When, coinciding with the arrival of 'Abdu'l-Bahá in America in 1912, a second edition of the book was released, Phelps was, however, unable to make the corrections because he was in India. Instead, the problematic sections were simply removed from that edition.

Phelps's book was very well received and is indispensable for understanding the popularity that 'Abdu'l-Bahá had gained among Americans and the background of much of what was written about Him in later years – especially during His travels in the West – by many authors who were not Bahá'ís. The publication of *The Life and Teachings of Abbas Effendi* was followed by dozens of reviews and advertisements in the press. It is impossible to include in this volume all these materials but a brief survey of some of them is worth presenting here.

In August 1903 *The New York Times* announced the forthcoming publication of the book and summarized portions of its introduction.[28]

Advertisements in the same journal and in the *New-York Tribune* show that the book was released on 21 November 1903.[29] Soon afterwards the *Brooklyn Daily Eagle* published a lengthy review which opened with the remark:

> Babism, or Beha ism – do ye ken it? if not, lose no time. Investigate. It is not merely one of these fashionable esoteric fads which society (not forgetting Brooklyn society) cultivate along with the solemn mysteries of palmistry and crystal gazing, but it is – possibly – a future world religion.[30]

In a similar vein the *New York Herald* stated in its review that 'if you are one of the many people now in search of a religion . . . Babism is the latest and most up to date of all the creeds. In its capacious bosom it embraces every predecessor.'[31] A review in *The New York Times* concluded by asking,

> Are we to decry Abbas Effendi because he wears a fez and long flowing robes and discredit him as an interpreter of the living truth? Mr. Phelps's volume impresses one with the idea that here is an Oriental possessed of unheard-of liberality and breadth of thought.[32]

Outside New York, *The Minneapolis Journal* recommended that 'after a study of this book, it would be very interesting to religious students to see the views of some Christian missionary in Persia'.[33] The *Springfield Daily Republican* (MA) published two reviews of Phelps's work. The first noted that 'Abdu'l-Bahá 'lives gladly among the poor, and converting foes into friends by the gentleness and sanctity of his daily life';[34] and the second stated that 'from whatever viewpoint one approached the book he will find in the simple life of self-sacrifice of the present Bab, Abbas Effendi, a great deal to be interested in and to admire, and in his words of wisdom many thoughts conducive to high living'.[35]

Like other Christian magazines, the reviewer for *The Record of Christian Work* (Northfield, MA) expressed some scepticism over the subject of the book and claimed that whatever was good in the Bahá'í Faith could already be found in Christianity. However, the author concluded the review by stating that 'this is a most fascinating subject and a most interesting book. Few can read it without a desire to visit Akka, and see with their own eyes the man who seems to follow so closely in the footsteps of the Master.'[36]

The judge Ernest Crosby (1856–1907), a Christian anarchist and promulgator in North America of Tolstoy's ideals, published a lengthy and sympathetic review in the monthly magazine which he edited with Benedict Prieth (1870–1934), *The Whim* (Newark). 'I have been reading an extremely interesting book which I strongly recommend to all who are concerned with the spiritual development of the race,' Crosby opened his review. He quoted some of the words of 'Abdu'l-Bahá found in the book, then concluded, 'This is true religion by whatever name it may be called, and in thought and expression . . . it evidently has that distinction and dignity which are the marks of all great religions in their inception. It is this dignity of word and idea which are so conspicuously lacking in recent religious movements in this country.' Crosby, who had visited Tolstoy and corresponded with him, closed his review with words of regret that on a one-night visit to 'Akká in 1894 he had failed to see 'Abdu'l-Bahá. 'Abbas Effendi was there and I might have passed one of the evenings of my life.'[37]

As mentioned above, many other reviews, articles and announcements about Phelps's book were published in the United States[38] but also in England,[39] Germany[40] and probably other countries. Phelps's book also raised press interest in 'Abdu'l-Bahá's followers in America and was the basis of many articles published at the time on the Bahá'í Faith and the early American Bahá'í communities.[41]

Soon after the publication of his book Phelps wrote a series of articles for *The Theosophical Forum* (New York)[42] which contained abundant references to the Bahá'í Faith and he also gave some lectures on his book.[43]

The Commission of Inquiry

The year 1905 witnessed the failed revolution against Tsar Nicholas II of Russia, which forced him to establish modest but important changes in the state, including the formation of a consultative assembly, the Duma, and the instauration of certain rights that had been non-existent for Russian citizens up to that time. Although in the end this revolution did not achieve the results it expected, the episode nevertheless became an example for many oppressed peoples and political movements around the globe and at the same time a warning, unheeded in most cases, for many despots.

Emulating the Russian revolution, there started in Yemen another uprising. Arab nationalists revolted against the government of the Sultan and their movement soon expanded to other regions of the Empire with Arab-speaking populations. Successive Ottoman troops sent by Sultan Abdul Hamid were defeated by rebels in a series of clashes that continued for several months and took the lives of thousands of people.[44]

It was in this context of political unrest that Muḥammad-'Alí, the half-brother of 'Abdu'l-Bahá, who up to that time had not spared any occasion to try to harm and eliminate his brother, announced to the authorities that 'Abdu'l-Bahá was also plotting against the Sultan. In his many calumnies Muḥammad-'Alí portrayed the shrine of the Báb, which with much effort was being built by 'Abdu'l-Bahá at Mount Carmel, as a fortress and an arsenal. The western pilgrims visiting the Holy Land to see the Master were denounced as a concourse of foreign spies financing and overseeing the plans for a revolution. Many other accusations were made in an attempt to profit from the paranoid state of the government, which was already very suspicious about 'Abdu'l-Bahá and the Bahá'ís for their religious activities and which kept them under surveillance.[45]

The immediate result of these accusations was that a commission was sent from Constantinople to 'Akká to investigate 'Abdu'l-Bahá and an order was issued for His exile to the desert of Fezzan, in Libya.[46] However, the order to exile 'Abdu'l-Bahá was not executed. According to Bahá'í sources, the commission that was to enforce the orders of the Sultan left suddenly for the capital on the very day it was meant to capture 'Abdu'l-Bahá: on 21 July 1905 the Sultan had been the object of a terrorist attack which killed 26 people.

The western press published some information about this incident. On 18 August 1905 *L'Écho de Paris* published information sent from Beirut about the work of the commission of inquiry.[47] *The Times of London* published that same information on 19 August:

> THE ARAB REVOLT
>
> A sort of peripatetic inquisition, composed of five Turkish Pashas from Constantinople, is reported by the Echo de Paris to be now visiting the Syrian towns to inquire into the present movement. Its

> proceedings are mysterious. The witnesses examined are forbidden under penalty of death to reveal the questions put to them. The Babist chief, Abbas Effendi, has been exiled because he was building a palace on Mount Carmel which commands the Turkish fortress of St Jean d'Acre. He was accused of erecting a fortress for the Egyptians or Arabs.[48]

In Alexandria *The Egyptian Gazette* of 26 August 1905 published the following news item:

> RELIGIOUS LEADER EXILED
>
> Abbas Effendi, the head of the Babist community, who has long been resident at Akka near Haifa, has been condemned to exile. It appears that the Babi Sheikh recently decided in an evil hour for himself to build a palace on the slopes of Mount Carmel. It unfortunately happened that the palace commanded the whole town of Haifa and the Kaimakam's house. Suspicion was aroused and representations were made to Constantinople that the Babist leader was building 'a fortress' for the benefit of the Arabs or the Egyptians!
>
> Abbas Effendi has therefore been exiled though the Babis, who are exiles from Persia, have been for the past forty years most excellent citizens. Religious quietists, their conduct has always been marked by toleration and charity, and since their settlement at Akka, they have abstained from all forms of political activity. The reputed wealth of the sect is no doubt the cause of Abbas Effendi's exile.[49]

Le Journal of Paris published on 21 September a letter from a certain correspondent in Beirut who, as well as describing events in cities such as Tripoli, gave information about the situation in Acre. Adding to information previously published in other journals, it inaccurately reported that 72 Babis (sic) had been expelled from Acre and mentioned that the commission of inquiry sent to the city had interrogated more than a hundred witnesses. The authorities feared, stated the correspondent, that the Bahá'ís, led by 'Abdu'l-Bahá, were planning an insurrection with the aim of uniting Egypt with Syria. The Governor, the general commandant and other local officials had been dismissed on the grounds that they were collaborating with 'Abdu'l-Bahá.[50]

The Liberation

Following the triumph of the Young Turk's revolution in July 1908, a general amnesty was decreed for political prisoners and prisoners of conscience. This amnesty included 'Abdu'l-Bahá, who after 40 years of incarceration in one of the worst prisons of the Ottoman Empire, was at last a free citizen.

In 1912, coinciding with the arrival of 'Abdu'l-Bahá in America, *The Evening Post* (New York) published a vivid account by a woman who was present at the moment the Master received the news of His liberation:

> It was in the spirit of reverent inquiry that I made the pilgrimage to Acca. I had heard and read much of the Bahai religion, and had been touched to admiration by the beautiful character of Baha'o'llah and the deep spirituality of his religion. I should not, however, have thought of seeking 'The Master', his son and successor, had I not happened to be in Palestine and Syria one summer just at the time a friend of mine was acting as governess in the family of Abbas Effendi, who urged me to look her up. I kept it idly in my mind until I found that the plans of our party gave us a whole day in Haifa, which is but a few miles from Acca. Now that the great Persian religious leader has arrived here on his way to Washington to take part in the second annual conference next week of the Persian–American Educational Society, the events of that day take on an added interest.
>
> The governess put me into the hands of Mirza Ameen, nephew of Abbas Effendi, who was to take me over to Acca. He demurred a little to the idea of presenting me unannounced, for Abbas Effendi usually set the time for his visitors, and sometimes eager pilgrims were kept waiting months, or even years, before they might look on the face of 'The Master'. Various reasons have been given for this hedging about of the presence, but an adequate one would be found in the leader's position as a political prisoner, continually under suspicion: and we, during our Oriental travels, had been made painfully aware of the atmosphere of tense, unhappy oppression and secrecy that seemed to [illegible] Turkey. It was the summer of 1908, mid July, during the last days of the old regime of Abdul Hamid, the tyrant.
>
> Mirza Ameen . . . hired an open carriage and we started for Acca.

SUDDEN OPPRESSIVENESS OF ACCA

Haifa is a port town, neat and Western in appearance, and containing a 'Cook's Office' and a German Hotel. It lies just between Mt. Carmel and the sea. The drive was along a curving shore, over firm yellow sand, with the waves of the Mediterranean washing our wheels. It is about four miles to Acca. We seemed suddenly to shed all the beauty of the shore drive and pass unto an atmosphere of oppression. As if feeling that, Mirza Ameen asked if I would be willing to remove my Western hat and wear a veil as Oriental women do, thus making myself less conspicuous. I complied, arranging the folds of my tourist veil over my head and hair and close to my face, as Turkish women do. Then he suggested that he should leave me at the entrance of the town and rejoin me within the prison, as it was better that we should not be seen together and he warned me, as I should await him in the courtyard, not to speak to anyone or answer any questions. It was indeed a queer sensation that seized me as I left the carriage before the high walls of the prison and walked into the square courtyard and for a moment stood there alone. Two elderly men addressed me, but I only shook my head.

Presently Mirza Ameen appeared and led me up the long outside stairway to the apartments of Abdul Baha. At the head of the stairs stood his wife, a plain stout woman, with a sweet expression and a most hospitable manner. Her dress was a loose muslin wrapper of the Mother Hubbard type. She took me into her room, which she assured me with many smiles, was my room, as indeed the whole house was my house, and her only desire was to see me feel at home. After I had laid off my wraps and sat awhile in the deliberate Oriental fashion, I was taken into the sitting-room. This was a plain, rectangular room with yellow matting on the floor, the only furniture being a row of straight chairs against one wall and a low seat running around the two sides of the room, covered with coarse red rugs. The view of the sea from the windows was the only touch of beauty, but all was spotlessly clean.

The Master entered.

INTERVIEW WITH THE MASTER

I greeted him reverently and shook hands. He looked deeply into my eyes and bade me a cordial welcome. I have heard of pilgrims who have fallen at his feet. But his manner to me showed no expectation of such a greeting, nor did he seem offended by my manner. I regarded him with deep interest. What I first saw was an old man, who had suffered. His clothes, the loose garments and white turban of the Oriental, were poor. His skin was like a piece of wrinkled parchment, and his gray locks fallen over his shoulders were scanty. His features were strong and dignified and as I looked longer I saw that his eyes were remarkable. They were large and blue and around the iris was a wide circle of black. They were the eyes of a mystic and the eyes of one who understands men. Calm and loving, they yet seemed to see all that I was and was not. He seated himself cross legged and invited me to ask him questions. Mirza Ameen sat opposite me and interpreted from Persian to English with unobtrusive perfection. The Master, for indeed he seemed such to me as he talked, a master of life and religion, said many beautiful things, some clear and simple, and some suggesting depths of thought and many full of Oriental imagery. He made no claims to unusual knowledge, indeed once he disclaimed such, but he is, without doubt, of profound insight.

Later his women folk came into the room [illegible]. As the room gradually filled with grave-eyed men and sweet-faced women, I received an impression of loveliness and happiness such as I never remember getting in any other home. It was as if the prison had become a hot-house for the flowers of the spirit. I dined with them, of course sitting at the head of the table and being offered the best the house afforded.

Then a curious element was introduced. Abdul Baha, who had been in the courtyard talking with the Governor of the town, came up with fresh news from Constantinople by official wire that the Sultan had granted a constitution to his beloved people and that all political prisoners were free. It was hard to believe and very wonderful. Abdul Baha said: 'This is a beautiful act of his Majesty: he was not forced to do it, but has given it of his own free will to the people. I honor him.' I was impressed with this charitable judgment of a monarch who had persecuted him and his people for a generation, and can still see the sweetness of his face as he uttered it, but it was historically wrong, for Abdul Hamid had most assuredly been forced at the cannon's mouth to cede the constitution to Young Turkey.

The news of that day has changed the life of Abdul Baha and his family. They are no longer prisoners, and it is due to the constitution that he is able to travel. He has many disciples in our country. He assured me that my coming to Acca had been auspicious and that they should always associate me with the coming of freedom. Mirza Ameen said, 'We can go out of the city openly for now we are free,' so I drove forth with my American hat on my head and my Persian escort by my side.[51]

2

WESTERN PILGRIMS

In the winter of 1898–9 the first western Bahá'ís were able to visit 'Abdu'l-Bahá in the prison-city of 'Akká.[1] Two of them, Edward and Lua Getsinger, had the opportunity of visiting the Master again from September 1900 to March 1901 and were soon followed by other American Bahá'ís. As pilgrims returned from the Holy Land the press would publish articles recording their impressions and experiences or reproducing their letters and pilgrims' notes. A survey of some of these articles is presented in this chapter.

It should be noted that there were serious misunderstandings about the station of 'Abdu'l-Bahá among some of the early American Bahá'ís and some wrongly considered Him to be the return of Christ. This fact is reflected in some of the articles published at the time.

As early as 12 August 1900 the *New York Herald* published a full-page article about the Bahá'í Faith which included the following comments about 'Abdu'l-Bahá:

> The life of Abbas Effendi is one of extreme simplicity. He puts forward no claims for himself, and discourages the more enthusiastic Babists, who would fain reverence him. He frequently waits upon the members of his household at table, spends much of his time in ministering to the poor, and many of his acts closely resemble those of Jesus. To the direct question, 'Are you the Christ?' he replies humbly, 'I am the Servant of God.' To his followers the fact that he does not deny his divinity is convincing proof of its existence, while the fact that he will not affirm it places him in a still more exalted light.
>
> Such a one is Abbas Abdel Beha, whom some two thousand intelligent Americans regard as being in very truth the reincarnation of Christ . . . Several of the New York members of the faith have

> 'tablets' or personal letters from Abbas Abdel Beha, and these they regard as more valuable than gold or precious stones.[2]

On 9 September the *Springfield Daily Republican* (MA) carried a caustic article about the progress of the Bahá'í Faith in America which stated that 'to see and worship ['Abdu'l-Bahá] American Babis have made pilgrimages to Acca, for they claim that he is the son of God. He is a man of singular beauty of countenance, and he plays the role of Messiah in a very graceful and gracious manner, being very attractive to women in search of new religious sensations, and there are many such in each generation'. The newspaper then quoted parts of Lua Getsinger's account of her first pilgrimage as well as accounts by other members of the first party of western pilgrims, including the following words attributed to Phoebe Hearst (1842–1919):

> 'We entered the garden, ascended one flight of stairs, and were shown into the hall, or reception room, where we removed our wraps, and were welcomed by the uncle, who told us to pass into the next room. Dr. Kheiralla went ahead, and by the violent beating of my heart I knew that we were soon to see the blessed face of the prince of the House of David, the king of the whole world. We reached the door and stopped – before us in the center of the room stood a man clad in a long garment with a white turban on his head, stretching out one hand toward us, while his face (which I cannot describe) was lighted by a rare, sweet smile of joy and welcome! We stood thus for a moment unable to move – when my heart gave a great throb and, scarcely knowing what I was doing, I held out my arms crying, "My Lord, my Lord!" and rushed to him, kneeling at his blessed feet, sobbing like a child. He put his dear hands upon our beloved heads and said, in a voice that seemed to our ears like a strain of sweet music, "Welcome, welcome, my dear children, you are welcome; arise and be of good cheer."'
>
> Truly there is yet faith on the earth, or rather let us call it credulity, when a handsome Persian, who seems to believe it himself, or at least plays the part very well, is worshiped as the Son of God.
>
> It might be thought that a woman like Mrs. Phoebe A. Hearst, who has so many millions of dollars at her command, a woman, it may be presumed, of good business judgment and sound, common

sense, would not easily be carried away into fanaticism, but she also is a worshiper at the shrine of the Bab Messiah. She says in a letter dated Washington, November 19, 1899:–

> The Master I will not attempt to describe; I will only state that I believe with all my heart that He is the Master, and my greatest blessing in this world is that I have been privileged to be in His presence and look upon His sanctified face. His life is truly the Christ life and His whole being radiates purity and holiness!
>
> Without a doubt Abbas Effendi is the Messiah of this day and generation, and we need not look for another.

In a letter written to a gentleman in Chicago she uses similar language, saying:–

> I believe in Him with all my heart and soul, and I hope that all who call themselves Believers will concede to Him all the greatness, all the glory, and all the praise, for surely He Is the Son of God – and 'The Spirit of the Father abideth in Him.'[3]

The *New York Herald* also reported Edward Getsinger stating that

> Abdul Beha lives in a small stone building of one story and basement. He has a wife and four daughters. He was exiled by the Turkish government in 1852. The court in which they live is for political exiles only. Abbas Abdul Beha is at times permitted to go out on parole, but he is not allowed to leave Syria . . . Although he has not had one day's schooling in his life it is said, there is no subject on which he cannot talk learnedly. He speaks many languages.[4]

On November 1900 a correspondent in Haifa of *The Egyptian Gazette* (Alexandria) wrote an article about the second group of western pilgrims. It was based on information provided by Edward Getsinger and also mentions the crisis caused by Ibrahim Kheiralla in the young American Baha'i community.[5]

> HAIFA, November 6. In the middle of the month of September

last, an American party composed of Mr. and Mrs. Gettsinger, the preachers of Babism in New World, two other ladies and gentlemen, came here on a pilgrimage. They arrived at night and early on the following morning they repaired to the abode of Abbas Effendi and offered up their homage and adoration. The party remained here for a fortnight during which time they paid repeated visits to this pseudo-Christ and also visited the tomb of his father, Beha Allah, which is situated three miles to the west of Acre.

At the end of the fortnight, three of the party returned home, leaving behind the preachers of this doctrine to receive the other pilgrims who were on their way to Haifa. In the first week of October, an American lady arrived, and is now living with the daughters of Abbas Effendi, who last year applied themselves to acquiring a knowledge of the English language. The sisters are four in number, two of whom are married. Towards the end of last month, three more ladies arrived, and are still here. Mr. Gettsinger expects to see two hundred pilgrims, who will arrive in parties during the ensuing winter and spring.

These American pilgrims believe in the Godhead of both Beha Allah and Abbas Effendi, his eldest son. The former they maintain to be the Almighty God, or the father, and the latter to be the Son, or Jesus Christ. There are about two thousand people in the United States, especially in Chicago and its vicinity, who believe in this dogma, though some of them deny the divinity of the son and believe only in the father. These believers have for their preacher Dr. Kiar Allah, a learned Syrian gentleman, who was the introducer of Babism to the States. This predicator had two years ago gone at the bidding of Abbas Effendi to America and taken with him several followers, amongst whom were Mr. and Mrs. Gettsinger. When here he differed with the Effendi upon certain points in the dogma, and this enraged Abbas Effendi, who ordered him back to America. He kept back Mr. and Mrs. Gettsinger, whom he imbued with a strong belief in his divinity, declaring that he was the true Christ. He supplied them with documents which called upon believers to look to them alone for light and leading, and to renounce all other teachings. Thus dissuasion has arisen in their ranks. Some adhere to Dr. Kiar Allah, whose teaching is that Beha Allah is the only divinity, while others follow in the steps of Mr. and Mrs. Gettsinger, who

> maintain that Abbas Efiendi must also be worshipped like his father, as he is the true Christ.[6]

Among the pilgrims who visited 'Abdu'l-Bahá in 1900 was Sarah Farmer, the founder of Green Acre. An article about her work published in *The Saginaw News* (MI) states:

> Two years ago Miss Farmer went – was led, she says – to journey to the Holy Land and to Akka, the headquarters of the Bahai religion . . . The present head of the order is Abbas Effendi, son of Beha. He is a man of overwhelming personality and of extraordinary power. The faith itself of the Behais is in many respects identical with Christianity, in it Miss Farmer believes she has found the common faith in which all devout souls may unite and yet be free. To establish this divine union on earth Miss Farmer will work henceforth – dreamer, enthusiast and idealist – like her father before her. To this end will much of the teaching at Greenacre this summer be directed.[7]

In a notice about a series of public talks to be given by Arthur Pillsbury Dodge (1849–1915) after his return from the Holy Land, *The Sun* (New York) stated that he 'has been on a visit to Abbas Effendi, better known among the "believers" as "Our Lord", and spent two weeks at Acca and at Haifa'.[8]

In November 1901 *The Sun* (New York) published a three-column article about Bahá'í pilgrims in which early American Bahá'ís such as Sarah Farmer and Phoebe Hearst were again mentioned. In an unsympathetic tone, the newspaper ridiculed the belief wrongly held by some Bahá'ís that 'Abdu'l-Bahá was an incarnation of Christ. The interest of the text, however, lies in the fact that it reproduces a letter sent from Egypt by Lua Getsinger summarizing some of her experiences in 'Akká:

> A VISIT TO ABBAS EFFENDI
>
> On the afternoon of March 20, I said 'Good-bye' to Dr. and Mrs. Kheiralla, Nabiha and Labiba in Haifa (for they were to leave the next day for Port Said) and set out by myself for Acca, the gardener, Abdul Hasim, who happened to be in Haifa, being my sole companion in the carriage, and he made the drive over very pleasant by telling me, in simple Persian, some of the tablets and words of the Manifestation.

When we reached the city, our Lord and Seyyed Yahya were standing near the gate, but we passed them without speaking or noticing them apparently, for there were many of the Turkish soldiers standing about – and went directly to the house, where I was most cordially welcomed by the 'Greatest Leaf' and the daughters of our master.

It was nearly dark – so we went to the apartment of the Holy Leaf, where we had tea and then sat talking, waiting for the 'King' to come. At last a servant announced that He was coming, so the two youngest daughters and myself ran out in the court to meet Him. I reached Him first and knelt down before Him, kissing the hem of His robe.

He thereupon took my hand, and, saying in Persian, 'Daughter, welcome', helped me to my feet, and, keeping my hand, walked with me into the house, where I sat down beside Him while He drank some tea – and asked me if I was 'well, happy and content', to which I could only reply that to be in His presence was health, happiness and contentment itself. Then He said:

'I am sending you back to America that you may work to gain a place beside me in the Eternal Kingdom.'

Soon after this dinner was announced and our Master seated me beside Him – then His wife, the 'Greatest Holy Leaf', and His daughters made up the rest of the party, while His sons-in-law waited upon us.

This meal was served according to the Arabic fashion – on a very low table, around which we sat on the floor upon cushions. Once during the meal our Lord took a piece of bread, and putting on it some honey, handed it to me to eat, saying as He did so:

'Let all of your words be as sweetly flavored with kindness to all people – as this bread is flavored by honey.'

When I swallowed this mouthful from His blessed hand I truly felt a great spiritual blessing – my heart was fairly melted by the power of love, and the tears fell like rain over my cheeks. The 'Greatest Leaf' took her handkerchief, and, wiping my eyes, said:

'You are blessed – be happy.'

Indeed I was happy – my tears were tears of joy! After the meal was over I poured the water on His hands while He washed His face (a custom in the Orient after eating); then He handed me the towel and I did likewise – He saying, after I had finished:

'Now you must go and wash from the faces of the people the clouds of ignorance, and from their hearts the love of this world – that they may receive the Spirit of Truth and shine as lamps in the Kingdom!'

NEW YEAR CELEBRATION

He then went out to see some of the officials and I spent the evening with the 'Greatest Leaf' and the daughters. We were chanting tablets and I was trying hard to tell them in Persian something about the Believers in America, and succeeded quite well for the little time I have studied the language, though sometimes we had a good laugh over my queer accent, especially on words containing the gutteral sounds. They never tire of hearing about the work in America, and the four daughters are studying English very diligently so they can speak to the pilgrims as they come to Acca in the future. We retired about 11 o'clock, and I was very happy indeed.

Next morning very early the Babis in Acca began to assemble at the house of our Lord, the ladies going to the room of the 'Holy Leaf' and the men remaining downstairs. The occasion of this gathering was on account of March 21st being New Year's Day, according to the Babis, so it was a feast day.

Our Lord came into the room and gave to everybody some sweets from His hand, after which Rooha Khanum, one of his daughters, chanted a beautiful tablet. Then He arose, and, saying a few words of welcome, went to the room occupied by the men.

There He gathered all of the children together and gave each of them a few coins, about ten or fifteen cents, which made them all delighted and very happy, of course, because He gave it to them. After drinking tea and visiting a little while, they all went away.

Then we had lunch, and directly after prepared to make my last visit to the tomb of the Manifestation. I went in a closed carriage with Rooha Khanum, and upon our arrival we went into a small room where we remained hidden until all of the others had made the visit with our Master and departed.

AT BEHA'U'LLAH'S TOMB

Then He came and told us to come out, which we did – the three of us then being in that sacred place alone! Immediately He led the way to the room where lies the precious casket which contained the most brilliant jewel that ever shone upon this earth – Beha'u' llah – and there He lifted up his voice in supplication for me – (worm of the dust that I am! Oh God, my heart burns like fire and my tears flow like rain when I think of it!) – asking that I should receive the confirmation of the Holy Spirit, and go forth to work in the cause of God, guiding souls to the Kingdom.

What this day was to me no one can ever know! My work, my words, my deeds must tell in the future whether or not He prayed for me in vain! I can only say I wanted to fall at His feet then and there, and give my heart, my soul and my life for the dear and sacred mouth that had spoken in my behalf!

I then prayed for our teacher who was the means of giving us the Truth in America, for I felt that if I should live a thousand years I could never ask God enough to repay him for what he has done for me and for those I love in my own dear native land. I can never do it; God only can pay my deep debt of gratitude by answering my supplications for his welfare.

As we turned away, my eyes lingered lovingly upon the sacred place – and in my heart I could only feebly thank God for His great mercy and many blessings which I can never deserve, though I give my life for His sake by shedding my blood in His cause – which I pray may be my happy lot – when His will in me is done!

ABBAS' EXECUTIVE ABILITY

It was dark when we reached the house of the Master in Acca, so we had dinner soon after. The Master was not present as He was obliged to go away on business directly after our return, to the house of one of the government officials.

We had a pleasant evening in the apartment of the 'Greatest Leaf' reading tablets, singing, visiting, etc. – after which we retired.

Next morning, March 22, Mr. Getsinger came and was welcomed by our Lord, who kissed him tenderly on both cheeks and bade him sit beside Him while He wrote many tablets, occasionally smiling and speaking a few words to him, asking after his health, if he were happy, etc. – though writing all the time. The great power of the Spirit is very apparent when He is thus occupied, and it is a blessing to be in His presence.

All the day long he was very busy as many people came to him, but in the evening he came into the room where His son-in-law, Mousin Effendi, Mr. Getsinger and myself were sitting (we bowing before him as he entered) and sat down upon the sofa, telling my husband to sit by his side, while he motioned me to my accustomed place at his feet.

A MESSAGE TO AMERICA

Then, putting one arm around him and laying Mr. Getsinger's head on His shoulder, at the same time gently stroking my head with His other hand, He began talking to us, His son-in-law interpreting what He said.

'My children,' He began, 'tomorrow you leave us, and while we would love to see you always, would always love to have you with us, it is better that you should go and work in the cause of God, for thereby He will open upon your faces the door of His gifts and shower upon you His blessings.

'Have no fears, God is with you, and with all those who are striving to advance His Truth throughout your country. You must say to all the Believers in America that I love them and pray for them, and in turn I desire that they love and pray for each other, ever seeking to be united together, living in harmony and concord, for where division is, God is not. The law of His whole universe is unity, and discord must in no wise enter in among you.

'You must be kind to each other and act toward each other like true children of the Kingdom – thus you will all please me and please our Father Who art in heaven.'

DIVIDED BREAD AND SYRUP

Oh, if you could have seen the expression of love and tenderness on His face as He uttered these words – it seemed that His whole great, noble soul was pleading for the complete union in every respect of the Believers in America.

Oh, I beg of all of you to love each other as He, our Lord, loves all of us. If you see faults in each other, overlook them quickly and forgive them – for His dear sake!

He then sent His son-in-law for some bread and syrup, made from the juice of pomegranates, which he brought and placed before

Him on a low table. Our Master took the bread and breaking it dipped it into the syrup and gave a piece to Mr. Getsinger, another to me, and took one Himself; then told us to eat it – which we did – it tasting most delicious, after which He, smiling sweetly, said:

'Now I send you out into the world to give to the hungry souls who are seeking to know their God – the "Bread of Life", which is the Word of God, and to show them how sweet is the "Water of Life", which is faith in God.'

Then He talked about our journey, inquiring most carefully how long it would take, and telling us, when we reached Cairo, that we should see Mirza Abdul Fazl and Abdul Karim, who would tell us some things we wished to know. (Mirza Abdul Fazl is, we find, a most learned man. He knows the Bible by heart and is a great historian.) He then told us that He wished us to be in America in six weeks after we left Acca, so our stay in Cairo must be short. Arising and bidding us 'good night', He went to sleep.

THE LAST DAY

Thursday, March 23rd, our last day at the Holy Household, was a beautiful day. Early in the morning Rooha Khanum called me and arising hastily I went with her to the room of the 'Greatest Leaf', where the Master was sitting.

He bade me welcome as I entered, and I knelt before Him, kissing His hand, and then sat down at His feet beside the 'Holy Leaf', and we drank tea together. As I looked at Him and thought 'I must leave Him today', the tears came to my eyes and my heart was very heavy, though I tried hard to conceal my feelings.

He noticed it and said: 'Do not cry – be happy. I will go with you in spirit –the separation of the body is nothing. I will go with you.'

I dried my eyes and went with Him to the room where He writes, and with Rooha Khanum sat down while He began His work for the day. He took up Mr. Chase's picture which was on the divan beside Him – also one of Mr. Clark and one of Mr. Struven (pupils of mine in Ithaca) – and, looking at them, kissed first one and then another, then turned and said:

'You must tell them that I kissed their pictures and am glad to have them; that they are my sons and my heart longs to see them so that I may kiss them.'

THE PARTING

Soon after He called Mr. G. into the room and gave him a bottle containing juice of pomegranate; also to each of us a small bottle of oil of roses.

Shortly before noon He went out and we watched Him as He walked through the court, for we wanted to see Him as much as possible. After a little time He returned and sat down to luncheon with us, one on each side of Him.

We could scarcely swallow for we well knew it was our last meal with Him, and the thought of parting was breaking our hearts! As we left the table, a servant said:

'The carriage is ready.'

So then began the 'good-byes' which were painful in the extreme, though everybody was trying to be brave, but it was impossible – we all cried – and when we went to our Lord I was faint and sick.

He came quickly from the room and, taking me by the hand, led me down one flight of stairs, and I pressed His hand to my lips, while He turned away and silently kissed Mr. Getsinger – then left us hastily.

When I reached the court below it seemed that the sun grew dark for I realized I would not see Him again, and the pain of it was awful!

We rode in silence back to Haifa and very soon went on board the steamer. From the deck we watched Acca fade out of sight, and then I knew that only my body was going away for I had left my heart there – at His feet.

Please give my love to all the Believers, and tell them to all be firm in the faith for this is the Glorious Truth and we will live forever and ever. I am yours faithfully in the cause of God.[9]

The Getsingers visited the Holy Land again in 1904 and at their return further articles relating their experiences were published in a number of newspapers. This excerpt from one of them provides guidance on Lua's personal habits:

For nearly a year Mrs. Getsinger remained at Acca, a member of the household of 'The Master'. While there she received daily instructions. When she was about to leave to take up her work, Abdul-Baha-Abbas gave her this charge:

> 'Never permit yourself to want what you do not need. When your wants become needs, you will always find them supplied, for your Father knows what is necessary and will give it to you. Dress in such a way that your outward appearance will be a comfort to the poor and an example to the rich. Let it be uniform, that your appearance may be a symbol signifying your recognition of material things as merely temporary necessities.'[10]

The *New York Herald* also published an account by Lua Getsinger which explains how 'Abdu'l-Bahá brought together people of all lands: '"The Master has never declared himself to be the Christ,"' stated Getsinger, after explaining how 'Abdu'l-Bahá brought together people of all lands, adding:

> He surely manifests the Christ holy spirit in his daily life, which is one of purity, simplicity, loving acts and godly counsel, and by such fruits can he best be judged. His is a life of divine servitude, and a glorious example for all who are desirous of promulgating brotherhood and peace among mankind. I have never known him to command another to do anything which he has not already fulfilled.[11]

The prominent North American Bahá'í Laura Clifford Barney also visited the Holy Land in 1900. Her social position in Washington made her and her family the subject of many newspaper articles which often mentioned the fact that she was a Bahá'í. An article published in *The Sun* (New York) on 28 September 1902 carried portions of her account of her pilgrimage:

> The Babs, or Behaists, look upon Acre as the followers of Mahomet do upon Mecca, as the Holy City, and all the believers who are financially able to go there do so.
>
> Among those who have been is Arthur Pilsbury Dodge, who has compiled a book about the 'New Holy City', to which Miss Barney has contributed an account of her interview with the Master. Miss Barney's contribution is interesting as showing the attitude of a woman follower of the head of this faith.
>
> She is a firm believer in Abbas Effendi, whom she calls 'a perfect

being'. Her account of her welcome at his home in Acre, or more strictly speaking, outside of the city, for he is a State prisoner, and the place of his semi-confinement is near Acre, was written to her cousin, Miss Goin, in this city.

The book has not yet been published. In her account of her meeting with Abbas Effendi. Miss Barney gives the following as the greeting she received:

'You brought me your soul and I took it. You will learn that it is mine. The spirit will come into you with increasing force, for your being must become as a temple in which the truth of God can dwell.'

Miss Barney was the guest overnight of Abbas Effendi, and the next day, before she took her departure, he said to her:

'Last night I dreamed of you; it was a beautiful vision, and I prayed God it might come true.

'Yesterday your greatest joy was to remain by my side; now you say that your greatest joy is to sacrifice this desire and to follow my bidding.

'I promised to send for you by a special messenger to come to me again, and I have done it. My spirit has entered your soul, but you must cut your body from the world; then your soul can grow rapidly.

'Verily, the spirit is strong, but the weak body must be cast aside. Soon your eyes will be illuminated.

'You should thank God and praise Him that he has allowed you to reach this sacred mount, and, as you are turning away with warmth, so do I love you deeply. It gives me joy to see you approach me, and from my heart I bless you.'

It seems that after Miss Barney made her first visit to the 'Master', she had only reached Paris on her way to New York when his messenger notified her that she was to return to Acre, and it is to this fact that Abbas Effendi refers in his remarks above. She was greatly touched by this proof of the interest taken in her by the 'Master' and she said to him:

'My Lord, how can I ever thank you for all the blessings you have showered upon me?'

'I shall pray the Father,' he replied, 'to multiply these spiritual gifts forever.' 'Master,' inquired Miss Barney, 'may I go and live with the lepers so that I shall be able to instruct them in your truth?'

'Their disease is not yet to be cured,' he answered; 'but you may give them money and go to their hospitals, but I do not wish you to go and live with them.'

'Master, what am I to do? My life is at your disposal; direct it.'

'Remain in Paris to teach Babism,' said Abbas Effendi.

'Shall I continue my study of art and theatricals with the aim of going on the stage?'

'If you wish to do so.'

'No, Master, tell me which is better; leave my studies or not.'

'Cut your heart from even your studies,' Abbas Effendi said. 'But continue with them if you desire to do so.'

'No Master. I will follow your command. But I will not have strength to teach in Paris; I am too weak to face that city. If I should live there surrounded by my past dreams and ambitions, its worldly attractions will have too great a hold upon my heart.'

'I need you in Paris,' insisted Abbas Effendi; 'sow the seeds of Babism there. I need you for that work.'

'But Master,' implored Miss Barney, 'I know my weakness and tremble at the task you set me.'

'It is hard,' replied Abbas Effendi. 'It is the most difficult place in which to teach Babism, and that is the reason I wish to place you there; and there you are to accomplish your task.'

'Then, my Lord, give me strength to fulfill your command, for now it is no longer your wish, but mine.'

'I will pray to the Father,' replied Abbas Effendi, 'that the light may shine through you – even into the darkest part of Paris.'

'Master, then will I stay, awaiting your further commands,' replied Miss Barney.

'You may go to other places,' Abbas Effendi continued, 'but your headquarters are to be at Paris.'

'Master,' said Miss Barney, 'then I shall be able to free myself from the restraint of my family and my position. May I mingle freely with the fallen?'

'Christ sat at meat with the publicans and sinners,' said Abbas Effendi. 'Follow Him.'

Miss Barney was thrown from a carriage several years ago and suffered a severe injury to one hip which has caused a lameness, and she was referring to this accident when she asked:

'Master, shall I continue to take care of my leg? It requires so much time and money.'

The answer was:

'No, when the proper time comes God will care for you. It is He that wished you to be injured. It is a great blessing given you in order to make you advance in Babism; it is a great blessing.'

'I am feeble for the task you set me. So, Master, you must always help me.'

'Fear not, for I am ever with you,' said Abbas Effendi. 'All that you ask for with a pure heart shall be given to you. Your stay here has been short but I pray that the result thereof will continue forever. A slight shower can fertilize the earth. Pray to have the strength to bear the worthless kingdom of men so that you may enter the Kingdom of God. Every day your face shines brighter with your spiritual development. I give you this precious letter. Keep it. In years to come all your family will be proud to know that you received it from me. You must not cry at leaving me. I am ever with you and love you very much.'[12]

Barney, accompanied by her mother, visited the Holy Land for a third time in 1904 and the press again wrote about her travels. On 30 October, for instance, *The Washington Times* published a half-page article about the Bahá'í Faith which included a portrait of 'Abdu'l-Bahá and a reference to the presence in America of Mírzá Abu'l-Faḍl-i-Gulpáygání (1844–1914), who had been sent to America by 'Abdu'l-Bahá to help in the consolidation of the Bahá'í communities. The article also reported Barney's efforts to improve conditions for 'Abdu'l-Bahá in 'Akká, whose situation had worsened since 1901 owing to the machinations of the Covenant-breakers in the Holy Land.

From the walled city of Akka, in far Syria, under the dominion of the Turkish Empire, there has come a story of the rescue from captivity of the head of the Babist faith by a prominent society girl of Washington. It is known that the Turkish government has relaxed its severe ruling against the person of Abbas Effendi, 'the greatest branch' of the Beha's faith, and that he is now permitted to visit the tomb of his father, Beha Ullah, several miles beyond the walls of

Akka, and to make short journeys in the neighboring parts of Syria, and rumor is insistent that the Ottoman government has made these concessions because of the pressure brought by the European governments at the solicitation of Miss Laura Clifford Barney, of this city.

The story is neither affirmed nor denied, but it is known that Miss Barney made a round of the embassies and legations before her departure from Washington last spring. The British ambassador, Sir Mortimer Durand, and Chekib Bey, the representative of the Turkish government, were among those visited. Since that time Miss Barney has been in Akka and it is said that her efforts have been energetically continued and finally crowned with success . . .

Three years ago word came to the followers of the master in this country by way of Port Said that the Turkish government, at the request of the heads of certain religious sects in close touch with the government, and having influence in Constantinople, had changed their conduct toward the master and had ordered his confinement to the city of Akka. This was the occasion of great grief to the members of the faith here in America. It is believed that Miss Barney has since that time devoted her energies to effect his release and have restored to him the liberty he had formerly enjoyed.

In a letter to a friend in Washington Miss Barney tells how the governor of Akka visited the master on the 6th of last August and invited him to drive in his carriage to the tomb of his father. This meant, of course, that his former liberty was to be restored. She was among the number of the faithful who immediately went to the home of the master and begged him to accept that invitation.

CONSIDERED WISHES OF AMERICANS

Abbas Effendi turned to her and asked if his going would give pleasure to the followers in America. Miss Barney assured him that it would, whereupon he immediately agreed to go. The present governor knew the master at the time of his stay at Adrianople and entertains a high regard for him as do all the Turkish officials who have been associated with him. It is believed that his influence was added to the efforts of Miss Barney and others to have the severe orders of the Turkish government modified . . .[13]

In 1906 the same newspaper published the following article after Laura Barney's return from 'Akká:

> When Miss Laura Barney, a leader in the Capital's smart set, returns from Syria to her home in this city about the middle of February, the beginning of a new era in the propagation of Bahaism, the strange new cult which has taken firm hold among the fashionable of Washington, will have dawned . . .
>
> Miss Barney went to visit the 'Master' at his home in Acre, and remained for some time a member of the household. On her return she was the most active of the members in town of the new cult, and at her own expense had many writings translated, even paying the expenses of a Persian teacher, who spent the whole winter here.
>
> About a year and a half ago, Miss Barney again went to Acre, and has since spent most of her time in the 'Master's' own home listening to his teachings and absorbing this faith which teaches that, as Christ was the Incarnation of God the Son, Beha-Ullah, the father of Abdul-Baha, was the Incarnation of God the Father, and that the whole world will ultimately accept this faith of Bahaism and thus bring about the millennium.[14]

Many other Bahá'ís also visited the Holy Land and some, for example, Colonel Nathan Fitz-Gerald[15] and Isabella Brittingham, were interviewed by the press.[16]

3

VISITORS IN HAIFA

With the amnesty for political prisoners and prisoners of conscience decreed by the new regime established in the Ottoman Empire after the triumph of the revolution of the Young Turks in 1908, 'Abdu'l-Bahá was now free to leave the walls of the city of 'Akká. He gradually moved His family into a new house in Haifa over the next year and was better able to oversee the construction of the Shrine of the Báb on Mount Carmel. On 21 March 1909 He was finally able to lay to rest the sacred remains of the Herald of the Bahá'í revelation which for almost 59 years had been hidden.

In Haifa, 'Abdu'l-Bahá continued to receive many visitors, including a number of westerners who wanted to know more about the famous prisoner of whom they have heard from Bahá'ís or read about in Phelps's book and in the many articles on the Bahá'í Faith published at the time.

Ethel S. Stevens

One such westerner to visit 'Abdu'l-Bahá in Haifa was the traveler, writer and scholar Ethel Stefana Stevens (1879–1972), later known as Lady Drower. In her travels she associated for over six months with 'Abdu'l-Bahá and the Bahá'ís in the Haifa-'Akká area. She afterwards published *The Mountain of God* (1911), a novel containing abundant references to 'Abdu'l-Bahá and the Bahá'í Faith. Proficient in Arabic and other Semitic languages, Stevens some years later became a renowned scholar in the Mandaean religion, which she was able to study while living in Iraq.

Coinciding with the release of her book, she wrote two articles in which, in vivid language, she described her meetings with 'Abdu'l-Bahá and confessed her deep admiration for Him and the teachings of the Bahá'í Faith.

The first, and longer, of these articles, was published in London in *The Fortnightly Review* in June 1911 and was entitled 'Abbas Effendi: His Personality, Work and Followers'. Stevens introduces her article thus:

> The proclaiming of the Constitution throughout the Turkish dominions brought a belated freedom to a famous Oriental prisoner, the living head of one of the most remarkable movements which have appeared in the last century. Imprisoned for forty-two years in the penal settlement of Akka in Syria, the prisoner, now a man of sixty-eight, is at last permitted to leave the precincts of that unhealthy little town, and take up his residence on the airier slope of Mount Carmel, across the bay. Any day in Haifa you may meet an old man whose flowing white hair, gathered up beneath his snowy turban, proclaims his aristocratic birth, accompanied at the slight distance prescribed by respect by Persian followers with folded hands. His long white beard, his blue eyes slightly flecked with brown, his commanding bearing, his dignified walk, his keen kindly face, all proclaim him to be someone of importance and distinction. He wears the simple robe of white linen and grey linsey customary in Persia. This man is Abbas Effendi, or Abdul Baha (the Servant of Baha), the recognized head of the Bahai movement throughout the world.
>
> Bahais have been accused by their Persian enemies of working an enchantment on those who visit them, so that an intoxication, an exultation like that of the hashish smoker, seizes their intellect and enchains their senses, lifting them into a dream-world of illusion. And anyone who has come into close contact with them, as I have been permitted to do during the past six months, is inclined to endorse this, for it is impossible to be with them long without feeling the infection of this strange enthusiasm, this spiritual hashish, which has sent men to martyrdom with smiles on their faces and joyous ecstasy in their hearts . . .

The article continued for some pages with a summary the history of the Bahá'í Faith. The rest of the article focused on the figure of 'Abdu'l-Bahá:

> Abbas Effendi, his eldest son, who during his father's lifetime had

been his untiring help and companion, had been carefully trained by his father to assume the leadership of the Bahai Community and to become the head of the movement. With selfless enthusiasm he devoted himself to his life-work, and was recognized by all the Bahais as their head and loved teacher. He was preeminently fitted for this important office. He has in the highest degree that great gift which we call personality. His readily-given sympathy, his understanding of human nature, his power of interesting himself in every human soul which asks his advice and help, have made him passionately beloved by his people. Above all, he has that subtler quality of spirituality which is felt rather than understood by those with whom he comes in contact. He receives the long stream of pilgrims, inquirers and pupils who come to Akka, and now in Haifa, with unfailing gentleness, geniality, and courtesy. He takes a personal interest in every one of the Persians in Haifa – there are now about thirty families, some of which were exiled with Baha U'llah, others Bahais who have voluntarily come to Syria in order to be near the Master. He names their children for them, helps to educate them when they are unable to afford education for themselves, and advises them in their material as well as their spiritual life.

It is his habit to receive the men of the community every evening an hour after sunset, and however long and tiring the day's work has been, he never refuses to admit them and talk with them. It has been my privilege to assist several times at these evening receptions. The Master's house is simply built and simply furnished. He loves two things: light and flowers, so that the room in which he receives his guests has many windows, and a vase full of flowers stands always on the table. For the rest, the walls are bare and white, the woodwork is painted white, and the chairs and divans ranged around the room are covered with an unpretentious light-coloured cotton holland material. At seven o'clock the Persians enter together, their hands folded and their heads bent, and, leaving their shoes outside in the Oriental fashion, seat themselves round the room. For each man as he comes in Abbas Effendi has a kindly greeting, a tactful remark, a personal inquiry, or sometimes a humorous sally which brings a smile to their grave faces. Among them is often a pilgrim, a believer who has travelled from a great distance to see and learn from the Master. Abbas Effendi will draw him out; and interesting discussion follow, for the pilgrim may be a Zoroastrian from North Persia, a Parsee from India, or even a Japanese. After a moment the talk invariably turns on the spiritual life, and upon the twin *Leit-Motive* of the Master's teaching – Love and Unity . . .

He is keenly interested in the political, social, and educational movements in the Western world which seem like the beginning of the fulfillment of Baha U'llah's predictions. He has discussed Esperanto with me, which may be destined to become the universal language prophesied by Baha U'llah; the efforts of Tolstoi and the Peace Conference towards the abolition of war, and the great philanthropic institutions of Europe and America. He speaks confidently of the day when Chauvinism, the wish to further the interests of one nation at the expense of another, which too often passes for legitimate patriotism, will be replaced by the endeavor to further the interests of humanity at large; of a time when the universal language will be taught in schools founded on an international basis whose educational system shall have no religious bias, no racial bias, no political bias; of an era when the attention of inventors, instead of being directed towards the construction of engines of war and destruction, will be exclusively devoted to the improvement and amelioration of the human race and the alleviation of its miseries. He discusses, too, the scientific questions of the day, and has opinions to offer which are of the most interesting nature.

And this versatility, this capacity to reason and form suggestive theories on any subject, is the more amazing when one reflects that Abbas Effendi has had no schooling at all. He was nine years old when he was exiled with his father to Baghdad, and during his forty-two years of close imprisonment in Akka there was little opportunity for study, cut off as the prisoners were from relations with the world and culture and science. The same might be said of his father . . .

A Frenchman of great intelligence who has lived for many years in Haifa in an official capacity, and who often goes to Abbas Effendi's house to discuss the questions of the day with him, said to me with admiration, speaking of such a discussion, 'What a mind! What intuition he has!' And in the early days at Akka, when Abbas Effendi was appointed by his father to receive the visitors who came to their house – for Baha U'llah rarely admitted any to his presence except the faithful – controversialists and religionists of all kinds would come to him with the purpose of confuting him with their arguments. But Abbas Effendi was able to answer them all; and so great is the respect in which he is held, even among the fanatical Mohammedans, that ceremonial visits have been made to him by most of the principal Moslem theologians who have come to Akka or Haifa.

Another side of his character is his charity. He never makes his charities openly, or even speaks of them; but you hear of them in roundabout ways. A devout Catholic once said to me: 'Abbas Effendi helps our work among the poor every year, and –', she paused – 'if I were only permitted to tell you of the secret good he has done!'

And once in Damascus I ran across a poor Persian, who asked me to take his respectful greetings and a letter to the Master. He spoke of him with emotional affection, and then told me that during the late Adana massacres his shop had been burnt down and his father killed by the Kurds, he himself being left for dead. Abbas Effendi sent him monetary help, wrote him kindly letters which gave the unfortunate man the courage to face life again, and started him afresh. Nor, in spite of his vast correspondence, does he cease to take an interest in his protégé.

And the Master himself lives in the utmost plainness. I have said that the furniture of the house is not rich. His own bedroom is of a Spartan simplicity. His food is very frugal: a little rice and a plate of soup will often represent his biggest meal, which, by the way, is always concluded by the ceremonial washing of the face and hands by water poured over them by a servant, and the rinsing of the mouth in the Persian fashion. His wife and his four daughters clothe themselves in the plain Persian house-dress of print in summer or merino in winter, wear no jewellery, and when they go out of doors dress themselves in the ordinary modest out-of-door habiliments of the Turkish and Persian women – the nun-like black chadder, or black mantle and hood-cape, which covers them completely, and the ruband, which falls like a thick curtain before their faces.

And this leads me to speak about the family of Abbas Effendi. He is an advocate of monogamy, which he thinks is the higher conception of marriage; and though his only son died in infancy and lies buried in the little Persian cemetery outside Akka, he has never taken a second wife, as Persian custom permits. His daughters address their father as 'Agha' (lord), speak of him as the 'Sarkar agha' (worship lord), and hold him in the very highest respect as well as affection. Their life is a very busy one, for from morning to evening their services are required for the entertainment of guests, or as translators should foreign ladies be amongst the visitors for they are good linguists, and for the superintendence of a very irregular household. Oriental hospitality is a duty, but when the visitors are so numerous and frequent as at Abbas Effendi's house, it must become a duty not without its burdens. 'We never know how many people to prepare for when ordering meals,' his daughter said to me once with a smile. 'We have to be ready for any emergency. Sometimes when a number of Persian pilgrims arrive we may have as many as twenty unexpected guests to our evening meal.' In the *anderun*, or women's apartments, the samovar is always boiling, for every visitor is served with a glass of tea in the Persian fashion, and this entails constant labour. But it is cheerfully performed, and though I have practically lived in the house during a very busy time, I never heard an impatient word or complaint.

No Bahai visits Haifa without first receiving a permission from the Master. He does not receive everyone who wishes to see him. Those who have nothing but idle curiosity to prompt their visit are not accorded interviews. Indeed, I am told that even to believers he is sometimes difficult of access, so that I have been doubly fortunate in seeing him almost daily and in having continual long interviews with him. During these interviews, one characteristic, not, I think, particularly noticed by those who have written about him, has particularly struck me. That is, his keen sense of humour. He has the Oriental habit of illustrating his teaching with stories, and sometimes these are of a delightfully ironical and amusing nature . . .

His philosophy is essentially human, in the highest and broadest sense of the word. He directs the attention of humanity not to the letter, but to the spirit of religion. I remember that once our discussion fell upon the question of asceticism, and I asked whether the crushing of the desires and needs of the flesh, in his opinion, helped the soul in its growth into the spiritual state.

He replied:–

Asceticism is not necessary. A soul grows by the exercise of

> human virtues, and the observance of human morals; and by the Divine Favour. The extreme asceticism of the saints was superstition . . .

On another occasion an American visitor asked a question about fasting, and whether it would not be beneficial to the spiritual life. He replied:–

> Fasting is a symbol. Fasting signifies abstinence from lust. Physical fasting is a symbol of that abstinence, and is a reminder; that is, just as a person abstains from physical appetites, he is to abstain from self-appetites and self-desires. But mere abstention from food has no effect on the spirit. It is a mere symbol, a reminder. Otherwise, it is of no importance. Fasting for this purpose does not mean entire abstinence from food. The golden rule as to food is, Do not take too much or too little. Moderation is necessary. There is a sect in India called the Jats, who practise extreme abstinence, and gradually reduce their food until they exist on almost nothing. But their intelligence suffers. A man is not fit to do service for God in brain or body if he is weakened by lack of food. He cannot see clearly.

The American then told him of experiments made in America, whereby the mind was supposed to benefit psychically by abstinence. He replied:–

> It is imagination . . . To sum up, God knows better than all. He has given us an appetite; therefore we should eat. If the body is deprived of what is necessary to it, the mind suffers. God asks of us according to our capacity. If a man who has only sufficient strength to carry fifty kilos be burdened with a hundred kilos, he will fall. Moderation and commonsense must be used.

He considers superstition and interest in miraculous phenomena as also tending to divert the mind from the pursuit of real and practical religion . . .

I once asked if prayer was necessary, since presumably God knows the wishes of all hearts. The Master replied:–

> If one friend feels love for another, he will wish to say so. Though he knows that the friend is aware that he loves him, he will still wish to say so. If there is anyone that you love, do you not seek an opportunity to speak with him, to speak lovingly with him, to bring him gifts, to write him letters? If you did not feel such a desire, it would be that you did not love your friend. God knows the wishes of all hearts. But the impulse to prayer is a natural one, springing from man's love for God.
>
> If there be no love; if there be no pleasure or spiritual enjoyment in prayer, do not pray. Prayer should spring from love, from the desire of the person to commune with God. Just as a lover never ceases from wishing to communicate with the beloved, so does the lover of God always wish for constant communication with the Deity. Prayer need not be in words, but rather in thought and attitude. But if this love and this desire are lacking, it is useless to try to force them. Words without love mean nothing. If a person talks to you as an unpleasant duty, with no love or pleasure in his meeting with you, do you wish to converse with him? Efforts should first be made to make attachment to God.

'But how is this attachment to be made?' I asked. 'How is the love of God to be obtained? There are many people in the world who admit the existence of a Deity, but without any emotion.' The reply was:–

> Knowledge is love. Study, listen to exhortations, think, try to understand the wisdom and greatness of God . . . The soil must be fertilized before the seed be sown.

Another time, speaking of love, he said:-

> Unity is love: it cannot be established without love. Therefore try, as far as possible, to be filled with love. Love is perpetual life, the most perfect vitality. Consider how love has gathered

us together from the East and the West! If there were no love between us, our friendship would have been concluded by salutations, such as 'Good Morning' and 'Good Evening'. Love draws us in friendship to the people of every race and religion. From whom we breathe the fragrance of this love again, he is a Bahai, of the people of Baha . . . The highest love is independent of any personal advantages which we may draw from the love of the friend. If you love truly, your love for your friend will continue, even if he treat you ill. A man who really loves God, will love Him whether he be ill, or sad, or unfortunate. He does not love God because He has created him – his life may be full of disaffections and miseries. He does not love God because He has given him strength of youth, because old age will surely come upon him. The reason for his love is not because he is grateful for certain mercies and benefits. No.

The lover of God desires and adores Him because He is Perfection and because of His Perfections. Love should be the very essence of love, and not dependent on outward manifestations.

A moth loves the light, though his wings are burnt. Though his wings are singed, he throws himself against the flame. He does not love the light because it has conferred some benefit upon him. Therefore he hovers round the light, though he sacrifice his wings.

This is the highest degree of love. Without this abandonment, this ecstasy, love is imperfect.

The Lover of God loves Him for Himself, not for his own sake.

This high, mystical fervor, these spiritual ideals, constitute the real life of Bahaism . . .

This, and the practical endeavor to bring about the Kingdom of love upon earth, occupies their energies. I have often commented to outsiders upon the atmosphere of radiating happiness which surrounds most Bahais. I have found them sincere, unlike other Orientals. And their warm hospitality and friendliness is unfailing. I cannot enumerate the many kindnesses which I have received, kindnesses which I have been totally unable to return in any way . . .

Once I asked him: 'What is essential in the belief of a Bahai?' We were in the low, white house of one of the Persian exiles at the foot of Mount Carmel, and the wind conveyed the scent of almond-blossom from the hillside. Abbas Effendi was seated on the divan by the open window, and was gazing towards the sea beneath us. The kindly face beneath the white turban was turned to me after a moment, and with a smile in his tired blue eyes he answered:–

> To be a Bahai simply means to love all the world, to love humanity and try to serve it; to work for the universal peace and the universal brotherhood.

I have said that Abbas Effendi is fond of flowers. He is, in fact, like his father, Baha U'llah, an ardent lover of nature. His favorite flower is the pink Persian rose, not unlike a larger Dorothy Perkins, with pink, fragile petals and an extremely sweet perfume. He likes to have these roses strewn upon the table whenever he has guests. He has a great love for Mount Carmel, and I have often met him with a few followers on the little platform, planted with rose trees, before the tomb of the Bab half-way up the mountainside; for the body of the martyred saint was secured by his followers and eventually interred on Carmel. From this little rose-garden, tended lovingly by the Persians, one has a wonderful view of the flower-covered slopes of the mountain, the little red and white town of Haifa below and then the wide blue bay with its long crescent of sandy beach, on the further side of which Akka lies close to the water's edge within her fortified walls, white as the breast of a sea-gull.

One April afternoon, when we had met by chance in the rose-garden and were afterwards drinking glasses of Persian tea in one of the cool, high ante-chambers of the tomb, he remarked:–

> This mountain is a holy mountain: it has always been a sacred place. The prophets have always loved this mountain. Christ has trodden on its paths; Elijah lived in it. The wind is sweet on it, the flowers are many, the view is wonderful. When you come up the mountain, there are many fragrances which reach you: the clean air gladdens you, the beauty refreshes you. So

> the mind is made pure on this mountain, the thoughts are cleansed, the spirit turns to God.

> Every Persian pilgrim visits Akka when he comes to Haifa, as it was the scene of Baha U'llah's long imprisonment, and the spot from which most of his teachings were given out into the world. I, too, went, curious to see the environments of Abbas Effendi's youth and manhood, and the spots which are regarded as hallowed by Bahais of the East and West. I went with a gentle old Persian and his wife and daughter in one of the high carriages used for the voyage between Haifa and Akka . . .
>
> There we visited the house in which Abbas Effendi lived before his removal to Haifa. His once carefully-tended garden in the fore-court had been trampled down ruthlessly by the lawless Arabs; but within the little garden was still sweet with flowers, and weeded and watered by the few Persians who take care of the place since Abbas Effendi and his family have left . . .

The article then described her visit to the former house of 'Abdu'l-Bahá in 'Akká and some of the Bahá'ís she met in the city, among them the renowned teacher Ḥájí Mírzá Ḥaydar 'Alí with whom she held a conversation, excerpts of which were included in the article. Stevens described some of the places associated with the life of Bahá'u'lláh such as the Citadel and the Garden of Riḍván and also details her visit to His Shrine. The article then concluded with the following words:

> I have spoken at such length of the followers of Baha and his successor, because each contributes by his personal enthusiasm to this other-worldly, fairy-tale atmosphere which constitutes the charm of converse with them. Haidar Ali, the Parsees, the twin gardeners, and my companions are all typical Bahais. And to judge of the strength and vitality of a movement, one judges it not so much by its head as by its followers. There is a power, there is a force in Bahaism which, at least in my opinion, may make it one of the elements to be reckoned with in the history of the future. Sooner or later it must become an important factor in the policies of the Near East. No movement, however rational, has any continued vitality among any Eastern people unless it be religious. Enthusiasm, romance, and

> impulse to action, to the Oriental, are centered entirely in his religious life. Even when he has ceased, under European influences, to believe in his ancient creeds, his subconscious ego is governed by this inherited sense. So that progressivism in the East must, in order to permeate the masses, be a religious progressivism. And this is exactly what Bahaism provides. It appeals to the religious sense. It makes converts in Islam, both Shiah and Sunni. It turns fanaticism into tolerance, retrogression into progression, Saul's fire and sword in their hands into Paul's preaching brotherly love and goodwill . . .[1]

Several publications in England, United States, Egypt and Australia reproduced, reviewed or simply mentioned this article.[2] Stevens's book *The Mountain of God* also received some attention in the press. *The Christian Commonwealth* (London), for instance, published excerpts from a section describing an interview with 'Abdu'l-Bahá.[3]

On December 1911 the second of the articles was published in *Everybody's Magazine* (New York), a literary monthly with a national circulation of 632,500 copies, under the title 'The Light in the Lantern'. The text was preceded by the following introduction from the editor, John O'Hara Cosgrave (1864–1947):

> For seventy years a religion without church, priest, creed, or fixed form of worship has been spreading through the Orient, claiming converts and martyrs by thousands. Love and Unity are its sole principles; and on this broad program believers in various faiths can unite. This movement, called Bahaism, has also extended to Europe, Great Britain, Hawaii, and the United States. In this country the Bahais number thousands, with large assemblies in Boston, New York, Washington, Chicago, Los Angeles, Oakland, Seattle, and Kenosha, Wisconsin. The Mashrak-el-Askar (literally, the Dawning Place of Mention), a great temple where all races and creeds may worship, is about to be built in Chicago. Miss Stevens's thrilling story of Bahaism in its years of persecution, and her sympathetic interpretation of the movement, gather an additional interest from the fact that the Bahai leader, Abd-ul-Baha Abbas, is now making a visit to the Western world. Her acquaintance with Abd-ul-Baha in his Oriental home makes her story authoritative – a first-hand, intimate study.

Stevens's second text about 'Abdu'l-Bahá had some parallels with the article published in *The Fortnightly Review* but most of its contents were original. The article was embellished with a series of drawings of 'Abdu'l-Bahá, Bahá'í holy places and different scenes, made from photographs by William Oberhardt and Neal A. Truslow.[4]

> This Abd-ul-Baha, or Abbas Effendi, as he is more generally known, is truly a remarkable man. That he is the greatest power for good among the two hundred millions of the Moslem world, there can be but little doubt. The success of his proselytism among people whose orthodox Mohammedanism is bred in the bone has been absolutely astounding. Already he has converted to his creed a third of the Persian nation, and in Asia, Europe, America, all the world around those who revere him as the True Light are numbered by the tens of thousands . . .
>
> Almost any afternoon you can see him for yourself if you will stroll in the streets of Haifa, that half-Syrian, half-Teutonic village, where ragged Turkish roustabouts load cargo from a pier which was built for the German emperor to land on, and where the shriek of the Mecca mail train echoes over the very slopes where once the Saviour trod. This servant of Baha is a man with shrewd, kindly, courteous eyes that seem to look into you instead of at you, but that instinctively make you like them and all that goes with them. A keen, sun-tanned, friendly face framed as in silver by his long, white hair and beard; an expression that is alert, intelligent, and serene; a walk that is dignified without being conscious; a carriage that is peculiarly commanding. In him you see an Old Testament patriarch personified. Always he wears the snowy turban, the robe of plain white linen, and the gray wool over garment peculiar to all Persians of high standing, while behind him, at the distance prescribed by respect, walks a group of his disciples with folded hands.
>
> Regard him well, my friends, for in him you behold one of the most significant figures in the religious world to-day; one who is perhaps doing more for the uplifting of the Oriental than any other force; one who has actually suffered for his faith; one whom nearly two millions of people hold in greatest reverence as the Light in the Lantern, the Knowledge within the Gate.
>
> Come with me now to the Master's home in Haifa, that you may

hear from his own lips the simple tenets of the Baha faith. We shall have scant trouble in finding it, for every dragoman, cab-driver, and street urchin in the town will vociferously urge his services as guide to the residence of the Persian Prophet, as Abbas Effendi is locally called. The hour when the sun sinks behind the Samarian hills is his time for receiving visitors; and, however long and tiring his day's work has been, he never refuses to admit and talk with those who have any just claim upon his time, though no Bahai would presume to visit Haifa without first obtaining his permission.

His white-walled, red-roofed, rose-smothered house, different in no respect from the dwellings of the Saviour's day, is as simple within as without, for he lives, though wholly without affectation, in the utmost plainness. Leaving our shoes without the door, after the Oriental fashion, we enter a reception room, spacious, airy, and spotless, its woodwork and undecorated walls painted white, and the low divans that encircle it covered in unpretentious linen. It is a room with many windows, and jars of blushing roses stand on every table, for, as a result of his long imprisonment, perhaps, Abbas Effendi requires a wealth of light and flowers.

Just at sunset, the pilgrims and disciples enter with bent heads and folded hands and seat themselves silently about the room. For each man as he enters, Abbas Effendi has a kindly greeting, a tactful remark, a personal inquiry, or sometimes a humorous sally, which brings a flittering smile to the grave faces – for with these pilgrims this is a solemn and impressive moment. Most of them have suffered for their faith, and many of them have traveled far for this meeting with the Master.

This lean-faced convert at our right is a Fire-Worshipper from the shores of the Caspian; beyond him, he of the yellow skin and silken coat is a Sart from Samarkand; over there is a hungry-looking Parsee from the Punjab, and, in the corner, a keen-faced Japanese. And for each of them the Baha has ready sympathy and sound, comprehensible advice. And therein lies his power. He possesses to a positively miraculous degree the faculty of interesting himself in every human soul that asks his spiritual or material aid, and it is this very power which has made him so passionately beloved by his disciples. But above all, he possesses that subtler quality of spirituality which is felt rather than understood by those with whom he comes in contact. Gentle, genial, and courteous always, he receives, instructs, advises, and assists with unfailing tact and understanding the cosmopolitan stream of pilgrims which flows so steadily and so increasingly toward this little Syrian coast town.

The charities of Abbas are bounded by no horizon of race or creed. The thirty-odd Persian families who followed Baha Ullah into exile have more than once had his son to thank for the clothes they wore and for their daily bread. 'Not a year passes,' a Roman Catholic remarked not long ago, 'that Abbas Effendi does not help our work among the poor, and' – she paused, for his charities are never open – 'if I were only permitted to tell you of the secret good that he has done!' Question them, and the *imams* of the Haifa mosques and the pastor of the German Lutheran Church, the foreign consular agents and the resident manager of the Hedjaz Railway, will tell you the same . . .

Religion aside, is it any wonder that a man with such sympathy for humanity has gained the blind faith and devotion of his people? . . .

That his theories have worked out among those who follow him is evidenced by the dozen nationalities which often sit down at his table in utmost harmony; and this, remember, in a land where religion and fanaticism are all but synonymous; where a true believer will rarely consent to use the dishes that an infidel has handled, much less consent to eat beside him. The Effendi is a keen and clever controversialist; his verbal parries and thrusts are quick as rapier-strokes, as has been learned to their discomfiture by theologians of all creeds who have visited Haifa for the sole purpose of confuting him with their arguments. So highly is he respected, even among the most bigoted followers of Islam, that many Moslem ecclesiastics of note have stopped at Haifa to pay him a visit of ceremony on their way to the Holy Cities . . .

Nor does he confine himself to things spiritual and theoretical. He takes a lively interest in those political, social, and educational movements of the Western world which he holds to be the beginning of the fulfillment of the prophecies of Baha Ullah . . . He discusses, too, the scientific questions of the day, displaying as remarkable a familiarity with the discoveries of Curie, Edison, and Peary as with creeds, dogmas, and beliefs . . .

I have shown you now, as best I am able, what manner of man is this Abbas Effendi who is variously held to be impostor, priest, and prophet. Whether he deserves the title of prophet I do not know; no one knows; that, the future alone can tell. That he is a good man and sincere, there can be no doubt. That the faith which he holds and the creed which he preaches might be followed with benefit by us all, there is no gainsaying. Be you Confucian, Buddhist, Zoroastrian, Christian, Moslem, or Jew, to follow the lantern which Abbas lights can bring you to no harm; to abide by his Rule of Love can be no heresy. He preaches a clean and wholesome creed, and though you may question the divine origin of his mission, there is no denying that he is a sincere, courageous man, a figure whose increasing influence is already world-wide in its significance.[5]

The Rev. Carl D. Case

Another visitor in Haifa was the Rev. Carl Delos Case (1868–1931) who at the time was pastor of the Delaware Av. Baptist Church, Buffalo, and also a leading member of Rotary and a member of the American Religious Education Association. A few days after the visit of 'Abdu'l-Bahá to Buffalo in September 1912, Case published in the *Buffalo Examiner* an account of his visit to the Master in 1910. In this article Case, without losing his sympathetic tone, expressed his disagreement with the Bahá'í teachings on the divinity of Christ:

A VISIT WITH ABDUL BAHA AT HAIFA

BY REV. CARL D. CASE. D.D.

The present tour of Abdul Baha in America recalls vividly a personal visit made two years ago on the venerable religious leader at his own home at Haifa. Armed with a personal letter of introduction from the leader of the Bahaist Assembly in Buffalo, upon arrival at Haifa inquiries were at once made whether it would be possible to have a personal interview. The first questions were answered a little suspiciously by a merchant in the town, but soon the merchant closed his store and went with me to the magnificent home of the Servant of God, as Abdul Baha styles himself, a gift, I understood, from a wealthy American lady.

A half dozen disciples were gathered in the receiving room, and soon the master, as he was called by all, came in and was greeted by the visitors standing. There was no formality, however, and through the interpreter a pleasant greeting was given to the stranger from America. The face was kindly, the eyes were mild yet expressive and searching, and the manners courteous. Later in the evening cake and coffee were distributed, which had the usual tendency of making all feel at home. The conversation of the evening, which, of course, consisted chiefly of questions and more or less lengthy comments by the leader, was upon topics presented many times during the present tour in America, and need not be rehearsed in detail. The Bahaist movement takes the essence of all religions. As Mohammedans respect Christ, Christians should acknowledge Mohamet as a prophet.

The next day was spent with the various other leaders and a visit was made to the great mausoleum of the Bab on the side of Mount Carmel. In the evening at a second interview I was given the honor of a private conversation. We were at once, although speaking on both sides entirely through an interpreter, struggling with the supreme question, which, if understood, forbids the Christian remaining a Christian and being a Bahaist – the Incarnation. Spirit cannot be body, he said, but is only its manifestation. No human being can contain God. Light is not iron, though iron becomes cold and hot, hard and liquid. Iron is iron. Christ was perfect, but now a new manifestation is needed. The rich young man said, 'Good Master', but Christ refused the title. Christ said, 'Thy will be done.' He (not God) was dead in the tomb for three days. God does not change. The divine reality cannot be incarnated. We say enthusiasm lives in such and such a man or justice is embodied in him. So the Word became flesh.

The interview closed with a hearty clasp of both hands. One could not help being impressed. But still the words kept repeating themselves, 'No man cometh unto the Father but by me.'[6]

The *Bible Review*

The *Bible Review* was the monthly organ of the Esoteric Fraternity in California and had a circulation of 800 copies. It was edited by Hiram Erastus Butler (1841–1916), an astrologer, palm reader and author of books on spirituality and esoteric issues. In July 1909 this magazine published in its editorial section a letter by 'Abdu'l-Bahá to Benedict Peeke, son of the Bahá'í Margaret B. Peeke, who had recently passed away and who was herself involved in the esoteric movement.

Reproduced here are the editor's introduction, a letter from Ali Kuli Khan enclosing his translation of the Tablet, and the translation itself:

> Mrs. Peeke was a mystic of the ancient order of the H. B. of L, but as all those great orders wherein reside knowledge have no narrow bigotries to support, she became the Inspectress General of the Martinist Order in America; and she likewise saw good in the Babist movement; she became an active worker in it. We also see good in this movement, for certainly if the teachings of Abdul Beha were followed by the American people we should be a far superior nation. The narrow-minded will say at once: 'I wonder if the editor of this magazine is a Babist; I thought he was an Esoterist.' It is hard for narrow minds to conceive of the possibility of a mind like the late Margaret B. Peeke's, loving goodness, righteousness and truth regardless of all personality, sect, denomination or society, and willing to work for the advancement of whatever will advance the public interest; and we are glad to see indications that she has a noble son who is disposed to take hold of the work where she laid it down and to carry it forward. It is our earnest prayer that God may strengthen him, make him wise and prosper him in the work.

> Washington, D. C. May 6, 1909
> Mr. Benedict Peeke
>
> My dear Mr. Peeke,
>
> A few days after your dear mother's departure, I wrote a long letter to our blessed Abdul Beha asking him to write a tablet in memory of my dear friend Mrs. Margaret B. Peeke. I have now received a Holy Tablet from Him to translate and forward to you. I advise that you write a letter of thanks to the Master and send it to me to forward to Him. I am glad that he addressed it to you. This tablet is so beautiful that I trust you will think it best to send copies to all of Mrs. Peeke's Beha friends and pupils and keep the original for your own self. I am indeed delighted that such a beautiful tablet came for your dear mother.

Trusting that I will hear from you soon, I am sincerely yours.
Mirza Kuli Khan (Persian Consul, Washington, D. C.)

He is God
O thou, daughter of the Kingdom! O thou, esteemed maidservant of God! O thou, Mrs. Peeke!

Pure and sanctified is the Lord of the Kingdom who released thee from this earthly world and led thee unto the Kingdom (Divine World) who took thee into the Pure World out of this world of dust, delivered thee from separation, longing and yearning, and caused thee to soar up to the rose garden of vision and meeting.

O thou, who art attracted unto God! Happy is thy condition! For in this world thou didst devote thy life to spiritual pursuits, didst call people unto the Kingdom with inner attractions night and day, and didst partake of Eternal Life, and of the Meeting of the Lord of the Kingdom. Before long the Queens of the world will be nameless and forgotten, but thou art shining and luminous, like unto a star on the Eternal Horizon. During future centuries thy name will be on all tongues, and thy Eternal Glory will be clear and manifest. Tho this bounty is not at present clear and manifest, but in the future, it will before long become visible and evident. Happy, happy is thy condition, for thou hast become a recipient of the favors of His Highness, the Merciful One, and hasten unto the Assemblage of Meeting, of the beauty of Abha.

O thou, Creator! Glorify this esteemed daughter of the Kingdom of the Divine World, and cause this longing one to attain unto the honor of Thy Union. Give this thirsty one to drink from the fountain of life, and cause this enraptured one to seek rest and peace in Thy Shelter. Grant the wishes of her heart and soul, and make her survivors firm and steadfast in the Right Way, and the Path of the Kingdom, so that they may light the lamp of that attracted one and walk in her footsteps. May her descendants be related to Thy Threshold in this world, and may they be known in Thy Name. Thou art the Clement, the Merciful, and Thou art the Beneficent, the Gracious, the Forgiving, the Powerful. Upon her be Behai Ullah-el Abha. (Sig.) E. E. Abdul-Beha-Abbas.

Translated by Ali Kuli Khan, May 6, 1909. Washington, D. C.[7]

PART II

4

FIRST VISIT TO EGYPT

August 1910–11 August 1911

In late August 1910 'Abdu'l-Bahá left Haifa for Egypt. Only a few knew His plans before His departure. Siyyid Asadu'lláh Qumí, a witness to those days, reported that 'The day he left he visited the Holy Tomb of the Bab on Mt. Carmel, and when he came down from the mountain of the Lord, he went direct to the steamer. This was the first anyone knew about the matter. Within two days he summoned to his presence Shoghi Effendi, Khosro [Áqá Khusraw], and this servant.'[1]

The first stage of 'Abdu'l-Bahá's stay in Egypt was in Port Said. After a few weeks He moved to Alexandria, staying there for most of His sojourn in Egypt except for a period of two months in Cairo.

Bahá'í accounts agree that His presence in Egypt attracted considerable attention from the local press. Mohammad Yazdí, a Bahá'í writing from Alexandria, reported that 'when he ['Abdu'l-Bahá] first arrived in Egypt, a great cry and clamour was raised by the representatives of the people . . . Facts were exaggerated and misrepresentations abounded in every paper.' The situation, however, changed completely as editors and journalists personally met the Master and were impressed by His personality. 'After short time,' added Yazdí in the same report, 'the clouds of misrepresentation were dispelled and the light of reality shone forth with great splendour. So much so that at present there is not one dissenting voice in the land of Egypt about the greatness of Abdul-Baha.'[2]

More than 120 journals were published in the region at the time, including some newspapers in European languages, and further research into the Egyptian press will undoubtedly unearth many previously unknown references to 'Abdu'l-Bahá.

Bahá'í accounts give the titles of some Arabic newspapers that wrote about 'Abdu'l-Bahá. One of them was the daily Muslim, nationalistic and anti-British newspaper *al-Mu'ayyad* (Cairo), one of the most popular Egyptian periodicals of the time. Its editor and founder, the influential Egyptian intellectual and politician Shaykh 'Alí Yúsuf (1863–1925), interviewed the Master in Alexandria and afterwards published an account of their meeting:

> The eminent Mirza Abbas Effendi, Head of the Bahai Faith in Acca, and the centre of authority [for Bahais] throughout the world, has arrived in the port of Alexandria. At first he stayed for a few days in the Victoria Hotel, Ramleh. Then he rented a house near Shatis, Safar. He is a sheikh revered throughout the world, an expert in Shariah and learned in the fluctuations and developments of Islamic history. He is aged seventy or older.
>
> Although he made Acca his residence, he has followers in their millions in Persia, India, and even in Europe and America. His followers worship him to an extent which is divine and holy, such that even his opponents disseminate his thinking. But everyone who sits with him sees a man of great intelligence, with beautiful speech. He attracts spirits and souls wholly to his belief in the oneness of mankind, which in its approach corresponds to a belief in 'the unity of being' in religious belief. His teaching and guidance revolve around the elimination of prejudice, whether that is in religion, gender, nationality or the comforts of temporal life.
>
> We sat with him a couple of times. His speech and thoughts reminded us of the demeanour of the respected Jamal Al-Din Al-Afghani, in his knowledge of his subject and how he captivates his audience. However, he is gentle in his approach and relaxed in his discussions. He listens to them [the audience] more than Jamal Al-Din listens . . . [*the rest of article is illegible*].[3]

Qumí quotes a comment made by 'Abdu'l-Bahá about the article and its author:

> A clipping from the newspaper Moaid [*sic*], which is the first newspaper of Egypt and its editor well known throughout the world for his learning, is enclosed. Formerly, this person, through the

> instigation of some influential resident Persians, wrote many articles against this Cause and called the Bahais infidels. But when Abdul-Baha arrived in this country, with one interview he was completely changed and contradicted all his former articles with this one. This is the type of the just man![4]

A Persian periodical published in Cairo, *Chihrih-Nimá*, is also reported as having published an account of the Master. Its author, Mírzá 'Abdu'l-Muḥammad-i-Írání, whose antagonism towards the Master also turned into admiration after meeting Him, is quoted to have written:

> Indeed, I was very much benefited in meeting Abdul Baha. The Arabic newspapers are now anxiously waiting to read my paper No. 20 and believe you will prize it very highly. There is no doubt that some people will slander and accuse me of being bought, but I do not care. I have seen the Truth, and I will write the truth, no matter what may happen.[5]

The pro-British *al-Muqattam* (Cairo)[6] also published a long article on 28 November 1910, which defended 'in most eloquent terms the Teachings of Abdul-Baha'.[7]

On 19 January 1911 *al-Ahram* (Cairo),[8] the first non-official newspaper in Egypt, published a report by a correspondent who twice visited the Master at His temporary residence in Ramleh on the outskirts of Alexandria. The reporter described 'Abdu'l-Bahá in positive terms and denied some of the accusations made against Him in other Egyptian newspapers. The text thus gives some clues as to the character of the attacks that appeared in the Arabic press of Egypt:

> ABBAS EFFENDI THE LEADER OF THE BAHAIS
>
> STATEMENTS REGARDING HIS MORALS AND RELIGION
>
> Continually, the greatness of the Leader of the Bahais, Abbas-Effendi, is the topic of conversation, among the men of affairs and statesmen. The wise men of Alexandria, and the nobility of that city are paying him great respect and homage. Lately he has received many letters from his numerous followers in the United States, requesting him to travel to those parts so that they may meet him. They have prepared a great house in New York in accord with his

station and position amongst them. However, it is probable that he will not respond to their invitation, on account of the remoteness of the country and the length of the trip.

We have received a letter from the celebrated scholar, Schokry Effendi, who has just arrived from Syria, in which he praises Abbas Effendi, explains his religion and produces certain arguments in his favor.

He says: 'The wisdom of Abbas Effendi, our respected guest, descends from a family which was noble in lineage and descent in the Kingdom of Persia. He is the son of the "Dweller of Paradise", BAHA'O'LLAH, the founder of the Bahai Movement, and he is the successor of his Father. In regard to his morality and character, he is the pattern of dignity and perfection. He is gracious, generous, noble-minded, philanthropic, charitable and full of benevolence. He is very kind to the poor and patient to the indigent. He does not make any difference between the followers of any religion, whether they be Christians, Jews, Mohammedans or Brahmans. To him all are the same, he looks upon them as part of the same family of humanity and not their particular religion. The aim of his movement is the unity of religions in the world and their equality among the children of men. He thinks that the differences of religions are impeding the progress of the world and he believes that the removal of these differences will benefit mankind.

'This religion has spread greatly and is carried to Europe and America so much so that today the number of Bahais has reached the number of fifteen million, men, women and children included. Many of these Bahais are in New York, Chicago and India, Persia, Egypt and Syria, and it is continually growing and spreading.

'The Tomb of BAHA'O'LLAH is in Acca, called Bahaji and every year the Bahais come from all parts of the world to visit it.

'Twice I have called upon Abbas Effendi while in Ramleh and have seen the poor and indigent gathered around his house waiting for him to come out and when he appears, they beg alms and he gives to them. This is just a short sketch of his generous qualities and I confess my inability to do it justice. His physical appearance is medium size, white hair, penetrating eyes, smiling face and wonderful countenance, courteous, and his manner, simplicity itself, disliking any ostentation and show. He is a wise man, a philosopher and his knowledge of Turkish, Persian and Arabic is unsurpassed.

'He knows the history of nations and understands the causes of their rise and fall.

'He is sixty years old and on account of certain nervous ailments he has come to Egypt for a change of air. He personally reads all the articles and letters sent him from all parts of the world, and answers the most important of them in his Persian handwriting which is famous for its beauty. Many of the great men of this country and delegates from other nations have met him and he gives a personal interview to each one of them. No one has visited him without leaving him impressed by his presence and praising his qualities and wondering at his magnanimity and his astonishing mind.

'Concerning the reports of his leaving Acca and the statement that he is against the Constitution, this was without foundation and the proof of this is his endeavor to unite the religions in the world and establish equality among nations. If such were his qualities, working against religions and Constitution, and on the other hand trying to bring union and harmony amongst them, how can we reconcile the two? This is indeed far from him, for he is a man who advocated the Constitution from the very beginning and before the Turkish people received their Constitution. But the real object of his coming to Egypt is for the change of air and his physical condition. This is the real truth we are proclaiming at the top of our voice and if there is any virtue in it, it requires no praise or blame.'

This is what our correspondent writes and we thought it advisable to quote it as we received it.[9]

It is reported that the semi-official *Wádí al-Níl* (Cairo), the first political newspaper in Egypt, published an article about 'Abdu'l-Bahá on 22 March 1911.[10]

The Egyptian Gazette

The Egyptian Gazette was founded in 1880, first as a weekly appearing in English and French, and later as a daily newspaper with a shorter French section. With its headquarters in Alexandria, *The Egyptian Gazette* was for many years the major non-Arabic newspaper in Egypt and the Middle East and it seems that it even launched its own Arabic edition which contained translations of the English one.[11] From 1899 until 1922 its editor was Rowland Snelling, a British journalist who had previously worked as the assistant of Andrew V. Phillips, the first editor and one of the founders of the newspaper.

As noted in previous chapters, *The Egyptian Gazette* mentioned 'Abdu'l-Bahá as early as 1900 and 1905 and further research will surely provide results from the years prior to His liberation and travels. It paid considerable attention to 'Abdu'l-Bahá's three visits to Egypt. Its first articles about Him were, however, not devoid of a certain amount of satire, which together with their inaccuracy made them quite unsympathetic. But once staff of the newspaper personally met 'Abdu'l-Bahá the editorial line about Him changed completely.

The first article giving the news of 'Abdu'l-Bahá's presence in Egypt appeared on Tuesday, 20 September 1910, just three weeks after His arrival. The note simply mentions the fact that He is in Port Said and repeats some of the topics about Him which were circulated at the time by Christian missionaries:

> THE ACRE DEITY
>
> Egypt is entertaining now a very interesting and extraordinary visitor. Abbas Effendi, a Persian living at Acre in Syria and who pretends to be an incarnation of Deity, is now at Port Said. Abbas Effendi has inherited the pretence from his father Bahaullah and has some followers in Syria and Egypt who call him a Prophet or an Apostle. But he has followers in the United States, most of whom look upon him as a god and many among them offer him handsome sums of money. There was a schism among his followers in the States some years ago owing to differences of opinion on his so called deity. Abbas Effendi usually employs a secret agent in Cairo who endeavours to see his American worshippers before they proceed to Acre and supplies him with all possible information about them. A certain American lady who worshipped Abbas Effendi is well remembered by some Cairenes and the awe which he inspired in her by recounting information about her gathered from his late secret agent in Cairo caused at the time a great deal of merriment among those who heard her story when she returned from Acre to Cairo.[12]

Just one week later, Tuesday, 27 September, a further article about 'Abdu'l-Bahá's arrival appeared in *The Egyptian Gazette* which echoed some of the rumors about Him that were circulated by His opponents:

> An interesting person has just arrived at Port Said, Abbas Effendi, the chief of the Batists, who is said to have come to Egypt to take refuge from the Young Turks, as he wants to be out of the reach of the clutches of the so-called Turkish Constitution, as he has annoyed the authorities by urging his followers to remain faithful to Abdul Hamid and the exiled Shah of Persia. Some of his followers, however, say that he has only come to Egypt for a change of air. The Bab, or Gate of Truth, Mirza Aly Mohamed, died a martyr's death at Tabriz in 1850, and his successor Mirza Yehia, Subh-i-Esel (Morning of Eternity) was found at the British Occupation of Cyprus a State prisoner at Famagusta. The Babus faith dwells on the endless progressiveness of Revelation, and aims primarily at a universal reign of peace, love, freedom, and unity of belief and effort. They are strong in Persia.[13]

Once the Master moved to Ramleh a reporter with *The Egyptian Gazette* – probably Sealing himself – interviewed Him. The article that ensued, one column and a quarter long, was published on 18 January 1911:

> A PERSIAN PHILOSOPHER IN EGYPT
> ABBAS EFFENDI AT RAMLEH
> MOSLEM CRITICISMS
>
> The prolonged stay in Egypt which the leader of the Bahais is now making has drawn some attention to this notable religious movement, having its rise in Persia. Abbas Effendi, as he is called, makes no supreme personal claim such as his followers do, but declares himself to be the protector and expounded of those teachings primarily revealed through his great father, Baha Ulla, the most renowned teacher in the East of recent times. Abdul Baha, for he prefers to be known by this title, claims for his teaching that he is but an interpreter of the eternal principles of divine truth embodied in the works of his predecessors and so far as we have been able to understand no active propaganda is being carried on in this country, but in Persia it is spreading greatly. It is feared that Bahais may be

subversive to the teaching of the Koran and consequently the reactionaries here are misrepresenting both his aims and his methods.

ACCUSED OF IGNORANCE

They charge him and his adherents with ignorance owing to their imperfect acquaintance with the classical Arabic. Nevertheless there are some notable converts already among the Egyptian Moslems. But the influence of Abbas Effendi is not confined to the Near East. It has already extended to Europe and the United States where he counts many illustrious and intellectual disciples and expanders. In Paris many translations and a treatise on the movement have been published by M. Hyppolite Dreyfus. The majority of Bahais are naturally to be found in Persia where one third of the population is said to have embraced this youngest of religions. The rapidity of its growth is surprising seeing that it is only sixty years ago since the movement first saw the light.

THE RELIGION OF TOLERANCE

Abbas Effendi does not concern himself with politics here and leads a very secluded life, though having expounded the doctrine of the unity of races and peoples, and preached peace, and the cessation of fanaticism in religion or politics, has brought down upon him the dislike of the Nationalists. He is sixty-six years of age and still enjoys vigorous health, but for a malarial infection contracted during his many years' imprisonment in the old Turkish fortress of Acca. We cannot on this occasion do more than just touch upon tenets of this faith, though the matter really justifies a more detailed account hereafter.

One general consideration regarding religion is that if it is to have any permanent impression upon those to whom it is revealed, it must firstly embody the ideals of the period in which the propaganda is first launched and secondly due regard must be had to the state of civilisation of the people whom it is intended to indoctrinate. This religion fulfils these two conditions. Its diction, metaphors and teachings are redolent of the Orient, though one perceives in the ideals expressed a certain measure of Christian or European influence. The teachings expound the theory of progressive revelation, as does the Koran, and advocate the brotherhood of nations, an era of universal peace, law, and language, doctrines some of which bear a striking likeness to arguments introduced in Mr. Hall Caine's recent work 'The White Prophet'.

A SPECIAL INTERVIEW

The following are a few brief notes taken down during a visit to Abdul Baha by one of our representatives. The conversation mainly turned on the necessity to arrive at a great unity of races and religions and how in these days God would appear to be inspiring humanity towards a universal brotherhood.

In reply to questions, Abdul Baha said:–

God has endowed man with freedom in thought. He has created one globe. Man has raised imaginary barriers to define varieties that are in name only. Race hatred is unnatural since all are members of the one human family. Political loves, patriotic claims, religious fanaticism all these are separative forces. They make for wars, egotism and disagreements. God's Politics are best. All were created by the One and He shows impartiality between all. The human will should endeavour to copy the Divine Will. Sooner or later the brotherhood of man will be established on earth, it must come. The Bahais are now demonstrating in their lives this ideal. In their homes, communities and countries they make the utmost endeavours to live in love and friendship with all men irrespective of race or creed.

'The Jews should believe equally in Jesus as well as Moses, and so should Christians acknowledge the Divine Mission of Mohamed.

THE FUTURE OF ISLAM

The question was put: Is the world of Islam capable of religious reform?

Abdul Baha – Certainly, even Moslems themselves acknowledge that the spirit of much of these teachings have got lost and they are seeking to reform the expositions of the Koran. The Koran teaches that there are no differences in the religions of the world. Before Christ came his world was split into many races and creeds, Romans, Greeks, Syrian, Egyptians, and yet through His spirit He drew a unity from all these varied elements that lived for many centuries after Him. When later there were separations and quarrels it was because the followers deviated from the original principles.

Those who live in accordance with the original teaching to-day are the friends and peacemakers of the world.

THE VICE OF PATRIOTISM

A remark having been made that though modern civilisation had done so much to restore Egypt yet its inhabitants were not satisfied, Abdul Baha replied:-

Your remark proves my former observations *viz.* that the mistaken or distorted views of patriotism and politics must inevitably lead to separating and discordant results. If the people show dissatisfaction here it is because they are now developing a so-called national or patriotic sense which creates in the mind the sense of desire and combat. Hatred reigns where love should be manifested. Individual egoism rules and man prefers his own interests to those of his neighbour or community. The Bahai principles if inculcated and applied will transform the outlook of man and create ultimately the power to view matters from a larger standpoint and raise the tone of the aspirations in the human breast.[14]

Some months after the publication of this article, *The Egyptian Gazette* carried a letter by a correspondent – presumably Thomas Atwood (see below) – clarifying that the writer Hall Caine (1853–1931) was not a Bahá'í:

> Those who have read Mr. Hall Caine's White Prophet and are also cognizant of the teaching of Abdul Baha (for so all the Bahaists I have ever met call him) must have been struck by the similarity in the doctrines of the Persian leader and those which Mr. Hall Cain puts into the mouth of the White Teacher . . . At a recent meeting held at Canton Hall last August, the Chairman read a telegram he had received from Mr. Hall Cain, who he had asked whether the similarity was a coincidence or not. Mr. Hall Cain replied: 'Sorry to say I had never heard of Bahai sect or doctrines until two years after the White Prophet was published.'[15]

On 27 March *The Egyptian Gazette* stated that 'Abbas Effendi, the present head of the Bahai movement, who is now staying at Ramleh, will be among those present at the Universal Races Congress at London in July next.'[16] On 1 April, however, it stated that 'We hear it is unlikely that Abbas Effendi, who as we stated in a recent issue was to accompany Suror Bey to England, will after all attend the meetings of the Congress.'[17] On 28 June the newspaper mentioned the 'interesting article' about 'Abdu'l-Bahá by Ethel S. Stevens published in *The Fortnightly Review* of London[18] and on 12 July stated that 'Abdu'l-Bahá would probably visit Europe soon.[19]

Among the English admirers of 'Abdu'l-Bahá in Egypt was a certain Thomas Atwood. In a letter sent from Alexandria, Sidney Sprague mentions that 'There are two interesting English persons here, a Mr. and Mrs. Atwood, at one time prominent spiritualists in London. As Mr. Atwood is slightly paralyzed, Abdul Baha went to see them, much to their great joy. They are now eager to serve the Cause.'[20]

Atwood mentions the Bahá'í Faith in several of his letters to the editor of *The Egyptian Gazette*. Probably the first of these was the one appearing in a letter dated 27 August in which Atwood criticizes the work of Christian missionaries in Egypt. In the course of his exposition he states that 'The Bahai movement, so rapidly extending both in the East and the West, is doing splendid work in bringing to the minds of men the great truth that real religion is not dependent upon creeds and dogmas but that all . . . may meet on one common ground and work together for the good of humanity hampered by no difference of race or creed, but simply recognizing the fatherhood of God and the brotherhood of man.'[21] As we shall see, while 'Abdu'l-Bahá was in Europe, Atwood wrote many other articles mentioning Him (see chapter 8).

Interview with William T. Ellis

A number of articles about the Master were published outside Egypt. In late 1911 the noted religious journalist William Thomas Ellis (1873–1950) managed to interview 'Abdu'l-Bahá in Ramleh. Ellis, who specialized in Christian subjects, had been the editor of various publications such as *The Christian Endeavour World* (Boston) and *Forward* (Philadelphia) as well as an editorial writer for *The Philadelphia Press*. At the time of his visit to Egypt he was also working for *The Continent* (Chicago), a Presbyterian weekly. Ellis was best known for his Sunday religious columns, which were widely distributed and published in American and Canadian newspapers. At the time of his meeting with the Master, Ellis was writing a series of articles for his column 'The Awaking of the Older Nations', in which he described his experiences during his travels in the Middle East.

The article reporting the interview shows that Ellis not only failed to grasp the meaning of some of the comments made by 'Abdu'l-Bahá but also misunderstood His position in the Bahá'í Faith, something which no doubt influenced his attitude. As many other Christian writers and journalists would do later and just as many missionaries in Persia and the Middle East did before, the author's purpose was to convey to the reader the idea that there was nothing in the Bahá'í religion that could not already be found in Christianity.

THE AWAKENING OF THE OLDER NATIONS

New World Religion – Syria Now Offers Another Creed for the Alliance of the Whole Earth, Called Behaism – Many American Followers

By WILLIAM T. ELLIS

Haifa, Palestine – Having given the world Christianity, the one most nearly universally accepted religion, Palestine has now become headquarters of a faith, Behaism, formerly called Babism, which its followers and some writers in Europe and America, claim to be the universal and final religion. Since I have found religion to be, in practice, fundamental to my main thesis in this series of articles, 'The Awakening of the Older Nations', I repaired hither to the home of the head of the Bahists and its 'Messiah', Abdul Baha Abbas.

It was somewhat a shock to be told, when I made inquiry at the large gray stone house here, that Abbas Effendi was away on a vacation for his health. The house was full of people, as I could tell by the voices of scurrying females in the echoing hall, when I succeeded in making my presence known at the knobless doorbell. There were several children playing in the large, unsodded yard, and doubtless one of these reported the stranger's coming. These were grandchildren; for Abbas Effendi has four daughters, but no sons. The whole family, or group of families, live in the one house, Oriental fashion. An English governess, who is not a Behaist, lives with them to teach the children.

A 'MESSIAH' AT A SUMMER RESORT

There are no disciples of the Behaist 'Messiah' in Syria, except the pilgrims who come here, and the number of these is regulated by Abbas Effendi himself. He is highly spoken of by his neighbours, and specially by the poor, to whom he gives presents sometimes standing on the corner, and giving away a hundred garments. He is enabled to do this by the rich presents of his followers, who are said to number several million in Persia. Abbas Effendi makes no claim to be a healer, and he himself occasionally needs the doctor's attention. He is simple in his manner of life, and has steadfastly refused to take more than one wife, despite the fact that he has no son, and that his father before him, 'The Blessed Perfection', had two wives. His teachings permit polygamy, but they counsel against it.

Incongruous though it seemed to find a 'Messiah' gone away to a health resort, I followed Abbas Effendi to Alexandria, in Egypt, where I trailed him by trolley car from a huge summer hotel to a magnificent private house which he has rented for his sojourn. There, hospitably received, for Abbas Effendi is fond of visitors, I had a most interesting interview with the man whom a considerable number of Americans and Britons, and millions in Asia, call 'Master,' and hail as the latest and fullest manifestation of the deity . . .

In an elegantly furnished modern house I found Abbas Effendi seated on a sofa, waiting for me. He is a striking figure in any garb, and when clad in a white tarboosh, or fez, with a white cloth wound around it, Moslem style, and a long gray outer cloak of mohair, like a motor coat and two white cloaks beneath it, he would attract attention anywhere. He resembles, in appearance and manner, General Booth of the Salvation Army, more than any other man I recall. He has the same Roman nose, the same restless, hawk-like eye, the same silver beard and shaggy iron gray locks, the same transparent skin.

As he speaks Abbas Effendi opens wide his big gray eyes beneath his bushy eyebrows, and looks directly at one, giving an appearance of unsimulated interest and sincerity. He is a restless person – doubtless those 40 odd years as a prisoner have left their mark on his nerves – and throughout the interview he wriggled and twisted his body, sometimes revealing the folded red bandana handkerchief upon which he sat; sometimes cocking his fez to the back of his head, and again to the side, and sometimes rakishly forward until it rested on the high bridge of his nose. All the while he was talking he twiddled in his long white hands a string of mother-of-pearls beads, such as gentlemen commonly carry in this part of the world. Altogether, he looks the part of a benevolent old gentleman with considerable force of character.

This positiveness was shown during the interview. A gentle-faced young Englishman, who looked fitter for esoteric discussions than for the football field, had been doing the interpreting, Abbas Effendi speaking in Persian. The most difficult form of interpretation is that of a discussion of abstract themes, and I early saw that the young man's renderings were inadequate; my host saw it also; and peremptorily ordered one other of his attendants to repeat what he said, sentence by sentence.

In the room during the conversation, besides the two men mentioned, was a Persian pilgrim, who wore the green turban that marked him as a descendant of Mahomet; a keen-eyed old fellow, who followed the discussion intently; and another Persian in long black cloak and turban; who looked as if he might sit for an illuminated edition of Omar Khayam; but he went sound asleep during the interview. The conversation lasted for over an hour, and I was cordially pressed to remain and partake of a Persian meal; but a journalist must be careful whose salt he eats, if he is to remain free.

BEHAISTS IN AMERICA

After the pleasant generalizations with which the conversation opened, I asked Abbas Effendi concerning the number of his disciples in America, for this has been put as high as a million. He himself avoids the use of the word 'disciples', but does not object to its employment by others. I could not get him to give even approximate figures; he contented himself with saying that he had many friends in America and that there are regular spiritual gatherings of these in Washington, Boston and Chicago. It is evidently with these centres that he conducts his correspondence, for the names frequently occurred.

As to the number of Behaists in the world he was equally vague, but wholly honest. When I said that a friend from Persia had told me that fully half of the people in Persia are Behaists, he promptly declared that he thought this number entirely too high. Equally candid was he in saying that there are practically no Behaists in Turkey; the following is found chiefly in Persia, and then in India, America, Great Britain, and a scattering in other countries. 'Quality,' he remarked, 'is more important than quantity; better five diamonds than a hundred pebbles.' Abbas Effendi has considerable aptness in the art of illustration; this was further shown when we got on the main track of the meaning of Behaism.

AN ALL-INCLUSIVE RELIGION

'All religions,' said Abbas Effendi, 'are substantially the same; there is no real difference. The difference is only in names. There were once a Turk, a Greek, a Persian and an Arab, to whom a piece of money was given in common. Each said in his own tongue what he wanted bought with it; and they had a long and angry discussion. Then along came a man bearing grapes – and lo, that was what they all wanted, but each had used a different name for it. So Moses, Buddha, Confucius, Christ, Mahomet, were all prophets of God. They merely had different names. Each should accept the other.'

When this important point was pressed, he affirmed that all Christians should accept Mahomet, as the Jews should have accepted Christ.

'Do you really mean that all religions are essentially the same, and that one is as good as another? Do you include paganism, and idolatry?'

'Yes, they were all right at first, even Buddhism, which has deteriorated, as all religions do.' At this point my host's knowledge of the ancient and so-called 'ethical faiths' proved so shaky that I abandoned this line of questioning.

He got onto firmer ground by saying: 'There have been a thousand unknown prophets in the world. They were truly prophets of God, but the world never recognized them.'

'Please tell me what you mean by prophet? That word is often used as meaning any man with a new or helpful message to this time; but you surely do not put the prophets you have named in the same class with the ordinary writer, teacher or preacher today?'

Here again the 'Prophet' of the Behaists showed his rare skill at evasion. He took up the figure of the mirror, and dwelt at great length upon that, and would not be diverted; the prophet is the man who best mirrors God. I could not get to him the suggestion that, after all, the mirror does not reflect or impart life, heat or power. Nor could I get past the interpreter the query whether this teaching is not a great comedown for those of Buddha, with his doctrine of man being part of the divine essence; and of Jesus, who professed to give life; and who boldly declared: 'I and the father are one', and of Mohamet, with his stern claim to be the very voice and representative of God. Interpreters are a great convenience when there are uncomfortable questions flying around.

WHAT BEHAISM STANDS FOR

A definition of Behaism, which to an unsentimental westerner seems rather vague, is a hard thing to secure; so I asked Abbas Effendi, frankly, to give me a categorical definition of the distinctive doctrine of Behaism, 'something with hooks to it, so that it will grasp the ordinary man'. This he patiently and kindly did.

'First. Behaism believes that all men are brothers, and should so act.

'Second. Behaism believes that there should be no strife of religious creeds. All are equal. No man need change his religion when he becomes a Behaist, whether he is a Moslem, a Christian or a Buddhist.

'Third. There should be no war between races or countries. There should be international brotherhood and international peace.' Incidentally, the retainer who had done the interpreting later told me that Abbas believes that there will be a great war, and then worldwide peace. He also advocates one language and one form of writing.

'Fourth. Bahais teaches its followers to love everybody. In Persia there are Jews, Moslems, Zoroastrians, Buddhists, Brahmins and Christians, who meet in love and concord as Behaists. It removes fanaticism from all sects.'

And I verily believe that Abbas Effendi practices his creed, for he is a gentle, kindly man; who, however, has no conception whatever of the high inexorableness truth. Gen. Lew Wallace's aphorism: 'Better law without love, than love without law' would not appeal to him. None the less, his high, fine ideals embodying as they do, the commonplaces of Christianity, are in consonance with the spirit of the age, and we may expect to see Behaist grow and prosper,

> especially among sentimental persons. Its claim to be the final and universal religion is scarcely tenable, since it has not bones enough to stand the scalpels of the scholars.[22]

Sidney Sprague, the 'gentle-faced young Englishman' mentioned by Ellis, was present at the meeting acting as translator. He sent a report to *Star of the West* offering another perspective on the interview:

> Two nights ago, an American journalist, Mr. William Ellis, representing *The Continent*, came especially to Alexandria to interview Abdul Baha. It was my privilege to be the translator on this occasion. One of the first questions Mr. Ellis asked was: 'How many followers have you?' The answer was: 'We have no statistics and we do not consider these things important. It is the quality of the believers we care for. If a few are characterized with the attributes of God and live according to the divine Teachings, it is praiseworthy. Five diamonds are worth more than five million stones.' Again the journalist asked: 'Have you not many followers in America?' 'I have a few friends in different cities who love me,' was the reply. 'Is it not true that half of Persia is Bahai?' persisted the journalist. 'No; it is not,' replied Abdul Baha, 'but many there who are not Bahais are influenced by our Teachings.' 'Are there not many followers in the Turkish Empire?' 'No,' and again Abdul Baha reiterated the non-importance of numbers. The journalist seemed very much taken aback. He evidently expected Abdul Baha to boast of a large following. What an example Abdul Baha has set us!
>
> Then Mr. Ellis asked briefly: 'What are the Teachings of the Bahai Revelation and in what does it differ from other religions?' Abdul Baha replied: 'While all the other religions are hating and denouncing each other, the Bahais are the friends of all religions and the lovers of all peoples, and their aim is to unite and harmonize all.' There were many other questions which drew forth wonderful, illuminating explanations from Abdul Baha. I have not the time to write them now, but be on the lookout for an account of this interview in *The Continent*. Mr. Ellis is on his way to Persia to write articles about that country, so he may write of the Cause there.[23]

This was not to be the last time Ellis wrote about 'Abdu'l-Bahá. He wrote about Him again in articles published during and after His travels in America (see chapters 36 and 38, vol. 2).

Meeting with W. Tudor Pole

Wellesley Tudor Pole (1884–1968), was a British businessman with a profound interest in esotericism and mysticism. He had in his possession what he believed to be the Holy Grail used by Christ in the Last Supper, a cup dated by some antiquarians as being some two thousand years old and which his sister found at Glastonbury following the instructions Tudor Pole, who claimed to have seen the object in a vision while in a trance.

A large and heterodox group of people sharing the idea that the cup was the Holy Grail soon emerged around Tudor Pole. Among these people we can find the names of Archdeacon Basil Wilberforce, Alice Buckton and others who either eventually became Bahá'ís or maintained close contacts with them and with 'Abdu'l-Bahá. For obvious reasons, however, the majority of the public opinion received Tudor Pole's ideas about his cup with severe skepticism and this prompted him to plan a series of travels to Europe and the Middle East to try to document the origins and provenance of his precious object. It was on a visit to Constantinople in 1908 that he first heard about 'Abdu'l-Bahá from a group of Persian Bahá'ís residing in the Ottoman capital and it can be assumed that soon afterwards he also acquainted himself with the British Bahá'ís, considering himself one of them.

On 1910 he started his third trip to Constantinople and also planned to visit Vienna, Damascus and Smyrna.[24] His first stop was to be Alexandria, where he expected to visit 'Abdu'l-Bahá. Tudor Pole arrived in Egypt in the second half of November 1910 and stayed there for nine days. His meetings with the Master made a profound impression on him and he experienced a personal transformation.

Before Tudor Pole left Egypt, and to his surprise, 'Abdu'l-Bahá instructed him not to follow his original travel plans but to go instead to Paris to find the young Bahá'í Tammaddun'ul Mulk and advise him on behalf of 'Abdu'l-Bahá to proceed to Egypt. With no contact details or any other information at all, Tudor Pole was able to find the Persian Bahá'í in the streets of Paris and deliver to him 'Abdu'l-Bahá's message and a sum of money He had sent for the travel expenses.[25]

It was probably while he was in Paris that Tudor Pole wrote the article describing his visit to 'Abdu'l-Bahá that appeared on 7 December 1910 in *The Christian Commonwealth* (London):

> A correspondent sends us the following account of a visit he has recently paid to the home of Abdul Baha, the great Persian religious and social reformer, who for so many years was a State prisoner at Haifa and Acre, on the Syrian coast. The movement which Abdul Baha directs is another sign of the world-wide awakening which is now taking place:–
>
> Details of the great master of men and his work for the brotherhood of East and West are, I expect, already familiar to your readers. I was a guest of Abdul Baba for nine days, and came into close contact, not only with him, but with other pilgrims who sat down with us at his table, including Christians, Jews, Moslems, Hindoos, Zoroastrians, and others. As the movement is a rapidly growing one, and its followers already number millions, and as the spiritual power behind Abdul Baha is so wonderful and arresting (even to a casual observer), it is certain to make its power and influence felt in this country, and will have to be fully reckoned with. There is nothing in the Bahai teaching that is not in full sympathy with your work and the Liberal-Christian League. Abdul Baha sends by me his greeting and prayers for Mr. Campbell and his fellow-workers, for the whole movement, and THE CHRISTIAN COMMONWEALTH. I should like people in England to realise that the spirit of brotherhood and love and progress that is beginning to make itself felt the world over is specially focused in a truly divine manner in this Persian seer and prophet, and that his influence the world over is far greater than any of us realise. A copy of THE CHRISTIAN COMMONWEALTH was on Abdul Baha's table when I arrived, and I found cuttings from your paper in most unexpected quarters, and amongst Easterners too![26]

Back in England, Tudor Pole was interviewed by *The Christian Commonwealth* and on 21 December the magazine announced that: 'In our next issue we shall print an interview with Mr. W. Tudor Pole, who has just returned from Egypt, where he visited Abdul Baha, the leader of the Bahai movement. Mr. Pole has an impressive story to tell of the growth and power of Bahais, of its ideals, and of the remarkable personality of the 'Master'. We shall also print in facsimile a fraternal message which Abbas Effendi has sent to the CHRISTIAN COMMONWEALTH and the movement we represent.'[27]

The article that followed the interview was published on 28 December and offered an extensive introduction to the Bahá'í Faith and its history – not reproduced here – together with Tudor Pole's account of his encounter with the Master:

A WONDERFUL MOVEMENT IN THE EAST

A VISIT TO ABDUL BAHA AT ALEXANDRIA

To most of us the world consists of modern Europe, North America, South Africa, Australia, and since the Russo Japanese war, in a lesser degree, Japan. Our daily newspapers keep us informed, more or less accurately, of movements social, political and religious, that occur within those lands, but of the rest of the world we are for the most part ignorant. In this there is a danger that we may fail to read the signs of the times, not because we are necessarily lacking in wisdom, but because we do not behold the signs. The Bahai movement is a good illustration of this. Not one Englishman in a thousand has heard of this religious and social uprising in the East, yet its adherents are estimated to number millions, and its power and influence are growing week by week! In order that our readers may be informed about this remarkable outpouring of the divine spirit, a representative of THE CHRISTIAN COMMONWEALTH recently called upon Mr. Wellesley Tudor Pole, who has just returned from the East, where he has been studying the movement at first hand . . .

'Did you meet Abdul Baha on your recent visit to the East?'

'Yes, I met Abdul Baha near Alexandria, where he was staying with some of his followers. Let me try to give you a word picture of him. He is sixty-five years of age, of medium height and of commanding presence; he has long silver grey beard and hair, blue grey eyes, a fine forehead, a wonderful carriage, and a sweet but powerful voice. He was dressed when I saw him, in cream white robes and a white Persian headdress. You feel at once that here is a master of men and a marvellous spiritual personality. He seemed to me to focus in a truly divine manner the spiritual ideal of the coming age. When one has come in contact with Abdul Baha's power, or rather

> the power behind him, one has no doubt that this movement will vitally affect the religious and social evolution of the whole world. At his table I met pilgrims who had come to receive his blessing from many parts of the world, and representing almost every faith the world knows. Jews, Mohammedans, Hindus, Zoroastrians and Christians sat around one table, all holding this one great belief that God has again sent one of his messengers to earth, and that the great call that was focused in Baha Ollah is the call for the unity of nations, the brotherhood of man, the peace of the whole world, and the realization of those fundamental truths that lie behind all faiths. Baha Ollah did not say to the Christian, "Come out of your religious order", nor did he say to the Mohammedan, "Turn your back on your faith." He said to every man, "Go and live out your faith in unity and brotherhood with all mankind, and thus show that behind all expressions of religion there is one religion and one God."'[28]

The same page carried some passages from the Bahá'í writings and the translation and facsimile of 'Abdu'l-Bahá's message addressed to *The Christian Commonwealth*:

> November 30, 1910
> *To the Editor of The Christian Commonwealth:*
>
> My Dear Friend: I have received your letter, for the contents of which I am extremely grateful to you. I understand the aims of your movement, and hope that with the greatest spirituality and by the pursuit of truth, it will succeed in bringing about the unification of mankind.
>
> Enclosed you will find some of the sayings of Baha Ollah: insert them in *The Christian Commonwealth.*
>
> Be so kind as to accept for yourself and your honorable society my kindest regards.[29]

After his return from Egypt and the publication of his interview, Tudor Pole delivered a series of lectures on 'Abdu'l-Bahá and the Bahá'í Faith. One of them was held on Saturday, 31 December 1910 at the headquarters of the Higher Thought Centre, a place where regular meetings on the Bahá'í Faith were being held by Ethel Rosenberg and Mary Thornburgh-Cropper and where 'Abdu'l-Bahá would give a public talk on 1 October 1911. Summaries of the lecture, which was advertised under the title 'The Glory of God as revealed in Persia', appeared in *The Christian Commonwealth*[30] and in *Light* (London) magazine. The latter magazine, referring to 'Abdu'l-Bahá, mentioned that 'Last autumn he visited Egypt and Mr. Tudor Pole met him there, becoming his guest, sharing many meals at his house, and enjoying friendly intercourse with Hebrews, Moslems, Christians, Hindus, Buddhists, Zoroastrians and Parsees, all of them pilgrims in sympathy with the great causes of World Brotherhood and Universal Peace. Abdul Baha Abbas (the Servant of God), as he is now called, who has the blue-grey eyes of a great seer, seemed to focus the spiritual ideal of the coming age.'[31]

Tudor Pole delivered another talk on the Bahá'í Faith at the request of the Bath Theosophical Society on 9 January 1911. The local press published an account of this meeting.[32]

In a further article for *The Christian Commonwealth*, Tudor Pole stated that 'Very considerable interest has been aroused throughout the country by the article that appeared in THE CHRISTIAN COMMONWEALTH on December 28 last, in reference to Abdul Baha and the Bahai movement' and added that 'a large number of enquiries for literature on the subject have been received at the office of the Bahai Press, 47, Vicarage Road, East Sheen, S.W.' The article continued with information about Bahá'í sacred literature and some general notes on its teachings.[33] While on a visit to Edinburgh, Tudor Pole was also asked by the Theosophical Society to lecture on 'Abdu'l-Bahá but he was unable to accept the invitation.[34]

Pilgrimage of Louis Gregory

The prominent Washington Bahá'í Louis Gregory (1874–1951) also had the opportunity of visiting 'Abdu'l-Bahá in Egypt. After his return he lectured in the capital on his experiences with the Master. The *Washington Herald* reported that a lecture was to be held on 12 June 1911 at the Lincoln Temple.[35] A short account of the lecture appeared in the black newspaper *The Appeal* (St Paul, MN) on 17 June, which reported that 'Mr Gregory is a forceful and eloquent speaker, and he held the attention of his audience for nearly two hours', adding that 'The Bahai revelation is gaining great headway in Washington, and at its basis is the absolute equality of all persons, regardless of color or creed, the most intelligent Afro-Americans in the city are encouraging the movement.'[36]

Contacts with the British Quakers

While He was in Egypt 'Abdu'l-Bahá received communications from several churches and prominent people in the West. Some of them were to be His hosts during His travels. Such was the case of Basil Wilberforce, Archdeacon of Westminster, who sent a message to 'Abdu'l-Bahá, and also of R.J. Campbell, who in a service at the City Temple (London) on 24 October 'Remarked that he had received a very gracious message from Abbas Effendi, who took great interest in his work in London.'[37]

Such was also the case with the British Society of Friends, or Quakers, who invited the Master to speak at their Westminster headquarters on 12 January 1913. They had established contact with Him as early as autumn 1910 when the Bristol Friends sent Him a message, to which He replied with the following Tablet:

> Convey to them my salutations. Tell them that the Spirit is encompassing and surrounding all. It is holy. It is sanctified from attachment to a special place. It is present everywhere and at every time. It exists in all places, yet, is place-less.
>
> The organisation of worshipping places is not simply for drawing near to God: but it is to concentrate the Word of God, and cause the power of unity and oneness among the peoples. The Temple is the symbol of the real Church, which Church is the Reality of the Christ. It is for this purpose:– that we should consider that, as the outward Temple can gather men of different nations in one place, likewise the Reality of Christ has united the great races of the world together. You have been labouring to establish this spiritual worship for yearly two hundred years.
>
> Come now, O ye Friends, and serve for the unity of the whole world of humanity: and ye shall behold the prevailing power of the Word of God. To-day the Word of God rules the whole earth. The Word of God is the only promulgator of the oneness of the world of humanity.

This letter, together with the following message 'To a Worker in a Crowded City', was afterwards printed as a pamphlet:

> Give to him my greetings. Tell him Christ is ever in the world of existence. He has never disappeared out of it. He is the source still of Christian life. But, to find Him is difficult.
>
> To be nominally a Christian is easy: to be a real Christian is hard. Read *Hidden Words* carefully. Rest assured that Christ is present.
>
> 'The Spiritual beauties we see around us to-day are from the breathings (breaths) of Christ.[38]

After the receipt of 'Abdu'l-Bahá's Tablet, John William Graham (1859–1932) was commissioned to sent Him a reply on behalf of the Society of Friends in the counties of Lancashire and Cheshire. The letter, reproduced below, was translated from English into Persian by Edward G. Browne and was 'addressed under cover for safety, to someone else, in Alexandria'.

> We have received and read your message of salutation to the Society of Friends, dated 1910, and sent by you to some of our Friends in Bristol. It is cause of great gladness to us to hear of those in other lands to whom the indwelling Spirit has been so mightily revealed, showing to you and to us that when we draw near to one another we draw near to God, and that in the happy recognition of human fellowship we find the bond which makes us one in the Eternal, in spite of diversities of race and language and of the externals of belief. This sacredness of the human soul makes us demand, for all, both men and nations, liberty of thought and of action, that we may follow our own guide, not another's. The tyranny of one nation over another is abhorrent to us. Every instinct of our being leads us to obey the teaching of our Lord Jesus Christ against war and violence, which lead to the submission of the soul and conscience to brute force. Our hearts go out to you under the fire of persecution which you are undergoing, such as fell upon our forefathers 250 years ago. Though both you and we may seem, to our critics who belong to Churches of elaborate doctrine and established ritual, to leave out much which to them is precious, we believe that we hold the absolute and simple religion which places no intermediary between God and man.

Written by instruction of the Meeting at Bolton, 19th January, 1911.[39]

A further letter from 'Abdu'l-Bahá was received and read at the Manchester Quarterly Meeting for Spring 1911:

To the respected members of the Friends' Assembly in Lancashire and Cheshire

He is God!
O Heavenly Friends! Your letter arrived, and its subject afforded me joy and gladness. Thanks be to God that such an assembly is organised which renders service to the unity of the world of humanity, and seeks equality among all men.

Although in Western countries, through justice, hatred and animosity amongst religions and nations have been abated; yet, in Eastern countries, quarrels and disputes, hatred and enmity, among religions and peoples, had reached to such a degree, that they used to drink each other's blood, like refreshing water. If they could, they would set on fire one another's houses, and burn their sacred books. While walking in the street, if it happened that the garment of one would touch that of the other, they would either wash or burn it.

The East was in such a troubled condition, and diseased with such darkness of superstition when Baha'ullah hoisted the banner of the unity of the world of humanity, and promulgated equality among all men. He extirpated the root of hostility, and founded unity in its place. By the power of the Word of God, and the brightness of the teachings, he expelled that gross darkness of hatred, and brought the light of love. The East was illuminated, and the star of eternal life did shine. Many of those contending people were gathered together in unity; meeting round the Manna of love, in perfect harmony and friendship. One would say that they are kindred, or sons and fathers, or brothers and sisters, even more close than these. For the taper of love was lighted, and the sweet melody of the unity of the world of humanity reached to the regions of the kingdom. The social gathering was adorned, and the festival of unity established. The light of union and concord shone, and the establishment of unity of humanity was settled in the hearts. The power of the spirit of Baha'ullah so influenced the hearts that the very enemy became friend, and strangers as acquaintances. The hated became beloved, and the rejected received honour.

Now Bahais do not look to men, but have their attention directed towards the Lord of men. Therefore they do not consider anyone as an enemy; on the contrary they count their enemy as a friend. They know no one as a stranger, they love even the outsider as an intimate friend. If they be oppressed, they count it fleeting, but when they see justice they deem it everlasting. If they meet with enmity, they think it like a shadow; but if they should see a kindness, they count it as the radiance of the sun.

Because the darkness of oppression cannot withstand the light of justice; yea, the sweetness of love will dispel the bitterness of animosity. Thus, they love and show kindness even to the oppressors, the cruel and bloodthirsty ones. We hope that the brightness of these teachings may illumine all the world, and the spirituality of these precepts make the East and the West to clasp their hands round each other's necks, like unto two longing and most dear lovers. So that this pavilion of the unity of the world of humanity may shelter the four corners of the earth, and make the five continents of the world as one continent, and its different nations as one nation, and the rival religions as one religion, remote native lands as one home, and the different languages into one tongue.

Upon thou be the Glory of the most Glorious. – 'Abbas Abdul Baha.[40]

Meanwhile, John W. Graham had read 'Abdu'l-Bahá's first letter at a Meeting for Sufferings held at London on 3 March 1911. He suggested on behalf of the Lancashire and Cheshire Quarterly Meeting that the London Friends send to 'Abdu'l-Bahá a further communication and mentioned the following about the Bahá'í Faith:

> . . . Their message was the indwelling Spirit of God in all men, and its proclamation had led – as in the early experience of Friends and of the Doukhobortsi – to great persecution. Since their rise, twenty thousand Bahais have suffered martyrdom. The main tenets of these people were the emancipation of women, peace, non-resistance, the supreme importance of prayer and the rooting out of all self-will.

> There are now in Persia not less than a million Bahais and the movement was spreading to other countries. A lengthy discussion ensued. Some Friends wished to know whether the Bahais were Christians, and also as to the political significance of this movement.
>
> A committee representing the different views expressed was appointed to make further enquiries into the movement and to draft a reply to the letter.[41]

The members appointed for that committee were Mary L. Cooke, Edward Grubb (1854–1939), John W. Graham, Samuel F. Hurnard, Charles E. Stansfield (1865–1945), Theodore Harris (1870–1958) and Metford Warner (1843–1930).[42]

In the Meeting for Sufferings held on 7 April, the commission reported that a draft had been prepared and a letter sent from Egypt by Henry T. Hodgkin (1877–1933), secretary of the Friends Foreign Mission Association, was also read out. Hodgkin had traveled to Lebanon and Egypt with Gilbert Gilkes (1845–1924), deputy chairman of the Friends Missionary Board, and in Egypt the two men met 'Abdu'l-Bahá. In his letter Hodgkin reported his interview with the Master in Cairo and requested that the reply to 'Abdu'l-Bahá be delayed until his return since he had 'information which may prove of value to our Committee'.[43]

According to *The American Friend*, once in London, Henry T. Hodgkin, at a meeting held on 9 June 1911, 'gave some information of this leader ['Abdu'l-Bahá] and his followers, speaking very highly of his private life. He had found him living a simple life and filled with a genuine desire to help his fellows. The Bab [*sic*] was in touch with Christian missionaries, who frequently visited him and his wife. Bahais was stated to be a very marked advance on the Mohammedanism from which it had sprung, but it was certainly not a Christian movement, and, if pressed, the Bab would probably say that his father had brought a message to the world more appropriate to the present age than that of Jesus Christ.'[44] From the reports of the meeting it is evident that part of the committee appointed by the London Friends was not comfortable with the idea of sending a letter to 'Abdu'l-Bahá. Graham, Hodgkin and probably others had a sympathetic view of the Bahá'í Faith and 'Abdu'l-Bahá, while other members were less open in their views:

> H. T. Hodgkin felt that there was much to say on both sides as to

whether or not to send an official reply to the Bab's communication.

The proposed reply was then read, and a prolonged discussion followed. Some Friends felt uneasy as to the future of any reply sent, as it would probable not end with the Bab himself, and the official reply, once sent, could never be recalled, and would be liable to inaccurate translation and also to be printed and used for purposes which Friends would not approve.

After the meeting had decided to send the reply, the epistle was read clause by clause and considerable amendments were made with the view to making the position of Friends absolutely clear, while at the same time retaining the character of the epistle as a greeting and not making it too doctrinal. Eventually the epistle was agreed to. To safeguard a proper translation, it is to be translated into Persian under the supervision of Isaac Sharp, and is to be sent in the English and Persian languages.[45]

The letter to 'Abdu'l-Bahá finally read as follows:

FROM A MEETING REPRESENTING THE RELIGIOUS SOCIETY OF FRIENDS, HELD IN LONDON THE 6TH OF SIXTH MONTH (JUNE) 1911

To ABBAS EFFENDI –
The message of Abbas Effendi addressed to the Society of Friends has been read among us, and, on behalf of the Society of Friends, we gratefully acknowledge it in the same spirit of love that called it forth. We have heard a little of the principles for which the Bahai people have suffered, and recognise in them some of the truths for which our own forefathers endured imprisonment and other terrible persecutions.

These truths have come to us through our Lord Jesus Christ, in whose perfect life, and in whose sacrificial death for the sins of the world, we see the complete manifestation of the eternal love of God. In leaving the world He gave the promise of His Spirit, who should lead us into the truth. We can testify from the experience of our own Society to the fulfilment of this promise, and we find that the message of Jesus Christ is interpreted to each age by the Spirit of God working in the hearts of men.

> He taught us that as the Father's love goes out to all the sons of men, so we too, if we would be true children of God, must love all men and not our friends alone. This teaching we have striven to follow, and to work for the day when all mankind shall live as brothers. He taught us the infinite worth of every human soul, whether that of male or female, bond or free, of every nationality; and we believe that all His followers should spend themselves in the endeavour, by peaceful methods, to right the wrongs of the downtrodden and to let the oppressed go free. It is our happiness to make no distinction in spiritual privileges, or place in the Church, between men and women.
>
> It is a joy to us to hear that the Bahai movement stands for universal love and purity of life, and that the education of the young of both sexes is a chief concern of its leaders.
>
> We conclude with cordial greetings, and the earnest desire that the Spirit of Christ our Divine Lord may rule the lives of men, bringing them to the knowledge of the love of God, Who hath made of 'one blood every nation of men for to dwell on all the face of the earth'. Signed, on behalf and by direction of the Meeting,
>
> Robt. A. Penney, Clerk.[46]

Samuel F. Hurnard, editor of the *Friends' Witness to Spiritual Truth* (London) and a member of the committee that had to draft the letter to 'Abdu'l-Bahá on behalf the London Quakers, was among those who opposed the Bahá'í Faith and were against the idea of writing a reply. On May 1911, one month before the letter to 'Abdu'l-Bahá was approved, the magazine carried an article on the Bahá'í Faith by Hurnard in which, among other things, he declared that Bahá'ís 'refuse to give Christ His unique and exalted place as the only begotten Son of God' and that 'such a claim as theirs is an outrage on Christian sentiment and an insult (if one may use the term here) to the Father who sent His Son into the world to redeem it'. To these statements he further added that 'If anyone is puzzled at the excellent moral teaching of this movement . . . let him remember Paul's warning . . . Even Satan fashioneth himself into an angel of light . . .'[47]

In the United States, *The American Friend* (Philadelphia) published on July 1911 an impartial article on the origins and tenets of Bahá'í Faith by the Arab Quaker Khalil Totah. The article also included details about the meeting at which the reply to 'Abdu'l-Bahá was discussed and approved.[48]

On 4 August the leading literary magazine *T.P.'s Weekly* (London) published a letter by one of its readers, Hubert W. Peet,[49] who reproduced 'Abdu'l-Bahá's Tablet to the Friends' Assembly of Lancashire and Cheshire. He had sent this letter to complement the information that had appeared in a sympathetic article about the Bahá'í Faith which had been published in the same magazine on 21 July:[50]

'This mystical religion is, I believe, making so much headway in the East' stated Peet, 'that it is worth the while of students of human development to make themselves acquainted with its characteristics and tendencies in relation to the general forward movement in religion and ethics the world over.'[51]

5

ARRIVAL IN EUROPE

11 September 1911

After almost one year in Egypt 'Abdu'l-Bahá left for Europe on 11 August 1911. He proceeded first to France, where He visited Thonon-les-Bains, on the shores of Lake Léman, and spent a few days resting and recovering His health.

Rumors about the expected visit of 'Abdu'l-Bahá to Europe were circulating in the press a few months before His actual arrival. On 28 June 1911 *The Near East* (London) announced that 'Abdu'l-Bahá would probably visit Europe: 'It is rumored that during the summer Abbas Effendi will come to Europe, probably to Switzerland. Till now he has never set foot on European soil, and has always retained his Persian dress and customs.'[1] Exactly the same statement was published on 12 July in *The Egyptian Gazette* (Alexandria).[2]

The Christian Commonwealth reported the rumor that 'Abdu'l-Bahá would attend the First Universal Races Congress that was to open on 26 July. The organizers had included His name among the speakers:

> There is a widespread belief in London that Abdul Baha Abbas, leader of the Bahais, will personally attend the Universal Races Congress in London next July and read a paper. There is no foundation for this report so far as can be ascertained, and the message to the Congress from Abdul Baha will be taken as read. It is hoped, however, that Abdul Baha may possibly be present at the Parliament of Religions, to be held in Holland next year. In the meantime interest in the Bahai movement continues to spread rapidly, and there is a large demand for the very useful and instructive penny booklet on

> the subject written by E. J. Rosenberg, and just published by the Bahai Press, Vicarage Road, E. Sheen, S.W.[3]

A few weeks later the same periodical stated: 'We understand that there is a prospect that Abdul Baha, the leader of the Bahai movement, will, health permitting, attend the Native Races Congress in London next month.'[4] When the arrival of 'Abdu'l-Bahá in Europe and His visit to Thonon-les-Bains were finally confirmed, Albert Dawson, editor of *The Christian Commonwealth*, sent Him a telegram which was published on 23 August:

> We have dispatched the following telegram to Abdul Baha, the great leader of the Bahais, to welcome him on his arrival in Europe: –
>
>> The Editor of THE CHRISTIAN COMMONWEALTH, London, on behalf of himself and readers, sends cordial greetings. We are anxious to cooperate in the great work for the unity and fellowship of all peoples. Accept our strongest thoughts and prayers.[5]

'Abdu'l-Bahá's reply appeared in the same magazine on 30 August:

> As mentioned in our last issue, Abdul Baha is now in Europe and in response to our greeting we have received the following telegram from the leader of the Bahais:–
>
> (The) first telegram upholding (the) unity of mankind received (in) Europe (was) yours. (It) caused great joy, and I send thanks. (I) hope (the) light (of the) teachings (of) Baha'u'llah unifying (the) nations will illumine these regions, and your paper will be (the) first shining lamp. Abdul Baha.
>
> We are proud to be the channel of communication from the great religious leader of the East, and rejoice that THE CHRISTIAN COMMONWEALTH is becoming increasingly a link between spiritual movements throughout the world. We call attention to the account of a meeting with Abdul Baha on page 820.[6]
>
> In reply to inquiries we have to say that we are not at liberty to make known Abdul Baha's whereabouts.[7]

On 31 August 'Abdu'l-Bahá visited Geneva, where He stayed until 3 September at the Grand Hotel de la Paix (Peace).

Some local newspapers timidly noted the arrival of the Master in Switzerland. The *Journal de Genève* mentioned on 4 September that 'Abbas Effendi, the spiritual head of the liberal Bahai religion, which has enlisted millions of peoples in all Asia, is currently in our city. He is staying in the Hotel de la Paix where he is receiving many visitors. Abbas Effendi is a great poet and has a good command of several oriental languages.'[8] On the following day *La Tribune de Genève*[9] and *ABC*[10] carried the same information.

6

FIRST VISIT TO ENGLAND

4 September – 5 October 1911

As mentioned above, since mid-1911 the British press had anticipated the visit of 'Abdu'l-Bahá in London. When, finally, His arrival was confirmed, some newspapers published articles introducing the Bahá'í Faith and the figure of 'Abdu'l-Bahá to the general public.

On 2 September, the *Daily Mail* (London) published a lengthy article on the Bahá'í Faith which expected that 'In London Abdul Baha, the chief of the faith, should attract a large amount of public attention by his personal appearance alone'.[1] Portions of this article were later used in at least one British newspaper[2] and were also reproduced in newspapers circulated in Australia,[3] Canada,[4] Egypt,[5] New Zealand,[6] Singapore,[7] and the United States.[8] Probably relying on the same information, the London correspondent of the *Glasgow Herald* announced that 'Abdu'l-Bahá 'is to visit London immediately and conduct a mission lasting at least a week', adding that 'he is described as a man of dignified presence and moving eloquence'.[9]

Meanwhile, the Unitarian minister Henry Harrold Johnson[10] wrote for the readers of *The Christian Commonwealth* an article on the Bahá'í Faith which included a lengthy introduction to its history and teachings.[11]

'Abdu'l-Bahá arrived in London on Monday, 4 September 1911. Lady Blomfield, a distinguished member of London's society, arranged accommodation for the Master and his party in her apartments at 97 Cadogan Gardens, she and her family staying elsewhere. Mary Virginia Thornburgh-Cropper, the first to become a Bahá'í in the British Isles, put her automobile at His disposal and also opened her house as a meeting place. Every day a torrent of visitors wishing to meet the

Master personally was cordially received by Him. Bahá'ís, seekers, religious leaders, politicians, journalists, social activists, or simply curious people, all would receive their portion of 'Abdu'l-Bahá's love and attention.

An editorial in the 6 September 1911 edition of *The Christian Commonwealth* carried the news of the arrival of the Master on British shores:

> The event of paramount interest in the religious world this week is the arrival in London of Abdul Baha, the leader of the great Bahai movement, particulars of which have appeared in our pages from time to time. We regard the visit of Abbas Effendi as prophetic of that union between the spiritual forces of East and West which will undoubtedly be consummated in the not distant future. We take special interest in the Bahai faith because its fundamentals are so much in harmony with the main principle for which THE CHRISTIAN COMMONWEALTH stands, namely, the solidarity of mankind and hence the essential unity of all religious aspiration . . .[12]

This information was reproduced on 6 September in the London *Times*,[13] which at the time had a circulation of 45,000 copies.[14]

First Interviews

During 'Abdu'l-Bahá's first week in London several journalists visited and interviewed Him. Wellesley Tudor Pole, a privileged witness of those days, reported that 'countless press correspondents have been received and they usually retire from the interview greatly impressed by his noble dignity and spiritual simplicity', also mentioning that 'the great majority of articles that have appeared are both restrained and dignified in tone and there has been a welcome absence of sensationalism in the descriptions of Abdul-Baha's appearance and accounts of his life and work'.[15]

Albert Dawson, editor of *The Christian Commonwealth*, was probably the first journalist who had the honour of interviewing 'Abdu'l-Bahá in the West. He was received by the Master on 5 September, the day after His arrival in England, and on the following day a short note in the journal announced the publication of an account of the meeting,[16] which appeared on 13 September:

TOWARDS SPIRITUAL UNITY
AN INTERVIEW WITH ABDUL BAHA

For years past word has been coming to the West that a new prophet has arisen in the East, and that a great religious movement, starting in Persia, was spreading far and wide. Reports were vague and conflicting, but gradually the main facts emerged. Particulars have been given in THE CHRISTIAN COMMONWEALTH from time to time, and in our last issue appeared in outline the story of the movement and its leaders . . .

Some months ago I received private information that Abdul Baha might possibly visit this country, and recently he dispatched from Switzerland the telegram published in our columns a fortnight ago. On Monday evening of last week 'The Master', as his followers naturally call him, arrived in London, and on Tuesday I had the privilege of meeting him. 'What is he like?' Let me quote the words of one who visited him at Akka a few years ago:–

'He is of middle stature, strongly built. He wears flowing light-coloured robes. On his head is a light buff fez with a white cloth wound about it. His long grey hair rests on his shoulders. His forehead is broad, full, and high, his nose slightly aquiline, his moustaches and beard, the latter full, though not heavy, nearly (now quite) white. His eyes are grey and blue, large, and both soft and penetrating. His bearing is simple, but there is grace, dignity, and even majesty about his movements . . . We see the benignity and the kindliness, of his countenance.'[17]

It was interesting to find Abdul Baha well acquainted with THE CHRISTIAN COMMONWEALTH. 'He is very pleased with what you write in your paper,' were the first words, after a cordial welcome, that came through the interpreter. 'Some of the papers write things that he does not like and are not correct, but you write about what you know.' The production of an early copy of our last issue caused some merriment. The fact that it was printed a day before the date it bore amused him, and when the paragraph, 'A meeting between Abdul Baha and the editor of THE CHRISTIAN COMMONWEALTH took place yesterday (Tuesday) afternoon. Some particulars will probably appear in our next issue', was translated to him, he said, with a twinkling eye, he was very pleased with our 'prophetic writing'. Of the preceding passage, referring to the fundamental unity of all religious faith, Abdul Baha said, 'You have written all that I can say to you. That shows that we are one in spirit.'

Alluding to his visit to this country he said he wished to gain strength and to see his friends; the length of his stay would depend upon the state of his health. After forty-two years' imprisonment he was glad to be able to travel. I asked whether it was correct, as has been stated, that he was born in prison. No, he said; he was born in Teheran, the capital of Persia, in the spring of 1844. I gathered that at that time his parents were of good position and dignity. When the boy was nine years of age, the family was exiled from Teheran to Bagdad. From the beginning, the movement had been under the ban of the civil power, and sometimes, through mistaken zeal, such as that of Peter when he struck off Malchus' ear, some disciples came into direct conflict with the government. It was the attempted assassination of the Shah of Persia in 1852 by a young Babi, who had lost his mental balance, that led to the arrest of Baha'u'llah and the banishment of the family and many of their co-religionists. From Bagdad Abbas Effendi, with his father, was transported to Constantinople and Adrianople, and, finally, in 1868, to Akka, in Syria. Here Baha'u'llah remained a prisoner until his death, in 1892, and here his son, Abdul Baha, spent forty years within the fortifications. Three years ago, on the proclamation of the Turkish constitution, he became free. During his long imprisonment he thought not of himself, but of others; he enjoyed continual communion with God, he ministered to the needs of his fellow-prisoners, and it was because he lived this unselfish life that he survived while many others perished. 'A captive for the cause of God,' his interpreter explained, 'his prison was to him as a palace. His body was suffering, but his soul was free.'

The invariable tendency on the part of the followers of a great religious leader is to attribute to him supernormal powers. Abdul Baha emphatically disclaims possessing any such, and even deprecates the description of himself as a prophet. He told me he had never spoken a single word implying that he had right to such an appellation. 'I am simply a servant of God,' he said, 'and I do not wish to be called anything more than that.' He assured me that he has no desire to found another sect. 'The foundation truth of

Baha'u'llah is the foundation truth of all religions. The principles of the prophets of Israel and of Jesus Christ and of other religious teachers have been largely forgotten; Baha'u'llah has renewed them. Therefore, the Bahais have for the followers of other religions the greatest love and yearning, because they know that mankind is one. Baha'u'llah seeks to promote and establish friendship and union. He addresses himself not to a sect, but to the whole world. We are all branches of one root, blades of grass in one meadow. It is misunderstanding that has caused divisions and differences between mankind. If the truth were brought to people they would understand that they are all one, and each would say: This is the truth I have been looking for. Because the principles taught by every true prophet are the same; there is no difference between them.'

'What is the distinctiveness of the Bahai faith? What is its special contribution to world-religion?'

'The proclamation of the unity of mankind, and, consequently, peace between all nations; and also the renovation of the teaching of the prophets whom God has sent to the world, and its presentation in a form suitable to our time. When Baha'u'llah appeared in the East proclaiming the unity of mankind all the powers of Persia were directed against him, but in spite of all opposition he spread his message. For fifty years he endured, often in chains, the greatest suffering; four times he was exiled from country to country; but his voice could not be silenced, his influence could not be stopped. As a result of his life and teaching the different sects of Persia are becoming one family of God; the Mohammedans, Christians, Jews, Zoroastrians who have accepted Bahaism are now in the greatest unity and harmony. There is no more any war between them; each honours the head of other religions; Mussulmans are honouring Moses and Christ; Christians are honouring Mohammed and Moses; Jews are honouring Jesus and Mohammed. They have learnt to love one another, and are becoming one. The cause of unity is the cause of life itself, it is divine; that which leads to division or hatred is satanic. Religion should make for unity. The prophets did not come to bring about distrust and separation. Ignorance is the cause of division and hatred. Religion is like medicine; it is meant to cure, but in the hands of unskilled or bad physicians what should effect a cure may create disease, what should give life may cause death.

Therefore we must strive with all our strength, with all our heart, to promote only that which leads to unity and life.'

It is not surprising that people in increasing numbers are attracted to the Bahai faith by its catholicity, the loftiness of its ethic, the simplicity of its teaching, its complete freedom from narrow and exclusive dogma. It has no organisation, no hierarchy, no ritual, no fixed places and times of meeting; in short, it is spirit and life. It does not seek to proselytise; you can be a Bahai without ceasing to be a Christian, a Jew, or a Mohammedan. There are adherents of the Bahai faith in every country in the world; in Chicago a monthly organ has appeared, 'The Star of the West', printed partly in English and partly in Persian. There is a considerable body of Bahai teaching of which some particulars have already appeared in THE CHRISTIAN COMMONWEALTH, and further accounts will be given from time to time; the essentials of the faith may be gathered from Abdul Baha's utterances given above and below. Following the practice of Baha'u'llah, Abbas Effendi issues from time to time written tablets for the edification of Bahais and all who care to read them, he volunteered to write one such for THE CHRISTIAN COMMONWEALTH; this, in Persian character, will be reproduced in facsimile in our next issue, together with a summary in English.

It has been my good fortune to meet Abdul Baha several times during the past week. In one conversation I sought his impressions of England. Coming straight through to London, and having so far had only a few motor drives in the West End, he has not had much opportunity of observing the life and habits of the people generally, but already he has been much impressed by the freedom we enjoy. 'I admire the liberty you have in England and the use you make of it,' he said. 'Every person in this country can go his own way and say what he thinks without anyone making him afraid; in fact, he is king of himself.'

'Do you consider we have too much liberty?'

'Oh, no; you all seem to be perfectly comfortable and perfectly safe. Freedom of thought and speech enlarges the circle of one's understanding and leads to progress and unity. English people ought to be happy.'

Abdul Baha is married, and has had eight children; four of whom are living. He was frequently urged, in accordance with

> Mohammedan custom, to take a second wife, the more so that he has no heir; but he is a believer in monogamy, and says that if it had been God's will that he should leave a son the two born to him would not have been taken away.[18]

On 6 September, the *Evening News*, a halfpenny Unionist newspaper with a circulation of some 300,000 copies, published a fake interview with 'Abdu'l-Bahá. A simple reading of the article clearly shows that its author constructed the fictitious conversation using information already published in other newspapers. It also contained many statements that could have never been made by the Master. He was quoted, for instance, as defining Himself as the 'third prophet' of the Bahá'ís and as dating the execution of the Báb to 1825 instead of 1850. The article even fabricated a message from 'Abdu'l-Bahá 'to the British public'.[19] Owing to the false statements published in this article, 'Abdu'l-Bahá emphatically stated in interviews with other journalists over the next few days that His station was not that of a prophet but rather of a servant.

On 7 September He received the young reporter Percy J. Philip[20] whose visit to the Master coincided with that of the psychologist and writer Gustav Spiller.[21] Philip was a reporter with the Liberal *Daily News* (London), which at the time had a circulation of some 320,000 copies. He wrote the following account of his meeting with 'Abdu'l-Bahá:

> He speaks no English, and another interpreter spoke for him. 'Some of your papers,' he said, 'call me a prophet. I am not a prophet, I am a servant of God.'
>
> Shortly, and with Oriental imagery, he told of his doctrine.
>
> 'The foundation of Divine religion is one,' he said, 'and cannot be changed. After a little time that is ever forgotten, and then God sends another servant to renew his message. The cause is one, but the Divine teachings are of two kinds. The one is spiritual, the other is material. The one which is spiritual is the principle; it cannot be changed. The other, which refers to material things, changes with the necessity of the times. Such was much of the teaching of Moses. When Christ came it was necessary that much of Moses' doctrine should be done away with.
>
> 'Divine religion is like spring. When it comes it gives life and

beauty to everything, and the world is renewed. Then comes summer, and then winter, and there is no sign of life. But spring comes again, for the principles of nature and of God are everlasting and fixed . . .'

Mr. G. Spiller, the organizer of the Universal Races Congress, told a little story which admirably illustrates the careful organizing power and attention to detail of the Abdul in the midst of his greater work. 'He dictates hundreds of letters', he said, 'to his adherents in all parts of the world, and one which came under my notice finished with a delicious phrase. After his exhortation he assented to a proposal that the letter should be printed and circulated, 'but,' he added, 'let the type be clear and readable.'

From a letter the Abdul sent to the Congress this extract is interesting as showing sound knowledge of men. 'It is well seen,' he wrote, 'that the British are firm, and are not lightly turned aside, being neither ready to begin a matter for a little while, nor prone to abandon it for a little reason. Verily, in every undertaking they show firmness.'[22]

A reporter with the *Daily Mail*, the most widely-read newspaper in the United Kingdom with a circulation of 900,000, published the following account of one of 'Abdu'l-Bahá's public audiences:

PROPHET OF BAHAISM

FIRST DAY AMONG HIS ENGLISH FOLLOWERS

Abdul Baha Abbas, the Persian prophet of the Bahai faith, which claims over three million devotees and has been likened to a spiritual Esperanto, spent his first day in London yesterday. Accompanied by a small retinue of disciples and secretaries the prophet is making his English headquarters at a house in Cadogan-gardens, the precise neighbourhood of which is being kept secret.

The prophet is a man of sixty years, of medium height and vigorous, with little outward sign of the years he has spent in a Turkish prison. His dress yesterday, when he gave interviews to many of his followers, was a simple cream-coloured Eastern robe, with a Turkish cap and turban covering his long white hair. He spoke a little in English, short sentences, such as 'How are you?' and 'It is a good heat', but his main address to a gathering of fifty followers was delivered in Persian.

> The message he gave was as follows: 'You are all one family; you are grown out of one root. Each of you is like a flower, a branch, a fruit. You must look on no one as a stranger. You should try to show the greatest love to all men and to every creature. I have come to you as to my own people – brothers and sisters, sons and daughters. My bond is with all mankind. So should yours be. Try to follow the teachings of Baha'u'llah, then each one will shine like a star. Since the time of Adam there has been no other teaching; until the end of time there will be no other.'[23]

Some of the words attributed to 'Abdu'l-Bahá in this article, together with those quoted by the *Daily News* on 7 September, were the basis of a short article that appeared days later in *The Christian Globe*, an independent weekly devoted to religious subjects.[24] Other portions were also published in *The Egyptian Gazette* (Alexandria)[25] and in some Australian journals.[26]

On 7 September news agencies released a note regarding 'Abdu'l-Bahá's movements in London, which reported that 'during his stay in London Abdul Baha is holding daily receptions at 31, Evelyn Mansions, Carlisle Place, S. W. Those of his followers who visit him pass before the prophet in single file, and he bows and shakes hands with them. A short address is subsequently delivered in Persian, for the prophet speaks no English.'[27] Similar notes were published in the *Evening News*[28] and in the illustrated newspapers the *Daily Mirror* (London),[29] with a circulation of 670,000 copies, and *The Daily Graphic* (London),[30] with a circulation of 50,000 copies.

The illustrated *Daily Sketch* (London), with a circulation of some 800,000 copies,[31] also sent a reporter to interview 'Abdu'l-Bahá. The article that ensued mentioned only a few superficial details. During the first days of His stay in London and despite the insistence of the newspapermen, 'Abdu'l-Bahá would not allow pictures of Him to be taken. The *Daily Sketch*, however, published with its article a furtive shot that portrayed Him entering a building followed by His attendants. The picture, supplied by the London News Agency, is probably the first taken of the Master in the West. The same picture was published days later in *The Observer* (see article below).

The prophet of world-love is in London town.

Abdul Baha is his name, his nationality is Persian, and in the bedroom of a fashionable flat in Chelsea he received a representative of the *Daily Sketch* yesterday. An old man of seventy years, clad in a biscuit-coloured robe, with biscuit-coloured slippers and fez to match, Abdul Baha has a benevolent, aquiline face on which trouble has scored many lines.

His religion is called Bahai, and to be a Bahai, he explained through his interpreter, it is not necessary that you should disavow the religion you profess. You can be a Protestant and a Bahai at the same time, for a Bahai, says Abdul Baha, loves his neighbours without distinction of race, creed or politics . . .

'The English people', he said, 'are a very good and a very wise people. I notice that the English are not inclined to levity; they are serious, and study things. The people have freedom; everyone is a law to himself.

'Your traffic – its roar and rush – I do not mind, because it is evidence that the people are serving one another.'

The Abdul delivered a tabloid sermon based on Bahai principles, and the interview ended.[32]

A reporter on *The Evening Standard and St. James Gazette* (London), a Liberal newspaper with a circulation of 160,000 copies, met 'Abdu'l-Bahá on at least two occasions, writing afterwards a sympathetic account:

ABDUL BAHA ABBAS

THE PERSIAN TEACHER'S ADMIRATION OF ENGLAND

SPECIAL INTERVIEW

(BY A CORRESPONDENT)

Abdul Baha Abbas, the leader of the Behai movement, whose arrival in England was reported in these columns a few days ago, does not claim the title of prophet, but he wishes to be regarded as he is – a simple man, who tries to make known the teachings of his father – Bahaullah, the spiritual descendant of the Bab – the founder of the universal religion which, since its inception in Persia, has found adherents in nearly every country in the world. Abdul Baha Abbas has a striking personality; the forty years of martyrdom spent in a

Turkish prison at Acre have not quenched the noble kindliness of his nature, and in spite of the lines which indescribable hardships have left on his face, his dark eyes are alive with the fire of understanding and sympathy.

His imprisonment was due to the fact that the Turkish Government feared that his liberal ideas might tend to subvert the power of the clergy.

To-day I have had the privilege of again having a long conversation with him, and he told me of the horrors of this prison which few can survive, even one year; but his certainty in his lofty mission enabled him calmly to bear tortures which would have broken the spirit of anyone less persuaded that their sufferings were for their faith.

OBJECT OF HIS VISIT

He told me that he has come to England at the desire of many disciples who are anxious to see him. He pointed out to me that Behaism is not a new religion but religion renewed. It recognises no clergy, no ceremonies, no dogmas; it is the religion of love in the highest sense of the fellowship between man and man; it asks that we should all consider each other as leaves of one tree.

When reason and intelligence guide us to further knowledge of these teachings, wars will naturally cease and the worship of God will be freed from sectarian strife. Like the light of day it will fill the world, so that no one can escape from it. When Behaism succeeds in further impressing its influence on humanity the position of woman as the first educator of man will receive in the East a recognition even beyond that which at present it obtains in the West.

I was astonished that Abdul Baha Abbas, notwithstanding the fact that he has passed the greater portion of his life in a prison, was able to show interest and sympathy about the details of the life of Englishmen. He asked me questions about my own life, and I described to him a journey which I had lately made to Russia. I found myself talking to him as to one who had been a friend always. It was strange, in a pretty London room filled with flowers, to see the Oriental figure of Abdul Baha Abbas, who was dressed in brownish white linen clothes and wore a white turban.

As he talked he moved his hands, and at the end of a sentence folded them and laid them on his knees. He spoke quickly in a deep voice, using simple words.

He likes England and greatly admires the liberty of thought of the English people.

VISIT TO EGYPT

Since his release he has not visited his native country, but before coming to England he went to Egypt, where the number of his adherents is rapidly growing.

A proof of the all-embracing nature of his teaching is that during even the few days which he has already spent in this country he has been visited by many clergymen of all denominations. Behaism welcomes all sects, all religions, all philosophies. It asks only that all mankind should unite in the great work of fighting evil by love, through the power of God.[33]

The weekly newspaper *The Observer* (London), with a circulation of some 175,000 copies,[34] published in its issue of Sunday, 10 September, an interview with 'Abdu'l-Bahá, who again requested not to be called a prophet:

BAHAISM

INTERVIEW WITH ABDUL BAHA

'A RELIGION OF UNIVERSAL BROTHERHOOD'

What manner of creed is the Bahaism whose leader is now in London, and which, started only sixty years ago, now, in spite of terrible persecution, numbers a third of the inhabitants of Persia among its adherents?

Abdul Baha, the leader in question, was good enough to make some points clear to a representative of THE OBSERVER yesterday. 'The keynote to Bahaism', he said, 'is the idea of the universal brotherhood and the interdependence of man. In this world there is an intimate relation between all existing beings, in the same way as the limbs of the body are united. If one of the body suffers all the body suffers.' All the world's great teachers or prophets are accepted as 'manifestations' of the Divine Light; types of the greatest of these prophets being Moses, Buddha and Christ.

The teachings of Bahaism are eminently practical and directed

> to the social welfare. Thus, it is commanded that every follower in every condition of life must practice some trade, art or profession that shall be beneficial to society as well as to himself. All begging is strictly forbidden, but it is incumbent on the community to provide work for all who need it. It is also commanded that every child shall receive the best education possible, an injunction which is likely to change the condition of the East as much as the equally revolutionary doctrine that women are the equals of men and have a similar right to education . . .
>
> One misconception Abdul Baha wished to correct was the idea that he claims to be a prophet. He is the son of a prophet, and devotes his life to carrying on the teaching of his father, a Persian nobleman, who afterwards became universally known as 'Baha ullah' meaning the 'Glory of God'. Abdul Baha's teachings were considered antagonistic to the faith of Islam, and aroused the antagonism of the Turkish Government, who imprisoned him within the walls of Acre for forty years, and he was only released three years ago. He is a man of patriarchal appearance, with keen, green eyes, and a beard of snowy whiteness.
>
> . . . In spite, however, of his many years in prison and a life of many hardships, the aged teacher is still hale and hearty. Abdul Baha is married, but has no son to carry on the propaganda.[35]

After the publication of all these interviews *The Near East* lamented in an article published on 13 September that poor information about the Bahá'í Faith was being published in the articles appearing at the time:

> The presence of Abdul Baha, the recognised leader of the dominant Bahai sect of the Babi religion, is to be welcomed as stimulating interest in an important and little-understood movement. His arrival has, of course, been exploited by the cheaper Press, which has published various interviews with him and his entourage, and a number of slipshod articles on the doctrines and progress of the mystic religion of which he is the head. That, however, is the inevitable result of modern developments in journalism. The public are not likely to be much enlightened by anything that has appeared about Abdul Baha, or about Bahaism, in the halfpenny newspapers, which aim, not at giving information, but at arousing and gratifying

a momentary and superficial curiosity. But perhaps some of the readers may be sufficiently interested to want to learn more about a religion that, although outwardly suppressed by revolting cruelty in its country of origin, still has its thousands of declared converts in other parts of the world. If they are led to seek this information in the works of Professor Browne and other serious writers, they will gain an insight into Eastern conditions and Eastern ways of thought that will amply reward them for the intellectual effort required to grapple with an abstruse and unfamiliar subject.[36]

Address at the City Temple

On Sunday, 10 September, 'Abdu'l-Bahá gave His first public address in the West. The scene of that historic occasion was the City Temple of London, a Nonconformist church built in 1874.[37] Its minister at the time was Reginald John Campbell (1867–1956), who had probably learned about the Bahá'í Faith through Lady Blomfield and Wellesley Tudor Pole and who had maintained some correspondence with 'Abdu'l-Bahá while He was in Egypt (see chapter 4).

Campbell was a very popular religious figure, a preacher of repute, a respected leader in Nonconformist circles and had a large following among Christian liberals. His sermons and writings were widely followed in the United Kingdom and abroad. He propounded what became known as the 'New Theology' and defined it as holding 'that we know nothing and can know nothing of the Infinite Cause whence all things proceed except as we read Him in His Universe and in our own souls'.[38] In the political field Campbell was a supporter of the Socialist movement and devoted many of his sermons to discussing and denouncing contemporary social problems. In June 1908 his followers founded the League of Progressive Thought and Social Service which by 1909 had four thousand members. In 1915, however, Campbell started to distance himself from his previous ideas and in 1916 he finally withdrew from the Congregationalist Church to become a member of the Anglican Church, the church of his youth.[39]

While the City Temple was the platform from which Campbell expounded his ideas, the weekly journal *The Christian Commonwealth*, self-defined as the 'organ of the progressive movement in religion and social ethics' and with a circulation of some 50,000 copies, was the publication that echoed them beyond the walls of the church, publishing every sermon preached by Campbell. Thus behind *The Christian Commonwealth* and Campbell there were thousands of liberal Christians of the time who were introduced to the Bahá'í Faith and to the figure of 'Abdu'l-Bahá.

Campbell was received by 'Abdu'l-Bahá on 5 September, the day after His arrival in London, and it was during the meeting between the two that the Reverend invited the Master to preach at his church on the following Sunday. Dawson kept for posterity notes of their conversation.

> I happened to be in the room when Rev. R. J. Campbell was announced. There were also present several English ladies. Mr. Dreyfus-Barney (who kindly acted as interpreter), Tamaddon-ul-Molk, Abdul Baha's secretary, an elderly Persian scribe who sat like a statue taking notes of the Master's words, and another Persian gentleman – altogether a picturesque mingling of East and West.
>
> MEETING BETWEEN ABDUL BAHA AND MR. CAMPBELL
>
> Immediately Mr. Campbell entered the room Abdul Baha rose from his chair and advanced to meet him with smiling face and arms extended. The elder man grasped both the hands of the younger, and, retaining them, warmly greeted him. His expression and manner showed that he regarded the occasion as no ordinary one. Standing face to face, linked hand in hand, in the centre of the room, these two spiritual leaders of world-wide fame – Eastern and Western, but essentially one in their outlook on life – formed an impressive picture that is stamped indelibly on the mind's eye of all who were privileged to be present. The meeting was so remarkable that I ventured to take notes of the conversation (conducted through an interpreter), and here reproduce them. It should be mentioned that the note-taking was quite unpremeditated. Neither speaker was aware that his words were being recorded. The conversation was private, and permission to publish was given with reluctance.
>
> Abdul Baha first inquired after Mr. Campbell's health, and said he had been very anxious to meet him. The conversation then proceeded as follows: –
>
> R. J. Campbell: I have long looked forward to this opportunity.
>
> Abdul Baha: That is proof that both our hearts are at one.

R. J. C. I think that is true.

A. B.: There is a Persian saying that hearts that are at one find their way to one another.

R. J. C.: I do not think that saying is peculiar to Persia.

A. B.: Often two people live in the same house in constant intimacy, but their hearts are not united. Here are two men, one living in the East and one in London, whose hearts were coming to meet one another long ago. Although in the material world we were far apart, we have always been near in the spiritual world. The real nearness is the nearness of the heart, not of the body.

R. J. C.: The spirit knows no nationality.

A. B.: Praise be to God that now there is between us a material as well as a spiritual tie, the union is perfect!

R. J. C.: I am so glad that you took the resolution to come to England, even though you can remain only a short time.

A. B.: From the time I left Egypt my purpose was to come here, but I remained a few days on the Lake of Geneva for a change of air.

K. J. C.: I know many of your friends who are also mine.

A. B.: I have read your sermons and speeches.

R. J. C.: And I have read yours.

A. B.: That is a proof of unity. As I have read your sermons (with a humorous smile), you have to read mine.

R. J. C.: I see on my left one who has spoken from my pulpit (Tamaddon-ul-Molk).

A. B.: We are all friends of one another (hands raised as in benediction). We have spread the proclamation of universal peace, therefore we are friends of people all over the world. We have no enemies; there are no outsiders; we are all servants of one God.

R. J. C.: That is good.

A. B.: Worshipers of one God, we are recipients of the graces of one God. Men have made differences and divisions; God did not establish them. God has created everyone, and treats everyone equally. He is merciful to all and gives food (lit. 'livings') to all. God knows everyone. To him none is a foreigner. We must follow his example.

R. J. C.: What is distinctive of the Bahai movement as compared with the faith out of which it came?

A. B.: The Bab foretold the coming of One after him who

would address the whole world. We are the followers of that One – Baha'u'llah. When he manifested himself, some of the followers of the Bab did not receive him. Those are called Babis; the disciples of Baha'u'llah are Bahais. The Bab came as a reformer of Islam, and foretold the coming of a greater one in his footsteps. Instead of confining his revelation to the Moslem world, Baha'u'llah gave it forth to all mankind. The narrow-minded ones, even those who meant well, could not understand so broad a movement, they were not strong enough to follow Baha'u'llah; they said, 'He is speaking a language we cannot understand.' Therefore they are called Babis.

R. J. C.: What a close parallel to primitive Christianity! The Judaising portion did not wish the Gospel to go any further.

A. B.: It has come about, by their narrow-mindedness and exclusiveness, that the Babis are now opposed to all the other religions; they want to keep rigidly to the teaching of the Bab, and convert everybody to it. The Bahais recognise the truth in all religions. They come from the same root, but there is now that difference.

R. J. C.: A difference of attitude.

A. B.: Their conduct is absolutely different.

R. J. C.: How many Babis are there?

A. B.: Very few.

Interpreter: Perhaps 200 or 300 in Persia.

R. J. C.: It is suggested that there are three million Bahais.

Interpreter: There are no statistics. The Babis are more politicians than anything else. Some Persians, who do not live the life, are not acquainted with the life, claim to be Bahais, because they know the Bahais are the advanced people.

R. J. C. (to Abdul Baha): I should like you to visit the City Temple.

A. B.: I should like to come. I know that the City Temple is a centre of progress in the religious world, and seeks to promote a universal understanding. As you have been a promoter of unity in the Christian world I hope you will strive to bring about unity in the whole world. A man first wants unity in his own family, and then as his intelligence expands he wants unity in his village, then in his town, then in his country, then in the world. I hope you will strive to unify the whole world.

R. J. C.: We are doing what we can. We believe that religions are many, but Religion is one.

A. B.: The principle of religion is one, as God is one.

A Lady: Mr. Campbell's reform movement in Christianity is helping the world of Islam. The attitude of the New Theology is one Moslems can understand; they cannot understand the divisions of Christianity.

R. J. C.: I have had some evidence of that.

When Mr. Campbell left it was with the understanding that there would be a further meeting.[40]

Five days after this meeting with Campbell, 'Abdu'l-Bahá gave His address at the City Temple.[41] Over two thousand people listened attentively to the words of the Master, who spoke for about eight minutes, and to the translation read afterwards by Wellesley Tudor Pole.[42] A note reporting the service was distributed through news agencies and was published in several London newspapers on 11 September:

> Abdul Baha (Abbas Effendi), head of the religion of Bahaism, attended the service at the City Temple last evening. The religion was started in Persia only sixty years ago, and now in spite of persecution, embraces, it is said, a third of the people of that country. According to the leader himself it is a religion of universal brotherhood. The visit to the City Temple had not been announced, and the fact that the Bahai leader was coming was known to a few. The service proceeded as usual until the hymn before the sermon, when the venerable figure of Abdul Baha, clad in Persian costume, was seen on the pulpit stairs.
>
> After the sermon the Rev. R. J. Campbell, welcoming the visitor, spoke of Bahaism as one of the most remarkable religious movements of this or any age. Abdul Baha then addressed the congregation in Persian, speaking for about eight minutes. A translation of the address was read by Mr. W. Tudor Pole. It was mainly an exhortation to spiritual unity and closer relations between East and West. This was the first time that Abdul Baha had addressed a large gathering in England, and he afterwards said in English: 'I am very happy.'[43]

The *Daily Express* (London), a Conservative halfpenny with a circulation of 330,000 copies, also published on 11 September a short report which stated that 'Abdu'l-Bahá's message 'was to the effect that the time was approaching when war would cease and peace be established throughout the world'.[44] On 17 September *The Observer* quoted in its section 'Sayings of the Week' a sentence from 'Abdu'l-Bahá's address: 'Enmity is the result of prejudice'.[45]

The most complete report on the presence of 'Abdu'l-Bahá at the City Temple was, however, the one published by *The Christian Commonwealth*, which included the notes of the address (not reproduced here) together with the introductory and closing remarks made by His host, R.J. Campbell:

> ABDUL BAHA AT THE CITY TEMPLE
>
> Abdul Baha attended the evening service at the City Temple on Sunday. No announcement of the visit was made, and, although the sight of the Persians and other members of the suite in the congregation excited curiosity, very few people were aware that the Bahai leader was expected. The service proceeded as usual until the hymn immediately preceding the sermon. Whilst this was being sung a venerable figure, clad in Persian robes, was seen slowly ascending the stairs of the pulpit. When the hymn was finished Mr. Campbell placed the distinguished visitor in his own chair, and then, addressing the crowded congregation, said:
>
> 'I propose to shorten my sermon this evening, because we have a visitor in the pulpit whose presence is somewhat significant of the spiritual drawing-together of East and West, as well as of the material drawing-together which has long been going on, and I think you would like to hear his voice, if only for a few moments.'
>
> Mr. Campbell spoke on 'The Use of the Will in Prayer' (Luke 18:1), closing with the story of wireless telegraphy . . . He then said: This evening we have in the pulpit of the City Temple the leader of one of the most remarkable religious movements of this or any age, a movement which includes, I understand, at least three million souls. The Bahai movement, as it is called, in Hither Asia rose on that soil just as spontaneously as Christianity rose in the middle territories adjoining, and that faith – which, by the way, is very closely akin to, I think I might say identical with, the spiritual purpose of Christianity – that movement stands for the spiritual unity of

mankind; it stands for universal peace among the nations. These are good things, and the man who teaches them and commends them to three millions of followers must be a good man as well as a great. Abdul Baha is on a visit to this country – a private visit – but he wished to see the City Temple; and I think I am right in saying for the first time in his life he has consented to lift up his voice in public. He does not address public meetings, he does not preach sermons; he is just a religious teacher. He spent forty years in prison for his faith, and from his prison directed the efforts of his followers. There is not much in the way of organisation, but simple trust in the Spirit of God. We, as followers of the Lord Jesus Christ, who is to us and always will be the Light of the World, view with sympathy and respect every movement of the Spirit of God in the experience of mankind, and therefore we give greeting to Abdul Baha – I do not know whether I could say in the name of the whole Christian community – that may be too much – But I think in the name of all who share the spirit of our Master, and are trying to live their lives in that spirit. Abdul Baha, I think, intends to say a word or two in response to these greetings that I address to him in your name.

ADDRESS BY ABDUL BAHA

Abdul Baha then advanced to the front of the pulpit, and addressed the congregation. He spoke for eight minutes in Persian, with considerable animation, his voice rising and falling as in a rhythmic chant. Towards the close he placed the palms of his hands together as in prayer. The translation was afterwards read by Mr. W. Tudor Pole . . .

Mr. Campbell: I think you will probably agree with me that this is an interesting as well as a unique occasion, and that what we have been listening to in that brief message uttered by a spiritual teacher from the East is in spirit the same message that you are listening to on the authority of Jesus week by week. It is a great time, a time of the drawing-together of all people. East and West join hands in the City Temple to-night

The service closed with the doxology and benediction.

The same article also reported that after the service 'Abdu'l-Bahá wrote a note in Persian on the pulpit Bible, which was translated thus: 'This book is the Holy Book of God, of celestial inspiration. It is the Bible of Salvation, the noble Gospel. It is the mystery of the Kingdom and its light. It is the Divine Bounty, sign of the guidance of God. – Abdu'l Baha Abbas.' A picture of the note in 'Abdu'l-Bahá's original handwriting accompanied the translation.

The account closed by stating that 'asked by Mr. H. W. Chapman[46] his impressions of the service, Abdul Baha replied: "It is an assembly which is turned to God. The light of guidance is shining luminous here. The bounty of the Kingdom was spread, and all hearts were praying to God." As he took his departure, Abdul Baha said in English, "I am very happy." So were we all!'[47]

On 14 September, *The Christian World* (London), a liberal evangelical weekly, published a summary of this article.[48] *The English Churchman* (London), a magazine that had published articles opposing the Faith, carried on 14 September a brief note criticizing Campbell's invitation to 'Abdu'l-Bahá (see chapter 36, vol. 2). *The Monitor and the New Era* (London), a Catholic weekly, also published a short notice about the address.[49]

'Abdu'l-Bahá's talk also reverberated outside the United Kingdom. In the United States at least three newspapers – the *Los Angeles Times*,[50] the *Buffalo Express*[51] and *The American* (Baltimore)[52] – published the talk.

In the Netherlands the *Nieuwe Rotterdamsche Courant* (Rotterdam) published an article which summarized the history and tenets the Bahá'í Faith, introduced the figure of 'Abdu'l-Bahá and quoted some parts of His address at the City Temple. The information was mainly drawn from Dawson's article in *The Christian Commonwealth*. 'The ethics of Bahaism are received with increasing sympathy in Theosophist and New Theology circles,'[53] stated the author. This article was afterwards published in Indonesia.[54]

In Spain, the Theosophist monthly *Sophia* (Madrid) published a Spanish translation of portions of 'Abdu'l-Bahá's address.[55]

Taking a Picture of the Master

As mentioned earlier, during the first days of His stay in London, 'Abdu'l-Bahá would not allow pictures of Him to be taken. That was also His norm in the Holy Land, where not even pilgrims were allowed to photograph Him.

After the repeated insistence of the newspapermen in London, 'Abdu'l-Bahá finally granted permission to a number of them to take some pictures of Him.[56] A report about 'Abdu'l-Bahá sent to America via agencies described the whole episode:

> Of course as soon as his arrival was known the house was besieged by newspaper interviewers and photographers. Abdul Baha consented to be interviewed and expounded his doctrines to the newspaper men, but when it was suggested that he should sit for his photograph he was horrified.
>
> 'I have never been photographed,' he said through an interpreter, 'and I don't intend to be. After my death people might make idols of these photographs and worship them and I don't intend to leave any such relics behind me.'
>
> Then ensued an amusing game of hide and seek. Dozens of newspaper photographers haunted the house. They hid in neighbouring doorways and areas and tried to snapshot the prophet as he came out. Abdul sent out scouts and when they reported that the house was beleaguered he refused to come out. The photographers refused to go away and finally they were invited into the house where his hostess and his secretaries implored them 'not to profane the prophet of God by making an image of him'. Some of the photographers went away but others remained in guard and finally Abdul consented to give one sitting. The result of that sitting, the first photograph ever taken of the leader of Bahaism, is reproduced herewith.[57]

The London News Agency distributed one of the portraits taken that day. On 12 September various London illustrated dailies published it with different captions.[58] In America *The New York Times* also published the 'first photograph ever taken of Abdul Baha Abbas' and stated that He 'may come to America'.[59]

Days later a series of portraits of the Master was taken at Lafayette studios in London.[60] Mary Thornburgh-Cropper held the copyright of the images and pictures soon circulated in a number of newspapers, especially in North America.

The Christian Commonwealth published on the front page of its 20 September issue a different portrait of the Master, having stated in its

13 September edition that the picture had been taken especially for the publication.[61] In ensuing weeks the magazine advertised their sale.[62]

Further Interviews and Articles

In the days following His address at the City Temple, 'Abdu'l-Bahá continued to grant interviews to the press. On 11 September *The Glasgow Herald* published a further letter from its London correspondent which presented some of the Bahá'í teachings. The author claimed to have seen 'Abdu'l-Bahá and described Him as a 'most genial and attractive personality'.[63] On 14 September the *Daily Mail* published a third article introducing the Bahá'í Faith and the figure of 'Abdu'l-Bahá. He was described as 'a man of medium height, but striking carriage, with kind, thoughtful eyes, high forehead, clear-cut features, white hair and beard . . .'[64] This article was later the basis for other articles that appeared in the United States.[65]

On 12 September *The Gloucester Citizen* also published a brief note about 'Abdu'l-Bahá which described Him as 'a patriarchal figure with a long snowy beard and piercing grey eyes'.[66] On 16 September the satiric London magazine *M.A.P.* (*Mainly About People*) published in its section 'Letters that were never posted' a letter attributed to Colonel W. J. B. Bird, who was at the time secretary of the National Service League, an organization created in 1902 with the aim of making military service compulsory in the United Kingdom. The editors of *M.A.P.* mocked Bird and his militarist ideals by inventing a letter addressed by him to 'Abdu'l-Bahá. In it Bird is portrayed as trying to convince the Master of the importance of military service: 'my dear sir, you cannot truly suppose that World-Love is anything more than a pretty dream? . . . I shall be delighted to see you if you would care to call at my office any day. We have one or two splendid little pamphlets which are bound to convince you that your whole idea of life is wrong.'[67]

On 24 September *The Weekly Budget* published a very interesting article by the American Bahá'í Isabel Fraser, which reproduced an account given by 'Abdu'l-Bahá Himself about His life. 'Freedom', 'Abdu'l-Bahá was reported to have said, 'is not a matter of place. It is a condition. I was thankful for the prison, and the lack of liberty was very pleasing for me, for those days were passed in the path of service, with the utmost difficulty and trials, bearing fruits and results. Unless one accepts dire vicissitudes, he will not attain.'[68] This article was later reprinted in the compilation *'Abdu'l-Bahá in London*.[69]

On 22 September the liberal halfpenny *Daily Chronicle* (London), with a circulation of 400,000 copies, also published a lengthy, sympathetic and well-informed article about the Bahá'í Faith which included the following statement about 'Abdu'l-Bahá:

> His method of life has been, and continues to be a luminous example of the fact that, here and now, despite all the surroundings of struggle for fame and wealth and material mastery, an existence guided and guarded by the Light of the Spirit, is a possible actual thing. Those who pray for the coming of the kingdom of God on earth may see in Abbas Effendi one who dwells in that kingdom consciously, and creates an environment pulsating with the peace that passeth ordinary understanding.[70]

Some American newspapers reproduced portions of this article.[71] Days later, the *Daily Chronicle* published the following account by a reporter present in one of the daily meetings held in London during the Master's sojourn in the city; it also included some biographical information (not reproduced here):

> Recently Abdul Baha rose from his chair in the London drawing-room and gave his hand to the interviewer – a long, thin, brown hand, with a tender, lingering clasp. The light from the window fell upon his white turban, and fawn-coloured cloak above white robes. It revealed the old man's face, with its aquiline nose and grey-blue eyes, soft as a deer's eyes, and the white beard that rested on his chest. It was the face of an Eastern prophet or teacher, whose skin has been browned by the burning sun of Syria, whose eyes have searched for God in the infinite blue of an Eastern sky, who has murmured his prayers in the shadow flung from a prison wall.
>
> A strange figure in a London flat! A Persian scribe in a brown turban and flowing robe sat silently by an English grand piano. A dark-eyed gentleman in a Turkish fez listened to the words spoken by Abdul Baha and repeated them in English.

'THE MASTER'

Some English ladies rose from their chairs when the man whom they call 'The Master' rose, and were silent when he spoke, though at other times they discussed his teaching and praised the beauty of his spirit. Among them was Lady Esther Blomfield, to whom the flat belongs, and whose reverence for the teaching of Abdul Baha is so great that she is proud to have him as her guest, and glad to give up her rooms to him, while she lives at a London hotel to save him from unpleasant publicity.

Abdul Baha deep in an arm-chair, with his hands folded across his chest, spoke to our representative, to whom a Turkish servant had handed a little glass of tea. The old man's voice was dreamy. But now and then a bright light burned in his eyes, and his aquiline face was illumined by the merriest of smiles.

He spoke of his gladness in coming to England. 'I love your people,' he said. 'They like to talk about the ways of God. They have welcomed me with beautiful friendliness. I thank them through you . . . This London of yours is a good city. It is full of well-behaved people. There is good order everywhere. I marvel at the silence of London.' He held up his hand and said: 'Listen! There is no noise! In the smallest village of Persia there is always shouting and tumult. The millions of London are quiet – very quiet. They are peaceful. The Government is good. London is perfect, but for one thing. Ah, the smoke of London!'

He spoke the word in English several times, 'Smoke! Smoke!' and then laughed.

A lady asked a question: 'Does the master believe in equality between men and women?'

Abdul Baha answered, and said: –

'Men and women were born with two eyes apiece, and one brain and one heart. God sees no difference between them. They may serve him with equal fidelity.'

He laughed again, enjoying his own merriment. 'In England men shave off their beards, so that all difference has vanished before our human eyes.' Then the spirit of the teacher stirred in him.

'My son, the world is not seeking now for differences. It is searching for unity. Peace among nations. The brotherhood of all races. Unity of faith in the worship of God.'

And that in brief is the teaching of Abdul Baha the Servant of God.

. . . Abdul Baha addresses himself to the whole world, and his message is for unity and love and peace under one great God. So, briefly, the spirit of his teaching was explained recently to 'The Daily Chronicle' representative, who, as he left the presence of the old man who calls himself 'The Servant of God', and heard his farewell in Persian speech, and received another lingering hand-clasp from a thin brown hand, went into the streets with the vivid impression of a personality with the dignity and courtesy of an Eastern patriarch, with the sweetness which belongs to old age that has not been embittered in spite of suffering and with eyes that look out upon life with a strange simplicity. It seemed like the memory of an Arabian Nights dream on a grey day, in modern London.[72]

In America the *Christian Science Monitor* (Boston) published on 21 October an article sent by its London correspondent who had the chance of interviewing the Master during a car drive through the city. The text included some historical information about the Faith, not reproduced here:

LEADER OF BAHAISM TALKS ABOUT ITS ETHICS

ABBAS EFFENDI, PRESENT HEAD OF PERSIAN PHILOSOPHY, IN INTERVIEW WITH REPRESENTATIVE OF THE CHRISTIAN SCIENCE MONITOR, COMMENDS THOSE NEWSPAPERS THAT TELL THE TRUTH

LONDON. A great national movement is a phenomenon which cannot fail to interest thinking people. Such is the Bahaism of Persia, which already numbers in its ranks some third of the population of that country. Entirely unsectarian, aiming at uniting in a common fellowship men of all races and all religions, it has spread rapidly through Persian where those differences are not so numerous and so strongly defined as in Europe.

In Europe and in America, however, it has found many sympathizers, but to what extent it will appeal to western civilization remains still to be seen. Even in the east it has still to make its way amid the discordances of the religions which existed before the day of the Prophet . . .

LEADER INTERESTED

It was in a London drawing room. The [illegible] old man, with his mobile face, white turban, and long brown robe, sat in the corner, talking easily and quickly, while his secretary, in his little black fez sat opposite, and translated. A moment later the motor was announced, as he walked down the long staircase, [illegible], with his hands clasped [illegible] his back to take his seat.

He asked several questions with regard to *The Christian Science Monitor* as the great motor rolled silently through the rush of the London traffic and expressed the greatest interest in all he had heard of its mission.

'Those papers,' he said, speaking with some of the picturesque imagery of the east, 'which strive to speak only that which is truth, which hold the mirror up to truth, are like the sun, they light the world everywhere with truth, and their work is imperishable. Those who play for their own little selfish ends give no true light to the world and perish on their own futility. In carrying out the aims of your paper you are adding to the light. Go on, and let nothing stop you.'

POLITICS TABOO

I spoke to him of Persian politics, but he smiled and shook his head. 'The government has forbidden us to discuss politics in public, and we bow to their wishes. We realize, of course, that the views we are disseminating are permeating the thought of Persia, and bearing fruit in a hundred ways to the advantage of the country and to its advancement, and we are content with the knowledge of this. After all, we are teaching the World views far above party strife and national animosities. We are teaching the universal brotherhood of man. We look down on all lesser ideas and aims, as from the mountain-top you look at the pigmies in the valleys. We strive not for Persia nor Turkey, not for France nor Germany, not for England nor America, but for humanity.'

We were passing down Constitution Hill, and he bent forwards from the depths of the motor and asked his secretary to find out what the great garden was. 'The palace,' he repeated, when he was told it was the garden of Buckingham Palace, and all along the route he continued to ask questions, yet always came back immediately to the subject he was explaining, without losing grip for one moment.

Suddenly his secretary produced a letter from his pocket, from a London paper, addressed to the secretary of the prophet. His eyes twinkled as the address was read out to him, and he laughed quietly. 'Why will your papers do it?' he inquired in amused protest. 'I am not a prophet. I do not claim to be a prophet. I am only the servant of humanity.'

MOVEMENT GROWS

I told him that sometimes papers seemed determined of insisting on titles the recipients repudiated altogether, possibly because they made better headlines. 'I think it must be that,' he said, 'You put it well, how I have told them, again and again, I am not a prophet, only the servant of striving humanity.' I asked him how large the movement in Persia was and in return he asked if I meant how many actually professed Bahaists there were, or how many people accepted its teaching. 'There are many more of the latter than of the former,' he explained, 'for it is not yet popular to accept Bahaism. Numbers, too, are hard to arrive at, for the government, as yet, takes no census. Still, there are perhaps two or three million of the latter which, in Persia, is not a bad proportion.'

The motor was passing along Westminster hall and under the Victoria tower. He inquired what the building was, and murmured thoughtfully to himself, 'the Parliament house'. A moment later he inquired about the Tate gallery, and, on hearing its history, exclaimed, 'The citizens of your London have indeed been generous to it.' On the embankment, the conversation turned into education. He spoke strongly of the importance and advantages of a sound and comprehensive scheme of teaching in all its branches. Persia, he said, had much to accomplish in that respect. Compared with Egypt, its schools, he admitted, were deficient, though at the present time much was being done to remedy matters. Egypt, however, had had the help of many years of English assistance, and England recognized fully the claims of a good educational system.

JOURNALISTIC TRUTH NEEDED

Battersea Park came to distract his attention for the moment. He was amused and interested by the flower beds and the little lake on which, though the evening was late, the boats were still crowding. Then he returned once more on his own pleasure, to the press. He spoke earnestly of the necessity for strong, disinterested papers, whose only object was to tell the world the truth of what was happening from day to day. 'How', he demanded, 'were people to know the truth of what was happening if it was veiled from them in their journals?' Bahaism, he explained, had suffered severely from ignorant misrepresentation in the press, when all it asked for was that the truth about it should be made known, yet that was the one thing withheld. A determination on the part of the press of the world, that nothing save the truth about it should be told, would have saved much suffering to many people. 'What was Bahaism,' he asked, 'but the attempt to teach people to follow and seek the truth, without attempting to interfere with their views of life. It was the permeation of mind with truth.'

The dusk of the evening had closed in darkness, and the little electric lamp in the roof of the motor was shedding its light faintly around. He pointed out to it with a smile.

GOOD ALL-EMBRACING

'The human view of good,' he said, 'was not unlike that light shedding its rays in some little cabined space, but good was like the sun, lighting the whole world. A man begins,' he said, 'with a little selfish view of good limited to himself; after a time, he learns more wisdom, and his view of good enlarges to his own household. Then with more wisdom comes the realization that good must include his family, no matter how large. Again more wisdom, and his family becomes his village, his village his city, and in turn, his city, his country. But this is not enough; as his wisdom grows, his country becomes his continent, and his continent, the world; his family has become mankind. It is the duty of the press to teach this wisdom to mankind, for it is the wisdom of God. You are doing this in your paper, because you are following the teaching of Jesus the Christ.' For the first time he spoke eagerly, pressing his hand upon my knee, 'It is the work of a true press to preach the wisdom of God.'

In another minute, we were at his door. 'Good night,' he said as he shook hands, 'in a few weeks I return to Persia. If it is God's will we shall meet again.'[73]

Visit to the Keshub Niketon

Among those who visited the Master at Lady Blomfield's residence was a delegation of London members of the Brahmo Samaj community. This was a movement started by Keshub Chandra Sen (1838–84) around 1866 as a split from Debendranath Tagore's Brahmo Samaj (later Adi Brahmo Samaj). Keshub saw himself as the bearer of what he called 'the New Dispensation' with universalist aspirations and incorporated into the religious practices of his group a series of rituals from other religions, especially Christianity.

Rev. Promotho Loll Sen,[74] the leader of the community in London, extended an invitation to the Master to visit their recently-opened headquarters in Hampstead, which He visited on Sunday, 17 September. An interesting account of the meeting was published in *The Christian Commonwealth*:

> . . . Mr. Loll Sen, who was conducting the usual service, which is held in the afternoon at 5 o'clock, had just said a few words before reading, as one of his lessons for the day, from THE CHRISTIAN COMMONWEALTH the short message of Abdul Baha delivered in the City Temple on the previous Sunday, when his arrival was announced. Mr. Sen greeted him in his Indian fashion with a 'ramaskar', and went on with the reading, matching the message of the present leader of the Bahai movement with a message from one of the Town Hall lectures of the last leader of the Brahmo Somaj.[75] . . . After the service, at the request of friends, a few words were spoken in Persian by the revered leader of the Bahais. These were kindly translated for the congregation by a lady who had accompanied him.[76] Rev. Promotho Loll Sen speaks of the occasion as the last of the jubilees they have had at the Niketon.[77]

'Abdu'l-Bahá requested the Hampstead Bahá'í Arthur Cuthbert to visit on his behalf the Brahmo Somaj centre on Sunday, 24 September, 'with a special message of his love for these earnest people in a strange land'.[78]

The Archdeacon Wilberforce

One of the distinguished visitors at 97 Cadogan Gardens was Archdeacon Basil Wilberforce, of Westminster, grandson of the famous abolitionist William Wilberforce.[79] He had become acquainted with the Bahá'í Faith as early as 1900 when the American Bahá'í Arthur P. Dodge contacted him on his return from a pilgrimage to the Holy Land.[80] In later years one member of his parish and personal friend, Lady Blomfield, became a Bahá'í. Since at least as early as 1907 he also knew personally Wellesley Tudor Pole who, as seen earlier, would eventually also become a Bahá'í.

Like Campbell, Wilberforce had also maintained some contact with the Master before His arrival in Europe. On 1 March 1911 he even spoke on the Bahá'í Faith in his church and later corresponded with some members of his parish to answer their questions on the Faith.[81]

Blomfield described Wilberforce's visit to 'Abdu'l-Bahá as 'a remarkable interview. Our dear friend, the Archdeacon, sat on a low chair by the Master. 'Abdu'l-Baha spoke to him in His beautiful Persian. He placed His hand on the head of the Archdeacon, talked long to him, and answered many questions. Evidently His words penetrated further than the outer ears, for both were deeply moved. On this occasion the invitation was given for 'Abdu'l-Baha to speak to the congregation of St John the Divine,[82] at Westminster, on the following Sunday.'[83] The invitation was accepted and on 17 September 'Abdu'l-Bahá delivered an address during the regular Sunday service.

In introducing 'Abdu'l-Bahá to the audience, Wilberforce referred to Him as 'Master' and 'wonderful visitor' and even invited Him to sit in the bishop's chair. Campbell and Dawson were also present among the numerous members of the public that attended the meeting. Dorothy Hodgson, a Bahá'í who was present at St John, recorded some of the introductory remarks about 'Abdu'l-Bahá made by Wilberforce on that occasion:

> Look at our wonderful guest of tonight who has suffered forty years imprisonment for the sake of humanity. Look at those hands which have felt the chains, those feet which have endured the gyves, because of his Message of Love and Unity to all peoples, and now he is free and has come to us from the East to bring that Message. Oh!

> Pray that God's blessing may descend upon him; send out vibrations of love to meet this Spirit of God who is in our midst.[84]

'Abdu'l-Bahá then delivered His address and afterwards a translation was read for the audience.[85] Peggy Scott, a reporter with *The Christian Commonwealth*, described in the following account what transpired on that evening:

> THE VANISHING OF THE VEIL
> ABDUL BAHA AT ST. JOHN'S, WESTMINSTER
> ARCHDEACON WILBERFORCE'S WELCOME
>
> Eighteen months ago Archdeacon Wilberforce, who had been watching the Bahai movement for some time with interest, sent a message to Abdul Baha. 'We are all one,' he said, 'there, behind the veil.' And Abdul Baha replied from his home in Akka, 'Tell him the veil is very thin, and it will vanish quite.'
>
> All who were present in St. John's, Westminster, last Sunday evening, could not fail to realise that the veil was vanishing. Archdeacon Wilberforce's beautiful intercessory service was a means to that end. He asked that each one in the vast congregation should at that time put away all selfish thought and use all energy in prayer for those in trouble. 'Will you bear upon your heart,' he said, 'a mother ill in India.' Then followed a graphic description of the circumstances, until each felt the loneliness of the sick woman and the keen anxiety of the daughter hastening to her side. So the spirit of unity was spread abroad.
>
> Then Dr. Wilberforce told of the teacher – 'Master' he called him – who had come to London to emphasise unity, and who was present that evening at St. John's to proclaim the meaning of it. 'Whatever our views,' the Archdeacon said, 'we shall, I am sure, unite in welcoming a man who has been for forty years a prisoner for the cause of brotherhood and love.' Abdul Baha is not an orator or even a preacher, but, in view of all he stands for, we are keenly interested in everything he has to say.
>
> Full of expectation, the congregation waited when the Archdeacon for a brief moment left the church. Divested of his white surplice, he returned with Abdul Baha. All eyes were fixed on the leader of the Bahai movement. In his customary Eastern robe and

head-dress, walking hand in hand with a leader of the West, it did indeed seem that the veil was vanishing.

Down the aisle they passed to the bishop's chair, which had been placed in front of the altar for Abdul Baha. Standing at the lectern, Archdeacon Wilberforce introduced the 'wonderful' visitor. He told of his life in prison, of his sufferings and bravery, of his self-sacrifice, of his clear and shining faith. He voiced his own belief that religion is one, as God is love.

Then Abdul Baha rose. Speaking very clearly, with wonderful intonations in his voice and using his hands freely, it seemed to those who listened almost as if they grasped his meaning, though he spoke in Persian. When he had finished, Archdeacon Wilberforce read the translation of his address.

His theme was the Character of the Manifestations of God. He said that God the Infinite could not be comprehended of man; that whatever man understands of God is born of his imagination. For illustration he pointed to the mineral, which does not comprehend the vegetable, as the vegetable cannot understand the animal. So the animal cannot reach the intelligence of humanity. Neither, he said, is it possible for man, a created being, to understand the Almighty Creator. Nevertheless, the perfection and qualifications of God are seen in every created being and in the most perfect beings in the most perfect manner. In the manifestations of God, Abdul Baha likened these qualities to the rays of the sun focussed in a mirror. If we claim that the sun is seen in the mirror, we do not mean that the whole sun has descended from the holy heights of heaven and entered into the mirror, that is impossible. The Eternal Nature is seen in the manifestations, and its light and splendour are visible in extreme glory. Therefore men have always been taught and led by the prophets of God. The prophets of God are the mediators of God. All the prophets and messengers have come from one Holy Spirit and bear the message of God, suited to the age in which they appear.

It is the *One* Light in them, and they are one with each other. But the eternal does not become phenomenal, neither can the phenomenal become eternal. St. Paul, the great apostle, said, 'We all, with open face, beholding as in a mirror the glory of God, are changed into the same image, from glory to glory.'

> Then, raising his hands, Abdul Baha prayed: 'O God, the Forgiver! O Heavenly Educator! This assembly is adorned with the mention of thy holy name. Thy children turn their face towards thy kingdom. Hearts are made happy and souls are comforted. Merciful God! Cause us to repent of our shortcomings! Accept us in thy heavenly kingdom and give unto us an abode where there shall be no error. Give us peace. Give us knowledge, and open unto us the gates of thy heaven.
>
> 'Thou art the Giver of all! Thou art the Forgiver! Thou art the Merciful!'
>
> The final note of a real chord of harmony was stuck when Archdeacon Wilberforce asked that Abdul Baha would pronounce the Benediction. 'I think we should take it kneeling,' he said.
>
> Who shall say that the veil is not vanishing?[86]

The visit of 'Abdu'l-Bahá to St John had some echoes outside England. In an article about Charles Wagner for *El Imparcial* (Madrid), the litterateur Constantino Román Salamero[87] briefly mentioned that 'in London, Archdeacon Wilberforce, chaplain of the Parliament and nephew of Cardinal Manning, invited Abdul Baha Abbas to go up the steps of the Cathedral of St. John in Westminster, causing scandal among the orthodox'.[88] In Egypt the *Wádí al-Níl* (Alexandria) published an Arabic translation of the talk.[89]

After the passing of Wilberforce in 1916, Constance Maud[90] wrote a tribute to him for the literary magazine *Nineteenth Century* (London) in which she stated:

> In his church of St. John's the archdeacon showed the same eclectic spirit as in his social life, the same desire for all helpful, beautiful and outstretching thought to have a hearing. Among those whom he invited to preach in his church after the Sunday evening service was the great Persian teacher Abdul Baha, head of the Bahaists, who number over six millions in Persia at the present time. To see the venerable white-robed Eastern walking hand in hand up the nave of St. John's with the silver-headed archdeacon was to realize that the miracle had come to pass – East and West had met, and fused. For they knelt as brothers before the same Father of all spirits; and

perhaps with few priests of his own Church was Basil Wilberforce in such close, inner sympathy as with this wise and beautiful Oriental, so humble and so simple, yet possessing such profound insight into human life and character, refusing utterly to stand on the pinnacle on to which his followers pertinaciously endeavoured to lift him, whether they were Zoroastrians hailing him as fourteenth incarnation of Zoroaster, Buddhists acclaiming him as another Buddha, or pseudo-Christians insisting he should be proclaimed as Christ of the Second Coming. To all he answered in his few words of broken English: 'Not Christ – not Zoroaster – Servant of the Glory – like you and you – Servant not Lord.'[91]

The National Brotherhood Conference

The Brotherhood Movement started in the 19th century as an attempt to increase the number of men participating in the life of the churches. Brotherhood societies in Great Britain proliferated rapidly at the turn of the century and at the time of 'Abdu'l-Bahá's arrival in England almost all Christian denominations had their own society for men. These societies were federated and celebrated yearly meetings. The aims of the Brotherhood Movement in England were:

> (1) to lead men and women into the Kingdom of God. (2) To unite men in Brotherhoods of mutual help. (3) To win the masses of the people for Jesus Christ. (4) To encourage the study of Social Science. (5) To enforce the obligation of Christian citizenship. (6) To preach the unity of social service.[92]

On 18–19 September 1911, a National Brotherhood Conference was celebrated at the Albert Hall. An article in *The Christian Commonwealth* mentioned the fact that 'Abdu'l-Bahá was invited to speak at the morning session of the second day of the conference:

> Slow as the race has been to learn and apply this elementary fact about itself, it is a hopeful sign that the spirit of brotherhood is stronger, more widespread, and more operative to-day than ever before. We see it at work in all parts of the world and in all relations of life. It was in every way appropriate that Abdul Baha should be

> invited, as he was to attend the International session of the Brotherhood Conference on Tuesday morning; for the fundamental principle of Bahai teaching is simply brotherhood. We are coming to see more and more how mutually dependent we are – individual upon individual, class upon class, nation upon nation.[93]

'Abdu'l-Bahá, however, was unable to accept the invitation. A telegram containing His reply was read at the closing of the morning session: 'Greeting. Cordial thanks for invitation. Deeply regret unable to be present. Our spirit and aims are the same. Hope to meet you on my next visit. Abdul Baha.'[94]

A Message to *The Christian Commonwealth*

As well as the full report of the Master's visit to St John's, Westminster and an account of His visit to the Niketon Keshub, on 20 September *The Christian Commonwealth* also published a facsimile of a Tablet 'specially written' for the magazine by 'Abdu'l-Bahá. The English translation was printed on the same page:

> A MESSAGE FROM ABDUL BAHA
> TRANSLATION (SUMMARY)
> BY TAMADDON-UL-MOLK
>
> God sends prophets for the education of the people and the progress of mankind. All the manifestations of God have raised the people generally. They serve the world of humanity by the bounty of God. The sure proof that they are the manifestations of God is in the education and progress of the people. The Jews were in the lowest condition of ignorance, and captive to Pharaoh, when Moses appeared and raised them to a high state of civilisation. Thus was the reign of Solomon brought about. Science and art were taught to all the world. Even Greek philosophers became students of Solomon's teaching. So was Moses proved to be a prophet.
>
> But after a certain time the Israelites retrogressed and became subject to the Romans and Greeks. Then the brilliant Star of Jesus rose from the horizon on the Israelites and brightened all the world. All sects and creeds and nations were united. There cannot be any better proof than this that Jesus was the Word of God.

So with the Arab nations. They lived in savagery, they were oppressed by the Persian and Greek governments when the Light of Mahomet shone forth. Then all Arabia was brightened. The oppressed and degraded nation became enlightened and civilised, so much so that the other nations came to learn of Arabian civilisation. This was the proof of Mahomet's divine mission.

All teaching of the prophets is one; of one faith, of one Divine light shining over all the world. Now, all people should, under the banner of the oneness of humanity turn away from prejudice, become friends and believers in all the prophets: as Christians believe in Moses so the Jews should believe in Jesus. As the Mahommedans believe in Christ and in Moses, likewise, the Jews and the Christians should believe in Mahomet. So all disputes would disappear, all would be united. Baha'u'llah came for this purpose. He has made one the three religions. He has uplifted the standard of the oneness, of the honour of humanity in the centre of the world. Now we must gather round it and try with heart and soul to bring about the union of mankind.[95]

Both the image of the message and a translation of the above summary were included months later in Spain as part of an article published in the theosophical magazine *Sophia* (Madrid),[96] which was probably the basis of a very similar article that appeared in El Salvador.[97]

The same issue of *The Christian Commonwealth* also contained a letter to the editor sent from Edinburgh by a certain William Marwich from Jamaica who shared his impressions of the Bahá'í Faith, explained how he was acquainted with it for the first time, and recommended some literature. 'As a Scotsman, who is in fullest sympathy with all movements towards spiritual unity,' stated Marwich, 'I venture personally, and I think I may add as expressing the desire of many like-minded fellow-countrymen, to send through you a respectful fraternal greeting to Abdul Baha, and expression of sympathy with his deeply spiritual message. Were he able to visit Scotland he would receive a warm welcome from many who have been influenced by the message of Bahaism.'[98]

Visit to the Pioneer Preachers' Hostel

As mentioned earlier, Campbell's 'League of Progressive Thought and Social Service' had several thousand members. By 1911 it had changed its name to 'League of Liberal Christian Thought and Social Service' and included among its members a contingent of preachers whose task was to spread Campbell's New Theology. 'Abdu'l-Bahá was invited to see two endowments associated with the work of the Liberal Christian League and He visited them on Friday, 22 September. *The Christian Commonwealth* gave the following account:

> ABDUL BAHA AT THE PIONEER PREACHERS' HOSTEL.
> A visit was paid by Abdul Baha last Friday afternoon to the Hostel of the Pioneer Preachers of the Liberal-Christian league, 28, King's Square, Goswell Road, E.C. He was received by Mr. Campbell, who gave him a very hearty welcome, as did also the preachers in residence. Abbas Effendi was charmed with the simplicity of the appointments of the hostel and expressed his delight that young men should choose to live in that way for the sake of preaching to people who could give them nothing in return. Going into the pretty little chapel, he said it was a true sanctuary, but it was the demeanour, the spirit of the men themselves that made it so. He felt that all the influences of the place were good. Then he sat and talked about religious revival, the preachers asking him questions. He considered that the immediate prospect for religion in the West was not outwardly hopeful owing to various influences, but that in religion as in everything else there were seasons of decay and resurrection. One of the young men having remarked that the religion of the West was now passing through the winter season, he smiled an affirmative, and went on to describe what the springtime of spiritual life in the West would be like. He thought it would be a recognition of the spiritual unity of the whole race. Someone present said, 'Then are these young preachers the snowdrops which herald the coming of the spring?' This apt remark greatly pleased him, and he said, 'Undoubtedly!' He added that he had seen in England many signs of true religious vitality; it is by no means a country that is spiritually dead.
>
> Abdul Baha afterwards went into the Home of Service, 36,

King's Square, and shook hands with the ladies. He said that women who gave their lives in the way these were doing were deserving of high honour from all their sisters everywhere, for they had surrendered what to most women was dear – the joy of the exclusive home circle.[99]

Visit to Bristol

During His sojourn in England, 'Abdu'l-Bahá also paid a short visit to Bristol on Saturday, 23 September, staying for two nights at the Clifton Guest House,[100] 16–17 Royal York Crescent, a facility run from 1909 by Wellesley Tudor Pole, who used to invite speakers to conferences on different topics, and which was aimed to be 'a Centre for those who take an interest in the forward Movements of the day and for the furtherance of true Brotherhood'.[101] 'Abdu'l-Bahá delivered a public address there which was listened to by some 80 people. A reporter with the western edition of *The Daily Chronicle* (Bristol) was present at the meeting and wrote the following account of it:

ABBAS EFFENDI

THE PROPHET OF BAHAISM IN BRISTOL

East and West came together in a Clifton drawing-room on Saturday night, and once again a new religious message was unfolded – or, rather, not a message so much as a point of view. In the name of that substratum of precept and ideal which is common to all religious faiths, let all the communions and all the sects work harmoniously in their own paths for the promotion of universal brotherhood, service, and peace.

Not altogether a new idea that may be objected, but as viewed, in the light of the thousand jangling creeds that go to make up our national theology, sufficiently so to arrest the attention of thoughtful men, especially when we take into account its picturesque presentation by a famous Persian leader who, by the purity of his faith and the long martyrdom of imprisonment which he has endured on account of it, has surely won the title of a holy man . . .

Abdul Baha has been in London – his first visit to Western Europe – for purposes of cementing the union of thought and sympathy which Bahaism has been the means of creating among friends of humanity in this country and in America with the Eastern advocates of the movement. Bristol is the only provincial city which he has honoured with his presence, and by the courtesy of Mr. Wellesley Tudor-Pole, who visited Abdul Baha at Alexandria, in 1910, a representative of this journal was present at the deeply interesting meeting of Saturday evening in Royal York Crescent, Clifton.

REGENERATION OF THE WORD

It was simply a drawing-room gathering, for Bahaism seeks no proselytes, aiming at the deeper spiritualisation of the existing creeds in the interests of the common task of the regeneration and uplifting of the world. Abdul Baha is 67 years of age, of robust build and a stately and reverend presence. He wore a Persian headdress, and a flowing gown of light brown material over vestments of white. His beard is iron-grey turning to patriarchal silver, and kindly blue eyes, full of the light of enthusiasm, look out from beneath overhanging brows. With him was his secretary and interpreter, Tamaddon-ul-Molk, who, after 'the master' had spoken, told us in occasionally halting English, of terrible episodes he had seen in the persecution of people of his faith in Persia.

The little congregation rose by one impulse as, after a few introductory words from Mr. Tudor-Pole, Abdul Baha entered the room. Through Tamaddon-ul-Molk he asked us how we were, and gave us a hearty welcome. And then rising from the sofa, that he might be seen of all, he began to speak in a voice of singular sweetness. His first sentence was from the Old Testament – 'Send out Thy light and Thy truth, let them lead me, and let them bring me to Thy holy hill.' It was a short address, full of imagery, in which he spoke of the world being enlightened and mankind spiritualized by the coming of Jesus Christ, but how there had followed a falling off and away, and that now the light was becoming strong and clear in the dawn of a new era, when the nations should dwell together in peace and amity and brotherhood in all good works.

And then he prayed and blessed us, not folding his hands in the conventional manner but holding them extended and slightly bent, with concaved palms, towards his breast, as though already gathering in the blessing for which he prayed. It was a moment full of feeling for those who realised, as he stood there, the gigantic sacrifice for conscience sake which his whole life exemplified. And not a vain sacrifice, since he can point to Mohammedans, Jews, Christians, Zoroastrians, Parsees, and members of many another faith, united and joined together in Persia in the bond of Bahaism.

A question elicited the fact that the new inspiration has many adherents in India, especially among the friends of the Brahmo Somaj movement.[102]

The Christian Commonwealth, always keeping its readers informed about the movements of the Master, also offered the following report of 'Abdu'l-Bahá's visit to Bristol, which included a summary of His public talk:

Last Saturday afternoon Abdul Baha arrived from London with a few friends to spend the weekend at the Clifton Guest House. After a rest he expressed the wish to see the country around Bristol. What impressed him most was the fresh green of the woods and fields, the spaciousness of the open downs, and the absence of smoke.

He was present at the evening meal and warmly greeted those who had gathered together to welcome him. After commenting upon the peacefulness of the house he contrasted the costliness of material feasts with the pure simplicity of this meal, where the all pervading spirit was that of love and friendship between East and West. There were nineteen at table and on hearing it Abdul Baha remarked that nineteen was a good number (held sacred by the Baha'is) and that this meal would go down to posterity as a matter of history. It was afterwards proposed to send to the believers at Teheran a message of united gratitude for the presence of Abdul Baha, in response to the generous greeting that they had sent on their part to the followers in England. The same evening about eighty friends assembled to listen to the words of the great Persian teacher. Mr. Tudor Pole took the chair and introduced him by a few words on the Bahai movement. Abdul Baha then rose and spoke with impressive dignity, Tamaddon-ul-Molk translating.

The master says that he has come from very far to see you, and that you are very welcome. He praises God that after forty-two years of imprisonment for the faith he is able to come to you. Abdul Baha then continued: 'These people are very spiritual, with hearts looking towards God, waiting for the glad tidings. They have come through the power of the Holy Spirit, therefore we thank God. May he send you straightforwardness to guide you to your holy mountains and blessed places; the Truth has come, let its holy springs water you. It is evident that day follows night, and after dawn the sunset. Just as the sun sets and rises and sets again, so Jesus Christ appeared on the horizon of this world like a sun of Truth, bringing light and joy to the whole world. But the people now are not in such close touch with his spirit; their religion and faith are not so strong. The people are searching after material things instead of looking forward to the kingdom. Again God has sent light and truth into the world. The heavenly star has appeared in Persia; a new spiritual illumination is now penetrating throughout the world (the result of Baha'u'llah's teaching). The great light shall spread through all lands.' Abdul Baha said that our hearts should become as mirrors and be ready prepared for the glad tidings of the dawning of a new age. Jesus Christ said that we should be born again through the spiritual fire and love of God and be baptized by the water of life and the Holy Spirit, that we may obtain everlasting life. Abdul Baha went on to say: 'Be very kind and serve everyone; become lovers of justice and pray for the whole of mankind; help the poor and the children; heal the sick; shelter the refugees; and be known by your lives as the children of God; so may that sun become the light of the world, casting its radiance upon East and West. May the world become a new world; may war and slaughtering cease and the most Great Peace come. God help you to spread this Divine teaching, and to establish everywhere the characteristics of Jesus'. He then prayed as follows: 'O God, these people are your servants; they turn their faces to you to receive the manifestations of your bounty. Brighten all these hearts and bless their souls. Give them new life to follow your teachings. Let them enter into your kingdom, and bestow on them the blessing of the Holy Spirit. Open their eyes to the light and help them to serve mankind. Thou art a powerful giver and merciful. God bless you all.'

> After asking the people if they were happy he left the room. Tamaddon-ul-Molk then gave a short account of the Bahais and the terrible sufferings they had undergone for their faith. He spoke of some of the martyrdoms which he had himself witnessed. Mr Tudor Pole then spoke of the great Persian lady, a poetess, Quarratul 'Ain, of whom an account appeared in *The Christian Commonwealth* of September 13. After a few questions were asked the gathering closed. Abdul Baha stood in the doorway and shook hands with everyone, wishing them Godspeed.
>
> Sunday being a glorious day, Abdul Baha went driving both morning and afternoon; he walked on the downs, and spoke with many of the little children whom he met. Later he gathered together the servants of the house, spoke to them of the dignity of labour, and thanked them for their work. He then went over the Clifton Guest House, and blessed it as a centre for pilgrims from East and West, saying that it would become truly both a guest house and a rest house indeed.
>
> Abdul Baha returned to London on Monday, and Bristol is the only provincial city that he visited during his present stay in this country. He leaves England early next week.[103]

Days later, the *Clifton Chronicle and Directory* published in its 'Arrivals' section a note giving the names of those who were staying with 'Abdu'l-Bahá at the Clifton Guest House.[104]

Farewell to 'Abdu'l-Bahá

On Friday, 29 September, a farewell reception was held in honor of 'Abdu'l-Bahá. The meeting gathered over two hundred friends of the Master and the Faith. Among the speakers that day were the writer and educator Alice Buckton,[105] Claude Montefiore,[106] Professor Michael Sadler[107] and Sir Richard Stapley.[108] *The Christian Commonwealth* published the following account:

> At the invitation of Mrs. Thornburgh-Cropper about two hundred representative people met in the hall of the Passmore Edwards' Settlement, Tavistock Place last Friday evening to bid farewell to Abdul Baha Abbas on the eve of his departure for Paris. Arriving in London

on Monday evening, September 4, he has spent a happy and busy four weeks in our midst. Except for a brief visit to Bristol last week, he remained at 97, Cadogan Gardens. His time was mainly occupied in interviews with people who wished to meet him. These included not a few whose names are household words in this country, and some travelled long distances to see him.

A beautiful spirit prevailed on Friday evening. The atmosphere was very different from that of an ordinary meeting or religious gathering. Everyone present was enriched by the lofty spiritual tone of the proceedings; the notes struck were all in the direction of Brotherhood, unity, peace. While a report of the speeches would give a very inadequate idea of the effect produced, yet they were so well-conceived, so sincere, so exquisitely phrased as to be all worthy of reproduction. Among others Ameer Ali Syed wrote regretting his inability to be present, and Archdeacon Wilberforce sent affectionate greetings.

After the Lord's Prayer and prayers for Unity of Baha'u'llah and Gelasius (V century), Professor Michael Sadler spoke as follows: –

> We have met together to bid farewell to Abdul Baha, and to thank God for his example and teaching, and for the power of his prayers to bring Light into confused thought. Hope into the place of dread. Faith where doubt was, and into troubled hearts the Love which overmasters self-seeking and fear. Though we all, among ourselves, in our devotional allegiance, have our own individual loyalties, to all of us Abdul Baha brings, and has brought, a message of unity, of sympathy, and of peace. He bids us all be real and true in what we profess to believe; and to treasure above everything the Spirit behind the form. With him we bow before the hidden name, before that which is of every life the Inner life. He bids us worship in fearless loyalty to our own faith, but with ever stronger yearning after union, brotherhood, and love, so turning ourselves in spirit, and with our whole heart, that we may enter more into the mind of God, which is above class, above race, and beyond time.

Prof. Sadler concluded with a beautiful prayer of James Martineau.

Mr. Eric Hammond said the Bahai movement stood for unity: one God, one people; a myriad souls manifesting the divine unity, a unity so complete that no difference of colour or creed could possibly differentiate between one manifestation of God and another, and a sympathy so all-embracing as to include the very lowest, meanest, shabbiest of men; unity, sympathy, brotherhood, leading up to a concord universal. He concluded with a saying of Baha'u'llah, that the divine cause of universal good could not be limited to either East or West. Miss Alice Buckton said we were standing at one of the springtimes of the world, and from that assembly of representatives of thought and work and love would go out all over the world influences making for unity and brotherhood. The complete equality of men and women was one of the chief notes of Bahai teaching. Sir Richard Stapley pointed out that unity must not be sought in the forms and externals of religion, but in the inner spirit. In Persia there had been such an impulse toward real unity as was a rebuke to this so-called Christian country. Mr. Claude Montefiore, as a Jew, rejoiced in the growth of the spirit of unity, and regarded that meeting as prophetic of the better time to come, and in some sense a fulfilment of the idea, expressed by one who fell as a martyr to the Roman Catholic faith, Sir Thomas More, who wrote of the great Church of the Utopians, in which all varieties of creeds gathered together, having a service and liturgy that expressed the higher unity, while admitting special loyalties. Mrs. Stannard dwelt on what that meeting and the sentiments expressed meant to the East, especially to the women, whose condition it was difficult for the West to understand. Tamaddon-ul-Molk testified to the unifying effect the Bahai movement had has in Persia, and of the wonderful way in which it had spread to America and other countries.

Then 'The Master' rose to give his farewell address. An impressive figure, the face rather worn, but the eyes full of animation, he stood for about fifteen minutes, speaking in soft, musical Persian. From time to time he gently stroked his white beard, and, with, hands extended, palms upwards, he closed with a prayer:-

> 'O noble friends and seekers for the Kingdom of God! God be praised! We see the light of love is shining in the East and the West; and the tent of intercourse is raised in the centre of

the world for the drawing together of hearts and souls. The call of the Kingdom is gone all over the world. The annunciation of the world's Universal Peace has enlightened the world's conscience. My hope is that by the zeal and ardour of the pure-hearted, the darkness of hatred and differences will be entirely abolished, and the light of love and unity will shine more brightly. This world shall become a new world. Things material will become the mirror of the Kingdom. Human hearts will meet and embrace each other. The whole world shall become as a man's native country; and different races shall be counted as one race. Then disputes and differences will vanish and the Divine Beloved will be revealed in the society of mankind. It is because the East and the West are illumined by One Sun, all races, nations, and creeds are the servants of the One God. The whole earth is one home, and all peoples are bathed in the ocean of God's mercy. God created all. He gives sustenance to all, He guides and trains all under the shadow of His bounty. We must follow the example God himself gives us, and do away with all these differences and quarrels.

'Praise be to God! The signs of friendship are appearing, and a proof of this is that to-day I – an Eastern – in the London of the West have received extreme kindness, regard, and love, and I am deeply thankful and happy. I shall never forget this time I have spent with you. I leave you with extreme regret, and with prayers for you, that all the beauty of the Kingdom may be yours.'

The translation of the valedictory having been read by Professor Sadler, Abdul Baha closed the meeting by giving his blessing in undulating rhythmic tones.

By the time these lines appear Abdul Baha Abbas will have left our shores, but the memory of his gracious personality is a permanent possession. His influence will be felt for many days to come, and has already done much to promote that union of East and West for which many have long yearned.[109]

The Christian World also published a brief note about the meeting and the contents of His talk: 'The visit of Abdul Baha, the leader of the Bahai movement, to England has come to an end. In a farewell address to his sympathisers he enumerated the leading tenets of the Bahai faith as the search for truth, the oneness of humanity, the equality and brotherhood of mankind, the eternal love, the dependence of religion upon science and of science upon religion, a social gospel, and the coming of the great peace.'[110] On 27 September *The Near East* also announced 'Abdu'l-Bahá's imminent departure.[111]

Address at the Higher Thought Centre

It is likely that 'Abdu'l-Bahá's last public appearance during His first visit to London was His address on Tuesday, 1 October, to the members of the Higher Thought Centre, which at the time was located at 10 Cheniston Gardens, Kensington.

Higher Thought was one of the first branches in England of the New Thought movement and had strong ties with the British Bahá'ís. Just before 'Abdu'l-Bahá's arrival in England, its London Centre was put at the disposal of Ethel Rosenberg and Mary Thornburgh-Cropper to hold regular meetings about the Bahá'í Faith. As described previously, Wellesley Tudor Pole gave a public talk at the Centre about his meeting with 'Abdu'l-Bahá in Egypt.[112] Other Bahá'ís were also invited from time to time to present the Bahá'í movement in events arranged by the Higher Thought Centre.[113]

An account of 'Abdu'l-Bahá's address was published in *A Quarterly Record of Higher Thought Work*, the official organ of the Higher Thought Centre. Its author mentioned the fact that 'Abdu'l-Bahá was 'visited privately by nearly every earnest Truth seeker and leader of high thought in London' and quoted a line of a message sent by 'Abdu'l-Bahá to the members of the centre:

> THE VISIT OF ABDUL BAHA
>
> One of the most interesting and significant events which has taken place this autumn has been the visit of Abdul Baha to London. It has given a new inspiration and deep satisfaction to his many immediate followers and has allayed the suspicions and misapprehensions which often attach to a great spiritual movement where overzealous disciples claim more for their leader than he does for himself.

The Persian Mage, whose life passed in prison, has been spent in promoting peace and unity by the one certain method of aiding individual spiritual development, must in a very real sense have 'tasted of the travail of his soul and been satisfied'. Not only was he visited privately by nearly every earnest Truth seeker and leader of high thought in London, but his Message was made known to thousands who had before but dimly heard his name. The Church of the Country, in the person of Archdeacon Wilberforce, received him with honour. Nonconformity, as represented by the Rev. R. J. Campbell, opened its doors widely. The Theosophical Society welcomed him with full recognition of his Mission, and other bodies sought his benediction on their work.

The 'Higher Thought' Centre was well known to Abdul Baha as the weekly meeting place of the Behais, under the direction of Miss Rosenberg, during the past few years, and their invitation to him was accepted just two days before his departure. There was little time given to make it known, but it was announced at both Sunday morning meetings, and by 3.30 the lecture room was full. Those committee members already in town received him in the members' room and after a short commune there he proceeded to the lecture room where after the singing of a Truth song Abdul Baha gave a kindly greeting and a short but impressive address through his interpreter, dwelling on the blessedness of such an assembly gathered in a spirit of unity and spiritual aspiration. He concluded with a lowly uttered fervent prayer in his own tongue and a benediction which all present felt to be very real.

On the following day a message was conveyed to the Centre from Abdul Baha signifying the fullest appreciation of all kindness shewn to Behais, and concluding with these words:

'It matters not by what name each calls himself – the Great Work is One.'[114]

The front page of the same issue carried a quote attributed to 'Abdu'l-Bahá: 'Christ is ever in the world of existence. He has never disappeared out of it . . . Rest assured that Christ is present. The spiritual beauty we see around us to-day is from the breathings of Christ. – *Abdul Baha*.'[115]

Articles Published after the Departure of 'Abdu'l-Bahá

'Abdu'l-Bahá reached Paris on 4 October. Meanwhile, in England, articles about Him and the Baha'i Faith continued to appear in the press. *The Near East*, for instance, published its own assessment of the repercussion of the visit of the Master to London:

> It is, perhaps, too early yet to form a just estimate of the effect that Abdul Baha Effendi's visit is likely to have upon this country. Whether Bahaism has any real chance of becoming 'a universal religion' remains to be seen, for, as yet, it is safe to say that, as far as England is concerned, it has only reached the stage of seed-sowing. Abbas Effendi has been in our midst, has made several new friends, won many fresh admirers, and certainly made at least a few converts. He has also been the subject of many inaccurate paragraphs and distinctly foolish articles in the cheap press – which, of course, knows the class of reader it caters for. And with all due respect, it may be added that he has been the object of not a little foolish gush and sentiment on the part of certain people who are always ready to 'take up' new movements, and of no little manoeuvring on the part of certain other people who miss no opportunity of advertising themselves. For these things, of course, he is no wise responsible. They are merely signs of the times. And probably they should be regarded as misfortunes rather than faults, even in those who are responsible for them.[116]

Just before 'Abdu'l-Bahá's arrival in Europe *The Near East* had published a review of D. S. Margoliuth's book *Mohammedanism* (1911) regretting that the Bahá'í Faith 'has passed without notice'[117] in the work. This statement prompted a series of letters to the editor by the journalist and writer Francis Henry Skrine in which he presented an introduction to the Bahá'í Faith as well as a comparison of its teachings with various forms of mysticism.[118] The publication of Skrine's letters prompted some readers to mention the Bahá'í Faith in their correspondence to the editor. On 27 September, for instance, the magazine carried a letter by a reader signing as 'Alex. Sefi.' who stated about the Bahá'í Faith that: 'although it is not new as an idea, its coming forward as an organization is a new feature worthy of warm support by all well-meaning people . . .'[119]

A further letter, signed by a certain M. M. Faulkner, appeared on 11 October and stated that 'it seems to me that even if Abbas Effendi "fails", the light kindled by his father, by both word and deed, will not die'.[120]

The monthly magazine *Brotherhood* (Letchworth), published an interesting article about the Bahá'í Faith in its October issue. This magazine was edited by J. Bruce Wallace[121] and was the organ of the Alpha Union of the Brotherhood Church. In all probability Wallace heard about the Bahá'í Faith through Wellesley Tudor Pole[122] and it is also possible that he personally met the Master during His visit to the Higher Thought Centre, of which Wallace was a member, or during His visit to Bristol. Regarding 'Abdu'l-Bahá, Wallace stated that 'His presence among us has probably done good by stimulating the realization of the large deep common ground there is in the faith of spiritually minded people the world over, irrespectively of their minor and superficial difference' and encouraged his readers to 'rejoice in the great work that our brethren the Bahais have done and are doing in the East. They are the means of a spiritual awakening, and their characters and lives stand well the great test, "by their fruits ye shall know them". They are men of universal Love, preaching purity and peace. We bid them "God speed".'[123]

The Christian Commonwealth continued publishing references to 'Abdu'l-Bahá after His departure. On 16 December, the magazine carried a special section entitled 'The Universal Movement Towards Unity', the purpose of which was to show how different movements and organizations – whether religious, social or political – were working in the same direction for the achievement of the unity of mankind. To this end the section included a series of messages from different leaders of opinion. The following one was attributed to 'Abdu'l-Bahá:

ABDUL BAHA ABBAS
BANNER OF DIVINE HARMONY AND SOLIDARITY OF NATIONS

Battles, murders, bloodshed, and strivings are the characteristics of the wild animal world. Loving kindness, friendliness, and justice are virtues belonging to humanity. But what do we find when we read the records of history from the beginning of the existence of man, whether in the earliest times, in the Middle Ages, or in our own day?

Constant tales of woe – the earth is ever stained with the blood of man, and human beings are in continual danger of being slain!

Now, praise be to God! We are living in an enlightened age; minds of men are becoming illumined, and their souls are reaching out towards the light. The sun of truth has burst forth from the horizon of Persia, and, little by little, its radiance is dispersing the dense clouds of superstition. The light of the unity of mankind is beginning to spread over the earth; soon the banner of divine harmony and solidarity of nations will wave aloft, and the breezes of the Holy Spirit will inspire and bring help to the whole world!

O, peoples and nations, arise and work, and be happy! And gather together with joy under the tent of the unity of mankind![124]

The same section also included a brief presentation of the Bahá'í Faith. On a different page the magazine carried a two-column article by Wellesley Tudor Pole introducing the Bahá'í teachings.[125]

In early January 1912 *The Christian Commonwealth* published an interesting letter on the Bahá'í Faith by one of its readers:

A. S. M. writes: –

Your readers cannot fail to have been interested in the accounts given recently in your columns of this movement, and of the visit of Abbas Effendi to this country. Four years ago I procured copies of the French editions of the Kitab-el-Ikan, or book of 'La Certitude', as well as of 'The Precepts of Behaism', and was much struck with the rich catholicity of the contents. About two years ago I had sent to me a lengthy review of the latter volume by one of our staid Scottish scholars (of St. Andrews), in which after enumerating the various practical features of the teaching he says:

'One, like myself, unacquainted with any other documents of this new religious movement, can only say that perhaps never before has excellent, clear good sense been hailed with such rather unaccountable fervour.

'There may be, I am inclined to think there must be, other things with which I am unacquainted to explain the extraordinary enthusiasm which leads to such exaltation of spirit, such readiness for martyrdom in the cause of fairly obvious, if highly desirable reforms. We have in the Bab, and in Baha 'U'llah a serene conviction of

> inspiration, in their followers a joyous acceptance of illumination which, as yet, appear somewhat out of focus with the apparent absence of any supernatural element, and with convictions and aspirations which are, after all, fairly common and perhaps just a little commonplace.'
>
> To this reviewer the enthusiasm is inexplicable in 'the apparent absence of any supernatural element', and we cannot deny that the history of religion has been a history of 'supernatural elements'. This is just where, it seems to me, the movement shows its unique superiority. The great truths on which it rests are in the fullest sense 'natural,' while they are at the same time essentially 'supernatural'. For in the end, of course, all nature is supernatural. 'Earth's crammed with heaven, and every common bush afire with God.' It is the perception of this truth and the assimilation of it in their spiritual life that explains the 'serene conviction of inspiration', in 'the apparent absence of any supernatural element'. It is a truth that does not depend on any single 'world-teacher'. Teachers innumerable have been helping forward this recognition. The air is full, as never before, of a passion for unity – unity of man with man and of man with God – which is the very backbone of Christianity, and the source of all religious enthusiasm. This Persian Renaissance carries in it lessons for our creed-bound churches that in all likelihood will take long to learn thoroughly. But that way lies the faith of the future. Its teaching is by no means new to thoughtful Christian men. Its present word to us is, 'Be thorough and fear not!'
>
> It would be interesting to know what Mrs. Besant, in her new role of 'John the Baptist' (to quote Dr. Horton), has to say as to this movement. Is this he that should come, or look we for another?[126]

On 31 January 1912 *The Christian Commonwealth* reproduced portions of a story in Mary Hanford Ford's *The Oriental Rose* (1910) in which 'Abdu'l-Bahá was mentioned.[127]

On 27 March the magazine launched a quest for its readers. Some sayings of Vivekananda regarding religious harmony were published anonymously and readers had to guess who the author was. The following comment, which appeared on 3 April, illustrates very well the degree by which the general public was familiarized with 'Abdu'l-Bahá and His teachings: 'Our readers are showing a delightful ingenuity in discovering the author of the seven sayings published in our last issue. They have attributed them variously, to Mr. Campbell, Leo Tolstoy, Abdul Baha, J. Krishnamurti, Mrs. Besant, and Keshub Chunder Sen. The great weight of opinion has favoured Mrs. Besant and Abdul Baha.'[128]

Months later Albert Dawson wrote to 'Abdu'l-Bahá in America requesting from Him that a Bahá'í delegate be appointed for the Liberal Christian League. The Master replied to Dawson, thanking him for his work and assuring him that somebody would be appointed to represent the Bahá'ís at the LCL. His reply was published on 28 August 1912.[129]

The Unitarian minister Henry Harrold Johnson wrote a second article on the Bahá'í Faith for one of the most important British magazines of the time, *The Contemporary Review* (London). It was a lengthy, detailed and objective introduction to the history and teachings of the Baha'i Faith which he considered 'calculated, as nothing else I know, to inspire and promote modern religious developments in the direction of a truly catholic [i.e. universal] religion adequate to meet the needs of the modern world'. The article also reproduced the text of the talk delivered by 'Abdu'l-Bahá at the Theosophical headquarters in London on 30 September 1911.[130]

On 27 March *The Christian Commonwealth* published a review of this article.[131] Portions of Johnson's text were also published in America in the *Dallas Morning News* and *The Christian Register* (Boston)[132] and in Australia it was the basis of a two-column article written by Muriel Chase[133] for the *West Australian* (Perth).[134]

In April 1912, another major and influential London periodical, *The Fortnightly Review*, published an article penned by the suffragist writer and personal friend of Lady Blomfield, Constance Maud, who gave an account of some episodes related to the visit of 'Abdu'l-Bahá to London:

ABDUL BAHA

(*Servant of the Glory*)

A great Persian teacher has recently made his first appearance among us, though the rumour of his teaching had reached many in this country through travellers and pilgrims who had visited the small fortress town of Akka, where Abbas Effendi passed the greater number of his forty years' imprisonment and exile.

Rudyard Kipling, voicing the feeling of most of his countrymen, sang:

> 'East is East and West is West,
> And never the twain shall meet.'

Abbas Effendi, or, as his followers love to call him, Abdul Baha, signifying 'Servant of the Glory,' has come to us with another song:

> 'East and West, North and South, men and women, all must join hands in one great brotherhood, uniting their voices in prayer for the Abbas Father, before the human race can rise to the divine heights and grow to the perfect stature to which the All-Father has destined it.'

'War must cease,' says Abdul Baha. 'There is something above and beyond patriotism, and it is better to love your fellowmen than to love only your countrymen.'

'When we see this, and know in very truth the brotherhood of man; war will appear to us in its true light as an outrage on civilization, an act of madness and blindness. If the hand fights against the foot, all the body must suffer, and no one part can possibly be the gainer. When the light drives away our present darkness, we shall recognize that we were like men in a dungeon, fighting and slaying ourselves.'

This is the key-note of the Bahai teaching, identical with that of the Founder of Christianity, but so forgotten by the Christian world that it came almost as a fresh and new illumination when the Persian prophet, Baha Ullah, father of Abbas Effendi, proclaimed it sixty years ago, and founded the great Bahai movement, which now numbers over three million followers in Persia alone . . .

To the house in London where Abdul Baha and his suite were received as honoured, welcomed guests, came a constant stream of all sorts and conditions of men and women. Christians of every denomination, Buddhists of every nationality, Theosophists, Zoroastrians and Mahometans, Agnostics and Gnostics. To all he spoke some individual message, and to their varied questions he gave a simple, direct, and quite spontaneous answer. A remarkable serenity, an atmosphere of peace and aloofness from this material world, pervaded his whole personality. Everything he said was characterised by a crystal-clear lucidity of thought, and a penetrating wisdom which cleaved through the immense difficulties of language and disadvantages of transmitting his speech through an Oriental interpreter, whose knowledge of English was of necessity limited.

In spite of having passed the greater part of his life within prison walls, Abdul Baha possesses an amazing power of going straight to the core of men and things. He sees people as Teufelsdröck tried to imagine them to himself, minus their trappings, whether coronets, mitres, orders or fine clothes. He looks straight through even the colour of the skin, right to the heart, to the soul. A look of wonderful love, joy and understanding comes into his visitor a pure heart, a soul of light; it is as though he had found a brother or sister, someone near of kin. But when he speaks of the discord, misery and sorrow of the world, his eyes take on an expression of unfathomable sadness, and visions rise up before one of the ghastly scenes of death and torture those same eyes have been forced to witness.

Still, sadness is far from the characteristic note of his face or character. He not only preaches happiness, but radiates it, and though he has learnt but a few words of English, he often repeats:

'No cry – no cry – laugh – be happy – that is good.' He could wear 'the glorious morning face' enjoined by Robert Louis Stevenson, even at seven o'clock in the morning, when his zealous followers and importunate visitors not infrequently began their daily visits.

His custom while here was to give short, informal addresses on various subjects to those assembled to hear him, and to answer any questions that might be put to him: afterwards to retire to his own room, where he received a succession of people requesting private interviews.

Though his own special theme was the Universal brotherhood of man, religious unity and the necessity for a universal language to be taught in every school, yet to the representatives of every different school of thought he gave a special teaching.

To the Theosophists who came greeting him as Master he preached a practical living of the truths to which they profess to have attained:

'To know the Truth, to have attained Knowledge, is good, but it is only the first step, it is not enough. The one thing that is of any avail for the soul, is to live the truth, to do the good. Of what use is it that we know for a fact there are ten thousand people cold and hungry if we do not feed and warm them – to know of the right road to the mountain top if we do not walk in it – to know there are bad laws if we do not mend them – or to know divine truths concerning God if we do not listen and obey His voice?'

'Granting that I know the truth,' one of the listeners asked in reply, 'how am I to acquire the right spirit and incentive to live the life?'

Abdul Baha answered: 'Faith in God will create in you that spirit and incentive. But by faith it must be understood the real, living, active faith. There are three kinds of faith. First, there is the faith of tradition, of the accident of birth; you are born in a Mahommedan home, you are a Muslim; in a Christian home, so you are a Christian, and so on. This faith is of a very weak, unstable quality – it does not touch the soul. Next there is the faith which springs from a mental conviction, a personal perception of the truth – you know God is, therefore you believe, but neither does this faith touch the soul, nor make it grow and bear fruit. Only one kind of faith can do this. It is as though there were a lamp which the first class of men believe to exist merely on reports of others; the second class on the evidence of their own eyes, though seen only from a distance; but the third class of persons believe in because, having approached near to the lamp they have become so illumined by the rays and warmed through and through by the heat that they are enabled to give out to others light and love, manifesting God. This alones is the real faith.'

Another inquired asked: 'Does the Master consider all religions equally efficacious, all the great Teachers equally divine?'

To this Abdul Baha replied:

'There is but one God and all the great Teachers and Prophets are sent forth into the world by Him, but all have not an equal amount of truth. They are like the various branches growing on one tree. Some are great branches bearing fruit and many leaves, others are far smaller and less important, yet all, even the smallest and weakest branch, draws its life from the same great stem and root. That Stem is God. But no man can say, for instance, that the branch of Mahomet can be compared to that of Jesus Christ, that most vital of the branches on the tree of Life, when we clear away the dogma with which the Churches and sects have encrusted it, and go back to the Divine Teacher Himself.'

He was asked whether he would rank Buddhism as high as Christianity?

He answered: 'Buddhism was once like a beautiful child, fresh and fair from the Hand of God, but it has now become a decrepit feeble old man – worn out and unrecognizable.'

A vegetarian questioned him closely concerning diet, whether, in his opinion, it was not right to abstain from all animal good?

He replied that though he hoped for the time when we should no longer kill animals in order to sustain our own life, yet the law that each Kingdom, animal, vegetable, and mineral, drew its substance from the others, was God's law for this world, and we cannot escape it if we would. He then told a story of a Hindoo who came to him one day, his ears and nose stopped up with cotton wool lest he should be the cause of death to some small insect or microbe. While they were talking the Hindoo asked for a glass of water. When he had drunk half the amount, Abdul Baha sent for a microscope and showed him the multitude of living organisms the water contained. The Hindoo left minus his cotton-wool.

'We should give our bodies a healthy, simple diet, just enough to keep them fit for good service – no more; to think too much of what we shall not eat is making too much of the material,' he concluded.

This subject led into the question of whether he did not think that the mind ought to be able to control and heal the body?

'Yes,' Abdul Baha answered, 'when the complaint is mental in its cause and source. Many diseases springing from inside the body (I give the interpreter's exact words) have a mental origin. These can be best healed by mind cure. But purely physical ills, such as a broken bone, a wound from a weapon, must be healed by physical remedies. God gives us such remedies in the natural world, even as He supplies our physical needs by physical means. You suffer hunger, you take food – you suffer cold, you put on warm clothes. You do not use a mental treatment for ills of the body that are not caused by mind. Still, there is no doubt the body and the mind act and react, the one on the other, and the mind can greatly aid and modify even the ills that are purely of a physical and outside origin.'

To women, especially those who are working for the uplifting of their sex, and better conditions for the children, Abdul Baha had a special message. 'Sixty years ago,' said he, 'Baha Ullah taught the perfect equality of the sexes. Essential difference in sphere, in point of view and service to their joint humanity, but each like two pillars supporting the arch of life, the necessary complement one of the other. What absurdity then to talk of superiority or inferiority, and what folly to base life on such a fallacy! It is as though a man tried to run a race with one leg tied up and crippled. So the race, with one half crushed and undeveloped, halts and is unable to progress.' The education of women he regards as of paramount importance. So much so that should the family funds permit only half the children being well educated, the girls, declared Abdul Baha, should come first, as being the trainers of the race. 'No nation,' he said, 'ever advances beyond the point of progress to which its women have attained – the two legs belong to one body.'

No wonder Baha Ullah's gospel found small favour with the Mahometan Persian of his day, whose womankind were degraded to the level of slavery, their bodies not their own, their minds kept as far as possible in the darkest ignorance, and the very existence of their souls considered a debatable point.

Asked by a leader of one of the Woman's Suffrage Societies whether he approve of the political vote for women, Abdul Baha answered:

'Yes, yes, of course I do. In all questions which concern the welfare of a nation is not a woman's view as important as the man's if one would get a just and true consideration of all sides of that question? Therefore I am in favour of votes for women on every subject. This great woman's movement which is stirring and vibrating all round the whole world is a sign of spirit awakening. Even in Persia they stir, they wake, and many have become Bahaists, and are freed from the old chains. That one who first awoke them, who gave her life for this noble cause, was Quarratu'l-'Ain. Blessed is she among women!'

According to Abdul Baha, the first Persian woman to preach the Bahaist gospel of the emancipation of her sex was the wife of a Mahometan priest. She was remarkable for her beauty and her intellectual gifts. One day from behind her barred windows she heard the Bab preach, and his words brought a flood of new light to her soul. From that moment she felt God had spoken to her and opened her eyes to the truth. Abdul Baha described her as shining like a bright lamp, giving out light and warmth by her very nature, her words kindling in others an extraordinary enthusiasm, so that all about her caught fire. Her husband, however, was horrified at finding sedition and heresy in his own wife, and shut her under lock and key. She escaped and joined the Bahaist camp under Baha Ullah, the Bab having been martyred some years before. One day it was reported that Baha Ullah lay dangerously ill in his tent, whereupon Quarratu'l'Ain flung aside her veil, crying aloud that the trumpet had sounded and the dead must arise – the dead soul of woman. The veil like the grave clothes, must be cast aside, as she did now. And to the scandal of many a Persian, even among the enlightened Bahaists, Quarratu'l'Ain marched unveiled into the tent of Baha Ullah, and there nursed and tended him till he was restored to health. Everywhere she preached, women, and men too, were drawn to her, and for a time the authorities forbore to touch her. But at last, urged by the indignant priesthood, she was arrested. The Governor, however, was lenient, and at first had her placed in his own house, where she promptly converted the men and women of his household. Her eloquence and zeal were so irresistible that again the priests interposed and insisted she should be handed over the executioners. But even in her dungeon Qurratu'l'Ain made conversions, and the very men sent in to torture and dispatch her came out of her cell with changed hearts and softened faces, saying they could not do this thing, for the woman was an angel of God and a saint. What she underwent during this time of captivity can only be darkly surmised; the end came at a moment when they professed to be releasing her, and by a treacherous plot she was assassinated. Qurratu'l'Ain gave her life gladly for the faith, thereby again by her death causing many conversions, and setting an example which numbers of her own sex rose up and followed. She inaugurated, in fact, a woman's movement in Persia, the consequences of which will be a vital import to the nation in time to come.

One of the most frequent subjects on which Abdul Baha was questioned was that of re-incarnation. In the sense of the same ego being educated and evolved through many lives, he may be said to hold this doctrine, but he gave clearly as his belief that we are here as human beings on this earth for the first and last time. When asked his reasons for this belief, he answered:

'We have grown up step by step, always to a state in advance of the last. God's processes are never retrogressive. No butterfly goes back into the chrysalis – constant change, never a repetition, is the fundamental law. So with what comes after this life. Here we are subject to the conditions of matter, after this will succeed life on the mental plane, a life freed from this material body. But according to the life we have lived here depend the conditions of life on that next plane. What we sow here, that we reap there. Even though on leaving this body we enter upon a life of the spirit, the conditions of that spirit-life must depend upon the degree of development to which the soul has attained.'

Questioned as to his ideas on the conditions of the next life, and whether we should be reunited to those who had loved on earth, Abdul Baha replied:

'Love will re-unite all those whom physical death has parted. But it must be remembered that we can only be in perfect touch with those on the same plane of development as ourselves. You can understand perfectly those below you but not those in advance of you, though *they* can come down to you. It is the same law as we find in this world. The mineral kingdom is distinct in its conditions from the vegetable – impossible for the mineral to comprehend the powers of the vegetable which grows and changes from a seed into a flower or tree, drawing its nutriment from earth and air and water. So, again, it is impossible for the vegetable to conceive of the kingdom above it – the animal whose powers and senses so entirely transcend its own. Equally the animal can never comprehend the working of man's brain. For man alone of all the animals is not governed by the conditions in which he finds himself. He has no wings, but he does not submit himself to this fact; he makes wings and conquers the air. He has no fins, but he conquers the sea. He conquers the night by creating for himself light; the cold by making heat; his heaven itself that he may rise to God his Father and Creator. To the animals other than man, the attainments of man are inconceivable, just as inconceivable as the nest plane above and beyond this is now to us. For there we shall find new powers, new senses, as far transcending those we now have, as they transcend the powers of those on the planes below us.'

Someone observed that since most of us make but a sorry business of life, our sins and shortcomings being many, and our good deeds few, it would be but a sad plane, that one which comes next in order.

Abdul Baha looked at the speaker, his whole face lit as though for a moment he saw beyond the mists of earth into that future, as he answered:

'It might be so if we were not in the Hands of the great Father Who is perfect love and endless mercy. The best among us will need that grace and mercy, and will find it joyfully awaiting him. God judges not as we judge, He looks at the intentions of the heart. Also his punishment is always to cure, to redeem, to educate, so that we may become radiant Sons of God.'

He was asked whether he thought those on the Other Side were able to see what happened to those they love still on earth.

To this he replied: 'They see all as it affects the spirit. A great joy, a great sorrow, a sin or a good deed – as these things darken or cloud the soul, or cause it to rise into greater light, so they see every earth event that touches you for good or ill, reflected in your soul. That is the meaning of 'the angels who rejoice over one sinner who repents'.

Concerning himself and his own mission Abdul Baha was very explicit.

Some people came to him asking if he were not a re-incarnation of the Christ. He laughed at the question in his kindly wise way. 'No, no, no,' he answered emphatically. 'I am not the Christ – I am not even a prophet – Baha Ullah was a prophet, but I his son am just simply this – the 'servant of God.' You also,' he added, 'must be servants of God.'

The Zoroastrians came to him asking if he was that One for whom they had been waiting, the Teacher, the Light. They hailed him as a re-incarnation of Zoroaster. He received them with his usual kindly courtesy and answered their philosophic and religious questions to their satisfaction. But when the chief representative present, insisted on performing a kind of ceremony he declared proclaimed Abdul Baha as head Master of their religion, and therewith proceeded to hang a symbolic garland round his neck, the 'Servant of the Glory' remonstrated with emphatic gestures to supplement his few words of English the only language they had in common.

'Enough, enough,' he said deprecatingly, waving them aside and hastening to remove the garland. Then at their earnest entreaty that

> he would at least accept and wear their flowers, he promised, lest their feelings should be hurt, that he would do so later.
>
> This is only a light pencil sketch of a most remarkable personality, a very inadequate suggestion of a great spiritual force. To do justice to Abdul Baha would require the inspired pen of one who had attained to his own spiritual stature. 'God screens us evermore from premature ideas. Our eyes are holden till the mind is ripened.'
>
> There is much in the teaching of Abdul Baha that most of his hearers of necessity miss, since 'we can only be in perfect touch with those on the same plane of development as ourselves.' For my own part I have not attempted to do more than gather up a few crumbs of this spiritual bread.[135]

This article, together with Harrold Johnson's article in the *Contemporary Review*, were the object of a review published in the June 1912 issue of the *American Review of Reviews* (New York) under the title 'Will Bahaism Unite All Religious Faiths?'[136]

In Australia, *The Register* (Adelaide) published on 20 May an article based on Maud's text.[137] The *Review of Reviews* (London), edited by W. T. Stead, published on April 1912 a brief note about the same article stating that she 'writes a most interesting account of Baha Ulla, whose Babism may be regarded as a better substitute for Christianity than any of the revolutionary makeshifts. Baha Ulla is sound on woman's suffrage, and the brightest page in Miss Maud's story is devoted to the first Persian woman who joined the Bab, and was martyred for her pains.'[138] In Canada a further review was published in the *Manitoba Free Press* (Winnipeg).[139]

In August 1912, at the midpoint of 'Abdu'l-Bahá's visit to America, the *African Times and Orient Review* (London) carried a lengthy article by Eric Hammond introducing the Bahá'í Faith which opened with the following words: 'The student of the Bahai movement finds himself engrossed by a personality of surpassing interest. In Abdul Baha he discovers the living heart and leader of the movement, and understands how sagaciously it is dominated and guided.' The article then continued with a summary of the teachings and history of the Bahá'í Faith and ended with a reference to the recent visit of 'Abdu'l-Bahá to Europe:

> We who had the happiness of greeting him in London met a man of patriarchal bearing. None could approach him without veneration,

> but each visitor was immediately set at ease by the beautiful graciousness which marked each reception with the impress of acknowledged and realised brotherhood. Patient with all questioners, eager and apposite in reply, bent from moment to moment upon the establishment of unity, his spiritual kindliness grasped the individual and the universal alike.[140]

Months after the departure of the Master from England, the *Daily News and Leader* (London) interviewed Lady Blomfield who also spoke about 'Abdu'l-Bahá. The article that ensued was reproduced in Australia:

> The lady who was Abdul Baha's hostess while he was in London told a 'Daily News and Leader' representative in tones of true reverence of the saint who had been her honored guest.
>
> 'Abdul Baha lives what he preaches,' she said: 'that is the secret of his power. A lady who had known many of the great ones of the earth – people of royal and noble birth – when asked how Abdul Baha impressed her, said, "Oh, all the people I had ever seen suddenly seemed so small in comparison with him. Yet he is of medium height, and he dresses simply and lives sparingly." The first night he dined with me I expressed the hope that the meal pleased him. He said with charming gentleness – "the flowers and the art are beautiful, but is it right to have six courses when so many poor people have not even one?" He never accepts money, and a lady, not being aware of this, presented a large sum for him. With his unfailing courtesy, he thanked her and took it, but returned it to her immediately, saying, "please give it to the poor for me." Not to offend the heart of anyone or to hurt any soul is one of the chief teachings of Bahaism' . . .
>
> 'Abdul Baha believes greatly in the power and influence of women. He continually spoke of this. He says that women have a stronger sense of religion than men, that they are more intuitive, receptive, and intelligent, and that day will come when the equality of the sexes will be acknowledged. He believes the education of the girl, because of her potential motherhood, is of more vital importance than that of the boy.'
>
> The spirit of the teaching is not an ascetic or solitary spirit. Its belief is that each person ought to have some trade or profession.

'All work is worship, whether art, science or daily manual labor,' said Abdul Baha on one occasion. When suffering comes, the Bahai meets it with a steadfast faith and determination to learn its lesson. 'Unless one accepts dire vicissitudes,' says Abdul Baha, 'he will not attain.'

It is interesting to know that Abdul Baha looks forward to a time of universal peace on earth. 'It will come about gradually,' he said. 'If a family lives in union great results are attained. When a city lives in intimate accord greater results will follow, and a continent that is fully united will likewise unite all other continents. Then will be the time of the greatest results, for all the inhabitants of the earth belong to one native land.' This is the opinion of a man of whom Tolstoy said – 'He holds the secret of the enigma of life.'[141]

Echoes in America

As mentioned earlier, agencies circulated in America news and pictures about the Master's visit to England. Some newspapers also received particular correspondence, sometimes from Bahá'ís. The information published did not generally offer details about 'Abdu'l-Baha's activities in London but rather a summary of His biography, some words about the history of the Faith, and sometimes extracts from the Bahá'í writings.[142]

At least two Bahá'ís who met the Master in Europe wrote articles about Him for leading American newspapers. One of them was Alice M. Buckton, who published an article in the *Washington Post* introducing the Bahá'í Faith and offering some details about the visit of 'Abdu'l-Bahá to London:

> Abbas Effendi, the subject of your notable article on December 31, whose presence is shortly expected in this country, has sent an open letter to friends in New York. In it he shows that he has no doubt as to his own mission and station. He writes:
>
> 'Abdul Baha (literally the "servant of God") is the manifestation of service, not the Christ. The servant of humanity is he, and not a chief. The herald of the kingdom is he, that he may awaken the people of the East and of the West. The voice of friendship, of uprightness, and of reconciliation is he, quickening all regions. Beware of disputes. By disputes the temple of God is razed to its foundations.'

Nothing can be clearer than this. Many have been the misrepresentations of this extraordinary movement.

The anxiety which missionaries have felt with regard to its rapid increase arises from the fact that it seems able to do for the Mohammedan world what they themselves have failed to accomplish . . .

During his stay in London, Abdul Baha was received with every mark of courtesy and respect. The lord mayor of London entertained him at the Mansion House.[143] Leaders of various circles of thought came to consult with him, among them Mrs. Annie Besant and Mr. George Gladstone. By invitation he addressed vast congregations in the City Temple and in the Church of Saint John. Abdul Baha has stood where no Easterner has ever before been allowed to stand, and the world has listened.

Before the Theosophists in Paris, he gave an address in which he said: 'The Great Light of Spirit has ever arisen in the East, but in the West it has found its greatest force of expansion. The Christ was like a star on the horizon of the East; but the light of his influence has had its deepest effect in the West. The people of the West are very faithful in their hearts; they do not easily forget.'

Abdul Baha's teaching rivals no creed. In an ancient Bible, hallowed by the use of many preachers, he wrote the following:

'This is the Holy Book of God. It is the Book of Salvation. It is the Noble Gospel. In it is the Mystery of the Kingdom and its Light.'

Is this a visitor that any Christian country should fear?

It was the writer's good fortune to be present at interviews between Abdul Baha and editors of papers, social workers, suffrage bodies, and clergy of many denominations. Specially noteworthy have been the words of the historian, the Rev. Prof. Cheyne of Oxford, Dean Kitchin of Durham;[144] Mr. Claude Montefiore, and Prof. Michael Sadler, vice chancellor of the University of Leeds, testifying to their sense of the import of Abdul Baha's mission to the West today. MISS A. N. BUCKTON, NEW YORK, JAN. 6, 1912.[145]

Buckton also offered a presentation at the Emerson College, Boston, and 'beautifully described a personal interview with the Persian leader, Abdul Baha'.[146]

In an article for *The Sun* (New York), Mary Hanford Ford also gave some details about the visit of 'Abdu'l-Bahá to England:

Abdul Baha is above all things an apostle of democracy. He loves a man for the spirit within him, not for the gifts of fortune he happens to possess, and frequently he honors more those whom the world esteems least. No one who saw him in England can forget his sorrow when a poor man was accidentally refused entrance to his house, nor the great pity that possessed him at sight of the poverty of an English village. He went to the postmaster, who was also the banker, and changed all his gold pieces into sixpences, so that he might comfort the hungry looking children who followed him everywhere and who treasured his gentle words and caresses even more eagerly than the sixpences. Afterward, when he was the guest of the Lord Mayor of London with all the titled smart folk who had been invited to meet him, this is what he said to them:

'Therefore my advice to you is: Endeavor as much as ye can to show kindness to all men, deal with perfect love, affection and devotion with all the individuals of humanity. Remove from among yourselves racial, patriotic, religious, sectional, political, commercial, industrial and agricultural prejudices, so that you may become freed from all human restrictions and become the founders of the structures of the oneness of the world of humanity. All the countries are one country, all the nations are the children of one Father. The struggle for existence among the ferocious wolves has become the cause of all the differences and strifes; otherwise the expanse of the world is spacious and the table of the Almighty is spread in all regions' . . .

In one of his London interviews he was questioned sharply as to his ideas in regard to the creation of a more liveable universe, and he replied that in this day new laws must be made in every country so that a greater degree of equality may be attained among men. He explained that men are so differently endowed as individuals that they can never be kept on an exact equality, but the laws must be so altered that it will become impossible for single person to control enormous wealth and impossible also for anyone to suffer dire poverty.[147]

7

FIRST VISIT TO FRANCE

5 October – 7 December 1911

'Abdu'l-Bahá arrived in Paris on 5 October, staying in an apartment that was rented at 4 Camoëns Avenue. The press in Paris started publishing articles about Him soon after His arrival.

On 6 October *Le Figaro*, a conservative newspaper with a circulation of some 37,000 copies,[1] carried an article written by Guy Darés who introduced in poetical terms the main tenets of the Bahá'í Faith and the figure of the Master, whom he described as 'unique and interesting'.[2] It was not the first time he had written about the Faith. Just two years earlier he had been present at a Bahá'í Naw-Rúz meeting held in Paris and afterwards published a lengthy article about it.[3]

On 7 October the conservative weekly *L'Opinion* (Paris) published in its editorial section some sarcastic comments about 'Abdu'l-Bahá's pacifist views: 'Poor good old man,' stated the article: 'he is not happy right now, without any regard to grieve Baha-Ullah, the guns are thundering at Tripoli, Persia struggles with Revolution and the most peaceful peoples are waving their arms. Apparently Paris has some Bahai followers. Mr. d'Estournelles de Constant should be one of them.'[4]

In Marseille, *Le Petit Marseillais*, a newspaper with a circulation of some 200,000 copies,[5] carried on 10 October an article, signed with the pseudonym of Caderoussel, which also reported the arrival of 'Abdu'l-Bahá and introduced the Bahá'í Faith. The text was similar to that in the article in *Le Figaro*.[6]

Interviews with the Local Press

In the weeks following the arrival of 'Abdu'l-Bahá in France many personalities of Parisian society, including several journalists, visited the Master. One of them was Myrtil Airel, a journalist and poet who contributed to several periodicals including *Le Figaro* and who attended one of the public receptions held at 4 Camoëns. His account of his visit to the Master was published on 13 October in the Catholic journal *La Liberté* (Paris), with a circulation of 63,000 copies, and included an introduction to the Bahá'í Faith (not reproduced here):

BAHAISM

WITH THE HEAD OF THE UNIVERSAL RELIGION

Avenue Camoëns, 4, beyond the Trocadero, on the first floor of a beautiful new building.

It is two o'clock in the morning. A large audience, in which one can distinguish the black caps of several Persians, has already filled two rooms.

Men and women talk in a low voice. The atmosphere is not that of a social gathering. The first impression one gets is that serious ideas float in the air.

We are at the residence of Abdu'l-Baha, the head of the Universal Religion . . . But let us be silent. A door opens, everyone rises and the Master – as his disciples call him – enters, gesturing a blessing. Medium size, white beard, long hair, regular features illuminated by the gaze of his particularly bright and shiny brown eyes. As for his costume, his dress is covered with a light green caftan; on the head he wears a white fez.

Abdu'l-Baha smiles to the audience. He shakes the hands that reach out to him, then he sits down and, in a refined voice, speaks Persian. As soon as it is pronounced, every sentence is translated by M. Hippolyte Dreyfus, the most zealous adept of Bahaism in Paris. He once lectured on its origins and development at the School of Advanced Social Studies [École des hautes études en sciences sociales, EHESS].

First, he wants to welcome us. The Master is delighted to be here. He comes to visit London, where he has found many admirable things, just like in our Paris, and pays tribute to the French character, always open to any high and generous idea. He loves all nations. We are all sons of Adam. God – the Lord of all – did not create English, Persians or French, but men, and the duty of these men – trees of the same forest, leaves of one branch – is to love and help each other. The world has made immense progress in material terms. Moral progress is less advanced. We have to work hard for it, without discouragement. We will make mankind better and, for that very reason, more happy.

All religions have tended towards this goal and the few differences between them are the result of man-made rites.

Bahaism focuses on the essentials. It has neither dogmas, nor priests, nor temples. It is a friendly religion, a happy one, which does not believe at all that God enjoys our privation, our mortification. No, no! God has granted us possessions to contribute to our earthly happiness . . . 'for the rich have to hear the midnight lamentation of the poor'.

We must also avoid idleness. Work and love, this is, in two words, the program of the Universal Religion which will lead us to the reign of universal brotherhood.

One feels that Abdu'l-Baha speaks with conviction, with absolute confidence in that future of happiness that he is preparing and expecting.

But, one of the assistants gently objected, it is not overly optimistic to believe in this new golden age, when current events brutally belie these magnificent hopes? A few years ago, at the Hague Conference, the powers reached agreements, on paper, to inaugurate international justice. What results they have achieved? As soon as two nations have conflicting interests, they unsheathe their swords.

– Do not be alarmed at what is going on, said the Master. The Hague Conference was an early effort which, considering the spirit of the rulers and the people, was doomed to fail.

And, clarifying his opinion in a humorous way:

– Those diplomats look like a congress of wine sellers deciding that we should not drink more wine, but as soon they separate, they begin again selling!

Time goes by. Abdu'l-Baha asks permission to return to his work. He maintains a considerable correspondence for the dissemination and defence of his doctrines.

While we retire, a photographer points his camera at a group which included westerners and easterners of different nationalities surrounding the Master, an image of the future harmony between the races and the peoples converted to the Universal Religion.[7]

This article was later reproduced in *L'Echo du Merveilleux* (Paris), a bimonthly review specializing in occult sciences.[8]

Jean Lefranc, a reporter with *Le Temps*, a newspaper with a circulation of 36,000 copies, attended a public talk delivered at the Theosophical Society on 26 October and on the next day had the opportunity of meeting the Master again and interviewing Him for his newspaper. Lefranc's comments and the general tone of the article suggest that 'Abdu'l-Bahá made a good impression on him. The description of their meeting was preceded by a lengthy introduction to the history and tenets of the Bahá'í Faith. 'Without doubt Christ has given us equally magnificent writings of guidance,' stated Lefranc after quoting some statements attributed to 'Abdu'l-Bahá by Bahá'í pilgrims.

BAHAISM AND ITS PROPHET

You whom life has disappointed, you who cry without cause, who suffer without injury, you who no longer believe but need to believe, you impious mystics, atheists without conviction, you anxious ones, pessimists, victims of boredom, weakened westerners, my brothers, rejoice! You will heal your ills, the imaginary and the real, by the Truth; and the talisman is Abdu'l-Baha who brings it to you.

Abdu'l-Baha, son of Baha'u'llah, prophet of Bahaism, has indeed come to visit the West.

In aristocratic lodgings, on the avenue de Camoens, in the shadow of the Trocadéro and the Eiffel Tower, Abdu'l-Baha receives his followers each day. He is a noble Easterner with a long white beard, wearing a white turban and dressed in ample robes of olive green. He speaks only Persian but his voice is sweet, and M. Hippolyte Dreyfus, a fervent Bahá'í who translates his words, expresses with faithful eloquence the biblical flavour of his inspired language.

Abdu'l-Baha was an exile in Akka until the recent proclamation of the new Turkish regime granting freedom to all political prisoners. He then undertook a great religious voyage, visiting Egypt and England, and has finally arrived in Paris . . .

I heard Abdu'l-Baha the other night in Paris among the

> Theosophists, who are not Baha'is but who admire the Bahá'í Faith. The audience was elegant. The prophet spoke and M. Hippolyte Dreyfus translated each of his sentences, with their poetic and harmonious tone. Abdu'l-Baha announced that he would pray for all those who had been listening to him. He then chanted a long prayer in which the guttural sounds of Persian intersected the prolonged and monotonous liturgical murmur.
>
> The next day I was received by Abdu'l-Baha. The salon was full of people standing and awaiting the blessing of the prophet. The majority spoke together in English. Abdu'l-Baha, in his office, took my hands and held them within his for some time. He told me that the press was one of the greatest powers in the world and that he had already proclaimed this truth in one of his books. He assured me that Parisians were friendly.
>
> The venerable face of Abdu'l-Baha, in which his young eyes sparkle, beams with intelligence and kindness. He is fatherly, affectionate, simple; he inspires trust and respect. His divine power comes no doubt from knowing how to love people and to be loved by them. He merely repeats, slowly, the great wisdom: love each other! Oh how beautiful religions are when they have just begun!

The same article also included the following comments about Hippolyte Dreyfus:

> M. Hippolyte Dreyfus, to whose kindness I am indebted for the opportunity to approach Abdu'l-Baha, is a Baha'i. He is a man of the world, dressed in meticulous Parisian style, and who, if he speaks Persian, clearly writes in French. He has translated numerous Baha'i books and is the author of an interesting 'Essay on Bahaism'. By what means did M. Hippolyte Dreyfus come to approach this prophet figure? Such is the question that every unbeliever must ask himself. The Parisian lawyer told me, without flourish, the story of his introduction to Bahaism. He had just finished his studies in Paris and he was a materialist. Nevertheless, he felt that 'there was something more'. He engaged in the spiritual sciences of the occult. These 'sciences' disappointed him. Those who were returning from Akka spoke to him of Abdu'l-Baha. He was persuaded by their words and went to Akka. His interviews with Abdu'l-Baha resulted

> in him joining the Bahá'í cause. But he did not understand Persian at all, and Abdu'l-Baha does not speak French. Lacking access to an interpreter, he therefore learned Persian. A young Bahá'í lady, Miss Laura Clifford Barney, who had also met the prophet and had even written a book about the Bahá'í Faith: *Lessons from Akka* [*Some Answered Questions*], is now Mme. Hippolyte Dreyfus.[9]

Lefranc's article was the basis of articles published in *Le Petit Marseillais*[10] and *Le Stéphanois* (Saint Etienne)[11] and also of a review in the *Mercure de France.*[12]

Outside France it was used at least on four occasions, all of them reproducing some of the words attributed to 'Abdu'l-Bahá. Spain's liberal newspaper *Heraldo de Madrid* carried under the title 'The Baha prophet' an editorial in its front page summarizing the article in *Le Temps*. 'Jean Lefranc says that Abdul Baha is superior to Christ,' commented the editor. 'Let him be crucified too and we will see.'[13] A further summary was written almost a year later by Fernando Araujo, a journalist writing for the leading Spanish magazine, *La España Moderna* (Madrid).[14]

In Latin America, the Mexican daily newspaper *El Universal* also reproduced portions of Lefranc's article.[15] In Argentina, the newspaper *La Nación* (Buenos Aires) included the text as part of an article by the Nicaraguan writer, journalist and diplomatic Rubén Darío (1866–1916), who was staying in Paris at the time of the Master's visit to the French capital and who, as a noted poet and litterateur, is considered one of the most outstanding Latin American writers. Darío added some information of his own about the history and the teachings of the Faith and, in keeping with his views on the role of religion, the general tone of his text was rather skeptical.[16]

The journalist, author and art critic Remy de Gourmont (1858–1915) visited 'Abdu'l-Bahá on 20 October. The following day, the newspaper *La France* (Paris), with a circulation of just 500 copies, carried a column in which, in a literary mode, he described his meeting with the Master:

> BAHAISM
>
> I have never seen that word written and I have never heard it pronounced according to the English pronunciation, but I have heard it

> so often that I am sure at least of how it sounds. This is the name of a new religion that has a few followers in Paris and [illegible], a handsome old Persian man, is currently amongst us. Persia is a home to religions. Many religions of the past came from there, including the founders or reformers Zoroaster, Mani, and Ali the Bab, who was so persecuted. Bahaism extends Babism, but with even fewer rites, forms, or external aspects. It comes in the guise of a very sweet and simple philosophy that wants to unite men in peace and love, a philosophy at once naive and sweet, against which one may look for objections in vain. This religion was taught to me yesterday by the Master, in a language rich with oriental flourish that MD [Monsieur Dreyfus] translated into French with an ease that amazed me almost as much as Bahaism itself. The eloquent patriarch spoke to us of the simple joys experienced in the Bahai city, of pleasures designed to delight the docile hearts, where spring is eternal, ever-flowering with the perpetual blooming of lilies, violets and roses, where women smile and men are happy in the perfumed air of love. And we spoke of the great truth that excels all the previous truths, in which our little human errors are melted and transformed, as such quarrels disappear in the shade of the greatest Peace. And we felt a deep passion in the faintly halting voice, roughly punctuated by the guttural sounds of the Persian language, but also gently punctuated by the phrasing of his musical laughter. For the prophet is joyful and we all feel within him the gaiety of being a prophet, upon whom forty years in prison have left no trace. He had with him a bouquet of violets, offering one to each of his visitors; to the most resistant to his teachings and to those who had the audacity to stubbornly oppose him, the parma violets serve as his arguments, as do his hearty laugh, his beautiful and poetic arguments, and the simplicity of his Persian dress. We will hear him, it seems, in a debate at the Sorbonne, where he will partner with Mr Loyson, an abbot and an independent. You must not miss this occasion.[17]

On 23 October, the journal *Gil Blas* published a brief note based on this article. 'This venerable Oriental possesses a very special charm', stated the author.[18] A few weeks later, Gourmont under his pseudonym R. de Bury, published in the celebrated *Mercure de France* (Paris), a magazine of which he was a co-founder, a review of his own article in *La France* and of Lefranc's article in *Le Temps*, reproducing large portions of the latter.[19]

The *Paris-Journal*, a socialist newspaper with a circulation of 40,000 copies, published on 8 November an article one and a half columns long by the author, journalist and art critic Camille de Sainte-Croix (1859–1915),[20] who apparently also had an opportunity to meet 'Abdu'l-Bahá. Judging from the contents of the article, the meeting was rather short. Most of the article was dedicated to describing the history of the Bahá'í Faith, with the few words of 'Abdu'l-Bahá quoted by the author being taken from Lefranc's article in *Le Temps*. Sainte-Croix concluded his article by asking, 'at the very moment when the question of Islam stands armed before Europe, is it not symbolically edifying to see in Paris a thinker – an old sage, powerful and gentle, who gives us the most lively, most radiant, most fruitful form of thought and social action that has yet acted in the world – coming to us from the depth of that same Islam?'[21]

A reporter with the daily illustrated newspaper *Excelsior* (Paris), a journal with a circulation of 110,000 copies, also visited the Master and on 7 November the newspaper published an article summarizing in a few lines the history and moral teachings of the Bahá'í Faith. It also included a description of the Master:

> . . . We visited Abdu'l-Baha in the apartment where he is staying at 4, Avenue du Camoens. There is an atmosphere of laughter and repose. White woodwork and luminous drapes; here and there, wreaths of flowers. The Master receives with equal good grace disciples and those who are simply curious. As he speaks only Persian, Turkish and Arabic, a friend serves as his interpreter. To all he repeats that to transform oneself and to transform the world one must but desire it.
>
> Nothing in our western civilization seems to surprise him. He is erudite, and that which he has not had the occasion to see with his own eyes, he has learned in advance through study.
>
> He is interested in all matters of art and science, in all that brings to our lives spiritual delight, concord and beauty. He integrates himself in our daily life. The masterpieces of the museums charmed him and you could have seen him on Saturday circulating with ease through the flowery sumptuousness of the chrysanthemum exposition.[22]

Meeting Hosted by Herman Bemberg

On Saturday 11 November a reception for 'Abdu'l-Bahá was organized by the French composer of German background Herman Bemberg (1859–1931). Several Persians were also invited to the meeting at which the host performed portions of his opera *Layla* (1914), a work inspired by Persia and composed from a libretto by the French artist and literary critic Jules Bois (1868–1943) in collaboration with the archaeologist and diplomat Eustache de Lorey.[23]

A brief reference to the meeting was published in the *Excelsior* on 12 November[24] and some days later *Le Figaro* published an account by one of the guests:

> The Persia of today, in some slightly painful news, has been nicknamed 'The France of the East'. Also, Persians are fond of being around Parisians.
>
> The other night, the elite of the Iranian colony came together around a famous thinker, Abdu'l-Baha, in the home of Monsieur H. Bemberg, and today very interested in the land of Ferdowsi and Saadi because of the opening of a new opera.
>
> It was an interview where metaphysics alternated with excerpts of poetry and *ghazals*. To complete the depiction of the country where the rose is never separated from the nightingale, they played a few fragments of Leilah, with Persian lyrics, yet unpublished, composed from a poem by Mr. Jules Bois, by Messieurs H. Bemberg and Eustache de Lorey. The latter, during his stay in Tehran, as attaché to the French legation, made a thorough study of the music of the country and collected some melodies whose flavor is particularly unique. Through the phrasing of the instruments, Abdul Baha perceived, like a clairvoyant, the mirage of the desert, the nonchalance of the caravans, the intoxicating scent of the gardens where Sultanas pass their time.[25]

In 1925 Jules Bois recalled his meeting with 'Abdu'l-Bahá in 1911 in an article on the Bahá'í Faith for the literary magazine *The Forum* (Boston):

> Once during a journey through Syria I stopped at Mount Carmel to place flowers on the tomb of the Bab, but had not the good fortune

to meet Abdul Baha. In 1912 [sic] I was luckier. A few weeks before the production of my Persian dramatic poem at Monte Carlo I had the privilege of a conversation with Abdul Baha at the home of my musical collaborator. Thanks to a young diplomat, who had just returned from Persia and knew the language, we could exchange ideas. The old prophet was full of hope for the future. Through Baha'u'llah's doctrine, he declared, the world was on the way to becoming metamorphosed into a 'rose-garden' and a 'paradise'. I had already listened to paeans of universal peace and knew that not infrequently they could be a harbinger of universal war.

'Do you really believe,' I inquired, 'that the solution of so grave a problem is posited in such ephemeral instrumentalities as the Hague Tribunal or Esperanto?'

Abdul Baha lifted his clear gray eyes, which reflected the poignant weariness of life. 'This world is but one realm and one native land,' he replied. 'This twentieth century is the dawn of spiritual illumination, and it is evident that day by day its potency will assume greater and greater proportions.'

In this exalted and Daedalian Eastern soul I suspected a sincere over-confidence in our outwardly brilliant civilization. I reminded him that Asia has so little to gain from our intricate 'improvements', while we have so much to learn from the laws of the spirit which she intuitively discovered many centuries ago.

'Can peace exist among men,' I exclaimed, 'before man is at peace with himself? Psychology, not external collyria, may, in rebuilding the individual, heal social perversions and deficiencies. Man is immemorially soul-sick. Torn between his lower and higher self, he is not seriously determined to create in the world a harmony he fails to find in himself. Since he secretly longs for conquest, all that artificial mechanism of accord is but a plaything in a hand always ready to grasp the sword.'

Abdul Baha shook his head majestically and, with oriental impressiveness, replied: 'Let us heed the gentle voice of the dove and the melody of the nightingale.' Then, closing his eyes, he added: 'Be admonished, ye who are possessors of intelligence.'

Two years later all Christian Europe was a battlefield.[26]

Visit to the Foyer de l'Âme Reformed Church

The reformist pastor Charles Wagner (1852–1918)[27] was one of the leading religious figures in France. Like Campbell in the United Kingdom, Wagner was the French exponent of Christian non-conformism and liberalism and his sermons and writings had an important following even in the United States.

'Abdu'l-Bahá was invited by Wagner to speak at his Foyer de l'Âme church, 7 bis rue Daval, during the morning service held at quarter past ten on Sunday, 26 November.[28]

The weekly magazine *Le Christianisme au XXe Siècle* (Paris) published on 5 January 1912, an unfriendly four-column article about the Bahá'í Faith over the by-line of the rather orthodox Benjamin Couve (1844–1928).[29] The text began with a sympathetic account of the meeting written by Bernard Le Gouis,[30] one of the participants:

> We personally witnessed, on Sunday November 25, at Foyer of the Soul, an impressive service. Mr. Pastor Charles Wagner received at his temple the representative of the sect known as Bahaism, Abdu'l-Baha Abbas . . .
>
> Commenting with particular emphasis on the passage 'That all may be one', Mr. Wagner read excerpts from his new book, *Ce qu'il faudra toujours* . . . Then, in a grand gesture of evangelical proportions, he left the floor to Abdu'l-Baha. In a few sentences, which an interpreter translated simultaneously, he urged men to stop their quarrels and their political and dogmatic struggles, to try to solve social and moral problems without regard for sect or caste. It was a touching sight to see this Christian pastor and this Muslim unite in the name of the same divine love . . .[31]

This account was also published in the supplement of the medical magazine *Aesculape* (Paris). Introducing 'Abdu'l-Bahá, the author stated that

> . . . the presence in Europe of the Persian prophet Baha, has produced such a strong impression that we are naturally led to devote him a few lines. The physician cannot remain indifferent to the revival of idealism . . . The ideas for which this venerable Persian began his

> long journey around the world are not those of the founder of a simple new sect, but a real and important embryo of the Universal Religion. Its aspirations are not only very high but also susceptible of becoming practical and immediate.

The same article also included some lines about 'Abdu'l-Bahá's talk to Theosophists in Paris (see chapter 34, vol. 2).[32]

Outside Paris the magazine *Le Foyer Protestant* (Nimes)[33] also published the account. In Spain the writer Román Salamero used parts of it in an article for the daily newspaper *El Imparical* (Madrid).[34]

'Abdu'l-Bahá met Wagner again in a meeting held in Paris on 11 February 1913[35] and after his passing the *l'Univers Israélite* (Paris) mentioned in an obituary the invitation that Wagner extended to 'Abdu'l-Bahá and referred to the episode as a unique event.[36]

An Episode of Opposition

On 17 November the French Anti-Masonic League, a conservative, anti-Semite and ultra-Catholic organization, held its third congress in the Atheneum located at rue de Saint-Germain, the same place where a few days before 'Abdu'l-Bahá had addressed the members of the Spiritualist Alliance (see chapter 35, vol. 2). The proceedings of the meeting as published in the *Revue Anti-Maçonnique* show that a brief mention was made about 'Abdu'l-Bahá and the Bahá'í Faith in the report by the vice-president of the congress, Antoine Baumann (1860–1925):

> M. Baumann, Vice President, read his report on occultist Freemasonry . . .
>
> 'And finally, at the beginning of November, with great fanfare a conference was given in Paris by a Persian by the name of Abdul-Baha Abbas, who claims to be the founder of the universal religion. This Persian had been presented to the public by the Jews.
>
> 'We persist in the belief that these events, with their charlatan air, are intended to excite some crazy enthusiasts to be used subsequently in those tasks whose execution can only be entrusted to fanatics.' (Applause.)
>
> Commander Cuignet thanked Mr Baumann for his interesting report.

> DUHAMEL (Bourg en Bresse) expressed the wish that great vigilance should continue to be exerted . . .[37]

The Anti-Masonic League was founded by the journalist Paul Copin-Albancelli (1851–1939) who was also the director of *La Bastille* (Paris), a weekly magazine which in the previous year had published an article by Louis Dasté (pseud. of André Baron) in which the Bahá'í Faith was linked with a supposed Judaeo-Masonic conspiracy, a theory triggered by Hippolyte Dreyfus, one of the leading French Bahá'ís who was of Jewish background.[38]

Echoes outside France

In addition to the articles from Argentina, Mexico and Spain mentioned earlier, newspapers in other countries also published references to the visit of 'Abdu'l-Bahá to Paris.

Henry Meunier, writing for the colonial newspaper *Les Nouvelles* (Algiers), published a series of articles on 'Islamic modernism'. In at least two of them he mentioned the recent visit of 'Abdu'l-Bahá to Paris and quoted extensively from His address in a meeting of the Theosophical Society. It is interesting that while in America and England the Bahá'í Faith was many times represented as a Christian movement, in France the press preferred to depict the new religion as a sort of Islamic reform.

Meunier's articles are a clear example of this misunderstanding. Considering the Bahá'í Faith as the vanguard of Islamic reformism, he used the words of 'Abdu'l-Bahá to support his idea that new trends within Islam were modernizing certain aspects of that religion. 'In recent days,' stated Meunier, 'Abdul Baha gave a lecture in Paris in which he outlined the aspirations of Islamic modernism. Never had such a liberal voice been raised among the priests of the present religions and ironically these aspirations, so appropriate for the spirit of modern free thinking, rise from that faith [Islam] that is reputed as the most fanatical . . .'[39]

The second of the articles on Islamic modernism closed declaring that 'a single prejudice remains rooted amongst even the most advanced of our native friends: the prejudice of the physical and moral confinement of women. This painful point of Islam in contact with civilization is removed at once by the Bahais, by the energy of a powerful will animated by a boundless love for progress.'[40]

In England, *The Christian Commonwealth* carried on 1 November an article by Wellesley Tudor Pole summarizing some of the activities of 'Abdu'l-Bahá during the first weeks of His sojourn in Paris:

ABDUL BAHA IN PARIS

Abdul Baha Abbas has spent the month of October in Paris, prior to his departure for Egypt. In his quiet apartments in the Avenue de Camoens a large number of Persians have gathered round him, attracted from different parts of the world to meet their beloved master. The gatherings at his apartments have proved more international than were those in London, and have included Hindoos, Parsees, Persians, Arabs, English, French, Germans, and Americans. Pére Hyacinthe Loyson (Prédicateur), the well-known preacher and teacher; M. Remy de Gourmont, the writer; M. and Mme. Mardrus, the poets, M. Bonet Maurez de l'Institut, and many others, have been among his visitors. The French Press has commented favourably on his visit, and several papers have described with appreciation his recent activities in London. Interesting accounts of the Bahai movement have appeared in the 'Figaro', 'L'Opinion', 'La France', and 'La Liberté', and it is understood that Abdul Baha will be asked to speak at the Académie Française and the Sorbonne before he leaves Paris. Abdul Baha looks for great things from London, and expects that the gradual spiritual awakening now becoming so apparent the world over will in many respects find its focus in the British metropolis. He looks back with pleasure to his sojourn in England and sends greetings to the many friends he made during his visit.

W. TUDOR POLE[41]

In the United States, the International News Service distributed an article by Paul Pierre Rignaux, a correspondent in Paris, about the visit of 'Abdu'l-Bahá:

WANTS FAITHS UNITED

Paris, Nov. 13 – Abdul Baha Abbas, head of the Bahaian religion, is visiting Mr. and Mrs. Hippolite Dreyfus, formerly Miss Laura Barney, and other co-religionists in Paris. He is the son of the martyred Baha Oullah, who propounded the first principles of Bahaianism in 1853. The 40 years he was locked up in a Persian prison have left him old and feeble.

Thanks to the generosity of an American woman, Mrs. James Jackson, this white-bearded prophet has now a suitable home in which to spend his declining years. Speaking to a correspondent, Abdul Baha revealed for the first time the tenets of his faith:

'Our goal is a universal religion, which means first of all a union of the Orient and the Occident – between Islamism and Christianity. Universal religion means universal peace. All faiths and peoples must be made one: rumours of war and fruitless strife must cease; the man will glory not so much that he loves his country as that he loves his kind.

LOVER OF ALL MANKIND

'I am a lover of all mankind for the Bahaian religion is universal. The principal teachers of mankind have been the manifestations of God. They came when most needed. Moses came when Egypt was in darkness and gave the Jews complete civilization. When this began to be replaced by ignorance then came Christ, the Light of the World, and the nations were united under his teachings.

'Once again men began to forget and divine counsels disappeared. Then came Baha Allah, my father. He unfurled the flag of the unity of mankind. We need neither temples nor churches. Though we sometimes build houses of praise, we have no set forms of worship. We have houses of justice, each composed of nine members distinguished for learning and probity, to direct our social work. We have no beggars, as the community provides employment for all who are able to work. Everyone must have some art, trade, or calling. We insist upon equal rights for men and women, and the best education for all.

'I prefer to call myself a servant rather than a prophet of God. I ask men to make good their faith, not to give it up.'

Abdul Baha will remain in Paris until the end of November, when he will return to Akka. He has two daughters, but no son to succeed him.[42]

As mentioned in the previous chapter, Mary Hanford Ford wrote an article for *The Sun* (New York) with her recollections and impressions of her meetings with 'Abdu'l-Bahá in Europe. The portion dealing with 'Abdu'l-Bahá's movements in Paris reads:

> When Abdul Baha was in Paris he rented his own furnished apartment, to which everyone had free access, and many charming interviews were held within its confines. People began to come, it was said, at 9 o'clock in the morning, and kept it up frequently until long after midnight. Between times the traveler snatched a few moments for the beauty of Paris, which delighted him.
>
> Sometimes in the afternoon he would suddenly start off for a walk, followed at a respectful distance by one of his Persian friends, who realized that the stranger wished to be alone, but feared he might get lost! He never did, however, and found his way about the crooked streets of ancient Paris quite as if he had been born there. He walks very swiftly, and would return after a two hour tour with a shining face and evidently renewed sympathy for the Western world which had received him so gladly. The children would turn to gaze after his rapidly passing figure, his Oriental robe blown back by his quick movement, his white turban pushed up perhaps from the broad forehead which arose above his wonderful eyes. He is only of medium height, but his fine bearing gives the impression of loftier stature.
>
> It was interesting in Paris to watch his audiences and observe his effect upon his hearers. In London he had been surrounded from the first with famous and prominent people, who consumed his time and lionized him. In Paris he was not so loudly heralded, and people sought him out more gradually. Every morning from 10 to 12 o'clock they gathered to meet him, and at some moment between the two hours he would seize the interval allowed by pressing private interviews and come out to meet the crowd.
>
> There is something singularly inspiring about the presence of Abdul Baha. He so forcefully radiates faith in God and belief in mankind's power to do the square thing in all directions and make a better world that in spite of oneself pessimism disappears at his advent and is replaced by courage and the joy of life. Many persons came first to his receptions out of curiosity, but returned again and again, and as they reappeared their faces had lost the worn, hunted,

worried look of modern life. They dropped their feeling of class consciousness, discussed the events of the day with anyone who happened to be present, even if that someone wore a shabby coat or a dark face, and broadened into vivid sympathy with the positive 'unity' of the prevailing atmosphere.

This uplift he inspires is of course Abdul Baha's peculiar charm. No one who comes into contact with him fails to experience it. All leave the interview idealists, hopeful of the future, earnestly determined to make a better world and do one's part in it.

One day he defined swiftly the motive power of his movement. 'You are a society,' he said, waving his hand toward the group before him, 'banded together for the increase of friendship among nations and races and of brotherhood among men.'

Then continuing he traced the enormity of war and hatred, and insisted that the only remedy for such outrage lies in the gracious and forceful thought of each individual. 'So now while these men are creating death you think life, while they are guilty of cruelty you think tenderness, while they make destruction you think construction, while they create war you think peace.'

One little talk he gave on the Holy Spirit shows how lovely and intimate is his teaching on God the Glorious One, the Father. It was inspired by a group of French and American Buddhists, readers of Paul Carus and the *Open Court*. They had been discussing the action of the Holy Spirit, some of them questioning its existence, and asked Abdul Baha to explain it from his own point of view.

After a striking description of the 'Divine Reality, far removed from man,' the abstract and essential Cause, he finished in these words:

'So the Holy Spirit touches the heart of man and wakens him to eternal life. Like the sun to earth, it brings to man warmth, energy and perfection. It gives him all possibilities. The cause of life widens before his eyes, eternity opens to him and becomes his, he no longer knows fear, for the wealth of God is his and every moment is his inviolable possession. Limitations disappear and as he becomes more and more sensitive to the teaching of the Holy Spirit all things are his own.

'Without the sun the earth is only the habitation of death and would remain forever in its frozen clasp were it not for the intermediary of light and heat stirring its inert mass and transforming into budding energy and accomplishment all its repellent hardness.

'So without the intermediary of the Holy Spirit man would remain dull, helpless and deprived of all attainment. But touched by the Divine elixir he becomes tender, loving, responsive and capable of every perfection of life.'

The newspapers of Paris gave Abdul Baha a most cordial and respectful reception. Articles in the *Temps*, the *Figaro*, the *Journal*, the *Matin* commented sympathetically upon his mission to the West and reproduced his ideas. He spoke in many public places and notably in the pulpit of Charles Wagner, the famous advocate of the simple life, and in that of Père Hyacinthe.

Abdul Baha insists that in this day of unity the East and the West must come together. Perhaps, a great war may terrify us before this is possible, but it must be accomplished. From the East, as he so beautifully expresses it, comes the breeze of God, which is his breath speaking through all the prophets, and without this inspiration the world stagnates and men lose their spiritual life. The West receives this breeze of God as it did in the wonderful word of Christ and by its aid creates a splendid and forceful civilization. The East needs the great civilization of the West, which must stir all its arteries of practical life to renewed vigor, but the West needs now especially that reviving and recreating breeze of God that is blowing from the East, and that certainly touches all who approach Abdul Baha.

A part of his mission of peace lies in the reminder he brings us that we have forgotten to apply the word of 'His Highness the Christ' to our life and business. He meant it to be practical; we have made it into a beautiful theory, and Abdul Baha insists that we must restore its original intention and build out of it the lovely world the Divine One saw when he gave it.[43]

8

SECOND VISIT TO EGYPT

December 1911 – 25 March 1912

The Egyptian Gazette

During 'Abdu'l-Bahá's sojourn in England, *The Egyptian Gazette* kept its readers well informed about His movements. On 11 September 1911, for instance, the newspaper mentioned the article that appeared in the *Daily Mail* (London) on 2 September and announced to its readers that 'Abdu'l-Bahá 'is going to London very shortly in order to meet his English adherents'.[1]

On 22 September, the newspaper published the following article by Thomas Atwood in which he summarized in glowing terms some episodes of 'Abdu'l-Bahá's visit to London:

ABDUL BAHA IN LONDON

SERMON AT THE CITY TEMPLE

A Memorable Scene

After spending last winter in Ramleh and paying a visit of some weeks' duration to Cairo spring of this year Abdul Baha (to speak of him by the name by which he is best known, although it is understood that he prefers to be known as Abbas Effendi) embarked for Europe early in August and after a brief stay in Switzerland proceeded to London where he arrived on Monday the 4th inst.

Much interest was caused by the appearance of so distinguished a visitor and he was especially welcomed by that section of the religious world known by the name of Liberal Christians and embracing many advanced thinkers of all denominations, Anglicans, Roman Catholics, Nonconformists, Jews and others being members of the Liberal Christian League. The editor of the 'Christian Commonwealth' at once interviewed 'The Master', who, it is interesting to note, was during his stay the guest of Lady Blomfield, so well known and highly esteemed in Alexandria, who is herself an ardent Bahaist.

INTERVIEW WITH REV. R. J. CAMPBELL

A full report of this interview appeared in the 'Christian Commonwealth' in its issue of the 13th inst. which also contained a deeply interesting account of the meeting shortly afterwards between Abdul Baba and the Rev. R. J. Campbell, of the City Temple, London, who is as prominent a leader in the West of the Universal Brotherhood movement as Abdul Baba is in the East. The interview was a private one, but shorthand notes were surreptitiously taken and, a reluctant consent having been obtained to its publication, the dialogue which took place between these two remarkable men appeared in print. It was my great happiness shortly before leaving England in December 1902 to spend a day with Mr. Campbell and his family at Brighton and last winter Abdul Baha honoured me by paying me three visits at Ramleh, so I can well imagine the fervour with which they greeted each other and the spiritual power that was manifest on the occasion.

IN THE PULPIT

On the following Sunday the Master attended the evening service at the City Temple and after Mr. Campbell's sermon addressed the vast congregation in Persian for eight minutes, his utterance being afterwards translated to his hearers. What a scene! It was the first time in his life that Abdul Baba had addressed a public assembly of any kind and his emotions may be more easily imagined than described, while to the crowded assembly the spectacle of a stately, I might say majestic, venerable figure, dressed in Oriental flowing robes, pouring forth a stream of eloquence in a language not a word of which they could understand, must have left an impression equally indescribable. The published account of this unique service concludes thus. 'As he took his departure Abdul Baba said in English, "I am very happy." So were we all.'

Truly we have among us a great prophet, one possessing the true Missionary Spirit, that spirit that inspired Robert Moffat and David Livingstone, in their noble work for the furtherance of Christ's

> Kingdom on earth. Where is that spirit now? Do we see it in the bickering and jealousies that disgrace modem missionary 'enterprise'? I think not.
>
> But the dawn is breaking; Liberal Christianity with its gospel of brotherly love is advancing all along the line; and (forgive! the mixing of metaphors) new wine is being poured into the old bottles which are bursting in every direction.
>
> THOS. ATWOOD[2]

The author confused the Bahá'í Lady Blomfield with Lady Massie-Blomfield, a feminist who defended the rights of women in Islamic countries in some of her writings, including some articles published in *The Egyptian Gazette*. A note published days later clarified this confusion.[3]

In a further article published on 5 December, Atwood criticized Christian missionaries in Egypt and in the course of his argumentation asked the following rhetorical question: 'Who is the true follower of Christ, Archdeacon Wilberforce, leading Abdul Baha by the hand along the aisle of his church and placing him in the seat of honour in front of the altar, or the Bishop of London uttering slanders against Moslems at a missionary meeting?'[4] This statement embarrassed Snelling, who in his editorial column stated that 'we have no desire to be identified with Mr. Atwood's opinions of the subject of missions', and added that 'Archdeacon Wilberforce who is put today as the idea of "the true follower of Christ", as regards his dealings with other religions, is probably even less in sympathy with him in these matters than we are'.[5]

On 25 September *The Egyptian Gazette* carried portions of the interview granted by 'Abdu'l-Bahá to Percy J. Philip of the London *Daily News*.[6] On 27 September it stated that 'Last Sunday week Abdul Baha Effendi attended at St. John's Westminster and, at the invitation of Archdeacon Wilberforce, delivered a short address in Persian.'[7] On 2 October it announced that 'Abbas Effendi, the Bahai leader, left England at the end of last week.'[8]

On 4 October, the newspaper published an interesting opinion article about 'Abdu'l-Bahá. While its first part was a copy of what was published in the *Near East* (London) on 27 September (see chapter 6),[9] the second part carried the following comments about the potential role of the Bahá'í Faith:

> But what does seem remarkable in the case is that nobody has drawn attention (we believe) to the possible political value of the Bahaist movement. Rightly or wrongly, the West undoubtedly considers that Islam has always been, and remains even now, the implacable opponent of progress. If, therefore, Bahaism should succeed in engrafting the spirit of tolerance and friendliness towards progress upon the Islamic stock, it would undoubtedly become a factor to be reckoned with seriously in the political problems of the Near East. There are also, of course, plenty of opportunities for the Bahaist to preach tolerance to Christians. The West has its fanatics as well as the East, and it is to be feared that they will prove every whit as hard to convert to the Bahaist doctrine of universal brotherhood and universal peace. But the ideal is one worth striving for, and the Bahaists certainly are striving for it. And the point is that since they show clear signs of growing power it will be a strange thing if the West fails to watch their growth with interest, even if that interest be of a purely selfish character. In the best interests of Bahaism it is to be hoped that it may never take on a political colouring. In view of past experience, however, that seems almost too much to hope for.[10]

A curious discussion, not devoid of personal attacks, took place among readers of *The Egyptian Gazette* after the publication on 27 September of a letter to the editor signed by a certain Abbas from Alexandria who, regarding Atwood's article published on 22 September, stated that 'the real surname of Abbas Effendi, as he prefers to, and therefore should, be called, is Abou'l Baha, or Father of Splendour, not Abdul Baha, Servant of Splendour, as Mr. Atwood would call him.'[11] Atwood's reply to this letter was published on 29 September and in it he stated that all accounts spell the name as 'Abdul Baha' and added that 'To those who know Abdul Baha the idea of his claiming to be called '*Father* of Splendour' is simply ridiculous. 'Servant of Splendour', yes. His whole life has been devoted to the service of mankind and he has no higher ambition than to be known as the Servant of God and Man. His followers have every right to speak of him as Abdul Baha instead of as simply Abbas Effendi.'[12]

Abbas struck again in a long letter in which he stated to be a Syrian 'closely acquainted with many Bahais' and put forward a number of linguistic arguments to defend his thesis that the Master's title was actually

'Abou'l Baha'.[13] Simultaneously, a third reader signing as 'H.' referred Abbas to an article about Bahá'u'lláh by Clément Huart in the *Encyclopaedia of Islam* (1913) in which the name of the Master was correctly spelled.[14]

Atwood's final letter on this subject was published on 5 October and closed with this interesting statement:

> I ought to be grateful to Mr. Abbas . . . for the help he has given in directing attention to the Bahai movement. In a recent letter to the Gazette on another subject I alluded to this movement and a correspondent at Port Said wrote to me asking what it was. I told him and in his reply he said, 'There must be a very great number of people who are Bahaists without knowing it.' And indeed I feel sure there are.[15]

On 6 October it was announced that 'Abdu'l-Bahá was 'expected to arrive in Alexandria shortly from Europe. He is now in France.'[16] A note appeared a few days later reporting that those readers 'who may wish to know more of the Bahai movement, of which frequent mention has of late been made in our columns' could request pamphlets from a certain postal address in London.[17]

A few days before the return of the Master to Egypt, the Bahá'í Jean Stannard wrote a letter to the editor of *The Egyptian Gazette* calling for a fairer treatment of 'Abdu'l-Bahá, especially in the Arabic press. 'The world of Islam', she stated, 'should open a wide door of hospitality to this great teacher with his message of peace and religious unity for through the beauty of his teachings and philosophical knowledge he has done more in Europe and America to remove obsolete intolerance against the Mohammedan Faith than any reformer of our days.' Stannard's letter ended by stating that it remained 'for the friends of Islam to pay a just and generous tribute to this brave worker in the cause of peace and unity . . .'[18] The same issue of *The Egyptian Gazette* carried an editorial by Snelling concerning Stannard's letter. In a sympathetic tone, the article regretted the lack of attention that the Egyptian public opinion, especially Muslims, was paying to the 'mighty teacher':

> THE RETURN OF ABBAS EFFENDI
>
> The letter from Mrs. J. Stannard, which we publish in another column today, recalls the fact that Abbas Effendi, the leader of the

Bahai movement, is shortly expected to return to the country where he has spent such a large part of his time since the Young Turks released him from his long imprisonment at Acre. His presence here last year did not arouse the curiosity that such an interesting and commanding personality might have been expected to evoke. His venerable figure might have been observed by the initiated, a quietly amused spectator at aviation meetings and the like, or gently expounding his doctrines to a few eager disciples in the shady walks of Nouzha Gardens. But his doings attracted less public notice than those of comparatively unimportant officials and infinitely less than those of Farid Bey. Islam remained indifferent – if we disregard the early revilings of the local Moslem press – and the greater part of the Christian community, it is safe to say, was entirely ignorant of the fact that we had such a mighty teacher in our midst, a man whose followers are said to number over a million in Persia alone, and whose doctrines are spreading in America and elsewhere with astonishing rapidity. The indifference, or hostility, of Islam is the more remarkable since, as Mrs. Stannard observes, Abbas Effendi has probably done more in Europe and America 'to remove obsolete intolerance against the Mohamedan faith than any reformer of our day'. Bahaism tolerates all faiths, apparently believes in all faiths up to some point never very clearly defined; and it has done Islam the service of explaining to the Far West that Mohamedans are not merely the Mormons of another hemisphere. Tolerance so sublime as Abbas Effendi's is not easy to understand, even in the Twentieth Century, and though Mrs. Stannard tells us that the followers of every known religion were to be found in the Bahai circle we cannot help doubting whether any very orthodox Mohamedans – or Christians either, for that matter – were numbered among them. As far as Egypt is concerned, at all events, the new religion has made little perceptible progress and has met with nothing but indifference or active hostility from the representatives of the older faiths. The voice of the Eastern Tolstoy, with his doctrines of peace and good will, has been drowned in the present outburst of patriotism and militant religion, just as the Western Tolstoy was shouted down in Russia, just as the Master from whom both derive their teaching, was shouted down by the patriot Pharisees of Jerusalem.

But to Christians, at all events; and English Christians in

> particular, Abbas Effendi's return on the present occasion should arouse a real interest. He returns from a remarkable visit to London and Paris, from conferences with the leaders of religious thought in England and France, from addressing vast audiences at the City Temple and elsewhere, on all of which occasions his personal triumph has been striking and complete. No one who has had the privilege of meeting and conversing with the Bahai leader can be surprised at this, and it needs but little imagination to be impressed by the dramatic picture of this venerable Oriental in his white robes speaking to crowded congregations of London 'City men,' expounding in the Persian language those 'high ideals of love, charity and compassion,' which, as Mrs. Stannard remarks, Western Christians have been too apt to regard as their own special prerogatives. Such scenes were reported at length by our London contemporaries and reproduced from time to time in these columns during last summer. Yet, we must frankly admit, that to us this is the least attractive side of the Bahai movement. If Bahaism has found favour in the United States it cannot be forgotten that countless other 'religions' have become popular there which would not have been taken seriously in any other country in the world. About the London meetings, also, there was a certain air of gush and self-advertisement – not on the part of Abbas Effendi, but on the part of his enlightened friends – which was quite patent to all who are familiar with that kind of religion which will listen to anything so long as it is unorthodox, new, sensational. We cannot help regretting the 'lionizing' of Abbas Effendi. In the East his religion will find its true home and exercise its beneficent influence upon nations newly awaking to a sense of their unity and power. We can, then, the more heartily welcome him back to Egypt, fresh from achievements in the Western capitals which have afforded yet another proof of his remarkable personal and intellectual powers.[19]

On 16 December *The Egyptian Gazette* published the news that 'Abdu'l-Bahá 'has arrived in Alexandria on his return from Europe and is again residing at Ramleh'.[20] Several weeks later the newspaper gave further details about 'Abdu'l-Bahá's stay in Ramleh and reported that

> Abbas Effendi, the Bahaist leader, is taking a house at Ramleh,

> Alexandria, to which his wife, daughters, and grand-children will migrate shortly. The fact that the electric light is to be installed in the new residence is evidence, if further evidence be required, that Abbas Effendi is a firm believer in progress – of the right kind. He intends, we understand, visiting the United States in March.[21]

Finally, on 28 March, *The Egyptian Gazette* reported that 'Abdu'l-Bahá, 'left for the United States on Tuesday'.[22]

The Wádí al-Níl (Wadinnil)

The Egyptian Gazette was not the only newspaper in Egypt to give news about the movements of 'Abdu'l-Bahá in London. On 23 December 1911 the *Wádí al-Níl* (Alexandria), a newspaper founded and directed by Muhammad A. Kalza in 1910, published an Arabic translation of 'Abdu'l-Bahá's address at the Church of St John the Divine of Westminster, which was preceded by this introduction:

> We came upon a copy of a great sermon on the subject of prophecy. In it Sheikh Said Abbas Effendi, Imam of the Bahai, talked about the essence of divinity. When he visited the capital of Britain he was living in Ramleh, Alexandria. His sermon in Arabic was heard by a large number of people from all religions. They were so affected by what he said that they all rushed to get the sermon translated into English.
>
> Since the name of this great and pious Sheikh has been talked about so much since the day of his arrival here last year, we have tried to convey this speech in writing. This is so that it can be read and Egyptians can respect this pious man, who commands respect the world over, and was welcomed wherever he went on his trip to Europe last summer.[23]

Reactions among Christian Missionaries

The presence of 'Abdu'l-Bahá in Egypt and the success of His visit to Europe aroused some opposition among Christian missionaries in Egypt, as can be gathered from information appearing in *Blessed be Egypt* (London), a quarterly journal of the Nile Mission Press (NMP).

An article about the annual meeting of the NMP gave the details of a report delivered by Arthur T. Upson, its superintendent, who reported the recruitment of an Egyptian writer who had converted to Christianity. His name was 'Sheikh Ahmed Abdullah' and of him Upson reported that 'at one time he joined the sect exactly similar to the Behâi sect' and added that 'Abdul-Behâ Abbas has occupied Mr. Campbell's City Temple pulpit; he is a force you have to deal with.'[24] The report contained this interesting statement:

> Sheikh Abdullah has just written a tract upon the Behais, otherwise called Babis. Abdul-Beha is the son of Beha-allah, who was exiled by the Turkish Government to Acre. He was kept there for some time, but when the Turkish Constitution was proclaimed it was made possible for him to come to Egypt and other lands. It is estimated that he has about 500,000 adherents in the United States, and he is getting a growing body in this land. And so Sheikh Abdullah wrote a tract, at my suggestion, upon 'The truth about the Behai sect', from his own personal knowledge of them. That is just ready in Arabic and English.[25]

According to announcements published in the same journal, the work produced by Sheikh Abdullah was a little booklet of 17 pages in the English version and 24 in the Arabic. One thousand copies were made of the English edition and two thousand of the Arabic[26] and were sold at the price of half a piaster.[27]

The International Congress of Moral Education

In 1897 the Moral Education League, an institution of interreligious character, was created in London with the aim of introducing moral education as part of schools' curricula. In a short time the institution gained considerable influence in the United Kingdom and other countries. Its president was Professor J. S. Mackenzie and the secretary of the organization for ten years was the Rev. Harrold Johnson, the Unitarian pastor who wrote articles about the Baha'i Faith for the *Contemporary Review* and *The Christian Commonwealth*.[28] Another close associate of the organization was Dr Michael Sadler, who, as indicated above, met 'Abdu'l-Bahá during His first visit to England and was one of the speakers at the farewell ceremony held in His honor in London just before leaving for Paris.

The Education League organized the first Congress of Moral Education, which was held at London University on 25–9 September 1908. The success of the event prompted the convention of a second congress which was held in The Hague 22–7 August 1912. The aim of the Congress was 'to enlist the active co-operation of all, irrespective of race, nations, and belief, in promoting the work of moral education'. Twenty-three governments sent official delegates, over a thousand delegates registered as participants and over two hundred papers were read.

One of the delegates summed up the topics discussed during the Congress:

> The subjects dealt with and under discussion at the various sessions were: Moral Education and Character Building considered from the Denominationalist, the Undenominationalist and the Independent–Moralist points of view; Moral Education considered from social and national points of view; Formation of the Will; Physical Training as a means of Character-Building; Moral Education considered from a Practical Point of View; the Moral Education of Adolescents; Character-Building in family life and in society at large; Character-Building of young people at educational institutions not dedicated to the ordinary primary education; Character-Building of Abnormal Children.[29]

'Abdu'l-Bahá was invited to participate but owing to His planned visit to America, He was unable to attend. Instead, He sent the text of His lecture, which was read in one of the sessions. This paper was written in Alexandria, during 'Abdu'l-Bahá's second sojourn in Egypt.

One of the participants at the conference, Jean Devolvé, wrote a review of the event for the *Revue de Métaphysique et Morale* (Paris) in which he mentioned 'Abdu'l-Bahá and briefly summarized His Tablet to the congress. 'His paper . . . was more the haranguing of a prophet than a pedagogical presentation,'[30] stated Devolvé who, in discussing the lecture by Harrold Johnson, stated that the minister and organizer of the congress 'has developed the subject of 'Abdu'l-Bahá'.[31]

At the end of the year the proceedings of all the lectures delivered at the Congress were published in a lengthy volume edition that also included the text contributed by 'Abdu'l-Bahá:

O respected gathering of the world of humanity!

Such noble intentions and excellent purposes as are shown by your Congress, should receive the world's greatest gratitude and pleasure; for you are tirelessly engaged in such efforts that are conductive to the peace and tranquility of humanity, because the promotion of comfort and happiness in the realm of creation depends upon the general upliftment and moral refinement of the human world.

The great objects of moral education are to inculcate a lofty ideal, to induce broadmindedness and noble efforts, and humanity may therefore be well appealed to in the interest of such a great work.

Consider! The predominating principle of life today seems to be one that urges to self-interest or welfare – to self-protection and selfish gratification – to egoism and self-aggrandizement; such ideas in the majority of individuals lead ultimately to utmost degradation, misfortune and base thought.

When man has developed further in knowledge and his efforts become correspondingly nobler, then he will desire and seek for the higher good for his own household and their protection, since he will realize that the comfort and prosperity of his home assures his own happiness; advancing still further in reflection and lofty aspirations he will ultimately strive to seek the welfare of his fellow-countrymen and the nation; yet notwithstanding these very efforts and ideals, beneficial to himself, his home and his countrymen, he may still prove injurious to another nation, for his utmost endeavours are to draw all possible benefits for himself and usually strive to particularise and monopolise for his household and nation the general prosperity of the world. He imagines that when other nations and neighbouring Powers are degraded, the greater will be the progress of his own country and people, until through supreme power and opulence he will dominate victoriously all other races.

But the godly man and heavenly personage is absolutely free from such bondages; the mobility of his thoughts and superior aims are above this: for the circle of his thoughts (ideas) becomes sufficiently broadened to realise that universal benefits are the foundation for individual happiness, while injuries to other nations and powers must be reckoned as affecting his own country, nation, household and himself. Therefore he sincerely exerts himself to draw happiness and benefit for the whole world and protects the welfare of others generally, seeking for the upliftment, enlightenment and prosperity of all. He knows no distinction, for he considers the world of humanity as one and the nations as individuals of one household! Nay more! He views the collective community of humanity as a single being and each nation as a bodily member thereof.

The loftiness of aim in man should become so developed that he may help and serve universal morality and be a means of glory to the human race. But today the reverse is apparent; for the nations of the world are only considering their own aggrandizement while desiring the downfall of others; nay, even they strive to draw away to themselves the prosperities of others and injure them and they count this strife as winning immortality and declare such conditions as the natural basis of humanity, but this is a gross error; indeed there is no greater mistake than this.

Praise be to God! In some animals solidarity and mutual co-operation for life is frequently seen; when in the time of danger, each will try to surpass the others in help. One day as I was standing near the borders of a little stream. I noticed some grasshoppers that had not yet developed full wings. These insects, wishing to pass from my side of the stream to the other in order to procure some food, threw themselves forward each one trying to emulate the other in flinging itself in the water, so that a bridge was formed, in order that the others might pass and this was accomplished; yet those who gave themselves as a bridge for the others finally perished!

Now consider how such solidarity makes for life as compared to the fighting for oneself which generally destroys it! As long as insects have admirable instincts, how much more should man possess them, who is the noblest of created beings; especially when Divine Laws and Heavenly Teachings instruct man how to acquire the virtues. In the sight of God national distinctions, patriotic differences, family-fame and self-interest are abhorred and condemned.

The appearance of the Holy and the revelation of all Divine Books have been for the purpose of practising these principles and to be characterised with such virtues and perfections. All the sacred teachings can be summed up into this, that the lower conceptions of self-interest should be eliminated from the human mind, the general morality in the race reformed and exalted and enabling equality and solidarity universally established, to the extent that an individual will readily sacrifice his life for another. This is the divine foundation and the heavenly Law; but such a solid basis cannot be established except through a supreme Power, influencing the sentiments of humanity; no other force is capable of developing such characteristics except the Power and the Breaths of the Holy Spirit, which transforms man to such an extent that his morality becomes entirely changed and he is born again and baptised with the Fire of the Love of God – which means Love Universal and the Water of Eternal Life.

Ancient philosophers who sincerely strove to promote the refinement of morals, were chiefly capable of influencing themselves individually but not universally. Reflect on the histories of the past and this truth will be clearly evident. Only by the Power of the Holy Spirit can the universal morality be improved and advanced, the world of humanity be enlightened, obtaining an ideal upliftment and receiving true education. Therefore the sincere well-wishers of the world should ceaselessly endeavour, that through their power of faith they may attract the confirmations of the Holy Spirit.

My hope is that your honourable Congress and meeting of well intentioned minds for human progress may be compared to a mirror reflecting the rays of the Sun of Truth and be the cause of elevation and education of the universal morals!

Pray accept my high esteem and regard for this inestimable gathering.[32]

Visit of Platon Drakoules and Felicia R. Scatcherd

In early 1912 'Abdu'l-Bahá received in Ramleh the British journalist and spiritualist Felicia R. Scatcherd whom He had met earlier in London (see chapter 35, vol. 2). Scatcherd was accompanied by Platon Drakoules and his wife.

Drakoules (1860–1941) was the founder and leader of the Greek Socialist Party (1909) and in 1910 became its first representative in the Greek parliament. Before moving to England, where he lived for 20 years, he founded the first Greek socialist newspaper, *Ardin* (1885–7). In London he became acquainted with Scatcherd, who was eventually appointed as the vice president of his party.

Scatcherd's account of their visit to 'Abdu'l-Bahá in Egypt appeared on January 1913 in *The International Psychic Gazette*, as part of a larger article on the Bahá'í Faith. In their meetings Drakoules, who besides being a Socialist was also a member of the International Vegetarian Union, posed questions to 'Abdu'l-Bahá regarding his areas of interest, and notes of some of the Master's answers were included in the article. Scatcherd also mentioned the fact that the renowned Greek artist Thalia Flora Karavia (1871–1960) made, at their request and after gaining permission from 'Abdu'l-Bahá, a portrait of the Master:

> *Alexandria, Sun. 21 Jan., 1912.* A beautiful morning, my second Sunday in Egypt. We are on our way to see Abbas Effendi, Dr. and Mrs. Platon Drakoulès and myself. I had met this leader and inspirer of his fellows many times before under the grey skies of London, when his smile of sunny welcome seemed to atone for the absence of the sunshine, due even on an English autumn day.
>
> Years ago, Mr. Sidney Sprague had been the guest of Dr. Drakoulès, and had held a Bahaist meeting in the Doctor's Oxford home, when he had ardently desired that the Greek Reformer should make the personal acquaintance of the 'Great Teacher from the East'. And now by a strange coincidence this wish was to be realised, and Mr. Sprague was to be the interpreter between these two devoted souls – the younger standing for the Social Regeneration of Mankind, the elder representing Spiritual Illumination and Unity.
>
> In London, surrounded by the leaders of Western thought, Abdul Baha had rendered null and void Kipling's dictum: 'For East is East, and West is West, But they twain shall never meet.' Here, in the East, I wondered what effect would be produced upon us, where his picturesque personality had no longer the charm of uniqueness.
>
> We found him in a villa, opposite the new Victoria Hotel, Ramleh. Although only 10 a.m., he had been astir for hours, attending to his enormous correspondence, and receiving visitors. Again, in his presence, the old sense of goodness and simplicity overwhelmed one. The venerable figure in its Persian costume, was just as unique in its Eastern setting, as in London.
>
> Of middle stature, and broadly-built, he yet strikes one at times, as if he were tall, and is undoubtedly imposing. Oval-faced, and large-featured, with heavy eyebrows, a nose resembling that of General Booth, he has the compelling personality of all born leaders of men. His grey eyes are unusually expressive. In moments of

excitement they become dark and deep in the piercing intensity of their gaze. I have seen them dash as if generating a kind of lightning, and then they soften and brighten and change expression with all the varying moods of his active mentality. But whether under the influence of sorrow or joy, indignation or pity, they are always surcharged with sympathy. One who knows no word of Persian can share the emotions of his soul by watching the lights and shadows in his eyes. When, as often, he closes them, then one need only follow the movements of his no less wonderful hands.

I will not dwell on the details of the glad welcome, the oriental hospitality, the fragrant Persian tea, and the groups of waiting disciples from all quarters of the globe. I will only summarise the points in the discussion not generally dwelt on: –

Dr. Drakoulès asked whether Abdul Baha did not think that injustice in industrial arrangements, resulting in antagonism between classes, owing to the existence of extreme poverty and excessive riches, militated against his teachings of love and unity.

He replied that he could assure him on the authority of his father, Baha Ullah, that the legislators of the world were approaching a time when it would become illegal to own more than a certain amount of wealth. He added that the principle of unity was asserting itself more and more, and that under its influence, class antagonism will be recognised as immoral. This led the conversation to the subject of ethics, especially in relation to the lower animals.

Dr. Drakoulès asked whether he did not hold it to be immoral to exploit the sub-human races for our benefit, either in the domains of science, diet, or amusement?

Abdul Baha gave a definite reply in the affirmative. That is, he emphasised his belief that the destruction of humble life for the benefit of human life was inconsistent with the principle of unity. He said that this teaching would become accentuated later on. At the present time mankind is not ripe for certain aspects of truth. Even as Jesus, the Christ, refrained from saying to the world at large what he deemed it necessary to impart to his esoteric circle, so he, Abdul Baha, felt his general teaching circumscribed by the same necessity. But further manifestation of the Divine would lead to freer and fuller exposition of the fact of the Oneness of all Life – the basic principle of unity or love.'

> While in Cairo we made the acquaintance of other members of Abdul Baha's family. His daughters came to see us, and we visited the Bahai centres there, as well as the home of our good friend Mr. Sprague, who had married a niece of the Master, to whose cause he is devoting his life.
>
> On our return to Alexandria, I went again to Ramleh, to obtain permission for a Greek painter, of great talent (Madame Thalia Karavia), to make a painting of the Master. This permission was accorded, mainly, I believe, owing to his daughter's persuasion. You see, I felt unless the prophet adopted the veil the women were casting on one side he could not avoid portraits being taken. One fine one had already been made, and he had been photographed several times without permission . . .[33]

Echoes in America

On February 1912 the Associated Press released an article about the Bahá'í Faith from a correspondent in Cairo who basically summarized the lives of the Báb, Bahá'u'lláh and 'Abdu'l-Bahá, adding a few lines about the Bahá'í teachings. 'In some respects the Bahai movement is the most remarkable of modern times,' stated the author. 'The foundation principle of the Bahai doctrine is universal brotherhood. It seeks to reflect the best of the various religions and to find a common ground for worship and service for all mankind.' The article also announced that 'Abdu'l-Bahá would sail from Egypt on 1 March. As a separate section it also included His farewell words to the Bahá'ís of Europe spoken before He returned to Egypt in late 1911[34] and a portrait of the Master taken in Paris and distributed in the media by the Harris & Ewing Studio in Washington. Several newspapers across the United States reproduced this article in their pages.[35]

9

'ABDU'L-BAHÁ EXPECTED IN AMERICA

The American press reported the news that 'Abdu'l-Bahá would visit Europe and the United States long before His actual arrival in the West. The *Los Angeles Times* mentioned on 1 November 1910 that 'that Abdul Baha may arrive in the United States and make himself known to his followers in the immediate future is a possibility now stimulating those of his faith to an intense excitement . . . A few weeks ago he left his home in the Orient to startle his followers in France by his unexpected appearance at Paris.'[1] Just a few days later the *New York Herald* reported that it 'is now said that he ['Abdu'l-Bahá] will not reach these shores from Persia this year'.[2]

Almost one year later 'Abdu'l-Bahá was finally able to travel to Europe. As has been shown earlier, the American press kept its readers informed about the Master's presence in London and Paris. When the news of 'Abdu'l-Bahá's planned visit to America was definitely confirmed, further opportunities arose to familiarize the general public with the fundamental principles of the Baha'i Faith as well as to provide new details about the success of the Master's travels in Europe.

The Persian–American Educational Society engaged several Bahá'ís in the task of writing articles on the Bahá'í Faith, hired a press agent and started sending copies of those articles to the leading newspapers. As a consequence, across the United States several articles announcing the upcoming visit of the Master were published and also a large number of news items appeared in the local newspapers of some of the cities where 'Abdu'l-Bahá was expected. This chapter will focus on some of the articles that appeared on the national stage or in the major newspapers in North America.

One of the earliest articles about the expected journey of 'Abdu'l-Bahá to America was published in late December 1911 in several newspapers. It carried a picture of the Master and offered a positive description of Him and the Bahá'í Faith:

COMING TO CONVERT US

'THE LIGHT IN THE LANTERN'

ABDUL BAHA, the head of a religion which is spreading over the world, is soon to visit this country. Out of the mystic Orient, out of the land of the Arabian Nights, comes this turbaned teacher to convert the New World. From the land which was old when Abraham walked the earth, from the deserts across which flitted the Wise Men two thousand years ago to worship the Babe of Bethlehem, will now start a crusade to this, the youngest of modern nations, a crusade which will tell of a new Dispensation, that the coming of the father has been fulfilled in Baha'Ullah who was an incarnation of the deity and whose worship is destined to harmonize and unite all believers in one God.

Bahaism has grown so rapidly in America that most of the big cities contain many of that faith. In Chicago they are planning to build a mighty temple to be known as Mashrazk-el-askar (The Dawning Place of Mention), while in Washington many of the exclusive Smart Set are adherents. One of the most prominent of these is Mr. Charles Mason Remy, son of Admiral Remy, a young man, who in spite of his position as head of an architectural college, gives a great deal of his time to the spread of the faith, and has visited many countries as a missionary. It was to him that the Prophet recently made known his intention of visiting the capital at an early date.

While in Washington the Prophet will likely be the guest of Mrs. Christian Hemmick, better known to the world as Mrs. Barney. The Barneys were among the first American converts. Miss Laura Barney, now Mrs. Hippolyte Dreyfus of Paris, having spent many months at a time in visiting Acre, where the Prophet lived, and contributing her time and means to a spread of the faith . . .

This year he visited London, where he was warmly welcomed by many of the nobility, among them Lady Bloomfield. He also spent a few months in Paris where there is a large colony of the faith and where Miss Laura Barney was busy writing a play in which is depicted the martyrdom of a beautiful Persian girl who was a convert. After a visit to Egypt it is expected that Abdul Baha will

> then set sail for the New World, which he expects to bring under the sway of his faith.
>
> In appearance he is tall, with brown skin and a snowy beard; a white turban and linen robe of the same colour are his costume, this being surmounted with the gray overgarment peculiar to all high caste Persians. Around his simple cottage on the slopes of Carmel are gathered at sunset each day a band of pilgrims who listen for hours to the dignified discourse with which he entertains them.
>
> His room is plainly furnished, his food soup and rice, which simple meal is always followed by the washing of the hands commonly in use in the East. His conversation lies in the direction of his hopes to do away with the dissensions of the different religions, to unite Jew and Gentile, Buddhist and Mahommedan, the East and the West, all under the sway of a brotherhood in which there is no creed but the good of humanity . . .[3]

Beginning in 31 December 1911, some newspapers, among them the *Washington Post*, carried a half page article about 'Abdu'l-Bahá which was copyrighted by the *New York Herald*. Its information was largely based on accounts of the Master penned by Myron Phelps and Edward. G. Browne in their works and was illustrated with a drawing depicting 'Abdu'l-Bahá in the streets of 'Akká assisting the poor in the city, an image inspired by one of the episodes described in Phelps's *Life and Teachings of Abbas Effendi* (1903). While most of the contents of the article consisted of a general introduction about the origins and tenets of the Bahá'í Faith, it also offered the following comments about the Master:

> THE COMING OF ABBAS EFFENDI MESSIAH OF 6,000,000 SOULS
>
> MYSTERIOUS PERSONALITY OF THE PERSIAN WHOM NEW YORK BAHA'ISTS SOON WILL WELCOME
>
> When Abbas Effendi, known to millions of his followers as 'Our Master' and 'Our Lord', arrives in America within a few weeks there will be among us a personality as mysterious and strange as any that lives today on earth.
>
> For Abbas Effendi, manifestation of the Son of God, direct instrument on earth of the Divine Intelligence, as his followers

declare him to be, possesses an influence over the lives of his followers only comparable to that displayed by the great prophets of the race, from whom men died that might justify their faith.

Mohammed or Buddha had no more complete sovereignty over the minds and bodies of those that accepted their teachings than has Abbas Effendi, the Abdul Baha, or son of the Supreme One. Thousands have chosen death rather than deny his name and have died uttering his name, even as did the Christian martyrs while whispering the sacred name of the Founder of their religion. The Bahaist, of whose religion Abbas is the head, he is unquestioningly accepted as the reflection of God on earth, a being that is man, yet more than man; to touch whose robe is a consecration, to be blessed by whom a promise of Paradise!

Such is the leader of the Bahaist or Babist religion, whose following includes six million persons and whose purposes are toward a brotherhood among the nations, the abolition of wars, and the adoption of a universal language, all of which is in detail provided for in the Kitab'l Akdas, or book of laws, and was set forth in 1870 by Abdul Baha, father of the present prophet . . .

APPEARANCE OF ABBAS

Of Abbas himself some vivid pictures have been drawn by travelers who came to visit him from all corners of the earth during that period of 40 years when he was so peculiar a prisoner in Akka – for he has only been at liberty since the ascendancy of the new Turk party. So powerful is his influence on those about him that no governor was continued in office at Akka, for above one year. Several visitors tell of dinners at which the governor and his staff – actually Abbas' jailers – stood with bared head till the prophet has seated himself, and only then sat in deference to a gesture from him . . .[4]

On 8 January, *The Brooklyn Daily Eagle* reported a special service in the Hanson Place Baptist Church (Brooklyn) that was dedicated to peace. The pastor of the church, Rev. Theodore S. Henderson, invited among others H. H. Topakyan, the Persian Consul-General, Dr. W. A. Hunsberger, acting President of the International Peace Forum, the financier Henry Clews and the former Minnesota Senator Charles A. Towne. 'Abdu'l-Bahá was also invited to participate in the program of the service. According to the *Daily Eagle*, Henderson read at the meeting a message by 'Abdu'l-Bahá 'written in Arabic, a translation of which, divested of its ornate Eastern expressions, expressed regret at his inability to visit America at this time, and praised the work which is being done in this country in the interest of international peace'.[5] On 21 January the same newspaper published a lengthy interview with the local Bahá'í Howard MacNutt who shared his opinion about the upcoming visit to America of the Master.[6]

The news of the visit of 'Abdu'l-Bahá to the United States also reached the ears of the former President Theodore Roosevelt, who was a personal friend of the Washington Bahá'í Agnes Parsons. In its issue of 20 January 1912 the *New York Tribune* carried an account of a visit paid by Roosevelt to the Three Arts Club (340 West 85th Street), an institution for the artistic education of girls managed by his sister Corinne Roosevelt Robinson. During the meeting, one of the members asked him about the future visit of 'Abdu'l-Bahá to New York. His significant answer was reported in the following way:

> He made near a dozen little impromptu speeches to the girls as they clustered about him – told them how much in favor of the Three Arts Club he was, how he approved of its work, then branched out into more general remarks on conduct in general and conduct for girls in particular. He pronounced himself as wonderfully impressed with the teaching of Abdul Baha, the Persian teacher of a universal religion, just liberated from prison and expected in this country in May. He declared that Abdul's teaching would lift Mahometanism up spiritually into line with Christianity and would make for world peace. The important subject of Abdul Baha was called to his attention by a member of the club.[7]

On 25 January the national Unitarian magazine *Christian Register* (Boston) published an editorial on the Bahá'í teachings stating that 'It is interesting to note how fully abreast of the best modern thought and effort is the declaration of purpose put forth by Abdul Baha' and summarizing some Bahá'í teachings.[8] This editorial was later reproduced in other newspapers.[9] A few weeks afterwards the same magazine published an article on the Bahá'í Faith by Rev. Thomas Van Ness (1859–1932), minister of the Second Unitarian Church of Boston, who stated that the Bahá'í Faith 'should be welcomed as one more indication of the drawing together of races and the coming co-operation of man in the establishment of what in both Eastern and Western language is called the kingdom of God'.[10]

On January 28 *al-Hoda* (*The Guidance*), an evening Arabic newspaper published in New York, carried an extensive article about 'Abdu'l-Bahá that included a portrait of Him taken in London.[11]

In February the *Herald* (Boston) published a lengthy article about 'Abdu'l-Bahá and the Bahá'í Faith which was later quoted in other newspapers. 'That he practices what he preaches there can be little doubt,' stated the article, which continued with a series of statements attributed to 'Abdu'l-Bahá.[12]

The Advocate of Peace (Washington), organ of the American Peace Society, carried in February 1912 a lengthy article by Joseph Hannen summarizing some of the Bahá'í teachings on peace and also announcing the arrival of 'Abdu'l-Bahá in America and His expected participation at the Lake Mohonk Conference.[13] Another pacifist newspaper, *The Peacemaker* (Philadelphia), organ of the Universal Peace Union with 951 subscribers, also published in April 1912 two articles on the Bahá'í Faith.[14]

As mentioned in chapter 6, on 17 March *The Sun* (New York) published an article by the Bahá'í writer Mary Hanford Ford (1856–1937) who as well as giving details about 'Abdu'l-Bahá's sojourn in Europe also offered a lengthy introduction to the Faith. Regarding 'Abdu'l-Bahá the article stated:

> Since the World's Congress of Religions many interesting and famous Orientals have wandered from their mysterious shores to our own but none has come about whom are the romance and authority suggested by the presence of Abdul Baha. This name is in reality a titular one and is translated the Servant of God, or the Servant of the Glory. In the official circle of his own Orient he is sometimes spoken of as Abbas Effendi, which might be interpreted as 'Mr. Abbas'. He is the centre of the greatest religious movement of modern times, whose practical effect is seen in the constitutional reforms of Persia and Turkey, which have resulted merely from the deeply instilled principle of brotherhood, always the central point of Abdul Baha's teaching. His principle is non-resistant and never

revolutionary, but it generates a sentiment of mutual helpfulness which makes the presence of tyranny impossible.

He has been a prisoner for fifty years and more, having been incarcerated with his noble father, Baha Ullah, when he was but 6 years old, and he has suffered every ignominy that could be imposed by ignorant fanaticism, as the sole reason for the arrest of these admirable people was the fact that they endeavored to pour new life into the ancient mould of Mohammedan theology . . .

Abdul Baha is of charming presence wearing always the white turban and costume of a Persian scholar. He is gay and witty, wonderfully intelligent upon every phase of human progress, in which he is deeply interested. If you approach him with science or economics he is alert and responsive, believing all the progressive advancement of the day as a part of the predestined unfoldment of humanity at this time. It is not known that he has yet flown in an aero plane, but he has watched the gyrations of the air craft with profound interest and regards it as significant that man is now 'conquering the air'.

He comes to us especially to attend the peace conference at Lake Mohonk, which has been called to discuss the possibility of establishing an international court of justice which shall have authority to settle the quarrels of all nations, so that universal peace may at length be realized. It was a part of the teaching of Baha Ullah that such a tribunal must be created and if it becomes a fact in his time Abdul Baha says he shall feel that he has not lived in vain.

To those who have seen him in the prison town of Akka, which he left only three years ago, the name of Abdul Baha will always be associated with the tiny walled city which lies so white against the blue breast of the Mediterranean. There, his rambling old stone mansion, built around a court in Oriental fashion, was often filled with men and women of all races who had come to him from the Western world, and these cosmopolitan globe trotters rubbed elbows with Mohammedan, Jew, Persian and Hindu, who had sometimes walked trackless miles through the desert seeking truth from the lips of an inspired teacher. Here the unity which is the cohering word in the message of Abdul Baha found vivid illustration, and seekers of every color and race, of every religion made friends in hearty fashion and gained a new impetus from this concord of different individuals. Together they dined at the table of Abdul Baha, together they visited the tomb of Baha Ullah or the charming garden of the Rizwan, which is fragrant with the plants brought across the desert by loving hands. His followers had early learned that the great teacher would not accept money but that he delighted to cherish rare plants.

The flat roof of the big house was the refuge of Abdul Baha in those days. From its height one looked far over the blue Mediterranean, and there many counsels have been given to wandering strangers, while in this quiet spot the Seer has passed night after night in prayer for the martyrs of Persia, supplicating the peace of the world.

Abdul Baha knew well that the presence of these strangers was regarded with grave suspicion by his Turkish guardians, who suspected him of designs upon the throne of the Sultan, yet his generosity did not lessen. Each day that he seated his guests at his bountiful table and sent them away with a new ardor to serve their kind his own life was in danger, and I shall never forget the moment when his wife, 'the holy mother' as she is called, spoke to me of the sword constantly suspended over his head.

'It is nothing to him!' she exclaimed. 'He would glory in the thought that his blood was shed that men might be brought nearer to God; but think of our anguish, for we love him not only as the Messenger of God but as one personally precious to us; and each morning when I waken I think, "Before night he may be dragged into the market place and shot!"'

In Abdul Baha the seeker found a holy man who was a prisoner but not a recluse; who though under guard, touched all quarters of the globe in correspondence and who taught that men serve God best by serving their kind. His household was a most interesting one, including strangers from the West, the wives and children of martyred Persians and others who assisted in the labors of the home for the sake of its lessons, so that a snobbish inclination to snub the 'boots' could not be indulged with safety at Akka . . .[15]

Hanford Ford also lectured on the Bahá'í Faith on several occasions. One of these was reported in *The Washington Bee*: 'Quite a number of colored believers in the Bahai faith attended the lecture of Mrs Mary Hanford Ford last Friday evening at 1219 Connecticut Avenue. She spoke on "The Bahai Movement in the West". Abdul Baha the leader of the Bahai religion is expected to visit Washington in the spring. The chief exponent of the faith among colored Washingtonians is Mr. L. G. Gregory of the Treasury Department, one of the race's brightest young men.'[16]

In the last weeks before the arrival of 'Abdu'l-Bahá in America many other articles were published announcing the visit of the Master. The *Democrat and Chronicle* (Rochester, NY) published an interview with a New York Bahá'í, Mrs. W. Logie, that also included a portrait of the Master.[17] On 3 March the *New York Herald* published a long interview with Ahmad Sohrab about 'Abdu'l-Bahá[18] which was later reproduced in other newspapers.[19] The *Brooklyn Daily Eagle* carried on 19 March a picture of the Master distributed by Harris & Ewing[20] and on 7 April published one more report about 'Abdu'l-Bahá with lengthy information about the Bahá'í Faith which again included a picture of Him.[21] The same day the *Detroit Tribune*, in reporting the publication of Francis H. Skrine's *Bahaism* (1912), stated that 'The approaching visit of the noted Persian teacher, Abdul Baha, for the purpose of lecturing throughout the United States on the religion of brotherhood and peace, has started much discussion in cultured circles of this new international movement which will have a strong influence on civilization.'[22]

After his pilgrimage to Egypt to visit 'Abdu'l-Bahá, Louis Gregory wrote at least three articles for the press familiarizing the general public with the figure of the Master and Bahá'í Faith. The earliest appeared in the black newspaper *The Washington Bee* on 11 November 1911. It carried a portrait of the Master and was introduced with the following words:

> About two years ago the writer was asked by The Bee for an article on the Bahai Revelation, the so-called New Religion. We shrank from the task, for the reason that no newspaper articles can do more than call attention to so vast a subject. But now we find, in view of the recent visit of Abdul Baha to England, that the British press is teeming with the subject, and that many of the articles written have found an echo in America. So the time seems ripe to use every agency to acquaint, as far as possible, the people of the world with the movement, and this we hope to do in part through The Bee and its exchanges. May the Divine Light inspire hope and cause inquiry.

After giving a complete overview on the Bahá'í Faith, Gregory added that 'With the usual faith and courage shown in various parts of the world, the movement has grappled with the race problem in America.'[23]

A second article was published in the literary weekly *The Independent* (New York) on 11 April 1912, the same day as the arrival of 'Abdu'l-Bahá in America. Its editor, Hamilton Holt, who in all probability met 'Abdu'l-Bahá weeks later in Lake Mohonk, introduced Gregory's article:

> Abdul Baha, the distinguished Persian who leads the Bahai movement, will arrive in New York City this spring for a tour of America. He has recently visited in Europe, where he addressed many people on the subject of universal peace thru the unity of religions. The Bahai movement is attracting a larger and larger share of public interest and attention, as is deserving of a movement which in sixty-seven years has manifested enough power to unite Jews, Christians and Mohammedans, to the extent of several millions.[24]

A third article was published in the black newspaper *The Chicago Defender* on 12 April offering general information about the Bahá'í Faith along the same lines as the previous articles. The text concluded by stating that 'About fifty invitations have already been extended to Abdul Baba to address gatherings in the cities he will visit. It is to be hoped that people of all races and classes will embrace the opportunity to see and hear him.'[25]

The monthly magazine *Oriental Review* (New York) published in its April issue a lengthy and sympathetic article on the Bahá'í Faith. This magazine was the organ of the Oriental Information Agency, founded by the Japanese Embassy in the United States. Its editor, Masujiro Honda, was a few weeks later one of the speakers at the conference of the Persian–American Educational Society, where he probably met 'Abdu'l-Bahá.[26]

'It is interesting to record in connection with the coming visit to America of Abdul Baha, the inspiring leader of the growing Bahai religion', reported in April the *Unitarian Advance* (New York), organ of the Western Conference of the American Unitarian Association, 'that three of our churches have had the invitations they have extended to him accepted and that he will speak at the Church of the Messiah, at the Brotherhood Church in Jersey City and at the Montclair Church.'[27] At least four of the seven editors of this magazine later met 'Abdu'l-Bahá.[28]

10

ARRIVAL IN AMERICA

New York, 11–20 April 1912

'Abdu'l-Bahá's arrival in North America was to coincide with two major events that caught the attention of the media for a long time: the tragic sinking of the *Titanic* on 14 April and the ongoing presidential campaign. Despite this, as we shall see, 'Abdu'l-Bahá's visit to the United States aroused a very considerable interest in the press. In the city of New York alone the articles published about His arrival and the accounts of the many interviews He granted reached a potential readership of over 1.5 million people.

The Arrival

The *Cedric* reached the shores of New York on 11 April 1912.[1] Some passengers had fallen ill during the journey and owing to this circumstance the passengers on the ship had to wait several hours before they were permitted to go ashore.

At that time it was customary for the media to send reporters to vessels arriving in New York from overseas to interview important passengers returning to or visiting the United States. A number of these reporters boarded the *Cedric* and met 'Abdu'l-Bahá in His stateroom where He granted His first interviews in America. Among the newspapermen was Wendell Phillips Dodge (1883–1976), a local Bahá'í working for the New York City News Agency. As a privileged witness of the arrival of 'Abdu'l-Bahá, Dodge wrote an article describing those moments and recording some of the responses that the Master gave to the various questions raised by the journalists who whirled around Him. This article was probably circulated among major journals:

ABDUL BAHA, the eminent Persian philosopher and leader of the Bahai movement for the unification of religions and the establishment of universal peace, arrived April 11th on the steamship Cedric from Alexandria, Egypt. It is his first visit to America, and except for a brief visit to Paris and London last summer and fall, it is the first time in forty years that he has gone beyond the fortification of the 'prison city' of Acre, Syria, to which place he and his father, BAHA'O'LLAH, the founder of the Bahai movement, were banished by the Turkish government a half century ago.

He comes on a mission of international peace, to attend and address the Peace Conference at Lake Mohonk the latter part of the month, and to address various peace meetings, educational societies, religious organizations, etc.

When the ship news reporters boarded the Cedric down the bay, Abdul-Baha was found on the upper deck, standing where he could see the pilot, his long, flowing oriental robe flapping in the breeze. He was clothed in a long, black robe open at the front and disclosing another robe of light tan. Upon his head was a pure white turban, such as all eastern patriarchs wear.

His face was light itself as he scanned the harbor and greeted the reporters, who had been kept waiting at quarantine for three and a half hours before they could board the ship with the customs officers, owing to a case of smallpox and several cases of typhoid fever in the steerage, which had to be removed to Hoffman Island for isolation, and the ship then fumigated.

He is a man of medium height, though at first sight he seemed to be much taller. He is strongly and solidly built, and weighs probably one hundred and sixty-five pounds. As he paced the deck, talking with the reporters, he appeared alert and active in every movement, his head thrown back and splendidly poised upon his broad, square shoulders, most of the time. A profusion of iron grey hair bursting out at the sides of the turban and hanging long upon the neck; a large, massive head, full-domed and remarkably wide across the forehead and temples, the forehead rising like a great palisade above the eyes, which were very wide apart, their orbits large and deep, looking out from under massive overhanging brows; strong Roman nose, generous ears, decisive yet kindly mouth and chin; a creamy white complexion, beard same color as his hair, worn full over the face and carefully trimmed at almost full length – this completes an insufficient word picture of this 'Wise Man Out of the East'.

His first words were about the press, saying:

'The pages of swiftly appearing newspapers are indeed the mirror of the world; they display the doings and actions of the different nations; they both illustrate them and cause them to be heard. Newspapers are as a mirror which is endowed with hearing, sight and speech; they are a wonderful phenomenon and a great matter. But it behooveth the editors of the newspaper to be sanctified from the prejudice of egotism and desire, and to be adorned with the ornament of equity and justice.

'There are good and bad newspapers. Those which strive to speak only that which is truth, which hold the mirror up to truth, are like the sun: they light the world everywhere with truth and their work is imperishable. Those who play for their own little selfish ends give no true light to the world and perish of their own futility.'

Dr. Ameen U. Fareed, a young Americanized Persian physician and surgeon, who is a nephew of Abdul-Baha, and who acted as interpreter, then told of how Abdul-Baha spent most of his time on the way across standing beside the wireless operator, himself receiving numerous messages through the air from his followers in America.

Talking to the reporters in his stateroom aboard the Cedric, Abdul-Baha told of an incident which occurred in the Holy Land last winter, and it shows what a rare sense of humor this great world figure has. An enquirer, about to set off to Jerusalem, was one day discussing with Abdul-Baha the subject of pilgrimage:

'"The proper spirit", said Abdul-Baha in his quaint way to the enquirer, "in which to visit places hallowed by remembrances of Christ, is one of constant communion with God. Love for God will be the telegraph wire, one end of which is in the Kingdom of the Spirit, and the other in your heart."

'"I am afraid my telegraph wire is broken," the enquirer replied.

'"Then you will have to use wireless telegraphy," I told him,' said Abdul-Baha, laughing heartily.

When the ship was abreast the Statue of Liberty, standing erect and facing it, Abdul-Baha held his arms wide apart in salutation, and said:

'There is the new world's symbol of liberty and freedom. After being forty years a prisoner I can tell you that freedom is not a matter of place. It is a condition. Unless one accept dire vicissitudes he will not attain. When one is released from the prison of self, that is indeed a release.'

Then, waving adieu to the Statue of Liberty, he continued:

'In former ages it has been said, "To love one's native land is faith." But the tongue in this day says, "Glory is not his who loves his native land; but glory is his who loves his kind – humanity."'

'What is your attitude toward woman suffrage?' asked one of the reporters.

'The modern suffragette is fighting for what must be, and many of these are willing martyrs to imprisonment for their cause. One might not approve of the ways of some of the more militant suffragettes, but in the end it will adjust itself. If women were given the same advantages as men, their capacity being the same, the result would be the same. In fact, women have a superior disposition to men; they are more receptive, more sensitive, and their intuition is more intense. The only reason of their present backwardness in some directions is because they have not had the same educational advantages as men.

'All children should be educated, but if parents cannot educate both the boys and the girls, then it would be better to educate the girls, for they will be the mothers of the coming generation. This is a radical idea for the East, where I come from, but it is already taking effect there, for the Bahai women of Persia are being educated along with the men.

'We have only to look about us in nature', Abdul-Baha continued, 'to see the truth of this. Is it not a fact that the females of many species of animals are stronger and more powerful than the male? The chief cause of the mental and physical inequalities of the sexes is due to custom and training, which for ages past have molded woman into the ideal of the weaker vessel.

'The world in the past has been ruled by force, and man has dominated over woman by reason of his more forceful and aggressive qualities both of body and mind. But the scales are already shifting – force is losing its weight and mental alertness, intuition, and the spiritual qualities of love and service, in which woman is strong, are gaining ascendency. Hence the new age will be an age less masculine, and more permeated with the feminine ideals – or, to speak more exactly, will be an age in which the masculine and feminine elements of civilization will be more properly balanced.'

'What is a Bahai?' asked one of the reporters.

'To be a Bahai simply means to love all the world, to love humanity and try to serve it; to work for Universal Peace, and the Universal Brotherhood,' replied Abdul-Baha.

The ship now pointed its nose up the North River, and, gazing in a look of bewildered amazement at the rugged skyline of the lower city formed by the downtown skyscrapers, the 'Wise Man out of the East' remarked, pointing at the towering buildings:

'These are the minarets of Western World commerce and industry, and seem to stretch these things heavenward in an endeavor to bring about this Universal Peace for which we are all working, for the good of the nations and mankind in general.

'The bricks make the house, and if the bricks are bad the house will not stand, as these do. It is necessary for individuals to become as good bricks, to eradicate from themselves race and religious hatred, greed and a limited patriotism, so that, whether they find themselves guiding the government, or founding a home, the result of their efforts may be peace and prosperity, love and happiness.'

The ship now reached its pier, where were anxiously waiting several hundred Bahais, as the followers of Abdul-Baha are called, who had been craning their necks down the river for a first sight of him since early morning. The ship docked shortly after noon, but, fearing that a demonstration in public would not be the best thing for the Cause, and not liking that sort of thing, the venerable Persian Divine did not leave the ship until the pier had been quietly cleared of his followers, who were told to meet him in the afternoon at the home of Mr. and Mrs. Kinney, where he greeted them a few hours later.[2]

Meanwhile, the Associated Press also wired its own note:

NEW YORK, April 11 – Abdul Baha Abbas, the leader of the Bahai movement for world-wide religious unity, arrived here early today on the steamer Cedric from the Mediterranean. Preparations for his welcome at the pier were made yesterday by the Persian–American Educational Society and a number of local followers.

Abbas Effendi, as he is known by his official title, is the third of the leaders of Bahaism. He has been repeatedly imprisoned by the Moslems, who regard his liberal tendencies with the greatest distrust. The Bahai belief is that universal peace is possible only through the harmony of all religions, and that all religions are basically one. It is estimated that about a third of the Persians are now members of the cult.

The Rev. Dr. Francis E. Clark, founder of the Christian Endeavor Society, and Dr. John B. Robinson, bishop of Bombay, were passengers on the same steamer with Abbas Effendi.

Dodge's article and the note released by Associated Press were widely distributed across the United States. More than 20 newspapers are known to have published portions of one or the other in the days following the Master's arrival, reaching more than one million potential readers.[3] It is more than probable, however, that the actual number of newspapers that gave the news was considerably higher.

As well as the information received from these two sources, some newspapers in New York added information of their own. A reporter on *The Evening World*, a newspaper with a daily circulation of 401,000 copies, met 'Abdu'l-Bahá on board the *Cedric* and also interviewed some of the Bahá'ís who were waiting at the pier. The article that ensued included a picture of the Master and, after stating that 'Concerning woman suffrage he is as modern as Sylvia Pankhurst', quoted Him saying: 'The woman suffragists'

. . . are fighting for what must be. Their mental capacities are the same as those of men; they have the same civil offices; they are the equal of man. Some of them, of course, need further education, but that is all. There are as many ways to God as there are souls to His creatures, and the suffrage movement is but the hewing of another path to Him.'[4]

The Republican *New-York Tribune*, with a circulation of 92,000 copies, carried on 12 April a very similar article which also quoted some of His comments on women.[5]

The independent newspapers *The Evening Telegram*,[6] with a circulation of 150,000 copies, and *The Evening Post*, with a circulation of nearly 27,000 copies,[7] reported the following statements not recorded in other periodicals:

> 'To-day there is no more important and greater cause than the movement for peace,' he said. 'The world needs a uniting power to connect nations. The differences in languages are one of the causes of disunion between nations. There must be one universal auxiliary language. The diversity of faiths is also a cause of separation.'

The *New York Herald*, with a circulation of 100,000 copies, published on 11 April a brief note on its front page reporting the arrival of 'Abdu'l-Bahá[8] and on 12 April the same newspaper reproduced some general comments on the Bahá'í Faith by Amín'ulláh Faríd, 'Abdu'l-Bahá's interpreter.[9]

In an article on its front page *The Sun* (New York) added to the information released by agencies, saying that 'the Bahais of New York [city] were incorporated in 1907 as the First Bahai Assembly of New York'.[10] The *New York Times*, a Democratic newspaper which at the time issued 175,000 copies every day, published information about 'Abdu'l-Bahá very similar to that which appeared in other journals and gave the names of several of the notable passengers who travelled with Him on the *Cedric*.[11]

First Interviews

'Abdu'l-Bahá stayed in an apartment in the Ansonia building. The site had the optimum conditions of space to meet the rush of visitors that every day crowded to meet the Master. Among those who visited Him on His first day in New York was a group of reporters representing most of the major local daily newspapers.

One of them was Nixola Greeley-Smith,[12] a reporter with the *Evening World* (New York), whose articles were characterized by their caustic tone. In the account of her interview with 'Abdu'l-Bahá she displayed this feature of her journalistic style. After describing satirically 'Abdu'l-Bahá's figure, age and fatigue, the author quoted His words:

> The wearing of the veil by Oriental women is the cause and the symbol of their enslavement. Mahomet never prescribed that

women should veil their faces – that is one of the abuses which have crept into the religion he taught. I have come to America first of all to see your country and because I have heard that there is great popular interest in the cause of Peace here and I am the servant and the advocate of Peace. Human solidarity is what my religion urges – unity of nations and of religions.

Errors have crept into the religions of to-day and through those errors strife. All prophets are manifestations of Truth, but there cannot be multiplicity of truth. It is because errors have crept into religions that there is division and misunderstanding. To eliminate these errors we must get back to fundamental truth – return to the starting point.[13]

A reporter on the Democratic *World*, with a circulation of 362,000 copies, also met 'Abdu'l-Bahá and afterwards published the following account of the interview:

PERSIAN TEACHER OF WORLD-PEACE IS HERE

PHILOSOPHER HEADS CRUSADE TO UNITE NATIONS IN BROTHERHOOD AND RELIGION

'Khosohamadid.'

This is Persian, meaning 'Howdy' or 'Welcome'. It was spoken by Abdul Baha Abbas, Persian philosopher, teacher and leader of the Bahai movement, as he sat in the apartment in the Hotel Ansonia after his arrival here yesterday on the White Star liner Cedric.

Abdul Baha Abbas is accompanied by his nephew, Dr. Ameen Fareed, and two other philosophers, Said Assadullah and Effendi Shoghi.

Abdul spent most of his time at sea striding by the side or the wireless operator. He saluted the Statue of Liberty by extending his arms. 'There is the New World's symbol of liberty and freedom,' he exclaimed.

A steerage passenger of the Cedric developed Smallpox after the ship left Gibraltar, and 200 third class passengers were transferred to the retention Hospital in the lower bay. Among them was the Persian cook of Abdul. He will be held until his bill of health is perfect.

Abdul Baha Abbas is sixty-eight, but from his appearance you would judge him to be at least in the nineties. He has a snowy white beard and white hair which is twisted in a kind of queue at the back of his head, below his 'ammamah' or turban like skull-cap. This appearance of extreme age is due to the fact that forty years of his life were spent in the loathsome prison at Akka, Syria, over which it was commonly stated that no bird could fly without falling to the ground. His Voice is strong.

ADVOCATES WORLD-PEACE

Abdul Baha Abbas does not speak English and carried on his conversation with newspapermen through his interpreter and personal physician, Dr. Ameen Fareed. He said:

'I have two reasons in coming to this country. The first is to travel and see your places of interest, your large cities and your country as any ordinary tourist might do. I do not come to make converts to the Bahai movement. I will remain about a week in New York and then go to Washington. I want to meet your prominent people. I have heard of the numerous organizations in this country toward the establishment of universal peace and the popular interest manifested in this peace movement. I am an advocate of international peace and human solidarity because it is one of the fundamental tenets of the Bahai faith and all nations and all religions may become united and by that unity, perfect peace may reign among them all.

'All strife and animosity existing among the religions of the world is solely due to misunderstandings. If these misunderstandings are once removed, then unity can be accomplished. This quarrelling, which has existed for 6,000 years, will vanish and we will all become one family, as originally we were all one family.'

The Persian teacher said there might be about 2,000,000 persons of all religions who have accepted the Bahai teachings.

FAVORS WOMAN SUFFRAGE

He pronounced himself very emphatically in favor of woman's suffrage and said that the custom of wearing the veil in the East had been the very means of keeping women back. Monogamy was by all means the rule of his faith, and he said that divorce was permissible under certain conditions if the man and woman were hopelessly incompatible.

> Abdul Baha Abbas is not a prophet, but, as he expressed it, 'the servant of the Glory of God', his father, who founded the religion, having been the 'Glory of God'. He said he didn't want to be called a prophet.
>
> The Persian philosopher was given a reception yesterday afternoon at the home of Edward Kinney, No. 780 West End Avenue, where he gave a short talk to about one hundred and fifty persons from many parts of the country . . .
>
> Abdul Baha Abbas will remain in America four months and then go to Japan and China.[14]

As stated in the article, after receiving the press and other visitors at the Hotel Ansonia, 'Abdu'l-Bahá visited the home of the Kinneys, where He received many people wanting to see Him.[15] A reporter with *The Sun*, which at the time circulated 100,000 copies daily, who was present at both the press conference held at the Ansonia and the meeting in the home of the Kinneys, afterwards wrote an account which included a short summary of the origins of the Bahá'í Faith (not reproduced here) and which quoted 'Abdu'l-Bahá saying:

> 'Having heard of the numerous organisations in this country for peace and arbitration, and because of my great interest in those subjects, I have come here,' said Abdul Baha, 'to advocate human solidarity. That is the basis of my teachings. All nations and all religions may become united by that unity. Perfect peace might reign among them. Strife and animosity are due to misunderstandings. If these misunderstandings are removed, then unity can be accomplished.
>
> 'All of the prophets of God were manifestations of truth and reality, but because imitations have crept into religions, divisions and misunderstandings have resulted. These imitations cannot be found in the bases of religions. Human beings should refer to the original foundations, and then six thousand years of strife and warfare will vanish. My purpose is to bring about the oneness of humanity and to secure accord and fellowship among all mankind, so that they may dwell together finally as one family.'[16]

Some excerpts of this article were published afterwards in the *Evening Call*[17] and in the *New York Tribune*.[18]

In the afternoon of 'Abdu'l-Bahá's second day in New York, He visited the house of Howard MacNutt in Brooklyn where he addressed a gathering of friends and seekers on the subject of the purpose of religion and the necessity of unity.[19] After that meeting He addressed some two hundred people at the studio of Harriet S. Phillips where He talked about the importance of unity and love among Bahá'ís.[20] A brief account of both meetings was published the following day in *The Sun*:

LISTEN TO ABDUL BAHA

PERSIAN PHILOSOPHER ADDRESSES 200 DISCIPLES AT A STUDIO

Abdul Baha Abbas, the Persian philosopher and teacher who arrived here on Wednesday for a four months preaching tour, gave a short talk last night to 200 disciples at the studio of Miss Harriet S. Phillip, 39 West Sixty-seventh street. Fatigued from his travelling, the venerable priest did not speak long. He had spoken in the afternoon at the residence of Howard MacNutt, 935 Eastern Parkway, Brooklyn.

Abdul Baha was accompanied by Dr. Ameen U. Fareed, his physician, Mirza Mohammed, Mirza Ahmad Sohrab and Said Assadullah. He does not speak English but his sayings and parables were told to the audience through Dr. Fareed, who will accompany the priest in this country. The substance of his talk was universal love and peace, and he said that there is good in everything if only we put ourselves about to see it.

'It is perfect happiness,' the sage said, 'to be with you. There is no joy except when friends meet face to face. You know the first teaching of God is love, and serving humanity is the same as serving God.'

Stopping a minute while his eyes rested on the electric lights in the ceiling, he continued:

'May love radiate from you like the light from these electric lights; like the stars in the heaven.' He said that this is the century of blessed perfection; it is the cycle of light, it is the period prophesied by all prophets.

Abdul Baha is also a man of wit. In his talk in Brooklyn in the afternoon he said that the streets of New York were like theatres, therefore he could not see the reason why we have so many theatres.

'The English language,' he said later, 'seems to consist of one word, "Alright".'[21]

A reporter from the *New York Herald* interviewed 'Abdu'l-Bahá once He arrived back at His hotel after His address in Brooklyn. The article that ensued, not devoid of a dose of sarcasm, included a photograph of Abdul Baha descending from a taxi in front of the Ansonia:

> Abdul Baha Abbas, promoter of the new religious code which has about 20,000,000 adherents, was very tired yesterday after his speedy tour of busy New York. He crossed the Williamsburg Bridge and went to the home of Howard MacNutt, No. 935 Eastern Parkway, Brooklyn; thence to the houses of a few friends, to the Cooper Institute and back across Williamsburg Bridge to east side at the rush hour. Then he visited homes of friends and went back for a brief rest in his luxurious apartment in the Ansonia. And how he did relish that cup of coffee – Turkish coffee – as he sat down in a red plush chair
>
> New York is a beehive in the estimation of Abdul Baha Abbas, and all the busy men and women bees laboring and working for the drone. He was dazed when he saw the throngs of busy humanity walking and running with their intentions focused on one place – Brooklyn.
>
> Then he saw the east side, and to him that was wonderful. His automobile stopped for a few minutes on the Manhattan side of Williamsburg Bridge and almost before it had drawn up to the curb there were scores of children wondering who was the aged man with the long beard. He leaned out of the window and then decided to rest his head on the cushioned back of the vehicle.
>
> 'I like New York,' he told a HERALD reporter. 'It is interesting and it is clean. London is filled with smoke.'[22]

A reporter on the daily Democratic newspaper *American* (New York), which had a circulation of 250,000 copies, was received on 13 April and published afterwards the following account:

> Abdul Baha, leader of the Bahaists, a cult which has for its aim the inculcation of universal peace, was enthusiastic over the New World when seen yesterday after his arrival here.
>
> He comes from Persia to the United States to talk with men interested in international peace and arbitration. 'It is my highest desire,' he said, 'to see these societies and converse with their founders and

members. For the great object of life is the oneness of the kingdom of humanity and international peace.

'We have come to see and to associate with the societies, so that we may find a basis of cooperation and mutual assistance. This is my first object.'

'But you have the idea also in mind of spreading your teachings, have you not?'

'My religion is the religion of the unity of the nations, and the promulgation and spreading of the universe of peace, as well as the investigation of truth, and to demonstrate to the people of the world that religion and science have been and will continue working hand in hand.

RELIGION THE CAUSE OF UNITY

'Whenever a doctrine is contrary to science, it is merely superstition. For that which is contrary to knowledge is ignorance. If we say that religion is against science, then religion is ignorance.

'We also believe that religion should never become the cause of warfare and strife. Religion must be the cause of unity of the nations, the affiliation of individuals with each other and the creation of a larger understanding.

'If religion becomes a cause of hatred, of antagonism, of creating prejudice against each other, it is better to have no religion.'

'Can an individual with a religion – Christian, Mohammedan or Jew – follow your teachings without abandoning his religion?'

'Yes, for truth is always one. The prophets of God have always spread the one truth and have established the truth. Truth cannot accept plurality.

'If the followers of all religions returned to the original principles of their religions they will, immediately, become united. The foundation of religion is one. We are following the religions of all nationalities, for the basis of all these religions is truth.

'Truth is indestructible and a unit. Therefore, we are associating with the followers of all denominations and religions with perfect peace and fellowship. We consider the members of all humanity as servants of God. We liken children of men unto a family, and the world of man unto a tree and all the communities are like unto the leaves and blossoms and fruits.'

LOVERS OF HUMANITY

'We are the lovers of humanity wherever we go. We are the lovers of all light no matter from which lamp it shines.

'We are lovers of the sun no matter from what horizon it dawns. We have not these human prejudices. To be brief, our greatest hope and our highest aspiration is to establish unity among mankind and peace among the children of God.'

'Do you find men or women the more religious – quicker to accept the truths expounded by you?'

'Those who have intelligence and understanding accept our teachings no matter whether they are men or women. For they are all intellectual and logical principles, and they are for the good of all humanity . . .

'What do you think of the woman suffrage movement?'

'Today women, on account of certain reasons, have not yet attained to the vigor of men. But these differences are only accounted for on lines of education. In reality there is no difference between men and women so far as their rights are concerned. They are all the children of one God. Both of them have capacities for progress . . .

'Truly, America is facing toward progress. There is no question of this. America is also advancing wonderfully in spiritual and ethical principles.'[23]

This interview was reproduced in the *San Francisco Examiner* on 30 April 1912.

Filming 'Abdu'l-Bahá

In 1908 the Société Pathé Frères invented a new media product, the newsreel, a series of short documentaries, usually covering current news, which was played in theatres as part of regular cinema sessions. Owing to the success of this format, the precursor of the television news, in a short span of time several newsreel companies were created in Europe and America.

A few days after the arrival of 'Abdu'l-Bahá in New York, probably on 13 April, while He was leaving the Ansonia building, a cameraman approached 'Abdu'l-Bahá and requested to take a 'moving picture' – as films were known at the time – of Him. 'Abdu'l-Bahá replied with a 'Besyar Khub' (Very Good).[24]

The cameramen who filmed 'Abdu'l-Bahá was a member of the staff at the 'Animated Weekly', which at the time was distributed by the 'Sales Company', an independent film distribution company created in 1909 by Pierre Ernest Jules Brulatour (1870–1946).

The 'Animated Weekly' was a newsreel covering domestic and international news. It was first launched on 1 March 1912 and was owned by the famous French producer León Gaumont (1864–1945). The company claimed to have one hundred cameramen placed all over the world and had its offices at 31 East 27th Street, New York.

In its seventh edition, which was released in cinemas on Wednesday 24 April, the 'Animated Weekly' included the film of 'Abdul Baba [sic], a very reverend old man, on a visit to this country.'[25]

It should be noted that the 'Animated Weekly' was at the time distributed by nearly 60 agents located in Canada and in 24 American states and thus the first film of 'Abdu'l-Bahá was probably watched by thousands of people.[26]

It was not until 18 June that the Bahá'ís took the initiative of making their own film of the Master.[27]

Sunday, 14 April: Address at the Church of the Ascension and at the Carnegie Lyceum

'Abdu'l-Bahá had received no less than 14 invitations from different churches to speak on Sunday, 14 April. '. . . some of the clergy,' states Juliet Thompson, a privileged witness to those days, 'had even wired to Gibraltar offering their pulpits for that date!'[28] The Episcopalian Church of the Ascension was the one chosen by the Master for His first public address in North America.

Consecrated in 1841, the Church of the Ascension was the first church to be built on Fifth Avenue. The Harvard-educated Rev Dr Percy Stickney Grant (1860–1927) was its rector from 1893 to 1924. During his three decades of ministry at the Ascension he opened the church to several social movements and religious denominations in New York that used it as the center of their activity. He was also in close contact with the Bahá'ís and even exchanged some correspondence with 'Abdu'l-Bahá.

Grant was received by the Master on the afternoon of Saturday, 13

April. It was during that meeting that 'Abdu'l-Bahá accepted Grant's invitation to speak at the Church of the Ascension. It is said that when the Reverend was leaving the Ansonia accompanied by Howard MacNutt he commented, 'You can't help but love the old gentleman.'[29] On the same day *The New York Times* published a brief note announcing that the service was to be held at 11:00 in the morning and that the address was entitled 'Bahaism'.[30] *The Sun* published on 14 April another brief announcement, together with a short comment about a meeting held the previous day:

> Abdul Baha Abbas, the Persian philosopher, met a number of disciples yesterday at the home of Mrs. Alexander Morton, in East Twenty-first street, where he preached a little sermon on the text that God is love and that to serve humanity is to serve God. To-day Abdul Baha will speak at the Church of the Ascension at Fifth Avenue and Tenth Street.[31]

Wendell P. Dodge wrote a detailed account of the address of 'Abdu'l-Bahá at the Church of the Ascension which was partially reproduced in several newspapers.[32]

On 15 Monday, *The New York Times* published its own report which was penned by one of its reporters who was also present at the service in the Church of the Ascension:

> In the Church of the Ascension, toward the close of the services, yesterday morning the big congregation knelt in the pews or stood in the aisle spaces with heads reverently bowed, and before the altar. Dr. Percy Stickney Grant and his assistant, Mr. Underhill, knelt, while a venerable white-bearded Persian, clothed in his linen gaba and wearing his fez and his patriarch's tabouch, stood and offered up a prayer in his native tongue. This was Abbas Effendi, or, as his followers call him, Abdul Baha Abbas, the Persian philosopher and interpreter of the Bahai revelation, who has come to this country to speak at the Lake Mohonk Peace Conference the latter part of this month and to spread his gospel of the fundamental unity of all religions.
>
> Dr. Grant was not the first clergyman to invite the Persian teacher, but his was the first invitation that Abdul Baha accepted,

and there was little room left in Ascension Church when the 11 o'clock services began yesterday. As they progressed the venerable Persian took his place in the high-backed seat to the right of the altar, with Dr. Ameen Fareed, his nephew, standing by, ready to act as interpreter.

'It is to be our privilege this morning,' said Dr. Grant, 'to hear one who has come out of the East, a new and great herald of good-will, one bearing a message of love to all mankind. Abdul Baha Abbas is a master of the things of the spirit. He comes from that part of the world where men meditate, where contemplation was born. He teaches the fundamental unity of all religions – a truth in which this congregation believes profoundly – and we welcome here one who may help the material fervor of the Occident to gain a new peace by the infiltration of the harmonies of the Orient.'

Abdul Baha spoke in Persian, with Dr. Fareed interpreting a phrase at a time. Our material civilization, the Persian teacher said, has progressed greatly with the perfection of the crafts and the forward steps of material science, but our spiritual civilization, that which is based on divine morals, has declined and become degraded. We should strive, he said, to make our material civilization the purest possible medium, the most unclouded glass, through which the light of our spiritual civilization must shine.

One of the things that supports a spiritual civilization is peace, he said, and the body politic is in need of universal peace, but the oneness of humanity, the human solidarity, which has been the message of all the prophets, will be achieved only through the spiritual power, for neither racial distinctions nor patriotism can further it. The oneness of humanity will come with the supremacy of the spiritual civilization, and not while, as now, we are submerged in a sea of materialism. The cause is progressing in the Orient, he concluded, and the heavenly civilization is daily making itself more manifest.

These things Abdul Baha said in the few moments that he spoke, before he returned to his seat beside the altar. While the offering was being taken those seated near the front could see him delving amid his robes, and finally his hand emerged with a bill that found its way to the plate. During the prayer he stood with his forearms extended, the palms of his hands turned upward, and as he finished he passed

> these over his eyes in a gesture that ended with the stroking of the patriarchal beard. A sense of the strangeness of the scene seemed to be with many in the congregation, and not a few lingered afterward to see the Persian philosopher, in his costume of the Orient, as he stepped into a modern Occidental limousine, to be whizzed uptown to his apartment at the Ansonia.
>
> Abdul Baha spoke yesterday afternoon at the meeting of the New Thought Society in the Carnegie Lyceum, and on Wednesday afternoon he will receive those of his followers who have come from distant places to see him.[33]

This article was later reproduced in other newspapers.[34] The account published in the *New York Herald* shows how some members of the parish were uncomfortable with the fact that a non-Christian was invited to participate in a Sunday service and that as a result some opposition arouse against both Grant and 'Abdu'l-Bahá:

> Some of the congregation of the Church of the Ascension and members of other Episcopal churches expressed astonishment that a religious leader not professing Christianity should have been invited to preach and permitted to offer prayer within the chancel at a regular Episcopal service.
>
> The Rev. Dr. Percy Stickney Grant, rector of the Church of the Ascension, has conducted an open forum in the church on Sunday evenings, at which laymen of all denominations have made addresses, principally on socialistic topics, which were followed by open discussions after the congregation adjourned to the parish house.
>
> These meetings seem to have given no offence, but when the leader of an Oriental cult was invited to take the leading part in the regular Sunday morning service there was an outspoken criticism, and it was intimated the matter would be called officially to the attention of Bishop Greer, through the Committee of the Diocese of New York.
>
> It was said that Canon Nineteen of the Episcopal Church forbids anyone not episcopally ordained from preaching in the Episcopal pulpit without the consent of the bishop. There is no provision against a non-ordained person offering prayer within the chancel, it was said, because no such contingency was anticipated.

> Announcement that Abdul Baha would take an address drew so great a throng in the church that every seat was filled and many sat on the steps of the chancel. In the throng were many disciples of the New Thought movement, among whom the Bahai religion has gained its principal fold in this country . . .[35]

In a different section of the same issue of the *Herald* it was also stated that 'Members of Protestant Episcopal Church of the Ascension may protest to Bishop Greer because Abdul Baha, leader of an Oriental cult, was permitted to preach in the pulpit of that church'.[36] Days later the New York Presbyterian weekly *The Observer* stated that the 'extraordinary spectacle of a professor of an Oriental and a non-Christian religion speaking from the pulpit of a Protestant church was witnessed last Sunday morning by the overflowing congregation attending the Church of the Ascension'.[37] In an editorial published in the *Churchman* (New York) its author complained that a non-Christian was invited to speak from a pulpit:

> Bahaism is a reforming Mohammedan sect. It seeks to infuse into the religion of Islam, or perhaps more accurately to develop in Islam, a higher morality and a more mystic theology than the current beliefs and teachings of that religion now encourage. Its purpose is, no doubt, laudable; and it excites the sympathy of those who see in all the great, ethnic religions glimpses of that Light which lighteth every man that cometh into the world.
>
> But Bahaism is not Christianity; and Abdul Baha does not profess to be a Christian. What right, then, has he to preach in a Christian church?[38]

Commenting on this editorial, *The Independent* (New York) stated:

> The rector of a New York church allowed Abdul Baha, teacher of a reformed sect of Mohammedanism, to speak in his church, whereupon *The Churchman* rebuked him. Then the Rev. John H. Melish, another local rector, defended his neighbor, on the ground that the teachings of Abdul Baha are essentially Christian, and that he is 'by nature Christian', as his whole doctrine is that of love. *The Churchman* prints Dr. Melish's letter and makes this reply:

> 'The question is, What is the law of the Church, not, What is the character of Abdul Beha or the nature of his teaching.'
>
> The reply is correct, shockingly correct and conclusive; for there is a law of the Church which excludes one not episcopally ordained. Dr. Melish cannot defend himself except by the bold reply of Peter to the Sanhedrim which forbade him to teach in the temple.[39]

On 17 April the *Post Express* (Rochester, NY) dedicated a column to summarizing 'Abdu'l-Bahá's talk at the Church of the Ascension under the title 'Wisdom of the Orient'.

On 4 May the *Congregationalist and Christian World* (Boston), with a circulation of 20,000 copies, quoted parts of 'Abdu'l-Bahá's talk and warned its readers 'that the religion of the Bahaists has nothing of the eccentricity or faddism of so many modern religions and none of their shallow philosophy . . . we are quite ready to listen to this Oriental Messenger of peace.'[40]

On 9 May the *New York Age*, a weekly black newspaper with a circulation of 4,500 copies, published an editorial about the talk in the Church of the Ascension, quoting from it extensively. 'A remarkable man has appeared in New York from the East,' stated the article, 'who has a message for the people of the West. He is a philosopher who has spent forty years in prison. His name is Abdul Baha Abbas . . . It is refreshing to have an old man of the East come into the country and by simple and direct speech enunciate anew the truth that it is dangerous to neglect the dictates of the culture of the soul for the desires and delights of the heart, the cravings of the heart for the lusts of the flesh.'[41]

The July issue the *New Age Magazine*, a monthly organ of the Southern jurisdiction of the Scottish Rite of Freemasonry issuing 30,000 copies, carried an account of the same talk followed with an introduction on the origins of the Bahá'í Faith. The article was signed by Potter A. Reade:

> A chair had been placed for him in the chancel, but he did not sit while addressing the people. He merely stood on one side of the chair, with his interpreter on the other, and uttered a series of short statements in his own tongue, pausing long enough after each to permit of its being translated into English.
>
> This aged Persian – his face heavily lined by the sorrows and

privations of a forty year imprisonment – seemed often to be gazing far beyond the crowded audience, and the aloofness of his eyes made one think that the inner vision of the Perfected Kingdom of God must be ever before him.

The Eastern figures, the sonorous phrases in a foreign language, the striking poetic similes in which the interpreter gave them forth in English, as well as the strange, indefinable impression that here indeed was one to whom things of the spirit were the only reality – all this combined to make the beholders feel as though one of the seers of old stood before them and that the ages had again rolled back to the days of Daniel.

The alternating statement and interpretation seemed like some antiphonal service from the Orient with the scent of the lilies for incense.

Referring to one of the 'lessons' for the day which had just been read by the Rector of the church, Abdul Baha commenced his discourse very quietly and with no gesticulation. All that he said was remarkable for its simplicity and directness.[42]

George Fleming Moore (1848–1930), editor of the *New Age Magazine*, wrote in the editorial pages of the same issue a brief presentation of Reade's article. Moore had read an article by J. T. Bixby that appeared the previous month in the *North American Review* (see chapter 25). Provoked by Bixby's inaccuracy and misrepresentation of the history of the Bahá'í Faith, Moore stated that 'we believe we may claim for Freemasonry all that is good in Babism and Bahaism . . . We may go further than this in asserting the superiority of Masonry: We have no bloody persecutions in our history!'[43]

Outside New York, the *Los Angeles Times* published on 19 June an editorial about 'Abdu'l-Bahá that mentioned His talk at the Church of the Ascension:

Several of the magazines are printing photographs of Abdul Baha and are paying some attention to his visit at this time to the United States. He is described by one of them as a man of loving kindness, spiritual breadth and physical frailty. Perhaps his slender store of bodily strength is due to the fact that for forty years he was a prisoner in Persia, his father having died in prison there and his grandfather

> having been executed. His reception in America has been a compliment to Americans themselves for their gentle courtesy toward the eastern teacher. In New York he occupied the pulpit of one of the largest Episcopal churches and in introducing him its pastor said that his strange gray brother from Orient teaches the fundamental unity of all religions. When he spoke the Baha said that the bond which can unite all the human race and make for the progress of the world is the love of God, and that it is this oneness of reality which will overcome all the lesser forces in life and give the world of existence a true maturity. It is his vision that when this is the common consciousness of all people there can be no more hate or war. It will end all superstitions and dogmas, he says, when the essential reality underlying all religions and revealed by all the prophets is known to be the same in its essence. It is quite probable that Abdul Baha speaks far better for himself than others have spoken for him, and that his visit to America will be a help to the people here in a general way, quite regardless of its effect on the Bahaist movement. It is likely, too, that the practical application of this movement belongs more properly toward unifying the many sects of the Orient, but the unity of religious doctrine and purpose is a consummation to be striven for in all places.[44]

As in London, 'Abdu'l-Bahá was invited to speak at a reception arranged by the New Thought society, which took place on the afternoon of 14 April and was held at the Carnegie Lyceum.[45] *The Sun* mentioned the meeting and quoted some of 'Abdu'l-Bahá's words. Regarding His talk at the Church of the Ascension it reported that:

> The venerable Oriental made a striking figure against the dark background of the chancel at the Church of the Ascension . . . During part of the morning service he remained seated in the chair at the left side of the communion table and delivered a final prayer in Persian . . . In repose the face of the Persian teacher has a sad, almost melancholy expression, but it lights up when he speaks.[46]

Both the address at the Church of the Ascension and that at the Carnegie Lyceum were briefly mentioned on 15 April on the front page of the socialist daily newspaper *Evening Call* (New York), which had a circulation of 32,000 copies.[47]

Public Talk at Columbia University

On Friday 19 April, 'Abdu'l-Bahá delivered a public address at the Earl Hall of Columbia University. The meeting was attended by a large number of teachers and students who listened to His talk on the powers of reason and science.[48] The *Columbia Spectator*, the official daily newspaper of the university, announced on the same day that 'At 4.30 this afternoon Abbas Effendi, or Abdul Baha, as he is sometimes known, head of the Baha movement which has attracted widespread interest throughout Europe, is to speak in the auditorium of Earl Hall. He will be introduced by Professor A. V. William Jackson, of the Department of Indo-Iranian Languages, and he will explain briefly the fundamental points of this great movement which has attracted so much attention.'[49] The announcement also included an introduction to the Bahá'í Faith.

A further announcement published in the *New York Herald* also stated that 'Abbas Effendi has attracted much attention by his religious teachings'.[50] The same newspaper published on 20 April an account of the meeting:

> ABBAS EFFENDI AT COLUMBIA
>
> PROPHET FROM THE EAST SAYS UNITY OF RELIGION WILL BRING UNIVERSAL PEACE.
>
> Abbas Effendi, the prophet of the unified religion, spoke at Columbia University yesterday afternoon on the Bahaist movement. Through his interpreter Dr. Ameen U. Fareed, Abbas Effendi, or Abdul-Baha as he is sometimes called, said that only through the unity of man's religion could universal peace ever be brought about. 'This is the bond,' said Abbas Effendi, 'which is to unite the East and the West and which will check the six thousand years of warfare which man has waged.'
>
> Abbas Effendi was a picturesque figure on the platform, clad, as he was, in a long flowing white gown and a braided Persian turban on his head. His white beard fell over his chest and his long white hair hung down over his shoulders.
>
> Reality, according to Abdul Baha, is the fundamental religion. It is what was taught by Moses, by Jesus Christ, and by Mohammed, and embodies justice, love, family bonds, promulgation of the arts, advancement of science and the bestowal of help to the poor.[51]

Weeks later Professor William Jackson[52] was one of the speakers at a reception for 'Abdu'l-Bahá held by the New York Peace Society on 13 May.[53] While traveling in Persia in 1918, Jackson also met with some Bahá'ís in Tehran and recalled with them his meeting with 'Abdu'l-Bahá.[54]

Interview with Kate Carew

Kate Carew (Mary Chambers, 1869–1960) was one of the first woman caricaturists in America. Her permanent column in the New York *World* and later in the *Tribune* and other newspapers became famous for her interviews with the personalities of the time. She used an incisive and sarcastic language and her texts were decorated with her drawings and caricatures of the personages interviewed.

She met 'Abdu'l-Bahá on Friday 19 April after His return from His talk at Columbia University. The text of her interview appeared in the *Tribune* one week later. Not only did she have the opportunity to talk with the Master but she was also invited to accompany Him on His visit to the Bowery Mission, leaving for posterity a vivid description of that episode.

Carew's article described with sarcasm and humor the moments before her meeting with the Master and she ridiculed the reverent attitude of the Bahá'ís gathered at the Ansonia, the clothes of 'Abdu'l-Bahá's Persian companions and the comments she heard from the people around her (not reproduced here). However, her tone changed when she came face to face with 'Abdu'l-Bahá:

> I blinked my eyes. Everybody in the room was standing, breathlessly expectant. I rose mechanically.
>
> Abdul Baha entered.
>
> He is scarcely above medium height, but so extraordinary is the dignity of his majestic carriage that he seemed more than the average stature.
>
> He wore, over biscuit colored velveteen trousers girdled with white, a long, full robe of grayish wool. The Panama fez was wound with white folds.
>
> While slowly making the round of the room his soft, penetrating, faded eyes studied us all, without seeming to do so.

One and another he termed 'My child!' – and they were not all young who responded to this greeting.

He stopped longest before the young girls and boys, those 'blossoms on life's branch', as he speaks of them in Oriental imagery.

A blushing young woman introduced her escort – 'Master, we have just been married.'

Such a look of joy illumined the face that in repose looks like a sheet of parchment on which Fate has scored deep cabalistic lines.

He did not want to leave them. He held their hands a long time, then turned and blessed the young man.

My dears, if that young man ever thinks of straying from the path of loyalty, me-thinks the pressure of that hand will weigh heavy on his soul.

He patted several people on the cheek, an old man, an apple-cheeked youth and myself. I got a nice, paternal little pat which has made me feel, oh, so much more like folks.

We seated ourselves about him. A good-looking young Turk understudying Dr. Fareed explained modestly: 'You know it is very difficult to translate the Master literally. I can tell you the words, but no one could possibly interpret the beautiful soul that informs them.'

Rather nice that, I thought!

The Baha repeated a statement he had made that day to the students of Columbia University.

'The great need of this country is the spiritual philosophy, the philosophy of the language of God. Everyone wants to find scientific truths, but we should seek the scientific truths of the spirit as well.

'Natural philosophy is like a very beautiful physical body, but the spiritual philosophy is the soul of that body. If this body unites with this spirit, then we have the highest perfect society.

'What God gives us in this world is for a time, our body is for a time, our millions of dollars are for a time, our houses, our automobiles, the same. But the spiritual gifts of God are forever. The greatness of this world will come to an end, but the greatness of the spiritual world is eternal . . .

I can imagine repeating his phrases to some of my clever friends, who would be sure to say:

'Why, that's as old as the hills. I don't see anything to make a fuss about in that.'

But the time honored words, even repeated by an interpreter, are so fraught with the Baha's wonderful personality that they seem never to have been uttered before. His meaning is not couched in any esoteric phrases. Again and again he has disclaimed the possession of hidden lore. Again and again he has placed the attainments of the heart and soul above those of the mind.

After a few more questions and answers the meeting is declared adjourned. Abdul Baha rises and passes into the inner room, where he gives some private-hearings.

No one starts to go. He has actually made New York people forget the dinner hour.

That in itself is a victory, I think. Don't you?

From my corner I wait my turn, again absorbed watching the human current . . .

As I respond to Dr. Fareed's signal and pass into the inner room I notice everywhere symptoms of departure. I get the impression of a large masculine family migrating from one part of the world to another, bringing messages of good cheer and brotherly feeling. It is very inspiring. I find the Baha seated in a comfortable easy chair at the bay window. Dr. Fareed sits near him as soon as I have taken my place. His beautiful voice, like a golden echo, follows close the termination of each sentence.

The master looks very spirituelle. He is in a relaxed attitude, sometimes 'going into the silence'. So much more akin to the spirit world than this does he seem that I find myself often addressing Dr. Fareed personally, referring to him in the third person.

'Do you think our luxury degenerate,' I ask, 'as in the great hotel?'

Abdul Baha strokes his long white beard.

'Luxury has a limit. Beyond that limit it is not commendable. There is such a thing as moderation. Men must be temperate in all things.'

'Does the attention paid at present in this country to material things sadden you? Does it argue to you a lack of progress?'

'Your material civilization is very wonderful. If only you will allow divine idealism to keep pace with it there is great hope for general progress' . . .

'Do you believe, in woman's desire for freedom?'

He adjusts his turban – a frequent mannerism.

'The soul has no sex.'

'In a supreme moment, as in that of the Titanic disaster, should both sexes share the danger equally?'

'Women are more delicate than men. This delicacy men should take into consideration. That is their obligation. If the time ever comes when the average woman is a man's equal in physical strength there will be no need for this consideration but not until then.'

As he says this he shakes the wonderful full-domed head and the singsong recitation has a note of great sweetness.

I thought of his childhood, passed among such unspeakable scenes of distress early matured into knowledge of sin and sorrow. I marveled at his childlike simplicity, which is combined with a sort of ageless spiritual wisdom. I asked:

'Is it possible for us ever to rid ourselves of our grown-up illusions and become, as Christ said, "as little children"?'

'Certainly. There is such a thing as innocence due to ignorance, due to weakness. It is innate in the child to be simple, but when a person becomes matured there should be such a thing as innocence of knowledge, of strength. For instance a child, owing to certain weakness may not lie. Even if the child wishes to tell an untruth it is incapable of doing it. This is due to his impotence but when it becomes old and its morals receive rectitude, then through pure, conscious potency can it restrain itself from lying.'

'Do we most need suffering or happiness to open to us the door of spiritual understanding?'

'Trials and suffering for the perfect man are good. For an imperfect they are a test. For example, a drunkard may, through his sin, lose all his possessions. He is cast into a great ordeal. That is his punishment. But the man who is endeavoring along the paths of virtuous achievement may meet ordeals which are really bounties, for they will help him.'

'Why is a child near thc spirit land?'

'Because children are so innocent. They have no stratagems. Their hearts are like spring meadows.'

'Should we train the young mind with fairy tales or something more realistic?'

'Fairy tales will not help a child. Anything without a foundation of truth lacks permanence. We should begin early to cultivate in children virtues, to teach them the realities of life.'

'Is there any way of making this life in a commercial city less crude for the young boy and girl?'

'It would be well to get them together and say "Young ladies, God has created you all human; isn't it a pity that you should pass your energy along animalistic lines? God has created you men and women in order that you may acquire his virtues; that you may progress in all the degrees, that you may be veritable angels, holy and sanctified."'

'There are so many temptations put in their way,' I murmur.

The Abdul Baha looks very sympathetic, but his singsong tones are relentlessly firm.

'Let them try a little of the delicacy of the spiritual world, the sweetness of its perfection and see which life is preferable. One leads man to debasement, the end of it is remorse, the end of it is scorn, the end of it is confusion. "Praise be to God you are gifted with intellect," I would say to them. "God has created you noble, why are you willing to degrade yourself? God has created you bright, radiant, how are you willing to be steeped in darkness? God has created you supreme. Why are you willing to be degraded into the abyss of despair? Admonish them in this way and exhort them."'

I noticed a trembling of the eyelids and that the gestures of arranging his turban and stroking his beard were more nervously frequent. Dr. Fareed answered to my inquiry, 'Shall I go now?'

'He has been giving of himself to everyone since 7 o'clock this morning. I am a perfect physical wreck, but he is willing to go on indefinitely.'

Abdul Baha opened the half-closed eyelids to say:

'I am going to the poor in the Bowery now. I love them.'

I was invited to accompany them. The Baha met my assent with a most Chesterfieldian expression of pleasure.

Mr. Mills, president of the Bahaite Society in New York, had placed his car at the disposal of Abdul Baha . . .

When we were seated in the machine, every inch of space taken by some member of the suite, I caught myself thinking what an amusing little anecdote I might make of this happening. Just then the Master said to me in a gentle but firm voice:

'Remember, you press people are the servants of the public. You interpret our words and acts to them. With you is a great responsibility. Please remember and please treat us seriously.'

Often during the interview I had felt like saying: 'You dear old man! You fine old gentleman!' I felt more than ever like it now. As if anyone could hold up that pure white soul to ridicule.

There was another gasp of surprise at the Bowery Mission as, still hand in hand – he just wouldn't let me go – the Baha and I trotted through a lane composed of several score of the society's members. A few of the young ladies had their arms filled with flowers, which afterward filled the automobile. Some four hundred men were present, belonging to the mission.

Just before the services were concluded I saw the courier stealthy approach the platform and hand the Baha a green baize bag.

Of course, I wasn't going to let that go on without finding out all about it, and to my whispered inquiry the Baha said, smilingly:

'Some little lucky bits I am going to distribute to the men.'

What you don't expect!

I had the surprise of my life!

For what do you suppose those lucky bits were?

Silver quarters, two hundred dollars worth of them!

There!

Guess you didn't expect it, either.

Think of it! Someone actually coming to America and distributing money. Not here with the avowed or unavowed intention of taking it away.

It seems incredible.

Possibly I may be a little tired of mere words, dealing in them the way I do, but that demonstration of Abdul Baha's creed did more to convince me of the absolute sincerity of the man than anything else that had happened.

And it was all done so unostentatiously, so gracefully, without any fuss or fume.

The Master stood, his eyes always turned away from the man facing him, far down the line four or five beyond his vis-à-vis, so that when a particularly desperate looking specimen came along he was all ready for him, and, instead of one quarter, two were quietly pressed into the calloused palm.

Once a young Turk of the suite slipped in, and before the Baha recognized him got a coin. He explained that he wanted it for luck, and the Baha most benignantly patted his shoulder. When he got back to his companions they all laughed at the joke.

I imagine them a merry little family among themselves.

I had said good night on the platform so my last view of Abdul Baha was as he stood at the head of the Bowery Mission line, a dozen or more derelicts before him, giving to each a bit of silver and a word of blessing.

And as I went out into the starlight night I murmured the phrase of an Oriental admirer who had described him as

The Breeze of God.[55]

Visit to the Bowery Mission

The Bowery Mission was established in 1879 by Rev. Albert G. Ruliffson (1833–96) as a refuge from which solace and assistance was offered to the poorest among the citizens of New York. In 1912 this institution was managed by the 'Christian Herald Association'. Just a few weeks before the arrival of 'Abdu'l-Bahá, Juliet Thompson had been invited by the mission's superintendent, John G. Hallimond (1857–1924), to present a talk on the Bahá'í Faith there. After her talk, Hallimond proposed to the audience that 'Abdu'l-Bahá be requested to speak for them and the three hundred people attending agreed with the idea. In the meantime, Thompson continued visiting the mission on a weekly basis to speak about 'Abdu'l-Bahá and the Bahá'í Faith.[56]

The Master visited the mission on 19 April and addressed a large audience composed of the most destitute men in the area who with reverent attention listened to His loving and encouraging words on the high spiritual station of the poor.[57]

Before the meeting 'Abdu'l-Bahá had given Juliet Thompson and Edward Getsinger each a check for one thousand francs with the request that they change the money into quarters. After His address 'Abdu'l-Bahá stood at the door of the Bowery Mission and as each one of the men attending the meeting left He gave him a coin or two.

On 20 April, two weeks before the publication of Carew's interview, the *New York Tribune* published a detailed account of 'Abdu'l-Bahá's visit to the Bowery Mission. It is possible that this account was also penned by Kate Carew who, as we have seen, was present at the meeting:

FREE MONEY ON BOWERY

ABDUL BAHA VISITS MISSION AND DISTRIBUTES QUARTERS

MONEY BAG SOON EMPTY

NEWS SPREAD RAPIDLY, BUT THE PERSIAN PROPHET HAS TO DISAPPOINT MANY

An incident that might have been immortalized by O. Henry, were he still alive when Abdul Baha Abbas, the Persian prophet, attired in the flowing robes of the Far East visited the Bowery Mission. 'Bagdad-on-the-Subway', as O. Henry often called New York, has been the scene of countless incidents that might be woven into tales as fascinating as those related to Haroun-al-Raschid, and many of them have been enacted on the Bowery.

Until last night, however, probably none bore so much flavor of the original Arabian Nights. For did not the 'the good Caliph' appear in person and greet the four hundred or more men who filled to overflowing the capacity of the mission hall to hear him preach, and did he not reward each of them with a memento of himself that brought joy to the heart of more than a few of those who through the efforts of the Bowery Mission have become rich in faith, if they are poor in material wealth?

Abdul Baha Abbas is a philosopher and teacher of a Christian doctrine that embraces world-wide unity and love. Since his arrival here, a few days ago, he has preached at a number of fashionable churches and last night his desire to see the 'other side' at worship led him to visit the Bowery Mission. His coming had been arranged for and when the evening service was well begun he entered a door at the rear and marched with dignified step to the platform.

There was a craning of necks as the venerable old man, his brown face and snow-white beard and hair, topped by a white fez, proceeded down the aisle. The same interest was apparent later when he arose to address the gathering in his native language, telling them, as his interpreter, Dr. Ameen Fareed, who is his nephew, explained, that because they were poor they should be thankful, because Jesus had said, 'Blessed are the poor', while the rich had never been so recommended.

At the end of his address Abdul Baha said he would like to meet each man as he passed out of the building. He said he had a token for them. Again the eyes of all followed him as he passed down the aisle and took a station near the door, carrying a mysterious looking bag in his hand.

As each man passed the prophet he was allowed to grasp his hand, and as he withdrew it in his palm lay a bright silver quarter.

Four hundred men were in the hall, and there was a gift for all. After the last one had gone and the empty bag remained, Abdul Baha congratulated the leaders of the mission and expressed his pleasure at having been able to be there.

Outside, on the Bowery, the news that there was a 'guy givin' away quarters at the mission' spread like wildfire. A crowd soon collected outside of the iron lattice work that protects the door, but $100 in 25 cent pieces was all the change the good prophet happened to have about him.[58]

Excerpts of this article were published afterwards in other newspapers.[59] In 1913, coinciding with the anniversary of His visit to the Bowery, 'Abdu'l-Bahá sent a Tablet from Stuttgart to the Bowery Mission and a second one from Haifa in 1914.

When the Bahá'ís of New York celebrated the first anniversary of 'Abdu'l-Bahá's visit to the Bowery Mission the following was published in the *New York Press*:

DERELICTS PAY HONOR TO PERSIAN PREACHER

BOWERY MISSION FREQUENTERS REMEMBER ABDUL BAHA ABBAS'S VISIT

There is one place in New York at least where the memory of Abdul Baha Abbas is kept green. Abdul Baha is the leader of the Bahai movement who spent forty years in a Persian prison for preaching the faith of his father, Baha'u'llah, and who spent some time in the United States last year spreading the doctrine of the unity of all religious believers. The particular place where Abdul Baha's presence is revered is in the Bowery Mission, and it is remembered for reasons connected with 'honest graft'.

When Abdul Baha was in New York in April last he was taken by a party of his local followers one night down to the Bowery Mission, where 300 of the derelicts of that thoroughfare were gathered for the occasion. When the guest of honor had finished his address to the gathering of 'downandouts' he stood in the doorway, and as each man went out he handed him a quarter. The frequenters of the mission were dumfounded at this practical evidence of the unity of mankind.

This year the followers of Abdul Baha in New York decided to pay another visit to the Bowery Mission on the anniversary of the leader's first trip. They wrote to Abdul Baha, in Paris, telling him of what they intended to do and by the first return mail they received from the preacher a money order for $80, which he wished given to the men who attended the mission on the night of his anniversary visit. To each man as he passed out the door again was given a quarter.[60]

Other Interviews and Articles

Despite His strenuous schedule, 'Abdu'l-Bahá continued to accept requests to interview Him. Another journalist who met the Master was the famous poet and leader in New Thought circles Ella Wheeler Wilcox (1850–1919), whose syndicated articles were published across the United States and who probably met the Master at the above mentioned meeting organized by the New Thought Society at the Carnegie Lyceum on 14 April. Wilcox dedicated one of her articles to 'Abdu'l-Bahá.

ABDUL BAHA, TEACHER OF RELIGION, DEVOTES HIS LIFE TO HUMANITY AND A NEW FAITH

BY ELLA WHEELER WILCOX

America has entertained many native and foreign teachers of religion and philosophy. It has entertained two remarkable masters – selfless, simple, earnest, profound souls who came with great messages.

These two were Vivekananda and Anna Besant.

They came filled with a love for all religions and hate for none. With no self-interest, with no desire to proselyte. Only a desire to help. With no egotistical assertion of having discovered a truth, but with a humble gratitude that they were able to promote an eternal one. Now comes another great teacher like unto these two. Abdul Baha, the Persian philosopher.

> Abdul Baha's life is one of active service to humanity. He is working to serve God, yet by serving God he serves mankind. From his early childhood to his sixty-fourth year he was an exile and a prisoner, yet the light of his life and teachings has reached to the far corners of the earth. From many a country have gone to him people of different beliefs to receive spiritual help, and upon leaving him they have returned to their various homes to share with others the joy and assurance of his spiritual message and to follow in his path of service . . .

The article continued with various quotations from the Bahá'í writings and some proverbs. The last one of them was 'He that knows and knows that he knows – He is wise, follow him.' After quoting it Wilcox added that 'Abdul Baha belongs to the latter class even as do Vivekananda and Anna Besant – follow them!'[61]

A few weeks after the publication of this article, 'Abdu'l-Bahá mentioned Wilcox in an interview in Chicago (see chapter 12) and also mentioned her in 1917 in a Tablet to Louise Waite in which He stated: 'This respected lady [Ms Wilcox] has infinite capabilities. She is like a lamp filled with oil which no sooner comes in contact with fire than it is set aglow. Now it is thus hoped that she may become enkindled with the fire of the love of God, and her torch become so illumined, so luminous, as to illumine all directions.'[62] Wilcox was also honoured with a Tablet from 'Abdu'l-Bahá consoling her on the passing of her husband. Owing to the war, however, 'Abdu'l-Bahá's missive did not reach America until after her passing.[63]

Just before 'Abdu'l-Bahá's departure from New York, He granted an interview to the *New York Times* which was published as a one-page article in the Sunday edition of the newspaper, which at the time had a circulation of 125,000 copies. The account of the interview was preceded by a long introduction to the history of the Faith, not reproduced here. The article also carried a picture of the Master distributed by Underwood and Underwood:

> Within the last week there has come to New York an old man, with a worn and beautiful face, who wears a long, brown gown and a white turban, and speaks the strange-sounding guttural language of Persia. On the pier he was welcomed by hundreds of people, for

he is Abdul Baha, or 'The Servant of God', the head of the Bahaist movement, and he is known to tens of thousands of followers all over the world as the 'Master' . . .

Needless to say Abdul Baha is a much occupied man, and it was not easy to secure an appointment with him. He is not exclusive in his ideas by any manner of means. In his house at Acre all men and women are welcome at all times, but he has to be shielded a little by his friends that he may not over-exert himself in his desire to make all the world welcome.

The reception room in his apartment was filled with flowers. There was not long to wait, for Abdul Baha is prompt and business like. In two minutes a young Persian opened a door and asked the reporter to enter.

A rather small man with a white beard and the kindest and gentlest face in the world held out a hand. In his brown habit he was extraordinarily picturesque, but one did not think long of that, for he smiled a charming smile and, walking before and holding his visitor's hand, he led her to a chair. Then he seated himself in another chair, facing her, and spoke in Persian to the younger man, who interpreted.

'He says,' said the interpreter, 'that you are welcome, most welcome.'

The reporter said she was grateful to Abdul Baha for receiving her. To this, when translated, the Master said, politely, that he, also, was most happy at the meeting. The reporter had been told that she need not ask a question to begin the conversation, but that Abdul Baha would speak, so after the exchange of courtesies, she kept silent while the old man, who has spent his life in a Turkish prison, looked at her with the interest one feels in a new specimen of humanity.

Then he began to speak in short sentences, without waiting for replies. The interpreter translated them in perfect English.

'Praise be to God, the women of America are progressing.

'This is as it should be. Every day they are making more and more progress.

'I hope that they will be the peers of men. They should progress equally with men.

'This is according to the institution of Baha Ullah, that there should not be a difference between men and women . . .

'In idealism women are the superiors of men in kindness and in gentleness, but they are now their inferiors in intellectuality. This should not be.

'Women should progress intellectually until they stand side by side with men.

'The women of America are progressing toward this, and they will attain it, for it is just. Women shall indeed be the equals and the companions of men.'

The words delivered in this fashion, in short epigrams, took one miles and miles away from New York. Outside the window was Broadway; under the building the subway; downstairs was all the paraphernalia of a big hotel, but all these things were far less real than the picture the old teacher called up. The only things that seemed near were the mountains of Carmel, so near the Village of Nazareth, and the fields where the lilies grow more beautiful than Solomon in his glory.

The strangeness of it all, the manner of speaking, the curious language, the unfamiliar dress might well have made the listener awkward and ill at ease; but one does not feel awkward with Abdul Baha. The reporter had wondered just how to address him, but that seemed a foolish matter now. It really made no difference what you did or what you said, this kind old teacher would know that you meant well.

When he had spoken his words in the cause of women Abdul Baha paused and inquired graciously if the visitor wished to ask a question.

'Ask him,' ventured the reporter, 'for a message to Americans. Tell him that a great newspaper sent me, and that many thousands will read what he says.'

'When this was translated to him the Teacher's face lighted up with the charming smile. He was evidently pleased and interested that a big newspaper should have sent a woman – so, at least, the smile seemed to signify.

With some gestures and with his bright eyes now on his interpreter and now on his visitor, he began again to speak in short sentences.

'Praise be to God, the dark ages have passed.

'A new age of great brilliancy has been ushered in. The minds of men have developed. Man has made discoveries in the mysteries of nature. The great capabilities of the human world have become manifest. The susceptibilities of the heart have become more acute.

'The time has arrived for the world of humanity to hoist the standard of the oneness of the human world, so that solidarity and unity may connect all the nations of the world, so that dogmatic formulas and superstitions may end, so that the essential reality underlying all the religions founded by all the prophets may be revealed.

'That reality is one

'It is the love of God.

'It is the progress of the world.

'It is the oneness of humanity.

'It is the bond which can unite all the human race.

'It is the attainment of the benefits of the most great peace; it is the discarding of warfare.

'It is progressiveness; it is the undertaking of colossal tasks in life; It is the oneness of public opinion.

'Therefore strive, oh ye people, and put forth your efforts that this reality may overcome the lesser forces in life, that this king of reality may alone rule all humanity.

'Thus may the world of mankind be reformed.

'Thus may a new springtime be ushered in and a fresh spirit may resuscitate man.

'The individuals of humanity, like refreshed plants, shall put forth leaves and shall blossom and fructify so that the face of the earth shall become the long promised and delectable paradise, so that the great bestowal – the supreme virtues of man – shall glisten over the face of the earth.

"Then shall the world of existence have attained maturity.

'This is my message."

He ceased speaking. There had been no pause in the little sermon, one sentence had followed as fast as the reporter could write them down, though he was always careful not to speak too rapidly for her convenience. It had been for one so busy a long interview, and the reporter rose.

The master of the Bahais rose too, with all his benevolent and fatherly heart in his kind eyes. He gave a little but very humorous

> laugh and patted his visitor on the shoulder, speaking to the interpreter who smiled, too.
>
> 'He says,' translated the interpreter, 'that he is pleased with you.' Then, obeying a gesture, he took a rose from a vase and brought it to his master.
>
> Abdul Baha put it in the reporter's hand and gave his parting blessing.
>
> 'May the divine spirit help you to do great works in the world,' he said gently.
>
> In a minute the door had closed and the reporter stepped from Palestine to the conventional hotel sitting room.[64]

Other newspapers outside New York later reproduced portions of this article.[65] Arthur T. Bailey, a reader of the *Schenectady Gazette*, wrote a letter to the editor quoting some sentences of this interview regarding gender equality.[66]

From an announcement published in the *New York Times* we also learn that a few days after the departure of the Master from New York, Dr. Joseph Herman Randall, at the time pastor at the Mount Morris Baptist Church, offered a sermon on 'The Message of Abdul Baha' on Sunday 28 April.[67]

As noted above, news agencies released a number of news items about 'Abdu'l-Bahá that were published across the United States. As well as the above mentioned articles about His arrival and His first public address in New York, 'Abdu'l-Bahá's portrait was sent through the agencies. A picture of Him taken by a photographer from the Underwood and Underwood studio was widely circulated with the caption 'Specially posed photograph of Abdul Baha Abbas, taken in New York soon after his arrival from London on April 11. The venerable Persian is the head of the new Bahai religion, having more than 20,000,000 followers. The belief embraces the doctrine of world-wide peace and unity of religion.'[68] During 'Abdu'l-Bahá's sojourn in America many newspapers included this picture in their articles. One of them was the *Fort Wayne News* (IN) which also published two drawings representing the Master in imaginary scenes.[69]

Just a few days after the departure of 'Abdu'l-Bahá from New York, the Bain News Service distributed across the United States a further portrait of 'Abdu'l-Bahá which was afterwards published in several newspapers with a caption which briefly summarized some biographical facts about the Master.

Editorials and Other Comments

The interest and curiosity aroused by the arrival of 'Abdu'l-Bahá in America also generated a number of references to His teachings in editorials, letters from readers and opinion columns. These references offer a clear indication that the general public and the media were quickly familiarized with the figure of the Master and with some of the teachings He expounded during His first week in America.

An early example of this phenomenon is a letter to the editor that appeared in the *New York Tribune* on 18 April. Its author, who was probably a sympathizer of Theosophy, expressed his view that the Bahá'í Faith was one part of a world-wide 'movement for unification':

> ABDUL BAHA
>
> To the Editor of The Tribune,
>
> Sir: The papers at present have much in their columns about the Persian teacher, Abdul Baha. He is here to sound the great note of peace based on human solidarity and human love. Those who have heard him speak, who have heard his earnest plea for perfect tolerance, perfect co-operation in religions and other affairs must carry away in their hearts a high resolve to break down all barriers such as those of creed, dogma, narrow patriotism which keep out human brotherhood.
>
> If, as Sir Oliver Lodge believes, there are 'powerful, but not almighty helpers to whom we owe guidance and management and reasonable control', the next step they are planning for humanity spiritually should be apparent to the careful observer. It is this unification of the human race, which is a recognition of essential oneness, not a destroying of racial characteristics, this drawing together of the religions on the basis of the fundamental verities which they possess in common. This movement for unification is showing itself everywhere. It is being put forward by many organizations. Bahaism stands for it preeminently; it is the very heart and soul of Theosophy, which has proclaimed it untiringly for the last thirty-five years. Outside of any society are millions of people whose

> hearts have been touched by this great message and who are spreading it silently but effectively. The steamship, the railroad train, the telegraph, all those modern inventions that serve to destroy distance between men physically are also destroying it between them mentally and spiritually.
>
> In a few years the world will awake to realize that the day of peace has dawned, a day when men will look into each other's eyes and see shining there the light of the spirit, the same in all, no matter what the race, the creed, the sex, the caste or the color.
>
> M.L. New York, April 15, 1912[70]

Around the same dates, Dr Franck Crane[71] dedicated his syndicated editorial 'The Philosopher's Corner' to the Bahá'í Faith. Crane opened his text by confessing his interest in the Bahá'í Faith and, as a former Christian minister, he also expressed his view that the Bahá'í doctrines were basically a repetition of Christian ideals:

> I am very deeply interested in this religious philosopher, Abdul Baha, the interpreter of the so-called Bahai doctrines of universal brotherhood and peace. This end Abdul Baha would accomplish by harmonizing all religions, a task which, I imagine, he will find rather difficult to say the least. It is not, however, the teachings of this aged prophet who comes to us out of far away Persia that I find particularly interesting; for his precepts are basically those common to all Christendom. That is, they are common as precepts, but less common so far as practice is concerned. I am impressed rather with the story of the martyrdom of the founders of this movement. Thus is emphasized the fact that those who first boldly stand alone for a great truth are doomed to drink the poisoned cup, to tread the way of the cross, to be driven to some other form of death or into exile or, in more civilized countries, to be subjected to scornful indifference.

The editorial continued with a short introduction to the figures of the Báb and Bahá'u'lláh, after which the author expressed his opinion about some of the Bahá'í teachings. As can be inferred from the text, Crane's knowledge of the Bahá'í Faith was probably derived from information that appeared in the press on previous days or from pamphlets circulated by Bahá'ís. These limited sources made him misunderstand the Bahá'í tenets. As Crane understood it, Bahá'ís considered religious unity as the only requisite for universal peace, and he expressed the view in his editorial that this was a limited solution for the problem of war.[72]

The Evening Telegram (New York) stated in one of its permanent sections that 'if Abdul Baha can really effect a unity of nations and of religions, we are with him. But he must show results quickly.'[73]

A humorous comment published in the Binghamton (New York) *Press* stated that 'Abdul Baha of Persia is here to urge upon Americans the wisdom of having one religion for all men. He will find American churchmen in hearty accord with him – only each one thinks his own church is the one for all men.'[74] In a reference to the political divorce between President Taft and Theodore Roosevelt, the *Springfield News* mentioned that 'Abdul Baha has come all the way from Persia to preach peace to Americans. Perhaps he felt it his mission to reunite Messrs. Taft and Roosevelt.'[75]

The *Brooklyn Daily Eagle*, a Democratic newspaper with a circulation of 44,000, also commented that 'Abdul Baha Abbas would have been a B. A. by natural selection and Divine right, even if his art had never turned to starting a new Brotherhood of Man religion'.[76]

'Uncle Eph', columnist on the monthly *Illustrated Companion* (New York), mentioned 'Abdu'l-Bahá in his article for the April issue of the magazine:

> . . . the considerate man will stop and take thought before condemning absolutely such men as Abdul Baha, the leader of the Bahai movement, who comes here from Persia to teach us that all good men should devote their lives to the poor and unfortunate. I don't expect many of us will become enthusiastic Babists, but it would not be a bad thing for us to find out just what that interdenominational sect are trying to do. The more we try to find out about any world-wide movement, whether we approve of it or not, the more we know.[77]

Other editorials were published outside the state of New York. The *Oakland Inquirer* published comments about 'Abdu'l-Bahá's presence in America:

> It is admitted that Abdul Baha is a man of deep learning and thought, but he will be a wonderfully old man if he lives to see the adoption

of one tongue, one religion, one line of education, one code of morals, one method of work and one government. Pervading all of his teachings is the ideal of unity and a common world-family. This is beautiful in theory, but altogether too beautiful to work out in practice . . .

Abdul Baha is several centuries ahead of the times. His ideas are admittedly beautiful. The keynote of the utterances of the Persian who for half a century has been known to the East, but rarely heard of in Western Europe or America, is unity and universalism. But the difficulty will be in pointing out a religion upon which we can all agree; a language which will suit all races and a single code of morals which will be acceptable.

And besides all of that Abdul Baha is due to hit this country during a hot political campaign and it is more than probable that he will have considerable difficulty in making himself heard even though he uses several languages in preaching the practice of a one-language race.

We will be glad to see Abdul, but we feel that he is due to return to his Persian home a deeply disappointed advocate of advanced social, economic, educational, political and religious ideas.[78]

A Message to Glen Falls

On His way to New York, 'Abdu'l-Bahá conversed with many of the passengers on board the *Cedric* and even gave a talk for some five hundred of them. One of the passengers who met Him was the American Quaker Sarah Maria Paine from Glen Falls, New York, who was returning from a missionary trip in Egypt. When Paine arrived in her town, she participated in the annual meeting of the local branch of the Women's Missionary Society, which was held on 16 April. A local newspaper reported that in one the sessions Paine spoke to some 75 participants 'of her great privilege in meeting on the return voyage, Abdul Baha, the great religious leader of Persia'. The same report noted that 'the indubitable feature of the evening was a greeting sent by Abdul Baha to the Friends in Glens Falls, Mrs. Paine reading the message to those present.'[79]

11

WASHINGTON

20–8 April 1912

Long before 'Abdu'l-Bahá's arrival in America the press in Washington published articles about the Bahá'í Faith in which His expected visit to the capital was announced. The independent *Washington Post*, which at the time had a circulation of some 30,000 copies, published in early March a lengthy article announcing the visit to Washington of the Master, introducing to its readers the history and tenets of the Bahá'í Faith, and even quoting from the communications of the Master:

> . . . For many years he has been in the Orient, where the Bahai movement, of which he is the chief exponent, has made rapid progress. But until recently, when the visits of this noted Persian to London and Paris and a brief stay in Switzerland focused the attention of the people of Europe, comparatively little has been known among Westerners about this remarkable religious movement. And now with the prospective visit of Abbas Effendi to America, Bahais, as his followers are called, are inclined to ask their friends to watch the mysterious East, which in past ages has brought many wonders to light.
>
> In appearance Abbas Effendi resembles a venerable patriarch from the ancient world. His face and form present a study worthy of a great artist. His liberal and progressive views have cost him and his followers much suffering, it is asserted, for the Moslems of Persia, among whom the movement started more than 50 years ago, are known to be among the most fanatical of religious devotees on earth . . .
>
> And the many beautiful books and tablets that have emanated from his pen, to individuals and to organizations, are treasured by his friends in all parts of the world. So that when Abbas Effendi, the

> venerable teacher, lands in America, he will not find himself among strangers. Although his adherents here are not noisy or demonstrative, they do their work in a very quiet way, and few of the larger cities of America are without a Bahai assembly.
>
> These form a network stretching from Maine to California, and even include the Hawaiian Islands. So among the agencies at work for the wiping out of religious bigotry and racial prejudices at the present day, among peace conferences and tribunals of arbitration, it may be questioned whether any of them or all of them are half as effective as this simple man, who affects no state or ostentation, but teaches universal tolerance and the cessation of all strife . . .
>
> All accounts agree that he is a most interesting and striking personality, who seems familiar with the needs of humanity and has some remedy to suggest for every human woe. His efforts to promote peace, his tolerance of all religions, his sympathetic touch, doubtless will find a response in the hearts of good people everywhere. Arrangements have been made to have him make addresses in churches of many cities, as well as at peace congresses and other gatherings.[1]

Some details about the program of 'Abdu'l-Bahá in the capital were confirmed as early as 5 April when various newspapers announced that He would speak at one of the sessions of the Persian–American Educational Society and that He would give talks at the Church of Our Father, the People's Church and All Souls Unitarian Church.[2]

The Annual Convention of the Persian–American Educational Society

The Persian–American Educational Society was one of the first instances of a large-scale social and economic development project sponsored by the Bahá'í community in the West. Under the guidance of 'Abdu'l-Bahá this organization was born in early 1910 with the ambitious aim of assisting Persia by sending teachers and doctors, supporting the creation of schools and medical centers, encouraging commercial investments in the country, and sponsoring Persian youth to pursue their studies in America. Its initial success prompted this organization to enlarge its scope of action and include other oriental countries. Several prominent non-Bahá'ís were also involved in the work of this organization, among them Benjamin Trueblood, the General Secretary of the influential American Peace Society.

In 1912 the society celebrated its annual convention from 18 to 20 April and 'Abdu'l-Bahá was to address the participants at one of its sessions. In announcing the meeting and its program, the Persian–American Educational Society sent several press releases to the media and distributed in the press the compilation of Bahá'í writings *The Universal Principles of the Bahai Movement, Social, Economic, Governmental* (1912). The Associated Press news agency also distributed a note about the convention. Thus in the weeks prior to the arrival of 'Abdu'l-Bahá in America He was mentioned several times in the press in connection with the convention of the Persian–American Educational Society.[3] In England, *The Near East* (London) also published a note about the event which mentioned the participation of 'Abdu'l-Bahá.[4] Further notes were released on the day of the opening of the convention reporting that 'the conference this year is honored by the presence of Abdul Baha',[5] and He was further mentioned in accounts of the first sessions.[6]

After a five-hour train trip from New York, 'Abdu'l-Bahá reached Washington at 1.30 p.m. on Saturday 20 April.[7] From the train station He was taken to the home of Agnes Parsons, where He was to stay during His sojourn in Washington. From there, and despite His fatigue, He proceeded to the public library to attend the last session of the Persian–American Educational Society. At some point between His arrival in Washington and His address on that day, a reporter on the *Evening Star*, a newspaper with a circulation of 5,000 copies, had the chance to interview the Master:

BAHAI HEAD ARRIVES

ABDUL BAHA ABBAS GUEST IN NATIONAL CAPITAL

RECEPTION IS TENDERED

TO SPEAK BEFORE PERSIAN–AMERICAN EDUCATIONAL SOCIETY

OUTLINES HIS AMBITIONS

OBJECT OF LIFE TO PROMOTE ONENESS OF LIFE AND WORLD-WIDE PEACE

> Abdul Baha Abbas, world leader of the Bahai movement, who has been in the United States for a fortnight, at the beginning of a tour of the principal cities of the country, reached Washington this afternoon from New York. For at least a part of the afternoon he will be present

at Rauscher's at a reception and musical to be given in his honor, and in consequence of the general invitation which has been extended to the public to attend this function, it is expected many Bahais and their friends will take advantage of the opportunity to greet the distinguished Persian. Abdul Baha tonight will be one of the speakers at the closing session in the Public Library lecture hall of the second annual conference of the Persian–American Educational Society.

In an interview soon after he reached the city, Abdul Baha declared that his primary object in coming to America was to see the country.

DISCLOSES AMBITIONS

'Last year I went to London and Paris and saw those cities, and then returned to Egypt,' he said. 'Now I have come to America to see this country, for I have heard many wonderful praises and commendations of America; that it is a country well populated and well civilized. People here enjoy freedom and liberty.

'On the other hand I have heard that in America many great national organizations are being formed for international peace and arbitration. It is my highest desire to see these societies and converse with their founders and members. For the great object of my life is to promote the oneness of the kingdom of humanity and international peace.'

Replying to a question whether a person with a religion – Christian, Mohammedan or Jewish – could follow the Bahai teachings without abandoning his religion, Abdul Baha said:

'Yes, for truth is always one. The prophets of God have always spread the one truth and have established the truth. Truth cannot accept plurality. If the followers of all religions will return to the original principles of their religions, they will immediately become united. The foundation of religion is one. We are following the religions of all nationalities, for the basis of these religions is truth.'[8]

When 'Abdu'l-Bahá arrived at the Convention of the Persian–American Educational Society, six hundred people were sitting in the library hall and a hundred more were standing to listen to His words. At the morning sessions of the convention members approved a change in the name of the organization to 'Orient–Occident Unity' to symbolize the extensions of its work to other countries other than Persia.

'Abdu'l-Bahá spoke to His audience about the necessity of union and cooperation between the East and the West and encouraged the work of the Orient–Occident Unity as a paradigm of this future union. He also praised the American nation and expressed His desire that it may be 'the first nation to establish the foundation of international agreement'.[9] Other speakers that day were John Barrett, director of the Pan-American Union;[10] Samuel Gompers,[11] president of the American Federation of Labor; Prof. Herman Schoenfeld, of George Washington University;[12] and Rev. J. W. Frizzell, pastor of the Ingram Memorial Church.[13]

After His address 'Abdu'l-Bahá was approached by many participants. Among the audience there were also reporters from the four major local newspapers. The representative from the *Evening Star* interviewed Him and asked His opinion on the *Titanic* disaster and the situation in Persia.

> Abdul Baha, leader of the Bahai movement, who reached Washington yesterday afternoon and who plans a week's visit to the National Capital as a part of his tour of the United States, made the principal address at the closing session last night of the second annual conference of the Persian–American Educational Society. The meeting was held in the lecture hall of the Public library, and every seat and all available standing-room was occupied by an audience eager to hear the distinguished Persian. Abdul Baha spoke in Persian, and his remarks, were interpreted, phrase by phrase, by Dr. Ameen Fareed, his nephew and a member of his party.
>
> In an interview after his address, and giving answer to a specific question, the Bahai leader declared that the disaster to the White Star liner Titanic, much as he deplored it, was only an outward expression of the too rapid development of the age.
>
> PROGRESS TOO FAST
>
> 'Both Americans and Europeans seem to be possessed of the mania for speed,' he said. 'It is true in this country in particular that growth in all directions has progressed too rapidly. Moderation should be practiced in all things. Be temperate, even in the size of the ships you build and in their speed; in your railroads and the schedules you

expect your trains to maintain. It was a pitiful waste of life that came because of the effort to save a few hours, in time-rushing a great vessel at top speed when it was known there was danger from ice.'

When he entered the hall, Abdul Baha was greeted by the audience – all Bahais and their friends and guests rising. And after he had spoken and when he was seated on the platform, hundreds pressed around him, seeking to grasp his hand.

OUTLINES HIS PURPOSES

In his address the Persian leader outlined the purposes of his visit to the United States, and he declared he already has seen great possibilities for co-operation between America and Persia.

'It is an evident fact that for Persia there is no better government to use as a model than that of America,' he said. 'And for America there can be no better mart than Persia. It offers virgin soil for her commerce, because in Persia all the mineral resources, and indeed all of the material resources, are latent in the soil and in the people. Perfect amity should be established between Persia and America, whether it be in material bonds or in spiritual bonds.'

Other speakers at the meeting included Mirza Ahmed Sohrab, treasurer of the society, and Prof. Hermann Schoenfeld. Dr. Schoenfeld asserted the Persian people need modern education. Mr. Sohrab devoted his attention to the recent present-day conditions in Persia, and he made the emphatic declaration that Persia never will be a satrap of some neighboring power . . .

Announcement was made that Abdul Baha will participate in and make an address at a meeting this afternoon at 3 o'clock in the Universalist Church, 13th and L streets northwest.[14]

The Washington Herald which at the time had a circulation of just 15,000 copies, used a more caustic and satirical tone to describe the meeting. Despite the fact that the overall subject of 'Abdu'l-Bahá's talk was the unity of mankind, *The Herald* represented Him as simply defending the interests of Persia:

WOMEN AND MEN JOIN IN WORSHIP OF ABDUL BAHA

HEAD OF NEW RELIGION MAKES WEIRD IMPRESSION AT PUBLIC MEETING

'GUIDE LIGHT OF MAN'

PROPHET OF NEW SECT APPEALS FOR WORLD UNITY AND FLAYS TITANIC'S OWNERS

VIEWS OF ABDUL BAHA

The Titanic disaster was due to the too rapid progress of present-day civilization. Moderation would have prevented the holocaust. Persia is in a chaotic state. The people want a constitutional government but at present they have nothing not even a monarchy. George Washington was one of the rare souls known, who left behind his footsteps on the sands of time. I want to pay homage to him. Omar Khayyam was a master poet, and his teachings are believed by all the people of Persia. I myself am a teacher of his word. – ABDUL BAHA

The advent of Abdul Baha, leader of the Bahai movement, who is acclaimed by his followers to be inspired, by the Supreme Being, into Washington last night was a weird and impressive ceremony. The prophet, as he is called by his followers, attended the third session of the Orient–Occident Unity, held at the Public Library, last night. He was lionized, worshiped, and even the hem of his garment was sought by men and women in the audience that they might touch it.

Baha addressed the assemblage at length and his chief concern, although he is the supposed guide light of all mankind, centered in the future of Persia, his native country. He appealed to the members of the unity to lend their support in establishing friendly relations with the Oriental country, and prophesied a wonderful future for his native land.

The address of the aged philosopher, relating only to Persia, caused much comment among his following, who expected him talk to them of the affairs of the world, to adjure them to love their fellow men. Instead, he seemed to ask them to love only Persians.

MEN NEED CO-OPERATION

One salient fact he pointed out was that while trees and beasts of the forest can live alone, independent of their kind, men are not so constructed, it being necessary for them to co-operate with their fellow-beings in order to make a success of life.

> The only reference Baha made to his doctrine of universal religion was the hope that universal peace might be realized. But here he departed and said that he hoped to see America the first nation to promulgate the action. He also, commended the Union for its interest in the welfare of the Persian government.
>
> Baha is accompanied on his trip to this country by his interpreter Dr. Fareed; Mirza Seid Asseid Ullah, and two others. He will stay in Washington until next Sunday, and during his stay here will make his home with Mrs. Arthur Pesse Parsons, of Eighteenth and R Streets Northwest. Next Sunday he will leave for Chicago, where he will address a meeting in the Coliseum . . .
>
> PROGRESS TOO RAPIDLY
>
> In an interview at the conclusion of his address, Abdul Baha was emphatic in his denunciation of the men responsible for the Titanic disaster. He declared the people of today are inclined to progress too rapidly, and had moderation been considered in the building of the huge vessel the disaster would have been averted.
>
> He was very enthusiastic about his visit in Washington.
>
> 'Washington,' said Baha, 'is one of the most famous cities in the world. I am longing for the opportunity to pay tribute to the memory of George Washington, who is one of the rare souls who left his footprints on the sands of Time.'
>
> 'Is the Persian government in good condition now?' he repeated when asked the status of his native land. 'No, things are in a chaotic state. The people there are in favor of a limited monarchy, with constitutional government but thus far there has been no provision made in this direction. I believe that in time Persia will be one of the foremost countries in the world.'
>
> While the prophet was sitting in a chair on the stage, conversing with reporters, there was a concerted rush by the men and women in the audience to reach his side and take him by the hand. Those who failed to grasp his hand clasped the hem of his garment and with utmost reverence raised it to their lips.[15]

Another newspaperman present at the event was the reporter with *The Washington Post*. The next day the newspaper carried the following account of 'Abdu'l-Bahá's address:

BOW TO BAHAI LEADER

FOLLOWERS IN CAPITAL GREET HIGH PRIEST OF SECT

URGES BROTHERHOOD OF MAN

PERSIAN, IN ADDRESS AT PUBLIC LIBRARY, TELLS FASHIONABLE AUDIENCE OF ADVANTAGES TO BE GAINED BY UNION OF ALL RELIGIONS –

NEW SOCIETY IS ORGANIZED HERE

When Abdul Baha Abbas, the leader of the Persian Bahai movement for a universal religion, the brotherhood of man, and a universal peace, entered the lecture hall of the Public Library last night, nearly half of the 400 members and interested friends of the Persian–American Educational Society stood up and reverently bowed their heads as he passed them, which mark of worship he responded to with a right-handed salute. At the close of his address scores of fashionably gowned women rushed to the front of the hall to fondle his plain, light-brown gown, touch the hem of his skirt, or take his hand.

'I am an Oriental,' said Abul Baha through his interpreter, Dr. Fareed. 'I come to America in hopes of enlisting the aid of the various societies here in the Bahai movement founded by my father, which shall result in one religion, one human race, and peace for all time. I predict that Persia will become one of the greatest countries of the East. I desire to see a bond of religion and international peace. Persia has unlimited resources which I hope will be developed by Americans. We earnestly solicit their coming to our country.

FOR ONE HUGE BROTHERHOOD

'Cooperation is what is necessary. The intermingling of the races of the East and the West is needed to bring about this condition which we seek.

'We were placed on this world as one huge brotherhood. The oneness of the world is necessary to the progress of humanity. I was thrown into prison some years ago, and only on the solicitation of a number of crowned heads of Europe did I obtain my release. I ask assistance of all Persians in America and all others interested in education of our people. Education is what the Persian needs most now. My mission to America is to establish a bond between America and Persia and I am proud to address a gathering of Americans – the

> first to establish a conference for international peace.'
>
> Prof. Hermann Schoenfeld, of George Washington University, made a short address outlining the condition of the Persian government at the present day.[16]

The Washington Times, an independent daily newspaper with a circulation of some 40,000 copies, also published a brief account of the session:

> LEADER OF CULT URGES THE UNITY OF NATIONS
>
> Declaring for universal peace and the brotherhood of man, Abdul Baha, leader of the Bahai movement, through his interpreter, Dr. Ameen Fareed, delivered an extended address before the members of the newly launched Orient–Occident Unity, at the final session of the convention of the Unity, in the Public Library Saturday night.
>
> Scores of the followers of the beliefs promulgated by the Oriental philosopher crowded about his chair at the close of the meeting to press his hand, or touch the hem of his garment.
>
> Abdul Baha declared he came to America to enlist the interest of the country in his nation. He said the ancient grandeur of Persia was some day to be revived, and that again the 'Land of the Shas' would take its supreme place among the nations of earth. He enlarged upon the opportunities on the Orient for American capital and American industry.
>
> The leader of the Bahis will be entertained in Washington for a week, going next Sunday to Chicago, where he will address a large gathering of the cult.[17]

Writing for the *Ameriko Esperantisto*, Joseph Hannen, secretary of the Orient–Occident Unity, reported 'Abdu'l-Bahá's address at the convention, stating that 'the capacity of the Hall was taxed by an audience which overflowed into the corridors, representing probably the largest gathering ever assembled in the Library building'.[18]

In New York, the *Oriental Review* published in its May issue the text of 'Abdu'l-Bahá's talk. As noted before, the editor of this magazine, Masujiro Honda, was one of the speakers at the conference of the Orient–Occident Unity.[19]

Visit to the Universalist Church

The first church visited by the Master in the capital was the Church of Our Father, Universalist. The meeting was arranged for Sunday, 21 April, at 3:30 and the address was announced in local newspapers under the title 'Religious Unity and Philosophy'.[20]

Over one thousand people attended the meeting[21] to listen to 'Abdu'l-Bahá, who was introduced by the pastor of the church, Dr John Van Schaick.[22] In His address the Master explained that the purpose of religions is to educate mankind and to be the cause of unity. He also stressed the fundamental oneness of religions and called his audience to strive to establish peace and unity.[23]

Some reporters attended the service and on the following day accounts of it were published in at least two local newspapers. One of them was *The Washington Star*:

> ABDUL BAHA TO REMAIN IN CITY MOST OF WEEK
>
> LEADER OF BAHAI MOVEMENT WILL SPEAK AT HOWARD UNIVERSITY
>
> Abdul Baha, Abbas Effendi, leader of the world-wide Bahai movement, who reached Washington Saturday and attended the closing session Saturday night of the second annual conference of the Orient–Occident Unity, will remain in the National Capital most of the present week. He will speak tomorrow afternoon before the student body of Howard University and tomorrow night he will address an audience in the Metropolitan A.M.E. Church.
>
> Accompanied by his interpreter, Dr. Ameen Fareed, and by other members of his party, Abdul Baha yesterday afternoon visited the Church of Our Father, Universalist, and he was introduced to the congregation by the pastor, Rev. John Van Schaick Jr.
>
> TENETS OF THE MOVEMENT
>
> In an address expounding the tenets of the Bahai movement Abdul Baha said:
>
> 'It declares for the unity of all present religions, so that they may rest upon a common basis. The Bahai movement stands for the fatherhood of God and the brotherhood of man. It is very a simple religion; it is merely a faith in God free from misrepresentations.'
>
> Following the address the aged Persian held an informal

> reception, in which he shook by the hand the members of the local Bahai colony and their friends.
>
> Abdul Baha will leave Washington probably Saturday, proceeding directly to Chicago, where he is to participate in the fourth annual Bahai Convention, which opens in that city the last of this week.[24]

The *Washington Herald* published a similar account and detailed how 'All arose when, accompanied by Rev. Dr. Van Schaick, he ['Abdu'l-Bahá] ascended the platform. The pastor introduced Baha, and read to him first the confessions and tenets of his own church, which were translated to the patriarchal teacher of Bahaism, who nodded his head in silent assent.'[25]

The *Washington Times* failed to publish any reference to the address at the Church of Our Father but instead gave some information about the Master's schedule during the remaining days of His stay in Washington:

> ABDUL BAHA MAKES SIGHTSEEING TRIP OVER THE CAPITAL
>
> LEADER OF ORIENTAL CULT DELIGHTED WITH BEAUTY OF CITY
>
> Abdul Bahai, leader of the Bahai cult, after completing a thorough tour of the city, expressed himself as being delighted with the beauty of Washington. He spent most of the forenoon in seeing Washington, and this afternoon will hold the first of his afternoon meetings at the home of Mrs. Arthur J. Parsons, at Eighteenth Street, where at 4:45 followers of the Bahai cult will gather to hear their leader talk of the aims of the movement.
>
> Tomorrow at noon Abdul Baha will address the students at Howard University at chapel. Wednesday afternoon at 3 o'clock the children of Bahaists will give a reception for the leader at 1219 Connecticut Avenue. The fondness for children by the philosopher is marked, and many times in Washington he has alluded to them.
>
> The afternoon meetings will continue throughout the week, it is announced at the headquarters of the Orient–Occident Unity today, and Sunday or Monday Abdul Baha will leave Washington for Chicago, where he is to deliver addresses at the national convention of Bahai followers next week. It is expected that hundreds of followers of the oriental philosophy will gather at Chicago, representing every State in the Union.

Since arriving in Washington the Persian philosopher has received nearly a hundred cablegrams from followers in all parts of the world, congratulating him on arriving safely, and wishing him success in the propagation of the beliefs of the Bahai.[26]

Receptions at the Home of Mrs Parsons

As was the case in New York, every day in Washington large numbers would visit the Master at His temporary residence. Mrs Agnes Parsons's home was open every day from quarter to five in the afternoon to receive the many visitors wanting to see 'Abdu'l-Bahá. According to Hannen, 'The large parlor, seating 150, was crowded each afternoon, and the interest grew as the week advanced. Many persons prominent in social, official and diplomatic circles were present, besides numbers of well-known men and women of literary and scientific attainments.'[27] 'Abdu'l-Bahá would usually address His visitors collectively but sometimes He would also grant private meetings.

A reporter with the *Washington Post* was present at the reception held on Thursday, 25 April. The ensuing account revealed, among other things, that among the visitors that day was Alice Longworth,[28] the eldest daughter of former president Theodore Roosevelt.

PERSIAN PRIEST ATTRACTS SOCIETY WOMEN TO THE CULT OF BAHAISM

FOLLOWERS KISS FLOWING ROBES OF ABDUL BAHA AT HIS ADDRESS TO LEADERS OF WASHINGTON SMART CIRCLES, IN THE HOME OF MRS. ARTHUR J. PARSONS – MRS. NICHOLAS LONGWORTH AMONG THE LISTENERS – SAYS RELIGIONS MUST CONFORM TO SCIENCE.

Fashionable Washington is showing great interest in the Bahai movement since the advent of Abdul Baha, the aged leader of the 'universal' religion, who is holding daily receptions and meetings. Already he has addressed several thousand women and men. He has been reverently received, and according to people prominent in the movement, many converts have been gained since he arrived.

Garbed in flowing white robes, which contrasted strangely with the fashionable garb of his hearers, Abdul Baha talked to a large audience yesterday afternoon at the home of Mrs. Arthur Jesse Parsons, Eighteenth and R Streets Northwest, where he is stopping.

As he spoke his hearers listened with rapt attention.

Whenever Abdul Baha appears some of his followers flock to his side, seeking a chance to grasp his hand, or even to kiss his robe. To them he is inspired from Heaven. Several of the most prominent society women in the city were present yesterday.

Before beginning to talk yesterday afternoon he personally raised the shades to let in more light. As he talked he walked about the front of the large room, sometimes turning his back on the audience. Several times he evidently became warm, for he pushed his turban back on his head, and wiped his brow.

OUTLINES PURPOSES OF BAHAISM

Abdul Baha is of medium height, and wears his snowy white hair long so that it falls over his collar. His features are finely cut, and as he talks he peers into the faces of his listeners to see if they comprehend his words. He chuckles to himself frequently, when he makes a good point. His brow is high, and he has every appearance of a deep thinker. He speaks no English, and his words are translated for his hearers by an interpreter.

What Bahaism stands for was the subject he chose by request yesterday. It meant, he said, the unification of all religions. The principal point he made was that all religions which do not conform to science, and which are not reasonable, rest on superstition. He urged his listeners to cast aside everything that is not true. He declared that Jesus Christ would not have been persecuted as He was had the people of His time seen the truth clearly.

'The intellect is great and has no bounds,' he said. 'The senses of touch, smell, sight, hearing, and taste have their limits, but with the intellect men go far beyond the things their senses inform them of. With the intellect men can tell what is true, and what is good, and, therefore, it is on the intellect that they should depend.'

Abdul Baha's manner was that of a teacher, and he spoke of commonplace things as though instructing a class of children.

MRS. LONGWORTH A VISITOR

All yesterday afternoon women in automobiles and carriages arrived for private conservations with the aged leader. A few poorer people came, but most of the visitors were wealthy. He expected to take an afternoon drive, but so many were the callers that he had to postpone the trip.

Mrs. Nicholas Longworth occupied a seat far back in the audience with two other women, and seemed greatly interested in the afternoon's entertainment. She contented herself with watching Abdul Baha from a distance and listening to what he said.

The last of the afternoon meetings will be held at 4:45 o'clock today. Tonight at 8 o'clock a large public meeting will be held at the Memorial Continental Hall, when Abdul Baha, Samuel Gompers, president of the American Federation of Labor, and several others will speak. Saturday evening there will be a reception, and Sunday morning Abdul Baha leaves for Chicago.[29]

Last Meetings in Washington

Owing to the large number of people who wanted to see 'Abdu'l-Bahá, the Orient–Occident Unity arranged a further public meeting for Him on 26 April.[30] The meeting was held at the Continental Memorial Hall, an emblematic building which was built by and served as headquarters for the 'Daughters of the American Revolution'. It is thus interesting that 'Abdu'l-Bahá's address on that occasion focused on gender equality, a subject He had already touched on in an address to the Woman's Alliance held on the morning of the same day at the All Souls Unitarian Church.[31] Among the speakers who accompanied 'Abdu'l-Bahá on the platform was Samuel Gompers.

The *Washington Times* advertised the meeting in a short note which appeared on 24 April.[32] A similar note appeared on 26 April in the same newspaper stating that the meeting was to start at eight o'clock in the evening and indicating that 'The meeting will be under the auspices of the Orient–Occident Unity. Through Mirza Ahmad Sohrab, treasurer of the organization, and Joseph H. Hannen, secretary, invitations to the public to attend have been issued.'[33] Other newspapers also published announcements of the event.[34]

A reporter with the *Washington Star* who was present at the meeting wrote an account which, as well as mentioning the reception that was to be held in honor of 'Abdu'l-Bahá on His last day in the capital, also summarized the contents of 'Abdu'l-Bahá's address at the Memorial Hall:

TELLS OF BAHAI IDEALS

ABDUL BAHA PORTRAYS PRINCIPLES OF ORDER OF WHICH HE IS HEAD

The portrayal of the principles of the Bahai movement was the feature of a public meeting which was held at D. N. R. Continental Memorial Hall last night. Abdul Baha, world-leader of the Bahais, was the principal speaker, and the meeting, which was held under the auspices of the Orient–Occident Unity, marked his last public appearance in the National Capital on his present tour of the eastern states.

Abdul Baha will be the guest of honor at a reception tonight by Mrs. Arthur Jeffery Parsons at her residence, 18th and R Streets Northwest. With his suite he will leave Washington tomorrow for Chicago, where he will attend the sessions of the fourth annual Bahai convention in the United States.

DRAWS CONTRAST OF CONDITIONS

At the meeting last night Abdul Baha drew a distinct parallel between the advancement of the women of the west and the women of the east, and he cited the hall in which the meeting was held – a building constructed entirely by women – as an example of the progress of womankind in the western hemisphere.

The present advanced position of women in this country, he said, was due wholly to education. He predicted that co-education would be attained in the east, and that its accomplishment would mean that eastern women ultimately will attain the same plane as the men. Education for women in Persia was first instituted by the Bahais. Full equality of the sexes in all the walks of life was prophesied by the speaker as being certain of accomplishment.

OTHER SPEAKERS

Other speakers at the meeting were Samuel Gompers, president of the American Federation of Labor; A. C. Monohon of the United States Bureau of Education and S. E. Kramer, a supervising principal of the local public schools.[35]

In a brief report the *Washington Post* stated that 'Abdul Baha, leader of the Bahai movement, in his last public address in this city last night at the Memorial Continental Hall, made a plea for the equality of man and woman,' and added that 'Stephen E. Kramer, of the public schools, and Samuel Gompers also spoke. Mr. Kramer discussed the part which education is to play in the establishment of universal peace, while Mr. Gompers made a plea for the working classes.'[36]

The *Washington Herald*, attempting, as usual, to present a sensationalist side to the events related to 'Abdu'l-Bahá, provided further details about the meeting and reported a curious incident at its closing:

> FLAYS BAHA'S PREACHINGS
>
> 'PROPHETIC EVANGELIST' AWAITS AUDIENCE AT ABDUL'S FAREWELL
>
> Following a public meeting of the Orient–Occident Unity in Continental Memorial Hall last night, members of the audience, as they left the building, were handed printed slips by a well known local 'prophetic evangelist', in which he called attention to the danger of the Bahai movement. He said, 'of the many of this class of false Christs and Elijahs who have carried off the lame sheep from the churches, none is more deceptive than this one from the Holy Land, known as Abdul Baha.'
>
> The occasion of the meeting was the farewell address of Abdul Baha, the Bahai leader, who made his appearance later in the evening, when he repeated the underlying principles of his cult. William H. Hoar, of New York, president of the Unity, introduced the speakers.
>
> The most interesting feature of the meeting was an address by Samuel Gompers, president of the American Federation Labor, on labor conditions in America and abroad.
>
> In the audience were many Daughters of the American Revolution, with Mrs. Matthew T. Scott, president general of the society; her daughter, Mrs. Carl Krooman, and others, occupying a box.[37]

On 27 April, Agnes Parsons convened a reception and farewell dinner for 'Abdu'l-Bahá which was attended by over three hundred people. Among the participants were Admiral Peary, the famous explorer of the North Pole, and some relatives of President Taft. A brief note on the event was published the following day, 28 April, in the *New York Tribune*: 'Mrs. Arthur J. Parsons had a reception to-night in compliment to Abdul Baha, the Persian religionist, who has been lecturing here for a week.'[38] Similar information was also published in the *Washington*

Times,[39] which on a separate page also carried a note reporting 'Abdu'l-Bahá's departure from Washington and His schedule for the following weeks.[40]

An Adventist Sees 'Abdu'l-Bahá

Among the people who met the Master at His public addresses in Washington was Milton E. Kern,[41] a member of the Adventist Church and a regular contributor to the magazine *The Youth's Instructor* (Washington DC). In an article for this magazine Kern briefly mentioned 'Abdu'l-Bahá:

> A few evenings ago I stood in the aisle of a crowded hall. The audience was composed mostly of fashionable and well-to-do people of our national capital. An old man in priestly robes and Persian costume entered with his retinue. The people rose en masse to do him honor. The leader of this meeting, in introducing our Oriental visitor, expressed the opinion that the audience was about to hear such words of wisdom as had never before greeted their ears. Who was this wise man from the East? Abdul-Baha, leader of the Bahai Movement. It is said that he has six million followers, mostly in the East, but a considerable number in England and America. What is this Bahai Movement? Believing 'that creeds and dogmas of the past have lost their spiritual power, and the world is reaching out for a religion which will be a living, spiritual factor in the life of humanity,' this Eastern philosophy is offered as a universal religion, adapted to all peoples. It recognizes good in all preceding religions, heathen, Mohammedan, and Christian, endeavors to harmonize science and religion, and concerns itself with temporal matters mainly, peace and progress, a religion well adapted to the unregenerate heart, in love with modern culture.

As a convinced Christian, Kern's article went on to state that only Christ 'can satisfy the longing of the sin-sick soul'.[42] The article was reprinted years later.[43]

12

CHICAGO

29 April – 6 May 1912

As in New York and Washington, 'Abdu'l-Bahá's visit to Chicago was announced in the press weeks before His arrival. On 13 April, for instance, an article by Louis Gregory with some introductory notes on the Bahá'í Faith appeared in the *Chicago Defender*. The same day an editorial appearing in the *Chicago Post* called for an appreciation of 'the real worth of the venerable leader':

> ABDUL BAHA AND CHICAGO
>
> Abdul Baha, the leader of the impressive Bahai movement which has sprung up in the Mohatmmedan world, is coming to Chicago this month to attend – strange to say – the international conference of the people of his faith.
>
> It seems odd that a movement which is still, to most people, a Persian phenomenon should propose actually to hold its annual gathering in the heart of the United States. But that seems to be the case, and one can only judge of the real extent of its cosmopolitanism by observing the conference itself.
>
> It is a pity that Abdul Baha has to talk through an interpreter. It would be hard to find anybody coming out of the Mohammedan world whose views of Christianity and the Western world would be more interesting or even impressive. The Bahai movement, with its large generalizations of the universal brotherhood of man, the unity of all religions and creeds, and of universal tolerance and peace, affords a splendid scale upon which to measure Western achievements. But this can't be easily conveyed through an interpreter.
>
> While Chicago is hospitable to cults and movements, it is, at the

> same time, rather inclined to lump them all together, to judge them from the features which seem to our eyes to be bizarre. But it would be a pity if this habitual discounting of Eastern faiths should mean that in our local treatment of the Bahai conference the real worth of the venerable leader of that faith should be unappreciated. Nothing could be more inept, more discreditable to our own intelligence, than to put this venerable Persian teacher in the fakir class. At the Universal Congress of Races last year he seems to have made a deep impression upon the delegates, and they were men of the highest intellectual attainments. The Bahai faith will not silence the thousand raucous noises of the City of Chicago in this year of grace, but it will probably encourage some to reflect afresh upon the large irenic generalizations which inspire the Abdul Baha and his followers.[1]

In ensuing days, other articles announcing the arrival of 'Abdu'l-Bahá in Chicago were published in the local press.[2] Outside Chicago a syndicated article signed by O. Terence was published in some newspapers. Terence gave a general summary of the Bahá'í Faith, announced the presence in Chicago of 'Abdu'l-Bahá and closed the article stating the following:

> Abdul Baha, with his wonderfully penetrating eyes, his wealth of silvery hair and long white beard, and his thoughtful and philosophic air, would be a striking figure if clad in conventional garb. In the costume of the Persian scholar and in white turban on his head, he is more than striking. The doctrines he teaches are strictly modern. Science is the handmaiden of the new religion, declared Abdul Baha, and he looks to the inventors and thinkers to create a new heaven on earth. Although not a Socialist, he teaches many economic 'isms' that are akin to the Marxian gospel of cooperation. While holding economic equality between men, he asserts that the present wide gulf between rich and poor is of artificial creation and that the laws of nations must be changed so as to prevent alike extreme wealth and dire poverty. He believes that women should have the same political rights as men.[3]

After an entire day's journey by train from Washington 'Abdu'l-Bahá arrived in Chicago late in the afternoon of Monday, 29 April. During His sojourn in the city He stayed at the Plaza Hotel.

The program of the Master for His first days in Chicago was a strenuous one. On His first morning in the city He received a group of newspaper reporters, held receptions for large groups of people coming to the Plaza and visited some Bahá'ís at their homes. In the afternoon He addressed the public gathered in two sessions of the Annual Conference of the National Association for the Advancement of Colored People (see chapter 32, vol. 2) and in the evening He spoke at a session of the Fourth Annual Bahá'í Convention (27 April – 2 May) organized by the Bahá'í Temple Unity. In total, on Tuesday 30 April over three thousand people listened to the Master's words.[4]

Interviews with the Master

According to Maḥmúd, on the very same night that 'Abdu'l-Bahá arrived in Chicago some newspapermen telephoned asking for appointments to interview Him. They were invited to come on the following day and on Tuesday morning the Master received at the Plaza reporters from the major Chicago newspapers. However, a reporter with the *Record-Herald*, an independent newspaper with a circulation of nearly 205,000 copies, managed to see 'Abdu'l-Bahá the night that He arrived. The article that ensued was quite caustic and sensationalistic in its tone:

> BAHAIST LEADER OPENS ORIENTAL COURT HERE
>
> PERSIAN HIGH PRIEST OF UNIVERSAL BROTHERHOOD CULT GREETS HOST OF FOLLOWERS.
>
> FAITHFUL FLOCK TO THRONE
>
> ABDUL-BAHA, 'SERVANT OF INEFFABLE SPLENDOR', ADVISER TO 40,000,000 THROUGH WORLD
>
> An oriental court that sways the destinies of 40,000,000 persons throughout the world has been established temporarily in Chicago.
>
> Abdul-Baha, leader of the Bahaist movement, is the ruler. He has come to America to preach the doctrines of universal brotherhood and world-wide peace.
>
> The aged priest, attended by a retinue of Persians and Americans, arrived in Chicago last night. He had been 'lost' all day to local Bahaists, who were awaiting anxiously his arrival from Washington.
>
> The Persian's dislike for publicity led to strenuous but vain efforts on the part of his personal bodyguard to keep his arrival secret.

He was bundled into a limousine the moment he arrived and was whizzed away to the Plaza Hotel.

‘INNER CIRCLE‘ ADMITTED

None but Persians were permitted to enter the presence of the ‘Servant of the ineffable Splendor’ during his first few hours at the hotel. Later a favored few, comprising the ‘inner circle’ of the cult, were allowed to pass through the suite and to touch his hand.

The high priest sat in a big plush chair during the brief reception. He wore a long, flowing robe, striped with red and white. His beard reached almost to his waist. A turban of the same material as the robe was wound about his head.

A half dozen Persians stood about the ‘throne’. A dozen or more American women from Huston, New York and Washington, formed the background. Hardly a word was spoken.

After the reception the priest again went into seclusion. It was announced that he was dining. Abdul-Baha has his own native cook.

In the evening Abdul-Baha held another reception. One hundred followers flocked to his apartments, which were filled with costly flowers. The priest gave all a cordial welcome. He had changed his costume of the afternoon for one of cream color and wore a white turban.

‘I admire this great city from what I know of it,’ said the priest through his interpreter. ‘It is a city beautiful in a material way. The time is coming when it will be beautiful in a spiritual way as well.’

FOLLOWERS HOPE FOR SIGHT

Followers of Baha from all parts of the world, who are in Chicago for their annual international convention, are hoping that the high priest will honor their meetings today with his presence.

‘We hope that he will honor us by his presence,’ said Dr. Frederic N. Nutt, president of the executive board of the movement in Chicago, ‘but it is not for us to suggest anything to him. He does as he wills.’

The priest is expected to attend an open meeting of the cult to be held tonight in the drill hall of the Masonic Temple. Through his interpreter, who is his nephew, he may make a short speech. This morning he will receive all who care to meet him in his apartments.

> Abdul-Baha has come to Chicago principally for the purpose of consecrating the plot of ground in Wilmette where the Mashrak-el-Azkar (Dawning Point of Prayer), a house of worship, will be built this summer by local Bahaists. The ceremonies will be held Wednesday afternoon . . .[5]

By the time 'Abdu'l-Bahá received reporters from other local newspapers on Tuesday morning, He had already been informed about this article, its improper tone and its false statements regarding, for instance, His dress. Thus when He addressed the journalists He made some remarks about the mission of journalism and requested the reporters to be truthful and honest in their chronicles. He also presented for them some Bahá'í principles, announced His schedule while in Chicago, and offered an introduction to the history of the Faith.

One of the reporters that visited the Plaza was with the *Daily News*, an independent evening newspaper with a circulation of some 323,000 copies. While not devoid of a certain measure of satire, the account that ensued offers a vivid picture of the press meeting:

> BAHA IS PEACE HERALD
>
> APOSTLE OF CULT GREETS FOLLOWERS HERE AFTER THEY HAVE WAITED PATIENTLY.
>
> 'MARHABA' IS FIRST WORD
>
> 'REALITY, ONE AND NOT MULTIPLE', SAYS LEADER IN EXPLAINING PRINCIPLES OF BELIEF
>
> Abdul Baha Abbas, son of Baha'o'llah, whose coming was foretold by The Bab in the early days of Bahaism, to-day spoke of newspaper reporters and universal brotherhood and peace in his first Chicago interview. The venerable leader of the Bahaists arrived last night from Washington, D.C., after Chicago followers had passed an anxious morning and afternoon meeting inward bound trains and trying to account for his non-arrival. Some ceremony was necessary before a delegation of reporters was ushered into the presence of the son of Baha'u'llah.
>
> First, it was necessary to communicate with Ameen Fareed, his nephew and interpreter. A little later word was sent that the delegation would be admitted.

REMAINS OF FRUGAL BREAKFAST

Without the door of the Plaza hotel suite a dish of radishes and celery, sprinkled with water, was discovered. This was part of the breakfast of Abdul Baha, who has in company a Persian cook. On the door was a sign, which read:

'Don't ring the bell. Knock softly.'

One of the delegation knocked softly. Ameen Fareed opened the door and down a long corridor ushered the visitors to the room of 'the master'.

'Marhaba!' said a voice from the sunshiny room, speaking the Persian word of welcome.

Abdul Baha looked at each of his visitors intently from under white, bushy eyebrows. His dark skin was interlaced with numberless fine wrinkles. He wore a gray-white beard. His forehead was high and surmounted by a fez turban of fawn and cream color. His rather long hair hung in a single curl over the nape of his neck and to his shoulder blades. He wore a fawn colored robe with a cream sash, striped with a simple delicate pink and blue stripe, over which was a black garment. On his feet were congress gaiters.

He motioned his visitors to a seat and sat himself in a rocking chair near the bed. He allowed his glance to roam over the flower decorated room before he spoke through his interpreter.

REPORTER MUST PURVEY TRUTH

'A reporter must be a purveyor of truth,' he said in Persian and Ameen Fareed translated. 'The newspapers are leaders of the people and the people must be able to rely on what they read. Now, some reporter on a Chicago morning newspaper said that I wore a gown and turban with red and white stripes. I never wore such colors. He said my beard reached to my waist. Look at it.'

The beard in truth, came scarcely to the chest of Abdul Baha. As the leader spoke, several of his suite peered through the green curtains at the door. 'The master' spoke of the teaching of the Bahai.

First he spoke of the beginning of the movement in 1844, the coming of the Bab, his martyrdom and the life of exile inflicted on his father, Baha'o'llah. He passed over in a sentence his own imprisonment of forty years with his parent in the Turkish penal colony of Akka, in Syria, from which he was released with the change of government in 1908.

SUMMING UP OF TEACHINGS

The interpretation of his summing up of the Bahai teachings, in brief, is:

'First, that which concerns the investigation of reality; all prophetic foundations were considered by Baha'o'llah to be one in fundamental reality. Reality is one and not multiple, not divisible. His holiness, Abraham, was the herald of reality; his holiness, Moses, was the herald of this reality. His Holiness, Jesus Christ, was the founder of this reality. His holiness, Baha'o'llah, was the light of this reality. Therefore, the reality of all the divine religion is one. The difference is only in imitations.

'The second principle of Baha'o'llah is the oneness of humanity. All the people are the servants of God.

SCIENCE AND RELIGION TWINS

'Thirdly, science and religion are twins. Science is the reality and the religion is the reality. If religion differs from science it is superstition. Fourth, religion must be conducive to the unity of mankind. Fifth, religious prejudice, racial prejudice, patriotic prejudice, the prejudice of interests and political prejudice are the very destroyers of the body politic.

'Sixth, the establishment of a most great peace. Seventh is the equality between man and woman. Woman must be educated and trained in order to reach the status of mind equal to man.'

With a wave of his wrinkled, though powerful looking, hand Abdul Baha tokened an end of the interview. As he said farewell to each of his visitors he presented them with a red apple from a heaped fruit dish. 'To-day I shall pass looking about your city,' he said. 'It is such a great place. In this country the flag of universal peace must first fly. The American democracy is the one to cope with the problem.'

POSES FOR PHOTOGRAPHER

A newspaper photographer interrupted the solemn farewell. For him Abdul Baha changed his dull black outer robe to a lighter, fur lined covering and adjusted his turban in the mirror before posing.

'You said you wished just a minute,' he smiled after the camera had clicked some half dozen times. 'You have taken several, very good, very good.'

Then, with another shake all around the farewell was said. Out in the first room of the suite a crowd of Chicago Bahaists were waiting to gaze upon Abdul Baha.[6]

The Chicago *Evening Post*, a newspaper with a circulation of 60,000 copies, published the following account, which also included some lines – not reproduced here – about the Bahá'í Faith and the Bahá'í Convention that was being held at the time:

BAHA BRINGS WORD TO CITY

MYSTIC RELIGIOUS LEADER THANKS TOWN FOR WELCOME

HOPES TO SEE ESTABLISHMENT HERE THE 'DAWNING POINT OF PRAYER' AND BELIEVES WE'LL BE HEADQUARTERS FOR UNIVERSAL PEACE

Though East be East and West be West the twain clasped hands in Chicago in a ceremony more picturesque and more filled with the mysticism of the Orient than has fallen to the lot of a youthful city of the Occident in all past history.

Brilliant robes flashed and silent, dusky servitors made obeisance with oriental grace before their advancing master, Abdul-Baha, 'servant of the ineffable splendor', as he moved abroad from his apartments at the Plaza Hotel, turned for the nonce into an oriental court . . .

Cessation of all conflict, whether between nations, classes or differences of belief, was declared to be the main object of Bahaism, at the convention of Bahaists, which opened this morning in Corinthian Hall at the Masonic Temple.

Meanwhile, though Abdul-Baha did not attend the convention, he received newspaper men at his apartments at the Plaza. His attendants had spoken with anxiety of an important engagement which would take all of their master's time, but he showed truly oriental patience and diplomacy, without a trace of hurry, in his reception of the representatives of the press.

NO FOE TO OTHER CREEDS

He answered quietly all the questions relating to the faith for whose spread he has come to America, explaining that it is not opposed to any existing religious faith, that a man may be a Christian, and continue to worship as he has always worshiped and still join hands with others throughout the world in an effort to secure a more universal understanding and sympathy.

Though all his speech had to be translated from the Persian by his nephew, who acted as interpreter, he sat patiently during the long periods in which he had to be silent while his meaning was explained. When the interview was at an end, he good-naturedly agreed to pose while innumerable snap shots were taken of him, and when it was suggested that he don another robe that was considered more picturesque, he consented to that.

The ceremony of dedication of the temple grounds will take place tomorrow morning at 11 o'clock in Wilmette. A reception for Abdul-Baha will be given Thursday afternoon in the red room of the Hotel La Salle by the Bahai Woman's Assembly.[7]

The reporter with the *Evening American*, a Democratic newspaper of the Hearst Group with a circulation of 324,000 copies, was also present at the reception and wrote a shorter report in which it was observed that the Master 'displayed surprising up-to-dateness in commenting upon modern customs':

BAHAIST CHIEF FOR SUFFRAGE

Garbed in long, flowing robes and a white fez, Abdul-Baha, 'Servant of the Ineffable Splendor' and leader of 40,000,000 Bahaists, held an Oriental Court at the Plaza Hotel to-day at which he dispensed snow apples and Persian philosophy.

Here to attend a conference of the leaders of his cult in the United States, the venerable looking priest discussed the doctrines of universal brotherhood and world-wide peace which are the foundation stones of his religion. Also he displayed surprising up-to-dateness in commenting upon modern customs.

Abdul Baha, who is the son of Baha-Ollah, founder of the Bahaist religion, who died in prison because of his advocacy of universal peace, took exception to some of the speeches attributed to him and descriptions of his habits of living.

'The press is a wonderful thing, an amazing influence on the spread of thought,' he declared. 'Journalists wield the greatest of modern influences. Therefore the press should be a synonym of integrity; its veracity should never be questioned.'

He also pronounced himself to be in sympathy with the suffrage movement.

'Women should be trained so that they may become the intellectual and religious equals of men; they should be their political equals also,' he declared.

'If religion disagrees with science then it becomes mere superstition, and if religion creates discord then irreligion becomes preferable.'[8]

Another evening newspaper, *The Chicago Journal*, at the time the oldest newspaper in the city with a circulation of nearly 127,000 copies, published the following account:

THRONG HOTEL TO GREET LEADER OF BAHAISTS

FOLLOWERS GATHER AS ABDUL BAHA ABBAS ARRIVES, EACH GUEST BEING GIVEN AN APPLE

Long before Abdul Baha Abbas, 'great teacher' and ruler of the 40,000,000 Bahaists throughout the world, awoke today, many fashionably dressed men and women awaited in the corridors and the lobby of the Hotel Plaza to greet the 70-year-old leader of the cult started by Baha 'Ollah in far off Persia.

Abdul Baha granted to Mrs. M. A. True, 5338 Kenmore Avenue, the honor of the first official visit that he was to make to the homes of Chicago's society.

After holding 'court' at his suite for almost two hours, he and his secretary, Dr. Ameen U. Fareed, who is also his interpreter, were taken in an automobile to the True home, and after a brief visit there were taken to homes of other prominent Bahaists.

Abdul Baha came here primarily to attend the convention of his followers, now going on at the Masonic temple.

'I may attend the convention late this afternoon,' he said in Persian. 'I have no set program, even as to the time I am to remain in Chicago. I am moved by circumstances.

'I am not trying to hide, as some said, and I never will. I like to meet my fellow men, regardless of race, creed or nationality.'

The aged leader, dressed in the robes and fez of a scholar of the Oriental countries, was democratic in his reception to all.

He greeted each visitor with a hearty handshake, and gave each an apple when he excused him.[9]

The Day Book, a Scripps group journal with no advertisements, published the following editorial about the arrival of 'Abdu'l-Bahá in Chicago:

THE LEADER OF BAHAIST MOVEMENT IS IN TOWN

One of the kindliest, most lovable men in the world is in Chicago today.

He is Abdul Baha, leader of the Bahaist movement.

Bahaism has been called an Oriental cult, a new religion. It is neither one nor the other. It is merely Abdul Baha. And Abdul Baha is a man who loves his fellow men, and who carries his love for them into every word he utters, into his every deed.

Bahaism is just the practice of universal kindliness, universal brotherhood, universal love.

Abdul Baha is an old man now. He has many followers, and is accorded great respect by them. His paths are not hard.

But it was different in his youth: when first he began to preach his doctrine of love and forgiveness in his native Persia he was persecuted.

The Mohammedans of his native land hated him. How could they, worshipers of the sword as they are, do otherwise?

He was driven from city to city, from village to village. There were times when he had no food to eat, when he had not a place to lay his head.

He was driven from his native land. He took refuge in Stamboul and there again felt the lash of persecution.

Yet he never spoke bitterly of his enemies, never denounced them, never cursed them. He went his simple, kindly way, saying they knew not what they did.

Abdul Baha arrived in Chicago this forenoon. A limousine was waiting him and he was whirled to the Plaza Hotel, where he has been closeted in his room all day, resting after his journey from Washington.[10]

On Wednesday, 1 May, the *Chicago Examiner*, a Hearst morning newspaper with 215,000 daily copies, published an article about the Master in which He was described as having 'deep, penetrating eyes of a prophet of old, looking very much the sort of Biblical patriarch'. In the course of the interview 'Abdu'l-Bahá mentioned Ella Wheeler Wilcox, who interviewed Him in New York for one of her syndicated articles (see chapter 10 above).

PROPHET ABDUL BAHA HERE

CHICAGOANS HONOR PERSIAN APOSTLE OF WORLD-WIDE RELIGION

RECEIVES FOLLOWERS; DECLARES HIMSELF SUFFRAGIST; WILL CONSECRATE TEMPLE SITE

In sacerdotal robes of 'the master' of the Bahai movement, with the deep, penetrating eyes of a prophet of old, looking very much the sort of Biblical patriarch that Dore might have painted, Abdul Baha is in Chicago, making this city temporarily the capital of a religious movement that is said to have 15,000,000 followers throughout the world.

In his suite at the Plaza Hotel, the distinguished Persian teacher was the object of reverential obeisance on the part of Persian and American followers who gathered there. With women gowned in blue robes and turbans, the men garbed in flowing robes and fezzes, his rooms had the appearance of an Oriental court.

INTERPRETERS WITH HIM

When the apostle of world-wide religion entered the reception room there was a hush and all rose respectfully. He motioned them to be seated, accompanying the gesture with a few words in Persian. A lofty, deeply furrowed brow was surmounted by a cream-colored turban. His beard almost white. His eyes, deep sunken beneath his shaggy eyebrows, flashed the vigor of a man who, despite his seventy years, might be said to have no age. Though his followers call him the 'master', he named himself the 'servant'.

Dr. Ameen Fareed, his nephew, acted as interpreter when the 'master' received the newspaper men. Through him he explained that the teachings of Bahaism were the broad general principles of religion which all creeds and nationalities could accept.

'It has for its object a universal religion, a world-wide brotherhood of man and international peace,' he said.

Christian ministers yesterday opened their pulpits to Abdul Baha, and on the invitation of the Rev. Joseph A. Millburn he will preach next Sunday at 11 a.m. to the Plymouth Congregational Church, 2535 Michigan Avenue. Sunday evening he will occupy Jenkin Lloyd Jones's pulpit at All Souls' Church, Oakwood Boulevard and Langley Avenue.

TEACHINGS ARE BROAD

He explains that his teachings are not opposed to any existing religion, and that the movement does not concern itself with details that lead to doctrinal controversies. His teachings as to the 'fundamentals of progress', as explained through his interpreter, are 'the love of God in the love of Mankind in general, long suffering, steadfastness, truth, compassion, generosity, bravery, perseverance, activity, purity, cheerfulness, modesty, zeal, resolution, high-mindedness, wisdom, intellect, sobriety, true piety, and, above all, the fear of God within the heart'.

With a glance at his women followers, Abdul Baba declared his belief in equal suffrage for both sexes.

'He believes,' the interpreter explained, 'if women were educated with the same advantages as men their capacity would be the same; in fact, women are superior to men; they are more receptive, more sensitive, their intuition is more intense.'

CONSECRATES TEMPLE HERE

To the reporter for the *Chicago Examiner*, Abdul Baha said he recalled meeting in New York Mrs. Ella Wheeler Wilcox, whose writings on the subject of Oriental religions, following a tour of the world, attracted widespread attention and comment.

The high priest is a son of Baha'o'llah, founder of the Bahai movement. For forty years the son was held a prisoner by Abdul Hamid, then Sultan of Turkey. His chief mission in Chicago is to consecrate the ground on which a temple is to be built in Wilmette, the spot having been named Mashrak-el-Azker, the Dawning Point of Prayer.

> LOVE IS RELIGION
>
> 'Love is the universal religion,' said Baha in an address to the Chicago assembly of his followers last evening in the Drill Hall of the Masonic Temple. 'Love unites the East and the West. It is the invisible power that unifies all mankind. It transcends racial differences, it sweeps aside all differences of creed, and it is the great regenerating force of the world, bringing in its train all good things and making peace and amity among the nations.
>
> 'The Bahai philosophy is simplicity itself. It is expressed in this short quotation from one of Baha'o'llah's writings: "The root of all knowledge is the knowledge of God." Each of the world's great spiritual teachers has taught the same eternal truth. This truth has ever been the mainspring and source of human advancement and civilization.'
>
> Baha went about Chicago preaching love. He visited Hull House on the invitation of Miss Jane Addams and gave a talk in the assembly room.[11]

The *Evening American*, which shared ownership with the *Examiner*, published a summary of this article on the same day.[12]

Another morning newspaper, the Republican *Inter-Ocean*, which had a circulation of 80,000 copies, repeated some of the information about the arrival of the Master that had appeared the previous day in various evening newspapers.[13] This newspaper also published on 2 May a brief editorial note about the Master's comments on journalism: 'Abdul Baha, "Servant of Ineffable Splendor", has arrived in Chicago from Persia to establish a world-wide peace between religion and science, but feels a little doubtful of our newspapers because a reporter wrote that he wore a robe and turban of red and white stripes – which he never did; so there!'[14]

As a curious note of 'Abdu'l-Bahá's first days in Chicago, an anecdote involving the Christian Catholic Apostolic Church, could be mentioned here.

This cult was created by the eccentric John A. Dowie (1847–1907) in an attempt to restore primitive Christianity and had some followers in the Chicago area. One of them was Rupert Deveraux Jonas, who in an interview with the *Examiner* expressed his belief that 'Abdu'l-Bahá might be the 'teacher' they were expecting:

BELIEVE ABDUL BAHA MAY BE SECOND DOWIE

Asserting their belief that the mantle of the late John Alexander Dowie may have descended upon Abdul Baha, the Persian religious teacher and leader of the great Bahai movement, followers of the Dowie Church in Zion City invited Baha to visit their colony to-day. The master of Bahaism was uncertain whether to accept, but Rupert Deveraux of Zion City was certain he would come.

'Nineteen hundred and twelve is the year during which according to Dr. Dowie's prediction a new prophet is to appear in Zion,' said Deveraux. 'We believe that Baha may be the teacher who is appointed to lead us out of our troubles.'

Abdul Baha accepted an invitation to address a meeting of suffrage workers this evening at the Hotel La Salle.

'I believe in suffrage for women,' he said, 'but no, it should not be striven for by window-smashing, and by what are called militant methods.'[15]

Fourth Annual Bahá'í Convention

On 30 April, after His address at the closing session of the conference of the NAACP, 'Abdu'l-Bahá visited the evening session of the Bahá'í Convention. This national meeting had started three days earlier and the consultation of the delegates that arrived from different parts of the country centered principally on the construction of the future Bahá'í House of Worship.[16]

As mentioned earlier, 'Abdu'l-Bahá was expected to arrive in Chicago before He actually did so, and this caused some problems for the organizers. Using a sensationalist tone, the *Daily News* on 29 April mentioned this circumstance in an article for which several Bahá'ís at the Convention were interviewed.[17]

The session in which 'Abdu'l-Bahá participated was held at the Drill Hall of the Masonic Temple and was the last of the Convention's public sessions. Both journalists and the general public were allowed to attend. The presence of 'Abdu'l-Bahá attracted so much attention that no less than one thousand people were assembled to listen to His talk on the purpose of the houses of worship and on the theme of unity.[18]

A reporter on the *Chicago Tribune*, a Republican newspaper with a circulation of 220,000 copies a day, was present at the address and wrote the following account:

WANTS CITY BAHAIST CENTER

BAHA URGES FOLLOWERS TO TAKE LEAD IN WORLD PEACE.

SPEAKS TO BIG AUDIENCE

BAHAISTS BEGIN CONVENTION; DELEGATES FROM SEVERAL NATIONS ATTEND

Abdul Baha, prophet of universal peace and one religion, was greeted by a big audience of men and women last night when he made his first appearance in public in Chicago at a meeting of Bahaists in the Drill Hall of the Masonic temple. Every person in the hall, which was crowded to the point where it was difficult to keep the aisles open, rose when the Persian religious leader entered the room.

Baha was garbed in native Persian garments of tan color and a white turban. He does not speak English, so his address was translated, sentence by sentence.

SEES DAWN OF WORLD PEACE

'The ages of darkness have passed away,' he cried with a gesture, half to the interpreter, half to the audience. 'The century of light has arrived. The difference between the nations and between the peoples of the earth is soon to disappear and the oneness of the human race is to be established.

'Let this American democracy become glorious in a spiritual degree as it has in a material degree. Let this just government and this revered nation hoist the standard of oneness of all humanity. Let it become the most glorious and praiseworthy of all the world.'

WANT CHICAGO CENTER OF CULT

The prophet is in Chicago to attend the Bahaist convention, which began yesterday He was not present at the opening session, but sent the following message:

'Men and women of Chicago, your city was the first in all America to open its arms to those things for which Bahaism stands. It has long been the desire closest to my heart to see established here beside this beautiful sparkling blue lake the Mashrak-el-azkar, Dawning Point of Prayer, the inspiration for a peace and brotherhood that is universal.'

All day yesterday the leader received local Bahaists at the Plaza Hotel. Delegates from all over America and from several other nations are attending the convention. This morning at 11 o'clock the prophet will dedicate the site for the proposed Bahaist temple in Wilmette.[19]

The following editorial was published in the same issue of the *Tribune*:

THE BALM OF ABDUL

We have with us at present Abdul Baha Abbas, son of Baha'u'llah, Glory of God, third prophet of the Bahaists, on a mission. As missions go it is not an old one, in the specific form in which Abdul Baha brings it to us. It was declared first by Mirza Ali Mohammad, who was born in Shiraz, Persia, in 1819, and who was shot at Tabriz six years after he had become a prophet. It was carried on by Baha'u'llah, Glory of God, who passed most of a hard life in prison or in exile.

The mission thus tempestuously born is one of universal brotherhood and peace, a universal religion of inter-racial amity. From Baha'u'llah the torch was passed to Abdul Baha, his son, and thus it comes to Chicago, the prophet being on a tour which has carried him to the Bahaists in Europe and America.

It is a noble mission, even if one which will not progress according to its merits. The prophet finds us given over to wrath and contention, suspicious of our neighbors and vexed within ourselves. The mind is not slow to anger, nor are causes and provocations lacking. It is moving time, the Mexicans rage to the south, and politics bubbles as it were in a caldron over a hot fire. Possibly there will be a balm in Abdul Baha to soothe sore disturbed minds and iron out the kinks in tempers. That as it may be, but Abdul Baha is welcome to our midst with the mission declared by Mirza Ali Mohammad.[20]

Also on 1 May the *Record-Herald* published an account of the public session of the Bahá'í Convention at which details of the plans for the construction of the Mashriqu'l-Adhkár were discussed. The author of this article attributed to 'Abdu'l-Bahá statements that were actually taken from other newspapers.[21]

Wednesday, 1 May 1912: Dedication of the Bahá'í Temple

The highlight of the Bahá'í Convention was to be the dedication of the site for the erection of the first Bahá'í house of worship of the West. On 1 May the *Daily Journal* announced that 'Abdul Baha Abbas, "great teacher" and ruler of the Bahaists, now in convention in Chicago, is to dedicate the site at Winnetka today for the proposed temple to universal peace and brotherhood'.[22] A brief account of the ceremony of dedication appeared on the same day in the *Evening Post*:

BAHAIST SITE DEDICATED

PROPHET OF UNIVERSAL PEACE CONSECRATES PLOT TO CAUSE

BRIEF CEREMONY MARKS EXERCISES ON NORTH SHORE AFTER

DISCOURSE ON AMERICA IS GIVEN AT THE PLAZA HOTEL

Chicago turned back the hands of time today for a pastoral spring epic on its North Shore hills that might have graced the shores of the Mediterranean.

His patriarchal beard waving in the wind on the crest of a wooded and grass covered hill overlooking Lake Michigan at the mouth of the drainage canal, Abdul Baha, prophet of universal peace and the brotherhood of the races, dedicated the site of his western temple this afternoon.

Hundreds of women in gaily colored spring costumes, and here and there Persians with heads covered with oriental fezzes, added to the picturesqueness of the general tableu. A brilliant white tent, pitched to guard against the threatening rain, flapped in the wind.

Abdul Baha was in somber European garb on his arrival at the temple grounds, which are on a commanding knoll, overlooking the new and handsome bridge by which Sheridan Road crosses the drainage canal. To the northeastward there was presented a broad view of the lake, sparklingly blue in spite of the cloudy skies, while to the west there stretched grassy meadows, across which knots of belated pilgrims were hurrying to the temple grounds.

The ceremony by which the Mashrak-el-Azkar (Dawning Point of Prayer) was dedicated was simple and brief. Abdul Baha spoke a brief ritual in Persian, waved his hands and the ground was turned over to its future use. Early in the day, however, he had received his followers at the Plaza Hotel and had given them for the first time a glimpse of American civilization through his eyes.[23]

The following day the *Record-Herald* briefly reported that: 'The high priest closed the Unity Convention yesterday with the consecration of the plot at Wilmette, where the Bahai temple is to be erected. The ceremony consisted in turning of a spade full of earth and a short address by the Persian.'[24]

The schedule of 'Abdu'l-Bahá prevented Him from arriving at the dedication at the expected time. The *Daily News* reported only this circumstance in its article about the event.[25] News of the dedication of the Bahá'í temple was also echoed outside the United States. In England *The Christian Commonwealth* (London) published its account of the event:

ABDUL BAHA IN AMERICA

DEDICATION OF THE MASKRAK-EI-AZKAR

The culminating event of Abdul Baha's visit to the United States – the dedication of the site of the first temple of Bahaism in America, 'the Maskrak-El-Azkar' (literally, 'the Dawning Point of the Mentions of God') – very fittingly took place on May 1, a day devoted, the world over, to the spirit of international brotherhood. The spot chosen for the temple is in the neighborhood of Chicago, where the ground slopes down to meet the waters of Lake Michigan. The ceremony in the great amphitheatre afforded by the thick woods, the fields, and the expanse of water was very beautiful, and symbolic at the same time of the Bahai movement, which has arisen to proclaim the day of 'the Most Great Peace' and the solidarity of humanity.

With an axe and shovel, tools of the everyday workers of the world, Abdul Baha and his friends excavated a resting place for the foundation stone, which had been brought to the spot as a living contribution by earnest Bahais from both east and west. No formal programme had been prepared in advance, but under the immediate inspiration of the moment this initial labour was made typical of the united and harmonious voluntary services of every nation, kindred, and tongue, as some native son or daughter, called by name by Dr. Fareed, in turn took hold of axe or shovel. Persia, Syria, Egypt, India, South Africa, England, France, Germany, Holland, Denmark, the Jews of the world, the North American Indians, were among the races and countries thus successively represented. Finally, Abdul Baha did the closing-work, and consigned the stone to its excavation on behalf of all the peoples of the world.

During his stay in Chicago the Prophet of the Bahais made his headquarters at the Plaza Hotel. It was his delight to stroll morning and evening in the beautiful Lincoln Park, which extends northward from the hotel for several miles along Lake Michigan. From Chicago Abdul Baha proceeded to Cleveland, Ohio.[26]

A translation of this article was published in *Sophia* (Madrid), the organ of the Spanish Theosophical Society.[27]

Sunday, 5 May 1912: Address at All Souls' Church

'Abdu'l-Bahá accepted invitations to speak at two of Chicago churches, the Plymouth Congregational Church and the Unitarian All Souls' Church. The *Record-Herald* briefly reported that 'Abdul-Baha will remain in Chicago until Monday. Christian ministers have opened their pulpits to him and on the invitation of Rev. Joseph A. Milburn he will preach next Sunday morning in the Plymouth Congregational Church at 2535 Michigan Avenue. Sunday evening he will occupy Jenkin Lloyd Jones' pulpit at All Souls' Church, Oakwood Boulevard and Langley Avenue.'[28] As described above, the *Examiner* and the *Evening American* also announced His visit to the All Souls' Church in their articles of 1 May.[29]

None of 'Abdu'l-Bahá's addresses seems to have received attention from the local press. Months later, however, *Harper's Weekly* published a general article on the Bahá'í Faith by Charles Johnston that included portions of 'Abdu'l-Bahá's talk at All Souls'.[30] The Unitarian magazine *Unity* (Chicago), edited by Lloyd Jones and with a circulation of some 2,250 copies, published on May 16 an article on the Bahá'í Faith based on Harrold Johnson's article in the *Contemporary Review* which briefly stated regarding 'Abdu'l-Bahá's visit to All Souls' that 'a large assembly gathered to hear him, representing a wide range of races, intelligence and geographic locations', but criticized His message as too simple.[31]

It is interesting to note here that Jenkin Lloyd Jones[32] had heard about the Bahá'í Faith as early as 1893 when, as one of the organizers, he was present at the session of the World Parliament of Religions where the name of Bahá'u'lláh was mentioned in public for the first time in North America. On 27 January 1918, Lloyd Jones devoted his Sunday sermon to an introduction of the Bahá'í Faith to his parish.[33]

Articles Published after the Departure of 'Abdu'l-Bahá

On the morning of 6 May 'Abdu'l-Bahá left for Cleveland. After His departure at least one more article was published about His visit to Chicago. On 12 May, the society writer of the *Chicago Tribune*, Mme. X (Caroline Kirkland),[34] published a short article in which she recalled the first time she heard about the Bahá'í Faith. 'The spectacle of the reverend, white robed and white turbaned figure of the new Persian Prophet, Abdul Baha, riding around our teeming, modern streets in an automobile, was rather startling last week', stated the author, 'It was as if some personality of the Old or New Testament had appeared in our midst. Much has been written about him and his mission here, so I will only call attention to the fact that many thoughtful and intelligent people have been drawn into his following.'

13

CLEVELAND

6–7 May 1912

'Abdu'l-Bahá arrived in Cleveland on the afternoon of Tuesday, 6 May. He stayed in the city for only one day, during which He gave an address for the local Bahá'ís and a public talk in the hotel where He was to stay, the Euclid.[1]

Weeks before His arrival the local press had already announced that it was possible that 'Abdu'l-Bahá would visit Cleveland. On 15 April the *Plain Dealer*, a Democratic newspaper with a circulation of 90,000 copies, published a portrait of 'Abdu'l-Bahá as part of a biographical article in which His forthcoming visit was mentioned.[2] On 22 April the *Leader* mentioned that 'members of the Bahai belief here have requested the prophet to visit Cleveland'.[3] The same newspaper reported a few days later that 'Cleveland followers of Abdul Baha, Persian prophet, who have gone to Chicago to greet him, will make an effort to induce him to visit this city . . . He has a considerable following in Cleveland. The delegation to Chicago from this city, headed by Mrs. C. M. Swingle, 8304 Wade Park Avenue, consisted of nine members.'[4] On 4 May the same newspaper reported that 'Dr. C. M. Swingle . . . received a telegram last night informing him of the coming of Abdul Baha'.[5]

On 5 May the *Plain Dealer* published an article about 'Abdu'l-Bahá in which it was reported that He 'will come here tomorrow night, when he gives a lecture in the auditorium of the Hotel Euclid'.[6] On 6 May the same newspaper published a lengthier article introducing the Faith to its readers and offering further details about the imminent arrival of the Master in the city. 'Dr. C. M. Swingle', reported the newspaper, 'is one of the leaders here and he is largely responsible for having Abdul Baha come.' In referring to the Master, the author stated that 'He wishes to be known as the servant of humanity. He seeks no higher station than this. Caring for the sick and protecting the oppressed form a large part of his daily duties . . .' Publicizing 'Abdu'l-Bahá's public talk at the Euclid, the article also stated that 'The lecture by Abdul Baha tonight will be the real introduction of the new Persian religion in Cleveland. Its followers are enthusiastic and feel that it is not unlikely that in time this city also will have a temple.'[7] Also on 6 May the *Leader*[8] and the *Cleveland News*[9] announced the Master's arrival in the city at four o'clock and His public address at the Euclid.

Meeting the Local Press

When 'Abdu'l-Bahá's train arrived in Cleveland the Master was welcomed by many Bahá'ís who were waiting for Him at the station. With them was a group of reporters. After having dinner with the local Bahá'ís at the residence of Dr Charles Swingle and addressing them, 'Abdu'l-Bahá proceeded to His hotel where a public meeting was scheduled at eight o'clock. Between two and three hundred people had gathered to hear Him. In the course of His talk, 'Abdu'l-Bahá spoke on international peace[10] and the accounts in the local press indicate that afterwards He also privately addressed a smaller group of attendants and touched on the subject of racial unity.

'Abdu'l-Bahá's presence in Cleveland coincided with a meeting arranged by the local Theosophical Society to hear F. B. Houghton speak about the physical form of mental processes or 'thought-forms'. The *Plain Dealer* noted on 6 May that 'The visit to Cleveland today of Abdul Baha, messiah of the Persian Bahai movement, wakened interest in unfamiliar ethical and religious movements, and a large number who were not Theosophists were in the audience at the Medical Library auditorium.'[11] The same issue carried a new article on the Bahá'í Faith which also mentioned the arrival of 'Abdu'l-Bahá.[12]

In an article that included a picture of Him, the Republican *Cleveland News*, with a circulation of 50,000 copies, quoted 'Abdu'l-Bahá: 'You have a beautiful city . . . You have a beautiful country and your people are the great people of the future.'[13]

The *Leader*, a Republican newspaper with a circulation of 55,000 copies, sent a cameraman to the train station to take some pictures of the Master and His retinue upon their arrival. A reporter for this newspaper was also present at the Master's address held in the auditorium of the Euclid Hotel and after the meeting was able to visit 'Abdu'l-Bahá in His hotel room. The article that ensued appeared on 7 May and contained a detailed account of 'Abdu'l-Bahá's activities in the city as well as photographs of Him and two members of His retinue:

WOMEN OF FASHION GREET ABDUL ABBAS

SOCIETY GASPS AND SILKS BUSTLE AS PERSIAN PROPHET FACES THEM

Abdul Baha Abbas, supreme prophet of the Bahai cult, the latest religion to come out of the Orient, with difficulty climbed down the steps of a Pullman car in the Union depot yesterday afternoon.

He wore the flowing Persian robes, champagne in color, but they were almost concealed by an American tailored raincoat. However, a snow-white turban and his long curling hair and flowing beard made him a conspicuous figure.

Perhaps it is the full grayed beard, perhaps the forty of his barely sixty three years spent in prison, that gives him the appearance of a man a score or more years older. Perhaps, too, his long imprisonment was responsible for his evident bewilderment as he turned to his followers amid the hustle and bustle of the Occidental railway crowds, to be led to the waiting motor cars.

APPEARANCE OF AGE

Slightly stooped, he gave the impression of being immeasurably frail and old as he leaned for support on the arm of his nephew, Dr. Ammen U'Fareed.

With the exception of one, Mirza Mahmood, who is even older than the prophet, all other members of the party which is accompanying him on his short tour of America wear European attire.

Those who came with Abdul Baha from Chicago were his nephew, who also acts as interpreter; Mahmood, Siyad Assad'Ullah, Dr. and Mrs. E. C. Getsinger and Mrs. W. C. Ralston, of Chicago.

The visitors were dinner guests of Dr. and Mrs. C. M. Swingle, 8304 Wade Park Avenue, leading exponents of the cult in Cleveland.

At 8 o'clock Abdul Baha, with his nephew and retinue, made his entrance at the Euclid Hotel auditorium, a rustle of silks and a series of but half suppressed gasps of delight from 300 fashionably attired women greeted him. A score or two of men were sprinkled through the crowd under the soft multi-colored radiance of shaded electric globes. It was a fashionable function.

Abdul Baha is a prophet not above chuckling joyously over his own jokes. The jokes probably were lost by his nephew in the translation, for which he paused after each sentence, but the crowd, nevertheless, giggled politely with him.

Were it not that he is the propagandist of a new religion Abdul Baha would be known first as a great advocate of universal peace. It is to deliver one of the leading addresses at the Lake Mohonk peace conference, at Lake Mohonk, N. Y., that he came to America two weeks ago.

His talk last night was almost wholly one of advocacy of international peace. Though making frequent reference to 'religious civilization and the spiritual civilization to come', in contrast to present 'material civilization', he did not define the former. The nearest he came to doing so was in saying the first two are based primarily on righteousness and the last wholly on greed.

In his apartment in the Euclid Hotel, after the lecture, he told of the aims of the Bahai movement. Lying back on a divan, his eyes half closed in fatigue, he said:

EXPLAINS MOVEMENT

'Listen to me and I speak. The teachings of the prophets of old are diverted or buried with forms or their meaning lost, even until their very foundations have been lost. It took Jesus to revive the teachings at that time from which you date years.

'At the bottom of all religions there is right, the spiritual, the teachings of the prophet. We must investigate. We must revive the spiritual, and then, when it has been done, it will be found all are one. Then will be a divine or spiritual civilization, an equality of rights.

'Womankind will have its powers established; the rich will have their luxuries, but the poor their abodes and necessities. There will be a readjustment of economic conditions; the mysteries will be revealed and greater discoveries than those of this material civilization will be made.

'All mankind will be of one great brotherhood. There will be no distinction between men who are red and yellow, black and white.'

The prophet of the Bahais will leave Cleveland this morning for

Pittsburgh. Staying there one day, he will continue to Washington, D. C. He will return to Persia immediately after the peace conference.[14]

The *Plain Dealer* also sent a photographer and a reporter to see 'Abdu'l-Bahá. On 7 May the newspaper carried a lengthy article quoting some of His words on the subject of racial unity and also printed three pictures of 'Abdu'l-Bahá taken on the previous day.

BAHAIST APPROVES UNION OF RACES

PERSIAN TEACHER TELLS CLEVELAND WOMEN INTERMARRIAGE RESULTS IDEAL.

ONE NEGRO BISHOP HEARS PLEA FOR AMALGAMATION WITH WHITES.

HERE AS LIVING MESSIAH

Abdul Baha, Venerable Leader of Movement for Universal Religion, Touring United States Draws Society to Hear Doctrine – Secretary Acts as Translator – Appears in Long Robes of Different Colors and White Slippers – Arrives Without Show of Churchly Pomp.

Abdul Baha, a venerable Persian now touring America as leader of the Bahaist movement for a universal religion, declared last night for an amalgamation of the white and negro races by intermarriage.

This was at a reception in his apartments at the Hotel Euclid last night, following his public address to an audience of about 200. He addressed his convictions on the amalgamation of races to a negro clergyman who gave his name as Bishop M. F. A. Eastern, and to about twenty women, who formed a circle about the room, some of them sitting on the floor, for there were not chairs enough for all.

'All men', said Abdul Baha, 'are progeny of one – Adam. They are of different color, but color is nothing. Men of all races are brothers. God is neither black nor white.

'Doves are of different colors, but the white and the gray and those which are almost black dwell together in amity, and unity. So should men of all races and creeds.

'Perfect results follow the marriage of black and white races. In my own family in Persia was a negro slave who was freed. She married a white man and her children married white men. These children are now in my household. The results of the union were beautiful. They were wonderful – perfect.'

TALKS IN PERSIAN

Abdul-Baha's talk was in Persian, as was his lecture. Sentence by sentence, as he proceeded, it was translated into English by Dr. Ameer Fareed, also a Persian.

Abdul Baha, who arrived late in the afternoon from Chicago, where women of fashion made up a large part of his audience, came as the messiah of the Bahaist movement. It is known as the only religion with a living messiah.

That the venerable Persian takes that view of his leadership was indicated last night by a reply he made to a question, why his movement, which is designed to include followers of all religions, but is still Christian, was needed?

'The teachings of Moses were almost forgotten – had almost disappeared', he said, 'when Christ came and gave it life again. Now in this materialistic civilization of ours, religion is again dying out. The need of a new spiritual civilization is evident.'

Abdul Baha's beard is nearly white, as is his thin, long hair, which he covered with a white cap of a Persian sort – half turban, half fez. He wore a cream colored robe, covered by an outer robe of darker shade. The outer robe he wore on the train and during his public address last morning was black. He had changed this for a robe of tan when later he received in his apartments at the hotel the company of followers and other visitors who came to him there.

On his feet were long, white slippers. A vase of lilies and a bowl of fruit stood on the table in the center of the room. Abdul Baha sat on a lounge, at one side.

There was no churchly pomp in his manner, either on his arrival in Cleveland, when he addressed his audience, or when he received the disciples who came to his apartments. His manner was one of benevolence and gentle humility.

When he sat at one side of the crowded hotel lobby early in the evening he gazed out over it sadly, as if in melancholy contemplation of the lack of spirituality he found in all the material civilization of America. He sat with his hand to his forehead.

HAS BENEVOLENT ASPECT

When he talked to those who found him in his apartment his face lighted with smiles. But all the time his aspect of venerable benevolence was curiously joined to an expression and manner so simple and unaffected that it seemed almost childlike.

Another aged Persian, Mirza Mahmoad, was one of the Bahaist messiah's party. There were four of them: Abdul Baha Abbas, Dr. Ameer Fareed, Mirza Mahmoad and Said Assadullah.

Dr. E. C. Getsinger, Mrs. Getsinger, and Mrs. W. C. Ralston, all of Cleveland, had attended the meeting in Chicago and accompanied the party to Cleveland. The Cleveland followers of the Bahaist movement number about 100. Several met the party at Union station. From there automobiles carried Abdul Baha and the others to the home of Dr. C. M. Swingle at 8203 Wide Park Av. North, where about forty had gathered for a reception.

Refreshments were served there. As they ate Abdul Baha spoke, Ameer Fareed translating. For the advertised meeting at the Euclid Hotel the main dining room had been cleared. Most of the audience were women. There were a number who are identified with the Theosophical Society and various Spiritualistic organizations in the audience, and most who came were fashionably gowned.

That Abdul Baha's approval of marriages between whites and negroes is but a natural part of his movement for a universal religion was indicated by extracts from a stenographic report of his sermon.

'Humanity', he said, 'will be bound together as one. The various religions shall be united and the various races shall be known as one kind.'

This is to be when the spiritual civilization which the Bahaist movement is to bring about is achieved.

'The material civilization', he said, 'has now reached its pitch, and there is need for a spiritual civilization. Material civilization alone will not satisfy. Its benefits are limited to the World of matter.

'There is no hindrance for the spirit of man, for spirit itself must progress, and if the divine civilization shall be organized then the spirit will advance.

'Real discoveries will then take place. The divine mysteries will be revealed. The power of the holy spirit will become effective. The influence of the great guidance will be experienced, and all that is conducive to the divine form of civilization. That is what is meant in the Bible by the descent of the New Jerusalem. The heavenly Jerusalem is no other than the divine civilization, and it is now ready. It can be and shall be organized, and the oneness of humankind will be a fact.

'Humanity will then be bound together as one. The various religions shall be united, and the various races shall be known as one kind. The Orient and the Occident shall be united and the banner of international peace shall be unfurled. The world shall find peace and the equality and rights of men shall be established. All the nations of the world shall then be relatives and companions.'[15]

Another account was published in the *Cleveland Press*, a newspaper with a circulation of 160,000 copies, and included two drawings of 'Abdu'l-Bahá:

An old man sat in the corner of the bustling hotel lobby. His bronzed face, furrowed by wrinkles, seemed to have a redder hue under the electric lamps. A long, white beard fell over his white robe, covered by a long coat of black broadcloth. A high white turban covered his gray hair that rambled in straggling locks over his shoulders.

Abdul Baha, Persian religious teacher, leader of the Bahaist movement, an oriental doctrine slowly spreading over the western world, was in the midst of the [illegible] with his oriental message.

But he seemed utterly oblivious of the little group of disciples in the Hotel Euclid lobby, of old Said Assadullah, his Persian companion, who sat gazing devotedly up into his face, of the fashionable men and women passing into the auditorium where he was to lecture.

He toyed with a string of black beads, and stared ahead of him. His faded blue eyes seemed filled with an unutterable weariness, a weariness and patience nourished by his 40 years in the prison at Akka, Persia.

'He wants you to get paper and pencil to take down accurately what he says,' his secretary, Dr. Ameer Fareed, a young Persian, with silky black beard, explained.

With Dr. Fareed translating, Abdul Baha spoke of his mission in hailing words.

'The Bahai movement teaches the oneness of humanity,' he said, 'and of international peace, the union of religion with science and the equal rights of all nations . . .'

'Above all,' Abdul Baha continued, 'our movement seeks to

remove from all minds religious and racial prejudices, and to show that the essentials of all religions are one and the same.'

The Bahaist movement endorses woman suffrage.

'We want womankind educated,' the old man went on, 'so that equal suffrage may become possible. We also want an economic and social readjustment whereby abject poverty cannot prevail.'

The amalgamation of white and negro races by intermarriage is another of his teachings.[16]

On 7 May the *News* published an article by the columnist and writer Edna K. Wooley containing an interview with the local Bahá'í Mrs. Swingle apropos of the comments made by 'Abdu'l-Bahá regarding racial unity.[17]

The Master left Cleveland by train on the morning of 7 May. Before His departure, 'Abdu'l-Bahá received copies of some of the articles published during His stay in Cleveland. According to Maḥmúd, 'He received a letter from a dignitary of the city, who stated that after reading the newspapers and reflecting on the teachings of the Cause, he was convinced of its truth and greatness . . .'[18]

The local press continued to publish references to His visit to Cleveland. The black newspaper *Gazette* (Cleveland), for instance, dedicated part of its editorial to comment on the ideas expressed by 'Abdu'l-Bahá at Hotel Euclid regarding racial unity and interracial marriages:

> The doctrine of the amalgamation or union of all the races being preached throughout the north of this country these days by Abdul Baha, the venerable and learned Persian leader of the movement for a universal religion, is no new one as all South America and many countries of southern Europe attest. The mixture has been going on there for centuries and will continue. It has steadily grown in this prejudiced country, before, during and since the days of slavery, and will continue to do so in spite of all the south and its cohorts, north and south, can do and say to prevent it. It is natural.[19]

The satiric section of the *Day Book* (Chicago) carried a short note that also commented on 'Abdu'l-Bahá's public talk at the Euclid: 'Abdul Baha, leader of Persian universal religionists, told society women and negro bishop at reception at Cleveland that inter-marriage of whites and blacks is natural and results ideal.' The *Plain Dealer*, published on 12 May a general article about the Bahá'í Faith that also reported on the plans for the construction of a Bahá'í House of Worship in Chicago.[20]

14

PITTSBURGH

7–8 May 1912

'Abdu'l-Bahá arrived in Pittsburgh from Cleveland at noon on May 7 and stayed at the Hotel Schenley where He addressed a public meeting in the evening.[1] Weeks before His arrival, the *Gazette Times* (Pittsburgh) had reported in an article about the Bahá'í Faith that 'in Pittsburgh he ['Abdu'l-Bahá] will address an audience in Rodeph Shalom Temple, Rabbi J. Leonard Levy, and before the Bahai Assembly'.[2]

The exact time of 'Abdu'l-Bahá's visit to Pittsburgh was confirmed while He was in Cleveland and immediately the local press published further articles reporting His approaching arrival. The *Pittsburgh Dispatch* reported that 'On Wednesday he ['Abdu'l-Bahá] will meet any who may wish to talk with him, and he will probably speak publicly again on Wednesday [*sic.*]. Several schools have invited him to address them. He advocates the Bahai principles of universal peace.'[3] A brief note in the *Pittsburgh Post* announced His address at the Schenley.[4]

The evening *Chronicle-Telegraph* was the first local newspaper to give details of 'Abdu'l-Bahá's arrival and the party that accompanied Him:

> Abdul Baha, a native of Teheran, Persia, and leader of 15,000,000 Bahais, arrived in Pittsburgh from Cleveland at 12:15 and will speak at 8:15 o'clock tonight in the ballroom of the Hotel Schenley. He is at the Hotel Schenley this afternoon receiving informally any who wish to talk to him. He leaves tonight for Washington. He was imprisoned 40 years for advocating the ideas for universal peace which now the western world hears with interest. Representatives from Evangelical churches, the Vedanta Society, New Thought

Association and the Theosophical Society met yesterday at McCreery's to arrange for the meeting tonight.

The party that came from Cleveland today included Abdul Baha, Dr. and Mrs. Edward Getsinger, of Washington, D.C.; Mrs. Ralston, of California; Miss Grace Roberts, from Boston; Dr. Fareed and Mirza Said Assadullah, of Syria, and Mirza Mahmud of Teheran, Persia.[5]

To this information the *Pittsburgh Sun*, with a daily circulation of 50,000 copies, added that 'Dr. J. Leonard Levy and several pastors offered their pulpits to him for tonight's meeting'[6] and that 'Director Arthur A. Hamerschiag, of the Carnegie Technical Institute, called on Abdul Baha at 2 o'clock today and invited him to deliver an address before the students.'[7]

Owing to His short stay in Pittsburgh 'Abdu'l-Bahá was unable to accept all the invitations to speak He had received. Instead, His only public meeting in Pittsburgh was convened jointly by several local organizations and was held at the ballroom of the Hotel Schenley. In His talk 'Abdu'l-Bahá presented some of the Bahá'í social principles and spoke about the need for a spiritual civilization.[8] Over four hundred people, including some reporters, were present at the meeting and on the following day several accounts of it were published in the local press.

A reporter with the *Pittsburgh Dispatch*, an independent morning newspaper issuing 67,000 copies daily, published the following account:

PICTURESQUE PERSIAN PROPHET LECTURES HERE

ABDUL BAHA PREACHES GOSPEL OF UNIVERSAL BROTHERHOOD AT THE SCHENLEY

AUDIENCE IS ATTENTIVE

Preaching a gospel of the union of the East and the West, on the common ground of universal brotherhood; the readjustment of economic conditions for the benefit of the poor; the abolishment of war, the equality of the sexes, and the adoption of a universal language, Abdul Baha, leader of the Bahai, addressed a large and attentive audience in the ballroom of the Hotel Schenley last evening. The fundamental doctrine of all Oriental thought, the oneness of life, was the keynote of the wisdom of this Persian prophet, whose appearance is picturesque enough to satisfy those in whom his romantic history had awakened an interest; and his patriarchal and saintly air was satisfying to his devoted followers, some of whom accompany him on his tour of America, and a small group of whom are residents of Pittsburgh.

In appearance Abdul Baha is venerable. He wears a long white beard, and his long-white hair falls to his shoulders beneath a white turban. Over his white robe he wore last evening a black cloak. His deep set eyes are large, dark and expressive. He spoke through an interpreter, who with several other Persians, accompany him.

Among other things he declared that 'Science and religion must correspond, and all religions which do not correspond with science and reason are absolute superstition and not worthy of the consideration of mankind. All religions may be divided into two parts; one the spiritual not subject to change; and the other the practical, concerned with the deeds done in the body and changing with the exigencies of the times.'

. . . In the audience last evening were representatives from the Vedanta Society, the two Theosophical Societies of Pittsburgh; the New Thought classes, and from many of the churches.[9]

Marion Brunot Haymaker,[10] a columnist for the *Chronicle-Telegraph*, a Republican newspaper with a circulation of 89,000 copies, was also present at the meeting and wrote a detailed report that included the names of women prominent in local social circles who were present at the gathering:

BAHA EXPOUNDS HIS RELIGION

HEAD OF THE BAHA MOVEMENT ADDRESSES A BIG AUDIENCE AT HOTEL SCHENLEY

BY MARION BRUNOT

'The noblest of all is he who serves mankind.' 'Truth is the same the world over.' 'Religion and science must correspond – if they do not the religion is only a superstition.' These are some of the ideas that were given by Abdul Baha, the head of the Baha movement hailing from Persia, in his talk in the Hotel Schenley last night.

Perhaps one of the most interesting figures of the time is Abdul Baha. Only 70 years ago was the Bahai movement started – called the universal religion, and based upon the Golden Rule, and today over 15,000,000 followers are found, including mostly Persians and Turks. Imagine the personalities, the doctrines, the testifying, that such an outcome would require, and especially when some of the truths preached were as follows, being direct heresy in the eyes of the Moslems:

Religion should be represented by no creed, no dogma, no set rule, it should have but one God, a universal one.

Man and woman are equal – and until such is established, peace and brotherhood cannot exist.

War and rumors of war should be done away with – arbitration is what should be used.

Education for everyone should be demanded. Until there are schools for all, there will be bigotry and superstition.

Politics, war, rule by selfishness, the rich over-striding the poor, all this does not stand for religion – what the world wants is a faith based upon truth service and love.

Abdul Baha, for 40 years, was imprisoned for his belief; but, even so, he managed to spread his ideas – to permeate the people with his religion. The Bab, in 1844, proclaimed the coming of one who would establish a universal brotherhood of man, just as John the Baptist foretold the coming of Christ.

And as John was persecuted, so was the Bab. Shortly after his martyrdom the promised teacher appeared in Baha'o'llah from whom the movement takes its name. His mission lasted 40 years, during which time he was subjected to all manner of imprisonment and suffering. Abdul Baha is the son of Baha'o'llah and was constantly at the side of his father during all his hardships.

Abdul Baha says he is the servant of humanity. 'I seek no higher office,' he declares. 'Such holds both humiliation and exaltation.'

This man has the power of penetrating the souls of men, at least so his followers say. He understands the need of each individual soul. He is a spiritual physician. Many and beautiful are the touching incidents told of him as he went through the East, healing the suffering, scattering kindness, clearing away prejudice, and making friends of those who formerly were his enemies. And as you sit and watch him as he speaks, noting his sad, kind eyes, his body, old before its time, his nervous hands, so full of sympathy, you cannot help but feel the personality of the teacher, and you believe, that truly he does represent hospitality, and truth, and that to be humble, to be reverent, to love all mankind are parts of him.

The audience was, indeed, a representative one, including Mrs. Charles B. McClain, Mrs. L. P. Seeley, Miss Suzanne Beatty, Madame Blanca de Ovies, Mrs. Ralph Flinn, Mrs. Henry W. Fisher, Mrs. J. I. Buchanan and Mrs. J. T. Manning.[11]

A further account was published in the *Pittsburgh Press* which at the time had a circulation of over 85,000 copies daily:

ABDUL BAHA LECTURES ON THE RELIGION AND PEACE

HEAD OF BELIEF APPEARS BEFORE LARGE AUDIENCE OF ALL CREEDS

Abdul Baha, aged 68, leader of the Bahai religion spoke last night in the Hotel Schenley to an attentive audience of about 400 persons. He is of absolute simplicity of manner: is unostentatious and unpretentious and delivered his message cheerfully, earnestly and quickly. The Bahai religion, emanates from Persia and is promulgating an era of peace, and unity in language, politics and spiritual creeds. The Universal Brotherhood of Man is the doctrine of this religion and it has about 15,000,000 followers, numbering Jews, Mohammedans, Christians, Hindus, and people from almost every other faith. Abdul Baha is the son of Baha-O'llah, who founded the religion. He is venerable in appearance, with long white hair and beard, and with strong, kindly, peaceful, expressive features. He is garbed in Persian costume and his address was interpreted, sentence for sentence, by Dr. Fareed, an attending Persian.

Abdul Baha said the Bahais believe in the equality of women with men, for until women have an equal voice in the affairs of the world, war will not be abolished. They believe in the harmony of science and religion; in the oneness of life with all good; in religious adjustment of political economical conditions; in temperate, reasonable living; in being happy and contented; and in following the teachings of the founder of the religion of love, Jesus of Nazareth.

Various churches and societies of Pittsburgh were represented in the audience. New Thoughtists, Theosophists, Christian Scientists and Unitarians met with the most orthodox of religious denominations.

> Today Abdul Baha left for Washington. D. C. where he will speak this week. He also will address the Mohonk Pence conference in New York State this month.[12]

The *Pittsburgh Post*, a Democratic newspaper with a circulation of 50,000 copies, offered the following summary of the talk in an article that included a portrait of 'Abdu'l-Bahá:

> He said it was incumbent upon all to investigate truth, for the different religions have one truth underlying them. He mentioned religious, sectarian, racial and patriotic prejudices as destroyers of human foundations. The equality of men and women was emphasized.
>
> He said peace was most necessary, and when woman reached the same status as man war would he dispelled, for women would not be willing to have their young killed on the battlefields. He believes women are the ones who will best serve in international arbitration and eliminate warfare. He held that universal peace would not come through racial or patriotic force, but through a force which would execute the oneness of humanity and destroy the foundations of warfare and strife.[13]

A similar account was published in the *Pittsburgh Sun*.[14]

Several months after His departure from America, 'Abdu'l-Bahá received in Paris a visit from Arnold William Rosenthal, a publicist and correspondent with the *Pittsburgh Spectator*, who interviewed the Master on 8 May 1913.[15] Rosenthal requested from 'Abdu'l-Bahá a message for the readers of the newspaper and on the following day He wrote a Tablet for publication in the *Spectator*.[16]

15

SECOND VISIT TO NEW YORK

11–22 May 1912

'Abdu'l-Bahá left Pittsburgh on the morning of Wednesday, 8 May, reaching Washington on the night of the same day. He spent some days in the capital and on 11 May proceeded to New York where He stayed at the Hudson building.

From New York the Master made several visits to nearby cities and towns, and the local newspapers in some of these places wrote accounts of Him. He also attended the Lake Mohonk Conference on International Arbitration, an event that elicited very great attention from the press on a national scale.

Visit to Montclair and Meeting of the International Peace Forum

During His stay in New York 'Abdu'l-Bahá made a short visit to Montclair, New Jersey, on 12 May, where He met the local Bahá'ís and addressed the Sunday service of the Unity Church. The minister of the Unity Church from 1906 was Rev. Edgar Swan Wiers (1882–1931). As well as being one of the directors of the American Unitarian Association, Wiers was also the organizer of the Unity Forum, a series of Sunday lectures, started in 1909, at which notable speakers such as David Starr Jordan and Reginald Campbell were invited to talk at his church about social issues. It was through Charles H. Edsall, a local Bahá'í, that Wiers invited 'Abdu'l-Bahá to speak to his congregation.

In introducing 'Abdu'l-Bahá, Wiers stated that 'to stand in the presence of the prophets of old is great, but to stand in the presence of the prophets of our own generation is far greater'. Afterwards 'Abdu'l-Bahá spoke on the fundamental unity of religions and closed His address with a prayer.[1] On the following day, the Republican *Montclair Times* published an account of the meeting and the notes of His talk (not reproduced here):

PERSIAN PROPHET IN TOWN

ABDUL BAHA ABBAS SPEAKS AT UNITY CHURCH ON SUNDAY

Abdul Baha Abbas, prophet of world-peace and brotherliness, whose followers number about 20,000,000, of which over fifty are in Montclair, visited this town last Sunday and spoke in Unity Church. The venerable religious leader was accompanied by his interpreter, Dr. Ameen U. Fareed, of Isphahan, Persia; Dr. Zia M. Bagdadi, of Beirut, Syria, now of Chicago; Mirza Waliallah Khan; of Teheran, Persia; Mirza Mahmoud, of Shiraz; Said Assadullah, of Gom, and Mirza Ahmad Sahral, of Isphahan.

Abdul Baha was entertained at the home of Mr. C. H. Edsall, of No. 37 The Crescent, where he met many of the local members of the cult of which he is the recognized leader.

The prophet is a picturesque figure. He wears a long iron gray beard, a white turban and flowing Eastern garments which make him look taller than he really is. Through his interpreter he spoke to those that greeted him at the Edsall residence. He referred to the general use of the expression, 'All right', by the people of America. 'Everywhere I go I hear it,' he said, 'and it seems to be characteristic of this country.'

At Unity Church, in the morning, Abdul Baha spoke on 'Divine Unity'. He was introduced by Rev. Edgar S. Wiers, the pastor of Unity Church, who referred to the need of fraternalism in religion.[2]

After the service at the Unity Church the Edsalls invited 'Abdu'l-Bahá to their home for a lunch organized in His honor. Some 20 people were present, including Rev. Wiers and his wife who were seated at either side of the Master.[3] As stated in the above article, 'Abdu'l-Bahá made a humorous comment on the English expression 'All right'. This anecdote was taken up by news agencies and reproduced in different newspapers across the country.[4] *The New York Times* was one of the first newspapers to publish this note:

BAHA LIKES 'ALL RIGHT'

PERSIAN PROPHET THINKS IT IS OUR MOST CHARACTERISTIC EXPRESSION.

> MONTCLAIR, N. J., May 12. – 'All right' is regarded by Abdul Baha, the Persian prophet of worldwide peace and human brotherhood, as the most characteristic expression of the people of this country.
>
> 'Wherever you go you hear it,' he said to-day at the home of Charles H. Edsall, where he was entertained after he had spoken to a large audience in Unity Church. 'You ask the bell boy at the hotel to do something and he responds, "All right"; you inquire as to the health of a friend and he answers, "All right"; everything is "all right". I have never heard the expression used in any other country, and I believe that it reflects the optimism of this great country.'
>
> Abdul Baha came to Montclair to-day accompanied by a retinue of beturbaned retainers and interpreters, and the presence of the prophet and his entourage in Unity Church gave a picturesque aspect to the Sunday morning service. A number of Bahaists from New York were in the congregation that heard the master of their cult speak. Montclair has about fifty Bahaists, and all were present.[5]

On the evening of the same day, 'Abdu'l-Bahá addressed the participants of a meeting of the International Peace Forum – of which Taft was its honorary president – held at the Grace Methodist Church, New York.[6] No account of this meeting seems to have been published in the press but some announcements gave some details about it. The *Tribune*, for instance, offered the names of other speakers: 'At the Happy Sunday Evening service, the International Peace Forum, of which President Taft is the head, will hold a meeting in its interests. Abdul Baha the great peace leader of Oriental countries, will speak. The Baha is a wonderful man and this is a marvellous chance to hear him. Senator Charles A. Towne, of Minnesota, will speak. The Rev. Dr. W. A. Hunsberger will preside.'[7] According to *The New York Times* His address was to begin at eight.[8]

Some weeks after this meeting the executive president of the International Peace Forum, Rev. John Wesley Hill (1863–1936), was the chairman of a reception at the Metropolitan Temple at which 'Abdu'l-Bahá was the main speaker.

The Lake Mohonk Conference on International Arbitration

One of the highlights of 'Abdu'l-Bahá's visit to North America was His participation at the eighteenth Lake Mohonk Conference on International Arbitration, which was held from 15 to 17 May 1912.

Albert K. Smiley (1828–1912) was the mind behind the organization of the conference. A Quaker, Smiley bought with his twin brother, Daniel, a piece of land near Lake Mohonk where they built a summer resort. Their interest in social work and the rights of the Native Americans prompted them to put their property at the service of their ideals. In 1883 they arranged the first conference on the rights of the Indian nations and in 1895 Smiley convened the first Conference on International Arbitration, which had as its aim 'creating and directing public sentiment in favor of international arbitration, arbitration treaties and an international court'.[9]

While in Egypt 'Abdu'l-Bahá held some correspondence with Smiley[10] and also with Harry Clinton Phillips, secretary of the conference.[11] Portions of the latter missive were published in an extensive article by Joseph Hannen announcing the visit of 'Abdu'l-Bahá in America and published on February 1912 in the *Advocate of Peace* (Washington), organ of the American Peace Society with a circulation of 7,500 copies.[12]

In a letter dated 10 November 1911, Phillips invited 'Abdu'l-Bahá to participate at the Lake Mohonk Conference: 'Remembering with great respect your impressively courteous letters to himself and the writer, Mr. Smiley would be very much gratified, should your expected visit to America extend to that time, to welcome you as his guest at the approaching meeting of this Conference to be held May 15th, 16th and 17th, 1912, formal invitation to which meeting will go to you later.'[13]

The conference of 1912 assembled over 180 personalities from various fields. Judges, presidents of universities and of chambers of commerce, editors of leading newspapers and magazines, diplomats, labor leaders, politicians, religious leaders and future prime ministers and Nobel prize winners, had the chance to meet the Master during the three days He stayed at the conference. The sessions were presided over by Nicholas M. Butler (1862–1947) who at the time was president of Columbia University and president of the Carnegie Endowment for International Peace and who in 1931 received the Nobel Peace Prize.[14]

In the weeks before the opening of the Conference news agencies released several notes announcing the event and in most of them mention was made of the participation of 'Abdu'l-Bahá.[15] On the opening day of the conference, a further press note was released from Mohonk in which again the participation of the Master was mentioned as one of the noted speakers coming from abroad.[16] The American Press Association distributed a picture of the Bahá'í delegation at Lake Mohonk. Besides the Master the photograph included Edward C. Getsinger, Lua Getsinger, Amín Faríd, Ahmad Sohrab, Mírzá Varqá, Siyyid Assad'u'lláh and Dr Zia Bagdadi. This picture was published in several newspapers across the United States.[17] A further portrait of the Master was released by the Press Association. Its caption read: 'Abdul Baha Abbas, of Persia, is perhaps the most picturesque figure at the conference on international arbitration being held at Lake Mohonk, N. Y. There are delegates from nearly all nations, and many of those from foreign countries wear their native garb. Abdul Baha Abbas wears flowing robes, and his long white beard gives him a patriarchal appearance. He is the head of a new religion of peace, and he is making a tour of the world in an effort to unite all churches in the interest of arbitration as a means of settling disputes.'[18]

'Abdu'l-Bahá's participation was scheduled for the second session of the conference, at 8 p.m., and was announced under the title 'The Oneness of the Reality of Human Kind'.[19] The Master's address was published in the proceedings of the conference:

THE ONENESS OF THE REALITY OF HUMAN KIND

ADDRESS OF ABDUL BAHA ABBAS

When we consider history, we find that civilization is progressing, but in this century its progress cannot be compared with that of past centuries. This is the century of light and of bounty. In the past, the unity of patriotism, the unity of nations and religions was established; but in this century, the oneness of the world of humanity is established; hence this century is greater than the past.

Sixty years ago Asia was in great turmoil of wars; England, Russia, Turkey and France went to war. There were wars in Persia, wars among the religions and wars between nations, especially in Persia on account of the existence of the different nationalities, such as Turks, Persians, Arabs and Kurds, and the various religions, namely, Mohammedan, Jewish, Christian and Zoroastrian. Among these different religions the greatest enmity and rancor were extant.

At such a time as this, His Holiness, Baha'o'llah appeared. He proclaimed the oneness of the world of humanity and the greatest peace. He wrote to all the kings and addressed epistles to all the religionists of Persia, and all the souls who accepted his platform and emulated and followed his teachings – whether Christians, Mohammedans, Jews or Zoroastrians – were united, and attained the greatest amity and unity. Through those teachings, the Kurd, the Arab, the Persian and Turk freed themselves from the prejudice of race and were people agreed to an extent which is indescribable, indeed, in such a manner, that were you to enter their meeting you could not distinguish between the Persian, the Christian, the Arab or the Turk, and you would not observe any differences of religious opinion. Among those people the utmost of love and oneness of peace now obtain, for the great teachings of Baha'o'llah make for the oneness of the world and for humanity, universal peace and arbitration. The following are a few of the principles of Baha'o'llah.

First, that all must investigate reality. It is incumbent on all nations to investigate truth. For Baha'o'llah declares that the foundations of the divine religion are one and that one is reality and reality is not multiple but indivisible. But the imitations which have come in, being different in character, have caused divisions and separations. If we forsake the imitations and revert to the original foundations of the divine religion, we shall find that the foundations are that reality which is one and not multiple.

The second principle of Baha'o'llah is the oneness of human kind. All humanity belongs to one family, inhabiting the same globe; all are beneath the providence of God; God has created all and has nurtured all and provideth for all and preserveth all. This is the policy of God. God is kind to all and why should we be unkind? Is there any policy wiser and better than God's policy? No matter how keen the human mind may be, it cannot surpass the policy of God. The policy of God is perfect and we must follow it and not our own self-interest.

The third teaching of Baha'o'llah is that religion and science are twins. If a religious question be not in accordance with science, it is imagination. All religious matter must correspond with science, every question which meets the criterion of science shall be acceptable and those questions which do not come to the standard of science are not to be given credence.

The fourth teaching of Baha'o'llah is that religion should be the one bond which shall unite society, which shall cement together the various peoples, which shall cause a unity among all the creeds. If religion should be productive of strife and division, if it should cause bloodshed and war and rapine, irreligion is preferable to religion. Religion was meant to be a bond of love among mankind.

The fifth principle is that racial bias, religious prejudice, patriotic prejudice, political prejudice, are the destroyers of the very foundations of the body politic. All humanity is one in kind, the surface of the earth one home, and the foundations of the divine religions one. All the wars which have taken place since the inception of human history have emanated either from religious prejudice, racial prejudice, patriotic bias or political greed and interest. As long as these prejudices last, so long will the foundations of humanity tremble. When such prejudices pass away the world will at last find peace.

The sixth principle of Baha'o'llah is equality between mankind and womankind. Woman and man are both human and both the manifestations of God's grace. God has created man and has endowed him with knowledge and intelligence. The difference which now exists between man and woman is only a difference of education, and when woman shall receive the same education no doubt her equality with man shall become a reality.

The world of humanity is composed of two organizations the male and the female. If one organ be defective, that defect will affect the other. Until perfect strength shall obtain in both, and woman shall attain equality with man, the happiness of humanity will not be insured.

The seventh principle concerns the readjustment of the economic questions in the social body. The rich now enjoy the greatest luxury, whereas the poor are in abject misery. Certain laws must be made whereby the rich cannot become over-rich and the poor shall not starve, both rich and poor enjoying the comforts according to their respective deserts.

The eighth principle of Baha'o'llah is that philosophy sufficeth not and is not conducive to the absolute happiness of mankind.

> Great philosophers have been capable of educating themselves, or a few who followed them, but generally education, ethical education, they could not endow. Therefore, the world of humanity is evermore in need of the breadth of the Holy Spirit. The greatest peace will not be realized without the power of the Holy Spirit. It is the Holy Spirit of God which insures the safety of humanity, for human thoughts differ, human susceptibilities differ. You cannot make the susceptibilities of all humanity one except through the common channel of the Holy Spirit. (Applause.)[20]

Other speakers at the same session were Salvador Castrillo, Nicaraguan Minister to the United States; J. P. Santamarina, of Argentina; Baron Eduard de Neufville (1857–1920), from Germany, member of the German Peace Society and nominated for the Nobel prize in 1913; John Lewis (1858–1935), editor of Toronto's *Standard* and years later member of the Canadian senate; and Andrew B. Humphrey, secretary of the American Peace and Arbitration League.

Abdu'l-Bahá's address was afterwards mentioned in various periodicals. The *Washington Herald*, for instance, stated that He 'attracted considerable attention as he delivered, through an interpreter, a message of good will to the audience. The leader of the new born cult spoke on "The Oneness of the Reality of Human Kind" and created a profound impression upon his hearers.'[21]

George Perry Morris (1864–1921), staff at the *Christian Science Monitor*, briefly mentioned the presence of Bahá'í delegates in a report sent from the conference to his newspaper.[22] The *Montgomery Advertiser* carried the comments of another participant, lawyer Fred S. Ball (1866–1941), who mentioned 'Abdu'l-Bahá's presence.[23] *The Christian Register* (Boston), organ of the American Unitarians, published on 23 May a report of the conference by Bradley Gilman (1857–1932), editor of the newspaper, in which He was also mentioned.[24]

In a letter for the *Advocate of Peace*, Charles E. Beals, field secretary of the Chicago Peace Society, reported that 'The presence of Abdul Baha and his retinue in Oriental costume lent color to the scene. One irrepressible punster was wicked enough to remark that at last universal peace seems assured, since it is now decreed by the law of the Medes (Meads) and Persians.'[25] Another article in the same issue also mentioned the presence of 'the distinguished Persian leader'.[26]

Another participant at the conference was Samuel Chiles Mitchell (1861–1948), president since 1908 of the University of South Carolina. In an address at the University of Tennessee entitled 'The Ethics of Democracy', Mitchell stated that 'I had the pleasure of hearing at Lake Mohonk recently the great Persian religious leader, Abdul Baha Abbas, a patriarch after the order of Abraham, I fancy, who has endured imprisonment for his views. He has millions of followers in this and other lands who rejoice in the discovery of this new sense of human brotherhood. The oneness of mankind is the cardinal tenet of this Persian prophet.[27]

13 May: Reception at Hotel Astor

Established in 1815, the New York Peace Society was one of the oldest peace organizations in America and one of the leading branches of the American Peace Society. The executive secretary of the organization, William H. Short, visited 'Abdu'l-Bahá soon after His arrival in America and had an interview with Him.[28] During the meeting Short formally invited 'Abdu'l-Bahá to a reception in His honour that was to be held on Monday, 13 May at the Hotel Astor which was arranged by the Woman's Social Committee of the New York Peace Society, of which the Bahá'í Mary S. MacNutt was a member.[29]

Despite illness, 'Abdu'l-Bahá attended the meeting and addressed the large audience which had gathered to hear His words.[30] The guest speakers represented various nationalities and religions including Rev. Percy Grant; Persian Consul Topakyan; William H. Short; Professor William Jackson of Columbia; Stephen Samuel Wise (1874–1949), rabbi of the Free Synagogue and a prominent Jewish reformer and political activist who was involved in the cause of civil rights and was also a cofounder of the NAACP;[31] Anna Garlin Spencer (1851–1931), a Unitarian minister who was also a renowned educator and journalist; and the feminist writer Gertrude Atherton (1857–1948), who in her work *Julia France and Her Times* (1912) had mentioned the Bahá'í Faith several times.

On the previous day the press had published announcements of the event. The *New York Times*, for instance, reported that the meeting would start at four in afternoon and finish at seven and added that 'Andrew Carnegie and other prominent peace advocates are expected to be present'.[32] Other announcements were also published in the *Brooklyn*

Daily Eagle,[33] the *Evening Call*,[34] the *Evening Post*,[35] the *Evening Telegram*,[36] the *Press*[37] and the *Tribune*.[38]

Some reporters were present at the meeting and over the next few days the press published accounts of it. The *Tribune* published the most detailed report quoting some of the words of the Master and also reproducing some of the comments made by other speakers:

BAHA TALKS ON PEACE

THRONG OF WOMEN AT MEETING TO HEAR PERSIAN PROPHET

SAYS U. S. WILL TAKE LEAD

MANY CREEDS REPRESENTED AT GATHERING UNDER AUSPICES OF SOCIAL COMMITTEE

So many worshipers came to sit at the feet of Abdul Baha yesterday afternoon, at the Hotel Astor, that the white turbaned prophet himself had considerable difficulty in even getting into the room. There was not even standing room an hour before his entrance was expected, and all the aisles had been filled in long since.

The woman's social committee of the New York Peace Society had estimated the number of guests by the number of acceptances they had received, which did not begin to represent the amount of popular interest in Abdul Baha. The crowd was unusually cosmopolitan. There was a group of Japanese students from Columbia University, the men following the lead of a trim little maid in a stay silk kimono. Here was a little knot of swarthy men from the Persian brotherhood in this city. Here were many of the members of the cult of the Bahai, followers of Abdul Baha waiting with rapt attention for the coming of their leader. Here were club women, philanthropists, ministers and college professors.

All rose to their feet with one accord when the prophet appeared. They stood in silence while a wave was made for him through the crowded little gilt chairs. His gray beard brushed against a woman's lace gown as he passed, and one saw her lip tremble. He reached the platform finally and stood looking into the hundreds of watching faces. Then he settled back with a sigh in his big chair and buried his face in the pink flowers he carried.

Rabbi Stephen S. Wise presided over the ceremonies, which included an address by one woman, Mrs. Anna Garlin Spencer, and by Dr. Percy Stickney Grant, Consul General Topakyan of Persia, and Professor William Jackson, of Columbia University.

Abdul Baha spoke last, his interpreter reciting each sentence after him:

Although I feel weary and ill this afternoon, because I attach great importance to this meeting and because I have been longing to see your faces, here am I. I am most grateful for the expressions of kind feelings on the part of my interlocutors, and I am thankful for the susceptibility of your hearts, for I discover that the greatest susceptibility of all of you is for international peace. Truly there is no greater glory for man than the service of the most great peace.

Peace is light, war is darkness, peace is life, war is death. Peace is guidance, war is misguidance. Peace is founded on good, war is a satanic institute. Peace is conducive to illumination, war is destructive of light. Peace and amity are factors of existence; war is decomposition, or lack of existence.

Wherever the banner of peace is raised it is conducive to the welfare of the world.

Consider the essential oneness of humanity. His holiness Adam was the parent of all. He was the trunk of the tree. You are all leaves of the tree. You must be united and consort with one another in perfect amity and accord.

No doubt this revered democracy will be the foremost among nations to champion the cause of peace. The banner of international peace will be unfurled here. Thus will the sun shine on the East and the West. The clouds will pass away. Your thoughts shall take an upward flight.

Rabbi Wise spoke of the meeting as a 'miniature religious congress' because so many creeds were met together and 'not in a spirit of tolerance only, but of fellowship'. 'Tolerance is Insult,' he quoted from Goethe.

'The term religious war,' he continued, 'is a misnomer, because there can be no war where religion is. We still have war in the world because we have no religion. All we have is a hollow sham, a pretence. When once we have real religion war will cease.'

Mrs. Spencer was greeted with applause when she said no one people could declare themselves the children of God and the others only stepchildren.

'Our honored friend,' she said, 'comes to us with the same

message proclaimed by our own Emerson that there are as many roads to the Infinite as there are travelers upward.'

After the addresses, Abdul Baha divided his pink blossoms, giving the finest ones to Mrs. Spencer and the rest of the other speakers. His interpreter, a romantic looking person with coal black hair and a scarlet tie, presented a rose to Mrs. Howard McNutt, of the reception committee.

Those who sat on the platform with the speakers were Mrs. Gertrude Atherton, Mrs. Samuel Untermyer, Mrs. Lua Moore Getsinger, a disciple of Abdul Baha; Mrs. Ernest Thompson Seton and Mrs. Frederick Nathan.

The reception committee included Mrs. Howard McNutt, Mrs. William H. Hotchkin, Miss Maud Wyman, Mrs. Katharine A. Martin, Mrs. William W. Beales, Mrs. George. T. Colter and Mrs. Frank E. Hadley, chairman.[39]

The *New York Times* also published an account of the meeting and quoted the Persian Consul saying, 'Our guest of honor has stood as a prophet of enlightenment of peace for the Persian empire and a friend and well-wisher of Persia may well honor him.'[40]

An article in *The Sun* also quoted some of the words of the Master and stated that some five hundred people attended the meeting. 'When he finished speaking,' stated the article, 'the refreshment tables were neglected as men and women pushed their way to the platform to get at least a nearer view of the head of the faith which has had for several years a considerable following in this city.'[41]

The account in the *New York Herald* estimated that one thousand people attended the meeting and mentioned that 'Abdul Baha shook hands with almost every person present'.[42]

The account in the *New York Press* raised the number of attendants to two thousand people.[43]

In its June issue the *Advocate of Peace* (Washington), the official organ of the American Peace Society, also published a short report of the meeting, reproducing some of the information already published in other journals.[44] The same issue included a brief reference to the meeting penned by William H. Short.[45]

In California, the *Oakland Tribune* reported in a short note that 'among the guests from California were Mrs. Edwin Goodall and her daughter, Mrs. Charles Minor Cooper, formerly Miss Ella Goodall'.[46] Weeks later, the American Press Association released a picture of the Master with a caption reproducing a portion of 'Abdu'l-Bahá's address.[47]

In Cuba the *Diario de la Marina* (Havana) published a brief account of the meeting on its front page.[48]

Address in the Church of the Divine Paternity, New York

'Abdu'l-Bahá spoke at the service of the Universalist Church of the Divine Paternity held on Sunday, 19 May 1912. A brief announcement in the *New York Herald* related that the title of the talk was 'Religions are many; religion is one.'[49]

Rev. Frank O. Hall (1860–1941), minister of the church from 1901, introduced 'Abdu'l-Bahá, who delivered a lengthy and sympathetic presentation of the Bahá'í Faith. In His talk the Master introduced to the audience some of the Bahá'í principles.[50] The *Sun* published on the following day a short report of the service:

ABDUL BAHA HEARD

THE PERSIAN PHILOSOPHER RECAPITULATES HIS DOCTRINE

Abdul Baha, the Persian philosopher filled the Church of the Divine Paternity Central Park West and Seventy-sixth street, yesterday morning, where, after the regular form of service, followed a short address by the pastor, Dr. Frank Oliver Hall, in which he said that Bahaism, Abdul Baha's doctrine, is in effect Universalism.

The Baha was dressed in Eastern garb and was attended by an interpreter. 'Today in Persia,' he said, 'the Christian, Jew and Mohammedan, those representing every denomination, who have followed my teachings have obtained unity. Strife has passed away. The principles of my faith are:

'1. The oneness of humankind.

'2. Truth of reality. The reality of divine revelation is one.

'3. Religion must correspond to science and have the foundation of science.

'4. Religion must be love and unity. Religion is at the base of all progress by humanity.'

To-morrow night Abdul Baha speaks at the Metropolitan Temple, Seventh Avenue below Fourteenth Street.[51]

Visit to the Brotherhood Church, Jersey City (NJ)

Also on Sunday, 19 May, 'Abdu'l-Bahá visited Jersey City in response to an invitation by Rev. Howard Colby Ives to speak at the Brotherhood Church.

Ives (1867–1941) was a Unitarian minister who up to this time had been pastor of various churches in Massachusetts, Connecticut and New Jersey. He became acquainted for the first time with the Bahá'í Faith and 'Abdu'l-Bahá in 1911 through reading an article that appeared in *Everybody's Magazine* (New York).[52] Soon afterwards Ives started attending some Bahá'í meetings and from these his interest in the Bahá'í Faith grew increasingly and prompted him to open his church to Bahá'ís. On 4 February 1912, for instance, Mountfort Mills delivered at the Brotherhood Church an address on the Bahá'í Faith.[53]

On 11 April Ives traveled to New York to see the Master on His arrival in America and the following day he had a personal interview with Him at the Ansonia. That was the first of many interviews and visits to 'Abdu'l-Bahá, the accounts of which he later penned in a moving way in his memoirs *Portals to Freedom* (1937). Ives remained a Bahá'í for the rest of His life and became one of the pillars of the American Bahá'í community.

On 18 May the Republican *Jersey Journal*, with a circulation of 22,000 copies, published an article announcing that 'Abdul Baha, who has been styled the Peace Missionary and who is spending some time in this country, will be a visitor in this city to-morrow night when he will speak on the need for universal peace and the teachings of the brotherhood of man at the Brotherhood Church service in Bergen Lyceum.' The article continued with some biographical information of 'Abdu'l-Bahá and concluded by stating that 'He has come at the invitation of the Rev. Howard C. Ives.'[54] A portrait of the Master accompanied the text.

'Abdu'l-Bahá spoke on the unity and brotherhood of mankind.[55] On 20 May the same newspaper offered an account of the service:

> FOUR HUNDRED HEAR ABDUL BAHA
>
> Nearly 400 people were present last night at the Brotherhood Church service in the Bergen Lyceum to hear the message of peace and spiritual brotherhood brought from the Orient by Abdul Baha,

the famous Persian prophet and reformer. After the message had been delivered most of those present were guests at an informal reception held in the church parlor and shook the hands of the distinguished speaker of the evening.

They saw a man of about 65, short in stature, with a dark brown face, of benign and spiritual aspect, but marked with lines that spoke of the forty years he had passed for his principles in a Persian jail. On his head was a white cap that seemed at a distance to be a bandage. A white beard and mustache gave the aged man a venerable appearance, he was dressed in some light fabric, coat and trousers being partly hidden by a long dark coat with flowing sleeves.

Accompanying Abdul Baha were his nephew, Dr. Fareed, who acts as interpreter, for the famous Persian speaks no English, and several other Persians, all wearing the Persian black fez, and two wearing the scholar's black robe over their American costumes.

Howard Colby Ives, pastor of the church, introduced Abdul Baha in a brief address in which he spoke of the life of the guest of the evening, of the fact that Abdul Baha came not to get money, but rather to give it.

Through his interpreter the venerable Abdul said:

'Because this church is called the Church of Brotherhood, I wish to touch on the subject of brotherhood. There should be perfect brotherhood underlying all humanity. We are all servants of the one God; we are all beneath the providence of God. There is brotherhood because we all belong to one family; we all belong to the unity of truth; we are all sensitive beings; we are all beneath the dome and canopy of heaven; we all inhabit one earth; we all see the necessity of co-operation; we all belong to one sociology; we are all as the waves of one sea; we are as the branches and fruit of one tree. Material things insure material happiness, and as material happiness becomes greater brotherhood becomes stronger and the world will advance accordingly. But the real brotherhood is the spiritual brotherhood, because material brotherhood is subject to separation and division, and that is why there are wars and strife. The spiritual brotherhood is eternal and does not accept the separation of the material brotherhood, but is the breath of the Holy Spirit. Like the lights in the lamps, there may be many of them, but they are all of the one light, and such is the light of the spirit.'

Next Sunday night's service will be the last at the Brotherhood Church till fall. Rev. William Sullivan, formerly a Paulist Father, but now a lecturer for the New York Ethical Culture Society, will be the speaker.[56]

The *Christian Register* (Boston), in an article dedicated to the Brotherhood Church and the efforts of Ives to maintain it, stated that 'On May 19 Abdul Baha, the Persian prophet of the wonderful world organization of all sects and creeds, under the banner of Brotherhood spoke.' The same article also mentioned the fact that Mountfort Mills spoke in this church on the Bahá'í Faith.[57]

16

BOSTON

22–6 May 1912

'Abdu'l-Bahá left New York on the morning of Wednesday, 22 May. His train reached Boston some six hours later and there He was received by the local Bahá'ís and representatives of different organizations and societies in the city. From the station He proceeded to Hotel Victoria where He stayed during part of His sojourn in Boston and where He received many of His visitors.[1]

As early as December 1911 Bostonian Bahá'ís informed a local newspaper of the upcoming travels of the Master. In an interview for the *Boston Journal*, Bertha Sythes, a local Bahá'í, stated that 'It is true that we expect the Abbas Effendi in Boston early during the coming year. A cablegram was received last week saying that he expected to be in the city some time during March.' Regarding the plans for 'Abdu'l-Bahá's visit to Boston, Sythes further declared that 'We have already had the offers of many churches in Boston, where the Abbas Effendi may preach while he is here, but we have felt that for many reasons it would be difficult to accept these kind offers, and I expect we shall use Ford Hall.'[2] One of these invitations came from the Mayor of Boston, John Francis Fitzgerald (1863–1950), grandfather of President J. F. Kennedy, who invited 'Abdu'l-Bahá to address the local government at a public meeting.[3]

Reporting on the celebration of the Naw-Rúz feast, the *Lowell Sun* (MA), a Democratic newspaper issuing some 15,200 copies daily, further reported that 'Plans were made at the observance for the reception which will be rendered Abdul Baha, 'Servant of God', present leader of the sect, who will come to Boston sometime in May. Mrs. Breed expects to leave Cambridge for Washington and New York early next month with a number of other prominent Bahais of America to greet him on his arrival in this country.[4]

The American Unitarian Conference

The same day that 'Abdu'l-Bahá arrived in Boston, He attended the festival of the annual American Unitarian Conference which was held at the Tremont Temple.[5] The event gathered a great number of Unitarian ministers from the United States and Canada, and different testimonies show that the audience was greatly impressed by the Master. David Rhys Williams (1890–1970), one of those present on that day, recalled years later in his memoirs that 'Abdul Baha visited this country several years ago. It was my privilege to see and hear him at a large gathering in Tremont Temple of Boston during my seminary days. I shall never forget the mental picture I have of him, a picture of a man of simple dignity and spiritual beauty with a resonant voice that commanded dignity.'[6]

The participation of 'Abdu'l-Bahá at the conference was reported in various newspapers on the preceding days as the highlight of the event. On 16 May the *Christian Register* (Boston), announced that the session at which 'Abdu'l-Bahá would speak was to start at 6 p.m. and detailed the prices of the tickets for participants.[7] On 18 May, the *Boston Transcript* carried an article announcing the visit of 'Abdu'l-Bahá to the city and introducing the Bahá'í Faith. Most of its information was probably gathered from the book *The Universal Principles of the Bahai Movement*. Regarding His visit to Boston the article related that 'in addition to his addresses before the Unitarians here, he will appear before the Twentieth Century Club, the Massachusetts Suffrage Society, the Second Church of Christ, Scientist'.[8]

On 20 May the *Boston Post* declared that 'nearly 1000 delegates from outside greater Boston' were expected at the Unitarian festival and that 'Two of the principal speakers of the evening will be Abdul Baha, the Persian prophet and founder of the new universal religion and Prof. William S. Morgan, a prominent member of the faculty of the University of California.'[9]

Interestingly, most of the reports published in the press about the festival centered their attention on the presence of 'Abdu'l-Bahá, who spoke on the unity of religions and the elimination of religious prejudice.[10]

Estimates of the number of attendants given by the press ranged from 700 to 1,500 people. Among the participants in the program were Robert Luce (1862–1946), Lieutenant-Governor of Massachusetts; Hon. George Hutchinson of Newton, who held various offices in the American Unitarian Association; and the ministers Howard M. Brown and Frederick Robertson Griffin of Montreal, who months later met 'Abdu'l-Bahá in Canada and from whose pulpit 'Abdu'l-Bahá delivered His first public address in Canada; William Rodman-Peabody (1874–1941), chairman of the festival; and William L. Sullivan (1872–1935).

The account appeared in the *Boston Post*, a Democratic morning newspaper with a daily circulation of 340,300 copies, quoted some of the words delivered by 'Abdu'l-Bahá and reported the following:

> PERSIAN PROPHET AT UNITARIAN FESTIVAL
>
> Abdul Baha Abbas Effendi, the Persian prophet, spoke for the first time in this city last night to more than 1000 delegates of the American Unitarian Association at the annual Unitarian festival in Tremont Temple.
>
> Attired in the flowing robes of his native land, the apostle of the Bahai movement made a great impression on his listeners, many of whom were clergymen from all over the United States and Canada. His remarkable face, long white beard and his expression of thought was in keeping with the universal principles of peace which the new religion stands for . . .
>
> Lieutenant-Governor Robert Luce presided at the festival introducing the aged Persian and he was given a great ovation. Baha dwelt on the universal principles of the Bahai movement, social, economic and governmental.
>
> He declared that religion must undergo an immediate change. 'Industrialism, law and legislation, the ethical world', said he, 'have been reformed. The sciences of past ages are in a measure useless today. The rules of the past century cannot be applied now. Old thoughts and ethics will not do for the present day. When you compare all of the achievements of the past they are infantile with those of the present.
>
> 'Religious differences have been the cause of strife and war. If the nations of the world forsake imitation and seek realities and realities are one, then all nations of the world shall be one.

'A Jew is a Jew because his father was a Jew. A Buddhist is a Buddhist because his parents were Buddhists. So the new generation is one of imitation, and because they never investigate they continue in imitation. Unity and amity will never be realized as long as imitation exists, but when imitation ceases, then we shall have universal peace.'[11]

The *Boston Transcript*, a Republican newspaper with a circulation of 30,100 copies, also reproduced notes of 'Abdu'l-Bahá's talk and described His audience as an 'attentive throng of Unitarians':

HEAR PROPHET FROM ORIENT

ABDUL BAHA CONTRIBUTES TO UNITARIAN FESTIVAL PROGRAMME

Abdul Baha, Abbas Effendi, apostle of what is called the Universal Religion represented in the Bahai movement, stood on the platform of Tremont Temple last evening and addressed an attentive throng of Unitarians. The venerable man, attired in silken robe and white turban of the Orient, was accompanied by Dr. Ameen Fareed, also a Persian, and a graduate of Johns Hopkins University, who translated the address sentence by sentence.

'All creation', said the prophet, 'expresses motion, for movement is the expression of being, whereas stagnation is the expression of death. Every moving object is a living object, and every object which is stationary is as dead.

'Among the great realities which must be living and therefore moving is religion. Day by day it must be progressive and expressive of motion. If religion be stagnant, motionless, it is dead.

'Science and the arts have undergone reformation, so have industry, crafts and laws. The ethical world has been reformed. The sciences of the past ages and the past forms of knowledge are useless today. The rules of the past centuries will not apply to present exigencies. Old thoughts, old ethics, will not do for the present time

'Religious differences, therefore, have been a cause of strife and warfare. But if the nations of the world investigate the realities, all the nations will agree, for reality is not multiple, but one. It is imitation that has proved to be a hindrance to this unity, the cause of the dispersion of mankind, the cause of strife and warfare. The new generation is one of imitation, it does not investigate. As long as man is bound by and subject to these imitations, the unity of mankind and unity among men will not be realized.

'And these imitations will not pass away without a reformation in religion, in other words, the reality of all the religions must be renewed. Fraternity will not hinder warfare until spiritual brotherhood comes through the breath of the Holy Spirit, and then it will not only hinder, but uproot warfare – will unite all the nations of the world: and make them one.

'This century, which has gone beyond the past and made all things new, is worthy to witness the great solidarity of human kind and the great service of universal peace . . .'[12]

Parts of this article were later included in an article about the Unitarian Annual Meeting that appeared in the *Springfield Daily Republican* (MA), a local newspaper issuing 16,000 copies daily.[13] The *Christian Science Monitor*, which had a national and a state edition with a combined circulation of 185,000 copies, reported the following:

About 700 men and women attended the seventy-first annual Unitarian festival in Tremont Temple yesterday and hundreds more were in the balconies at the close of the dinner to hear the speaking. The attendance was larger than for several years.

. . . Abdul Baha Effendi spoke of the necessity of progressiveness in religion as well as in every other phase of human life. He spoke in his native tongue, his remarks being translated into English by an attendant.

He deprecated 'religion by tradition' handed down from father to son, because, he said, it can bring to mankind neither unity nor amity. He hoped for the time when all nations will be united in loving fellowship, under a reformed, broadened and intellectual religion.[14]

A further account appeared simultaneously in the *Boston Journal*, with 95,000 copies, and in Springfield's *Daily News*, 11,000 copies, contained information similar to that published in other journals and stated that 1,100 people were present at the meeting:

NOTED PERSIAN GIVES ADDRESS

ABDUL BAHA PLEADS FOR RELIGIOUS UNITY AT UNITARIAN FESTIVAL

Abdul Baha Effendi, head of the Bahai movement, or universal religion, made his first public appearance in Boston last night when, dressed in a somber tunic and white turban, he stood upon the platform of Tremont Temple and told nearly 1100 members and guests of the American Unitarian Association on the occasion of their annual festival, that all countries must be one, all men brothers, worshiping God together.

'All things that live are realities,' said he. 'Religion moves, if it be a true religion, it is alive and, therefore, is a reality. This is the century of light as exemplified by progress in science, art and ethics.

'It is the clinging to the old order and reluctance to sympathise with one of the followers of another old order which is responsible for all the upheaval in the world. This separates men. With these imitations cast aside men seeking the realities shall receive it. Men will now seek out fraternity and through the power of the holy spirit understand God's will that all men shall be as one. There shall be no happiness and no prosperity until that day when all nations are one.'[15]

An account that appeared in the *Boston Advertiser*, a Republican newspaper with a circulation of 22,500 copies, also quoted portions of the talk and stated that 'Abdu'l-Bahá 'made a deep impression on his hearers':

ABDUL BAHA EFFENDI TALKS TO UNITARIANS

Abdul Baha Effendi, the picturesque leader of Bahaism, the Persian cult devoted to religious unity, international peace and universal brotherhood, was a speaker at the Unitarian festival at Tremont Temple, last evening. The old man, with his snow white beard, gray robes and white turban, made a deep impression on his hearers and was very cordially received by the large gathering. He delivered his address through an interpreter. 'All creation,' said he, 'is the expression of motion, for motion is the expression of life while stagnation is the expression of death. Every moving object is a living object and every stationary object is dead. Among the great realities which must be moving and therefore living is religion. If religion be stagnant, motionless, it is dead.

'The divine prophets have founded the divine religion. They have taught and promulgated the knowledge of God. They founded ethics worthy of the admiration of the world. Those realities which the prophets labored to inculcate in the human mind now vanished away. Religious differences have been the cause of strife and even bloodshed. The divine prophets have been the foundation of reality.

'If the nations of the world will forsake imitations and seek reality all the nations of the world shall agree. All are servants of God. All are sheltered under His providence. God provides for all. God is the giver of all.

'The spirit of brotherhood which obtains through the holy spirit hinders warfare, nay it uproots it. True fraternity shall be realized and through the holy spirit be established.'[16]

Another account was published in the *Boston Herald*, an independent morning newspaper issuing 70,000 copies daily. The article, which was accompanied by a drawing representing 'Abdu'l-Bahá while delivering His address, stated that when He arrived at the Tremont Temple He 'sat for several minutes, without exciting much attention, at the rear of the platform' but later, when 'he moved forward to the head table, the whole audience of 1500 people rose to welcome and applaud the Persian guest'.[17]

The Boston Daily Globe published an article in which no mention about the presence of 'Abdu'l-Bahá at Tremont Temple was made but which included a portrait of Him.[18] The *Christian Register* (Boston), monthly organ of the American Unitarians with a circulation of 6,600 copies, carried on 30 May a detailed account of the convention, including the words of Frederick R. Griffin in introducing 'Abdu'l-Bahá:

'We are to listen to-night to a man whose presence is a benediction, a man who has arisen as prophet and master of the largest spirit of internationalism, – one whose writings give a better spirit unto all who read them. When the time comes for us to welcome the leader of the Bahais, Abdul Baha, we shall find in him the embodiment of the American ideal of internationalism, and, as the world is being brought closer together, may its moral forces so marshal their strength that there may be not only internationalism through trade in material things, but a spiritual internationalism which will bind the hearts and the souls of men in one great family.'

At this point the distinguished Persian visitor, clad in white robes, his long white beard lending a patriarchal aspect to his benignant face, ascended the platform, attended by his interpreter and his secretary. Lieutenant Governor Luce introduced him with a few words of explanation of his late arrival, due to the fatigue of his journey from Mohonk. With one accord the audience rose to greet the Persian sage, who motioned them to resume their seats. He spoke in a voice the musical cadence of which was peculiarly charming, even though unintelligible, and each sentence was rendered into English by his interpreter.

He emphasized the truth that religion to live must be progressive. As the science of past ages and the rules of past centuries have become inapplicable to present exigencies, so religious differences among men ought no longer to be perpetuated. The essence of the teaching of the divine prophets has been lost sight of. Reality is one and not multiple, but imitations have proved a hindrance to this unity. The Jew, the Mohammedan, and the Buddhist are these because of their parentage. The prophets of God have all promulgated the true fraternity of brotherhood; and the spiritual brotherhood, which obtains through the breath of the Holy Spirit, uproots warfare and serves international peace. Until all humanity be united and all nations become one, progress and prosperity will not be realized by man. Inasmuch as this is the century of illumination, sciences have advanced, industry has progressed, liberty has been obtained, justice is established. Therefore this century is worthy of witnessing the great solidarity of mankind and the great service of universal peace.[19]

The *Unitarian Word and Work* (Boston) further related that 'Abdul Baha, the prophet of the Bahaist movement, spoke through an interpreter at the Festival and before the Religious Education Association and attended various other gatherings. His utterances were quite familiar in sound to Unitarian ears and his form of universal religion is congenial to the Unitarian habit of mind.'[20]

Several accounts of the meeting were also published outside Boston. The philosopher Ellen M. Mitchell,[21] who was probably among the participants at the conference, a few days later wrote her own impressions of the Master in an article for the *Post Standard* of Syracuse (NY), a Republican newspaper with a circulation of 42,400 copies daily:

> The most picturesque figure at the Unitarian Festival was the Oriental prophet Abdul Baha, leader of Bahaism, the Persian cult devoted to religious unity, international unity, international peace and universal brotherhood. Bahaism has many followers in Europe and in this country. It does not ask people to leave their churches. Abdul Baha simply urges on all the highest degree of morality and spiritual life. I know little of Bahaism but recall in this connection the words of Dr. Cuthbert Hall, who says that in the highest realm of thinking Christianity supplements Oriental philosophy and that the deepest mysteries of Christ may not be unfolded until East joins West in their interpretation.[22]

In Canada, the Icelandic monthly *Heimir* (Winnipeg, MB) published a report of the festival which also mentioned the participation of 'Abdu'l-Bahá and summarized His words.[23]

As for other events, 'Abdu'l-Bahá went to the Tremont Temple accompanied by His translator, Amín Faríd, and by Ahmad Sohrab, who was frequently in charge of taking notes of His words. Sohrab had developed a system for rapidly taking notes from the Persian and this caught the attention of some of the stenographers present at the event. One of them, Bates Torrey, associate editor of the monthly magazine *The Stenographer* (Philadelphia), interviewed Sohrab on the following day to inquire about his technique. The report that ensued offers interesting information about a little-known aspect of the process employed for recording the Persian words of the Master and also identifies the name of the stenographer who took the notes of the English translation of 'Abdu'l-Bahá's talk:

> One of the 1,000 delegates to the convention in Boston of the American Unitarian Association was Abdul Baha Abbas Effendi, who came to voice the principles of the Bahai Movement, that new and progressive religion of brotherhood and peace.
>
> When Mr. Frank H. Burt started to report the interpreted address of Abdul Baha he found by his side a dark complexioned person taking down the original Persian in the most fluent fashion, writing from right to left and keeping up with the procession.

Abdul Baha spoke only in Persian, having with him his own interpreter, a very scholarly man, and his secretary, Mr. Mirza Ahmed Sohrab, of Ispahan. It was this latter gentleman we next day went to interview; for Persian shorthand writers do not often reach Boston – to tell the truth, we had never heard of this Oriental branch of the craft. Mr. Sohrab said that his writing was not really a system of shorthand, but a sort of condensed Arabic longhand, something that any educated Persian could read. He stated that when Persia had a Parliament the speeches of the delegates were reported by a variety of so-called systems devised for the purpose; but that he had been away from home nine years, and had developed his own style of brief writing from reading the books recently printed in Persia in regards to it. We saw Mr. Sohrab write; we present herewith a page of his notes with their translation, and having before us so clear a notion of their fluency and legibility we come to the decision that if this is not shorthand in a practical sense, then we do not know what shorthand ought to be.

The magazine published a photograph of one page of Sohrab's notes. These notes recorded the comments made by 'Abdu'l-Bahá clarifying some points of His address at the Tremont Temple:

Last night I made a short address, and in the papers read this morning hardly a quarter of what was said was reported. From this my aim is not fully comprehended.

My object was this, that all things are constantly in a state of reformation. Every object is moving, for motion is a proof of life, and stagnation a proof of death.

All existing objects are in a state of evolution and progress, and among them is religion; and this should be in a state of motion and should progress continually.

If it has no motion it will fade away and become dead. The foundations of the teachings of the prophets of God have been a continued resuscitation of the religions of the world.[24]

Visit to Clark University

On 23 May 'Abdu'l-Bahá had lunch with Professor George Hubbard Blakeslee (1871–1954) who afterwards personally accompanied Him to Worcester where He visited the university and delivered an address to students and faculty members.[25] Blakeslee was the founder of the *Journal of Race Development* (Worcester) and launched a series of conferences at Clark University at which he would invite personalities of his time to speak about social and peace issues. He was quite famous for this, and his conferences were, after the Lake Mohonk Peace Conferences, second in importance for the peace movement in the USA.

'Abdu'l-Bahá's address was publicised in advance in two local newspapers.[26] On 24 May, the *Worcester Evening Gazette*, the city's oldest daily newspaper with a circulation of 17,400 copies, published the following account of the meeting:

> BAB RELIGION'S LEADER TALKS TO CLARK STUDENTS
>
> ABDUL BAHA ABBAS OF THE ORIENT ALSO PLEADS FOR SCIENCE
>
> Clothed in Oriental costume of rich colors and his head ornamented by a glossy white turban, Abbas Effendi, or Abdul Baha Abbas, head of the new Bab religion recently arisen in the Orient, spoke to an audience of 500 yesterday afternoon in Clark University. He was a man of striking and stately bearing, and made a picturesque figure as he talked in his Persian robes.
>
> He had an interpreter with him, Dr. Ameen Ullah Fareed, as he was not himself familiar with English. He was introduced by Dr. George H. Blakeslee, head of the department of history of Clark College, who arranged for the address. The Bab, as he is known officially by his followers, said little about the religion he professes, but he was rich in praise of science and the universities, declaring that in science lay the hope of ultimate solidarity for the human race.
>
> He said that science enables man to go beyond natural law, and it has given to the world its great array of scholars distinguished above their fellows, to whom he paid tribute. The scholar's sovereignty, he declared, is superior to that of the king. 'May science proclaim the wonders of humankind,' said the Bab, 'may it bring about universal peace, may it cement the hearts of men together, may it make of all countries one fatherland, and may it unite all religions according to

> the fundamental conceptions of reality; and all religion is founded on one reality.'
>
> The Bab gave a reception in President Hall's home after his talk, and a number met him there.[27]

The *Worcester Post*, a local Democratic newspaper with a circulation of 11,600 copies, published a shorter report which also included a biographical sketch of the Master (not included here) and a portrait:

> About 500 persons interested in theology and philosophy listened to an interesting talk given in Clark college gymnasium yesterday afternoon by Abdul Baha Abbas, head of the Bab religion, a new oriental faith that is said to have gained hundreds of thousands of converts in the United States and millions in the near east . . .
>
> The present Bab, Abbas Effendi, or Abdul Baha Abbas, does not speak English, and his remarks yesterday were interpreted by Dr. Ameen Ullah Fareed, his interpreter.
>
> He was introduced by Prof. George H. Blakeslee, head of the History department of Clark University. His talk was devoted more to science than a description of the new religion.[28]

A brief account published in the *Clark College Monthly* also stated that 'Abdu'l-Bahá 'spoke of science and its achievements in enabling man to solve mysteries and make intellectual progress, and expressed the hope that science will one day cement together by uniting the various religions, which are all ultimately based on one reality.'[29] The *Worcester Telegram*, a Republican newspaper circulating 23,700 copies, published on 24 May an article on the Bahá'í Faith.[30]

Interview for the Boston Traveler

According to Maḥmúd, a journalist who interviewed 'Abdu'l-Bahá in Boston became a Bahá'í as a result of this meeting.[31] Perhaps this newspaperman was the reporter with the evening Republican newspaper *Boston Traveler*, with a circulation of some 30,000 copies, which on 24 May carried an interesting interview with 'Abdu'l-Bahá that also included a picture of Him taken while He was leaving His hotel:

ABDUL BAHA HAS CREED HE DECLARES WILL FINALLY ELIMINATE CRIMINAL

PERSIAN DOES NOT BELIEVE IN CAPITAL PUNISHMENT AND THINKS THAT, IN EDUCATION, WOMAN SHOULD HAVE PREFERENCE OVER MERE MAN

'No, I do not believe in capital punishment,' said Abdul Baha, founder of the new Bahai religious movement, today in an interview with the Traveler.

'If the Bahai movement is widely successful it will hold such sway over the moral, intellectual and physical character of the race that there will not be a criminal to be found.'

When Abdul Baha was questioned regarding his views on capital punishment and the recent electrocution at the Charlestown state prison he would only say, 'Some other punishment more humane ought to be instituted. We should forgive. There is a distinction between retribution and revenge.'

Although the Oriental leader has been in Boston but a few days he is thorough acquainted with the religions of all parts of the country and thinks that Boston has more denominations and sects than any other city in the United States.

'BOSTON LIKE A ROSE GARDEN'

'Boston is like a rose garden,' he said, 'made up of variegated colors, all lending a charm and attraction to the various elements in that garden. The many religions of this city form the component parts of the garden. If you go into a garden where there is but one kind of flower, but of different colorings, the effect is much more beautiful than if it is made up of many different varieties.

'This sums up the religious situation of Boston. "Boston" means "garden" in the Persian language, and, as regards religion, lives up to its Persian tradition. There are many fruitful flowers and trees of religion here. There are many different sentiments and new thoughts of religion; there are many creeds and denominations, but no matter how many of them exist, there is bound to be a spark of good in each one which will contribute to the general good.'

When Abdul Baha speaks before the Free Religious Association in Ford this afternoon he is expected to touch on his favorite theme, that of woman suffrage. He is a most enthusiastic supporter of woman's rights, one of the principal laws in his religion embodying the rule of the equality of sexes. [*portion illegible*]

SHOULD EDUCATE MOTHERS

'Girls are to be the mothers of our race and they are the ones who should be educated. The result will be the education of the whole race. The father is only educated for himself, and he cannot teach his children. Of course I believe in woman suffrage. The women should have their freedom. We are all servants of God and he has blended men and women alike with the idea of equality, although unhappily this has not been demonstrated to any high degree as yet. That is the true religious atmosphere – equality of the sexes. I do not mean by that statement that womankind is better than men.

'Universal peace and international arbitration are impossible without universal suffrage. Women will eventually abolish war when they get the ballot and will accordingly refuse to let their sons go on the battlefield. Why don't you free the women?

'One of the most essential things of God's work is the future life. I believe strongly in the immortality of the soul. Bahaism does not differ materially from other religions in this respect. Death is the result of composition just as life is.

'Eventually humanity will advance to such a perfection that people will not commit any crime. When that time comes we will love our neighbors as ourselves [*portion illegible*].'[32]

Address to the Free Religious Association of America

Boston was the headquarters of the American Free Religious Association, an organization established in 1865 as an interdenominational and later interreligious non-conformist movement. From 23 to 24 May 1912, the organization held in Boston its forty-fifth annual meeting and its main topic was 'State and Church in America'.

'Abdu'l-Bahá was invited to speak at the public session of the conference which took place at the Ford Hall on Friday, 24 May, at 1 p.m. As usual, the press announced His participation some days in advance. On 16 May the *Christian Register* carried three references to 'Abdu'l-Bahá in relation to the conference.[33] On 20 May the *Boston Journal* mentioned that 'The Free Religious Association will be addressed at its annual meeting Friday in Ford Hall by Abdul Baha, the Persian leader of the Bahai movement, who will arrive in this city Wednesday. Saturday afternoon he will speak before the Twentieth Century Club.'[34] A further announcement was published in the *Boston Post* on 24 May as part of an article on one of the executive sessions of the conference.[35]

In His address 'Abdu'l-Bahá spoke on the need for peace and presented some of the Bahá'í principles.[36] His talk and the comments of other participants were recorded by the press. On 25 May the *Transcript* briefly mentioned the name of 'Abdu'l-Bahá among the speakers.[37] The same day the *Boston Herald* published the following:

> Moses, Zoroaster and Buddha taught the same principles as Christ and had the same purpose, Abdul Baha, founder of the new Bahai movement in religion, told the Free Religious Association at its conference in Ford Hall yesterday afternoon. He deplored the differences between followers of different cults and said there was no reason why all should not be at one.
>
> 'The essences of the teachings of these great and blessed souls are one and the same,' he said. 'The reality of their law is one. Zoroaster was a prophet precisely as was the Messiah. There is no difference whatsoever between the teachings of Zoroaster and those of Christ. The teachings of Buddha were not at all opposed to the teachings of Christ and likewise all the prophets.
>
> 'But, alas, after their days certain dogmatic motives crept in and those motives caused division, for the motives which crept in were not reality, but were purely superstitious, and directly inimical to the law laid down by them. Instead of the spirit of co-operation and solidarity taking possession of them they all began to cause greater strife, and jealousy existed among them.'
>
> He announced that the religion of God was the cause of united humanity, the cause of love.
>
> Other speakers were Edwin D. Mead, Jenkin Lloyd Jones, the Rev. Nicholas Van der Pyl, Alfred W. Martin of New York, Prof. Daniel Evans of Andover Seminary and Prof. William S. Morgan and the Rev. Frederick L. Hosmer.
>
> Rustom Rustomjee, editor of the Oriental Review of Bombay, India, outlined the dejection of the priestly class in India. Prof. L. P. Sacks of Oxford spoke of Great Britain and the church there.[38]

The following account in the *Boston Post* was also published in the *Daily News* (Springfield):

> Abdul Baha, the Persian prophet, who addressed his first Boston audience in Tremont Temple Wednesday evening, was graciously received. The large audience rose as he entered the hall, and that his simple teachings of universal peace and brotherhood were in accord with the feelings of the assemblage was evidenced by the applause which followed this distinguished eastern prophet's remarks.
>
> Abdul Baha dwelt on the principles of the new religion. 'This is a century of light,' said he, through his interpreter, 'a century in which enmity and strife must cease. The policy of God is a humane policy. Just as God deals with us, let us deal with one another.
>
> 'For thousands of years strife and enmity has been among mankind, each religion considering the other its enemy, and each denomination thinking the other false.'[39]

The *Christian Register* published on 4 July the following comment on 'Abdu'l-Bahá as part of a general evaluation of the conference: 'At the festival in the afternoon, in the lower hall, some two hundred and fifty places were reserved at the tables. So great was the additional attendance, however, that it was thought best to adjourn to the larger hall above for the remaining addresses. A unique and gracious feature of the occasion was the presence and word of Abdul Baha, Abbas Effendi, of Persia, the venerated leader of the Bahaist movement of that country. As he entered, leaning on the arm of the President of the Association, the audience rose in token of their respect.'[40] These comments appeared also in a report published with the proceedings of the conference.[41] The proceedings also included the introductory remarks to 'Abdu'l-Bahá made by Edward D. Mead (1849–1937), chairman of the conference and director of the World Peace Foundation, who met 'Abdu'l-Bahá for the first time at the Lake Mohonk conference:

> MR. MEAD. – It is a great pleasure to join in welcoming to Boston, and to welcome to the platform of the Free Religious Association, the living head of the great Bahai movement of Persia and the East. I could not think of any more fitting place for such a teacher of religion to come. If there is one thing for which the Free Religious

Association has conspicuously stood from the beginning, it is for the sympathy of religions and for giving a sympathetic and loving hearing to representatives of all the great religious movements of the world. There is surely no movement in the East to-day which has commanded more seriously and earnestly the attention of the religious people of this country than the movement represented by our friend whose presence here is so grateful to us. We welcome him for more reasons than one. We have been inspired, many of us, since he arrived in this country, by his noble and outspoken words in behalf of many of the movements which are to us of cardinal importance. The first time that I saw him, the only time that I have seen him until now, was at the Arbitration Conference at Lake Mohonk last week, where he spoke in behalf of the commanding movement for universal peace.

It chanced that yesterday, at the same time that the Free Religious Association was holding its annual Business Meeting, there was being held in another room in the same building the annual meeting of the Massachusetts Men's League for Woman Suffrage; and we remembered there that, as it was said by the great apostle that 'in Christ Jesus there is neither male nor female', so our friend has constantly here in America emphasized the equal rights of woman and the imperative duty of conferring that equality upon her in our modern society. We welcome him, therefore, for the conspicuous aid which he brings from a new point of view to the great social causes which are peculiarly sacred to us. But we welcome him chiefly as spokesman of religion and of a form of religion which is so nearly our own. The best tribute which I have heard paid to Abdul Baha in Boston was paid yesterday morning by a leading Unitarian as I walked with him across Boston Common. 'After all,' he asserted, – speaking of the night before, – 'all that he said was simply what we have been hearing here all the time.' My friends, that is the noble thing about it all, that under different environment, under an entirely different social system, with a history so unlike ours, proving their faith by willingness for martyrdom and by actual martyrdom, the representatives of this movement have stood in the East for the first principles of those forms of religion which we hold loftiest in the West. It is a notable tribute to the unity of the religious spirit and the unity of deep religious thought. And because we feel that we are one with him and that he is one with us, we welcome this representative of the great Bahai movement. I have pleasure in presenting to you Abdul Baha, the Abbas Effendi.[42]

'Abdu'l-Bahá's talk was also included in the proceedings:

[*Abdul Baha, who had entered leaning on the arm of the President of the Association, was received with great applause and the rising of the audience. He spoke in Persian, being interpreted by his secretary sentence by sentence.*]

REMARKS OF ABDUL BAHA

The divine religions have descended for love and amity among mankind. They have been founded for unity and the purpose of affinity among mankind. They have descended for the purpose of cementing together the human family. But alas! the religions of the world have made use of religion as a pretext for discord, considering each prophet as against the others. For example, the Jews consider Moses to be opposed to Jesus Christ. The Christians consider Zoroaster to be opposed or inimical to His Holiness the Christ. The Buddhist considers His Holiness Zoroaster as opposed to Buddha. The Mohammedans consider all of them as inimical to their religion; whereas, these great ones were founding the same principle. Their aim was one, and all of them were united and agreed. The essentials of their teachings are one and the same. The reality of their law is one. All of them have served the one God and they have all summoned people to the same Maker. For example, His Holiness Zoroaster was a prophet, precisely according to the Messianic example. There was no difference whatsoever between the spirit of the teachings which Zoroaster gave and those which His Holiness the Christ gave. Likewise the teachings of Buddha are not at all opposed to the teachings of the Christ, or to the teachings of any of the prophets. These great and blessed souls had for their aim the same principle. Their purpose was one, their law was one, their teaching was one.

But alas! after their days certain dogmatic imitations crept in, and these imitations caused division. For the imitations which crept in were not reality but were purely superstitious and utterly inimical to the law laid down by the founders. They were distinct from the teachings given by the prophets because they were inimical; therefore they caused enmity and strife and division. In place of the unity which was intended to bind together the religionists, these imitations caused a regrettable separation. Instead of loving fellowship which was to animate them, the spirit of strife and discord animated them. Instead of the spirit of co-operation and solidarity taking possession of them, they began to cause greater envy and jealousy to exist among them. Therefore, the world of humanity from its inception up to the present day has not found peace and rest. There has ever been warfare and strife among religions; discord and bloodshed have been extant among them.

If we refer to history we shall find such deplorable events as to cause us to lament and to mourn. For the law of God which was meant to be a basis for loving fellowship and unity was used for purposes contrary to the original intention. The law of God may be likened to a remedy. If a remedy be used in a proper manner it is curative. But alas! these remedies or curative agents were cast into the hands of unskilled physicians, who used them without skill and for purposes wholly selfish. In place of these remedies proving to be of healing properties, they proved the opposite. Instead of their conferring life they caused death. Instead of their causing illumination they caused darkness – simply because these remedies were placed in the hands of unskilled physicians. An unskilled physician cannot confer life; his prescriptions are ever futile; nay, they are harmful.

His Holiness Baha 'Ullah appeared about sixty years ago in Persia, at a time when among the peoples of Persia there was strife and enmity unspeakable, to the extent that each considered the other religionists as outcasts. They even went so far as using unseemly language, each thirsting for the blood of the other. His Holiness Baha 'Ullah proclaimed the oneness of the world of humanity. Secondly, he proclaimed that the religion of God must be the cause of unity and amity – the cause of life must it be. If religion be the cause of enmity, he declared, its absence is better than its presence, for the purpose of religion is love of mankind, and if religion yields enmity surely its non-existence is preferable.

Thirdly, Baha 'Ullah proclaimed that religion must correspond with science, for religion is reality and science is reality, and reality corresponds. It is not multiple, there is no difference in any reality. If a religious question be opposed to reason and science, it is pure imagination and baseless, for the opposite of knowledge or science is ignorance. This is as evident as the sun at mid-day.

The fourth principle he inculcated was that all humanity is in the estimation of God equal; all are the servants of God; all are beneath the mercy of God. God has created all, God provideth for all, God nurtures all, God protects all, God is kind to all; – why should we be unkind? God gives provision; why should we suspend that provision? God loves all his servants; why should we be inimical? God is at peace with everybody; why should we be warring? God has created us for love and amity and not for strife and enmity. Why should we oppose such an attribute of divine mercy? Why shall we becloud such radiance and effulgence with darkness? Why shall we oppose such love divine with hatred and jealousy?

For six thousand years humanity has been tormented with these baser qualities; strife and enmity have been extant among mankind, each religion considering the other as its enemy, each sect considering the others as inimical to it and each denomination considering all other denominations as false, each religion pronouncing anathema on all the others. Is it not sufficient? What result has come from that attitude, what fruit has it yielded to humanity?

Now, this century is a century of light. It is a century wherein such superstitions must be cast away. This century is one in which enmity and strife must cease. This is a century wherein all the peoples, all the religionists, must associate with each other with perfect spirit of love and fellowship. For all are the servants of one God. They have come to be through the same mercy, they are illumined by the same light, they are revivified by the same light. At most, one may be sick – he must be treated, he must be shown kindliness. One may be ignorant – he must be taught. One may be childlike – he must be assisted in order that he may reach maturity, until he may reach the age of majority. No one shall be considered as opposed, nobody shall be shown enmity. All are brothers, all are mothers, all are daughters, all are sisters, and that which God has meant to be united, those whom God has bound together, why shall we disunite and disband? That which God's hand of mercy has built, why shall we destroy? Oppose not the will of God. Think of no policy inimical to the divine policy.

> Think of how liberal God's policy is. Act in accordance therewith. Surely the policy of God is above human policy. For no matter how far human policy shall advance or how intelligent the human mind may be, the policy of God forever remains the perfect, the complete. We must emulate the divine policy. Just as God deals with his creation let us also deal with one another. Let us follow His example. There is no better example than God. We observe the traces of God, we observe the phenomena of his wisdom. Is it meet for us to leave aside the wisdom of God and to create certain imaginary distinctions and to hold tenaciously thereto and to cause enmity among humanity? God forbid. Never have the prophets of God been willing that such shall be the status. The prophets of God have all promulgated the same foundation; they have given fundamentally the same teachings, and the teachings of the prophets of God are pure spirit, are pure religion, are pure love, are pure unity. Therefore we must emulate the prophets of God.[43]

The next to speak after 'Abdu'l-Bahá was the Unitarian Minister Rev. Jenkin Lloyd Jones (1843–1918) who, as noted in chapter 12, had invited 'Abdu'l-Bahá to address his congregation at the All Souls' Church on 5 May. Jones spoke in favour of the social and religious role of the Catholic Church and in the course of his address asked that the Free Religious Association 'put the Catholic Church in the same favorable light into which it puts Buddhism and Zoroastrianism and Bahaism'.[44]

Some months after the celebration of the annual meeting of the Free Religious Association, the Catholic weekly *America* (New York) published an article criticizing the event and the fact that a group of mostly foreign men or second generation immigrants discussed the subjects of religion in America and Catholic clericalism. In the course of the article the author briefly mentioned 'Abdu'l-Bahá, reproducing some of the information published about Him in the proceedings of the meeting.[45]

Saturday, 25 May 1912

The date of 'Abdu'l-Bahá's birth, 23 May 1844, coincided with the declaration of the Báb in Shiraz and owing to this circumstance the Master instructed that this date be celebrated only as the day of the declaration of the Báb. Despite this, the Bahá'ís of Boston organized a birthday celebration for 'Abdu'l-Bahá on Saturday 25 May. 'Abdu'l-Bahá stayed for a while at the meeting, at which He again requested that in the future His birthday not be celebrated. An account of the meeting appeared in the *Boston Herald*:

> ABDUL BAHA IS BIRTHDAY GUEST
>
> In commemoration of the declaration of the Bab and the 68th birthday of Abdul Baha Abbas of Persia, now in Boston, a feast was given under the auspices of the Boston Bahai Assembly at the home of Mrs. Alice Ives Breed of Cambridge yesterday. About 100 friends from Boston and other leading cities of the country were present. Flowers were sent by Mrs. Joseph H. White of Brookline in memory of her sister, Mme. Jackson of Paris, and a personal friend of Abdul Baha.
>
> There was a big birthday cake adorned with 68 tiny candles and three flags, the American flag in honor of the Boston Bahai Assembly, the Persian flag and the English flag, in honour of Miss Alice M. Buckton of England, author of the 'Eager Heart', and the daughter of the famous scientist. It was the wish of Abdul Baha to have the flag of every country on the cake, as he is universal and considers every country his own, but there was not room for all. Abdul Baha made a short address at the conclusion of the feast.[46]

A brief notice of the meeting was also published in the *Boston Advertiser*.[47]

At lunch time 'Abdu'l-Bahá was expected to speak to a meeting arranged at the Twentieth Century Club, which was founded by the above-mentioned Edwin Mead.[48] Owing to His poor state of health, however, He was unable to attend and instead sent Dr Fareed to speak on His behalf. Accounts of this meeting were published in the *Boston Sunday Globe*[49] and in the *Boston American*, an evening newspaper with a circulation of 343,200 copies.[50]

A third meeting was scheduled for eight in the evening in the spacious Huntington Hall, located at the Rogers Building, the first permanent building of the Massachusetts Institute of Technology (MIT). The event was organized by the Bahá'í Assembly of Boston and announced on the same day in various newspapers.[51] Despite His illness, 'Abdu'l-Bahá was able to give the address Himself and spoke on the importance of religious unity.[52]

On 26 May the *Boston Herald* published an account of the meeting and quoting selections of the Master's talk:

BAHA SPEAKS IN EVENING

APPEARS FATIGUED AT HUNTINGTON CHAMBERS MEETING

A large and reverent audience gathered at Huntington Chambers last night to hear and see Abdul Baha. Mrs. Alice M. Buckson presided and unfolded the significance of the new religion of unity and peace, while awaiting the arrival of the speaker.

The eastern mystic entered late, leaning upon the arm of his secretary and interpreter, Dr. Fareed. He appeared far older than his 68 years, and spoke in a feeble voice, as if talking aloud were a considerable effort. The priest of the Bahais wore a loose caftan of brown linen and a snow-white turban. His face is brown and emaciated, and his beard and hair long and straggling. He spoke in short, guttural sentences leaning his head upon the back of the chair, and occasionally pointing upward with one finger.

The Baha told his congregation through the interpreter, that he was not feeling well but had come out of the great love he bore them and because it was his last evening in Boston. Using considerable repetition he went on to declare that in its achievements the present century was equal to the hundred years that had passed, and as its discoveries were making the theories of the past useless, there was need also of a new religion to take the place of the old dogmas.

'If we remain fettered by dogmas,' Abdul Baha prophesied, 'enmities will increase day by day until they have caused the destruction of the entire human race. If a city, if a family, is filled with the spirit of discord, it scatters and perishes day by day. We must band ourselves together to increase friendship among nations and races and brotherhood among men. God wishes man to establish just equality, not to transgress laws; to help each other and to live together in love. Do what God asks; be the cause of unity and peace, wipe out the horrors of war and hatred.

'We must be eager to suffer for such an end. Baha Ullah, my father, spent 60 years of his life in prison. In prison he unfurled the banner of universal peace, writing to kings and rulers of the earth. So his face became radiant, and among all the countries of the earth the bond of Bahai was established. Be dissolved in love, so that you may lose consciousness of everything except the good of all.'

The address concluded with a weird chant, during which some of the members of the audience knelt in prayer and the Baha left the hall, giving his benediction right and left and receiving greetings from the faithful.[53]

The *Post* also published an account of the talk:

FAREWELL MESSAGE OF ABDUL BAHA

PERSIAN PROPHET SEES COMING OF GREATER BROTHERHOOD

Abdul Baha, the Persian prophet and expounder of the Universal religion, which seeks to supplant all the religions of today, after twice disappointing his many followers in Boston last night delivered his farewell message to an appreciative and sympathetic audience gathered at the Huntington Chambers on Huntington Street.

DRESSED IN NATIVE GARB

The prophet, dressed in native garb, appeared very tired as he began by telling his hearers that only his great and unbounded love for them enabled him to come and bid farewell, as he was not feeling well.

The message of Abdul Baha consisted in telling his hearers of the wonderful achievements of the century, which exceed the human efforts of all the past centuries. With all that has been acquired, if all the world but learned the great lesson of universal love and brotherhood, he said, prosperity would be the reward of all, peace and happiness would reign supreme.

'A new condition must come,' he said. 'Everything must change and undergo reform.'

Abdul Baha said he was leaving today for New York City, but that his heart and his spirit remain here among his faithful followers. Nowhere, he said, was he received so kindly and treated as hospitably as in this country, for which he prayed God would reward it.[54]

A further account was published in the *Christian Science Monitor*:

ABDUL BAHA GIVES HIS LAST TALK TO BOSTON AUDIENCE

Abdul Baha was unable to be at Twentieth Century Club Saturday, where he was down to speak, but sent his interpreter and nephew, Dr. Mirza Ameen Fareed, a graduate of Johns Hopkins University. He told of the 40 years' imprisonment of the leader, son of the first Baha or founder of this movement.

Abdul Baha spoke at Huntington Hall on Saturday evening, bidding farewell to Boston and thanking the people for his kindly reception. He said that the twentieth century will do more than all the other centuries put together, that the achievements about to be seen now are beyond those of all the past heaped in one. He spoke for universal love and brotherhood and said that his father, the first Baha, had lifted during his 60 years' imprisonment the standard of national unity and peace and had called for the nations of the earth to meet in arbitration of their difficulties. If the people will hear the voice of God, he said, and determine to love one another and to live for unity instead of separation, then all the blessings of God will follow, for the law of the universe is union and the discordant, disintegrating force is separation.[55]

Last Day in Boston

Before leaving Boston, 'Abdu'l-Bahá received a number of believers and seekers at His hotel. Among them was a reporter from the *Boston Herald* for whom 'Abdu'l-Bahá spoke on family and the rights of women. The article that ensued was accompanied by a portrait:

The Herald representative was received, along with half a dozen disciples of the teachings of Abdul Baha, in his quiet apartments at the Charlesgate early yesterday morning. In spite of the many fatigues of the day before, the stately old man was up betimes – for 8 o'clock is certainly betimes on a Sunday morning in the city. A sound of voices from the bedroom preceded his entrance, and suddenly the audience seemed to 'sense' his approach, for every one rose and remained standing before he came into the room.

It has been said and written that Abdul Baha has a kindly smile. It is more than kindly; it is genial – there is almost recognition in it, even for complete stranger, and it has at moments an infectious gleam of humor. He shook hands with everyone present, repeating a certain phrase with each handshake, and then sat down with a general remark which Mirza Ahmad Sohrab interpreted: 'You are all welcome.'

There was a respectful silence; and then Abdul Baha – otherwise 'The Servant of God,' whose real name and rank, although he has repudiated them for the former, is Abbas Effendi – began to talk of the principles for which he stands. They are familiar to the public here, thanks to his many addresses of last week, although they seemed to take on a new significance, uttered in the quiet atmosphere of the little drawing room, by the old man, leaning back in his chair, to a group of hushed devotees.

The gleam of humor was evoked when the equality of the sexes was under discussion.

CHILDREN OF ONE GOD

'They are all one kind of creature – all children of one God, all have bodies and souls, and human instincts. There is no real distinction, except that men have beards and women do not; and American men', he added with a twinkle, 'shave their faces; so that even that distinction does not exist in this country.' Responding to a general smile, he laughed heartily.

He had something to say also about the newspapers, objecting that many of them had quoted him too briefly, while others had printed things he never said.

'One paper,' he declared, 'said that I wore a red turban. Can you think of anything more contrary to truth? In all my life I never had a red turban. I dislike them very much!'

He was wearing at the time a mode fez, with a long, loose robe of the same color, lined with soft fur. The fez, wound with a white cloth, got slightly askew from time to time as Abdul Effendi, in the animation of discussion, turned his head first to the right and then to the left, against the high back of his chair. He would laugh, put up his hands and straighten his head dress. His speech was accompanied for the most part with tappings of his hands on the arms of the chair.

The latter part of the interview was interpreted by Dr. Ameen

Fareed, who brought to The Herald representative, after the audience was closed, a fascinating little glass of Persian tea, strong but delicate, sweet and hot. Abdul Baha had to make preparations for an address to the Syrians down town, but he went about it in a leisurely way, and was in and out of the room several times while little groups lingered and talked. He seemed to take the invasion of his apartments as a matter of course, and his cordiality never flagged. Each time that he entered, he had a courteous little foreign speech to make, accompanied with a handshake. And when the visitors left each received a handful of bonbons; for it is a little ceremony to present the departing guest with a gift, to signify that he has not been to see a 'dead one'. A pretty custom, but not at all necessary in the case of Abdul Baha.[56]

17

NEW YORK, NEW JERSEY AND PENNSYLVANIA

26 May – 23 July 1912

From Boston, 'Abdu'l-Bahá returned to New York, arriving on 26 May at 6 p.m. He stayed in the city till the end of July. In the meantime, He also paid several visits to towns and cities in the New York area as well as in New Jersey and Pennsylvania.

Interview with Sophie Irene Loeb

On 24 May, two days before the return of 'Abdu'l-Bahá to New York, the *Evening World* (New York) published an interview conducted by Sophie Loeb,[1] which was probably granted before the Master left New York for Boston.

Loeb, a reporter who specialized in social and woman issues, began her article with an account of her conversation on the Bahá'í Faith with some members of the Master's retinue (not reproduced here). The rather sarcastic tone of the text changed when she started to describe her meeting with 'Abdu'l-Bahá. The conversation with Him focused on the importance of family unity as a first stage towards universal unity, the importance of a good partnership in marriage and the need for equal rights for women.

> At last, after two of his secretaries had told me that I would soon see him, another Persian, who was introduced to me as Dr. Ameen Fareed, his interpreter, led me toward an adjoining room and at the door I was met by a white-haired, white-bearded man who extended his hand and led me to a seat.

He has a kindly smile and speaks slowly and deliberately to the interpreter, who in turn translates into English. So here was the man whose father before him and he himself had for forty years been a prisoner on account of the beliefs he cherished, in which solitude he had perhaps figured out ways and means for carrying out 'his work', which he is now talking about throughout the country.

Whatever his religion may be, whatever construction is put upon him by his peace seeking followers, at least this old man of the East, coming from the land of the philosophic Omar, is keenly alive to things about him and has some sane ideas on the subject of everyday living.

'So you want a message for the Evening World,' he said. 'You can tell your readers, then, that in all principles of international peace that are being promoted throughout the world there is none so important as peace in the home. The first form of peace and unity emanates from this.

'First comes the united family, then the unity of the city, after which the unity of a country and then the whole world. But the foundation must begin in the home. A realization of peace loving attributes must be rooted there first of all.

The thoughts will be directed aright then along these lines for further universal peace. But if you don't educate the child along peaceful lines, how can you make the man, the leader or the ruler able to grasp it in the broad civic way?

EQUAL RIGHTS AND PEACE IN THE HOME FIRST

'First of all there should be equal rights in the home. Each should respect the wishes and needs of the other. The idea of serving in either case never can bring about unity. An equal partnership must exist, with the rights of each firmly recognized.

'Of all freedoms that exist in your country, the freedom of marriage is abnormal. There is not enough importance attached to it. Anybody can get married. It seems to be one of the easiest things you can do here. The coming existence is hardly considered. It is a case of one romance after another, and romance is indeed a very shaky thing to build from. If you would promote peace in the home, marriage must be made more difficult. The purpose of the present day marriage is haphazard in its conception.

'Given a little romantic stage setting and the thing is done. There is very little realization of the great importance of the couple's future together. They go into it willy-nilly and find it difficult to go out of it in the same way.

'There should be perfect understanding with respect to habits, temperaments and peculiarities. The great mistake is that people try to reform after marriage to conform to each other, which causes the trials that they have not calculated they would be called upon to bear.

'Too much of this is hidden before the marriage ceremony. People do not speak plainly nor do they give an account of each other. This is most important. Further, the state should demand this accounting.'

'What accounting would you suggest?' I asked.

'The purpose of two contracting parties as to a reasonable basis of livelihood, to insure comfort; a physical certificate of health so that progeny does not suffer, and a general assurance that the parties have hopes and ambitions in common. On account of these lax marriage laws your country is overwhelmed not only with granted divorces, but those taken for granted, the naturally divorced.

FAVORS WOMEN'S SUFFRAGE AS REFORM ELEMENT

'And what I mean by the naturally divorced is that the people are incompatible, which is the prime reason for divorce. I found many married American men traveling in Europe without their wives who did not seem to make any secret of the fact that they would rather be away from them, which is fundamentally due to the hasty, uncalculated marriage that is allowed in this country.'

Abdul Baha is a strong advocate of woman suffrage and thinks many of these reforms will come about when woman vote. 'Absolute equality of men is a mere dream and impracticable,' he said. 'But equality of the sexes must come. If absolute equality existed the whole order of the world would be destroyed. In mankind there is always a difference in degree. Since creation men have never been the same. Some have superior intelligence, others are more ordinary and some are devoid of intellect. How can there ever exist equality between those who are clever and those who are not?

'Humanity is like an army. An army must have a general,

captains, and soldiers, each with their appointed duties; it cannot exist of generals only, or captains or soldiers only; there must be degrees in the organization.

'But equality of the sexes must come. If women were educated with the same advantages as men their capacity is the same and the result would be the same; in fact, women have a superior disposition to men, they are far more receptive, more sensitive; their intuition is more intense. The only reason for their present backwardness in some directions is because they have not had the same educational advantages as men.

AS THE MOTHERS ARE, SO WILL CHILDREN BE

'If a mother is well educated her children will also be well taught. If the mother is wise the children will be wise; if the mother is religious the children will be religious. The future generations depend, then, on the mothers of today. Is not this a vital position of responsibility for women?"

And with this remark the interpreter informed me that the audience was at an end, as there were so many others waiting. Abdul Baha arose, reached to a table for an apple and gave it to me.

He readily discerned my look of surprise, whereupon he spoke to the interpreter, who in turn told me that it was an old Persian custom to go away carrying something, as otherwise it was significant that the visitor had been to see a dead one. I assured him that it did not need an apple to prove that Abdul Baha was very much awake in the garden of life.[2]

Excerpts of Irene Loeb's article were afterwards reproduced in other newspapers.[3]

Address at the Metropolitan Temple

On Tuesday 28 May, two days after 'Abdu'l-Bahá's arrival in New York, He addressed over one thousand people at a reception arranged by the International Peace Forum and held at the United Methodist Metropolitan Temple (Seventh Avenue and West Fourteenth Street, Manhattan). Short announcements of this meeting had been published on the previous days in local newspapers.[4]

'Abdu'l-Bahá spoke on the unity of religions, their purpose and the need of peace.[5] A reporter on *The New York Times* was present at the meeting and his account mentioned the names of some of the participants:

> BAHA POINTS TOWARD PEACE
>
> RELIGIOUS UNITY WILL BRING WORLD AMITY, SAYS PERSIAN TEACHER
>
> Abdul Baha Abbas, head of the Bahai movement in Persia for the unification of all religions, who has been lecturing in this country the last month, explained his religious theories yesterday afternoon to an audience which filled the Metropolitan Temple on Seventh Avenue, near Fourteenth Street, to the doors.
>
> Abdul Baha addressed the audience in Persian, and his remarks were rendered into English by an interpreter.
>
> 'Bahai means to love all the world and all humanity; to work for universal peace and universal brotherhood,' he said.
>
> Abdul Baha went on to explain that the unification of religions among all races would quickly bring about universal peace.
>
> The Rev. Dr. J. Wesley Hill, former pastor of the Temple, who has returned to this city temporarily from the West, where he has been campaigning for President Taft, presided at the meeting. He introduced the Rev. Frederick Lynch of the New York Peace Conference, who spoke on the subject of universal peace. Rabbi Joseph Silverman, who followed Abdul Baha, said that he believed that the distinguished Persian was right in stating that the world was coming nearer and nearer to universal peace and a common faith.[6]

The Herald simply reported that 'Prominent Clergymen and several of the countrymen of Abdul Baha Abbas, the Persian who came to this country as the exponent of a universal religion, attended a reception at the Metropolitan Temple, Seventh Avenue and Fourteenth Street.'[7] Some newspapers published editorial comments about 'Abdu'l Bahá words. The *Post-Express* of Rochester, New York, stated that 'The Persian religious leader and advocate of peace, Abdul Baha, has, whatever may be said as to his orthodoxy, influenced public opinion in the United States. Speaking recently in New York, he said his religion meant love of humanity, universal peace and universal brotherhood. In some respects at any rate Bahaism is an exalted creed, for human brotherhood and universal peace, are the ideals not merely of Christianity but of all great religions.'[8] The *Democrat and Chronicle*, also from Rochester, disagreed with the ideas expounded by 'Abdu'l-Bahá stating that 'With all due respect for Abdul Baha Abbas, it may be said that something besides the unity of religions will be necessary to bring about universal peace. An increase in brotherly love, which may exist utterly apart from religion, would have an influence worth considering.'[9] The *Times* of Brooklyn in a reference to Roosevelt and the presidential campaign stated that 'If Abdul should listen to some of the colonel's speeches he would admit that love and unity are not at the base of all progressive politics.' To this the Salt Lake *Evening Telegram* replied stating that 'The Times is behind the times. Anyone, to listen to one of the colonel's speeches, will have to admit that love and unity are at the base of all his speeches. The love, however, is all for Roosevelt, and the unity is in the same fix.'[10]

Visit to Fanwood, New Jersey

William H. Hoar (1856–1922), one of the first and most active Bahá'ís in America, invited 'Abdu'l-Bahá to visit Fanwood, a New Jersey town of which he had been mayor from 1912 to 1917. 'Abdu'l-Bahá traveled to Fanwood on 1 June, stayed in the town for one day and gave two talks, the last one a public address held at the local fire house.[11]

At least two articles were published at the time about this visit. The first one appeared on 31 May, and announced that the talk was to be held on the following day.[12] The second article contained the notes of His talk:

> Residents of Fanwood borough had an opportunity Saturday evening to hear Abdul-Baha, a Persian, who has come to this county to visit, after spending nearly forty of his seventy years in prison in the Holy Land for exploiting the doctrine of universal brotherhood, the doctrine for which his father suffered martyrdom.
>
> While in Fanwood he was the guest of Mr. and Mrs. W. H. Hoar. He will make his home, for a time at least, in Montclair.
>
> After highly complimenting the citizens of Fanwood for their beautiful homes and stating that the town ought to be named Spiritville, because of its spiritual atmosphere, he turned to a discussion of the eternal verities, a synopsis of his address being as follows:

'Material objects in the material world are subject to change, but the cause of the Kingdom is never-ending. Therefore it is the most important. But alas! alas! day by day the power of the kingdom is weakened, the material forces of nature gain the ascendency. The divine signs are becoming less and less and the material powers more and more. It has reached such a degree that the materialists are daily progressing and advancing, and the divine are vanishing.

'Irreligion has conquered religion. The reason for the chaotic condition lies in the differences among the religions themselves, and animosity and hatred among the sects and denominations. The materialists have availed themselves of this difference amongst the religious and are constantly attacking them so that they may uproot the tree of religion. As the religious are contending among themselves they are being vanquished. If the general is at variance with his army on account of military tactics there is no doubt that he will be defeated by the enemy. Now religions are at variance; war and strife exist among them, and they are back-biting each other, shunning each other's association – nay, rather, if necessary, they engage in shedding each other's blood. Read history and see what horrible events have transpired. All the prophets were sent for the sake of Christ, but alas! that the Talmud and the superstitions contained therein could veil Jesus to such a degree that they crucified their promised Messiah. Had they forgotten the Talmudic traditions and investigated in reality the religion of Moses there is no doubt that they would have become believers in Christ. But imitations deprived them of their Messianic bounty. They were not refreshed by the downpour of rain of mercy; neither were they illumined by the rays of the sun of truth.

'Imitation destroys the foundation of religion. Imitation kills the spirituality of the human world. Imitation has changed into darkness the heavenly illumination. Imitation has deprived man of the knowledge of God. Imitation is the cause of victory of irreligion over religion. Imitation is the cause of the denial of divinity. Imitation refuses the law of revelation. Imitation sets aside prophethood. Imitation denies the Kingdom of God.

'When the materialist compares these imitations with the intellectual criterion they find they are all superstitions; therefore they deny religion. The Jews have two ideas of purity and impurity of different religion. When you compare them with the criterion of science you will find that they are without foundation.

'Is it impossible for us to receive the infinite bounties of God? Is it impossible to discover the virtues of the spiritual world because we are not living in a day in the past ages – the era of His Holiness Moses – the era of the prophets of God and the era of His Holiness the Christ? Those periods were spiritual periods of the world; therefore, is it impossible for us to become perfect in spirituality as those in the past ages because we are far from them and are living in a materialistic age? But the same God is able to bestow the same favors – nay, rather greater favors upon the present century. For example, in past ages He granted to His servants reason, intelligence and understanding. How can we say that He is not able to bestow the same favors upon His people in this day? Is it just that He sends His Holiness Moses for the guidance of the past nations and forgets entirely those who are living today? Is it possible that this age has become deprived of the bounties of God, when the ages of tyranny and conflict of the past ages received an inexhaustible share of divine bounties? The same kind God who has granted His favors in the past has opened today the doors of the Kingdom. The rays of His sun are shining, the breath of the Holy Spirit is encircling, that omniscient God is still able to assist and confirm us by His spirit, to illumine our hearts and to gladden our souls, to perfume our nostrils with the fragrance of holiness.

'Divine wisdom has encircled all, has spread His heavenly table before us, and we must take a bountiful share of this divine favor.

'The work of the shepherd is to bring together the scattered sheep and to collect the dispersed sheep. If, on the contrary, he scatters the united flock, he is not the shepherd. As the prophets fulfilled their mission in this respect, therefore they are the true shepherds. His Holiness Moses came at a time when the Israelitish tribes were like scattered sheep; discord was rampant among them, enmity and hatred increased their disunion.

'Moses, with divine power, collected and united these scattered flocks. He set within the shell of their hearts the pearl of love. He freed them from captivity and carried them from Egypt to the Holy Land. In science and art they made wonderful progress. Sociology and bonds were established between them. Their progress in all the degrees of human virtues was so rapid and marvelous they founded the Solomonic sovereignty. Is it possible to say that Moses was not a real shepherd and did not gather together these scattered flocks?

'His Holiness Christ was a real shepherd. At the time of His manifestation the Greeks, Chaldeans, Assyrians, the Egyptians and the Europeans were like so many scattered flocks. Christ breathed in them the spirit of unity. He harmonized.

'Therefore it is established that all the prophets of God have come to unite the children of men and not to disperse them, and to put in action the law of love and not enmity. Consequently we must throw aside all these prejudices, forget the racial prejudice, the patriotic prejudice, the religious and political prejudice. We must become the cause of unity of the human race. Work for universal peace, sing about the means of love and destroy the basis of enmity so that this material world may become the divine world, the world of matter become the world of the Kingdom and humanity may attain to the world of perfection.'[13]

Second Address at the Church of the Ascension

Despite the attacks directed against Percy S. Grant by some members of his congregation for having invited 'Abdu'l-Bahá to speak at a Sunday service at his church, Grant invited the Master to speak to his parishioners a second time on Sunday, 2 June. This time the meeting took place at the parish hall of the Ascension Church, where Grant conducted a series of weekly debates on social issues known as the Ascension Forum. While no accounts of 'Abdu'l-Bahá's address seem to have been published in the local press, a few announcements appeared in the *Evening Post*,[14] the *Times*[15] and the *Tribune*.[16] According to these, the address was entitled 'How Can the Orient Help the Occident?' and was scheduled for 8 p. m. At 9 p.m., after 'Abdu'l-Bahá had spoken on the purpose of religions, their unity and the need for a spiritual civilization, participants were invited to ask Him questions.[17] The notes of His answer to one of the questions appeared in the *Theosophic Messenger*:

Is it not a fact that Universal Peace cannot be accomplished until there is political democracy in all the countries of the world? (Asked of Abdul-Baha at the end of a public address.)

It is very evident that in the future of all the countries of the world, be they constitutional in government or Republican or Democratic in form, there shall be no centralization. The United States may be held up as the example of government in time to come; that is to say, each province will be independent in itself but there will be a union concerning the interests of the various independent states. It may not be a Republican or a Democratic form. To cast aside centralization which promotes despotism is the exigency of the time. This will be productive of international peace. Another fact of equal importance in bringing about International Peace is Woman's Suffrage. That is to say, when perfect equality shall be established between men and women, peace may be realized for the simple reason that womankind in general will never favor warfare. Women evidently will not be willing to allow those whom they have so tenderly cared for to go to the battlefield. When they shall have a vote they will oppose any cause of warfare. Another factor which will bring about universal peace is the linking together of the Orient and the Occident. *Abdul-Baha*[18]

Lunch at the Brooklyn Union League Club

On 6 June 1912 the Union League Club of Brooklyn held a children's parade in honor of Admiral Peary, whom 'Abdu'l-Bahá had met weeks earlier at a meeting at the Persian Legation in Washington. After this parade a lunch was given for some of the guests of the Union League Club, including Major General Daniel E. Sickles (1819–1914).

The Master was invited to speak at this lunch. *The Standard Union* (Brooklyn), a Republican newspaper with a circulation of 56,000 copies, published an account of the whole event that included the following lines about the presence of 'Abdu'l-Bahá:

Among those who attended the luncheon were Abdul Baha Abbas, the Persian philosopher, and several of his disciples. The famous Persian spent forty years in prison for his religious beliefs, but now he is hailed as one of the mightiest men of learning of his day. His influence for good is recognized in America. He preaches the gospel of universal brotherhood.

Abdul Baha was called upon by Toastmaster Berri. He spoke

through an interpreter and discussed the natural laws which govern life, declaring that system and education were the things which made civilization what it is.

With his white beard and hair, Abdul Baha made quite a picturesque figure, attired in his native costume, and addressed the company in his native tongue.

He pointed out that a tree would go crooked if planted crooked, but straight if planted straight. He said it was the same way with children – that if they were taught righteousness in their early days, when their minds were open, they would become good men and women; but on the other hand, if no guiding spirit properly took care of their education, no one could tell how they would act.

'I hear that this organization is taking the right steps,' said the Persian. 'That is well, your country will be the better for the education. I ask the blessing of God upon this association for what it is doing.'[19]

Visit to Milford, Pennsylvania

During His stay in New York, 'Abdu'l-Bahá paid a two-day visit to Milford, Pennsylvania, starting on Tuesday, 4 June. He had been invited by the reformist politician Amos Pinchot (1873–1944) and by the renowned conservationist and politician Gifford Pinchot.[20] 'Abdu'l-Bahá stayed at Grey Towers, the summer estate of the Pinchot family, and there He met many prominent guests who had been invited by the Pinchots to hear Him.[21] Zia Bagdadi, who was present at the occasion, wrote a few years later an account of some of the questions that were put to 'Abdu'l-Bahá.[22]

In order to reach Milford, 'Abdu'l-Bahá had to take a train to Port Jervis (New York) and from there He and His retinue were taken by car to Milford. Despite His short stay at Port Jervis, a local paper published an account of the event:

DID YOU SEE ABDUL BAHA? HEAD OF PERSIAN RELIGIOUS MOVEMENT IN PORT JERVIS, TUESDAY

ON HIS WAY TO GREY TOWERS, MILFORD, AS THE GUEST OF AMOS PINCHOT – CAME TO AMERICA TO SPEAK AT PEACE CONFERENCE – PRESENTED CONDUCTOR CARPENTER WITH $5

Abbas Effendi or Abdul Baha, the leader of Bahii religion, which claims fourteen millions of members although it has only been preached for 68 years and who is one of the most talked of men in the world, was in this city Tuesday evening and this morning on his way to and from Milford where he was the guest over night of his friend Amos Pinchot, at Grey Towers.

Abdul Baha, as he likes to be called, arrived in town on Erie train 27 at 5:30 o'clock, Tuesday afternoon. He was attired in flowing garments of expensive Persian linen and wore a turban cay of silk and linen. His appearance impressed one at first glance. He is 68 years of age and has a long white beard and his countenance is friendly. Abdul Baha does not talk the English language, but speaks through an interpreter, who accompanied him with a party of Persians.

Conductor Benjamin Carpenter had a conversation with the foreigner, who said Americans should praise God for having such a delightful country in which to live. When he left the train at this station, Abdul Baha presented conductor Carpenter with a five dollar gold piece of the Turkish government. The party were conveyed to Milford and back in automobiles of Mr. Pinchot . . .

Baha will make his home in Montclair. The Persian prophet, who has spent forty of his seventy years in prison because of his religious beliefs, has taken the house at 11 Bradford Place, in Montclair, and will live there after 15 June.

Abdul Baha recently spoke in Unity Church in Montclair and was so impressed by the reception he received and by the physical aspects of the town that he expressed a desire to take up his abode in the town. There are about fifty Bahaists in Montclair.[23]

Soon afterwards the local press in Milford briefly reported the visit of 'Abdu'l-Bahá to the town. The *Milford Dispatch*, a Democratic newspaper with a circulation of 1,000 copies, reported that 'Abdul Baha, a venerable Persian philosopher, scientist and religious leader . . . attracted much attention in this village Tuesday afternoon on his arrival by auto en route to Grey Towers, where he was a guest of Amos R. E. Pinchot over night. The noted Persian . . . was accompanied by his secretary and interpreter, Dr. Ameen U. Fareed. Mrs. W. C. Ralston of San Francisco and Mrs. E. C. Getsinger of Washington were members of the party.'[24] The Republican *Pike County Press*, with a circulation of 750 copies, informed its readers that 'Abdu'l-Bahá 'was a guest at Grey Towers over Tuesday night. He was a venerable figure looking man and was attired in a turban and Oriental costume.'[25] The *Tri-States Union* of Port Jervis, a Republican journal with a circulation of 8,800 copies, published similar information.[26]

Visit to Philadelphia

'Abdu'l-Bahá visited Philadelphia on Saturday, 8 June, where He stayed for two nights. His state of health was not good at the time of His arrival. As noted earlier, in Boston, only two weeks before, He had had to cancel an appointment owing to health problems. Since then His daily program continued to be strenuous, not allowing time for a proper recovery. The signs of fatigue at His arrival in Philadelphia were noted by some journalists.

Several articles were published reporting His arrival in the city. The Democratic *Philadelphia Record*, whose Sunday edition had a circulation of 126,000 copies, published on 9 June a short note announcing His scheduled address at the Baptist Temple (Broad and Berks Streets) and stated that 'Although not one who has studied books, his wisdom is a marvel to all who have met him. He shows the greatest familiarity with the Bible and all the holy books of the different religions, and his explanations of their mysteries are very clear. He devotes his life to succoring the poor and unfortunate.'[27]

When the Master arrived from the North Philadelphia station at His hotel, the Rittenhouse Hotel, 2100 Chestnut Street, journalists representing the major newspapers in the city were waiting for Him. Despite His fatigue 'Abdu'l-Bahá patiently answered their questions, which centered on the issue of suffrage. The *Philadelphia Press*, the Sunday edition of which had a circulation of 160,000 copies, published the following account:

ABDUL BAHA HERE FOR FULL SUFFRAGE

PERSIAN NOBLEMAN SAYS UNIVERSAL PEACE WAITS ON VOTES FOR WOMEN ONLY

Abdul Baha Abbas, Persian nobleman, who endured forty-two years' imprisonment as the head of the Bahai movement, which expounds the unity of mankind, religion and education and, therefore, universal peace, arrived in Philadelphia last night and will preach twice to-day. He made a new statement shortly after he settled down in a hotel.

'Unless women receive their full liberty and the right to vote, universal peace is impossible,' he said, 'because woman by nature is against war. She will never give twenty years to her son and then willingly send him to war to be killed. When she votes then – and then only – war will end. The dreadnaught and the army then will have passed into history.'

Abdul Baha is an ardent suffragist. Since he arrived in the United States on April 11 his convictions on this subject have become more and more pronounced until, he said, he was impelled to make the statement quoted above.

PREACHES TO-DAY AND TO-NIGHT

He will preach this morning at the Spring Garden Unitarian Church, Girard Avenue and Fifteenth Street, and tonight at the Grace Baptist Temple, Broad and Berks Streets. Each address will be given through an interpreter, and each is expected to be a remarkable discourse.

When the teacher arrived at the Rittenhouse Hotel shortly after six o'clock, clad in his native costume and followed by three young men, also clad in bright silks and satins, there was a decided stir, for patrons of the house were just entering the dining-rooms. The dignified appearance of the leader, and the respect and awe of his followers, made a profound impression upon those who witnessed the arrival.

Abdul Baha is sixty-five years old. His dark Oriental complexion contrasts decidedly with his snow white beard. He is tall and dignified, and there is a sharpness about his features and eyes which makes all who behold him stop to compare him with their mental pictures of men of profound learning. On his head he wears a tall Persian fez of great height and as black as can be. It is made from a fine glossed cloth. He wears a great cloak of dark blue which extends to the ground and under this is a robe of fine thin yellow silk of almost equal length.

The men with him maintained a military bearing last night as long as he remained with them in the lobby. They stood at a respectful distance like soldiers at attention. Their garments were similar to those of their leader, though not of equal length and there were more bright colors.

CONFUSION ABOUT SUITE

There was some confusion about a suite for the priest. Only tentative arrangements had been made by Mrs. Louise D. Boyle, of Washington, a follower of the movement for eighteen years. She went to the desk to perfect these, but Abdul Baha was impatient and gave rapid orders to the men who communicated them to Mrs. Boyle and the clerks. He was so exhausted before he reached the suite that he was on the point of falling. In a half hour he had retired for the night.

The Bahai movement, of which he is the chief priest, takes credit for the great wave of sentiment for universal peace which is sweeping the world to-day. He and his predecessors have been teaching universal organization since 1844, but they have had to teach them through prison walls the greater part of that time. The movement teaches that the only way to reach perfection, the aim of all sects, is the unification of all religions, and that the world must be united in one great cause and for universal peace and education.[28]

A reporter of the *North American*, a Democratic newspaper issuing 160,000 copies daily, also had a chance to see 'Abdu'l-Bahá on His arrival in Philadelphia:

PERSIAN BAHA URGES VOTE FOR ALL WOMEN

DECLARES UNIVERSAL BALLOT WILL BRING ABOUT WORLD PEACE AND LOVE

TO LECTURE HERE TODAY

HEAD OF NEW RELIGIOUS MOVEMENT WILL MAKE TOUR OF UNITED STATES

'Universal peace, universal love, universal religion are all impossible until universal woman's suffrage is recognized; until women enjoy perfect political rights with men.'

That statement was made last evening by Abdul Baha Abbas, head of the Bahai movement or religion, which, starting in Persia two score years ago, has spread throughout the world. He is in this city in the interests of the movement, and will deliver two lectures here today.

'Humanity is composed of two organs,' continued the Baha. 'One, man; the other, woman. If one of these organs – woman – is not given the power of working properly it is impossible for the other to perform properly its functions. The perfect equality of men and women is a fundamental principle of universal love and peace, and the latter cannot exist before the former.'

The noted Oriental arrived at the Rittenhouse last night, coming from New York, where he was accorded a brilliant reception a few days ago. He is very striking in appearance, his venerable white locks and beard, his piercing gray-blue eyes and majestic carriage easily proclaiming him a personage of importance. He speaks little English, delivering his lectures through interpreters.

The Baha has a wonderful personal history, having spent forty-two years of his life in a Syrian prison in Akka or Acre, because of the fear his teaching created in the hearts of Turkish officials. He was released four years ago, when the 'Young Turks' went into power and since that time has been traveling over the world delivering his message.

Teachings of the Bahai movement comprise, as its chief doctrine, universal love, universal peace, universal education and a universal auxiliary language. The Baha stated last night that before any of these conditions would come to the world, racial, patriotic and religious prejudices must be wiped away and women placed on an equal footing with men. His work and his teachings have as their objective the wiping out of those prejudices.

This morning he will speak in the Girard Avenue Unitarian Church, the Rev. K. E. Evans having relinquished his pulpit to the distinguished teacher for the day, while in the evening he will address the congregation at the Baptist Temple, Broad and Berks Streets. He is planning a tour of the United States visiting every large city from Maine to California, and will start from New York on this tour in two weeks. He will be here until Tuesday afternoon.[29]

In New York City the black newspaper *The Age* reported apropos of these comments that 'Abdul Baha Abbas, the Persian leader of the popular Bahai movement, who is now in this country preaching the gospel of religious toleration and universal peace, speaking in Philadelphia last week, said that he was willing to predict that woman would ultimately win the suffrage all over the world before the end of the present century, but that they must do it by their own efforts – "must endeavor to acquire the mental ability of men in science, arts, crafts and inventions".'[30]

On Sunday, 9 June, 'Abdu'l-Bahá spoke to the congregations of two Philadelphia churches. At 11 a.m. He spoke at the Unitarian Church, 15th and Girard Avenue.[31] The address was announced the day before in a short notice published in the *Inquirer* that included a biography. 'Even through an interpreter,' stated the text, 'he is an elegant speaker.'[32] In His address 'Abdu'l-Bahá spoke on the knowledge of God, the purpose of religions and the mission of Bahá'u'lláh.[33] Various reporters were present at the meeting and on the following day different accounts were published in the local press.

A reporter with the Republican *Evening Bulletin*, Philadelphia's most read daily newspaper with a circulation of nearly 254,000 copies, attended the talk and wrote the following report:

OLD PERSIAN MYSTIC STIRS BY TEACHINGS

ABDUL BAHA ABBAS, HEAD OF BAHAIN CULT, SPEAKS IN TWO CITY CHURCHES

WOULD UNITE HUMANITY

Abdul Baha Abbas, world head of the Bahain cult, a gentle speaking old Persian with a fine intellect, wonderful eyes, a long-white beard and a philosophy sweeping enough to enfold the world in its beneficent influence, is in this city at the beginning of an American tour and delivered the first of his important addresses here yesterday.

The mystic, whose persecutions in the East make a tale unequaled in romance, is believed by a quarter of a million people in this country to be the redeemer foretold by all religious prophets since religious prophecy first began.

His followers believe that his coming in the first decade of this century has been made clear as day in the Old and New Testaments. Bahais are firm in the belief that within the next few years the teachings of Abdul Baha Abbas will spread like fire throughout the world, unite all humanity, wipe away strife, discontent and trouble, and create a peaceful revolution in society and industry that shall have its end in happiness for everybody.

The first of the notable visitor's addresses was delivered yesterday morning before a large congregation at the First Unitarian Church, 15th St. and Girard Ave., and the second was given last evening in the Grace Baptist Temple. Each address was delivered through an interpreter, and was an exposition of religious philosophy that is both wide and kindly.

HERE TO UNITE ALL PEOPLE

'I have come,' said Abdul Baha Abbas, 'from a part of the world wherein the manifestations of God were first made plain, and out of which the radiance and power of God first shone through man, his Son. The intention and purpose of my visit is in that a bond of understanding and agreement may be established between us.

'All humanity is surely the creation and the servant of God. All came into being through one Creator, who is kind to all. He rears all. He provides for all. He protects all, and He deals lovingly with all. Inasmuch as God is kind to all, why should we be unkind to any of his creatures? Inasmuch as God is loyal to all, why should we be disloyal? Inasmuch as God deals in mercy with all why should we deal in animosity and hatred?'

Six thousand years of unrest and unhappiness, says the Bahai head, has been due to social and religious and racial prejudice. Latterly have come unfair industrial conditions and war of one kind and another has been linked with business. In a word the Baha is attempting to change and remodel the foundations of human nature.

FIGHT TO COME SOON

'This country,' he says, 'is the country in which many mysteries will be solved. The mystery of the universe may be among them. The world was made to be the seat of transient happiness. Untold misery has defiled it only because man has failed to realize responsibility to the Creator of his spirit and to his kind.'

When all private and personal ambition has been made secondary to the thought of what he calls the Oneness of humanity, said Abdul Baha Abbas, man will suddenly come upon absolute happiness and peace as a lost and wandering explorer finds the goal of his desire – suddenly and without warning.

Abdul Baha Abbas is close to sixty years old and wears the garb and turban of Persia. With him are two companions who translate his utterances and keep careful journal of them all. He has been imprisoned times innumerable in the East, where his father, the founder of the cult of the Bahais, was a prophet before him.

All told Abdul Baha Abbas has served something like forty years in Persian prisons for questioning, in his general teaching, the infallibility of any one accepted religion and for the reiterated assertion that all religions in their present state represent the instinctive desire of all people to serve their common Creator.[34]

The Republican *Philadelphia Inquirer*, with a circulation of 172,300 copies, also published an account of the morning's address and reproduced several notes:

ABDUL BAHA ASKS FOR WORLD PEACE

FAMOUS PERSIAN MYSTIC ADDRESSES TWO CONGREGATIONS IN NATIVE TONGUE

FAVORS COMMON STANDARD OF EDUCATION AND ETHICS AND SEX EQUALITY

Clad in the garments of his native Persia, from which he was exiled because of his teachings, Abdul Baha, head of the Bahai movement, preached the gospel of the universal brotherhood of man to two large congregations of this city yesterday. The famous Persian spoke in his native tongue, but his words, repeated in English by a clear-voiced interpreter, held his auditors in rapt attention.

Baha, in his address, explained the views which have for some time attracted the interest of thousands throughout the world. Using the expression 'oneness', he urged that but one religion prevail throughout the world and that man's holier nature be developed so as to prevail over his materialistic instincts. He declared himself as favoring universal peace, a common standard of education and ethics throughout the world, and the equality of the sexes.

The visitor spoke at the First Unitarian Church, Fifteenth Street and Girard Avenue, in the morning, and in the evening delivered an address at the Baptist Temple, Broad and Berks Streets. In the morning address he said:

WANTS BOND OF UNITY

'I come here from distant countries, from the Oriental climes, from countries wherefrom the lights of heaven have ever shone forth, from climes wherein the manifestations of God have ever come forth, countries wherein the radiance and power of God have become manifest, and my intention and purpose of this visit are that perchance a bond of unity and agreement might be established between the east and the west, the divine love may encompass all, the divine radiance shall enlighten both continents, and the bounties of the heavenly spirit shall revivify all. Therefore I supplicate at the threshold of God that the orient and the occident may become as one, that these peoples shall become one people, and that all souls may become as one soul.'

Baha told in detail of the teachings of Baha'o'llah, his father, one of the early leaders of the movement, in whose steps he is following.

'Baha'o'llah appeared from the eastern horizon promulgating the oneness of mankind, and the oneness of the divinity,' he said, 'he taught that all humanity was the servant of one God, all have come into being through the bestowal of the one Creator, who is kind to all. God provides for all. He rears all, he protects all and He deals lovingly with all races of people. Inasmuch as God is kind to all, why should we be unkind? Inasmuch as God is loyal to all, why should we disloyal? Inasmuch as God deals with all in mercy, why should we deal with animosity and hatred?'[35]

Back at His hotel, the Master gave at least two interviews which were published the following day. One of them was granted to a reporter on the *Philadelphia Press*, the daily edition of which had a circulation of 80,000 copies. The article that ensued included two pictures of Him, one seated and another surrounded by His assistants:

PERSIAN PRIEST TELLS BELIEF

AMERICAN WOMEN SUPERIOR MENTALLY TO ALL OTHERS, SAYS ABDUL BAHA ABBAS

Women's suffrage, universal peace and unity of religion will become general all over the world before the end of the present century, but women must bring this about by rising to equality with men in science, arts, crafts and inventions, according to Abdul Baha Abbas, Persian nobleman, head of the Bahai movement, which has as its principal objects the spread of religious toleration and universal peace.

The leader made this assertion in an interview yesterday afternoon after his address in the forenoon at the Spring Garden Unitarian Church, Girard Avenue and Fifteenth Street. He talked readily of the meaning of the movements, which his followers declare are fermenting the entire world to-day. Last night he spoke in the Grace Baptist Temple, Broad and Berks Streets, of which Rev. Dr. Russell H. Conwell is pastor. Both of his addresses were delivered through an Interpreter.

'Women must attain the right to vote through their own efforts,' he asserted in the interview. 'They must endeavor to acquire the mental ability of men in science, arts, crafts and inventions, or they cannot win the confidence of men in their efforts to gain the ballot. But when they have attained this mental state suffrage will become a natural result and men themselves will become a factor in spreading suffrage.

AMERICAN WOMEN FAR AHEAD

'I have watched the rise of women throughout the world with a great amount of interest and I am willing to predict that in nearly every part of the world they will attain equal suffrage during the present century. The women of the United States are far ahead of the women of the rest of the world in their learning, but this is because they have been encouraged and assisted. General suffrage will be granted women in all parts of the United States long before it will be granted in any other country because the American woman is more nearly the equal of men.

'In Oriental countries, where woman was formerly little more than a slave, there has been a great change, which substantiates my prediction that this century will see the change. Revolutions in all lines are phenomenal.

'No one can deny that this is the century for the solution of mysteries. You only need to make a brief review of the astounding progress of the century. What was mystery a few years ago is perfectly plain to-day.'

RELIGIOUS UNIFICATION COMING

'This century will also see the unification of the religious movement under one great plan. The great progress demands it, and all people who think deeply admit that the various forms of religion must be founded on one central idea or about the one fundamental truth of God. It is only a matter of interpretation – of true, accurate and correct interpretation. It is only a question of how many years it will take the great leaders to get together on the situation.

'Science will bring about this service to the human world. Through science it will become evident that these prejudices are like clouds which hide the sun. They prevent knowledge, interpretation and belief from being accepted. Science will prove that we are wrong in the imitation of our ancestors, and when these are proved to be imitations the truth will stand out. Science has done enough to show that it will soon offer proof for the central belief.

'When this unification comes about there will be no religious rulership as at the present time. He who has the ability and capability will naturally be the herald.'[36]

To the reporter of the *Public Ledger*, an independent newspaper with a circulation of 60,000 copies, 'Abdu'l-Bahá gave advice on the mission of journalism. The article that ensued also included brief accounts of His two addresses in Philadelphia:

PERSIAN SAGE PAYS VISIT TO THIS CITY

ABDUL BAHA ABBAS, PHILOSOPHER AND POLITICAL MARTYR, TALKS IN TWO CHURCHES

MAXIMS FOR NEWSPAPERS

Abdul Baha Abbas, Persian philosopher and martyr, who is today revered as the head of more than 3,000,000 followers in his gentle and kindly religious cult, paid a flying visit to this city over the weekend, attended by Dr. Ameen U. Fareed, Mirza Ali Akbar and Mirza Ahmed Sohrab.

To learn the significance of the visit, a reporter of the PUBLIC LEDGER hastened to the Rittenhouse Hotel yesterday afternoon and was immediately ushered into the philosopher's suite of rooms, where an informal audience was in progress.

A dozen women were sitting at the feet of the master – metaphorically speaking. As a matter of fact, they were sitting, very erect and self-conscious, on the edge of straight-backed chairs, dotted here and there about the room. Over by the window the venerable philosopher leaned back in a deep armchair and surveyed his visitors benignantly. Close at hand was a Persian member of the staff, an open copybook on his lap, eagerly gathering in pearls of philosophy and fragrant flowers of speech. Finally there came a lull in the proceedings. Guttural murmurs in Persian and Arabic were exchanged at length. The interpreter switched round on his chair.

'Abdul Baha asks how many newspapers you have in this city?'

'Nine or ten, I think.' The information was transmitted.

The philosopher nodded and made a comment.

'Abdul Baha says that is very good,' volunteered the interpreter.

And there and then Abdul Baha, who is only a few months free from 40 long years imprisonment for the expression of his progressive teachings in the fever-racked penal settlement at Akka, in Syria, delivered himself of a series of maxims for American journals and journalists. They were punctuated by impressive pauses, and this is how interpreter Ahmed Sohrab passed them across from the vernacular:

'Newspapers are the mirrors that reflect the progression or the retrogression of the community.

'We may ascertain the progress or the retrogression of a nation by its journalism.

'If journalists should abide by their duties, they would be the promoters of many virtues, among the community. Truth and the virtues would be fostered. This would be so if they carried out the duties incumbent upon them.

'Journalists must serve truth.

'Newspapers must investigate the means for the progress of humanity, and publish them.

'Journalists must write significant articles, articles that shall foster the public welfare. If they so do they will be the first agents for the development of the community.

'From the days when newspapers were first published they have been the cause of progress; if they abide by their duties great will be the benefit forthcoming.

'Journalists must endeavor to make their organ a trustworthy agent, in order that their articles may be effective in the hearts of the people and that the readers of these articles may be edified.'

Abdul Baha went on to discuss the parks of Philadelphia; he was gratified to hear of the open-air opportunities offered by Fairmount Park. He told how struck he had been on this, his first visit to America, with the self-sufficiency – in the highest sense of the word – of the American city, with its own parks and museums and libraries and educational institutions. In the East, he said, the capital city of the nation is a model city, but squalor and lack of the concrete amenities of life characterize the towns of the provinces.

The philosopher gave his views on the much vexed question of Sunday amusements for the people.

'Man must have one day to rest from everything, to have composure, with neither body occupied nor mind. This is necessary. Therefore on Sunday all affairs shall be at a standstill and man must be occupied with the contemplation of God.' 'Nevertheless,' he added, 'the reading of books on Sunday is a good thing, and if edifying moving-picture shows be available on Sunday, it is a good thing to go to them.'

Abdul Baha spoke yesterday morning at the Spring Garden Unitarian Church on the unity of all mankind. He said woman should be so educated as to place her on an equal footing with man and he even goes so far as to suggest that where a man cannot afford to educate both son and daughter he should educate the daughter, for the woman is the mother and the teacher of the race.

The philosopher compared humanity to a bird, one wing man, the other woman. Both wings are needed for flight. If one wing be defective the unharmed wing will not be capable of flight.

Abdul Baha delivered an address last night in the Grace Baptist Temple. Many years ago the Rev. Dr. Russell H. Conwell visited him in the penal settlement of Akka and asked him to visit Philadelphia

> if ever the opportunity presented itself. Then, two years since, with the ascendancy of the Young Turks and the overthrow of Abdul Hamid, came his release. For awhile the venerable philosopher took up his residence at Haifa at the foot of Mount Carmel of Biblical fame. Thence he visited Paris and London. He visited friends in America in April and is just now living in New York whither he will return today.[37]

The second address of the day was delivered at the Baptist Temple. 'Abdu'l-Bahá was invited by Dr. Russell H. Conwell who was the founder of the church as well as the university adjacent to it and who years before had met Him while traveling in Syria.[38] Conwell called on 'Abdu'l-Bahá at 4 p.m. and is reported as having said to Him: 'We believe in your doctrine and our church is your home, our people are your family, and I hope that you will accept this.' He also offered 'Abdu'l-Bahá to pay the expenses of His visit to Philadelphia. The Master thanked him for his gesture but refused his offer answering, 'Your love is my fee. If I have your love, I have everything.'[39] The talk started at 8 p.m. and 'Abdu'l-Bahá spoke about materialism and the purpose of religions and also presented some of the Bahá'í principles.[40]

The *Philadelphia Record*, which had a daily circulation of nearly 157,000 copies, stated in its account that over two thousand people had gathered at the church to listen to 'Abdu'l-Bahá:

> PERSIAN FOR SUFFRAGE
>
> AGED LEADER OF BAHAI MOVEMENT PREACHES EQUAL RIGHTS
>
> In the quaint Oriental language of his mother country Abdul Baha Abbas, Persian nobleman, suffragist and chief priest of the Bahai movement for the unification of all mankind, told an audience of more than 2000 people in the Grace Baptist Temple last night that woman, if given the same education, is the superior of man, and that the happiness of the world will never be secured until the female of the species is privileged equally with the male.
>
> 'In the animal and vegetable kingdoms,' said the Bahai priest, 'male and female depend in equal proportions one upon the other; mankind alone denies its mate, womankind, proper and deserved privileges. Woman is weak only when man makes her weak. Because a child is a child, do we blame it for so being? No, we train it and

educate it. We do not blame a patient for being a patient; we seek to cure and heal. So must we remedy the age-long differences between man and woman.'

Turning for a moment from his appeal for woman's rights, the aged Persian referred as follows to the question between capital and labor:

'Readjustment of the economic condition,' he said, 'is imperative. Until it comes there can be no true equality, and true equality is necessary because finally it must be assumed before the judgment seat. Six thousand years of unrest in the world has been due to prejudices – political, religious and otherwise. When they have passed away the great destroyers of the human foundation will have passed away, and warfare and animosity will be known no more.'

As chief priest of the Bahai movement, a distinction bequeathed to him by his father, Baha O'Allah, who, after writing the book of laws known as Kitab Akdas, died in a Turkish prison in 1892, Abdul Baha Abbas stands for the unification of all races and sects through a universal enlightenment.

'The schools of the world,' he told his audience last night, 'should be put upon a common basis. In them should be taught only two languages, the one the national tongue, and the other the international or auxiliary language, which should be agreed upon by a congress of the world's teachers. Efficiency in the auxiliary tongue should be made compulsory.'

Religion's attitude towards science he explained to be the same as the attitude of knowledge towards teaching.

'Religion,' he said, 'is the cause of everything; it represents the unification of men because it represents love and the mercy of God. It must be in accord with science; if it conflicts then it is wrong, for science is the opposite of ignorance and ignorance is the enemy of religion.'

Abdul Baha Abbas arrived in Philadelphia Saturday night and while here he is under the direction of the Philadelphia branch of the Bahai movement, of which Miss Jessie Revell, of No. 1429 Mayfield Avenue, is the leader . . .[41]

After the departure of 'Abdu'l-Bahá from Philadelphia, *The Telegraph*, a Republican newspaper with a circulation of 120,000 copies, published a rather skeptical comment about 'Abdu'l-Bahá and the Bahá'í teachings:

ABDUL BAHA'S MESSAGE

Whatever may be said of the practicability of the religion of brotherhood preached by Abdul Baha, no one will deny that his is a beautiful conception of how all peoples of the earth might and should dwell together. This venerable Persian spoke before two audiences in this city on Sunday last. His plea was simple and direct, being merely a restatement of the part of the ethics of Christ which is best known. Unhappily the same incredulous spirit which exclaimed 'impossible' when the Nazarene said 'Love thy neighbor as thyself' is alive and dominant still upon earth.

In the coming of this bearded man from the East asking again in effect, 'How can a man love his father in Heaven, whom he hath not seen, if he love not his brother on earth, whom he hath seen?' there is a powerful appeal to the spiritual emotions. Abdul Baha preaches as preached his father and his father's father. He is 65 years old. For preaching the brotherhood of all men the Turks kept him in prison for 41 years. With the triumph of the Young Turks he was released and at once took up again the work of his fathers. This wise man from the East is a sign of the times. In him is embodied in large degree that new spirit of world-wide unity which so powerfully moves all races in this age. The world is riper for his message than it was in the days of his dead parents. He is an effect more than a cause; without him the world was already turning toward peace and will continue to turn.[42]

A Poem by Edith M. Thomas

Edith Matilda Thomas (1854–1925) was a famous poetess who contributed some of her poems in leading periodicals of her time including *Scribner's Monthly*, *Harper's Weekly* and *The Evening Post*. By the time 'Abdu'l-Bahá visited America she had already published at least 15 compilations of her poetry. On 15 June *The Evening Post* carried in its pages a poem by Thomas dedicated to 'Abdu'l-Bahá:

ABDUL BAHA SEEKS IN MANHATTAN

Where these centuries has slept Firdusi?
Where Saadi? – or Hafiz, golden-tongued?
Dropped asleep while singing – waked, a dreamer.

Seeking body for his dream divine.
Love-of-God and World-round Kinship Teaching
Wandering Westward, thus our city greets
Mildly wonders at our vaunting fabrics –
At our granite shafts that aim to stay,
Vistaed lamps in diamond diminution,
Air-swung bridges, marts and palaced Wealth –
All the tideless, daily, urban pageant!
Marvels at our churches – not averse,
Opening doors, as to a looked-for pilgrim!
Pilgrim not to any Mecca bound,
Bearing in his heart a shrine of holies –
World-round Kinship, Love-of-God – his Word!
Goes he up and down our brave Manhattan,
Unbewildered through its soundful maze;
Childlike seeker – child and seer in challenge,
Subtlest when most simply he demands –
Affable yet penetrant inquirer!
Asked by someone, 'Have you seen our Parks?'
Softly he makes answer, 'I have seen them,
Very noble Garden for a king
But no rose therein have I seen blossoming,
And no nightingales therein I heard!'
Wistful smiling, turns he on the questioner
Eastern eyes with mystic seal aglow!
'Is there anyone that in the garden
Lists to be a rose – a rose-in-bloom?
Is there anyone that in the garden
Lists to be a nightingale and sing?'
Thus, the pilgrim goes his way among us,
World-round Kinship, Love-of-God – his Word.
What finds he of lack in brave Manhattan,
What, forsooth, the 'rose' and 'nightingale?'[43]

Central Congregational Church in Brooklyn

On Sunday 16 June, 'Abdu'l-Bahá spoke at the services of two Brooklyn churches, the Flatbush Unitarian Church (Beverly Road and East

Nineteenth Street) and the Central Congregational Church (Hancock St. and Bedford Ave.). The minister of the first church was Rev. Leon Harvey, who on the previous week had dedicated part of his Sunday sermon to speak about 'Abdu'l-Bahá. Announcements of this talk, which had the title 'The Unity of the Great Religions of the World' and started at 10:45 a.m., were published in the local press.[44]

In His talk at the Congregational Church, which was held at 7:45 p.m.,[45] 'Abdu'l-Bahá spoke on the unity of religions and the abolition of religious prejudice and called for better relations between Christians and Muslims.[46] On the following day the *Daily Eagle* published a short account of this meeting including the text of the talk:

ABDUL BAHA ABBAS IN DR. S. PARKES CADMAN'S PULPIT

UNIVERSAL PEACE BY ABDUL BAHA ABBAS

Last evening in the Central Congregational Church, Abdul Baha Abbas from Persia, who is making a tour of the principal cities of this country for the purpose of explaining 'The Baha Spirit' religion, delivered an address to a large congregation. The Rev. Dr. S. Parkes Cadman, the pastor, introduced him, and after the address, thanked him warmly for his message.

Abdul Baha Abbas does not speak enough English to enable him to make an address in that language, and so speaks in his native tongue, and sentence by sentence his interpreter, Dr. Ameen U. Fareed, translates what he says into most excellent English. Besides the interpreter, several other Persians accompany him. The object of the mission to this country is to unite the Orient and the Occident in bringing about universal brotherhood and peace, and to set aside once for all those prejudices among religious bodies which stand in the way.

Abdul Baha Abbas said: This is a good temple, and this is a good congregation, for, praise be to God, this is a temple wherein the conscience has free sway. Every religion and every religious aspiration may be freely expressed here. Just as in the world of politics there is need for free thought, likewise in the world of religion there is need for freedom of religious thought. Consider what a vast difference exists between democracy and the old forms of despotism. Under despotic government the thoughts of men are not free, but because under a democratic government thought is free, the greatest progress is made. Even so is it in the world of religion. In a democratic country the platform is open to every religion for the conveyance of its ideals, and I am most grateful to the reverend doctor, whom I find to be a servant to the oneness of human kindness. The holy, divine manifestations are all united and agreed, and they are the heads of religion. For example, his holiness Abraham, his holiness Moses, his holiness Christ, his holiness Mahomet, Buddha, are all united and agreed. Every former prophet foretold the coming of the latter, and the latter sanctioned the former. For example, Abraham foretold the coming of Moses and Moses sanctioned it. Moses prophesied the Messianic time and Christ fulfilled the Mosaic law. It is evident that they are all united and agreed. All the holy manifestations are agreed. They are all founders of reality, and they are all promulgators of the religion of God. The religion of God is reality, and the reality is not multiple, reality is one. Therefore the foundations of the divine religions are one; because all are based on reality and the reality is not multiple. But religion has discord, strife, enmity, rancor. Wherefore? because they have forsaken the foundation of the divine religion, holding to religious imitation. And inasmuch as imitations differ, strife and enmity have crept in. The foundation laid by Christ was reality, but after His time many sects sprang up. What caused this? They were, no doubt, called up by imitation. The various sects are investigating the foundation of Christ, which is reality and will unite them all. If they will emulate the one reality, forsake imitation and seek to find the real meaning of the Sacred Book they will all unite. But as long as they follow these counterfeits, or imitations, undoubtedly this discord will continue. Let me illustrate: His holiness Moses prophesied regarding the Messiah, but when his holiness Christ appeared they rejected Him. Why? Because they had followed imitations and had not investigated the reality. They had not apprehended the significance of the Holy Bible. The prophets had given certain signs and conditions regarding His coming. He was to come from an unknown place, whereas they said, 'We know He has come from Nazareth and we know His father and mother.' Secondly, He was to rule with a rod of iron; but this Christ had not even a rod of wood. Thirdly, He was to sit upon the throne of David; and this Christ had not even a mat. Fourthly, He was to conquer the East and the West; this person had not even conquered a village. How could He be the Messiah? Fifthly, He was to promulgate the laws of the Bible; but He not only did not, but He broke the Sabbath law. Sixthly, the Messiah was to gather together all the scattered Jews; but this person rather degraded the Jews and did not gather them together. Seventhly, under His sovereignty the Jews were to enjoy bliss; the lion and the bear were to pasture in the same meadow; justice was to reign; warfare was to cease, and He was even crucified! How could He be the Messiah? This Messiah was not the promised Christ. But the Jews had not comprehended the meaning of the prophecies. All these prophecies were fulfilled, but because the Jews were captives of imitation they were holding the imitation and did not comprehend the meaning of the Bible. The purpose of the prophet was not an outward literal meaning, but they spoke in symbology. For instance, they mentioned that the Messiah was to come from an unknown place. They did not refer to the body of Christ; it had reference to the reality of the Christ. That is to say, the Christ reality was to come from the invisible realm, for the Christ reality had sanctified the birth place. He was to conquer through a sword; He conquered through the sword of the tongue. He did conquer the East and the West. He was to sit upon the throne of David; but the sovereignty of Christ was not that of a Napoleon or a Hannibal, but an eternal sovereignty, an everlasting sovereignty; there is no end to His sovereignty. As to promulgating the laws of the Bible, it meant the reality of the laws of Moses, which are the very foundation of the reality of Christianity. He subdued the East and the West through the breath of the Holy Spirit illuminating the East and the West. The lion and the lamb were to drink from the same fountain. This was realized in this sense: the fountain referred to was the gospel whereof the waters of life gushed forth. The wolf and the lamb are the nations and races thus symbolized. Those who were wolves and lambs were united through the words of the gospel. All the meaning of the prophecies was fulfilled, but because the Jews were captives of imitation they did not realize the meaning of the prophecies.

We must investigate the reality; we must lay aside selfish purposes; we must banish heresies. The Jews considered Christ the enemy of Moses, but had it not been for Jesus Christ you would never have had the Old Testament. His holiness, Jesus Christ, fulfilled the Mosaic law and in all cases did He praise Moses; but the Jews, because of blind imitation, considered Christ the enemy of Moses. Among the contemporaneous religions is Mohammedanism. About 300,000,000 believe in that religion, and from olden times there has been enmity and distrust between Mohammedans and Christians. This has been due to misunderstanding. Were imitation to be forgotten and forsaken, there could be no enmity between the Moslem and the Christian. Now, I wish to call your close attention to this: The Koran, the Mohammedan Bible, contains this text: That his holiness Christ was the very Word of God; that He was the Spirit of God; that Jesus Christ came into this world through the resuscitation of the Holy Spirit, and that His birth was through the Holy Spirit; that Mary was holy and sanctified. In the Koran a whole chapter is devoted to the story of Jesus Christ, and it is recorded that Manna descended from heaven day by day for the sustenance of the infant Christ. And in the Koran there is a remarkable eulogy regarding Christ, such as you do not find in the gospels. Marvelous to relate the first petition to his people by Mahomet was this: 'Why don't you believe on Jesus Christ? Why have ye not believed in the Bible and the prophets of Israel and in the disciples of Christ? Ye must know Moses as the prophet of God; ye must know Jesus Christ as the Word of God; ye must know Jesus Christ as a product of the Holy Spirit.' His people said: 'Very well, we will become believers, but our fathers, our ancestors, were not believers, and we are proud of them. What is going to become of them?' And he said: 'I say unto you that they occupy the lowest stratum of hell, because they did not believe in Moses; because they did not believe in Christ; because they did not accept the Bible, and they are my own ancestors, yet they are in hell.' This is an explicit text in the Koran. If both parties should investigate the reality of conditions they would know, and this strife would pass away. How much blood has been spilled; how many cities have been destroyed; how many children made fatherless! All these things were due to imitations and misunderstandings. If the Holy Bible were to be understood in reality none of these things would have existed.

The divine manifestations of God are all founded upon fellowship. The religion of God is the cause of love, but if it be the cause of enmity and strife, surely its non-existence is better than its existence, because then it is a catastrophe in the human world. In the Orient various nations were in a state of discord. Darkness had encompassed all nations. When He appeared He removed all imitations, and laid the foundation of the one religion of God. When the imitations were dispelled, the Mussulman, the Christian, the Jew and the Buddhist were united, and they have become revivified through the breath of the Holy Spirit. Praise be to God, this love has come forth from the East, and eventually there shall be no discord and enmity in the East. Through the power of Baha, all will be united. When he was the subject of banishment he wrote to all the kings, summoning them to international peace. He made it incumbent on them to call a board of arbitration for all international disputes. I was in prison forty years until the Young Turk and the Committee of Union and Progress proclaimed liberty. Were it not for these, I should have been in prison to the end of my life.[47]

Second Visit to Montclair, New Jersey

'Abdu'l-Bahá visited Montclair for a second time on 20 June, staying in the city for eight days.

Soon after His first visit to the city, news had been distributed by agencies stating that 'Abdu'l-Bahá 'will make his home in Montclair', 'has taken the house at 11 Bradford Place, in this town, and will live there after June 15'. The articles further added that 'Abdul Baha recently spoke in the Unity Church here and was so impressed by the reception he received and by the physical aspects of the town that he expressed a desire to take up his abode in the town'.[48]

A few days after this note was released, agencies also distributed a picture of 'Abdu'l-Bahá with the title 'Persian Prophet to Remain in US'. The caption stated that 'he is so pleased with this country that he has determined to remain here the rest of his days'.[49]

During His stay at the residence of Gifford Pinchot in Milford, one of the guests asked the Master regarding these reports. 'Abdu'l-Bahá answered, 'They are right in their report, but they did not understand what kind of a home it is. All the world is my country and I am living everywhere. Wherever such souls as you are found, there is my country. Hearts are the real country. Man must live in the hearts and not on the earth. This earth belongs to no one. It will pass away from the hands of all. It is an imagination. But the hearts are the real country.'[50]

When He returned to Montclair, the newspapers again reported that 'Abdu'l-Bahá intended to reside there permanently.[51] Some reports also mentioned an anecdote that occurred during His departure:

> ABDUL BAHA MANAGES TO CATCH A TRAIN
>
> BUT FOR TWO PERHAPS FORTUITOUS INCIDENTS HE WOULD HAVE BEEN LEFT
>
> Montclair, N.J., June 29 – The departure of Abdul Baha, leader of the Bahaist cult, from Montclair to-day was attended by excitement that was strikingly at variance with the peaceful character of the religious prophet. Abdul Baha and a retinue of ten fez-wearing Persians have been making their home at 11 Bradford Place for several weeks. Arrangements were made for the departure of the aged prophet to-day for West Englewood, where he addressed a meeting of Bahaists.
>
> Several members of Abdul Baha's retinue left for the Lackawanna railroad station in advance of their leader. When the time for the train to depart arrived he was not in sight. He had been delayed in leaving the house. The baggage was aboard the train and as it moved out of the terminal there was a great excitement among the retinue, who appealed to the trainmen in several Oriental languages to defer the departure for a few minutes. Some of the excited followers of the prophet, when they realized that the train was leaving, got aboard. One of them in swinging his arms about, incidentally or otherwise, pulled the bell rope. At the same instant Abdul Baha came in sight in an automobile that moved swiftly in the direction of the railroad station. To add to the excitement another one of the Persians at this moment, accidentally or with purpose, knocked off the conductor's hat. The train came to a halt and Abdul Baha leaped from the automobile and was hustled aboard.
>
> Abdul Baha will be in New York City for a while. About the middle of July he will go to Boston. He had intended to make a long Western trip, but it was feared that the exertion at the season of the year would be too much for one of his age, and the tour was cancelled on the advice of physicians.
>
> During his stay here Abdul Baha has attracted considerable

attention. There are about fifty Bahaists in Montclair, and they made the stay of the prophet as pleasant as possible. They showered him with gifts of fruit and flowers daily. These are the only gratuities that the leader would accept at the hands of his followers, as he is wealthy. Last evening at the home of Mrs. Charles H. Edsall of The Crescent a farewell reception was given to Abdul Baha and his intimate disciples.[52]

VISIT TO THE HOUSE OF THE PERSIAN CONSUL, MORRIS PLAINS, NEW JERSEY

On Sunday 30 June, 'Abdu'l-Bahá was invited to a lunch at the house of Haigazoun H. Topakyan, the Consul-General of Persia in the United States. This social meeting was announced in *The Sun* (New York) on 28 June: 'Consul-General Topakyan of Persia will give a Persian barbecue on Sunday at 2. p. m., at Persian Court, Morris Plains N. J., in honor of Abdul Baha of Persia.'[53] Besides the prominent guests, at least one reporter, the representative of the New York *Sun*, was also present at the meeting. The article that ensued included these passages:

The Consul had prepared a list of the more prominent people at his barbecue, and typewritten copies of this same list he distributed generously from point to point and from time to time. Someone noticed that there were crosses after several of the names, but the Consul when approached could not remember whether the marks indicated who was present or who absent.

Here is the list in its integrity: Henry Clews, Gen. Benjamin F. Tracy, Col. George Clinton Batcheller, Frederick D. Underwood, Baron Schliffenbach, Mr. and Mrs. W. E. D. Stokes, Youssouff Zia Pasha, Mr. and Mrs. John Ford, Mr. and Mrs. Lincoln Peabody, Rabbi Joseph Silverman and Mr. and Mrs. C. C. Moss.

The guests came out of New York in automobiles early in the morning; that is, early for Sunday morning, and they did not leave until the shadows of evening began to darken the lawns of Persian Court. The young people left the tables and went for a romp, leaving their elders to the discussion of themes of national significance.

Mr. Topakyan spoke of the need for universal peace and of the prevalence of injustice in Persia . . .

After the feasting was over the Consul escorted Abdul Baha to a

> waiting automobile and whirled him away to the house where the Consul really lives for a little rest and refreshment. On the lawn a large chair was placed for the teacher and he was treated to some real Persian music produced by two phonographs. The air sounded strangely in the ears of the outsiders but they brought smiles of appreciation to the face of the teacher.[54]

The *New York Herald* published on 1 July a brief note about the meeting and also offered the names of some of the guests: 'A Barbecue in honor of Abdul Baha, leader of the new Babist movement, was given by Hagizoun H. Topakyan at his country place, Persian Court, this afternoon. There were more than one hundred persons present, including Mirza Ali Kuli Khan, the Persian Charge d'Affaires at Washington; Charles O. Maas and H. P. Dispecker, of New York, Dr. and Mrs. Britton Devans and Mrs. Homer Davenport of Morris Plains. Abdul Baha made an address.'[55]

Interview for *The Sun*

On Sunday 7 July, the New York *Sun*, which, as mentioned earlier, had a circulation of 90,000 copies, published an interview with 'Abdu'l-Bahá. The article was accompanied by a portrait taken by the renowned photographer Gertrude Käsebier.[56] In the course of the interview 'Abdu'l-Bahá summarized the purpose of His travels and His impressions of America and underlined the need for spiritual civilization:

> ABDUL BAHA GIVES HIS IMPRESSIONS OF NEW YORK
>
> LEADER OF BAHAISTS FINDS THIS CITY BEAUTIFUL AND GREAT, BUT ITS CIVILIZATION IS TOO MATERIAL
>
> WAS HAPPY TO TALK TO THE MEN OF THE BOWERY – HE HAS DONE LITTLE SIGHTSEEING IN AMERICA
>
> Abdul Baha Abbas, leader of the sect of Bahaists and head of a religion which is said to have several hundred thousand followers, has recently finished a pilgrimage in search of disciples which stretched from the Atlantic to the Pacific. In the course of his journey the Master, as he is called by his converts, has visited Chicago, San Francisco, Cleveland, Detroit, Washington, Philadelphia and other cities.

At the request of THE SUN the prophet of the Bahai religion dictated a statement concerning his impressions of New York and other cities he visited. At the outset he explained that in his travels the material things he has seen have interested him but little. He hasn't cared to see any of the notable buildings of New York and has not visited the museums and art galleries.

While he has seen a bit of Central Park, his time, when he has not been with his disciples, at his temporary residence, 809 West Seventy-eighth Street, or speaking at meetings in various parts of the city, has been spent in walking through Riverside Park, near his place of abode. It is in this way that he takes his rest and he usually goes alone, because he finds no rest when there is someone along with whom he might converse.

For these reasons he has seen less of New York and this country than the average traveler from abroad, and although he is to remain here until fall, there is little likelihood that he will see much more before he departs for the East. While Abdul Baha had picked up a few English words of greeting while in this country and is acquainted with various foreign languages, he speaks most expressively in his native tongue. THE SUN is therefore indebted to his interpreter, Dr. Ameen U. Fareed, for the translation of Abdul Baha's account of his impressions, which follows:

'New York is very well built and it is very costly, but too many people reside in it. I like small towns and cities and I like Washington very much. New York is very prosperous and I can see it is a great commercial center.

'As one approaches the harbor, New York looms up in the horizon as a colossal statue symbolic of all America. From every standpoint it exhibits extraordinary advancement. Likewise all the other cities of America are in the utmost order. The continent is a garden in the utmost state of freshness and rapture.

'But it needs a melody of the kingdom in order that it may become the paradise of the world of humanity. The Government is a fair one; the nation intelligent. The liberty of the world of humanity, like an eagle, has unfurled its royal feathers and overshadowed this clime. I hope that it may achieve the utmost of progress.

'It is my hope that the banner of universal peace may be first hoisted in America and that the tabernacle of the oneness of mankind shall be pitched hither. The oneness of language may first radiate from here and spread throughout the world.

'What is the melody of the kingdom? To be free from the world of matter a bit. In the Orient, through the effective power of Baha Ullah, the foundation of divine and heavenly civilization was laid, and in the Occident its material civilization is day by day advancing. If divine civilization be united, then it shall be light upon light, and the utmost happiness will secure to the body politic.

'Consider that the body politic in these countries is day and night exerting itself to the utmost in order to obtain wealth. But you do not have happiness, love and unity among hearts such as ought to obtain. They do not exist because cordial love, save through the emanations of the conscience and spiritual susceptibility, cannot be realized.

'Material love is an exigency of the animal world, but the love of the conscience is an exigency of the world of man, and the latter cannot be attained save through heavenly means.

'His holiness Christ endured all hardships and ordeals in order to found the spiritual love and that the world might be illuminated. No matter how far material civilization shall have advanced it will not prove the cause of fellowship love; but divine civilization has for its fundamental basis absolute love. That is why God has sent prophets in order that they may found divine civilization and connect the hearts of men with one another.

'The foundation of all the divine religions is love, but alas, that the religionists have used the religion as the cause of enmity and the cause of murder and rapine, whereas his holiness Baha Ullah states that "if religion be the cause of enmity surely the lack of religion is better than its presence.' Because religious teachings are as remedies, if the remedy be productive of disease, surely its lack is better than its presence. To forsake that treatment is better than its use.

'The divine religions are all capable of commingling because they are all reality and reality is one. Subsequent imitations, which have nothing to do whatsoever with the divine religions, have proved to be the cause of warfare and battle. If the nations of the world forsake all these subsequent imitations and investigate the fundamental groundwork of religion they will all arrive at the reality and will exercise fellowship and love, and this warfare of 6,000 years duration shall be removed from among mankind.

'What I have seen of New York is very beautiful, beautiful. The people of this country are very intelligent and quick to grasp.

'Washington is small, but it is a good city. It is most delightful and refreshing, like a garden. While the capitals of Europe are very much larger, I like Washington the best.

'I like New York better than Chicago, but I did not go into the buildings in either city, and I do not know that the buildings are higher in New York than in Chicago.

'I am not interested in things that are merely beautiful to look at, but I am interested in the soul. I have nothing to do with mortar and clay. I wish to view an edifice that is never to be destroyed. But I am pleased with the people of America. They are noble people.

'From the beginning of human society the means for advancement may be reduced to two. One is philosophy and the other is religion. Philosophy serves the material world, but religion serves the world of morality. For example, Aristotle, the great philosopher, served material civilization, but Christ illumined the world and founded the spirit of civilization. The world of humanity is in need of both.

'These two civilizations are like two wings for man wherewith he can soar. To soar with one wing is not possible. The civilizations must be united in order that mankind may soar and reach the height of perfection.

'The earth's sphere, however much it may ignite lamps, nevertheless is ever in need of the effulgence of the sun. Matter, however much is refined, is in need of the spirit. Consider the great philosophers who have come. Their efforts at most were confined to a limited circle, but the holy, divine manifestations exercise an influence in an unlimited circle.

'The philosophers were able to educate a few souls, whereas the divine holy manifestations educate a republic. The effect of the philosophic instruction is lasting only for numbered days, but the effect of holy divine manifestations is everlasting and never ending.

'I find here how material civilization has progressed. The crafts have been perfected, the agricultural sciences have improved, and material science has been established. But the civilization of the spirit must not be left behind.

'The material civilization is like a glass in a lamp chimney. The spiritual civilization is the light in that chimney. The spirit civilization cannot be accomplished through ordinary means for the interests of matter and spirit differ. It is evident that it cannot be accomplished through patriotism; this human solidarity is impossible save through a spiritual power.

'Humanity is submerged in a sea of materiality and the light of the sun of truth can be seen but dimly. The heavenly civilization is daily making itself manifest, and it is my hope that the foundations of this solidarity may be established so that the hearts of the East and the West may be a divine unit and that this world may find peace.

'May the hearts of men become as mirrors and may the light of truth shine on those mirrors.

'The social unit of the world is like the ocean and each individual is like a wave and each wave belongs to that ocean. The most important thing is to polish the mirror of the heart so that it can reflect the sun. In the mirror that is polished you will see the sun in all its majesty, but the mirror full of dross is incapable of refulgence. But the sun is always the same.

'The center of the light is the sun, and the center of the sun is God. Therefore we must try to make love take possession of the heart so that all humanity of the East and the West may be one, for we are all recipients of the bounty of the sun.

'In the Orient there were great differences. The various peoples hated each other and the divergent sects were inimical to each other until Baha Ullah appeared from the Eastern dawn and connected the people by his love until the former enmity gave place to love, and a new spring appeared. And through this new spring appeared meadows with flowers of inner significance, and the real spring became visible.

'I talked to the men of the Bowery and I was happy then, for I was talking to my friends. I consider the poor my brothers, my companions. One who is poor should be thankful to God, for He never said, "Blessed are the rich." Happiness does not depend upon wealth. The rich are remorseful, never peaceful. We come to this world naked, and we must leave it naked. All possessions have to be left behind, therefore the poor have no regrets.

'When I leave these United States in a few months for the East

I can repeat the loving farewell I gave to the people of France and England. I am very much pleased with all countries I have visited.

'I counsel them all that they may day by day strengthen the bond of love and amity to this end, that they may become the sympathetic embodiment of one nation, that they may extend themselves to a universal brotherhood to guard and protect the interests of all the nations of the East and the West, that they may unfurl the divine banner of justice, that they may realize and treat each nation as a family composed of the individual children of God, and may know that in the sight of God the rights of all are equal.

'It has made me happy to visit New York and the other cities of these United States, and I would say let us all become as one so that each may become representative of the bounty of God.'[57]

All Souls Unitarian Church, New York

At the invitation of Rev. Leon A. Harvey who, as well as the Flatbush Unitarian Church, was also temporarily in charge of the All Souls Unitarian Church in Manhattan, 'Abdu'l-Bahá spoke on Sunday, 14 July, at a service at All Souls. Announcements had been published in various newspapers.[58] The *World*, for instance, published the following note:

> Abdul Baha Abbas, the Persian prophet, will speak at All Souls Unitarian Church, Twentieth Street and Fourth Avenue, to-morrow morning at 11 o'clock. This will probably be his last public address in New York, as he soon starts for the West on his way back to Egypt by way of Japan and India. This leader of the great Bahaist movement is reputed to have fourteen million followers. Abdul Baha's propaganda is absolutely universal and in no way restricted to party, sect, denomination or creed.
>
> Everywhere his addresses have been followed by a strong wave of influence toward Christian harmony and Christian recognition of a wider unity which is to comprise a real brotherhood and reconciliation among all religious systems of East and West. They reflect the essence of Christianity, Mohammedanism, Buddhism, Brahmanis, Judaism and Zoroasterism. The services to-morrow will be conducted by the Rev. Leon A. Harvey. His mission is one of unity, peace and brotherhood.[59]

Owing to these announcements in the press many people, including journalists, attended the service. 'Abdu'l-Bahá spoke on the oneness of humanity and mentioned some of the requirements for its achievement.[60]

The *New York Press*, a Republican newspaper with a circulation of 100,000 copies, published a lengthy account which quoted some of the words of 'Abdu'l-Bahá:

PERSIAN PROPHET FAVORS EQUAL RIGHTS FOR WOMEN

SUFFRAGE FOR ALL WILL END STRIFE, HE SAYS.

MAKES ADDRESS IN CHURCH

CULT OF WHICH HE IS HEAD SAID TO HAVE FOURTEEN MILLION FOLLOWERS

Equal rights for women were advocated fervently by Abdul Baha Abbas, Persian prophet, said to be at the head of a cult embracing fourteen million followers, at an address made before a large congregation in All Souls Unitarian Church, Fourth Avenue and Twentieth Street, yesterday morning. The keynote of the Persian's sermon was that all mankind sprang from one root, and that sectarian beliefs should not be a barrier to a religion of universal peace and brotherhood.

'We were all made equal, yet woman is said by ignorant persons not to be the equal of man,' he continued. 'The result is strife. But there will be no strife and the two will be equal in the eyes of the whole world when woman is educated as highly as man, for there can be no doubt they were created equal.'

After his talk, which was given in Persian through an interpreter, Abdul Baha held an informal reception for the members of the congregation. Questioned as to his views on woman suffrage in this and other countries, the prophet replied he had not given the subject exhaustive study, but that he certainly believes that if women are the equals of men in business and social life they should be in politics.

The Persian said in part:

'It will be seen and known that all humanity come from one family, Adam and Eve, who were made by God. All have been made by God, and all are protected by God, and God loves us all. God is kind to all. That is the basis for universal peace and religion of mankind. For 6,000 years before we had universal peace can be seen the ghosts of war. Look back and everywhere you will find warfare among men. It is religious warfare or party warfare, or it is national warfare or political warfare. The world of unity has not found rest at all. There has ever been unrest of one kind or another.

'Let us all strive for unity, so that it may be given a trial. If there be unity to greet God great things will be done. It is thought that some of us spring from different trees, the Merciful and the Satanic tree. That is the thought of many religions. Those of the Merciful tree were the religious; those of the other tree the people of warfare and strife.

'We all come from one tree, however, the Merciful tree, the tree made by God, the Adamic tree. All are of God and God is kind to all, and there is no interference of the Satanic tree. God alone is the creator, and all the universe is the result of His might. Therefore we must love all mankind. God has given all; we are the result of the grace of God, not wrath of God.

'In Persia all the followers of Christianity, Mahometanism, Buddhism, Judaism and other religions have followed the belief in the unity of God and the foundation of universal peace and mankind, and are living quietly together without strife. You can do the same.'

Abdul Baha, through the interpreter, also made the closing prayer of the service.[61]

A shorter but similar account appeared in *The New York Times*.[62] A brief note in the *New York Herald* stated that 'Abdu'l-Bahá addressed 'a large congregation' and added that 'He declared that differences in sectarian beliefs should be no barrier to a universal religion of peace and brotherhood'.[63] A short comment on the event published in the *Unitarian Advance* (New York), stated that 600 people listened to 'Abdu'l-Bahá and that His address 'was thoroughly enjoyed'.[64]

In a report about Unitarian activities in New York, a correspondent with the *Christian Register* (Boston) made the following remarks about the meeting:

On July 14 Abdul Baha preached at All Souls for Mr. Harvey, and the church was well filled, although the heat was great.

Americans are becoming devoted to the ideals of this Persian teacher. Chicago is to build a church for him, and there is something appealing to Unitarians in his belief. 'The Oneness of Humanity' was his topic July 14, and this 'oneness' includes women. The female is regarded as equally human with the male, and Abdul Baha preaches that men and women should share the same in ideals and responsibility both in Church and State. This is a refreshing phase of any religious belief.[65]

In the course of His address at All Souls, 'Abdu'l-Bahá quoted Bahá'u'lláh saying that, 'If religion and faith are the causes of enmity and sedition, it is far better to be nonreligious, and the absence of religion would be preferable . . . '[66] and developed the idea that if religion produces an outcome contrary to its essential purpose, it is better for it not to exist. This comment, or a similar one made in earlier addresses, was distributed by agencies for its inclusion in the religious section of various newspapers. The sentence prompted in turn different comments and editorials. The Charlotte (NC) *Daily Observer*, for instance, stated that

> Abdul Baha, the Persian philosopher and teacher, lately come to America, preaches the doctrine that all religions are at bottom one. He says: 'If a religion be the cause of hatred and disharmony it would be better for it not to exist.' The truth underlying his philosophy always appealed immensely to me. I always held that it was not so particularly a matter of what the particular belief was, so long as it was good enough to believe, and live and die by. I mean by that, it doesn't make much difference about the outward form of a man's religion. Religion, outwardly, is a man-made institution and creeds do not have souls any more than churches do.[67]

A similar note was published in *The Ohio State Journal* and reproduced in other newspapers:

> Abdul Baba, in his preaching on a universal religion, says this: 'If a religion be the cause of hatred and disharmony, it would be better for it not to exist than to exist.' He contends that at the bottom, all religions are one – that the divine speaks as well through one creed as another.
>
> But his idea that a religion that creates hatred is no religion at all

is right. There are several men in the world, and we see them quite often, whose religion makes them dislike men who hold different views. Of course, such men have no religion at all. They are just as irreligious as a man who doesn't believe anything. For the basis of all religion is love, and it is paganism if it hasn't that element in it.

And that is the force religion uses to make the world better. Where a reformer comes out hating his opponent, one might as well distrust that reform from the start. And it is that way all through life – the only way to make society, politics, religion, business better is to treat men and women in a sincere and brotherly fashion.[68]

Interview for *The Independent*

The Independent was a weekly liberal newspaper published in New York. Its editor was Hamilton Holt (1872–1951), who in all probability met 'Abdu'l-Bahá at the Lake Mohonk Conference, and perhaps also at the annual convention of the NAACP, an organization of which he was one of the founders. Holt was also a member of the New York Peace Society and used his magazine to promote his ideas on international peace and governance, and in later years the periodical voiced many of the ideas of the League to Enforce Peace.

Holt also probably met 'Abdu'l-Bahá in New York soon after His arrival in America and was in contact with Bahá'ís. As shown in chapters 9 and 10, coinciding with the arrival of 'Abdu'l-Bahá in America, this magazine published an article on the Bahá'í Faith by Louis Gregory and soon afterwards reviewed various comments in the press about 'Abdu'l-Bahá's talk in the Church of the Ascension. A further article introducing the Bahá'í Faith was published on 18 July and was probably penned by Frederic Deann. The text described the figure of 'Abdu'l-Bahá in the following words:

> He is an aged man now, with a long white beard and a saintly face, worn but peaceful. His bearing is simple and dignified, unembarrassed by unaccustomed surroundings, giving his message from a Christian pulpit to a strange audience in a foreign land with the same earnestness and naturalness as tho he were addressing his disciples in Acre. To say 'from a pulpit' is hardly correct, since he dislikes to occupy such an exalted position, preferring to put himself upon

> a level with his audience. Standing upon the floor or walking to and fro, he speaks quietly in Persian, which, sentence by sentence, is translated, tho at times his expressive features and gestures make the services of the interpreter almost superfluous. He wears a small white turban and a black robe over a white girdled garment. He greets the audience by touching his forehead repeatedly with the palm of the right hand and closes his sermon with a half-chanted prayer, standing and holding his hands upward and open, as tho ready to receive the blessing he beseeches.[69]

The day after the publication of this article 'Abdu'l-Bahá was interviewed for the magazine, and the article that ensued was published on 12 September together with a compilation of 'Some sayings of Abdul Baha' (not included here):

AMERICA AND WORLD PEACE

BY ABDUL BAHA ABBAS

Abdul Baha Abbas, Persian prophet and teacher, courteously replied to the questions of a representative of THE INDEPENDENT by means of an interpreter. In spite of the lofty position ascribed to him by his followers, his interest in ordinary human affairs is keen. He was dressed in flowing robes and turban, which accorded well with his square cut gray beard. His blue eyes are frank, lively and humorous, his figure of medium high and slight, but erect and graceful in spite of his sixty-eight years. When he was in London he preached in the City Temple and in St. John's, Westminster, and in the United States he has been invited to the pulpits of various denominations. In our issues of April and July 18 some account has been given of the leader of the Bahaists. – EDITOR

I AM very pleased with America and its people. I find religion, high ideals, broad sympathy with humanity, benevolence and kindness widespread here, and my hope is that America will lead in the movement for universal peace.

The people of this land enjoy many blessings. Day by day they are advancing and progressing, their fortunes are in their own hands, their patriotism is strong, they enjoy freedom in a superlative degree. They are not restrained by ignorance or the weight of old customs, nor are they tyrannized over by circumstances or fear of neighboring nations. In a hemisphere they are supreme, and as kindness is their natural disposition, the world will expect them to bear the banner of the peace movement.

Such leadership would be in accord with their own history and the principles on which their government is founded. Never in all the annals of the world do we find such an instance of national self-sacrifice as was displayed here during the Civil War. Americans who had never seen a weapon used in anger left their homes and peaceful pursuits, took up arms, bore utmost hardships, braved utmost dangers, gave up all they held dear, and finally their lives, in order that slaves might be free.

In Washington recently I addressed the students of Howard University – about fifteen hundred of them – and I told them that they must be very good to the white race of America. I told them that they must never forget to be grateful and thankful. I said to them: 'If you want to know really what great service the white race here has rendered to you, go to Africa and study the condition of your own race there.' But at the same time I said that the white people here must be very kind to those whom they have freed. The white people must treat those whom they have freed with justness and firmness, but also with perfect love. America's example in freeing the slaves has been a power for freedom everywhere. Because America freed her slaves, even at the cost of one of the bloodiest wars of modern times, other nations have felt themselves bound to free slaves. America's leadership in humanitarian and altruistic matters is generally acknowledged. Instead of robbing the weak, she helps them. The nations look to America to lead them in good works.

I am here in this country making an appeal on behalf of universal peace, unity, love and brotherhood. I do not know how many Bahaists there are in America or in the world. There are no statistics in regard to this matter. If figures have been published they are without authority. Bahaism has no creed, no ritual, no dogma. Its principles are:

1. Love of humanity, shown more in act than in word.
2. Kindness to all the nations of the world.
3. Service to fellowmen.
4. Day and night love for all men must be shown so that the foundations of war and strife will be utterly destroyed.

5. The Bahaist must be the embodiment of truth, sincerity and faith.
6. The Bahaist must be free from religious prejudice, patriotic prejudice, racial prejudice, national prejudice.
7. The Bahaist must consider humanity as one tree, of which the various nations are the branches, leaves and fruit.
8. The Bahaist's religion must agree with reason and the true findings of science.
9. The Bahaist must live and act in accordance with the principles and teachings of all the prophets.

If a man does and believes these things then he is a Bahaist, no matter whether he calls himself Shintoist, Confucianist, Buddhist, Hindoo, Jew, Mahometan, Zoroastrian, Parsee or Christian. No matter in what church or temple he worships. All men are brothers. All have the same great Father. They have had different teachers, different views of the same great Light, and they quarrel about these little differences. It is all very wrong. They must cease quarreling, love one another, as Christ has commanded, and unite for good works for the glory of God.

One of the principles of Bahaism is the perfect equality of men and women, therefore the women of this country interest me greatly. They have advanced far, they have high ideals. They have demonstrated their right to the suffrage, and it has been accorded to them in many of the States, while the other States seem likely to follow this example. The women of America, then, will be a world force, and humanity everywhere will look to them for leadership in the movement for universal peace. The women of America are facing great problems, but seem to have the wisdom and strength necessary for their solution.

Is peace always desirable? Undoubtedly it is. What is best in a family – peace or strife? Every good man will answer that family peace is best. So it is also with a nation, and so it is also with the whole world. In the United States of America forty-eight countries or States are gathered, living in peace with each other, and their enlightenment, happiness, progress and civilization serve as a model and inspiration to all men. It was not always so. Before Washington freed this country there were many wars and much strife and jealousy among the colonies. All that has gone, and peace, happiness and progress have come with union. The States support, love and are proud of one another, and what America has done, the rest of the world can do, following the example of America.

But would it be practicable for a country to lay down its arms and submit itself to the will of its neighbors – would not such a country be robbed and abused? Assuredly it is not practicable for a single country to disarm and trust the other nations to do justice for the sake of justice. Universal peace must be brought about by means of agreement among the great powers. They must assemble in convention, represented by their best and wisest men, and they must bind themselves by the strongest pledges and promises not to make war. Each should maintain an army and navy, but very small, merely enough to enforce order in its own territory.

Do not nations degenerate in peace? No. Again I refer to the example of America, which has prospered, grown strong and enlightened in peace and because of peace. I was in Africa and found warring tribes and much degradation. From there I went to Switzerland and found peace with high enlightenment, intelligence, justice and respect for the rights of fellow men. There can be no question as to the blessings of peace.

But nature is full of war. Beasts, birds, reptiles, insects, rob and destroy each other. Surely; there is much in nature that seems not good. But man has mind and soul. He has knowledge of good and evil, and his relations with God and duty to his fellows. He has free choice, and surely it is better for him to be as the peaceful lamb or dove than as the ferocious wolf or eagle. There are many things in nature that seem evil, as the venomous serpent and the scorpion, but we who are men must choose the good.

What is good? That which bestows or preserves life and happiness is good. That which destroys life and happiness is evil.

The cities here are wonderful and interesting, but the great height of the buildings oppresses me. They seem like beehives, with their crowds of inhabitants. The rooms are so small, like cells. I would feel stifled in such a building. We Orientals like low houses and plenty of room, with a garden in the middle and a fountain playing in the garden.

I will be in this country another month, but am going north now, for I find the heat here distressing. I will return to Syria by the way of England and France. The voyage here from Alexandria lasted fifteen days and the long confinement on shipboard was tedious. The return voyage to England will only last about five days, and that will not be so bad. Then I can journey in leisurely fashion thru England and France, tarrying at times with friends, and when I reach the Mediterranean I will be but two or three days' journey from home.

New York. July 19, 1912[70]

Armenian Federation Society

On Sunday 21 July, the Armenian Federation Society in New York held a memorial service in honor of the Armenian General Yephrem Khan Davidian (1868–1912), a leader of the Persian constitutional revolution who had been killed months before. 'Abdu'l-Bahá was invited to the services along with other prominent people such as Henry Clews, Judge John Ford, Dr W. A. Hunsberger and Rabbi Joseph Silverman. The meeting was chaired by Consul General Topakyan, himself an Armenian. The *New York Herald* published a brief announcement of the meeting on 20 July.[71] An account published in the *New-York Tribune* also mentioned 'Abdu'l-Bahá:

PERSIANS HOLD SERVICE

HONOR MEMORY OF GENERAL KHAN, KILLED IN BATTLE

H. H. Topakyan, Persian Consul General, presided last night in the Murray Hill Lyceum at the memorial services held there by the Armenian Federation Society of New York in honor of the late General Yephrem Khan, who was killed in battle about two months ago.

After a prayer by Father Manigan, Consul General Topakyan, in the course of his remarks, referred to the dead general as the greatest and bravest man the Persian Empire had ever known. After having gained a great victory, he said, over a larger rebel force, he was killed by an enemy bullet in Persia, sacrificing his life for a great cause. In the battle, he said, which lasted ten hours, three hundred were killed and many wounded.

'We are here to-night,' said the speaker, 'with heavy hearts, mourning for our victorious general, but it is gratifying to know that the memory of this noble man will never die.'

The other speakers included Abdul Baha Abbas, an old man with long white whiskers, clad in Persian costume, who was referred to by the chairman as 'the father of Persia'. He spoke through an interpreter and paid a glowing tribute to General Khan, whose deeds, he said, would illuminate a brilliant page in the history of Persia. Colonel Nevdon Khan, Kader Bey and William H. Hoar also spoke. Moses Gutterson's band played Chopin's Funeral march and other selections. Mrs. John Ryan sang the 'Ave Maria' and Miss M. Tateossian sang two numbers in Persian. Miss Yergarian recited in that language. Letters of regret were read from the Mayor, Charles A. Towne and Henry Clews, also a telegram from Mirza Ali Kuli Khan, the charge d'Affaires of Persia.[72]

Editorial Remarks in the *New York Press*

Before departing for Boston and Dublin, 'Abdu'l-Bahá received Jane Stone, a columnist with the *New York Press*, who in her column 'Through the Lorgnette' wrote critically about Him:

ABDUL BAHA

It seems that Abdul Baha intends remaining with us another winter. He has taken a house in the Seventies and with a retinue will live there again after his return from Dublin, N. H., where he is resting. Someone took me to call on this distinguished Easterner the day before he left New York. Through a most remarkable interpreter, a highly Europeanized Persian, Abdul Baha invited me to ask him one question which should include many. It was rather a weighty moment. The leader of Bahaism, in his Oriental robes, sat waiting, his head bowed, the friend who took me there smiled furtively wondering what I would ask, and the interpreter, the only other person present, beat time softly on the rug, that really didn't look as if it came from Persia. Said I, 'What is man's chief duty in the course of his earthly life?' Said Abdul Baha, by means of the interpreter, 'Man's chief duty in this life is to prepare for the next.' I wonder! I would have said that man's chief duty in this life was to get every last thing he could out of it, as the very best and only preparation for life in the next. I can't see what some religionists have against this life just because it happens to be here. For myself, I think it's a very good sort of life, created for our benefit, just as any future lives shall have been created.[73]

18

BOSTON, DUBLIN, GREEN ACRE, MALDEN

23 July – 29 August 1912

Second Visit to Boston

'Abdu'l-Bahá left New York early on the morning of Tuesday, 23 July, reaching Boston about 3:30 p.m. He remained in the city for two nights and stayed at the Hotel Victoria. On the day of His arrival He delivered a public address at His hotel, speaking on the economy and spiritual values.[1] The following day at least one local newspaper, *The Boston Evening Transcript*, carried the news of this meeting:

> ABDUL BAHA ABBAS COMES AGAIN
>
> PERSIAN SCHOLAR GREETED BY MANY FOLLOWERS AT RECEPTION IN THE HOTEL VICTORIA
>
> Many followers of Abdul Baha Abbas greeted him at the Hotel Victoria yesterday, where he made a brief stay after a tour of many large cities. All in the company are devotees of what this Persian scholar calls the new religion, which means world unity and universal peace. He expressed pleasure, through an interpreter, regarding his American travels and said that this country should lead in the peace movement. He added that this will not be brought about until there is wider interest in the religion of brotherhood. He is to visit friends in Dublin, N. H., during the next few weeks, after which he will return to his native land.[2]

In a similar article the *Boston Herald* reported that 'Abdu'l-Bahá

> . . . was at the Hotel Victoria yesterday, en route to Dublin, N. H.

> where he will rest for two or three weeks preparatory to his return to Persia. His apartments at the hotel last evening were thronged with visitors, mostly women, many of whom are followers of Bahaism . . . He declared that America should be the leader in the movement for universal peace, but deplored that hitherto efforts in that direction were merely verbal ones that produced no actual results. He hoped that America might prove to be the centre of the movement, but that if the promoters of the movement desired actual results their endeavors must be more extensive.[3]

A brief note about His arrival was also published in the *Boston Post*.[4]

On His first visit to Boston, 'Abdu'l-Bahá had been the guest of the Golden Links Society, a literary Syrian club of which Khalil Gibran was a member. On His return to the city the society invited 'Abdu'l-Bahá again.[5] The *Boston Herald* published a short report about the meeting which included the names of some of those present:

> SYRIAN MEAL FOR PERSIAN PROPHET
>
> ABDUL BAHA ENTERTAINED IN EASTERN STYLE WHILE IN BOSTON
>
> Abdul Baha, Persian prophet, and preacher of world unity, left Boston yesterday after a two-days' visit, and took a train early in the afternoon for Dublin, N.H. He was accompanied by Mirza Ahmad Sohrab, treasurer of the Persian Educational Society in Washington and Dr. A. U. Fareed, his interpreter.
>
> During his stay in Boston, the preacher was entertained by Nasim Khouri, publisher of the New Syrian, Dr. George Jureij and Rasheed Ab Delnour, who gave him a dinner Wednesday afternoon in the rooms of the Syrian Golden Links Society, 23 Hudson Street. Here he sat down to such a meal as might have been served to him in the distant East. He came to the table in full eastern costume and was greatly pleased when 'Kibby', the national Syrian dish made up of wheat and meat, was set before him. Next came some bread baked in Arabic style and when a bowl of laben – curdled milk was set before him he smiled happily and said that it all recalled to him Syria, 'the land of milk and honey'.
>
> Following the dinner, Abdul Baha, according to eastern custom, took a short nap, after which he addressed the company, predicting the coming unity of east and west. In addition to the Syrian guests,

several Americans were present.

After dinner the party was taken in two automobiles for a ride through the Fenway.[6]

Dublin, New Hampshire

From Boston, 'Abdu'l-Bahá went to Dublin, New Hampshire, a summer retreat to which He was invited by Agnes Parsons, who, as seen earlier, had also been His host in Washington. 'Abdu'l-Bahá stayed in the town from 25 July to 16 August and was able to recover to some extent from His fatigue and health problems after several months of strenuous activity. Some newspapers in the area published news about His presence in Dublin. The *Concord Monitor*, a Republican newspaper with a circulation of 2,500 copies, published on 26 May a note reporting the Master's arrival the day before:

> Abdul Baha Abbas, the remarkable Persian sage, who has been touring this country to promote the unification of religions and the attainment of universal peace, is at Dublin, this state, 'to rest for a few weeks'. Straightening out some of our New Hampshire political tangles would be right in his line of business, but probably he would esteem it too strenuous an undertaking for a vacation rest.[7]

In following weeks other references to 'Abdu'l-Bahá were published in the local press. The *Keene Evening Sentinel*, a Republican newspaper with a circulation of 2,100 copies, publicized on 9 August the address of 'Abdu'l-Bahá at the Unitarian Church of Dublin.[8] The *Peterborough Transcript*, with a circulation of 1,300 copies, published on 15 August a curious note stating that 'The venerable Persian, Abdul Baha, bears so much resemblance to Santa Claus that two little tots begged to take out their go-cart and get it filled with presents from him. They had espied the supposed Santa Claus sitting on the piazza of the Wilcox Inn and felt that the opportunity was too good not to be improved.'[9]

Green Acre, August 16 to 23

From Dublin, 'Abdu'l-Bahá proceeded to Eliot, Maine, to participate in the activities at Green Acre. On their way from Dublin to Green Acre,

'Abdu'l-Bahá and His party made a stop of two hours in Nashua, New Hampshire, where they rested at Tremont Hotel.[10]

Green Acre was an institution created by the Bahá'í philanthropist Sarah Farmer with the purpose of serving as a center for the work towards the unity of religions. Over the previous years the press had published dozens of articles about the place and its association with the Bahá'í Faith. When 'Abdu'l-Bahá arrived in America, Sarah Farmer was in bad health and at the same time different parties were disputing the leadership and control of the Green Acre institution and its properties. These issues were also covered in detail by the press.

'Abdu'l-Bahá's visit to Eliot was announced as early as 27 July. The *Springfield Daily Republican* (MA) published an article by a correspondent who was attending the conferences at Green Acre. The report, which dealt mainly with some of the problems surrounding the institution, offered details about the conference program at Green Acre and mentioned the expected participation of 'Abdu'l-Bahá as a circumstance of 'singular importance'. The correspondent of *The Republican* personally met the British Bahá'í Alice Buckton, who had been at Green Acre for several weeks attending conferences and performing her play *Eager Heart*. He reported that 'Miss Buckton informed us that Abdul Baha (accent on the last syllable) is in New England this week, and has promised to visit Greenacre before the 10th of August, though somewhat pressed for time.'[11]

On 14 August, two days before the arrival of 'Abdu'l-Bahá at Green Acre, *The Portsmouth Herald* (NH), with a circulation of 2,500 copies, also carried an article announcing His participation in the conference program:

> The great Persian teacher, Abdul Baha (literally 'Servant of God') is to spend several days at Green Acre, Eliot, arriving on Friday afternoon Aug. 16, about 4 with his interpreters. The sight of these visitors from Persia and the Holy Land, in their flowing Eastern dress, will be a remarkable one among the Western Pines . . .
>
> Abdul Baha has for many years, from within the walls of his captivity in the Holy Land, followed the work for Unity instituted by Miss S. J. Farmer at Green Acre and he has long desired to visit the place. It is hoped that he will briefly address the friends at the close of the Eliot day exercises in the Eirenion, at 4:30 o'clock on Friday next,

> and that he will hold a discourse every morning and evening during his three days' stay. Friends desiring to speak with him are asked to communicate with the interpreters, Green Acre Inn, Eliot.
>
> A large gathering is expected at the evening reception on Friday at eight o'clock, at which some notable figures will be present. All friends of Unity and Peace are welcome.[12]

While in Green Acre, 'Abdu'l-Bahá was scheduled to speak every day at 7:30 p.m. A reception for Him was also celebrated on Mount Salvat at 4 p.m. on Wednesday 21 August and He also gave a talk to over one hundred people at the home of Sarah Farmer.[13] During those days many people also had the opportunity of having private interviews with Him. One of them was the above-mentioned Boston correspondent of the *Springfield Daily Republican*, who wrote the following for his newspaper:

> Returning from Old Orchard, I stopped over at Greenacre in Eliot and had a pleasing interview with Abdul Baha concerning Miss Farmer and the writings of his own father, Beha Ullah, of which a partial translation exists in English. His interpreter, Dr Fareed (said to be his nephew) is well versed in English medicine and literature, and proposes to remain in America. Abdul Baha goes to Canada tomorrow, but will be in Massachusetts for a while in September. He has made a most favorable impression at Greenacre – not so much as a thinker, as in the rarer capacity of a good, devout and unselfish person, sincerely desirous of reforming the world, especially in Syria and Persia, and more likely to aid in doing it than the keen-witted but not unselfish Swamis from India, who are this year almost wholly absent from Greenacre. Abdul Baha has increased the audiences there, which have been very large for a week past, so that the Inn, which had a large deficit last year, may even have a surplus, September 1.[14]

A further account of 'Abdu'l-Bahá's visit to Green Acre appeared in the *Biddeford Weekly Journal* (ME), a Republican newspaper appearing every Friday and with a circulation of 1,000 copies. As stated in the article, five ladies from the town attended the conferences at Green Acre and had a chance to meet 'Abdu'l-Bahá. It is probable that one of them was the author of this detailed article about the Master:

ABDUL BAHA AT GREEN ACRE CONFERENCES

IMPRESSIONS MADE BY EASTERN MASTER UPON HIS HEARERS

The week of August 19 was the really important week at Greenacre this season, for the great Persian leader, Abdul Baha, who has been visiting all the important cities in this country this summer, was there all the week, speaking every day, and giving private interviews to many people in addition. The principles for which Abdul Baha stands, 'peace and unity', have always been the principles of Greenacre; the white 'peace' flag has always greeted all who approach the place. Here have come, in years past, great teachers of all faiths and from all parts of the world, but perhaps none of as wide-spread interest as this latest foreign guest, whom his followers, the Bahai, call the master. Gatherings of Bahai have been held at Greenacre regularly each week, for many seasons, and when it was known that their leader was to come to this country to attend a great peace convention it was understood that he would pass some time with his friends there.

Picture a tall, commanding figure, with white hair and beard, eyes that, though blue, give the impression of dark eyes, so deep and keen are they, with a haunting something in their depths; a long black robe, and white fez; a firm, fine hand; this is the outward appearance of the master. His personality impresses those who meet him in various ways, according to their own temperaments; but all feel the power of the man. He is always ready to give his time to people who wish to meet him, even planning an audience for the colored servants at the inn. When they were assembled before him, he addressed them somewhat as follows, the report is from memory: 'Friends, I have asked to see you that I may talk to you of your relations to your fellowmen and to God. Though your skins are black and you are different from the people around you, your souls are not different . . . I thank you all for your kindness to me; you have worked hard to prepare pleasant food for me; you have labored for my comfort, while I have been at ease. I thank you, and I will supplicate God for you, that he may help you.'

Abdul Baha speaks always through an interpreter; three young Persians are with him in that capacity . . .

Five ladies from Biddeford and Saco recently passed a very pleasant day there, and all were granted an interview with Abdul Baha.[15]

The Republican *Lewiston Evening Journal*, with a circulation of 7,400 copies, also reported that one local citizen, Mrs. Ella F. Neal, 'recently had the pleasure of hearing the illustrious Persian teacher, Abdul Baha, in a lecture which he gave at Monsalvat, Eliot'.[16]

Visit to Malden, Massachusetts

On Friday, 23 August, 'Abdu'l-Bahá left Green Acre for Malden, a town near Boston, where He stayed at the home of the local Bahá'í Marie P. Wilson, 68 High Street. His arrival was announced on the same day in newspapers in Boston[17] and Malden.[18]

The following day He received several visitors, among them the president of the New Thought Forum, who invited 'Abdu'l-Bahá to address its members at their regular meeting. On Sunday, 25 August, 'Abdu'l-Bahá spoke to the New Thought members on the spiritual regeneration of mankind[19] and on the following day the *Boston Transcript* reported that He 'spoke before the New Thought Forum and the president J. K. Hicks, presided. Through his interpreter, Abdul Baha, addressed an audience, which thronged the hall, in the characteristically calm and serene manner about the spiritual forces of life and the many manifestations, on all sides, of the close relation between the unseen and the real.'[20]

On 26 August 'Abdu'l-Bahá spoke at the Franklyn Square House, an institution created in 1902 by the Universalist minister Rev. George Landor Perin (1854–1921) as a shelter for poor women and their children. In His talk the Master spoke about the equality of woman and men[21] and a brief article in the *Boston Post* reported 'Abdu'l-Bahá as stating that 'If, as philosophers have argued . . . man is superior to woman because he has a brain weighing 125 grams, whereas hers weighs about 117, then surely the donkey must be the wisest of all of us, for his weighs more than man's.'[22]

On 27 August He spoke to the Metaphysical Club at their headquarters in 30 Huntington Avenue and this was also announced in local newspapers.[23]

On Thursday, 29 August, a meeting was arranged in Malden at the house of Mme. Morey (1850–1931),[24] a famous musician in the Boston area. Over one hundred people assembled to hear 'Abdu'l-´Bahá speak about the unity and purpose of religions.[25] On 31 August the *Boston Transcript* published a brief account of the meeting:

> ABDUL BEHA ABBAS A GUEST
>
> PERSIAN LEADER GAVE INTERESTING TALK AT RESIDENCE OF MME. BEALE MOREY IN MALDEN
>
> Abdul Beha Abbas, the Persian scholar and leader, was the guest of honor at a reception given on Thursday evening at her residence in Malden by Mme. Beale Morey, the musician. There were nearly a hundred guests present, for whom Mme. Morey played at the piano an introductory musical programme, following which Abdul Beha gave a talk on the 'Religions of the World', showing the points of similarity of beliefs of different nations and their relations in the forming of a universal brotherhood. The hostess, Mme Morey, in her travels in the Far East studied into the various religions, including that of the Hindoos, Buddhists, the fire worshippers and others.[26]

The same information was published in the *Malden Mirror*, a newspaper with a circulation of a thousand copies.[27]

'Abdu'l-Bahá was also invited to participate in the wedding of Ruby Breed, sister of the Bahá'í Alice Breed (wife of Ali Kuli Khan), which was held in Cambridge on 28 August. A short article published the following day in the *Boston Evening Transcript* gave some details about the ceremony:

> At the residence of Mr. and Mrs. Francis W. Breed, 367 Harvard at Cambridge, last night, occurred the wedding of their daughter, Ruby Constance, and Clarence Watson Johnson of Lynn. The ceremony was performed by Rev. Ernest Denne, rector of St. Stephen's Church, Lynn, after which a blessing was asked by Abdul Baha Abbas, the Persian leader, who is touring this country propagating his new religion, based on the brotherhood of man, and who is a friend of the bride's sister, Mrs Ali Kuli Khan, wife of the Persian charge d'Affaires at Washington.[28]

The Master's departure from Malden was briefly reported in the *Malden Mail*.[29]

19

CANADA

30 August – 9 September 1912

As noted in previous chapters, 'Abdu'l-Bahá had already met some influential Canadians during His travels. At Lake Mohonk He certainly met, among others, William Lyon Mackenzie King (1874–1950), former Minister of Labour in Canada, who in 1914 became director of the Rockefeller Foundation and who in 1921 was elected prime minister of Canada; and John Lewis (1858–1935), editor of the Toronto *Star* and in later years senator.[1] In Boston He met the Unitarian minister Frederick R. Griffin of Montreal who introduced 'Abdu'l-Bahá at the public session of the Annual Convention of the American Unitarian Association at which He was invited to speak. In addition, Bahá'ís from Canada had visited 'Abdu'l-Bahá in New York.

On Wednesday, 28 August, 'Abdu'l-Bahá cabled May Maxwell (1870–1940) confirming that He would travel to the city of Montreal on Friday. She immediately made the arrangements for His arrival and contacted the press to inform them of His imminent visit to the city.[2] Thus in the ensuing days various articles about 'Abdu'l-Bahá were published in the local press[3] and also in Burlington, Vermont, a city that had been recently visited by May Maxwell.[4]

After travelling almost 12 hours from Boston, 'Abdu'l-Bahá reached Montreal at 8 p.m. on Friday, 30 August. At the station He was received by Sutherland Maxwell, who accompanied the Master and His retinue to his home on 716 Pine Avenue where He was to stay during part of His sojourn in the city and where He would also hold most of His public talks. Among the people who were waiting to welcome 'Abdu'l-Bahá was the above mentioned John Lewis.[5]

First Interviews

The day after His arrival in Canada, on Saturday, 31 August, 'Abdu'l-Bahá received many visitors, among them two journalists. One was Archibald Eddington, one of the early Bahá'ís of Canada, who at the time worked for the *Montreal Daily Star*, an evening newspaper with a circulation of 76,400 copies. The article that ensued was published on the front page of the newspaper, included a portrait of 'Abdu'l-Bahá, and gave a telephone number for those interested in visiting Him. In the course of this interview, 'Abdu'l-Bahá spoke in clear terms of an imminent great war in Europe:

APOSTLE OF PEACE HERE PREDICTS AN APPALLING WAR IN THE OLD WORLD

EUROPE HEADING STRAIGHT FOR A TERRIFIC CONFLICT, ABDUL BAHA DECLARES.

THE BAHAI LEADER ARRIVES IN MONTREAL

CANADIANS SHOULD BE HAPPY IN THEIR FREEDOM FROM GREAT ARMAMENTS, SAYS EASTERN SEER

'Be happy! You in Canada live in a magnificent, peaceful country. Be happy!'

This was the kindly greeting of Abdul Baha, messenger of peace from the Orient to the Occident, who as head of the Bahai movement has a following of three million people in Persia, when he arrived in Montreal from Boston last night, to remain in the city for a week. Accompanying him were two Persian interpreters, Mirza Ahmad Sohrab and Mirza Mahmoud. The party drove at once to 716 Pine Avenue West, where they will remain during their stay. Dr. Ameen Fareed, the chief interpreter, will arrive on Monday.

Abdul Baha, whose appearance is that of an eastern patriarch, with white turban and long white robes, expressed himself to a representative of the Star as delighted to be in Canada, whose people should be very happy to live in such a splendid country. He expressed himself as greatly pleased with the mission to the United States, where the message of peace and international unity had been given a splendid welcome. The people of America he had found to be wonderfully keen and alert. In fact we on this side of the Atlantic were a very wonderful people.

PEACE MESSAGE WELCOMED ON THIS SIDE

The people of the United States, Abdul Baha said, he had found to be remarkably receptive to the movement, which was, he declared, making good headway on this side of the Atlantic, in most marked contrast to the condition of affairs he had found to prevail in Europe.

GREAT WAR BEFORE UNIVERSAL PEACE

Apparently the era of universal peace would not be ushered in before a war of colossal proportions had been fought. Such war would be the most appalling in the world's history. Europe to-day was heading straight for this. The men at the head of affairs in the various countries seemed to have lost all thought of divine things, and they really walked in darkness. Practically the whole of what the people earned was taken away from them to be applied to the forging of weapons of war by which the peoples of various lands were prepared to slay one another. In Great Britain, Russia, Germany, France, Austria, and Italy, it is all the same. Every country in Europe was to-day spending fabulous sums of money in preparations for murderous warfare, and that was why there was so much misery among the masses of the people. The very flower of manhood was taken from productive employment and trained to slay one another. It was supreme madness.

A GREAT CONTRAST PRESENTED BY CANADA

'What a great contrast,' said Abdul Baha, 'is presented in your country. Canada should be a very happy land. So far removed from such a condition of strife. On this side of the Atlantic the peace message is well received; but in Europe, there is an apathy, a listlessness that is distressing.'

Abdul Baha will preach at the morning service, 11 a. m., in the Church of the Messiah, Sherbrooke Street West, on Sunday. During his stay he will welcome all visitors interested in his movement, if arrangements are made by telephoning Uptown 3015.[6]

'Abdu'l-Bahá was also interviewed by a reporter from the weekly newspaper *The Standard*, with a circulation of 29,000 copies. The article that ensued included a portrait of Him.

PERSIAN PEACE PROPHET GIVES MESSAGE TO CANADA THROUGH THE STANDARD

COMMENTS ON GREAT PROSPERITY OF THIS COUNTRY – HIS REMARKABLE, VARIED AND ROMANTIC CAREER

A venerable, gray haired man, older than his years, with flowing locks and patriarchal beard, the furrows of suffering on his still handsome and striking face, and lines telling of deep and anxious thought upon his brow, this is Abdul Baha, leader of the Bahai peace movement, who has come to preach his gospel of universal brotherhood and love to the people of Canada.

Abdul Baha Abbas, sometimes called Abbas Effendi, and whose name signifies the 'Servant of God', has had a career marked by privations such as fall to the lot of but few men. He has been imprisoned, exiled, ostracized, yet he has never faltered in carrying the mission he believes it his destiny to fulfill – the mission handed on to him by his father, Baha'o'llah, the founder and first great leader of this remarkable movement. With the firm conviction of a man who has unalterable faith in his mission, and in the Divine inspiration underlying it, Abdul Baha has gone forward fearlessly giving to all nations and all men the teaching he himself received from his father and predecessor.

EXTENDS CORDIAL WELCOME

Clad in a gown of grey canvas with an inner cloak of creamy texture, and an outer cloak of some black material, the whole surmounted by a white turban, Abdul Baha gave a cordial greeting to a representative of The Standard, who called on him. 'Welcome,' said he, the only English word he used during the interview, as he shook the Standard man warmly by the hand. But though he does not himself speak English he is well served in the matter of an interpreter by Mr. Mirza Ahmad Sohrab, who accompanies him. As the Persian philosopher spoke in clear resounding tones carrying the ring of sincerity with them, his words were quickly translated into fluent English by Mr. Sohrab.

MESSAGE TO CANADA

'You have a very beautiful country and you must be very happy here,' Abdul Baha began and then intimated that he had a message for the people of Canada. 'My message to the Canadian people,' he said, 'is this: Your country is very prosperous and very delightful in every aspect; you have peace and security amidst you; happiness and composure are your friends; surely you must thank God you are so submerged in the sea of His mercy.'

A VARIED CAREER

He then proceeded to speak of himself, and of his movement. The greater part of his lifetime, he said, had been spent in captivity at Acre, in Syria, where he was confined at the instance of the Turks and Persians, who objected to his teachings, and was only liberated on the fall of the old Turkish regime and the advent of the Young Turks to power. But though a prisoner he was allowed a certain amount of liberty and went on teaching all who came to visit him. In this way many thousands were won over to the cause, and Abdul Baha, in prison, was almost as big a thorn in the side of the religious bigots of the East as Abdul Baha, a free man. After his release he found the movement had spread wonderfully through Asia Minor and Persia, and he soon decided to visit the Occident as many Europeans and Americans had been amongst his visitors during the period of his incarceration. He accordingly made a tour through Europe last year and was well received, especially in Paris and London. In the latter city he spoke at the City Temple at the invitation of Rev. R. J. Campbell, and in St. John's Church by permission of Canon Wilberforce. He next turned his attention towards America, and arrived in New York in April last. Since then he has toured the greater part of the Republic, but there are a few important places he has not yet visited and these he intends to take in, after leaving Montreal next week end . . .[7]

Address at the Church of the Messiah

Frederick R. Griffin was also among the people who visited 'Abdu'l-Bahá on Saturday, 31 August. He offered his church, the Unitarian Church of the Messiah, to 'Abdu'l-Bahá for His first public address in Canada. The same day a note was published in *The Montreal Gazette* announcing the event and offering a biography of the Master.[8]

'Abdu'l-Bahá's talk was delivered on the morning of the following day,

Sunday, 1 September. He spoke on the brotherhood of mankind, international peace and the requisites for its achievement.[9] Some reporters were present at the meeting and several accounts of it were published in local newspapers. The *Montreal Daily Star* wrote the lengthiest report:

PERSIAN PREACHER IN FLOWING ROBES CALLS FOR UNITY

ABDUL BAHA, VENERABLE APOSTLE FROM ORIENT, DELIVERS MESSAGE TO MONTREAL

GOD'S ONE RELIGION FOUNDED ON REALITY

IMAGINARY LINES CAUSING BLOODSHED SHOULD BE FORGOTTEN, HE SAYS

Clad in flowing robes, and with a turbaned head, the great Persian apostle of peace, Abdul Baha, made a majestic appearance in the pulpit of the Church of the Messiah Sunday morning when he preached his message urging the oneness of religion and doing away with strife and hatred over imaginary things.

'The religion of God,' declared the venerable leader, 'is one. Abraham, Moses and Christ, were all founded on reality and were all servants of reality.' The burden of the preacher's message was that all racial hatred and bloodshed over imaginary lines should cease and that people should regard themselves as belonging to one family.

'Man has set up imaginary lines,' he said, 'only to have them become the cause of strife. A river is made a boundary, one side is called France and the other Germany. What a superstition! An imaginary line to become a cause of bloodshed.'

Preaching in Persian, his words were swiftly translated, sentence by sentence, into English by Mirza Ahmad Sohrab. The Rev. F. J. Griffith welcomed the preacher as a veritable prophet of God. Abdul Baha's sermon was a powerful plea for peace and unity among the nations.

REALITY IN ALL RELIGIONS

God Almighty, said he, had created all humanity from earth. All mankind came from the same elements, all were descendants from the same race and all had to live on the same globe. All of us had the same susceptibilities and in every essential there was no difference in the human family whatsoever. God created all mankind, maintained and protected all. His kindness extended to all, and there was no difference in His bestowal of mercy among His children. From age to age, He had sent forth His prophets with divine teachings, in order to establish unity and fellowship among the children of men. These prophets had proclaimed the oneness of the Kingdom of humanity, and had rebuked all things which brought about difference and discord. Their mission had been to proclaim the goodness of God and to work for the solidarity of the race.

All the prophets of God had been inspired with a message of love, and all the books of God taught fellowship and union. Reality was one and all of God's prophets had given forth the same revelation of the essence of reality. God's religions all had the same foundations, yet a thousand times, alas, imitations and innovations had come creeping along having nothing to do with the original teachings of the prophets of God. In this way there arose strife and contention. Warfare became rampant and everywhere there was bloodshed. Men became destroyers of the foundations of God and like beasts of prey engaged in each other's murder, wiping out homes and laying waste each other's country. Neglecting the law of love as announced by the prophets, men hated each other, turned the earth into a scene of strife and allowed themselves to be governed by racial and religious prejudice, or patriotic and political bias.

These unhappy prejudices were stronger in the Orient than in the Occident. The Orient had not achieved the freedom of the Occident and so powerful were the prejudices among peoples that the countries of the East had been constantly restless and in a state of commotion. Warfare had been incessant and hatred spread among all nations. [*illegible*]

RELIGION MUST AGREE WITH REASON

Baha Oullah had proclaimed anew that religion must be love and fellowship. If hatred arose, it could never be the product of religion but of irreligion. All hatred was unacceptable to God, while whatever produced love was beloved of God. If war arose from religion, then no religion was better: If a remedy produced sickness, then it were better to have no remedy. When religion became a cause of warfare and bloodshed it was worthless and it were a thousand times better to have none of it.

Religion must be in accord with science and reason, if not, it was only superstition. God has granted us reason to comprehend the realities of things. If religion came to be against reason and science, then confidence in it was impossible. Superstition could not be allowed to take the place of religion, nor racial or sectarian prejudices, patriotism or political bias, to drive out religion.

'The religion of God is one,' said Abdul Baha. 'Abraham, Moses and Christ, all founded on reality and were all servants of reality. All were promulgators of reality. Prejudice is unattainable for it is against reality. What foundation is there for racial and religious prejudice, when we are all the children of God, of the same race and of the same family. Since we are all the sons of Adam, what significance is to be attached to non-essential differences?

'Before God all mankind are one. There is no Germany, and no England, Frenchmen, no Turk and no Persian. All are equal before God and man, not the creator, made the divisions among them. Animals had no racial prejudice. A dove or a sheep from the Orient would consort at once with a dove or a sheep from the Occident, in perfect fellowship. Why could not men do likewise?

IMAGINARY LINES CAUSE BLOODSHED

'Man has set up imaginary lines only to have these become causes of strife. A river is made a boundary, one side called France and the other Germany. The river was in reality created for both. What a superstition! An imaginary line to become a cause of bloodshed!

'All this enmity and discord is the fruit of ignorance and a lack of mutual understanding. Get instruction, so that all this may be banished. Drive all this away, so that all mankind may become united.'

Universal education, said Abdul Baha, was now a necessity, and so was the recognition of the equality of the sexes in everything, political and social. Of the first importance, too, was the invention and use of a universal language. All should be instructed in this, so that everyone would have two languages, his native tongue and this international auxiliary language. With mutual understanding, strife would disappear and Orient and Occident embrace each other. The time had now come, too, for international arbitration of all disputes and the governments of the world must be called upon to make use of a tribunal to reach a settlement of all their differences. War must cease, and all mankind must live to unity and love, no matter whether they be Buddhist, Mohammedan, Christian, Zoroastrian or Hebrew. The broadest spirit must prevail.

'I have come to America,' said Abdul Baha, in conclusion, 'to speak a message of peace and good-will to you. You are a noble nation with a just government. I beg of God that this just and fair land may assist in working for the peace of the world.

'Let the people of this young and noble nation assist in the great movement for the peace and unity of the world. Let the people light a lamp that will illuminate the whole universe. Let us put love in the hearts of all the children of man. Let all mankind labour for this, that the favour of God may descend upon the Orient and the Occident.'[10]

The Conservative *Montreal Gazette*, which at the time had a circulation of 16,200 copies, published the following report:

RACIALISM WRONG SAYS EASTERN SAGE

STRIFE AND WAR CAUSED BY RELIGIOUS AND NATIONAL PREJUDICES

RELIGION MEANS PEACE

ABDUL BAHA CLAIMS WOMAN IS EQUAL TO MEN OR CAN BE SO WITH EQUAL EDUCATION

Both in matter and in style the message which was delivered in the Church of the Messiah yesterday morning by Abdu'l-Baha was unique and it had a picturesque setting all its own. A venerable looking figure with a long white beard, just streaked with a dark shade, the leader of the Baha'i movement wore a white silk turban, white vestments to match, over which was a loose brown robe; the whole fulfilling the usual conceptions of the Eastern sage. His address was uttered in the Persian tongue, and was interpreted sentence by sentence by a compatriot who wore European black clothing and a black turban of the Turkish type. The effect of the interpretation was to give the address a yet more Eastern sound, as the sentences, many of them, had a ring of the proverb and wise-saying. The chief points brought out by the speaker were the equality of the human race and the unnaturalness of the division of nations and countries, the horror of religious or any warfare whatever, and the equality of the sexes.

In introducing Abdul Baha, Rev. F. R. Griffin said he came not to unfold a fresh mystery, or to teach a new theology, and much less to establish a new church. 'The strangest part of all about him is that nothing is strange. He seeks to be the embodiment of that which is most natural. Is this not turning back to religion itself? Venerable in years, he is young as a child in the purity of his outlook on life; disciplined by long years in prison, his spirit has never yet been crucified by pain.'

Abdul Baha speaking through his interpreter, in his opening sentences said: 'God the Almighty has created all humanity from earth, from the same element. All men are descended from the same race and live on the same globe. As members of the human race He created them equal in all susceptibilities. He left no difference whatever. He provides all, He trains all; He protects all; He is kind to all.' Then passing on to the revelation of the Divine to man, the prophet said: 'All the prophets of God have been inspired with messages of love and unity to the sons of men. All the books of God have been revealed for the sake of fellowship and union. All the prophets of God were the servants of reality. All their teachings were the essence of reality. Reality is one, it does not admit multiplicity. Therefore, we conclude that the foundations of the religions of God are one. Yet, alas, a thousand differences have been creeping in which have nothing to do with this foundation. As these differences vary, therefore we have strife among the children of men; contention and warfare are rampant, and bloodshed and strife reign, everywhere. All the bloodshed and strife of the past have been induced either through religious or racial prejudices or political or patriotic bias. These prejudices are greater in the Orient than in the Occident, for freedom is less. All religions and nations of the Orient were in constant warfare with each other when Baha Oullah appeared and proclaimed that all the teachers are the servants of God, all religions but the shadow of the Almighty.'

'All lambs,' continued the speaker, 'are under the same shepherd. If one lamb is separated from the flock, all thoughts must be to bring it back. Baha Oullah proclaimed that religion must be the means of love and fellowship. If religion is the cause of hatred it has no meaning; it is not religion, but it is irreligion, for it produced opposite results. If religion become the cause of strife, then irreligion is better. The remedy must be health. If this remedy produces sickness then it is better to have no remedy whatever.

'Baha Oullah has taught that religion must be in accord with reason and science. If religion does not correspond with science and reason it is superstition. God has granted reason so that we may comprehend the realities of things and adore them. If religion is against reason and science, then confidence is impossible. Where faith and confidence are not created we cannot call that religion, that is superstition. All religious systems must correspond with intellect and science, so that the heart may obtain faith and assurance. The religion of God is one for all. His Holiness Abraham summoned the people to reality. His Holiness Moses proclaimed the reality. His Holiness Christ founded the reality. Likewise all the prophets were servants of reality.'

ALL ALIKE BEFORE GOD

Reverting to national prejudices again, the speaker asserted: 'Before God there is no Germany, no England, no France, no Turkey. All these people before God are equal. God did not make these divisions. There is no racial prejudice among the animals. There is no difference between an eastern or a western sheep or a dove. Europe is a continent. It is not divided, but we have created imaginary lines.'

After touching on the duty of parents or the community to give instructions to children, Abdul Baha spoke of woman's status. 'Women,' he said, 'were very much degraded in the Orient. Baha Oulllah proclaimed the equality of the sexes. Men and women both belonged to the human race, and both were the servants of God. Before God there is no difference or gender. Whosoever has a human heart is nearer to God and more favored, whether man or woman. These differences exist only for the present and only on account of education. For woman has not had the same instruction. If women receive the same curriculum they will become equal in all degrees, for both are human and receive the same share of powers. God has not made any difference whatever.'

In his closing sentences Abdul Baha pointed out that a universal language was needed and that this would help the cause of international peace and good-will. When all nations could talk with each other they will understand each other better. Certain peoples in the

East to whom Baha Ollah had written fifty years ago had adopted his teachings, and now all sorts of different tribes and creeds were living together in unity. The speaker expressed the wish that the governments of America would further the cause of international peace, thus bringing rest to the world.

Abdul Baha will address a meeting this evening at 716 Pine Avenue West, and tomorrow evening will speak at a Socialist gathering to be held at 8 o'clock in Corinthian Hall.[11]

This report was the basis of an article published on the same day in the Protestant evening newspaper *Montreal Daily Witness*,[12] which at the time had a circulation of 21,800 copies, and of a much shorter account which appeared in the French independent newspaper *La Patrie*, with a circulation of 40,300 copies.[13]

Interview with the Toronto *Star Weekly*

A reporter with the Toronto *Star Weekly*, probably John Lewis, was present at 'Abdu'l-Bahá's address at the Church of the Messiah and on the following day, Monday, 2 September, met Him again and was granted an interview. The weekly edition of the *Star*, with a circulation of 15,800 copies, published on 11 September the following article about 'Abdu'l-Bahá:

ABDU'L BAHA'S WORD TO CANADA

GREAT PERSIAN PEACE PROPHET INTERVIEWED IN MONTREAL FOR THE STAR WEEKLY

PROMOTION OF LOVE AMONG MEN

IS THE OBJECT OF HIS VISIT – 3,000,000 ADHERENTS IN PERSIA ALONE

MONTREAL, SEPT. 7

It was an impressive service, especially the closing part. For there on the platform, to the left of the little Unitarian minister, stood the venerable, grey-haired Persian Prophet of Peace, Abdul Baha, praying to the God of all nations in his native tongue, for greater benevolence, greater charity, greater tolerance, greater love among all man; while, to the right, almost motionless and likewise devout, stood the cultured interpreter, Mr. Mirza Ahmad Sohrab, translating the holy words of his country man to the congregation.

Picture to yourself a grey-haired man, older than his years, with patriarchal beard and face stamped by much suffering and serious thought, a yet handsome man with a high, intelligent forehead and the idealistic eyes of a dreamer, a man of power, determination, too, who will tread one path when he knows that it is the right one, yea, though he should lose his life for so doing. Clothe your man in Eastern garb. Put a white turban on his head and hang a gown of grey canvas over his stately shoulders. Then you will have Abdul Baha, who has come among us to preach his religion of peace.

What is it that strikes one most in this remarkable man? Is it his message, his simple doctrine of peace and love among all people? Is it his power of thought, his manner of expression, the privations he has endured? No; it is none of these. It is his great sincerity. He is a man with a mission, and he believes in it with all his soul. He looks upon himself as a servant of God whose duty it is to go out to many peoples, proclaiming the great truths he has long perceived.

MANY YEARS IN PRISON

ABDUL BAHA ABBAS, otherwise known as Abbas Effendi, and whose name signifies the 'Servant of God', has spent the greater part of his life in prison at Acca in Syria. He has also been exiled, ostracized and met with hardships and cruelties such as would have quelled the spirit of many brave men. But he never faltered; he never turned from the straight path, the path that to him spelled duty. Had not his father trod it before him? Had not Baha'o'llah, after Bab had been put to death, who had founded Babism, which created much stir in the Orient during the middle of the last century, arisen to preach the doctrine of universal peace, and had he not handed on the leadership of the Bahais to his son, Abdul Baha? So, come weal or woe, he would go forward fearlessly proclaiming the belief that was in him. And even when in captivity at Acca, he went on teaching all with whom he came in contact, and these in turn taught others. Thus it was that when he was liberated, on the advent of the Young Turks to power, he found that he had a goodly following both in Asia Minor and in Persia, and now, in Persia alone, his adherents are said to number three millions.

Last year he toured Europe and was favorably received. In

London, he spoke in the City Temple, the Rev. R. J. Campbell's church and in St. John's Church, by permission of Canon Wilberforce. Then he turned his attention to America and, since April last, he has toured the greater part of the United States. He is now in Canada, and he spoke in the Church of the Messiah (Unitarian) in Sherbrook Street West, Montreal, on Sunday last.

OLD DOCTRINE IN NEW SETTING

It was not a new doctrine that he proclaimed, just an old one with a new setting. He emphasized the oneness of the kingdom of humanity, and man's duty to the Supreme Being. What was that duty? The stirring up of contention and warfare? [*illegible*] 'God has created his servants to love and associate with each other,' said he. 'The God of the creation of the world is love. But man has arisen to oppose the will of God. He has attacked the very foundation of God's teachings. He has stirred up prejudices, feelings of racial enmity. And these prejudices are greater among men in the Orient than elsewhere, because there is less freedom there.'

There was wonderful breadth and depth of feeling in that sermon. It was not the message of a fanatic or a hermit, or a man unconversant with modern thought and modern life. It was Eastern, and yet it was Western. It was delivered as only an Oriental of pure blood can convey a message, yet it contained truths applicable to everybody. It was an embodiment of the oneness of humanity, of the oneness of religion, of the power of reason, reality, love. 'All prophets,' said Abdul Baha, 'are inspired by the power of love, unity. They are all servants of reality, and their teachings are the essence of reality. Reality is one; it does not accept multiplicity. And the religions of God are one.'

Dealing with the question of warfare and bloodshed, he said that 'where there is hatred there is no religion. For true religion means love, fellowship. It is the drawing together, not the pushing apart of people. It is life according to reason, science. Therefore, religious prejudice, racial prejudice, alien prejudice, must be destroyed if the foundations of humanity are to remain strong. All religions must become one and be based on reality. Races must give up their superstitions and join hands in friendship, all being equal before God, who made no divisions. Prejudices are falsehoods disliked by God.'

SEXES MUST BE EQUAL

But how to effect this reformation? By means of instruction. That was the simple, all-embracing answer given by Abdul Baha. Let fathers teach their children, let people teach people, let race teach race. Then misunderstandings will pass away.

And in noble words he referred to the place of woman in the universe. He showed how she had been degraded in the Orient, and pleaded for equality of sexes, purity of heart and equal educational facilities for both man and woman. 'Differences will be overcome by education,' said he. 'Our women have not had the same privilege of education as our men. Both must become equal. There must be no differences.' And he urged the furtherance of a universal language, so that there might be no barrier between nations and that peoples might readily communicate with each other. 'When all know the same language, association will become natural.'

But what are we to do in the meantime? Organize an international tribunal for the settlement of all disputes. That is Abdul Baha's solution. And who is to do this? Who is to be instrumental in bringing about this happy state of affairs?

Abdul Baha looks to the nations of which Canada is a part. He says our Government is a just Government, and that he expects us to play our part nobly in promoting unity among nations, in serving humanity.

He granted me an interview the following day, and I asked what was his opinion as to the increase in armaments that was going on in the world to-day. Would such continue? 'Yes,' he said, 'nations will go on arming. They are afraid of each other. [*illegible*] great war. This will take on the continent of Europe. After that there will be peace.'

WARFARE IS CONTINUOUS

Then he offered a further explanation: 'In reality,' he said, 'warfare is continuous to-day. It is bloodless but continuous, for the common people are ground down to provide its sinews. All over the world, the blood of the working man is being sucked to keep up a show of naval and military power. But Europe to-day is like a great powder-house, and a single spark will cause an explosion.'

I then referred to the fact that the organized workers of the world were beginning to declare themselves in favor of universal peace, and that a time might come when the general strike would be employed to prevent warfare between nations.

This raised the question of Socialism, and he told me how such doctrine was spreading rapidly over all the world. 'But it implies force, resistance,' he said, 'and we are out to promote the cause of peace and fellowship among man.'

'Have you got any Socialists in your country?' I asked.

'Yes,' he replied, 'but the movement is only beginning there.

'Do you think it will spread?

'It is bound to spread,' he answered. 'It is approaching everywhere. It is a humanitarian movement, and it is the grinding down of the people that gives it life.'

I then enquired if he intended to visit Toronto or any of the Canadian cities in the West, but he was afraid such would be impossible at this time. 'But you may tell your people,' he said, 'that I am very pleased with your country. It is a prosperous and delightful land. You have peace and security in your midst. Happiness and composure are your friends. Surely, then, you should thank the good God for all his mercies to you.'

He then took my hand in both of his and blessed me as a father would bless a son, with the same sincerity, the same depth of feeling, the same lofty purpose. For if this Persian dreamer, preacher, prophet, is anything, he is sincere, and his sincerity springs from a great sense of love and fellowship for man. He is a humanist of a high type; his church is the world.

'I cannot succeed,' were his parting words, 'without your help and the help of everyone who believes in the cause of universal peace and good fellowship among men; and, that you may not forget me and my cause in the days to come, I will ask you to accept a little gift from me.'

So saying, he handed me a small parcel, which, later, I discovered contained a handsome gold ring. It fitted perfectly; and, as I placed it on my finger, I felt that, coming from such a man, it would bring good luck.[14]

This article was partly reproduced in Alberta in the *Cayley Hustler*[15] and in the *Redcliff Review*.[16]

Talk on Materialism

The residence of the Maxwells was open every day for visitors. As was customary, 'Abdu'l-Bahá would receive them personally but public addresses were also held in the afternoons. On His third day in Montreal, Monday, 2 September, 'Abdu'l-Bahá spoke to those present at 716 Pine Avenue about materialism and the need for spirituality.[17] Some journalists were present at the meeting and at least two accounts of it were published on the following day. The *Montreal Daily Star* reported the following:

> MATERIALISM NO PHILOSOPHY, SAYS ORIENTAL SEER
>
> PHILOSOPHY FOUNDED ON NATURE IS BANKRUPT, DECLARES ABDUL BAHA, PERSIAN PREACHER
>
> That the godless, materialistic philosophy of the present age is hopelessly bankrupt and of no benefit whatever to the human race, was emphatically declared by Abdul Baha, leader of the Bahais, at a largely attended drawing-room meeting at 716 Pine Avenue West, last evening.
>
> Philosophers, said Abdul Baha, would spend twenty years of brain-racking study at the universities and then come forward to announce that God did not exist, that there was no moral order in the universe, that mankind had no souls, and were not much better than the animal.
>
> 'Well,' said Abdul Baha, 'that is not a very lofty message. The animals themselves have reached the same plane of intellectuality without so much deep cogitation. They have never been to the university, yet, strange to say, they have, without study, reached the same conclusions as our philosophers. To them God is non-existent, and they have no souls, and no spiritual aspirations. They are mere creatures of the senses, and our philosophers glory in that they too are mere creatures of tangibility and of the five senses.'
>
> 'The imperfection of Nature,' was the subject of Abdul Baha's discourse and he showed that the earth if left to itself without the application to it of human intelligence and labor would remain forever a barren wilderness. In the same way, man, unless touched by the divine rays would remain a savage.

MUST IMPROVE ON NATURE

'Looking at the material world,' he said, 'we see clearly it is imperfect and dark. If we leave a piece of land in its natural condition, thorns will grow thereon and parasites will become rampant. So we must illumine this world of nature. We must clothe and take care of the ground so that flowers may grow. If we leave man in his natural state, he will become lower than the animals. He will remain imperfect like the cannibals of Central Africa, who are in a natural dark state. If we desire to illumine the world of man, we must educate him, so that from a state of ignorance, he may become wise. If we leave him, it is sure he will become lower than the beasts of the jungle, for we see that the people of Central Africa, not having received education, are lower than the animals and remain in a state of cannibalism.

'So long as man remains ignorant and wild he remains in a state of nature, but when he begins to rise to receive instruction, he begins to rise toward perfection. It is to get away from the state of the natural man that we educate our children. The difference between the learned philosopher and the ignorant man is this: the ignorant man is left in his natural condition, but the great philosopher had been going through long training and education until he has reached a state of comparative perfection. Otherwise both are human.

'It is to lift man up out of his natural state and imbue him with a sense of the divine that God has sent his holy prophets to give their messages. They are the gardeners of God, and mankind are the wild growths that are objects of their cultivation out of the natural state. Without the message from God from age to age man would relapse into a state of barbarity and become like unto the wild animals.

CHRIST HAD DIVINE MESSAGE

'His Holiness Jesus Christ was divine. His message was from God and he unfolded the magnificent possibilities of human betterment and the spiritual perfectibility of the human race.

'No, the material world is not perfect and despite all the sayings of contemporary philosophers, nothing but the divine message, the ray from the sun of reality, such as was brought to us by His Holiness the Christ, will ever lift up mankind.'

Abdul Baha will speak to-night to Socialists and labor men at Coronation Hall, 204 St. Lawrence Street; tomorrow night at 716 Pine Avenue Street West, and on Thursday night at St. James Methodist Church when his subject will be 'The Happiness of the Human Race'.

So many enquirers have been seeking interviews with Abdul Baha that he has removed from the private house at 716 Pine Avenue into the Windsor Hotel, where he will be more accessible to visitors.[18]

A similar account was published in the *Montreal Gazette*:

MATERIALISTS LIKE ANIMALS

ABDUL BAHA SHARPLY CRITICIZES MODERN SCHOOL OF PHILOSOPHY

NATURE IS IMPERFECT

WITHOUT AID OF FAITH AND INTELLIGENCE PEOPLE WOULD SINK LOWER THAN ANIMALS

Agnostic philosophers were the subject of some measures of scorn and sarcasm at the hands of Abdul Baha, the visiting Oriental prophet and leader, last night. He said that animals knew nothing of God and could not because of their living in a natural and uneducated condition, and philosophers after ages of study saw nothing more than the animals did.

The talk which the prophet gave last night to a drawing-room meeting at 716 Pine Avenue West was devoted to showing that the world of nature is dark, and materialism is dark and degraded and needs to be illumined by intelligence being applied to it. Nature the speaker interpreted as the material world. 'When we look on the material world,' he said, 'we see clearly it is imperfect and dark. If we leave a piece of land in its nature condition, thorns will grow thereon and parasites will become rampant. So we must illumine this world of nature. We must clothe and take care of the ground so that flowers may grow. If we leave man in his natural state, he will become lower than the animals. He will remain imperfect like the people of central Africa, who are in a natural and dark state. If we desire to illumine the world of man we must educate, so that, being ignorant, he may become wise. If we leave him, it is sure he will become lower than the animals . . .

'In these days the new schools of philosophy blindly claim that the world of nature is perfect, and all the discussions are carried along that line. Why then do they put children in school? As long as the world of nature is perfect, why all the sciences?' All these sciences and discoveries have been produced through education, for they were not known from the world of nature. The difference between the learned philosopher and the ignorant man is this: the ignorant man is left in his natural condition, but the great philosopher had been going through long training and education until he has reached a state of comparative perfection. Otherwise both are human.

[*Illegible*] Abdul Baha described the prophets sent by God as the gardeners, and said that had the world of nature been perfect, there would have been no need of a revelation, nor indeed of God. Wild animals, he said, were not in touch with God. All animals were materialistic and had no other susceptibilities. 'All animals are a denial of God. They are not informed of the prophets of God nor of the holy books. They are like the philosophers of our time; they are entirely ignorant of the spiritual; they do not know the bounties of the Holy Spirit, they are not in touch with the supernatural power. [*Illegible*][19]

Talk to Socialists

On Tuesday, 3 September, 'Abdu'l-Bahá addressed a socialist organization in Montreal. It was certainly unique for Canadians to see a religious leader coming from the East speaking to a meeting of militant socialists about economics and social justice.[20] The event caught the attention of the local press and on the following days several accounts of the meeting were published in local newspapers. The most detailed report was published in the *Daily Star*. Its reporter estimated that some five hundred people had attended the meeting:

EARTH SHOULD BE PARADISE, SAYS SEER ABDUL BAHA

TELLS SOCIALISTS ABOUT HIS SCHEME FOR A GENERAL DISTRIBUTION OF WEALTH.

UPHOLDS DISTINCTIONS IN PEOPLE'S SOCIAL POSITION

That poverty could and should be abolished, and that every member of the great human family, without exception, had a right to live in comfort and happiness by sharing in the general welfare, was declared by Abdul Baha to be the economic expression of his teaching, in an address delivered last night in a gathering of Socialists in Coronation Hall, St. Lawrence St.

About five hundred people were present, many of them women, and they seemed to represent almost every nationality under the sun. Mr. H. A. Goulden presided and he welcomed Abdul Baha as a great messenger of love and brotherhood from the East to the West. The title of Abdul Baha's address was: 'The Economic Happiness of the Human Race'.

MAN ESSENTIALLY GREGARIOUS

'All phenomena seemingly can live solitary and alone,' he said. 'Trees, animals and birds can live the solitary life. But man cannot. He is necessarily ever in need of co-operation and mutual help.

'In reality, all mankind represent one family. God desired that each individual member of the body politic should live in the utmost comfort and welfare.

'If all do not so enjoy life, there is a lack of symmetry in the body politic.

INDIVIDUALS SHARE IN GENERAL WEALTH

'Let us look after ourselves,' the selfish say. "Let others die; so long as I am comfortable, everything is going well." Such a callous attitude is due to a lack of control and a lack of a working law.'

Abdul Baha then outlined a scheme which had been formulated by Baha Oullah, the great Bahai prophet, for ensuring the economic happiness of the people. The farmers were the first to be dealt with, for the agricultural industry was the most important and most useful in the national life. In every village community there was to be a general storehouse to which a number of revenues would come. This income for the general income would include tithes, a certain revenue from the number of animals, and one-third from mines and minerals. If anyone died without an heir, all his wealth went to the general storehouse. Any treasure trove picked up became public property.

ADVOCATES TITHE SYSTEM

The tithes were to be collected from the farmers on a graded scale. If a man's expenditure equaled his income, he could pay nothing; if one had an expenditure of one thousand dollars and an income of two thousand, he would pay one-tenth; from one having an income of ten thousand dollars and expenses of one thousand, two tenths would be exacted. If one had an income of twenty thousand dollars and his expenses were two thousand the taxes would amount to one-fourth. If the income was two hundred thousand dollars and the expenses ten thousand, then the community would exact just one half.

From the general storehouse, the less fortunate members of the community would draw to secure their share of the general welfare. If a man's expenses were ten thousand dollars and his income five thousand, he drew five thousand dollars from the store to even up.

WOULD ABOLISH POVERTY

There would be no poverty in the community. Orphans, cripples, the poor and the aged, the blind, the halt, the deaf, all would be looked after. The people themselves would elect trustees for the administration of the public trust. Whatever surplus there might be, after all were looked after, would go to the national exchequer. For big cities such a system would be carried out on, of course, a much more extensive scale.

By this system, said Abdul Baha, every member of the body politic would live in comfort, without fear, and without being under obligation to anyone.

UPHOLDS SOCIAL DISTINCTION

Degrees or grades would not be abolished. These were necessary, as in an army it was necessary to have marshals, generals, colonels, sergeants and foot soldiers. But, notwithstanding grades, all had the right to share in the general well being.

'The earth can be made a paradise. Let all the servants of God ever strive that such a great happiness may accrue to the world of humanity.'

Prolonged applause greeted Abdul Baha at the close of the address. Tonight he will speak at 716 Pine Avenue West, and to-morrow night he will speak in St. James Methodist Church.[21]

Parts of this article were quoted in the weekly *Le Nationaliste*, organ of the 'Ligue Nationaliste' with a circulation of 11,000 copies, which on 8 September published an editorial signed as 'Calibano' in which 'Abdu'l-Bahá's address to Socialists was criticized. 'If you or me had used this language, we would have been called Calino, La Palisse or Joseph Proudhon. But if it is used by Abdul Baha, he speaks gold.'[22]

The *Montreal Gazette* published the following account:

APOSTLE OF PEACE MEETS SOCIALISTS

ABDU'L BAHA'S NOVEL SCHEME FOR DISTRIBUTION OF SURPLUS WEALTH

MAN NEEDS COMMISSION

ADVOCATES GRADUATED DISTRIBUTION OF GENERAL WEALTH, BUT SOCIALISM COULD NOT OBVIATE SOCIAL GRADATIONS

Passing from the inviting atmosphere of a drawing room meeting held in a Pine Avenue residence on Monday night to a socialistic and very cosmopolitan gathering held in Coronation Hall, associated with Jewish strikers, Abdul Baha, the Oriental Apostle of peace and concord, exhibited his catholicity of spirit last night, and also developed in his address something more in the shape of practical politics, as he unfolded a scheme for dealing with the superfluous wealth of a nation. His style was quite in contrast to the violent and denunciatory methods usually followed by the group for whom he lectured. He confined himself to stating that the human race was not acting as though all were members of a family, and he then expounded his father's scheme for the distribution of surplus wealth in a village community. The crowded hall was too good an opportunity for the chairman, Mr. H. A. Goulden, to miss and he preceded the address of the visitor by a brief but vivid picture of the inequality and misery existing in big cities and the evident need that existed for this prophet to come from the East to teach the West the meaning of love and brotherhood.

How to obtain economic happiness was the theme of Abdul Baha's address. Speaking as usual through an interpreter, he said: All phenomena seemingly can live solitary and alone: a tree can exist alone on a mountain or in a valley, and a bird can live a solitary life in the air; these creatures are not in need of co-operation or solidarity. Man on the contrary cannot live a solitary live but is ever in need of co-operation and mutual help. If left in a wilderness he will ultimately starve, therefore he is in need of co-operation and reciprocity. The reason is that man originated as one family. For this reason each member of the race should remember that he is part of the body politic, and if anyone is afflicted, all the other members must suffer. Yet, although the body politic is one family, through lack of symmetry some members are well fed and clothed, while others exist in misery and go hungry and unsheltered. Why? Because the household is not well arranged and is under imperfect laws. Therefore a law must be given which shall ensure that each member of the human family shall enjoy happiness. Baha Oullah gave instruction concerning such problems.

Outlining this scheme of his father's, Abdul Baha enumerated the following principles: That all the members of the body politic shall be apportioned a share of the utmost welfare and well-being. That the problem has to be solved first with the farmer or peasant class, which stands first in importance and number. In every village there shall be a general storehouse. This shall have various revenues, including tithes, revenue from animals, from mines and mineral resources, estates with no heirs, treasure trove. The tithes would be collected on a graduated basis; thus, a farmer having expenditure of a thousand dollars and income of two thousand would pay a tenth but if his income were ten thousand and his expenditure one thousand, he would pay two-tenths. If income and expenditure just balanced he would not be taxed. The income of the general store would be devoted to helping the needy farmer who had expenditure of ten thousand against income of five thousand. Also the widow, cripple and orphan. All would live in comfort, yet, said the speaker, there would be no flaw which would affect the general body politic. Each individual would live in comfort without being under obligation to anyone. Notwithstanding there would be a conservation of degrees, because in the world of humanity there must be degrees, just as in the army.

Tonight Abdul Baha will speak at a meeting to be held at 716 Pine Avenue West, and tomorrow night he will address a gathering in St. James Methodist Church. He is now staying at the Windsor Hotel, where those interested will be received.[23]

A brief portion of this account was published in the *Daily Witness*.[24] French newspapers in Montreal also published versions of it. The Liberal *Le Canada*, with a circulation of 17,100 copies, published the following summary of what transpired at the meeting:

> A CONFERENCE BY ABDUL BAHA
>
> THE PHILOSOPHER SPOKE YESTERDAY ON THE 'ECONOMIC HAPPINESS OF THE HUMAN RACE'
>
> Bahai, in favor of peace, was in town yesterday. Abdul Baha is a Persian philosopher who is preaching his doctrines from town to town. He teaches that all men are brothers and should all love each other. He is in favor of international arbitration, the disappearance of racial differences, the establishment of a universal language and of women's suffrage.
>
> Abdul Baha is a venerable man who has some resemblance to Muslim saints. He spoke last night at the Coronation Hall, St. Laurent. The subject of his lecture was: 'Economic Happiness of the Human Race'.
>
> The philosopher believes in socialism.
>
> He is against those wealthy ones whose fortunes are the product of theft, selfishness and hatred towards their fellow men.
>
> His beliefs on the existence of God are however somewhat similar to those of the Catholics. He believes in the divinity of God. The proofs that God is a divine being, he said, are his miracles. He also says that evil is caused by ignorance. The primal cause of crimes is ignorance, and that's what he is combating.
>
> In summary, the theories professed by Abdul Baha are a mix of socialism and Christianity.[25]

Another French newspaper, *La Presse*, Montreal's most read newspaper with a circulation of 100,400 copies, stated that 'He wants that there be only one religion and to establish a socialism through which the surplus of wealth be distributed among the poor. The audience was greatly interested. He will give a new talk tonight. He retired to the Windsor.'[26]

On Wednesday, 4 September, the day after His address to Socialists, 'Abdu'l-Bahá gave a new public address at the home of the Maxwells in which He further developed some of the points He had touched on in His address at the Coronation Hall and clarified His position with regard to socialism. Some journalists were also present at this meeting and at least three accounts of it appeared in the press on the following day. The *Daily Star* reported the following:

SOCIALISM IS NOT CURE FOR EVILS OF PRESENT DAY

ABDUL BAHA SAYS ONLY SPIRITUAL BROTHERHOOD IS EFFECTIVE

KINGS ARE NOT AT EASE, NOR ARE THEIR PEOPLES

SAYS TO BRING EARTHLY PARADISE OUT OF THE POTENTIAL AND INTO THE REAL

The establishment of a great spiritual brotherhood worldwide in the extent of its operations and through whose activities the economic ills of the nations might be permanently settled was urged by Abdul Baha in an address to a well attended drawing-room meeting at 716 Pine Avenue West, last night.

The great question raised by the Socialists, he said, was one of paramount importance and the governments of the world had failed to give it the earnest attention it deserved. It had to be met, otherwise disorder everywhere would be the culmination. Socialists, however, would not be able to bring any permanent settlement because of their extreme radical views. Grades in society would not be abolished. A president must remain a president, a minister must remain a minister. There must still remain an industrial class and an agricultural class. Public order was impossible without this conservation of degrees.

ADVOCATES TRUE BROTHERHOOD

True brotherhood among all the peoples of the earth was the only remedy. A spiritual bond would have to bind all men. Brotherhood based upon the same parentage, or the same nationality failed to meet the situation for families quarreled and nations often had civil wars. The socialistic brotherhood was not perfect, for even Socialists fought each other. No brotherhood could be lasting save that of spiritual type.

Such a great brotherhood for the illumination of the human heart had been planned by Baha Oullah, the great prophet of the Bahai movement. It was not founded on physical or material interests yet the material ills of the world could never be solved, save through the activities of such a brotherhood.

ALL COUNTRIES IN A TURMOIL

'In reality,' said Abdul Baha, 'you cannot detect any semblance of that brotherhood in the world to-day. All countries are in a turmoil. Kings are not at ease, nor are their peoples, all are afflicted. But if a great spiritual brotherhood is founded, all sorrows will be transformed to happiness and all problems solved. A man will lay down his life, if need be, for his brother, or forfeit all his possessions if by so doing he can succor those who may be unfortunate. We must all strive for the establishment of this divine brotherhood on the earth. There is no remedy save this.

'Strive, then, for the establishment of such a brotherhood throughout America. Let us bring the kingdom, the earthly paradise, out of the potential and into the real. All other brotherhoods are perishable. The spiritual brotherhood alone will bring to you happiness upon earth, the life everlasting and the radiance of God's kingdom.'

A reception followed the address.

To-night Abdul Baha will speak to St. James Methodist Church on 'The Bahai Principles for the Happiness of the Human Race'.[27]

The account in the *Gazette* read as follows:

SOCIALISM MUST BE MET

ABDUL BAHA CONTINUES LECTURES ON MODERN CONDITIONS

As if to repair any possible misinterpretation of his appearance before a Socialist audience the previous evening, Abdul Baha last night plainly intimated to a Pine Avenue gathering that his principles did not call for any disorganization of the existing order of things, and did not propose to abolish the gradations of society. A president must remain a president, a minister a minister, and there would still remain an industrial class and an agricultural class and so forth. 'Because order,' he declared, 'is impossible without the conservation of degrees in a community.' Nevertheless, the question of socialism was one which governments would have to face, and if it were left in its present status there would be disorder.

As a continuation of his exposition of the scheme of 'Baha'o'llah' (his father), Abdul Baha last night elaborated the principles of brotherhood. Brotherhood based on the fact of one's parentage, he submitted, was not sufficient as there was often strife between brothers of one family. Equally, brotherhood founded on racial and national lines was unsatisfactory. In France 'fraternite' did not produce agreement, and civil war was common. Even the brotherhood of socialism was not absolute, because socialists sometimes fought each other. Hence the only lasting and possible brotherhood was that of the spiritual type. This was not for defensive purposes, but for the illumination of the human heart. Real and spiritual brotherhood was that which was ready to endure hardship, suffering and sacrifice, as exemplified in the lives of the prophets. If the problems of socialism were to be solved, it must be on the lines of establishing this spiritual brotherhood. In humanity today there could not be observed any sign of real brotherhood; the rich were not at ease, and the poor were not in comfort. The speaker concluded by expressing the wish that the ideas of Baha'o'llah might become universally adopted. The address was interpreted by Dr. Ameen Fareed.

Tonight Abdul Baha will address a meeting in the lecture hall of St. James Methodist Church on 'The Bahai principles for the happiness of the human race'. This will be the last appearance of the Oriental apostle of peace.[28]

Portions of this article were used in a brief note published in the *Daily Witness*.[29]

Talk at St James Church

On Thursday, 5 September, 'Abdu'l-Bahá delivered His last public talk in Montreal at the St James Methodist Church where He spoke on the unity of mankind, presented some of the Bahá'í principles and again mentioned that a great war in Europe was near.[30] The meeting was an interdenominational one. While the church was Methodist, 'Abdu'l-Bahá was introduced by the Rev. Dr. Herbert Symonds (1860–1921), who was the vicar of the Christ Church Cathedral of the Church of England. As a promoter of relations between Christian churches, his progressive religious views were followed by many. The meeting was closed by Judge Robert Stanley Weir (1856–1926), a Congregationalist, who since 1899 had been the recorder of Montreal and who is best known for having written the lyrics of Canada's national anthem

'O Canada'. Also present was Rev. Edward Bushell, of the Anglican St Matthias Church in Westmount. Several reporters from the local English and French newspapers were at the meeting and wrote accounts of it. The *Daily Star* published the following:

WORLD PEACE URGED BY ABDUL BAHA IN CLOSING MESSAGE

PERSIAN SAGE ADDRESSED LARGE AUDIENCE, IN ST. JAMES METHODIST CHURCH

Abdul Baha brought his peace mission to Montreal to a successful close last night when in glowing language and simple yet picturesque gesture he pleaded the cause of international peace and brotherhood before an audience of about twelve hundred people in St. James Methodist Church. On the platform with him were the Rev. Dr. Symonds, vicar of Christ Church Cathedral, Mr. Recorder Weir, the Rev. E. Bushell, rector of St. Matthias Church, Westmount, Dr. Ameen U. Fareed and Mirza Ahmad Sohrab.

Dr. Symonds, in introducing Abdul Baha, said the distinguished Persian teacher did not come to ask people to join a new religion but he came to the cause of human unification. It was a great mistake to imagine the West had everything to teach the East, on the contrary the East had a very great deal to teach the West.

The title of Abdul Baha's address was 'The Bahai Principles for the Happiness of the Human Race'. Dr. Fareed translated the speaker's words, in admirable fashion.

PLEASED WITH OUR PEOPLE

'I feel a sense of deep joy,' said Abdul Baha, 'at being present at such a revered assembly. Praise be to God for I see before me the earnest countenances of searchers for reality, an evidence that the people long to become acquainted with eternal verities. God created man and endowed him with reason with which to reach valid conclusion, therefore man must in all pursuits investigate reality.

'I am greatly pleased with the people of America, because they seek to know the reality of everything. Their reason is ever actively engaged and I find them independent investigators.'

Abdul Baha outlined under six headings the main points of the teaching of Baha Ollah.

'1st. – It is incumbent upon all humanity to make an independent investigation of truth, lack of investigation is the cause of the creeping in of error and subsequent dissensions.

'2nd. – The oneness of all humanity. All mankind formed one great family and all are immersed in the ocean of God's eternal mercy. So long as God is kind to all why should we be unkind, why should we not love all? Can we formulate a policy superior to the divine policy? No, we must emulate God, and if a soul is sick give him a remedy. If one is ignorant educate him, and if one has imperfections strive to make these disappear.

'3rd. – Religion must be the mainspring of love in every community. No true religion can cause strife. If enmity arises out of religion surely that religion's non-existence is better than its existence.

'4th. – Religion must correspond to science and reason, if not it is merely superstition. Reasoning ever leads us to the verities of things.

'5th. – It is necessary that all prejudices should disappear. Religious, racial, sectarian, patriotic and political prejudices are all destroyers of the foundations of God, and the denial of the divine truth. For God's prophets were sent with the sole purpose of creating unity and love upon earth. All mankind descend from Adam, all humanity are essentially one family, and before God there is no distinction of race. The earth has by man been divided up imaginary, and such divisions have been the cause of incessant shedding of innocent blood. The time has now arrived when all such differences should be laid aside.

'6th. – The world of humanity is ever in need of the emanations of the Holy Spirit. If man did not receive this he was only an animal.'

The Bahai teaching, said Abdul Baha, also inculcated the necessity of universal education. Illiteracy must pass away, and with it untold misunderstandings would disappear.

THE PEACE OF THE NATIONS

'Then,' said Abdul Baha, 'the time has come for us all to work for international peace. No catastrophe can be greater than war, and in preparation for it man is taxed beyond the limit of endurance. Europe is today nothing but a storehouse of explosives, it is ever on the edge of war, and a spark only is needed to ignite a blaze that will wreck that continent.

'The time has come for the establishment of an arbital court to settle all international disputes, and the nations must make use of such a court, and obey its just decrees.'[31]

The account in the *Gazette* read as follows:

APOSTLE OF PEACE SAID FAREWELL

ADVOCATED ESTABLISHMENT OF INTERNATIONAL ARBITRATION COURT WITH PLENARY POWERS

EUROPE POWDER HOUSE WHICH ANY SPARK MIGHT EXPLODE – MESSAGE OF SAGE ENDORSED BY CLERGY AND BENCH

'Europe today is nothing but a storehouse of explosives, to which if a spark were applied the whole continent would be in a blaze,' declared Abdul Baha in urging the cause of international peace and amity last night before a large audience in St. James Methodist Church.

Although the Oriental visitor had addressed meetings every night since Sunday, he had not really been heard by those who are only attracted by a central assembly. His final message was a comprehensive one in which he summed up all the tenets of his late father, Baha'o'llah, founder of the Bahai movement, which, in the words of Mr. Recorder Weir, covered international peace, the doctrine of the All Father, the proper distribution of wealth, equality of sexes, an international language, and other points.

Rev. Dr. Symonds presided, and in introducing the speaker emphasized the fact that he did not come with the idea of setting up a new cult or religion, but only desired to see the unification of Christendom and of all religions in regard to international peace. It was a great mistake, said the chairman, to believe that the West had nothing to learn from the East. Civilization had its shortcomings, and there were certain departments of human life in which the spirit of Christianity and good will were sadly lacking.

Abdul Baha told his audience that their presence meant that they were seeking the reality. He argued that it was a fallacy to believe that at certain times the divine bounties were poured out and then ceased for a season. 'That was a denial of God. If the heat of the Sun ceased, then it would no longer be the sun. The potency of the Holy Spirit was not temporary. Divine teachings had been given from time immemorial and continuously.

The eastern prophet proceeded to reiterate the teachings of Baha'o'llah under a number of headings. Investigate independently the realities, he said, for dissensions result from lack of that. The oneness of the race, the necessity of education, the folly of racial, national and patriotic strife, and the cultivation of the spiritual life were all briefly touched upon. Then the prophet came to the question of international peace, and depicted the growing armaments in Europe and their burden on the people. His remedy was the establishment of an international tribunal, which would apparently have greater powers than that of The Hague.

In concluding Abdu'l-Baha expressed his appreciation of the justice and amity enjoyed on this continent and hoped the governments in America would play a leading part in establishing such a tribunal.

Mr. Recorder Weir, in moving a vote of thanks, said some people believed the race of prophets had become extinct, but it was a pleasure to listen to one who was in the lofty succession of the long line of prophets. He had brought a message that would not be speedily forgotten.

Abdul Baha closed the gathering by an invocation which was interpreted. He leaves for Chicago today.[32]

The *Daily Witness* published another report in which it was wrongly stated that 'Abdu'l-Bahá would leave that day for Chicago and in which some of the closing remarks by Judge Weir were recorded:

INVESTIGATE THE REALITIES

POWER OF REASON ONE OF GOD'S MOST PRECIOUS GIFTS, SAYS ABDUL BAHA

STRIVING FOR UNITY

EQUALITY OF RIGHTS BETWEEN MAN AND WOMAN ESSENTIAL TO PEACE MOVEMENT

Abdul Baha, the Persian preacher, attracted a large congregation to St. James Methodist Church, in spite of the disagreeable weather last evening, to listen to his opinions about the principles on which the happiness of the human race might be founded.

He presented this argument in vivid language, brightly illuminated with passages of Oriental imagery. His manner gave the audience the impression that, while he insisted that his fundamental doctrines must be accepted, he was anxious that the details of his philosophy should be made as easy and attractive as possible to its disciples.

The speaker was introduced by the Rev. Dr. Symonds, who reminded the audience that Abdul Baha was not in Montreal to found a new sect, but was there as a sincere apostle of universal unity and peace. It was a great mistake to imagine that the West could learn nothing from the East. We ought to listen to the preacher's view with that point in mind.

Abdul Baha told his audience of the teachings of his father, a great Persian prophet, Baha Oullah, and gave a remarkably interesting and lucid resume of his principal doctrines.

He opened by paying a compliment to the Canadian people's desire for independent investigation, remarking that such a desire was praiseworthy inasmuch as the power of reason was one of the most precious gifts of God. Man, to achieve permanent happiness, must in all pursuits endeavor to investigate the realities of things. It was a mistake to say that at any time the human race was to neglect so to investigate, because in neglecting they refused to make use of it, the gift of reason.

He impressed his hearers with the continuity of God's bounties, and suggested that the great power of the Holy Spirit lay in the fact that its influence was not temporary, but everlasting, else it would cease altogether, even as the sun would cease to be the sun were it to stop but for a moment the shedding of its comforting rays of heat and light.

He further exhorted his audience to get at realities of life just as the teaching of all the old prophets taught them to do. Abraham strove for reality, Moses partly achieved reality, and Christ founded reality, and, he added, the teachings of Baha Oullah are all in all reality.

In his doctrines they had the solution of all the problems of life, and that solution was Absolute Unity of all nations and of all men. If unity was to be achieved, he said, all must investigate individuality, for dissension in every case followed from lack of getting to the realities of life.

Arguing in favor of the unity of the human races, he suggested that one had not far to look for incentives to the achievement of that end; because God created all, therefore, he loved all; because he protected all, therefore, he loved all. Surely that meant that he wanted unity.

Education must be given to all that they might be endowed with sufficient knowledge to think accurately for themselves. He condemned religious prejudices and racial alienation; sectarianism and political strife must be banned.

That this unity should be achieved, he further urged that some great international tribunal should be established, so that universal peace might be permanently attained. Redistribution of wealth would further stimulate the movement, while another essential was the equality of rights between men and women. Both, he said, were capable of education, therefore, both must receive an equal amount of it. With Oriental vividness he conjured up a picture of humanity as possessed of two wings, one man, the other woman, restrained from higher flight by the fact that one wing was crippled or undeveloped.

In conclusion, he urged that a universal language would enable all men much more readily to see eye to eye. He said that he had come to America after traveling long distances, and he gladly found noble nations, having fair governments and great ideals. He fervently hoped that amity between the United States and Canada would continue, and that that would prove a mighty power in the permanent establishment of universal peace.

Mr. Recorder Weir, in a graceful speech thanking Abdul Baha, said that it was a fallacy to think that the days of the prophets were gone, as all would appreciate who had been privileged that night to sit at the feet of one who was in such lofty succession of the long line of prophets.

Abdul Baha leaves to-night for Chicago.[33]

Some French speaking newspapers also reported the talk. *La Presse* published a short report that was probably based on the above account in the *Witness*.[34] The account appeared in *Le Devoir*, an evening liberal and nationalist newspaper, contained a summary of what had been published in the morning newspapers.[35] Another report appeared in the conservative *La Patrie*, which added some critical remarks in the line of those published a few days earlier in *Le Canada*. 'The doctrine he enunciated last night,' stated the article, 'contains nothing that has not been preached before by the apostles of universal peace and the propagation of socialist theories, except that it imposes belief in God and the biblical prophets' teachings of the universal principles of equality, moral progress and intellectual refinement.'[36]

Further Interviews

Before leaving Montreal 'Abdu'l-Bahá granted a further interview to the *Daily Star*. Its reporter asked 'Abdu'l-Bahá about the arms race between Germany and the United Kingdom. 'Abdu'l-Bahá stated again that a great war was approaching and insisted that only through an international agreement for disarmament could the military buildup of the countries be stopped. Countries are entitled to self-defence and thus, in the absence of an international agreement, they have no other choice than to prepare themselves in the face of a potential danger.

CANADA SHOULD PREPARE FOR A GREAT WAR COMING,
SAYS APOSTLE OF PEACE

UNIVERSAL PEACE ONLY POSSIBLE BY COMMON DISARMAMENT

That Abdu'l-Baha is under no illusions about the ushering in of a reign of peace all over the world by merely talking about it, was made abundantly clear by him in a special interview accorded to a representative of the Montreal Star.

The venerable apostle of peace emphatically declared that in the temper of the world today it was futile to hope for any slackening of the present race of the nations to increase their armaments. He reiterated his absolute conviction that a great war in Europe was a certainty before permanent peace would be established in the world.

Briefly, Abdu'l-Baha said the permanent peace of the world could only be established by international agreement, voluntarily entered into by all the nations; that for any single nation to disarm at present, or to fail to strengthen its armaments while the neighboring nations kept on adding to theirs, was simply out of the question, and, in fact, would be supreme folly, that Great Britain was justified at present, in view of menacing conditions in Europe, in increasing her armaments in order to safeguard her existence; and that the people of Canada, under such circumstances, could not well do otherwise than assist her Motherland in the task of defense.

THE INTERNATIONAL SITUATION AS IT CONFRONTS CANADIANS

The case was put to Abdu'l-Baha thus: –

'Granting the truth of all you say in regard to war – that it is wicked and cruel and a barbarous anachronism which ought to be swept away and replaced by arbitration – the fact stares us in the face that all the nations in the world are arming, and you have stated yourself during your stay in Montréal that an appalling war in Europe is inevitable. Undoubtedly the principals will be Great Britain and Germany. The victor in such a war would be in command of the seas and so become, for a long time, the dominant power in the world. We Canadians prefer to live under British institutions. We are bound by ties of blood and affection to the British Empire. In view of the apparent certainty of this struggle, what are the Canadians to do?'

SIMULTANEOUS ACTION NECESSARY

In reply to this Abdu'l-Baha said:

'As to the question of disarmament, all nations must disarm at the same time. It will not do at all, and it is not proposed, that some nations shall lay down their arms while others, their neighbors, remain armed. The peace of the world must be brought about by international agreement. All nations must agree to disarm simultaneously.

LOOK OUT FOR YOURSELVES

'In the case of Great Britain, so long as other nations are adding to their naval armaments and increasing the strength of their military forces, surely you are entitled to look out for yourselves. Were you to do otherwise, that would be folly: you would simply find yourselves bereft of the means of defense.

'No nation can follow a peace policy while its neighbor remains warlike. For example: If France should cease to maintain her armaments while Germany should maintain hers, France would not be able to offer resistance to attack and would simply invite her own destruction. If France added to her armaments and Germany did not do the same, France would be the victor as soon as the armed nation fell upon the disarmed one.

'There is no justice in that. Nobody would dream of suggesting that the peace of the world could be brought about by any such line of action. It is to be brought about by a general and comprehensive international agreement, and in no other way.

BRITISH AND CANADA JUSTIFIED

'So long as Germany is adding to its fleet of dreadnoughts, nobody can expect that the British people can or will do anything else but increase their own armaments. Disarmament, as I have said, must be by international agreement and it must be done at the same time. The nations must agree to abandon the ancient pursuit of war and lay down their arms simultaneously.

'Then, in view of the warlike state of affairs in Europe, the people of Great Britain are under no blame for adding new warships to their already powerful fleet,' Abdul Baha was asked.

'No, not at all,' he replied. 'They cannot well do anything else.'

'And Canadians cannot do otherwise than stand by their Mother Country and render her every material assistance possible,' the interpreter pursued.

'That is manifest,' said Abdul Baha.

'Simultaneous action,' he went on, 'is necessary in any scheme of disarmament. All the governments of the world must transform their battleships and warcraft into merchant vessels. But no one nation can by itself start in upon such a policy and it would be folly should one power attempt to do so.

WOULD SIMPLY INVITE DESTRUCTION

'If England, for instance, should decide that the time has arrived for her to disarm and set the world an example of a really peaceful nation, what would happen? Germany would at once pounce upon her and her power would be destroyed. In the absence of any international agreement, and while Germany is adding dreadnought to dreadnought, the British people can do nothing else than they are now doing – that is they are perforce obliged to add to their armaments – for self-defense of course.'

Abdu'l-Baha then told a little story to illustrate his point of reciprocity of action.

THE TURNING OF THE OTHER CHEEK

'One man slapped another on the face. When the man who had received the slap made a move to retaliate, the other reminded him of the precept concerning the turning of the left cheek after one has been smitten on the right. 'So you must let me slap you again,' said the aggressor. He allowed the surly one to do so. Next day, the same two men met, and the surly man struck the other on the right cheek once more. 'Now let me have your left cheek,' said the assailant. The blow was received, and the injured man quietly went his way. On the third day, the two met again, but by this time the man who had been smitten, thinking he had pretty well carried out both the letter and the spirit of his Master, said to the aggressor: 'Now, my friend, it's your turn to carry out the holy precept.' And so he went for him and gave him a good sound thrashing.

'So you see,' said Abdu'l-Baha laughing heartily, 'there must be reciprocity in carrying out a policy of peace and good-will. As with individuals, the nations must live up to the spirit of amity.

'In the meantime, all people of good-will must ever strive to make international peace the great issue. They must work unceasingly to turn public opinion in favor of this line of action. In the absence of a universal agreement, armament must continue to be piled up against armament and the nations cannot hope for release.'

A GREAT WAR COMING

'And a titanic war would seem to be approaching?'

'All Europe is an armed camp. These warlike preparations will necessarily culminate in a great war. The very armaments themselves are productive of war. This great arsenal must go ablaze. There is nothing of the nature of prophecy about such a view,' said Abdu'l-Baha; 'it is based on reasoning solely.'

'Are there any signs that the permanent peace of the world will be established in anything like a reasonable period?' Abdu'l-Baha was asked.

'It will be established in this century,' he answered. 'It will be universal in the twentieth century. All nations will be forced into it.'

GETTING BEYOND HUMAN ENDURANCE

'Economic pressure will tell?'

'Yes: the nations will be forced to come to peace and to agree to the abolition of war. The awful burdens of taxation for war purposes will get beyond human endurance. Practically the whole of the substance of the peoples, all the fruit of their labor is now taken away from them to be devoted to the forging of armaments everywhere. [*illegible*]

'No,' said Abdu'l-Baha in conclusion, 'I repeat, no nation can disarm under these circumstances. Disarmament is surely coming, but it must come, and it will come, by the universal consent of the civilized nations of the earth. By international agreement they will lay down their arms and the great era of peace will be ushered in.

'In this and no other way can peace be established upon the earth.'[37]

The same issue carried the following editorial regarding the warnings made by 'Abdu'l-Bahá:

WAR MUST PRECEDE UNIVERSAL PEACE

Abdul Baha has preached Universal Peace for fifty years. One third of the people of Persia are numbered among his followers. In London and in Paris, thinking men and women of all creeds have heard him gladly. In New York, Berlin, Vienna, even in St. Petersburg, the vigor of his thought and the value of his teachings, as well as the simple sincerity of his life have been recognized.

In a word, Abdul Baha is the great protagonist of Peace in the world today. To bring about its accomplishment is the practical corollary of the two tenets which are the foundation of his creed – the Fatherhood of God and the brotherhood of man. For forty years he was persecuted for preaching it, for twenty years imprisoned.

Yet the universal peace for which he hopes and in which he believes has no resemblance to the fantastic chimera of slack-thinking sophists who, on the easy assumption that all things are as they ought to be, would have Great Britain expose to the rapacity of any enlightened but well-armed competitor the fruits of the centuries of her striving for justice and liberty and freedom of opportunity by laying down her arms and abandoning her armaments.

For Abdul Baha, with all his hatred of war and horror at its moral and material results, has no delusions as to the conditions in Europe today or the trend of political events. 'It is futile to hope for any slackening of the present race of the nations to increase their armaments,' he says. 'A great war in Europe is a certainty before permanent peace can be established. International peace can only be reached by an international agreement entered into by all nations. For any single nation to disarm at present or to fail to strengthen its armaments while the neighboring nations kept on adding to theirs would be supreme folly.'

Strong words, those, from a teacher whose life has been spent in preaching peace on earth. There is no smug complacency about them, nor any blinking the facts that one's fragile fabric of assertions may not be rudely destroyed. Abhorrent as war is to Abdul Baha and his followers, they have the moral courage to recognize and acknowledge the probability of its occurrence.

In an interview printed elsewhere in this issue Abdu'l-Baha elaborates more fully his views on the question of national responsibility in the face of the present disheartening combination of circumstances. Great Britain, he says in view of the present menacing conditions in Europe, is justified in increasing her armaments to safeguard her existence and the people of Canada cannot well do otherwise than to assist the Motherland. 'No nation,' he says, 'can follow a peace policy when its neighbor remains warlike.' So long as Germany is adding to its fleet of Dreadnoughts, nobody can expect that the British people can or will do anything but increase their armament.[38]

A shorter account was also published in the *Montreal Daily Herald*, a liberal newspaper with a circulation of 28,000 copies.[39]

A further interview with 'Abdu'l-Bahá was published in the *Manitoba Free Press* on 19 September:

MESSAGE OF THE GREAT PERSIAN REFORMER

Abdul Baha Abbas, the head of the great Bahai movement for the unification of religions and the establishment of universal peace, is at present travelling in eastern Canada, and last Sunday preached in Montreal. He is a firm believer in woman's suffrage and indeed declares that universal peace will not be a reality until women have the right to vote.

'What is the difference between man and woman?' he said in the course of the interview. 'Both are human. In all the functions and powers they are partners. At the most it has been this: That woman has not had the opportunities which man has so long enjoyed, especially education. She has not had military tactics. If she cannot go for the battlefield and kill, is that a shortcoming? Supposing she has not used a gun, she has not worked the cannon. If we present a cannon to a woman and ask her to fire it and she should fail, is that an imperfection, or praise to her, that in the hardness of the heart she is inferior to man. My hope is that in the five continents where this is not fully established, it may be established, and the banner of equality may be raised. And let it be known once more that until womankind and mankind realize this equality, progress is not made possible. The world of humanity consists of two divisions, of two parts. One part or member is woman, the other is man. Until the two are equal in strength, the oneness of humanity cannot be realized and the happiness of humankind will not be a reality. God willing, this is to be so.'[40]

Echoes outside America

The visit of 'Abdu'l-Bahá to Canada was also echoed outside the country. *The Christian Commonwealth* (London) published a report by Joseph Hannen about the activities of the Master in the last weeks of the summer and His visit to Montreal:

ABDUL BAHA IN CANADA

Subsequent to the preparation of the recent report to THE CHRISTIAN COMMONWEALTH upon the subject, 'Abdul Baha in America', and in response to many urgent invitations the tour has been extended, and Abdul Baha with his party will visit points on the Pacific Coast before returning to Egypt via London and Paris.

July 23 and 24 were spent in Boston, Mass., where addresses

were delivered before large and enthusiastic audiences. Abdul Baha was then en route to Dublin, New Hampshire, the beautiful estate of Mr. and Mrs. Arthur J. Parsons. At this ideal place, several miles from the railroad and commanding a view of the White Mountains somewhat comparable to the scenes in Haifa and Akka, Syria, about two weeks were spent. Beside addresses to the Summer Colony, Abdul Baha by invitation spoke at the Unitarian Church, Dublin (Rev. Josiah L Seward, pastor), Sunday, August 11, on the subject: 'The Two Pathways of Education – Spiritual and Material'.

The next point visited was Green Acre, Eliot, Maine, where the annual Green Acre Conferences have been a noted factor in liberal religious thought for many years. This place was reached August 16. A number of gatherings were addressed, important receptions given, and here as everywhere a profound impression was created making this occasion, although unannounced in the original programme, by far the most important event in Green Acre for the season.

August 23 Abdul Baha left Green Acre for Malden, near Boston, Mass. On Sunday, August 25, an address was given at the New Thought Forum, Huntington Chambers, Boston; on Monday about 400 young lady students were present at an enthusiastic gathering held in Franklin Square House, and on Tuesday about an equal number of well-known people were addressed at the Metaphysical Club.

On August 30 Abdul Baha, with his party, reached Montreal, Quebec, Canada, where his coming had been widely heralded. The pulpit of the Church of the Messiah (Unitarian, Rev. F. R. Griffin, pastor) was occupied by Abdul Baha on Sunday morning, September 1. The subject of his discourse was 'Religious Unity'. Drawing-room meetings, largely attended were held each evening during his sojourn in Montreal at 716, Pine Avenue West. On Monday the subject was 'Materialistic Philosophy – Bankrupt'; on Wednesday, 'Principles of Brotherhood'. On the Tuesday a large gathering of Socialists was addressed by invitation. To them Abdul Baha conveyed the plan embodied in the teachings of Baha'o'llah, looking toward a more uniform distribution of wealth, on a basis which respects alike the rights of capital and labour, encourages industry by affording scope for ambition, and yet offers a remedy for every evil of our present economic system. The subject of this address was 'The Economic Happiness of the Human Race'.

On Thursday an audience of about 1,400 persons gathered at St. James's Methodist Church in what proved to be a farewell meeting. On the platform, with Abdul Baha, were Rev Dr. Symons, vicar of Christ Church Cathedral; Mr. Recorder Weir; Rev. E. Bushell, rector of St. Matthias Church, Westmount; beside the secretary and interpreter, Dr. Ameen U. Fareed and Mirza Ahmad Sohrab. The title of Abdul Baha's address was: 'The Bahai Principles for the Happiness of the Human Race'. The Church and the Bench united in his farewell, and Mr. Recorder Weir said at the close of the address that Abdul Baha was one in the lofty succession of the line of prophets, adding that his presence was proof that the race of prophets was not yet extinct.

From Montreal, Abdul Baha left on September 6 for Buffalo, New York, en route to Chicago, Illinois, and the West. Reports of the tour will be given in further articles.

A notable feature of Abdul Baha's work in the churches has been his generous contributions, sums ranging from 25 dollars to 100 dollars having been given in each instance.

Jos. H. HANNEN. Washington, D.C., September 19, 1912[41]

20

BUFFALO

9–12 September 1912

The visit of 'Abdu'l-Bahá to Buffalo had been anticipated months in advance of His arrival. The press reports reveal that it was originally planned that 'Abdu'l-Bahá would visit Buffalo in early May. An article in the *Buffalo Express* published on 28 April reported that 'a number of those interested in the movement for universal peace and unity in religion met last evening at the home of J. H. Mills, of no. 494 Elmwood Avenue, to make arrangements for the reception of Abdul Baha, its chief exponent, who is expected in this city the early part of next week. Nothing definite will be done until the day of the arrival of Abdul Baha, who is now in Chicago, it is learned.'[1] Judging from the comments published in the same newspaper on 5 May, the visit of 'Abdu'l-Bahá seemed imminent: 'Word has been received by John Harrison Mills that Abdul Baha . . . is coming to Buffalo on Wednesday of this week, to meet the disciples of Bahaism in this city. He went last week from Chicago to Pittsburgh and telegraphed Mr. Mills from the latter city to expect him here on Wednesday.'[2] The *Buffalo Courier* even reported that a meeting to greet 'Abdu'l-Bahá was arranged for May 8.[3]

When plans, however, changed and 'Abdu'l-Baha went from Pittsburgh to Washington, the *Buffalo Express* informed its readers that 'Abdul Baha, the Persian prophet, projector of plans for universal peace, will be unable to fulfill his engagement to lecture in Buffalo. Word was received yesterday that he is now in Washington. It was expected that he would lecture here this week.'[4]

On 1 September, while 'Abdu'l-Bahá was in Canada, the *Express* published a one-column article on its front page introducing the Bahá'í Faith to its readers and confirming the news that 'Abdu'l-Bahá would visit Buffalo.[5]

'Abdu'l-Bahá finally arrived in the city on the evening of Monday, 9 September, after a 14-hour trip by train from Montreal. Local Bahá'ís were not informed of His arrival until the following day, and as soon as His presence in the city was known, local journalists visited Him at the Hotel Iroquois where He was staying. The newspapers published very similar articles about 'Abdu'l-Bahá, quoting Him extensively.

The Republican *Commercial*, an evening paper with a circulation of 7,500 copies, was one of the first newspapers in the city to publish an interview with the Master who, among other things, explained the purpose of His travels:

> 'The object of my mission is to establish international peace; to spread the unity of the human world; to correspond religion with science and reason; to explain the essential unity of the religion of God; to enunciate the purpose of the prophets; to teach the people to leave behind their religious prejudices, their racial prejudices, their patriotic prejudices and their political prejudices; to enunciate the idea of the unity of the country, unity of the races and the unity of phenomena; to establish divine civilization; to teach heavenly philosophy; to readjust economic conditions of the world so that each member may live with perfect peace and comfort; to urge the establishment of international tribunals so that nations may resort thereto for the settlement of disputes; to remove entirely the feeling of hatred and animosity among the children of man, and to insist upon the establishment of a universal auxiliary language.'
>
> 'Are you the leader of this movement?' ventured the reporter.
>
> 'I do not like the word leader,' said Abdul Baba Abbas through the interpreter. 'I am servant of the servants of God. Often the papers call me the Oriental prophet. I am not a prophet. I am a servant. I am a disciple of the teachings of Bahai love . . .'[6]

A reporter with the Democratic *Buffalo Times*, with a circulation of 54,100 copies, was present when 'Abdu'l-Bahá addressed some words to the Bahá'ís who gathered at Hotel Iroquois to meet Him:

> Abdul Baha is within our gates!
>
> The long expected visit of the Prophet of peace is consummated,

and Bahai believers may well be content.

'I am glad to be with you. The Buffalo Bahai are among the staunchest branches.

'To this end I have traversed mountain passes, surmounted seas and rivers, covered many rivers in my desire to meet you.

'I am glad that you hold fast. Some are like a tree, which takes no root. At the first storm it falls and without nourishment it dies.

'Others are like a strong tree. Its roots sink deep, it has nourishment and grows, and leaves. When storms come it does not heed, but bends to the winds which pass over, leaving it stronger for the test.

'I love children and hope to see and bless these little ones whose parents are believers . . .'[7]

The Democratic *Buffalo Enquirer*, with a circulation of 30,000 copies, also sent a reporter to interview 'Abdu'l-Bahá. A lengthy article and a picture of the Master were published on the front page of the newspaper which called Him a 'prophet and prince'. As well as a general summary of the history and teachings of the Bahá'í Faith, the text included statements of 'Abdu'l-Bahá about universal peace, unity and 'the end of the world':

> Some folks have the impression that Abdul Baha forecasts the end of the world. He said he doesn't. Asked directly if he predicted the end of the world, he smiled in dissent and through his interpreter answered:
>
> 'I know the world has no end. It always will continue as God has created it. If anything is to end, as prophecy relates, it refers to present conditions.'
>
> 'Is the world growing better?'
>
> 'Much so. It has progressed and will continue to progress.'[8]

The *Buffalo Evening News*, a Republican newspaper with a circulation of 93,500 copies, interviewed Fareed, who gave a general presentation on the birth and progress of the Bahá'í Faith.[9]

On the evening of Tuesday, 10 September, 'Abdu'l-Bahá addressed a public meeting arranged at Hotel Iroquois. On the following day, at least five local newspapers published accounts of it. Some of them quoted some the words of 'Abdu'l-Bahá. A comparison of the different texts gives a glimpse of the message that He conveyed to His audience. It is apparent, for instance, that 'Abdu'l-Bahá warned again of an imminent war in Europe.

The account in the *Buffalo Times* simply offered its readers some biographical information about 'Abdu'l-Bahá and reported that 'Local Bahaists were addressed last night at the Iroquois Hotel by Abdul Baha Abbas, "the apostle of peace" from Persia declared that a great European War was imminent and endeavored to enlist his hearers and the people of the United States in the cause of peace that they might do all in their power to avert the conflict. He said that the continent of Europe was one great arsenal and that it would become a vast wilderness if one spark penetrated its foundations.'[10]

An account appeared in the *Buffalo Courier*, a Democratic newspaper with a circulation of 44,000 copies:

PERSIAN PEACE APOSTLE PREDICTS WAR IN EUROPE

ABDUL BAHA URGES LOCAL BAHAISTS TO DO ALL IN THEIR POWER TO AVERT TERRIBLE BLOODSHED WHICH HE SAYS IS PENDING IN EAST

Warning against a great European war and pleading that the people of this country do what they can to avert terrible bloodshed, Abdul Baha, Persian peace apostle, addressed the local body of Bahaists at the Iroquois Hotel last evening. Of the seventy persons in attendance about sixty were women . . . He said:

'The very cause of life is due to the Supreme One's love, for by His grace we move, we see, we hear, we feel, and all phenomena is based on His love. The prophets are sent to bear a message of holy love and the philosophers and all the wise men of by-gone ages have sung with sweet melody the theme of love. But, alas, the shadow obscuring the sun of affection. Alas, that on earth should breed a contrary spirit in the hearts of men. Alas, that hatred and enmity should spring forth to make a hell of war and bloodshed.

'Even now in the orient are widows weeping, children lamenting and fathers bereaved for the bloodshed of their dear ones. The continent of Europe is one vast arsenal, which only requires one spark at its foundations and the whole of Europe will become a wasted wilderness.

'And what flimsy, what impudent pretexts they use. Patriotism, say they; glory, say they; the upbuilding of the continent, say they. What a travesty of God's truth.'

Abdul Baha will speak again this evening at 8 o'clock at the Church of the Messiah, Mariner and North Streets.[11]

The *Buffalo Enquirer* published another report which also quoted some of 'Abdu'l-Bahá's 'beautiful words':

> You who comprise a large and peaceful nation, who are prosperous, who enjoy so just a government, shall try to cease these quarrels among nations, that these factors of tyranny and oppression shall pass away. Rather, may this dreadful state be transformed into one of peace and love.[12]

A similar article appeared in the *Buffalo Commercial*, including 'Abdu'l-Bahá's comments about the futility of war:

> The earth is not the man's life, it is his ultimate cemetery, and it is not becoming for men to quarrel over a cemetery. All this generation will have this land for graves not for a place of enjoyment. If it be a temporary place of life, it is an everlasting graveyard, and it will swallow all mankind, and all that inhabits it will be within its very bowels.[13]

The most detailed account was the one published by the *Buffalo Express*, with a circulation of 36,900 copies. After the talk the reporter for this newspaper had a chance to briefly interview the Master. As was the case with the article in the *Enquirer*, the *Express* called 'Abdul-Bahá 'A Persian prince', a comment that displeased Him.[14]

> Religious unity and world peace will come within the present century, by all means, said Abdul Baha in reply to a question by an Express reporter last evening, after the Persian prince, known in America as the Prophet of Peace, had addressed a small audience in the Iroquois parlors.
>
> 'Is that an inspired prophecy, or plain human opinion?' ventured the reporter.

'It is a divine prophecy,' said one of Abdul's brown-robed and black-turbaned interpreters, through whom the interview was being had. He spoke with solemnity and did not venture to repeat the question to his master, as if he feared the implied doubt might give offense.

'Many of his prophecies have been proved in Persia,' added the interpreter.

Asked to cite an instance for illustration's sake, he said Abdul Baha forecast the present trouble of Persia; with Russia and England. He had written to Bahaists in Persia not to interfere with political events; that they were not permanent; that the government and the nation must go hand in hand in harmony and unity; that if they did not do so other nations would step in and dismember Persia.

It has been proclaimed by Bahaists that Abdul Baha is of princely blood and of the seed of Mohammed.

'Are you a prince?' was another question asked to him in last's night's interview.

'I am a servant of God,' was his answer.

And that is what Abdul Baha means – the Servant of God. It is the title which he uses in front of his family name which is Abbas – Abdul Baha Abbas it reads on the hotel register. Whether or not one believes that the Abdul's predictions are the emanations of divine inspiration, as his attendants or disciples evidently believe, one who listens to his addresses is bound to credit him with perfect sincerity and good faith in his mission of promoting religious unity and world peace . . .

During the forenoon and early afternoon, the Abdul received small groups of Buffalo Bahaists in his rooms on the third floor. Though in New York he had extensive suites that occupied one quarter of a floor at the Ansonia, in Buffalo he has two ordinary rooms. One of the facts to which his followers point as proof of the good faith of his mission is that he bears all the expenses of his touring, supposedly from the increment from his princely estates in Persia; always pays for entertainment of his meetings when entertaining is done, and never solicits contributions to his cause.

In the early afternoon the Abdul Baha and his secretary and interpreters took an automobile drive to Niagara Falls. It was the first time he had ever seen the mighty cataract. On their return to the hotel his interpreters were asked what impression the sight had upon him. One of them quotes him as exclaiming:

'Nothing can surpass it. Its grandeur and majesty are awe-inspiring. Any of the grandees of Persia, could they but see it, would make their home near it.'

'We urged him to stay overnight and rest at this beautiful spot,' said the interpreter, 'but he said no, he must continue his work among the poor and to teach the gospel of peace.'

They returned to the hotel shortly after 8 o'clock. The hotel parlors were occupied by 50 or 60 persons, nearly all women waiting to hear him speak at that hour.

The venerable missionary was too fatigued to attend just then, but in less than half an hour he came down from his rooms, attended by his secretary, and interpreters.

The article closed with the words of 'Abdu'l-Bahá:

> Praise be to God! He is kind, He is generous. His treasures are overflowing. Hence we must never fail to put forth every effort, so that the talents He has given us may be used in such achievements as those of long ago. The God who moved others of long ago with the Holy Spirit can resuscitate us with the Holy Spirit. I hope that He may open the doors of His Kingdom to you, that His bounties shall ever be vouchsafed to you and that He will suffer you to grow in spiritual strength and in the life material; that your eyes be illumined by Him; that your ears be made attentive; that your hearts be sanctified; that you may be the cause of rendering this world better by helping to end warfare and battle, disease and discord, and bring about unity, love and peace.'[15]

On Wednesday, 11 September, 'Abdu'l-Bahá gave an address at the Universalist Church of the Messiah at the invitation of Rev. Leon O. Williams. At least three different accounts were published the following day. The article published in the *Express* was again the most detailed, quoting extensively from the words of 'Abdu'l-Bahá:

> Several hundred men and women assembled in the Church of the Messiah, at North and Mariner Streets last night and listened to a

most [*illegible*] and eloquent discourse by Abdul Baha, the Persian prince, prophet of peace and missionary for religious unity. At the close, at the request of the pastor, the Abdul Baha invoked the divine blessings in a prayer whose form, though Oriental, was not unlike in spirit and [*illegible*] the prayers of our Occidental preachers. There followed an informal reception in which the turbaned and robed leader of the far-famed Bahai movement shook hands with everybody present.

This morning the son and spiritual [*illegible*] of the martyred Baha'o'llah, founder of the Bahai movement, will leave Buffalo for Chicago, where is to be established a permanent religious, educational and charitable center. This will be known as Mashrak-El-Askar which means, 'The dawning points of the mention of God'. It will be surrounded by hospices, hospitals, asylums, schools, universities, etc. The name Mashrak-El-Askar applies to the whole group of buildings. In Russian Turkestan there is such a group, and now Bahais throughout the world have united to build one for America near Chicago. Abdul Baha said last night that the ground has been bought and the erection of the building is expected to begin about a year hence.

At present the business affairs of the movement are conducted by 'assemblies of consultation' in various localities. Buffalo has had such an assembly for seven years. It meets on Sunday and Thursday nights at the home of J. Harrison Mills, an artist, at No. 494 Elmwood Avenue. Eventually, the leaders of this movement for religious unity and world peace expect to establish a general assembly composed of representatives from all parts of the world, to be known as the universal house of justice.

In his address last night, the Abdul Baha, through one of his interpreters (while another took it down in Persian shorthand), gave an outline of the movement and the teachings of Baha'o'llah. He repeated and elaborated upon some of the thoughts he imparted in his address in the Iroquois parlors on Tuesday evening. Again he emphasized the absurdity of men warring for dominion over the earth, which is to be their everlasting graveyard. He enlarged upon the heavy burden of war imposed upon the masses of many nations, particularly in the East, where the very income of the peasant is taxed for the building of dreadnaughts, new guns and other implements of war . . .[16]

The account in *Commercial* included 'Abdu'l-Bahá's statements on the equality of women and men, and the education of children:

> 'We also believe in the equality of men and women. God has created them all equal, has made no distinction of gender. They are all endowed with the beautiful attributes of God. How is it possible for humans to make a distinction? The human world has two hands. One is man, the other woman. If one hand is defective, the body of the world is unbalanced. The world of humanity has two wings. If one is crippled, flight is impossible. Unless the two wings fly together the flight will not be high, and progressive, and all mortality cannot be reformed.'
>
> Another teaching referred to by Abdul Baha is universal education. The Bahais hold it incumbent on all parents to give liberal education to their children, except where the parents are unable to do so, in which case the body politic should see to it that each child shall have a goodly portion of the knowledge of the world.[17]

A shorter report in the *Enquirer* stated that 'Last night the Baha spoke at the Church of the Messiah before an audience of several hundred persons, explaining his gospel that peace and love should supersede strife and enmity in the world, and that a common belief in God should weld Christians, Jews, Mohammedans and followers of other faiths in a world-wide peace movement.'[18] The *Buffalo Courier* reported in a brief note about the meeting that 'He ['Abdu'l-Bahá] declared selfishness and hatred have brought Europe to the verge of revolution that will besmirch the entire continent with blood unless immediate reform is effected.'[19]

'Abdu'l-Bahá left Buffalo from the Lehigh Valley train station (Washington Street) on 12 September, at 5 a.m. A few days after His departure the *Examiner* published an article contributed by the local priest Rev. Carl D. Case describing his meeting with 'Abdu'l-Bahá years before in Haifa (see chapter 3 above).[20]

21

EN ROUTE TO CALIFORNIA

Chicago

On His way to California 'Abdu'l-Bahá made brief visits to several cities. His first stop after visiting Buffalo was Chicago, where He arrived on Thursday, 12 September.

Upon His arrival *The Day Book* (Chicago) briefly stated that 'Abdul Baha Abbas, Persian leader of the Bahaist religious movement arrived here from Buffalo, N. Y. He will speak here, then go to Pacific coast.'[1] On 13 September, *The Examiner* (Chicago), also reported that 'Abdu'l-Bahá 'arrived in Chicago last night to be the guest for several days of Mrs. Corinne True' and that He 'is on his way to California to spread his religion along the Pacific Coast. Many Chicagoans have taken up the movement. He believes if women were educated with the same advantages as men their capacity would be the same. He favors suffragism.'[2]

On the evening of Friday, 13 September, 'Abdu'l-Bahá addressed a meeting held at the house of Corinne True in which He spoke about the power of the Holy Spirit, the Covenant and the need for unity among Bahá'ís.[3] One local newspaper, *The Examiner*, which as mentioned earlier was part of the Hearst group and had a circulation of 215,000 copies, published an account of the meeting, describing it as an 'impressive scene'. A reporter from *The Examiner* also had a chance to interview the Master after the meeting. The article that ensued mentioned the names of some prominent figures who were received by 'Abdu'l-Bahá on that day: Esther Falkenstein, a social worker who since 1900 had opened her house as an educational center for children and women; Baroness Bertha von Suttner (1843–1914), a renowned Austrian pacifist and writer who in 1905 had received the Nobel Peace Prize; and Professor George Burman Foster (1858–1919), head of the Department of Systematic Theology in the Divinity School of Chicago University.

RICH CHICAGOANS PAY HOMAGE TO ABDUL BAHA

BAHA'O'LLAH'S SPIRIT DRAWS SOCIAL LEADERS TO PERSIAN SHRINE

PRIEST PRAISES SUFFRAGE

CROWD SITS ON FLOOR TO HEAR DISCOURSE ON GOLDEN RULE DOCTRINE

Seated on the rug-strewn floor, with legs crossed in Oriental fashion, 100 men and women of social prominence in Chicago paid homage last night at a perfumed shrine temporarily established in the home of Mrs. Corinne True, 5338 Kenmore Avenue, by Abdul Baha, the Persian apostle of universal peace and the golden rule.

Among the worshipers were Baroness von Suttner, Mrs. True, Dr. Fred Nutt, Mrs. H. H. Roe and others interested in the Bahaist cult. The True home was packed with society people who kept coming and going all the evening in automobiles. In a corner, on a Persian rug, sat H. S. Fugeta, Bahaist delegate from Japan, and near him was M. T. Basheer, a Bahaist leader from Port Said, Egypt.

It was an impressive scene as the Bahaist leader opened the ceremonies.

SPEECH IS TRANSLATED

Attired in a loose cream-colored robe, with sandals of scented wood on his feet and a snow-white turban on his head, he descended the great stairway of the True mansion and strode majestically about the parlors, talking volubly in Persian, while Dr. Ameen Fareed of Teheran, Persia, translated his words into excellent English.

The leader's utterances proved to be a sermon or exhortation embodying his message to the Bahaist devotees in Chicago and the Middle West. Its keynote was the golden rule, amplified and developed to include all the great spiritual, moral and ennobling ideals of all the religions and ethical systems of the world. The words of wisdom were received with rapt attention, and when the exhortation ended the devotees reverently touched the sleeve of the preacher's robe as a manifestation of their belief that its wearer is considered holy.

Early in the forenoon Abdul Baha established his shrine in the True home.

BAHA ADVOCATES SUFFRAGE

Here, in the heavy atmosphere of oriental perfumes, the aged teacher lay propped up on a divan, surrounded by his interpreters, scribes and servitors. The house was packed with wealthy and socially prominent men and women, standing in line at the staircase waiting their 'interview', and automobiles were coming and going all day.

Abdul Baha, son of Baha'o'llah, has committed himself to woman's suffrage. As he lay pulling tangles out of his beard with long and seemingly lifely fingers, Mirza Sohrab translated a dissertation on women, the two talking simultaneously and almost continually.

'Man must impartially investigate the reality,' he said. 'He must not be prejudiced. What is the difference between men and women. Both are human. In all functions and powers they are equals and partners. If we should investigate perchance we would find the woman superior to man.

'The male fig tree is fruitless, whereas the female is fruitful. The male type of animal does not glory in its being male and its being superior to the female. Is it meet that man should deprive himself of those qualities which animals enjoy? That distinction which God has not made we must not observe. It is a superstition.

NATIONAL PROBLEMS DISCUSSED

'One of the great things which was hidden in the realms of existence was the potential capability of womanhood. Through the light of the Sun of Reality the capacity of womankind has become manifest to the extent that the equality of man and woman is an established fact.

'You now are meeting perplexing questions as to your Panama Canal and other international affairs. Under the reign of universal peace a tribunal at which all the nations of the world will be represented would settle those questions equitably and beyond that decision there would be no appeal.

'Why could not such a body have some of the same relations to the countries of the world as your national government has to the states of your Union? The knowledge is spreading rapidly in the Orient and satisfactorily here.

'Why is the growth so slow here? Because it is complete. One bush with fair roses is better than a thousand with shrunken buds and thorns, one lighted candle is better than a thousand smoldering wicks.'

While the prophet was speaking the telephone rang and an appointment was made with Esther Falkenstein, the settlement worker, for an interview during the evening. The Baroness Suttner was announced and swept into the shrine room for half an hour's communion with the spirit of Baha'o'llah.

PROFESSOR FOSTER AT INTERVIEW

Professor George Burman Foster of the University of Chicago, whose renunciation of the divinity of Christ startled theological institutions of two continents, recently had arranged an interview. There were Bahai from Japan, Persia and Turkey, Honolulu and a dozen states.

Abdul Baha is sixty-eight years old and expects to return to Acca to die on the spot where he and his father were exiled for forty years. This is expected to be his last visit to this country and he may appoint his successor while here.

He goes to Minneapolis, Denver, San Francisco and will tour the Pacific coast before his return to the Orient.[4]

Kenosha

On Sunday, 15 September, 'Abdu'l-Bahá left Chicago to make a brief visit to Kenosha, staying there only one night. He received many visitors and at half past seven in the evening spoke at the Congregational Church.[5] The only daily newspaper in the city, the Republican *Kenosha Evening News* with a circulation of 2,500 copies, had announced His arrival on the day before. 'It is not often that Kenosha people have the opportunity to see and hear the head of any great religious movement and it is expected that there will be a large crowd at the services tomorrow evening,' stated the article, which also added that 'The Bahaist assembly in Kenosha was one of the first centers of the religion in this country and the assembly is one of the strongest in the smaller cities of the country.'[6]

The same newspaper published the following account of the address at the Congregational Church:

HEAR GREAT LEADER

ABDUL BAHA SPEAKS TO LARGE CROWD AT CONGREGATIONAL CHURCH SUNDAY

An audience which filled the entire auditorium of the church gathered at the Congregational Church Sunday evening to listen to an address by Abdul Baha, head of the Bahaist religion. The Bahaist assembly in Kenosha was one of the first formed in this country. The speaker of the evening filled all the preconceived ideas of what the leader of a religious movement should represent in his own person being a man of commanding presence and great personal magnetism. Although he spoke in Persian and his remarks had to be translated to the audience he held the closest attention of his hearers to the end of his address and his exposition of the scriptures was clear and concise from the standpoint of the believers in the new religion. Abdul Baha has been in this country since spring and his lectures and addresses have greatly strengthened the Bahaists in America. The spread of Bahaism is one of the wonders of the modern world, and already the new faith or rule of living numbers its converts by the tens of thousands in the Orient and is gaining in numbers rapidly in the western world.[7]

Minneapolis

From Kenosha 'Abdu'l-Bahá returned to Chicago and on the morning of Wednesday, 18 September, He left for Minneapolis. His visit to the twin cities of Minneapolis and St Paul was announced months in advance in the local press of St Paul. A note published on 5 June stated that 'The entertainment committee of the Commercial Club has completed arrangements for the reception of Abdul Baha, the Persian disciple of the propaganda of "peace and unification of the world", who is touring the United States. He is expected in St. Paul the latter part of this month.'[8] A similar announcement was also published in the black newspaper *The Appeal* (St Paul), which stated that 'Abdul Baha is the leader of a religious cult that knows no man by his race or color and his advent here will be hailed with joy by any who believe in the brotherhood of man'.[9]

The same day as 'Abdu'l-Bahá's arrival in Minneapolis local newspapers announced His visit to the city. According to some, His arrival was expected at 10:30 p.m.[10]

Early in the morning of the following day a reporter with the *Minneapolis Journal*, with a circulation of 78,200 copies, was able to interview 'Abdu'l-Bahá. The following account was published on 19 September:

BAHAIST LEADER IN MINNEAPOLIS, TELLS OF MISSION

TIME TO WIPE OUT RELIGIOUS SURFACE DIFFERENCES, ABDUL BAHA SAYS

TURBANED FOLLOWERS TRANSLATE MESSAGE

LEADER SAYS AMERICA IS IN NEED OF BREATH OF THE HOLY SPIRIT

Long before the other guests at the Hotel Plaza in Minneapolis were astir today, Abdul Baha Abbas, head of the Bahaists of the world, who believes and teaches the eventual harmony and unity of religious mankind, and who arrived last night in Minneapolis for a two-days' stay, was up and about in parlor 603, pacing quietly across the room and back, and pausing occasionally to look meditatively out across Hennepin Avenue into Loring Park. At 7 a.m. the five members of his party called at his parlor to pay their respects. Dr. Clement Woolson of St. Paul called on behalf of the St. Paul Bahaists, Dr. H. S. Harper and Albert H. Hall of Minneapolis came next. Mrs. R. M. Passmore and Mrs. H. G. Harrison, who have visited the country where Baha's influence is greatest in their foreign travels, and who had known well in advance of his coming, sent him messages of welcome to Minneapolis. Dr. S. N. Deinard of the Jewish Reform Temple called to see if it would be possible to arrange for the Bahaist leader to address the Jewish people of Minneapolis. About a dozen men and women, who are local followers of Bahaism, came into the room.

TURBANED INTERPRETERS

Turbaned, dark-visaged gentlemen of the visitor's party stood about ready to interpret. They were Dr. Ameen W. Fareed, who is Persian born, but who gained his physician's diploma at the University of Illinois and took a later postgraduate course at Johns Hopkins University, Baltimore, and who is thoroughly Americanized and speaks English with pleasing nicety of accent; Mirza Ahmad Sohrab, Mirza Mahmood, and Ali Akbar, the later really a Russian, governmentally speaking, since the part of Persia that he comes from is partially Russianized.

'I have not breakfasted nor did I eat last night,' said Abdul Baha, speaking through Dr. Fareed. 'It is spiritual food, not physical food, that I most crave.' He smiled faintly, and two beautiful large, hazel eyes looked about the room. He rose from the divan on which he had been sitting and walked towards the window. Except that his complexion is dark and he is short of stature, he looked not unlike the portraits of General Robert E. Lee, the contour of the nose being particularly striking.

ONLY INCIDENTALS DIFFER

'All the religions of the world are the same fundamentally,' said Dr. Fareed, stepping forward to offer to epitomize the Bahaist teaching. 'The essentials are the same, but the incidentals or accidentals differ. We believe the day has arrived where we can agree on the surface differences. Religious prejudice, racial prejudice and limited or nationalistic patriotism must be eliminated. The world can be unified.

'I do not offer this as a full exposition of the principles of Bahaism, but merely by way of guidance.'

SPEAKS TWICE TODAY

Mirza Mahmood had spoken of the Bahas, pronouncing it Bay-highs. But Dr. Fareed said it more like Bahhees. The correct spelling Dr. Fareed said, is Beha, but the Americanization of it has become Baha and is now commonly used. Dr. Woolson pleaded with Abdul Baha to visit St. Paul. Mr. Hall presented his program for approval. It was suggested that the distinguished visitor lunch at the Commercial Club at noon and speak in the assembly room after lunch.

'Will there be many there?' he asked through his interpreter.

'Not as many as if we made it tomorrow and the people knew Abdul Baha would be present,' said Mr. Hall.

The leader considered. He walked about. He shook hands with several visitors, and his hand felt like a silken glove. H. S. Fugeta, a Japanese from Cleveland, who had joined the party at Chicago, came in and knelt beside a window chair where Abdul Baha had seated himself, and the leader placed his hands on the head of the kneeling man and uttered a prayer in Persian. The syllables were strangely effective and rhythmetrical. Mirza Ahmed Sohrab translated it aloud.

'Your spiritual growth is noteworthy; you are becoming stronger your spirit is awake and you will be happy,' was the less poetic English rendition of part of it.

It was finally arranged that Abdul Baha should speak at the Commercial Club at noon, call during an automobile trip today at the home of Dr. Woolson in St. Paul, and at the residence of Albert H. Hall, 2030 Queen Avenue S, and speak tonight at the Jewish Reform temple, Tenth Street and Fifth Avenue S, admission to be free to all. There will be a short reception after the address at which people interested in Bahaism will have an opportunity to meet the leader of the movement. It was a program with physical effort enough in it to tax the abilities of a political campaigner, but Abdul Baha made light of that part of it.

He drew aside and stepped into another room. Those in parlor 603 sat waiting for him to return. In the other room he said, with traveler's phrase book accent:

'How do you do? I hope you are well.' The words came with surprising distinctness, but did not seem to carry with them indication of much more to come, nor did Abdul Baha make any pretension in that direction. To a question as to his mission, he waved his hand toward Dr. Fareed, who had entered the room. Mirza Mahmood had also come in silently. One sat upon the bed, the other, in a cane chair; and Abdul Baha seated himself at a window that looked out upon the blank wall of the Plaza enclosure. He looked long and silently at the wall.

Dr. Fareed rose and said:

'He is about to give a message to the people of Minneapolis.

'May I ask,' continued Dr. Fareed, 'that this message be taken exactly as he gives it? I ask this because, while it is not the case that any great numbers of the American people might as yet be interested in it, the people of Persia are profoundly interested, and all that is done by Abdul Baha on this journey and all that he says is sent back to Persia.'

He bowed very courteously, reseated himself and Abdul Baha began.

'I was in the orient and I learned that the western regions had advanced and I thought it opportune to visit these parts,' he said, his musical accents passing to Dr. Fareed and thence back in the harsher

English. 'Here I have come, to find, in reality, that material advancement has assumed noteworthy proportions.

"Day by day this country is advancing. The government is fair and the people are a noble people. I pray that this nation may advance day after day, that education may advance, that industrialism and commercialism may advance, and that the arts and literature shall advance.

'I pray that happiness may daily become greater. But all these are advances in the world of natural civilization. It is more favorable that there be advances in divine civilization.

'Natural philosophy is progressing, but divine philosophy is also necessary, because natural civilization is like the body, whereas divine civilization is like the spirit. Natural civilization serves the world of bodies. Divine civilization serves the world of morality.

'The body without the animus of the spirit is dead."

The word animus, as used commonly in America, seemed scarcely the right word here, but Dr. Fareed translated it so. He then said it meant animation spiritually. 'Without the spirit the body is lukewarm," the leader continued.

Abdul Baha stared long at the blank wall. His eyes were open, but he seemed to be looking afar. For some time he waited, then he said:

AMERICA'S SPIRITUAL NEEDS

'The American democracy is most beautiful, but it is in need of the breath of the holy spirit, in order to become exhilarated and that its beauty may become manifest.

'The holy men of God, like Christ, were founders of divine civilization. His (Christ's) life illustrated the world of morality. He adorned it. Christ was not an engineer, a geographer, a geologist, a mathematician or a natural philosopher, but he thought of the beauties of the holy spirit and illumined the world of morality.

'His holiness, Baha'o'ullah, through the bounties of heaven and the effulgence of the Son of Israel in the orient, illumined the world of morality and founded divine civilization. He ignited the lamp which will never be extinguished. He laid a foundation which will never be destroyed.'[11]

This account was the basis of a shorter article that appeared in the *St. Paul Dispatch*, a Republican newspaper with a circulation of 64,500 copies.[12]

The *Minneapolis Morning Tribune*, a Republican newspaper with a circulation of 91,800 copies, was also one of the first local newspapers to report 'Abdu'l-Bahá's movements in the city:

'PROPHET OF GLORY' VISITS MINNEAPOLIS

'ABDU'L-BAHÁ, WHITE OF BEARD AND GENTLE OF MIEN, GREETS FOLLOWERS

HIS SPEECH IS ARABIC, HIS WALK LIKE THAT OF KIM'S LLAMA

HE PREACHES THE GOSPEL OF UNIVERSAL PEACE AND LANGUAGE

Groups of curious people watched the progress through Loring Park this morning of an aged man with a white turban and a flowing white beard, who walked with his hands behind his back, and was followed by a group of fez-crowned men, who spoke in low voices and paid the aged man great deference.

Passersby who were attracted by the strange group followed through the park at some little distance.

The aged man was Adbul Baha, from the Far East, 'Prophet of the Glory', and head of the new religion whose followers seek universal peace. Abdul Baha arrived in Minneapolis late last night and is stopping with his four disciples at the Plaza Hotel. Two of his disciples are from Persia, one from Russia and one from Japan.

Abdul Baha is one of the most picturesque religious figures in the Orient. He is 68 years old and was imprisoned for 50 years, for his beliefs. The Baha has several hundred followers in the Twin Cities and thousands in the United States. Albert H. Hall of Minneapolis is one of the principal followers, and Mrs. H. McCutcheon and Dr H. S. Harper of Minneapolis are also numbered in his following.

The Baha and his disciples, including some Twin City followers, took a half-hour's constitutional in Loring Park. Under a loose coat of flannel the Baha wore loose-fitting trousers and white rough woolen socks that had rolled down over low shoes, which were like the bedroom slippers of the Western world.

The Baha walked slowly, contemplating the beauties of the park and watching the swans float on the mirror-like lake in Loring Park. He seemed to be absorbing the sunshine. The knots of followers were a few paces to the rear. They spoke in low voices and approached the Baha with deference. To his interpreter the Baha spoke in Arabic. His only words in English are 'Very nice' and 'Very good'.

'Newspapers,' said the Bahá, 'must be the first means of amity and understanding amongst men. All men must be the servants of one God, all must be united. Newspapers must be the heralds of the oneness of humanity. Morality must be reinstated in the world.

'The time has come for the world of humanity to hoist the standard of the oneness of the human world, so that unity may connect all the nations of the world, so that dogmatic formulas and superstition may end, so that essential reality underlying all the religions founded by all the prophets may be revealed.'

'Abdu'l-Bahá recognizes all the different saviors and prophets. Jesus, Mohammed, Buddha, Confucius, Bah Ullah – all were necessary to their time and place. He believes in monogamic marriages and woman suffrage and in a universal language.

'Abdu'l-Bahá spoke at noon today at the Commercial Club and will speak tomorrow night at the Shaari Tov temple, Fifth Avenue South and Tenth Street. He will leave Minneapolis tomorrow night. He has visited all the larger cities of the East, and a temple is soon to be built in Chicago.[13]

Among those who visited 'Abdu'l-Bahá in Minneapolis was Rabbi Dr. Samuel Deinard (1873–1921), of the first reformist synagogue of Minneapolis, the Shaari Tov (today know as Temple of Israel), who was also the founder of the *Jewish Weekly* and its successor, the *American Jewish World*. In the course of their meeting Dr Deinard spoke of 'Abdu'l-Bahá in high terms and invited Him to speak in his synagogue on Friday, 20 September.[14] In His talk to the Jews, the Master touched on some of the same points He would address weeks later in the famous talk delivered at the Emanu-El synagogue in San Francisco.[15]

An account in the *Minneapolis Morning Tribune* summarized the contents and quoted extensively from the words of the Master:

TEMPLE SHAARI TOV

MOSES AND THE MISSION OF JESUS CHRIST

ABDUL BAHA

Speaking at the Hebrew Temple, Abdul Baha, the Persian teacher, gave his message from the Far East to his brethren of the Western hemisphere. The message dealt with Moses and Christ and was a plea for peace among all religions and sects. Dr. A. U. Fareed interpreted the sermon. Abdul Baha was introduced by Albert Hall. He spoke, in part, as follows: 'I wish to speak to you a few words concerning a reality. But that which I shall discourse on this evening I invite you to compare with reason. If you find that it agrees with your reason accept it, and if you find it disagreeable with reason accept it not.

'Therefore in my discourse this evening I wish you to compare carefully with your reasonable standard from the beginning of history up to this day of ours.

'Among mankind there has ever existed warfare and contention, strife and rancor have been rampant. Bloodshed and rampage have been prevalent.

'Why? Because misunderstandings among the religionists have existed. This misunderstanding has caused the destruction of the world of humanity; men thereby have shed the blood of each other and have taken in captivity the offspring of each other. Every weak religion and religious nation has been subjected to the tyranny and bondage of great religions.

'Enough of misunderstanding. Praise be to God a century of illumination has come, a century of science and precise knowledge of progressiveness and advancement. Among the great world religions is that of Moses, of Christ and Mohammed. Consider what a vast misunderstanding exists among these. All the religions sanctify and glorify Moses. This unique and single personage was appointed a guardian among the Israelites at the time when they were in the utmost of bondage. He was the cause of rescuing this people, and led them to the land of promise. Even the Greek philosophers were wont to come to Palestine to study with the student disciples of Solomon.

'But now listen to this fairly. Until the appearance of Jesus Christ, the name of Moses was confined to Palestine, and up to that time the Old Testament, The Torah, was only to be found in the Hebrew tongue. It was His Holiness Christ who was instrumental in having the Old Testament translated into 700 languages. Even if you go to the regions of Central Africa yon will find the Old Testament in their vernacular tongues.

'Who has done this? No doubt Christ has done this. But the Israelites did not know this. Here we are living in a century of reality. It is not a century of tradition. The people of Israel have certain traditions and certain heresy, the Christians have their history, the

Mohammedans have their traditions and narrations. What can you rely on, for they are all contradictory. All mankind is created as an image and likeness of God. In some that image is evident and in others it is potential. Some have been ignited and in some the likenesses are still to be ignited. We must not have contentions; we must not entertain enmity towards each other. We must not speak ill of each other. Let it be known that we are all the servants of one God.

'Praise be to God we are all the servants of one God. We adore one God. We turn to one God and we are the servants of Him, and we are immersed in His ocean. Let one be Mosaic, but free him from the prejudice, it is useless to have that. If a Christian should have prejudice it is nonsense. If a Mohammedan should retain prejudice that is nonsense. No doubt that these prejudices are caused by utter ignorance, and we supplicate and pray to the Kingdom of God, that He may confirm us to act in accordance with the teachings of Baha Ullah and to hoist the banner of the oneness of the world and humanity, and that racial prejudice and religions prejudice and patriotic prejudice and political prejudice, which are destructive, shall be removed from among men.'[16]

A much shorter account was also published in the *Pioneer Press* (St Paul), a newspaper with a circulation of 49,200 copies, quoting the following portions of the address:

'Jesus loved Moses,' said Abdul Baha, 'Joshua loved Moses and Jesus loved Joshua, Mohammed loved Jesus and Moses both, and Jesus loved all the prophets. Why should there be hatred?' Why should the Christians, Jews, and Moslems hate each other? If the founders of our great creed believe that there is but one God who created us all, who loves us all and in whom we all believe, why should we fight each other on the battle field, why should we hate each other?

'In all the world of humanity there is no bestowal greater than reason. If we reason we will have no wars. We can all live in perfect accord if we reason. Let us correct the misunderstandings in religion and we will have international peace.'[17]

On 20 September, the *Morning Tribune* published an article describing some prosaic scenes during a walk of the Master in the city:

ABDUL BAHA IN AWE, CONTEMPLATES STYLES

PERSIAN PHILOSOPHER STANDS LONG BEFORE NICOLLET AVENUE WINDOW

HE IS ATTRACTED BY THE LATEST FASHIONS IN FEMININE GOWNS

On Nicollet Avenue yesterday morning before a shop window in which were displayed the dashing, chic creations of the Parisian purveyors to woman's fancy, there stood an aged man, about whom fitfully there gathered from time to time, as is the way of passersby, a little knot of people. Behind the aged man, deferent, respectful, were several fez crowned Easternmen. This aged man was Abdul Baha, leader of the Bahaist movement, who has passed the last two days in Minneapolis greeting followers who live in the Twin Cities. The fez crowned folk were members of his retinue, and also there were several Americans conventionally garbed.

Abdul Baha was out, apparently to view the fall fashion show, and the show was there. Panniers there were and scant skirts and other materials of the mode, in brilliant color combinations. Here was a puzzling to-a-man-out of skirt, scalloped in front at the lower hem as if to reveal the silk-clad insteps of milady. The array was alluring, even to friend husband. And to a Baha!

WORE LOOSE BROWN COAT

The Baha wore a loose brown coat, like a very negligee kimono combined with a bath robe. It was mended about the pockets and it hung loosely about the figure. On his feet were rough, American-made shoes – no such shoes as your man of the business world wears, but suitable, nevertheless, for keeping out the cold and for withstanding wear. His long white hair was tucked up under his white turban; his long white beard swept his breast. To right or left he cast no straying glance; his whole attention centered, through his extraordinary sympathetic eyes, upon the silks and filmy textures in the window.

But those curiosity seekers who halted caught never a word from the Persian gazing at the fashion show. Contemplatively he stood there for a long time, it seemed to those who waited for comment. For Abdul Baha is a philosopher. And in this he had it on the men of the Western world who now and then tarry to wonder what woman will wear next. The Baha is a philosopher – and he keeps his own counsel.

SCORNS AUTOMOBILE

Finally he turned and gently motioned his retinue toward the next street crossing. He was to have returned to the Plaza Hotel by automobile, but seemingly he determined upon another modern form of conveyance, for he chose the street car instead. He walked slowly to the front of the car and took a seat by himself where he could think. His party seated themselves in groups of two behind him, keeping a watchful eye on him, but not interrupting his thought.

On the Walker Art Gallery, which he visited later, the Baha was more communicative. He said he had visited galleries of the Old World, but he deemed the Walker Gallery a remarkable one, comparing favorably with others.

'Opening a gallery with such wonderful treasures within it so that the rich and poor alike may come and see is putting something beautiful into life and giving service to humanity. I am pleased.'

The Baha and his followers went for a drive about the city and in the afternoon attended a 4 o'clock tea at the home of Mrs. Roy D. Herrick. In the afternoon the party visited the University of Minnesota. In the evening the Baha met his followers and those who were especially interested in his movement at the home of Mrs. Albert H. Hall, 2030 Queen Avenue South.

Abdul Baha left Minneapolis last night for Omaha.[18]

While in Minneapolis 'Abdu'l-Bahá made, at the invitation of the local Bahá'í Dr Clement Woolson, a brief visit to St Paul. The *St. Paul Dispatch* announced the visit on the same day and reported that 'Dr. Woolson expects a representative gathering in which will be members of the Theosophical Society'.[19] Another announcement was published in *The Appeal.*[20]

The Pioneer Press (St Paul) published an account of the meeting at the home of Dr Woolson that also included some general notes about 'Abdu'l-Bahá and the Bahá'í Faith not reproduced here:

URGES ALL RACES TO SINGLE FAITH

ABDUL BAHA TELLS ST. PAUL AUDIENCE OF HIS PLANS TO REGENERATE MANKIND HAS SUFFERED FOR OPINIONS

LEADER OF NEW CULT CITES COLUMBUS AS AN EXAMPLE OF VICTORY THROUGH SACRIFICE

Abdul Baha, leader of Bahaism, which seeks to reunite mankind in its moral, spiritual and physical attributes addressed an interested gathering of those following his teachings at the home of Dr. Clement Woolson, 870 Laurel Avenue, last night. The 'Servant of Glory' as he styles himself, showed the wide variance between man in the animal state such as he is in when born and what he can attain to in spiritual life. He said in part: 'Man in the beginning is a habitant of a world of gloom and darkness. In the passage of time he finally becomes born into this world of nature from which he receives light. But he is still in the natural or animal state and as he attains maturity it is the purpose of God that he be born again from this natural world into the divine world. As Christ said: 'That which is born-of flesh is flesh and that which is born of spirit is spirit.'

CITES TRIALS OF COLUMBUS

'Consider Columbus and the trials arid tribulations he underwent in his efforts to discover a new world. Think of how he sacrificed all he had and suffered unspeakable hardships to carry out his purpose. The human race should emulate Columbus that it may strive with undaunted courage to discover this new world; the world of reality that it may come into a new light, a new life, a new consciousness and eternal station. This is the object which we should all strive to attain.'

In the course of his remarks, which were given through an interpreter, Abdul Baha referred to his own sufferings as a prisoner of Abdul Hamid, the deposed sultan of Turkey.

'I am an old man and have suffered much,' he said, 'but the light of divine attraction has brought me here to you tonight that we may associate in the utmost love and unity.'[21]

The day 'Abdu'l-Bahá departed from Minneapolis the *Journal* published the following summary of His activities in the city:

EDUCATORS MEET ABDUL BAHA ABBAS

CLERGYMEN ALSO INVITED TO TEA GIVEN BY BAHAIST LEADER – 400 HEAR HIM SPEAK

Abdul Baha Abbas, head of the Bahaists, whose arrival in Minneapolis was followed yesterday by a reception at the Plaza, luncheon at the Commercial Club, a trip to St. Paul and an evening address at the Jewish Reform temple, was the guest late today of Mrs. R. D. Herrick at a tea at her home, 1413 Harmon Place. Earlier today Abdul Baha and the members of his party accepted the invitation of T. B. Walker to visit the Walker Art Gallery. Mrs. Herrick's invitation list included Dr. and Mrs. George K. Vincent, Professor F. L. Washburn and Professor George F. James of the university, other university men and women and a number of the local clergymen, including Dr. Marion D. Shutter and Rev. C. D. Darling of Stewart Memorial church. Mrs. Herrick's sister, Miss Ethel Sanderson, who lives in Paris, is a follower of the teaching of Abdul Baha. Mrs. Herrick's entertainment was so planned and timed that opportunity might be given the university people and others who might not otherwise be able to hear the distinguished Persian.

Tonight Mrs. Albert H. Hall, 2030 Queen Avenue S, will receive informally for Abdul Baha.

SPEAKS TO 400

At the Jewish Reform temple, Tenth Street and Fifth Avenue S, before 400 people, Abdul Baha spoke last night, through Dr. Fareed, his interpreter, in outline of his teaching, and one basic principle upon which he and his followers are working was explained by him in the following words:

'Christ loved and venerated Moses and the Mosaic teaching, and Mohammed loved and venerated Christ and Moses. One great teacher loved and venerated that great teacher whose work had gone before. Yet where is there greater difference to be found today than that between Jew, Christian and Mohammedan? At the foundation of all are the same great basic truths.'

Unless his plans are changed by something unforeseen, Abdul Baha and his party will leave tomorrow morning for the west. He will go to San Francisco for a stay of probably a week or longer.[22]

After 'Abdu'l-Bahá's departure from Minneapolis the weekly local magazine *The Bellman* published a brief note to explain to its readers who was 'the venerable whitebearded and turbaned figure in oriental dress, who sat on one of the benches, apparently lost in the contemplation of the infinite', and who attracted the 'attention of pedestrians passing through one of the city parks on a morning of last week'.[23]

Omaha, Nebraska

From Minneapolis 'Abdu'l-Bahá travelled to Omaha where He arrived on Saturday, 21 September, just two hours after midnight. His visit to Omaha lasted only one day in the course of which two reporters interviewed him. At least one account of His arrival was published in the local *Daily News*, an independent newspaper with a circulation of 60,200 copies:

> PERSIAN, WITH TITLE OF PROPHET, IN OMAHA
>
> ABDUL-BAHA ABBAS, SON OF HEAD OF GREAT RELIGIOUS SECT, ADVOCATED WORLD PEACE
>
> HE HAS MANY SERVANTS
>
> Abdul-Baha Abbas of Persia, son of the head of a great religious sect in that country and a devoted advocate of the world peace movement, is in Omaha attended by a retinue of six secretaries and several servants. He is in this country to see what it is like and to learn present day reforms.
>
> Abdul Baha Abbas has found America very much as he had pictured it and said he is pleased with the people and their customs.
>
> The Persian peace advocate looks to be at least 80, but is only 68, his look of age being caused by the many years he spent in Turkish and Persian prisons because of his teachings.
>
> Like his father he has devoted the greater part of his life to religious teaching, publishing many books even from his prison cell. He was in prison nearly 40 years.
>
> That universal peace is the most important question before the world was asserted by the Persian reformer. He said his coming to Omaha immediately after Theodore Roosevelt and the Baroness von Suttner, both winners of the Nobel peace prize, was a mere coincidence.

If we can secure universal peace, we will soon follow it with a universal religion and comfort and security will come to all, for the diplomats and statesmen will turn their thoughts to the needs of the people rather than to war and preparations of war, he said.

In his own country Abdul Baha is given the title of prophet and is believed by his followers to have supernatural powers, but this he denies and says he lays no claim to be aught but one of the workers.

He will be in Omaha until Tuesday when he goes to Denver and then West.[24]

Lincoln, Nebraska

From Omaha, 'Abdu'l-Bahá reached Lincoln early in the morning of Sunday, 22 September. He intended to visit the politician William J. Bryan, who years earlier had met the Master in 'Akká (see chapter 1). Bryan, however, was travelling to campaign for Woodrow Wilson. 'Abdu'l-Bahá nevertheless met His wife, Mary Bryan, and wrote a short prayer in Bryan's guest book: 'Bless this family and grant it happiness in both this world and the world to come. Confirm this distinguished person in the greatest service to the human world, which is the unity of all mankind that he may attain to Thy good pleasure in this world and obtain a bounteous portion from the surging ocean of Divine outpourings in this luminous age.'[25]

'Abdu'l-Bahá also received reporters from Lincoln's two local daily newspapers, the Republican *Daily News* and the independent *Daily Star*. The article published in the *News*, which at the time had a circulation of 32,100 copies, was the most complete and quoted abundantly from the words of the Master:

> PERSIAN PEACE ADVOCATE PAYS VISIT TO LINCOLN
>
> Abdul-Baha Abbas, Persian exponent of the doctrine of international peace and son of Baha Ollah, who paid with his life for doctrines advanced in his native country, arrived in Lincoln this morning accompanied by his interpreter and four other traveling companions. Arriving in Lincoln at 9 o'clock, the party remaining only a few hours and took advantage of the time to call upon the family of W. J. Bryan, whom Abdul-Baha met while the latter was touring the world.
>
> Following almost identically the line of work that brought

Baroness von Suttner to Lincoln last week, the elderly Persian is conducting his work by a different means. He is the follower of a religion of his father, a religion in which the doctrine of peace among nations, among all people and among religions is predominant. Speaking no English, Abdul-Baha is conducting his work with the aid of an interpreter, and numerous addresses have been delivered in America since the Persian's arrival in this country last spring.

VISITED BRYAN HOME

Clothed in flowing robes and white cap and wearing the long white beard of the patriarchs of his native land, Abdul-Baha was to be seen for a few hours this morning, previous to motoring to the Bryan home. Kindly and smilingly, he received visitors in his room at the hotel and with the aid of Dr. Ameen U. Fareed, the interpreter, he carried on a brilliant conversation in which he set forth his work, his plans and his ideals. In true oriental courtesy, he expressed sorrow at the parting, bade the visitor Godspeed and slipped a token, a bit of jewelry, into his hand as a token of his pleasure and as a souvenir of himself.

A large part of his conversation was about his favorite theme, peace between nations and the abolishment of all warfare, but he also expressed his views on religion as well as other topics. That religion of the moderns is out of date, is not in harmony with the modern keeping of things, is his opinion, but nevertheless Abdul loves God in his own way and insists that the Hebrews made the gravest error of their race when they crucified Christ. On the matter of religion, the elderly Persian would have but little to say, merely stating that he realized that in doing so he might offend the people of the country he was visiting. His work was outlined for him, he said, and he was here solely in the interests of international peace, a doctrine advanced by his martyred father fifty years ago.

WORKING FOR PEACE

'I am Persian, I am a Bahai. I have come to America to visit the country, for I have heard that the American people are a peace loving people and I believe in peace. Therefore, I have come to see to what extent this peace propaganda has expressed itself in America,' said Abdul-Baha this morning.

'Being a Bahai means to be a follower of Baha-Ollah. When his holiness appeared in Persia, He enunciated certain teachings which people in all parts of the world have followed and are following. Among the teachings of Baha-Ollah is one relative to international peace. Again it is peace between religions; universal peace between races; peace between countries of all the world.

'Baha-Ollah founded these teachings in Persia fifty years ago. He wrote to many kings, and rulers of the world in regard to these principles. Innumerable souls from among the various nations, different religions and different communities became his followers, united and agreed.

'They expressed great love and fellowship for each other, while formerly they were most hostile toward each other. They killed each other; they stole each other's property, taking in captivity each other's wives and children.

'Now they have become united as one great family. He – Baha-Ollah – illuminated the east with these lights. Among his teachings was the oneness of the world of humanity. Another of his teachings is relative to the harmony of science and religion. Again it is to leave behind religious prejudice; to quit racial prejudice; to overlook patriotic and political prejudice.

'Fifty years ago he wrote to kings and rulers that an international tribunal should be organized to which representatives from all nations in the world should be sent; such a tribunal as should be ratified by all parliaments of the world and to which all international disputes should be taken. If any nation goes contrary to the tribunal's final judgment then all nations may combine to force that one to abide by its decision. Such a tribunal will be under the protection of all humanity. Then international peace will be proclaimed and humanity will thereby find rest and security.

'In reality the warfare in the present century is beyond endurance. Everything which is earned by the farmers is taxed for the preparation of armies and navies. Therefore war is continuous and although souls are not lost yet it is a constant financial drain which in the end equals the dire results of the loss of life.

'For example, there is a war going on between Turkey and Italy. So many lives are destroyed: so much wealth is wasted! If the international tribunal were organized this problem would have found solution, and there is no doubt that this tribunal would have arbitrated and the bloodshed would have been stopped.

'From the beginning of history, wars and battles have been waged between nations. How many countries of the world have been destroyed, how many millions killed, how much property and how much wealth pillaged, how many women and children taken into captivity!

'Now it is enough. This century has lightened. Thoughts are expanded; education has spread; these evils of war have become manifest. Therefore that which is befitting this illumined century is the proclamation of peace and all ferociousness wiped away entirely, for the ferocious beasts are characterized by these attributes.

'His holiness Baha-Ollah, like unto the Sun, appeared in Persia and promulgated these teachings in the orient. The governments of the east rose against him and oppressed himself and his followers most violently. He was fifty years in banishment, exile and imprisonment and he at last departed this world while in prison.

'I was a prisoner myself up to the time that the young Turks proclaimed freedom in 1908. They dealt justly with me. The government realized that I had not committed crime except by doing a service to humanity. Therefore they gave me freedom.

'Now I am traveling over the world spreading the principles of international peace; the oneness of the world. I am trying to dispel the clouds of misunderstanding so that all peoples of the world may find happiness and peace.' Although former governments of the orient, which were tyrannical and despot strove to extinguish the lamp of Baha-Ollah, Baha, with the powers of the Holy Spirit, spread his teachings and while in prison raised the standard of the world of humanity.

The party is working westward and this afternoon left for Denver. Abdul-Baha spoke in Omaha last night, arriving in that city from Minneapolis. Accompanying him in the party besides Dr. Fareed are Mirza Ahmad Sohrab, Mirza Ali Akbar, Mirza Mahmood and a Japanese servant. All in the party are cultured and well educated, two speaking English with little accent.[26]

The *Star*, which at the time had a circulation of near 19,400 copies, published the following account:

ABBAS BRINGS NEW CREED TO LINCOLN

Advocating the teachings originated by his father, tending toward the unification of humanity, and known as the Bahaollah movement, Abdul Baha Abbas and his retinue of interpreters arrived in Lincoln Sunday evening and spent the major part of Monday in the city. A visit was paid by the elderly apostle of the religious movement to the home of William J. Bryan, but the commoner was out of the city and he was disappointed at not being able to see him.

Bahaollah is a religious movement founded many years ago by the Abdul's father, and since his earliest childhood he has been advocating the teachings of which he conversed freely through the medium of an interpreter. Without the least hesitancy Abdul Baha carried on a conversation Monday afternoon with his interpreter in Persian and with his Lincoln countrymen he conversed in Arabic, directing one sentence at the interpreter and following this with another to his Lincoln visitors.

Of his teaching he spoke through his interpreter, stating that Bahaollah aims towards the unification of humanity, the oneness of nativity, and declared that all humanity was the servant of one God and was of one species.

'All people belong to one nativity,' declared Abdul Baha. 'For the earth's sphere is one, and all humanity is the progenity of one. We are all submerged in the sea of the mercy of one God.'

PREJUDICES DESTROYED

'According to the teaching of Bahaoallah, racial prejudices, political and patriotic prejudices are destroying the foundations of humanity. So long as the world is not free from these prejudices, construction, progress and peace is impossible, and the human world will not be composed and secure. Among the teachings of Bahaoallah is the fact that the fundamental principle of everything is one. This foundation of the world is one reality and this reality is neither multipliable nor divisible. Where the difference in religions is found is in the dogma, hence the difference causes enmity among religions. The difference in human physiognomy, though having a realistic basis, nevertheless it is the cause of strife which has only an idealistic basis.'

Abdul Baha advanced many other ideas regarding the religion which he advocated. For these he was forced to spend forty years of his life in a Turkish prison in Syria, where he was visited by Mr. Bryan on the latter's trip around the world. He is an aged man, 68 years of age, and when the Young Turks revolutionized the government of Turkey, Abdul Baha was given his freedom, as it was learned that he had committed no crime, but had only taught a religion contrary to the ideas of the government then in vogue.

He has been in America about six months, and of Lincoln he spoke very highly. He declared himself as being pleased with the Lincoln air, and the cleanliness of the city. The Abdul attracts attention wherever he goes. At the Lincoln Hotel Monday he was the center of all eyes because of his Persian dress, his long white hair and beard, and the spotless white turban which he wore.[27]

Denver

'Abdu'l-Bahá left Lincoln at 11:00 in the evening, reaching Denver at 2:00 in the afternoon of Tuesday, 24 September. It was a long trip by train but the Master preferred to occupy a seat cabin rather than more comfortable accommodation. When the party arrived at Hotel Shirley, where 'Abdu'l-Bahá was to stay, a group of newspaper reporters were waiting to interview Him and they were requested to come back a bit later and allow Him some rest after the long trip.[28] Days before, some articles had been published in the local press announcing His arrival and containing summaries of the Bahá'í teachings and history as well as interviews with local Bahá'ís.[29]

At least three journalists visited the Master requesting interviews with Him. One of them was Alice Rohe[30] of the *Rocky Mountains News*, an independent newspaper with a circulation of 29,000 copies. She described the Master as 'impressive' and confessed herself to have been 'thrilled for an hour by the flow of sonorous words that rolled from the lips of this man of the Orient':

NEW JOHN THE BAPTIST PREACHING UNIVERSAL BROTHERHOOD

Abdul Baha Patriarchal Head of Bahaists in Denver With Message of Love and Justice to All and for All

'Venerable Impressive and Imposing Figure From Oriental Lands Comes to Give Asking Nothing But to Be Heard'

BY ALICE ROHE

A venerable man – like a patriarch of old – his gray beard falling upon his breast, his white locks surmounted by a white turban, his erect figure draped in the flowing garments of Persia – this is Abdul Baha Abbas Effendi – 'Servant of God', teacher of universal religion, universal peace, universal brotherhood.

When I say this is Abdul Baha, the statement refers only to the first fleeting impression of this head of the Bahai movement who is in Denver spreading the message of brotherly love of the universal religion which will be the foundation of interreligious, interracial and international brotherhood.

For when this aged man – whose presence in the dominant personality defies age – speaks, when the keen dark eyes become afire with the words he utters, the first impression of Abdul Baha becomes but a superficial one. Yesterday afternoon at the Shirley Hotel, surrounded by a staff of attendants, chief of whom is the vividly intelligent and finely educated Dr. Ameen U. Fareed, I was thrilled for an hour by the flow of sonorous words that rolled from the lips of this man of the Orient who has a message for all this world.

Not understanding a word that Abdul Baha said in his native tongue, the calm of 'the master' broken at times by an impetuous ardor as he raised small slender hands in expressing a thought, his words quickly translated with a beautiful understanding by Dr. Fareed, gave to the interview an impressiveness that is seldom possible when interpretation from one language to another is necessary.

The son of Baha'o'llah, whose coming 'the Bab' foretold, Abdul Baha brings the message from his father, the founder of the Bahai movement.

UNDERLYING LOVE OF HUMANITY

The most impressive feeling that one receives in talking to this patriarchal messenger from Persia is his broad humanity, his love of humankind underlying the deep spirituality of his teaching and his deep love of God, in whom is all knowledge.

Yesterday afternoon, listening to the rolling sentences quickly translated by Dr. Fareed, the interruption of an afternoon tea drinking according to American custom would have been extremely incongruous.

But this man of deep sympathies, who shrinks from exploitation of his own personality, who wishes to get this message of brotherly, love of unity, to all mankind, is as simple as only dignity and nobility of character understands simplicity.

The conversation of Abdul Baha did not even stop even as we drank our Persian tea together. And for the benefit of tea drinkers let me add that until one has sipped this fragrant tea of Persia served in small glasses pored over two lumps of sugar and stirred with a tiny spoon on a plate of Persian design, one has never tasted tea. Then it was with the aroma of that fragrant tea permeating the room with a soft and subtle perfume that Abdul Baha added more light upon the Bahai movement of which he is the present head and which has witnessed the martyrdom of 'the Bab' and the forty years' imprisonment and exile of Baha'o'llah.

BROAD AND SWEEPING PHILOSOPHY

Questions concerning the actions of progressives and reformers of the woman's suffrage movement being but an outcome of the teachings of Bahaism were answered, but in broad sweeping philosophy of Abdul Baha's own style:

'The contingent world is typical of man as the microcosm the human organism. Just as the microcosm, the human organization goes through successive embryonic steps, beginning with embryonic origin through the fetal, to stages of maturity, likewise does this contingent world. In man we find in the period of maturity unfolding signs of intelligence and the virtuous characteristic of the world of humanity. Therefore we can say that the development of man from the beginning was a preparation for the laying of a foundation for the culminating event, which was intellection. All these physical processes expressed in metabolism are for the same purpose of ripening into a reasonable being. The reason of mind in the human world is the great goal toward which the organism works. The greatest of all reforming movements appeared bearing the same relation to the world at large as the mind in maturity bears to the human being. This was no other than the coming of Baha'o'llah. Bahaism appeared in the Orient and has founded the divine civilization because civilization is of two kinds, material and divine, natural civilization and the civilization of the kingdom. Inasmuch as these constitute a great issue which transpired in this century, the manifestation of Baha'o'llah in the East was like the dawning of the sun, was like the dawn of the great mind. And it revolutionized the Oriental world. The development is like unto a tree. It has put out leafage and branches and has blossomed. But like the tree, all these are only the beginnings preparatory to fruitage.'

TEACHES UNIVERSAL COUNCIL

As Abdul Baha spoke, leaning back in a chair drawn near the window of his room in this hotel, he glanced from the rain flecked leaves of a swaying tree skating its branches near the panes of glass. The gray bearded man with the message of universal religion wrinkled his high forehead at times and occasionally closed his eyes, as though looking into the future for the realization of the message which he believes is finding material ground for fruitage in America.

'Among the teaching of Baha'o'llah,' he continued, 'is that of a universal council.' Indeed the father of Abdul Baha – the promised one of whom the Bab prophesied to come bearing the divine truth – met imprisonment and exile through his teaching of universal justice.

'His teachings are for a universal council among all races for all nations for all religions.'

Abdul Baha then spoke of his father with an added reverence in his voice: 'Fifty years ago Baha'o'llah wrote to all the kings and crowned heads of the earth presenting the need of the world for a court of justice, the members of which shall be elected delegates representing all nations and governments of the world. The parliaments of every nation must have two delegates elected at large from each nation whereof the world's court shall be composed.

'All international disputes and intergovernmental problems shall be presented for settlement to this court of justice.

'If in case a nation should go contrary to the decrees and court, the world of humanity would arise against the rebel power.

'This was declared fifty years ago by Baha'o'llah. His addresses were published in India and were spread all over the continent. However the royalty of Persia arose against Baha'o'llah, being of the deepest despotic form of government. For fifty years he endured horrible ordeals. He was either in exile or prison but through the power of the Holy spirit he spread through the world his teachings.'

Abdul Baha was a young boy when his father was first thrown into prison and the gray-haired man who is now in Denver himself suffered forty years along with his father imprisonment and exile, receiving from the head of the Babism his instructions.

'Religion ought to be the cause of "love"', he continued. 'The foundation of Divine religion is love. Hence it must be ever the cause of love and fellowship among men. And if religion proves the cause of hatred and enmity and a factor in murder and rapine, it is better to do without it.'

The son of Baha'o'llah speaks always of his beliefs as being the teaching of his father. A favorite way of making his statements is:

'Among the teachings of Baha'o'llah is that relating to a universal language, which shall be the means of international communication. He speaks for a general spirit of education. It is the duty of a father to educate his children. If he cannot then it is the duty of the body politic to educate the child.'

PIONEER OF EQUAL SUFFRAGE

A system of social economy goes hand in hand with the Bahai movement and interesting it is to note the position of woman in their scheme of life entire. Indeed the Bahaists claim the forethought of the equal suffrage movement.

Abdul Baha, speaking of education, does not hesitate to say since women are the mothers of the race, a father who has not money enough to educate both boys and girls should choose daughters as the recipients of culture.

Speaking of civilization natural and divine, Abdul Baha says that the natural is not sufficient for it tends toward bodies while divine civilization is on the realm of morality. Were it not for divine civilization, the world of men would be akin to animals. All the divine holy manifestations were the founders of the godlike civilization. The first and foremost of such a civilization was Jesus Christ.

Asked whether he thought woman, with her awakened responsibilities and realization of her own individual rights, would be largely instrumental in the regeneration of society, Abdul Baha said:

The accomplishments of wonderful women in our own times gives us the keen anticipation of many extraordinary women in the future. So far as equality is concerned, both men and women must be equal. Men and women are as wings bearing humanity aloft. If one wing is weak the flight is hampered. Both wings must be equally strong in order that the bird may take its way to progress. Therefore as 'women become peers of men, the world of humanity will soar'.

And Abdul Baha sees no reason that woman is not man's equal. As the mind and the soul are sexless, so there should be no discrimination except those dependent upon frailer physique concerning women. Women, he believes, having finer sensibilities, finer intuitive powers, are often man's superiors.

Science and religion, instead of being conflicting, Abdul Baha compares to the same simile as that used for men and women – both are as wings of the same truth. The broadness of his views and the desire toward universal religion – a oneness of mankind accepts all religions. His philosophy is that as there is but one God which all religions worship – why not throw aside the symbols, the theories, the differences which but turn the straight path toward God in diverse directions.

Bahaism is not a cult, it is not a doctrine – it is a message, a desire to blend all religions to smooth away the rough edges of differences that creak. Abdul Baha has spoken in the big churches of New York City, he has addressed the men of the Bowery Mission, he has talked before the Theosophical Society in Chicago, he will talk in the Divine Science Church in Denver. Indeed he is a man of all religions, seeing good in all who worship God. He is a Christian in that believes in the teachings of Christ. Christ to the Bahaist is a manifestation of the divine spirit. This spirit manifests itself from time to time. Baha'o'llah is the last manifestation. Abdul Baha takes to himself no divinity. He is merely the messenger of his father's teaching of universal peace, brotherhood and religion. This patriarchal man of Persia, with the face that is now overcast with thought, was lighted by a kindly feeling

> of friendship, was born in Persia on the twenty-third of May 1844, the day upon which 'the Bab', prophet of the coming manifestations of the divine spirit, made his declarations to his disciples at Shiraz. His father Baha'o'llah was one of the richest and most noble families of Persia. Baha'o'llah never met 'the Bab', the prophet who told of the coming of the greater teacher whose mission would be that of establishing the universal religion, the Brotherhood of Man.
>
> HAS BEEN HEAD TWENTY YEARS
>
> The Bab suffered martyrdom along with thousands of his followers and, shortly after, Baha'o'llah appeared, his mission lasting forty years. He died in 1892 and since then the man who is now in Denver has been at the head of the Bahaist movement.
>
> This venerable man, whose only wish is to be known as the servant of humanity, has led a life which has been one continual dispensing of good. Charity flows from his finger tips. And the practical demonstration of brotherly love is his. Recently in New York, quite unostentatiously he gave away $200 in quarters to the poor at the Bowery mission.
>
> He teaches that the root of all knowledge is the knowledge of God. And when he teaches, it is not for gain.
>
> The remarkable thing about the Bahaist movement is that the teachings are altruist – Abdul Baha receives nothing – he gives always. He does not believe in a paid priesthood and his social and economic doctrine is that no human being should look to others for his maintenance.
>
> He gives freely of his teachings of a universal religion – a universal brotherhood – a oneness of the world.
>
> The followers of Abdul Baha number 200 in Denver. Last night he gave the first of his talks at the home of Mrs. S. E. Roberts on Sherman Street.[31]

The article also included a picture, especially taken for the *News*, portraying 'Abdu'l-Bahá accompanied by His retinue that now also included the Japanese Bahá'í Saichiro Fujita and 'Alí-Akbar Nakhjavání.[32] Two passages from the Bahá'í writings, one in Persian and one in English, were inserted in the picture.[33] Probably it was Alice Rohe herself who took the pictures.

Frances Wayne,[34] of the *Denver Post*, an independent newspaper with a circulation of 62,600 copies, also interviewed 'Abdu'l-Bahá and on the next day published the following account:

ABDUL BAHA ABBAS, PERSIAN TEACHER, TO CONVERT DENVER

A MAN OF GOD HAS COME TO TOWN

(BY FRANCES WAYNE)

With the arrival yesterday of Abdul Baha Abbas, a quicker spirit of tolerance, of brotherly love, of sincerer charity, of all those virtues which lift man above the beast was given wing and must, before his departure, have its effect upon every man and woman who comes within the radius of this wise man of the East.

Abdul Baha entered the city without any of the glitter or pomp which is the attribute of nobility. He came, a simple, stooped old man, his heavy figure clothed in a white coat, his venerable head swathed in a turban, companioned by five devoted servants of the faith he preaches and by a reputation for sanctity and holiness which makes of the most hardened cynic a respectful spectator.

It was with a sense of levity that I received the assignment to call on the Baha.

'Another of those Oriental teachers and prophets come to work on the emotions of women and long-haired men,' I thought. 'Another of those cunning gentlemen of Persia who have deep wisdom concerning the spiritual strivings and material cupidities of this, our native land.'

In such fettle I approached the presence in his apartments at the Shirley. In a far corner of the room, leaning back in his chair as though oppressed by a great weariness, his white beard flowing over his breast, his brown hands, carrying one simple jeweled ring, folded, and his eyes sending a kindly greeting toward the door, sat the Baha.

The women were there, too. Such women they were as one finds in all the forward movements by which the city is uplifted and advanced on its journey toward righteousness.

NOTHING SPECTACULAR IN THIS WISE MAN

There was nothing theatrical, nothing spectacular in the scene. The atmosphere was vital with that brand of religion which can emanate only from one who is utterly pure in heart; who has found the truth by mining his way through great tribulation and whose life has been purged of all dross by the length and unselfishness of it.

The story of this man is rich in romance. Imprisoned for twenty years, exiled after that because he proclaimed the doctrine of brotherly love, equality of all men and the need of a recognition of the value of a spiritual life, his estate confiscated, he set out to give the message to the world at large.

That he travels with a retinue of men and servants shows that somewhere and somehow he has stored goods against a rainy day. But the storing is done that he may give; give and again give.

This explanation is made by Dr. Ameen U. Fareed, the interpreter, who brings a flowing radiance and beauty to the Baha's sentiments expressed in Persian which can only be comprehended by hearing.

'Why was that man imprisoned?' I asked Dr. Fareed.

'Why was Christ crucified?' he answered quickly. 'The truth always has to fight the way . . . man suffering, and the truth that the Baha has to deliver is no exception.'

Abdul Baha is, first of all, a constructionist. He believes that the time of building is at hand, and to this end, war among the nations must cease. Looking upon his audience of visitors this morning he said, speaking through his interpreter:

'This is the Lord's supper. Material food is of little importance. It is knowledge, comprehension, good deeds, knowledge of God, the virtues of the human word, the perfection of the kingdom – this kind of food is acceptable. Whenever you desire to give a reception for me, prepare such a table. Such food of companionship gives enrichment to the spirit; makes men more heavenly and suffers the world of humanity to become illumined.'

That America shines on the vision of the Baha as a great Hope, but that it must wake to its shortcomings if its destiny is to be great, was indicated in this statement:

BLESSINGS OF GOD ARE UPON AMERICAN PEOPLE

'The country of America is a good country. From every standpoint material happiness has been prepared for the people. Vast and spacious is this continent and it is overflowing with the blessings of God. In this continent you find all blessings and freedom discovers its highest fruitage. It should be a continent of happiness and comfort, but it is in need, however, of influences of divine civilization. It needs the sun of reality. It is in need of spiritual culture, education, in need of the virtues of the ideal, in need of the effulgence's of the kingdom of God that its people may become reinforced to institute universal peace and become enabled to serve the world and humanity.

'America must wake up so this people may cause the spiritual progress of the world. Its lights may shine, hearts become illumined and virtue revealed.'

The Baha talks with a strong voice, sitting moveless as he speaks and waits for Dr. Fareed to pass on his message.

Remembering that David Starr Jordan in his 'Unseen Empire' had asserted that peace would only be possible when the 'pawnbrokers of the world agree upon it', I asked the Baha what part women must play in bringing about universal peace, and to this he answered without pause:

'If equal education is given to women; if they are trained according to the highest standards – that is if they are given the education of men and made equal in all human rights, even suffrage, then they will be enabled to serve international peace extraordinarily.

'These young men who go to war are trained by women during their early years. For at least twenty years women have the molding of men and go through many vicissitudes that they may educate them, undoubtedly women will come soon to the point where they will not suffer their children to go into the battlefield and be torn to pieces that the end of politicians and money changers may be served. For the son is well beloved to his mother, and she will not give her consent. Therefore when women receive the right to vote in all provinces they will strive so that warfare may be taken away from the world.'

GOSPEL OF BROTHERLY LOVE HIS TEACHINGS

The Baha movement, of which Abdul Baha is the apostle, does not aim to displace any of the accepted faiths by which mankind is striving to climb to redemption and happiness. It points out the big fundamental spiritual truths and the way to come at them and live by them.

Certainly Denver has not in the past been honored by the presence of a Godlier man than this simple hearted Persian, whose only weapon, whose only charm is the Word. This he gives unto his hearers in that ornate, courteous form that is like rich embroidery. Last night the Baha held a reception at the home of Mrs. Sidney Roberts, in Sherman Street. Tonight at the Divine Science church at West Thirty-eighth and Perry Street he will give an address and tomorrow night arrangements have been made for a meeting at the Shirley Hotel, to which the public is invited.

'If you have a word or an essence which a brother has not, offer it with the tongue of love and kindness. If it is accepted the end is attained. If not with regard to him, deal not harshly, but pray.'

The above is one of those delicate sentiments offered by the Baha in parting and which it might be well for every man and woman in this city of many strifes to cut out and paste in their hats or on their mirrors.[35]

A further interview with 'Abdu'l-Bahá was conducted by a reporter with the independent *Denver Express*, which at the time had a circulation of 17,100 copies:

MESSAGE OF UNIVERSAL RELIGION IS BROUGHT BY PERSIAN

Abdul Baha, Abbas Effendi – 'The Servant of God' – a venerable old man, son of a Persian nobleman, and the prophet of universal brotherhood and love, is in Denver, spreading the doctrine of the Bahaists.

A dignified old man with a flowing white beard and dressed in the pure white draperies of his native land, his wrinkled face beaming with kindness and charity – this is the head of a new religion, a faith which would do away with the strife of creeds and the wars of nations.

Perhaps it is not a new creed, for it teaches what men have long felt – that at the bottom of every religion there lies a foundation which is the same – but so enthusiastic is the venerable patriarch that the truths falling from his lips have a ring which is strange.

Abdul Baha is not the prophet of creeds; he does not seek to establish a new faith. His aim is a broader one. Its object is no less than to make every creed as one. He teaches the brotherhood of men, the universal scope of the love of God.

He does not pretend to be the Messiah or a prophet of God. In his native language his name signifies 'The Servant of God'.

'I am not a prophet. I am servant of God. You also are a servant of God.' This is the way he states his mission, taking care that you do not think him placing himself above you. He wants everyone to think of him as a brother.

Faithful to his doctrine that deeds and not words comprise the real service of God, he greets everyone with the utmost kindness. Perhaps he has been interrupted in the midst of his speaking, but as you enter his room he greets you with a smile and rises to shake hands. Through his interpreter he asks the health of his visitor and if he is happy. On receiving an affirmative answer his face gleams with gladness – and no one ever has the heart to tell this old man that he is not happy . . .

Abdul Baha does not urge his followers to give up their different faiths. He teaches that through the principles of his teachings they can become better Christians, stronger Buddhists and more faithful Moslems. But all the time their differences will grow smaller and soon they will be brothers of one faith, striving for one end – universal peace and the brotherhood of men.

Abdul believes that labor will be dignified through this love and that the working classes and the employers will reach one plane. He believes that strife will cease and that an eternal peace with happiness and content will succeed it.

In speaking of America, its possibilities and its needs, he said today: 'The country of America is a good country. From every standpoint there is natural happiness and prosperity for the people. It is a vast and spacious continent; it is a continent overflowing with the blessings of God; it is a continent in which you find all the blessings. It is a continent in which freedom finds its highest fruitage and is one of happiness and comfort.

'But it is in need of the influence of Divine civilization. It needs the splendors of the sun of reality. It is in need of spiritual culture and education. It is in need of virtues and ideals. It is in need of the effulgencies of the kingdom of God so that the people may become reinforced in the interest of universal peace, so that they may become able to serve humanity, so that they may cause the spirit of progress to spread through the human world.

'The lights may shine, the hearts become illuminated, and the virtues of the human world be revealed through this.'

Tonight he will speak at the Second Church of Christ, 38th Ave. and Perry. He is staying at Shirley Hotel and tomorrow night the management has consented to throw open the lower floor to him that he may address his followers.[36]

On the day after His arrival in Denver 'Abdu'l-Bahá delivered a public address at the home of Mrs Sidney Roberts, a local Bahá'í, where He spoke on the purpose of human beings, the knowledge of God and the need for unity.[37] A reporter with the *Republican*, a newspaper with a circulation of 42,800 copies, was present at the meeting and wrote the following account:

PERSIAN PROPHET PLEADS FOR UNION OF ALL RELIGIONS

ABDUL BAHA ASSERTS ALL FAITHS IN WORLD POINT TO BUT ONE SUPREME BEING

That today is the day of deeds and not words and that it is also the time for the various religionists of the world to cease their dissensions and combine, in one universal religion under one God, was the subject of a lecture delivered by Abdul Baha, the Persian prophet, at the home of Mrs. Roberts, 1851 Sherman Street, last night, before an audience of more than 100 people.

Abdul Baha, who is considered by his followers to be one of the world's greatest moral teachers, and who is traveling over the world preaching his doctrines, is stopping in Denver en route to the Pacific coast, from where he will go back to his native land. He came to this country last April to attend the Bahai convention recently held in Chicago.

'There must be a unification of nations and religions,' he said 'and the sooner we realize this fact the sooner will a great deal misery and unhappiness be abolished.'

He argued that religion has been given to man by the Creator as fast as man could comprehend it. A few hundred years ago man was in an unfit condition to be enlightened to any great extent, he said, but now he is ready for great revelations which will be forthcoming in their logical order and speed.

When all men can agree that there is but one God, then will great good be accomplished, he urged, but until then a few picked apostles will continue to preach that doctrine amid ridicule. But the time will come when those of that faith will predominate.

Those who believe in the various deities – the Buddhists, Brahmanists, Confucionists, Mohammedans and Christians alike – are beginning to see that there is but one Supreme Ruler, who governs every power and element in the universe, and it is unreasonable to attempt to reason otherwise, he declared.

After they all agree to believe in this one God there can be a union of forces, he said, and under a good leadership they can spend their energies toward the betterment of humanity. The only good in this world, according to Abdul Baha, is happiness. The greater amount each of us brings to those around us, the greater will be our reward in the world to come.

Abdul Baha will preach again tonight at the Second Divine Science church, 4231 West Thirty-second Avenue, at 8 o'clock. Thursday afternoon a reception will be given in his honor at the home of Mrs. Roberts, and Thursday evening he will leave for the Pacific coast.

Abdul Baha preached in many Eastern cities before coming to Denver including New York and Chicago. He does not speak well in English, but has an interpreter with him, and a scribe to record what he says. He will return to Persia after visiting the coast.[38]

Among the many people that visited 'Abdu'l-Bahá at the Shirley Hotel the day of His arrival was the pastor of the Second Church of Divine Science[39] who invited the Master to speak at his church. The Master visited the church just after the address at the house of Mrs. Roberts and spoke on the purpose of religions and their unity.[40] Interestingly, the *Denver Post* had placed a car at the disposal of 'Abdu'l-Bahá in front of His hotel that took Him to the church. On the following day the newspaper published a complete account of the meeting written by Frances Wayne, the same journalist who had interviewed the Master the day before:

WOMEN BACK ABDUL BA-HA; FEW MEN ATTEND SERVICE

PERSIAN TEACHER BELIEVES IN EQUAL RIGHTS AND THAT ALL NATIONS AND ALL CREEDS ARE ONE

(BY FRANCES WAYNE)

When the founders of Christianity appointed women to be the wick trimmers and cup bearers of the faith they 'unlidded the eye' of wisdom', as our distinguished guest, Abdul Ba-ha, would remark.

It was women, you remember, who furnished the enthusiasm and unswerving loyalty for the brief campaign of the lowly and beauteous Nazarene. Women washed the feet of the crucified with their tears and refused to leave the cross until its holy burden was delivered into their tender hands. Women were first at the tomb to witness with undoubting eye the resurrection of the Master, and women have ever since furnished a large percentage of audiences and sacrifices that the church might increase in numbers and multiply its power.

Looking over the crowd packing the church in which he made his first public appearance in Denver Wednesday evening, Abdul Ba-ha, Persian teacher and sage, must have reflected that history inclining always to repeat itself, remained consistent even in the shadow of the Rockies. The Divine Science church on Perry Street was packed to the doors, the throng overflowing to the sidewalks, when the aged prophet and optimist was assisted from The Post automobile and started to shoulder his way toward the pulpit, followed by his five disciples.

Ten women and one man formed the average. And those ten women were not driven by a love of sensation or emotional hunger to hear what the aged Persian had to say concerning 'Truth and the Way'. They were not of the bridge-playing, tea-drinking persuasion. Scanning the Blue Book, one looks in vain for their names in the list of high society.

The hands that have helped lift this city to its present high position; the large effort and achievement in charity, in education, in general betterment of social condition, belonged to the women of the Ba-ha's congregation.

WOMEN ARRANGED FOR SAGE'S VISIT

These women arranged for the visit of the teacher from the east. In doing this they could each of them remain true to the denomination to which their religious allegiance is given. The Ba-ha does not come to proselyte, but to efface lines and proclaim the imperative need of spiritual and human unity.

Since women do the practical work of maintaining the churches, they want to find the easiest way of making those churches effective in the community. They want to find why men are becoming indifferent and women slothful toward spiritual obligations, and they have a very definite impression that there is too much church-ianity and too little Christianity in the world today.

Thus they crowded to hear the Ba-ha, who spoke to them in Persian, which, being translated by his captivating voice into exquisite English by Dr. Fareed, was to this effect:

BA-HA OUTLINES RELIGIOUS TENETS

'There is a foundation truth underlying all religions. The principles of the prophets of Israel and of Jesus Christ and of Buddha and Mahomet and of Confuscius have been largely forgotten; Baha Ullah has renewed them. Wherefore the Bahais have for the followers of other religions the greatest love and yearning because they know that mankind is one.'

The surest way to force mankind to a realization of oneness is by way of influencing the women to preach this doctrine.

'We are all branches of one root,' declared the Ba-ha, seeming to gurgle in his beard, strange language being caught up and turned into light by Dr. Fareed. 'We are blades of grass in one meadow. It is misunderstanding that has caused divisions and differences between mankind. If the truth were brought to the people they would understand what they are, one and all, and each would say: "This is the truth I have been looking for, because the principles taught by every true prophet are the same."'

Holding that women should be given equal educational and political advantages with men, the Ba-ha is boosting their cause in his gentle way and in turn is going to rely on the mothers of the world to take from the 'pawn brokers' the right to send men into war.

Tonight at the Shirley Hotel Abdul Ba-ha will deliver an address to which the public is invited.[41]

On the same day, 26 September, a further account of the meeting was published in the *Rocky Mountains News*:

> UNIVERSAL PEACE AND RELIGION THEME OF PERSIAN NOBLEMAN, GUEST OF DENVER
>
> Abdul Baha Abbas, Persian nobleman, for twenty years in prison as a result of his devotion to duty and his stand for Christianity, who is in Denver with his family, and interpreter Dr. Ameen D. Fareel, and a Japanese servant, lectured last night at the Divine Science church on 'Universal Peace and Universal Religion'.
>
> It is to the study of this problem that Abdul devoted the twenty years he spent in prison, and it is to these two questions that he has since addressed his labors.
>
> Tonight Abdul Baha will lecture in the Shirley Hotel. His theme will be the same. Abdul speaks no English. His lectures are interpreted by Dr. Fareel, who speaks five languages.
>
> 'My association with Abdul has been sweet to think upon,' Dr. Fareel said last night. 'One cannot but observe him from day to day, much less hear his conversation, without getting a cleaner, a wider and an altogether better view of life.
>
> 'Abdul is getting old. He is now bent and gray and cannot stand before the world a living example of brotherly love many more years. Far better would the world be if there were more like him, in his simplicity, in his kindness and in his greatness.'[42]

Two weeks after the arrival of 'Abdu'l-Bahá in California, a note was published in various newspapers, relying on information sent from Denver on 8 October stating that: 'Abdul Baha Abbas . . . says the foundation of his belief is the brotherhood of man and the fatherhood of God, the establishment of universal peace, the prevalence of a universal language, and the establishment of a tribunal for settlement of all international controversies.'[43]

A few days after leaving Denver, the *Wet Mountain Times* (Westcliff), a Republican weekly issuing 400 copies, published a poem dedicated to 'Abdu'l-Bahá signed by La Eremita, the pseudonym of a poet who contributed regularly to the journal:

Coming from old Akka's fortressed walls,
Where Syrian shadows hid your trusting youth,
Coming from the clank of sentried halls,
Could not imprison mental gleams of truth.

In every walk of life, in soul of every nation,
That universal peace inter-religious creeds,
Urge brotherhood of man in true, heartfelt devotion,
Exemplified shall be thru shining deeds.

"Servant of God" is what he claims to be,
Resents attempts to adulate his name,
And all his services are given free,
Just as the glorious Jesus nobly came.

To the poor and needy he brings aid,
With golden coins disburses generous cheer,
Nor does incite to ridicule nor flayed,
Belief of any creed existing here.

One God Supreme Almighty living force,
Who dares imagine they control him here!
As well pretend to move the planets in their course,
Or mock His graciousness inciting fear.

Freedom of thot enlightenment for all,
Is what the blessed Jesus ever taught,
His voice rang not in gilded marble halls,
Where rank display destroys each noble thot.

The streets, the gardens and the hills rejoiced,
And gentle breezes bore his message on,
His thrilling depths of wisdom was not lost,
Down through the centuries in ringing tones,
Denounced hypocrisy in every guise,
Denounced all bigots who for selfish greed,
Enslave the toilers in a mesh of lies,
Denying them their rights and actual needs.

Thus Abdul Baha both sire and son,
Revealed the precious truths to willing ears,
On Persian soil their efforts were begun,
But Oriental despots voiced their fears,
Freedom of thot, enlightenment, if won,
Would shatter every fabric of their baneful lies,
Excited were they where grim old Akka's guns,
Mounted the fortress walls where freedom dies.

When Turkey's old despotic regime expired,
He was released, but heaven had claimed its own,
His father who had lived the life inspired,
Was led from prison bars to Angel home.

In France and Germany across Italy's land,
Down in Egypt his wandering feet have trod
Teaching the simple words of truth that message grand,
The root of every knowledge is the knowledge of God.

LA EREMITA[44]

Salt Lake City, Utah, 29–30 September

'Abdu'l-Bahá left Denver on the evening of Thursday, 26 September, en route to Salt Lake City.[45] The party decided to make a brief stop at Glenwood Springs, Colorado. After one day of rest in this town they took another train at midnight for Salt Lake City, arriving there on Saturday, 28 September. A brief note reporting the arrival of 'Abdu'l-Bahá and offering general information about the Bahá'í Faith was circulated in the local press. Some of the newspapers that published this article included a portrait of the Master.[46]

In Salt Lake City 'Abdu'l-Bahá sat on the stage of the Mormon Tabernacle during the Sunday service, which several thousand people attended.[47]

Echoes outside America

In a report sent to *The Christian Commonwealth* (London), Joseph Hannen summarized this phase of 'Abdu'l-Bahá's travels:

WITH ABDUL BAHA IN AMERICA

Abdul Baha reached Chicago Sept. 12. He and his party were entertained at the home of Mrs. Corinne True, 5338, Kenmore Avenue. Sept. 14 Abdul Baha visited Kenosha, Wisconsin, where he delivered an address at the Congregational Church. The Bahai Assembly at Kenosha, one of the first established in this country, was also visited. Arriving at Minneapolis, Minnesota, Sept. 18, Abdul Baha next day addressed the Commercial Club, and more than 400 persons at the Temple Shaari Tov, leaving Sept. 21 for Omaha, Nebraska.

Abdul Baha thus concluded his address in the Hebrew Temple: – 'We supplicate and pray to the Kingdom of God that he may confirm us to act in accordance with the teachings of Baha'o'llah and to hoist the banner of the oneness of the world of humanity, and that racial prejudice and religious prejudice, and patriotic prejudice and political prejudice, which are destructive, shall be removed from among men.'

From Minneapolis, Minnesota, Abdul Baha and his party journeyed to Omaha, Nebraska, arriving there September 21. Here, as in all the places visited, he gave interviews to the newspapers and received numbers who called at his hotel. The message given to the Press is typical. He said: –

'To-day the most important question is that of international peace. The world of humanity is in the utmost need of conciliation. Comfort and security are lacking because the thoughts of the diplomats of the world are devoted in the greater part to armaments and warfare. Many nations and governments are stepping forward in earnest to bring about international peace. And such nations will win the eternal respect and gratitude of humanity. When such peace as I speak of is brought about a universal religion will come, perfect in unity and love.'

From Omaha Abdul Baha proceeded to Lincoln, Neb., arriving there September 22. This is the home of W. J. Bryan, who visited Abdul Baha in Akka while on his trip around the world. Abdul Baha desired to return, his visit, but Mr. Bryan was absent.

Jos. H. Hannen, Washington, D.C., U.S.A., October 17, 1912.[48]

22

CALIFORNIA

2 – 25 October 1912

'Abdu'l-Bahá's journey to California had been anticipated in the press ever since His arrival in America itself. The *Oakland Tribune*, for instance, reported as early as 11 April that 'in California he will address an audience at Leland Stanford University'.[1] However, His visit to the West coast was not definitely confirmed until mid-August.

As the visit of 'Abdu'l-Bahá approached, the local press in San Francisco published articles about the Bahá'í Faith and biographical notes about the Master. On 25 September the *San Francisco Examiner* published a lengthy article about 'Abu'l-Bahá which carried a portrait of Him.[2] On 29 September the *San Francisco Chronicle* published an article that included an interview with Ella Goodall Cooper and details of the preparations made by local Bahá'ís for His visit. The text was accompanied by a portrait of 'Abdu'l-Bahá and also included excerpts from the Bahá'í writings and a summary of the history of the Bahá'í Faith (not reproduced here):

PERSIAN TEACHER COMING HERE TO PREACH BAHAISM

Out of prison comes the first missionary from the East to the West. He comes to preach the oneness of God, the oneness of religion, the oneness of humanity, the eradication of prejudice, universal peace.

Abdul Baha Abbas, the renowned Persian teacher and head of the Bahai assemblies, if they can be said to have any head, is on his way to San Francisco from New York, by way of Denver, and will arrive early this week. He will remain in the city for at least two weeks and most of the city's churches have extended invitations to him to address their congregations. A committee from the local Bahai Assembly, headed by Mrs. E. C. Getsinger and Mrs. Ella Goodall Cooper, will meet him at the railway station and escort him to the house at 1815 California Street, which has been prepared for his residence during his stay here. He will be accompanied by his secretary and two interpreters.

The local Bahai Assembly, which consists of nearly 500 members, is busy making arrangements to give everyone in the city who wishes to hear Abdul Baha a chance to do so, and expects large crowds to great him wherever he appears. He arrived in New York City last April and since then has visited Washington, Boston, Chicago, Philadelphia, Cleveland, Buffalo, Pittsburgh, Green Acre Me., Montreal, Denver, and everywhere has been most enthusiastically received by large audiences.

RECEPTION IN NEW YORK

In New York he was tendered a reception at the Astor House by the New York Peace Society and latter attended and spoke before the Lake Mohawk Peace Conference. He also spoke at Columbia University, the Bowery Mission and in churches of nearly every denomination in New York City. In all the other cities he has visited he has been received with marked cordiality and enthusiasm . . .

Last year Abdul Baha visited Europe. He was introduced to the Church of England by Archbishop Wilberforce, who invited him to occupy his pulpit at St John's Westminster, London. He spoke to a vast audience in the City Temple and at many other places. While in London, he occupied the apartments belonging to Lady Blomfield in Cadogan Gardens, and before leaving he was entertained by the Lord Mayor of London at a dinner. He also spent several weeks in Paris.

PREACHING ON UNIVERSAL PEACE

In discussing Abdul Baha's teachings yesterday, Mrs Ella Goodall Cooper said:

'He does not come proselytizing for any particular cult. He is preaching the doctrine of universal love, universal peace, the oneness of God and humanity. The adherents of any religions or the members of any denomination of any church can be a Bahai. Abdul Baha exhorts them to be better men and women, and act more conformably in their faith, no matter what it may be. His is a doctrine of love, of kindness.'

Abdul Baha speaks in Persian and Turkish and his sermons are repeated by an interpreter. Until he arrives no definite programme of his appearances in the different churches is possible, but it will be announced as soon as possible . . .[3]

The Arrival

After the long train journey across the United States, 'Abdu'l-Bahá finally reached Oakland on the evening of Wednesday, 2 October 1912.[4] He was received by the local Bahá'í Dr Frederik d'Evelyn who accompanied the Master and His party on the ferry that was to take them from the train station to San Francisco. Despite the inconvenient time of His arrival, several Bahá'ís were waiting for Him at a house rented by Ella Goodall Cooper, used as His temporary residence in San Francisco.[5]

'Abdu'l-Bahá's arrival was reported in the *San Francisco Bulletin*, which noted that the Bahá'í 'local assembly has already been notified by the Rev. Bradford Leavitt and the Rev. Dr. Meyer that their pulpits are at his disposal'.[6] This article also included a portrait of 'Abdu'l-Bahá and information about the Bahá'í Faith and the Master that was very similar to that published a few days before in the *Chronicle.*

During 'Abdu'l-Bahá's first days in California reporters from the major newspapers in San Francisco visited Him at the house of Mrs Goodall. One of the first to interview Him was the representative of the *San Francisco Chronicle*, an independent newspaper with a circulation of 70,000 copies. The reporter showed 'Abdu'l-Bahá news published in his journal about recent hostilities in Europe and the Master dictated for him a message for the American people. The article that ensued was accompanied by a portrait.

ABDUL BAHA ABBAS, NOTED PERSIAN TEACHER ARRIVES

APOSTLE OF UNIVERSAL PEACE AND BROTHERHOOD TO DELIVER SERIES OF LECTURES

Abdul Baha Abbas, the Persian teacher and disciple of universal peace, the oneness of humanity, the oneness of God, universal love, the eradication of prejudice, arrived in San Francisco early yesterday morning. He has been in the United States six months, and though his arrival here had been arranged for and expected for several days by the local assembly of Bahais, no one was at the railroad station to meet him. This was in accordance with the expressed wish of the venerable teacher. He had telegraphed that he desired to enter the city quietly. His train was eight hours late and he with his suite drove to the house at 1815 California Street, which has been prepared for his residence during his three weeks stay here.

Accompanying Abdul Baha were Dr. Ameen N. Fareed, Mirza Ahmed Sohrab and Mirza Mahmood of Persia, Mirza Ali Akbar of Russia and Mr. Fugita of Japan. They will act as interpreters to Abdul Baha in the series of lectures he will deliver in San Francisco and the transbay cities.

Abdul Baha's career is romantic. He went to the prison fortress of Akka, near Mount Carmel, in Palestine, with his father when only 8 years of age. With no schooling except the teaching of his noble father, he spent forty years in prison. Since his release four years ago he has traveled in Egypt, Continental Europe and England, pleading for the removal of prejudice and the establishment of universal peace.

At the house were a score of people, mostly women, a woman said she did not think Abdul Baha would see a reporter as he was going to Oakland in the afternoon. But he did.

IS STRIKING FIGURE

Abdul Baha is of middle stature, strong built, and wears long light-colored robes. His forehead is high, broad and full, his nose slightly aquiline and his beard and mustache gray-white. His eyes are gray and blue, large, soft, penetrating. His gray hair rests on his shoulders.

'My greatest happiness this morning,' said he, 'is this: That I have come to such a modern and progressive city. Praise be to God, everything is beautiful and there seems to be much joy here.'

After a few questions and answers he was shown a copy of the 'Chronicle' containing the full accounts of war preparations in the Balkan states and Turkey. He inquired if actual hostilities had begun and then asked:

'Will the "Chronicle" take a message from me to the American people?' Answered in the affirmative, he dictated an appeal for universal peace.

AN APPEAL FOR PEACE

'Praise be to God: The United States has in reality made extraordinary progress; day by day they are advancing toward the ultimate goal. The material virtues of the people are many; now they must think of the ideal virtues, so that the highest of the perfections of humanity may illumine the regions of America. Among the highest virtues is universal peace, the oneness of humanity. The chief ailment of humanity today is international strife; this militates against the advancement of the material and ideal virtues.

'The continent of America is isolated so far as other countries are concerned; the Government is not thinking of making conquests, of enlarging the circle of colonization. They are not thinking to contend with other nations so far as financial, commercial and political supremacy is concerned. They are not the rival of any other nation.

'Their utmost desire is this: That the continent of America be protected.

'They are engaged in the amelioration of internal conditions; they are not engaged in warfare with any nation. Therefore, they have the time and ability to raise the standard of universal peace and spread the doctrine of the oneness of God. May their influence spread and permeate to all parts of the world.

'Other peoples of the world have to contend with international difficulties. First, the nations are rivals with each other so far as commercial advantages are concerned. Second, they are thinking of national self-aggrandizement. Third, they are thinking of planting new colonies. Therefore, it is difficult for them to step into this field, to uphold international peace, because they are contending, warlike, victory-loving people. They cannot be instrumental in promulgating international peace.'

PRAISES AMERICAN DEMOCRACY

'But, praise be to God, the American Government is no warlike Government, the American democracy is not founded upon warlike doctrines. Hence, it becomes this democracy to uphold international peace and spread it throughout the world. Through the promulgation of this doctrine will be distributed the greatest blessings.

'It will eliminate the darkness of prejudice, the darkness of war, the darkness of rancor and hatred, the darkness of racial prejudice, the darkness of political prejudice. May this darkness be blotted out and the light become widespread universal. May the oneness of humanity become primordial, supreme.

'His holiness Baha Ollah fifty years ago spread broadcast this great movement, proclaimed the benefits of international peace. This took place at a time when the thought was not in the minds of men, nor the words upon the tongues of the people. At the time he summoned people from all parts of the Orient. He addressed letters to the sovereigns of Europe setting forth the results to accrue from the establishment of universal peace. He invited all to participate in a world's arbitral court of Justice to be composed of representatives of every Government in the world, the delegates thereto to be chosen and ratified by the Governments. Thereto would be referred disputes between nations for settlement. In case any Government or nation should prove rebellious concerning any decision of the court the other nations should coalesce to force it into obedience.

'A more fervent hope and fonder desire concerning the American people is that their instrumentality shall be such as to enlarge the scope of this scheme and that earnest concerted action from the nations of the world will result therefrom.

'This great cause, which alone insures the happiness of the world, must receive support throughout the world.'

Abdul Baha will remain in the city for two to three weeks. Many of the churches have invited him to fill their pulpits, and his first public appearance will be Sunday morning at 11 o'clock in the Unitarian Church at Franklin and Geary Streets. Sunday night he will deliver a sermon in the First Congregational Church in Oakland.

Abdul Baha has been invited to deliver a talk at Stanford University by Dr. David Starr Jordan, which he has accepted. Speaking of this yesterday, he said:

'The duty of educated men especially university presidents of the Nation is this:

'To teach in the universities and schools ideas concerning universal peace, so that the student may be so molded that in after years he may help carry to fruition the most useful and human issue of mankind.'[7]

The *San Francisco Examiner*, a Democratic journal of the Hearst group with a daily circulation of 116,200 copies, also sent a reporter to interview 'Abdu'l-Bahá:

ABDUL BAHA SUFFRAGE ADVOCATE
SEX EQUALITY NEED FOR PROGRESS
FAMOUS LEADER ASSERTS AMERICANS ARE LOVABLE, BUT SUBMERGED IN DOLLAR HUNTING

Surrounded by his Persian secretaries, Abdul Baha Abbas, one of the great leaders of modern times and spiritual adviser to fifty million followers, sat in an armchair at 1815 California Street last night, discussing American manners and ideals, suffrage and women's fashions, and told of the most wonderful things he had found in America.

The aged philosopher and head of the Bahai movement, which teaches the fundamental unity of all creeds, and the blessedness of universal peace, arrived in San Francisco on the Overland Limited late Wednesday night for a stay of three weeks. During this period he will speak from the pulpits of a number of churches of varying denominations, and on Tuesday he will address the students of Stanford University. Last night his interpreter was Dr. Ameen Fareed, a graduate of the University of Chicago.

SUBMERGED IN DOLLAR CHASE

'America is a prosperous country,' he said. 'The wealth of the nation is increasing, its development is phenomenal. It has civilized men and gracious ladies, but they are all submerged in materialism.

'The American people are a hospitable people, stranger-loving and very noble. I have found them quite courteous.'

'He has not ridden a great deal in street cars. He has been much in motors,' explained Dr. Fareed, laughing and translating his aside into the strange Persian for Abdul Baha, who sat with his shawl drawn tight up under his long white beard, his eyes closed in fatigue, and his white turban tilted forward. The teacher laughed, too.

'How about woman suffrage?' Dr. Fareed asked in the jerky Persian.

'The world of humanity is possessed of two wings, one represented by the male, the other by the female,' was the reply. 'Both must be strong in order that the world of humanity may fly. Equality of rights and prerogatives of men and women is finding foothold in America faster than in other parts. Until suffrage is established, the body-politic will not achieve its progress. Women are the first educators of man. Hence womankind must be educated until they reach the level of man.'

BALKS AT DELICATE QUESTION

'Do you regard American women as being at the level of American men? was asked.

'Let us not discuss that,' said Abdul Baha, hastily, through his interpreter.

The Persian philosopher was then asked about moving picture shows and theatres, and other phases of American city life.

'I have never seen any. I have come to America to advocate international peace and the oneness of humanity, not for sightseeing,' the philosopher explained, gently.

'We have paid no great attention to fashions and picture hats. We have no regard for the external clothes. If woman is virtuous, refined, near God, in our estimation she is praiseworthy and revered, in no matter what clothes.'

THIS NATION IS FREE

'The most wonderful thing I have found in America is its liberty. This nation is in reality free, and this government is fair.'

'International peace to-day is the greatest issue of humanity.'

Abdul Baha and his train have visited the largest cities of the United States and Canada since April. The aged teacher pays his own expenses and declines contributions. He will occupy the pulpits of the First Congregational churches in this city, besides speaking in synagogues, cathedrals and in private homes. Besides Dr. Fareed, who has addressed the Commonwealth Club and other San Francisco organizations on previous occasions, he is attended by Mirza Ahmad Sohrab, special correspondent of a Persian newspaper published at Cairo, Egypt; Mirza Mahmood, and Ali Akbar, a Russian, who act as secretaries. He also has a Japanese servant.

Abdul Baha urges the American people to develop a divine as well as a material civilization, adopting what is best of the creeds of

> Christians, Mohammeds, Buddhists, Shintos, or Jews. Out of Persia has come one to refute the fatalistic teachings of Omar Khayyam.
>
> 'He teaches for the Twentieth Century,' said Mirza Ahmad Sohrab.[8]

These comments were the basis of an article that appeared a few days later in the Fort Smith (AR) *American*[9] and in the *Fort Wayne Sentinel* (IN),[10] which also included a picture of 'Abdu'l-Bahá.

Ahmad Sohrab's notes of this interview were later published in *Star of the West* and presented a different version of what was published in *The Examiner*. According to Sohrab, 'the correspondent tried to ask a few more questions, but Abdul Baha interrupted him by this final statement while putting his hand on his shoulder and kissing his face: Consider how much I love thee, and to what extent I respect Mr. Hearst, that notwithstanding the fatigue coming over me as the result of a very busy day, I have answered all thy questions.'[11]

To the representative of the evening journal *Alameda Times* 'Abdu'l-Bahá spoke on the need for an international language:

> Although it was early in the morning, he was already astir. In reply to the question: 'Do you not feel fatigued by your long journey?' he replied, 'Ah, no, your great kindness and my longing to meet with the people in the west, caused me to "unknow" fatigue or discomfort. Your sunshine, your glorious skies, your brightness make me think of the Holy Land.' When jokingly reminded that the official entrance to this region is through the Golden Gate, he replied, 'Ah, not a golden gate, but diamond archway, studded with bright and beautiful gems. You are going to be a great people, but you must be sincere, you must be real, the spirit of Behai – that is the glorious, that is love – must be your title deeds to a greater capacity.'
>
> Abdul Baha takes a keen interest in every factor that can in any wise aid the betterment of man – his remarks upon the Irrigation Congress which was in session at Salt Lake City while he was there were most amusing and interesting. 'You have great lands; but you want more people, water is very necessary but more people is still more essential.'
>
> When asked if a common language was desirable. He answered by a strong, creative 'yes'. Strange power seems to center around his words.

'It is almost sixty years ago since Baha'o'llah, the manifestation of the teachings, urged the necessity for such a language. The races of mankind are not isolated as in former days. Now in order to be in close relationship with all countries it is necessary to be able to speak their tongues. A universal language would make intercourse possible with every nation.

'Thus it would be needful to know two languages only, the mother tongue, and the universal speech. The latter would enable a man to communicate with any and every man in the world. Esperanto has been drawn up with this end in view; it is a fine invention and a splendid piece of work, but it needs perfecting. Esperanto as it stands is very difficult for some people.

'An international congress should be formed consisting of delegates from every nation in the world, eastern as well as western. This congress should form a language that could be acquired by all, and every country would thereby reap great benefit. Difference of speech is one of the most fruitful causes of dislike and distrust that exists between nations which are kept apart by their inability to understand each other's languages more than by any other reason.

'If everybody could speak one language, how much more easy would it be to serve humanity.'

These statements are to be 'well-pondered over', he said, as there are few indeed amongst the present day students who realize the great significance of their activities as nascent factors in that universal peace so much to be desired.[12]

Besides these interviews, the San Francisco area press also published general articles about the coming of 'Abdu'l-Bahá which contained information about the plans prepared for Him. The *Oakland Tribune*, an evening Republican journal publishing some 39,700 copies daily, reported that 'At his temporary home, 1815 California Street, San Francisco, the Persian prophet will keep open house each evening when he is not engaged in lectures, and will discuss the great world questions in which he is interested.'[13]

Another evening Republican journal, the *San Francisco Bulletin*, which had at the time a circulation of 77,500 copies, gave the following details about the schedule of the Master in the city:

LEADER OF BAHAISTS MAKES LECTURE DATES

Abdul Baha, the leader of the Bahaists, a new Oriental sect that is making converts in the United States, will deliver a series of lectures in various cities about the bay this week. This evening he will speak at 8 o'clock at the Japanese Independent Church, 552 Syracuse Street, in Oakland; Tuesday evening at 3:15, at Stanford University, Palo Alto, and at 7:30 p.m. at the Unitarian Church, Palo Alto; Wednesday at 8 p.m. at Home of Truth, Berkeley; Thursday at 8 p.m. at Forum Club, Jefferson Hall; Friday at 8 o'clock at Theosophical Society, Yosemite Hall, Native Son's Building; Saturday at 10:45 a.m., at Temple Emanu-El, Sutter Street near Powell; Sunday at 3:30 p.m. at the Reading Room for the Blind, 1665 Jackson Street.[14]

First Public Addresses

The First Unitarian Church of San Francisco was the location of the first public talk of 'Abdu'l-Bahá in California which was arranged for Thursday, 6 October 1912, at eleven in the morning.[15] He had been invited by Rev. Bradford Leavitt, who had probably met 'Abdu'l-Bahá for the first time at the Unitarian festival held in Boston.

The Christian minister opened the service with a long sermon in which he presented 'Abdu'l-Bahá to the audience in the highest terms. 'Those who have met him,' he stated, 'bear witness to his loving kindness, and spiritual breath.' In the course of this presentation he read extensively from Harrold Johnson's article in the *Contemporary Review* (London). 'I need not', closed Leavitt, 'say there are very close affinities between this and all that we of this church profess, and what a special pleasure and privilege it is to me, in your name, to welcome this great religious leader to this pulpit.' After these words Faríd read a few of the Hidden Words of Bahá'u'lláh. Then 'Abdu'l-Bahá spoke on the need for unity and peace among mankind and on the purpose of religion and its essential unity.[16]

Several reporters attended the meeting and on the following days at least four accounts of it were published. The *Examiner* offered a detailed report of the service, including portions of 'Abdu'l-Bahá's address and some of the introductory remarks made by Rev. Leavitt. Leavitt was reported as having stated about the Bahá'í teachings that 'no religion is as significant as this one':

ABDUL BAHA BRINGS GOSPEL OF PEACE

FAMOUS PERSIAN RELIGIONIST TELLS CHURCH THRONG THAT UNITY OF NATIONS IS DAWNING

Abdul Baha, head of the Bahai religious movement, spoke at the First Unitarian Church, Franklin and Geary Streets yesterday. Dressed in a long brown robe and wearing a snow white turban, the venerable leader of the faith which now numbers more than three million followers looked like a patriarch of old as he stood in the pulpit and addressed the multitude in the church, on peace and love for all mankind.

Abdul Baha spoke in Persian and his remarks were translated into English. He was introduced by the Rev. Bradford Leavitt.

'There landed in New York a man, white turbaned and speaking a foreign tongue,' said Dr. Leavitt. 'Hundreds welcomed him at the dock and attended his lectures. That man is Abdul Baha, one of the most distinguished figures of the age. Bahaism has not less than three million followers throughout the world. It numbers its followers among all the great religions of the world. No religion is as significant as this one.'

STRIFE BRINGS DEATH

Abdul Baha spoke slowly and with a soft voice. He said in part:

'Love confers life. On the contrary warfare and dissension are ever productive of extinction and dissolution. Peace tends towards life wherefore warfare and dissension are the causes of death.

'We find that the domestic animals are in the utmost accord and fellowship. There is no dissension among them and all of them enjoy the utmost of accord among themselves. But among the ferocious animals you will find no fellowship. Here we learn that fellowship is a quality of peace. Warfare is a quality of the ferocious animals.

'How thoughtless and unjust a man is. In the Balkans now the general lays waste and destroys a hundred thousand men. All will honor him. Why? Because he has torn asunder a hundred thousand souls. Regard how thoughtless man is. If a man destroys property he is considered a criminal, but if a general lays waste a country, people praise him.'

TRUTH IS APPEARING

'The ray of the sun of reality is shining upon all of us. The breeze of God's providence is blowing on all of us. He is so kind to all that he will shelter all of us. Why should we not avail ourselves of this bestowal? Why should we transform this life into death and transform the fellowship into hatred and rancor?

'Verily he created us angelic. Is it becoming that we act as ferocious animals? Let us be loving. Let us proclaim international peace amongst all mankind.

'I have come from the distant Orient because I have loved you very much, having heard that you American people are peace loving. Therefore these noble thoughts of yours and these strivings of yours have afforded me great joy.'[17]

A similar article was published in the *Bulletin*.[18] To the information published in other journals the *San Francisco Post*, with a circulation of 47,200 copies, added that 'the speaker concluded with a plea for peace, international peace among all mankind'.[19] An account in the *Chronicle* also included some of the words of Rev. Bradford Leavitt:

ABDUL BAHA ABBAS SAYS OBJECT OF MISSION IS TO UNIFY ALL CREEDS

GREAT PERSIAN RELIGIOUS TEACHER EXPLAINS HIS LIFE'S AMBITION

'What Christianity has failed to accomplish Bahaism already has accomplished. It has 3,000,000 adherents throughout the world. It teaches the oneness of mankind and the fundamental unity of all religions. It has been said that no religious movement of the time is so significant as is this one, and you will hear today the greatest living exponent of this movement; a man who is a leading figure in the religious world today.'

It was in these words that Rev. Bradford Leavitt on Sunday morning introduced to an audience that filled the First Unitarian Church, Abdul Baha Abbas, who from prison in the far East has come into the West to preach the religion of his father, Baha Ollah, founder of the Bahai movement in Persia in 1844, and who, persecuted and imprisoned, died in the captivity that later claimed his son – the venerable man who yesterday for the first time spoke in San Francisco.

SEEKS NO CONVERTS

It was a message of peace and love and unity that Abdul Baha delivered to the people of this city. His address – or perhaps it would be more correct to call it a sermon – was a short one and spoken through an interpreter, but in it he sought to tell the people the fundamentals of his religion. It is not, he carefully explained, any new religion. He seeks no converts from other churches. Rather does he seek only to unify all churches of all creeds and of all denominations. He seeks, he said, to have men cull from each religion, be it Christian, Buddhism or the teachings of Confucius, the very best there is in it, making of them all one perfect whole. And he clearly pointed out that in so doing no man need forsake the creed to which he had given his allegiance. Rather would the acceptance of the Bahai faith strengthen one's allegiance to the church that he belonged to.

For the sake of his faith and the surety that his father's belief in the ultimate coming of universal peace, love and unity would be realized, Abdul Baha lingered in prison for forty years, his release not coming until 1908. Even then he remained in confinement at Akka, in Palestine, for two years longer, voluntarily and because his friends were there and he was loth to leave them.

A picturesque figure is that of Abdul Baha. His clean-cut, scholarly features framed by a patriarchal white beard and a white turban, he looks like one of the prophets of Biblical days. He speaks slowly and as one certain that each word he utters breathes the very spirit of truth.

WILL STAY TWO WEEKS

Abdul Baha will remain in this city for a couple of weeks. While here he is being cared for by the local Bahai Assembly, numbering some 500 members. He has spoken in London, where he was introduced to the Church of England by Archbishop Wilberforce, and the aged Persian spoke from the pulpit of St. John's, Westminster, London. The Lord Mayor of London entertained him at a great banquet, and the courtesies he was shown abroad he also received in New York, Chicago and other Eastern cities.

This afternoon Abdul Baha will speak at the Leland Stanford Junior University, Palo Alto; Wednesday he will speak at the Home of Truth, Berkeley; Thursday evening he will speak before the Forum

Club in Jefferson Hall, this city; Friday evening he will address the Theosophical Society in Yosemite Hall, Native Sons Building, this city; Saturday morning he will speak in Temple Emanu-El, and next Sunday afternoon he will make an address to the blind in the reading room at 1665 Jefferson Street.[20]

In the ensuing days, other journals, such as the *Sacramento Bee*,[21] published brief notices of the meeting. Two months later the *Pacific Unitarian* (San Francisco), organ of the Pacific Coast Unitarian Conference with a monthly circulation of 1,100 copies, also offered a vivid description of the visit of the Master to the Unitarian Church:

Coincidences are sometimes startling. Those who have attended the First Unitarian Church of San Francisco have not failed to be impressed with the striking mural painting that fills the gothic arch back of the pulpit. It is the work of Bruce Porter, a gift in the name of his mother as a memorial to Horatio Stebbins. Dr. Stebbins was fond of the passage, 'Lo, at length the True Light', and the painting depicts the artist's conception of the development of religious truth. Against a background of wooded hills, fine clouds, blue sky and mountain heights, are grouped four figures. In the foreground, prone, with covered face, a tawny form represents primitive superstition. At the left is seated a venerable sage, with snow hair and flowing beard. He is garbed in soft brown texture and is distinctly Oriental. His brow with closed eyes, rests upon his open hand, which is supported by his forearm. His attitude suggests weariness and relaxed severity. One thinks of Moses when he was tired and longing for relief.

At his right, with a harp that he is lightly touching, is seated a kingly figure that might typify the era of the Prophets, as Moses typifies the law.

At the right of these two, the commanding figure of the group, stands a majestic figure with left hand uplifted, strong, and glowing, seeming to proclaim triumphantly, 'Lo, at length the True Light'.

It is a very beautiful painting, restful, and uplifting.

A few Sundays ago Mr. Leavitt, with characteristic hospitality, offered the pulpit to Abdul Baha, the leader of the Bahai movement. The church was completely filled. When the distinguished

Orientalist arrived Mr. Leavitt left the pulpit and met him and his attendants at the door. They passed down the main aisle, an impressive group. Abdul is a substantial sort of a saint with a bearing of apparently conscious importance. He wore a white turban, had a flowing white beard and a soft, Oriental garb of light brown. His interpreter was black-bearded, with a black turban and gown.

As they passed into the space behind the pulpit, Abdul seated himself in a gothic armed chair in the right-hand corner, and almost immediately rested his head on his forearm, his elbow on the arm of the handsome chair. He closed his eyes in meditation and seemed lost to any interest in his surroundings.

The congregation was presented with a spectacle that aroused intense interest, for he represented in the flesh an almost exact likeness of the picture of the Moses above him. The color of his garment was the same. His attitude was absolutely true, and the facial resemblance was startling. The white turban differed little from the white hair, and the expression and atmosphere were identical. The living figure might have posed for the artist, and Abdul will perhaps never have a better likeness.

It was a remarkable instance of a happening of extraordinary similarity under circumstances that could be neither predicated or imagined.[22]

In the afternoon of the same day 'Abdu'l-Bahá spoke at the First Congregational Church in Oakland, whose minister was Herbert A. Jump. No accounts of the event seem to have been published but several announcements were published on the previous days in the *Bulletin*,[23] the *Call*,[24] the *Examiner*,[25] the *Oakland Tribune*[26] and other journals.[27] According to these, the address was entitled 'Universal Brotherhood' and the meeting was to take place at 7:45 in the evening.

Address at Stanford University

On 2 October, Dr. David Starr Jordan,[28] president of Leland Stanford University (Palo Alto), was among those who visited the Master at the home of Mrs Goodall. He had probably met 'Abdu'l-Bahá months before at the Lake Mohonk conference. Their first contact, however, took place as early as February 1912 when Jordan wrote to 'Abdu'l-Bahá in Egypt inviting Him to speak at his university.[29] Once 'Abdu'l-Bahá's visit to California was confirmed the meeting was arranged for 8 October 1912 at 10:15 in the morning and was announced in several journals in the San Francisco area.[30]

On 2 October the *San Francisco Call* carried an interview with Jordan in which mention was made of the upcoming visit of 'Abdu'l-Bahá to the university:

> Heralded throughout the orient as the head of a new world religion, Sir Abbas Effendi or Abdul-ul-Baha, the venerable Persian apostle of the Golden Rule and disciple of Bahaism, is coming to Stanford to speak at a special assembly of the student body. Sir Abbas is to arrive in San Francisco next week and will come immediately to Stanford. He will speak in Persian, which will be translated sentence by sentence by an interpreter. The aged Persian, who preaches universal peace, religious unity and the brotherhood of man, has traveled over all of Europe teaching his creed. He says that unity of religion should be the most powerful force in bringing men together, in breaking down the artificial bounds of creed, race, national and political antagonisms.
>
> Sir Abbas was imprisoned at Acre, Syria, for over 40 years by the deposed sultan Abd-ul-Hamid, the rebellion of the young Turks gaining him his freedom.[31]

Similar information was published in the *Palo Altan* on 4 October.[32] The *Daily Palo Altan*, the student journal of Stanford University, published the day before the meeting the following announcement, which included a picture of the Master:

> Abdul Baha, known as Abbas Effendi, the venerable Persian savant, will speak in a special assembly at 10:15 o'clock tomorrow morning. Sir Abbas' address will be followed at 11:15 by the welcoming assembly of the Australians.
>
> Owing to a misunderstanding, the San Francisco committee in charge of Sir Abbas' program scheduled his arrival on the campus for 3 o'clock tomorrow afternoon.
>
> At the time it was feared that it would be impossible to change the arrangements of the committee and a notice to the effect that

Sir Abbas would speak in the chapel at 3:30 o'clock was posted on the bulletin board.

However, when the San Francisco committee were appraised of the fact that only a limited number of students would be able to attend an afternoon lecture, the desired change was made.

The Bahaists of San Francisco have arranged elaborate entertainment for their leader from the orient, and his visit to the bay city is taken up with addresses before numerous organizations . . .[33]

'Abdu'l-Bahá traveled from San Francisco to Palo Alto by train. Dr Jordan was waiting for Him at the train station and accompanied Him to the university where some two thousand people had assembled to listen to the Master. The audience included professors, students, citizens of Palo Alto and other towns in the area and even a group of students from the Montezuma Mountain School, who were brought by Professor Ernest A. Rogers.[34]

In His address 'Abdu'l-Bahá spoke on the oneness of nature, the powers of man and the need for peace.[35] After the meeting Dr Jordan drove 'Abdu'l-Bahá around the university and showed Him the different buildings in the area.

Journalists were present during the talk and reports of it were published afterwards. On the same day the *Daily Palo Alto* published an account of the meeting that included portions of the talk as recorded in the notes of the Bahá'í Bijou Straun (not included here):

PERSIAN INDICTS THE FUTILITY OF WAR

ABD-UL-BAHA DECLARES INTERNATIONAL STRIFE UNSCIENTIFIC AND CONTRARY TO NATURE

An aged man, with a long white beard and a benign and saintly face, stood on the platform of the Assembly hall this morning and demonstrated the utter uselessness of war and its waste, with all the poetic beauty of oriental philosophy.

In a simple and dignified manner, with no more evidence of embarrassment that if he were addressing an assemblage of his native Persians, Abd-ul-Baha, or Abbas Effendi, brought the arguments of science, nature and philosophy together to show the universal brotherhood of man and the necessity for universal peace.

In the garb of his own country, a long brown toga which

> harmonized modestly with his dark complexion and the white turban, Sir Abbas presented a picturesque figure. Speaking quietly in Persian, his expressive features and gestures made the services of his interpreter seem at times almost superfluous.[36]

The *Palo Alto Times*, an independent journal with a circulation of 850 copies daily, reproduced this article and the talk on 9 October.[37] Similar information was published on 11 October in the *Palo Altan*,[38] an independent evening journal with a circulation of 350 copies. The talk was published again in the *Palo Alto Times* on 11 October and in the *Palo Altan* on 18 October. Both texts included the opening remarks made by Dr Starr Jordan:

> It is our portion to have with us, through the courtesy of our Persian friends, one of the great religious teachers of the world, one of the natural successors of the old Hebrew prophets.
>
> He is said sometimes to be the founder of a new religion. He has upward of three millions of people following along the lines in which he leads. It is not exactly a new religion, however. The religion of brotherhood, of good will, of friendship between men and nations – that is as old as good thinking and good living may be. It may be said in some sense to be the oldest of religions.
>
> He will speak in Persian. He will be translated by Dr. Ameen Fareed, a graduate of the University of Illinois and also of Johns Hopkins University.
>
> I have now the great pleasure, and the great honor also, of presenting to you Abdul Baha.[39]

Jordan closed the meeting declaring that 'we are all under very great obligation to Abdul Baha for this illuminating expression of the brotherhood of man and the value of international human peace. I think we can best show our appreciation by simply a rising vote of thanks.'[40] On 1 November the *Palo Altan* carried the following account of the meeting:

ABDUL BAHA, THE BAHAI PROPHET, SPEAKS AT STANFORD UNIVERSITY

A GREAT ASSEMBLY OF STUDENTS AND TEACHERS CROWD THE AUDITORIUM TO HEAR THE BAHAI PROPHET OF PERSIA EXPOUND THE DOCTRINE OF A NEW DAY FOR UNIVERSAL BROTHERHOOD, INTERNATIONAL PEACE AND RELIGIOUS UNITY. ORIENTAL SAVANT WITH ENTOURAGE OF TWENTY-NINE PERSONS SPENT THE DAY AT STANFORD UNIVERSITY AND ARE ENTERTAINED IN PALO ALTO

A crowded Assembly Hall, holding nearly two thousand people, awaited with eager expectancy the appearance last Tuesday morning, of Abdul Baha, Abbas Effendi, the world leader of the Bahai movement. The venerable prophet, with his long gray beard and Persian cloak and turban, gave a true impression of the reincarnation of the Far Eastern prophet of old. He spoke in Persian, and his remarks were translated by Dr. Ameen Fareed, a graduate of the University of Illinois and also of Johns Hopkins University.

Abdul Baha is revolutionizing the religion of Asia, bringing Mohammedans, Jews and Christians together on the basis of the laws of Moses, which they all ratify. He already has a vast host of followers and has aroused great interest by his present tour of America and England.

A pilgrimage through England and America undertaken by Abdul Baha has created great interest in the Bahai movement. The knowledge of this movement has been brought home to thousands of people who are willing and eager to spread its beneficent teachings. On this far western shore of America the seeds of peace find fertile ground and abundant fruitage. At Stanford there is a keen interest taken in International Peace on account of the prominent part taken by Dr. Jordan, one of the trustees of the Carnegie Peace Endowment.

After the address at the university some time was spent by the party in viewing the campus buildings and surroundings. In the evening another large assemblage gathered at the Unitarian Church in Palo Alto to hear the message to the church as the morning sermon had been addressed to the men of science. As before, the sermon was translated sentence by sentence by Dr. Fareed as uttered by the speaker. The venerable prophet was followed with close attention by the large audience of men and women present.

It seemed to be a notable day when Abdul Baha from the far country of the Orient, met Dr. David Starr Jordan of the far western shore, both carrying the standard of international peace and universal brotherhood. It was Persia, the oldest nation of the world, indeed the fabled country of the Garden of Eden and the birth-place of the human race, bringing a message to America, the youngest great nation of the world.

Abdul Baha carries the message of religion and Doctor Jordan carries the message of science, both aiming for one great result. As all men are the children of one God so are they all brothers and we are at the dawning of a new day when the relationship of world fraternity will be seen and recognized.

The prophets of Israel, Moses, Elijah and Christ, are firmly established in the heart and mind of humanity, as great teachers who delivered the message of God to the world. They lived and taught in one small country, never getting far away from the place of their nativity. In the case of Moses, who led the children of Israel up out of Egypt to Canaan, a notable journey in its day, would be a slight migration in the modern sense of people accustomed to traverse the globe. Our Savior lived and taught only in Palestine. Yet with all the differences which come in the stretch of two thousand years, one feels in the presence of Abdul Baha that he is a living embodiment of the old patriarchs and prophets. He has accomplished a great journey from the far East to the far West. Yet he was known before he came, and he will be long remembered.

In connection with these discourses, the wonderful skill and felicitous expression of the translator, Dr. Ameen Ullah Fareed, should not go unrecognized. To his ready learning is indebted the ability to fully appreciate the beauties of the discourses. They have been faithfully transcribed by the stenographer, Miss Bijou Straun.

The day, according to the wisdom of Solomon, is divided into three parts, whereof a part is for labor, a part for refreshment, and a part for repose. As fitting to follow the labor of a busy day, the company and a few guests enjoyed the hospitality of Mrs. I. C. Merriman at the home of her daughter on Waverley Street. An evening of profitable and delightful discussion of the Bahai movement was followed by the serving of a sumptuous dinner at which all the appointments of refinement and good taste pervaded. Mrs.

Merriman has taken a deep interest in the work of true benevolence best typified in the teachings of this universal religion and it was a pleasure to gather around her hospitable board on this occasion. The Company remained over night and the next morning returned to San Francisco.[41]

The following note released by agencies was published in some Californian newspapers:

PERSIAN APOSTLE OF PEACE MAKES PLEA

ABDUL BAHA ABBAS IN ELOQUENT ADDRESS AT STANFORD

SPECIAL DISPATCH TO THE 'CHRONICLE'

STANFORD UNIVERSITY, October 9 – In a simple and direct manner and with all the poetic beauty of the Orient, Abdul Baha Abbas, the venerable Persian apostle of brotherly love, addressed a crowded assembly of Stanford students and made a pointed talk on the uselessness of war. He unified arguments of nature, science and philosophy into one strong appeal for the brotherhood of man and universal peace.-

'Mankind, as the noblest creature of nature, has been endowed with a sound mind,' said the apostle. 'He is possessed of every other faculty of nature, and alone enjoys the extraordinary human quality, the human mind.

'How long can a being of such majestic intellect remain ferocious, like a wolf killing a fellow wolf? It is contrary to the laws of nature for man to kill man. Wolf kills wolf because of hunger. Wolves have no idea of humanity and justice and are excusable. But man kills man for greed.

'We are all the progeny of one man, Adam. All are of one family, one linage. Everything on this earth is dust. Must we behead our fellow men for dust? Earth merely is a graveyard for all eternity. Shall we fight over our own graveyard? What ignorance!'

The venerable Persian savant appeared in Oriental costume, with white turban and long flowing brown robe. He was accompanied by several interpreters, one of whom translated his address.[42]

In an article about Dr. Starr Jordan published weeks later, the *New York Times* also mentioned 'Abdu'l-Bahá's address at Leland Standford.[43]

'Abdu'l-Bahá's address was also mentioned in the *Annual Register* of Stanford University.[44]

Many years later Jordan recalled 'Abdu'l-Bahá in his memoirs with the following words:

> Another visitor of the same year was the Bahai, Abdul Bahas, son of Baha O'llah, the famous Persian devotee, founder and head of a widespread religious sect holding as its chief tenet the Brotherhood of Man, with all that this implies of personal friendliness and international peace. Through an interpreter the kindly apostle expressed with convincing force a message accepted, in name at least, by good men and women all through the ages. He asked for some of my own essays to be translated into Persian and cordially invited me to his abode of peace in the hills of Damascus.[45]

Address at the First Unitarian Church, Palo Alto

'Abdu'l-Bahá delivered a further address in Palo Alto at the First Unitarian Church. Its pastor, Rev. Clarence Reed, [46] spent the afternoon with the Master and then escorted Him to his church where the meeting was to start at 8:00. The text of this talk was published in the *Palo Altan* on November 1:

> Praise be to God, this evening I have come to a Unitarian Church. This Church is called Unitarian – attributed to unity. Hence I desire to discourse on the subject of unity, which is a fundamental basis of Divine teachings.
>
> In all the religions of God there is an exposition concerning unity. What is the basis of this oneness? It is evident that the reality of Divinity cannot be brought within human grasp. Man cannot comprehend the reality of Divinity, because man is accidental, whereas the reality of Divinity is eternal. Man is limited, whereas the reality of Divinity is unlimited. Assuredly, the limited cannot comprehend the unlimited, and the accidental cannot comprehend the eternal.
>
> When we observe and study phenomena we find a mineral kingdom, a vegetable kingdom, an animal kingdom, and a human kingdom.
>
> The mineral kingdom, however much it shall advance, cannot

be in touch with the vegetable kingdom. The vegetable kingdom, however much it advance, cannot be conscious in the sense of knowledge, cannot have knowledge of the animal kingdom.

For example, this flower, however much it may advance, cannot conceive sight and hearing. It cannot realize what constitutes hearing or seeing, what is meant by the spirit of man, what intellect signifies, because those subjects are beyond the pale of its grasp. It cannot, therefore, comprehend them. Although this plant and we are both accidental, yet the difference of degrees is a hindrance to comprehension. This plant belongs to the vegetable world or kingdom, whereas our kingdom is human, and because of this difference in the two kingdoms the plant cannot comprehend the human kingdom.

So long as differences in degrees hinder comprehension, to-wit: every inferior degree is incapable of comprehending the degree superior thereto, then how can we ever comprehend God Who is transcendental? We are accidental, whereas He is everlasting. We are weak, whereas He is almighty. We are poor, whereas He is rich. We are needy, whereas He is independent. We are finite, whereas He is infinite. We are mortal, whereas He is immortal. How can we, therefore, ever comprehend His reality, or even offer a word of praise or do homage?

All the homage we can proffer is only in keeping with our mental grasp and conception. All that comes within human conception is man's own creation. That is surrounded by man, and man is the surrounder, or infinite in relation thereto. But whereas a concept has only an ideal existence, man – the creator of such a concept – has both an ideal and an extraneous existence.

A Divinity which we can mentally grasp, which can be brought within the grasp of intellect, is not Divinity, because it has no existence extraneously. It is only a mental concept.

We, who are possessed of extraneous existence, who also possess the ideal existence, are greater than our own creation, because we are infinite, whereas our concept is finite, and assuredly that which is infinite is far superior to the finite.

If you ponder over this you will see how clear and evident it is. It is self-evident that the human powers of conception and perception cannot conceive of Divinity, but the bestowal of Divinity is all-encompassing; the lights of Divinity are shining; the qualities of

Divinity are evident and to be seen.

The holy verities, the divine prophets, are like mirrors, which are in a state of utmost purity and sanctity and polish, and because they are in an attitude facing the sun of reality, therefore that sun of reality, with its potency, effulgence and heat, is reflected therein, and all its virtues can be visible in the mirror.

If we say that the sun has shone upon these mirrors, or that it has become effulgent in the mirror, we do not mean that the sun has descended from its lofty state of sanctity and has chosen a habitat in the mirror, because that is impossible. For the sun there is no descent. It ever is in its high point of glory and majesty, but its light, and its heat, in a pure and polished mirror become revealed, and all its virtues are made visible, and these mirrors which thus reveal that light are the realities of the prophets.

Hence it becomes evident that the reality of Divinity is holy and sanctified above descent or ascent, even as the phenomenal sun, this material sun which can be reflected in the mirror, is holy above descent and ascent, is sanctified above egress and ingress, even as this sun is sanctified above egress and ingress, but the eternal bestowal of the sun, in this pure and sanctified and polished mirror has become evident and manifest.

The mirror says, 'Verily, the sun is in me, and if you do not believe, then look at me.' And the mirror is truthful, for the sun is seen in the mirror. Notwithstanding that, the purpose of such a statement, were it to be made by the mirror, is not that the sun has descended from its lofty state and entered and effected an ingress in the mirror, because, for the sun, there is no descent or ascent. But with all its bounties and characteristics it can become evident in the mirror.

That is why His Holiness Christ declares, or that is what He means when He said, 'Verily, the Father is in the Son.' That means that the sun in this mirror has become manifest and revealed. It does not mean that the eternal sun or verity has descended from the lofty heavens, when it is unlimited, and has become limited thereby, for were such a thing to be realized, it is a limitation.

This is the meaning of unity or oneness. This is the quintessence of this Divine subject. Consider how evident it is. It is as the sun at midday. It is reasonable and in conformity with science.

That is why we state that religious teaching must ever conform with science and reason. They must correspond with the mind. This is perfectly in conformity with science and reason. There is no doubt or uncertainty about it.

Now, inasmuch as the sun of reality has become manifest in this polished mirror, from this mirror, by processes of reflection, it can permeate throughout all regions.

The light of the sun is one, the heat of the sun is one, and these have become resplendent in all phenomena. There is no earthly phenomenon, no earthly form of life, which is bereft of the light and heat of the sun.

Likewise all humanity receives a portion of the bounty of God. All mankind are the manifestations of the signs of God. All phenomena are expressions of the might and power of God, and all phenomena reveal the handiwork of God. None of them are the handiwork of Satan. No man has ever been created by Satan. They are all the creation of God. These are the signs of God's power.

Hence we must ever reverence the creation of God. We must ever bow before the signs of the might and power of God. We must ever be kind and clement toward the signs of the power and might of God, and toward all humanity. All are the signs of His power. He has created them all. The devil has had nothing to do with it. At most, it is this: that some of us may be wise, some may be ignorant; the ignorant must be helped to become wise. Some are sick; they must be treated. Some are childlike; they must be helped to reach maturity. Some are asleep, they must be gently awakened. But everybody must be loved. That is it!

We must not hate a child just because he is a child and think he is imperfect when we compare him with maturity. But with the utmost of kindness he must be nurtured, be educated to reach maturity, in order that he may become reasonable, in order that he may attain to knowledge and wisdom, in order that he may be qualified to enter the Kingdom of God.

God is most kind. Consider what His Holiness Christ said: 'Verily, the sun shines upon the just and the unjust alike.' What a blessed statement this is! Even the sinner is not deprived of the mercy of God. What a sweet utterance!

Consider, although this earth is dark, all the earthly phenomena are dark; but this radiant sun, how it cultivates all, how it brightens all, how it heats all! Can we deny the efficacy of the sun? Not at all. It is evident.

Then shall we see the signs of God's kindness. Likewise we see how He educates us. We find that He bestows upon us all His bounties. Now, so long as we have such a kind God, why should we be unkind? He Who is our Creator, He Who is our Provider, He Who is our Resuscitator, He Who is so gentle and kind to all of us, then why should we not be kind to one another, instead of saying, 'This is a Jew, this is a Christian, the other is a Musselman or Mohammedan, this is a Buddhist.' This is none of our business. God has created us all and it is our duty to be kind to everybody. That is our duty. But as to their respective beliefs, that is between them and their God, and at the last day He will look out for their account. He has not appointed us as their expert accountants.

It is our duty to praise God and to thank Him that He has created all of us human. He has endowed us all with sight and hearing. He has destined us all to be after the image and likeness of God. What a bestowal is this! What a providence is this! What a glorious crown is this! Why should we lose these favors? Why should we be so self-occupied? Why should we deny the favors of God?

In thanksgiving for this glorious bounty we must all become unified as one family. We must all become as one people. We must all inhabit the same nativity. We must all become as one nation. Thus may the world of humanity prove to be the world of the kingdom, and this dark sphere become a bright sphere, so that these contentions and strife shall cease and the utmost of love and affection shall obtain.

Verily, this is the purpose of the mission of the prophets. Verily, this is the mission of all the books which have descended. Verily, this is the aim of the effulgence of the sun of reality. Thus may the fundamental oneness of the world of humanity become established, so that oneness of nativity shall be founded, the oneness of nationality shall be established, the oneness of policy shall be established, and the world of humanity become a mirror reflecting the Kingdom of God.

The lights shining in the kingdom – may they become revealed in the human kingdom. The virtues which are present in the kingdom – may they be revealed or become resplendent in the human kingdom. May the unity, or oneness, of the angelic state become manifest in the human state, so that humanity itself shall become angelic.

What is the meaning of the word 'angel'? It means no other than a holy soul, a bright and radiant soul, a perfect soul, a Divine soul, a soul who is the manifestation of love, a manifestation of reasonableness, a manifestation of knowledge, one who is not a captive of superannuated, blind imitations.

These superannuated, blind imitations, or religious dogmas, which are ever the cause of enmity, the cause of destruction, the cause of darkness, the cause of bloodshed, the cause of tyranny, the cause of despotism – these blind imitations must be cast aside, and the mysteries of reality shall be revealed.

That foundation which was meant to be the underlying principle of all the prophets, that foundation which Christ Himself laid – that is the basis of the oneness of the world of humanity.

That foundation is universal love.

That foundation is universal peace among the nations.

That foundation is universal peace among the countries.

That foundation is universal peace among all the races.

That foundation is the universal peace which shall weld together all the religions, and that foundation is to do away with all sectarianism.

At a time when the Orient was enveloped in the gloom of prejudice and fanaticism, and thick clouds had befogged the horizon of reality, among the nations of the Orient there was religious prejudice, sectarianism, political prejudice, racial prejudice and patriotic prejudice, and the Oriental nations were in constant conflict and state of war.

The religionists considered each other as contaminating and they shunned each other, exercising the severest enmities against each other. Darkness was so dense that not a trace of light was ever visible.

Under such circumstances His Holiness Baha'o'llah dawned from the horizon of reality, and He laid institutes and teachings which united all the nations, which caused fellowship among the various religions, which dispelled religious prejudice, which dispelled the political prejudice, which dispelled the patriotic prejudice and which dispelled racial prejudice, having ushered under the tent or tabernacle of the oneness of humanity all the peoples of reality. They were souls representative of the religions and of the denominations thereof who had hearkened to the call of Baha'o'llah and who had become informed of His teachings. Such souls, in Persia, are living together in the utmost of love and amity. They are in a state of the utmost kindness toward one another. It is just as if they were one household.

That is why His Holiness Baha'o'llah addresses humanity, saying, 'Ye are all the leaves of one tree and the drops of one sea.' That is to say, the world of humanity, representing all the religions, representing all the races, may be likened to a tree. Every nation of the nations is like a branch thereof, and every soul among them is like unto a leaf. But all of them belong to one tree, and that tree is the blessed tree, and that tree is the tree of life, and that tree is the tree of sacrifice.

Therefore, it is not allowable that among human individuals there should linger any strife. Let no sedition tarry. Let no hatred or rancor prevail. All must live in the utmost kindness, in the utmost love, the utmost of fellowship, and must pass their days pleasantly, for this will win the bounties of God and the bestowals shall surround them, and the Kingdom of God will become personified in the human kingdom. And this is our wish in its entirety.[47]

After the meeting 'Abdu'l-Bahá was invited to the home of the daughter of the Palo Altan Bahá'í Isabelle C. Merriman, 925 Waverly Street where a dinner for some 29 guests, including Dr Starr Jordan and Professors Samuel S. Seward and H. D. Gray, was held in His honor.[48]

Merriman had some social standing in the San Francisco area. Her sister Sarah was the widow of William Wirt Winchester, heir of Oliver Winchester, the founder of the famous weapons company. She was also well known for her social and charitable work. A journal stated that Isabelle 'has been unusually active as an officer of the juvenile courts of Santa Clara county in dealing with juvenile delinquents, many of whom she has brought into her own home in Palo Alto. At the present times it is stated that she has 11 girls and four boys in her care.'[49] It may have been because of this interest in working with children that the Master suggested to her that she continue her services in the Holy Land. This captured the attention of newspapers in the area.

An article published in the *Evening News* of San Jose stated that Merriman was 'seriously considering the advisability of abandoning her home and work in this country and entering into the service of Abdul Baha Abbas . . . "The offer was made to me only last night," said Mrs. Merriman. "And I am not sure just whether I will accept or not. Such an offer is an unusual tribute to my work in behalf of children."'[50]

Other journals published similar information which was probably part of a syndicated article. The *Oakland Tribune*, for instance, quoted Mrs Merriman as saying that 'although I have not fully decided whether I will return with him there is nevertheless the feeling that it is a chance to do good for humanity. I have for many years believed in the teachings of the Baha movement but not being in the heyday of youth I doubt the wisdom of going at this time into a strange land and to strange customs. I will consider the matter carefully and may return with the prophet to Persia.'[51]

Address at Berkeley and at the Open Forum

'Abdu'l-Bahá was invited to speak at Berkeley by its mayor, the socialist Jackson Stitt Wilson (1868–1942), who had learned of the Bahá'í Faith from Lua Getsinger and who had visited 'Abdu'l-Bahá in San Francisco on 7 October.[52]

A public meeting in Berkeley was arranged for Wednesday, 9 October. No accounts of this meeting seem to have been published in the press but 'Abdu'l-Bahá's arrival was announced some days before in local newspapers. The *Berkeley Independent*, a journal with a circulation of 2,750 copies, stated in a short article announcing the arrival of 'Abdu'l-Bahá in San Francisco that 'Berkeleyans interested in the movement are making an effort to secure the Greek theater for a meeting in the near future'.[53]

The Republican *Berkeley Daily Gazette*, with a circulation of 5,700 copies, stated that 'The theme for the lecture has not been announced, but it is expected that it will be on Baha's general subject, "The Peace of the Nation and the Unity of Religion".'[54]

In Oakland further announcements were published in the *Tribune* and the *Enquirer*. According to these the talk was finally held in the auditorium of the Berkeley High School, Grove and Allston Way, at 8 o'clock in the evening.[55]

On the evening of Thursday, 10 October 'Abdu'l-Bahá spoke at the Open Forum. Again it seems that no account of this meeting was published in the press. An announcement in the *San Francisco Bulletin* stated that 'Abdul Baha will address the Open Forum, 925 Golden Gate Avenue, on Thursday, October 10, at 8 p.m. He will expound the tenets of his religion.' The same announcement stated that the Indian nationalist and anarchist Har Dayal (1884–1939) 'will reply as an exponent of radicalism'.[56]

Address at Temple Emanu-El

On Saturday, 12 October 'Abdu'l-Bahá spoke in San Francisco's Temple Emanu-El, 450 Sutter Street, at the invitation of Martin A. Meyer,[57] who from 1910 was the rabbi of this reformed Jewish congregation. In an address that was followed by over two thousand people, 'Abdu'l-Bahá touched again on some of the subjects He expounded at the Shaari Tov Temple in Minneapolis, proclaiming, among other things, religious unity and the prophethood of Christ and Muhammad.[58] Reporters were present at the meeting and accounts of His address were published afterwards. The *San Francisco Post*, for instance, wrote on the same day:

> BAHAIST LEADER IN JEWISH PULPIT PLEADS UNITY
>
> 'CENTURY HAS COME WHEN ALL RELIGIONS SHOULD ENJOY UNIVERSAL PEACE'
>
> After expounding the unity of all fundamental religious beliefs and pleading for a universal faith, Abdul Baba, aged Persian leader of the universal religion movement, speaking today at Temple Emanu-El, rose to a dramatic climax in the emphatic declaration that the time has come for the unification of all religions when racial prejudice shall cease and when all the religions shall enjoy universal peace forever.
>
> 'The century has come,' he said, 'when all the religions are to be unified; the century has come when all the religions are to enjoy universal peace; the century has come when racial prejudice and religious differences shall be brushed away forever.'
>
> Abdul Baba spoke in Persian through an interpreter. He was introduced by Rabbi Martin A. Meyer and at once he plunged into a broad discussion of basic religious doctrines, attempting to prove

that the basis of all religion was to promote advancement and progress of man.

Dressed in a robe of tan, his head covered with a turban of pure white, the Persian gospel leader presented a unique figure as he stood before the altar with the sacred ark of the covenant as his background.

His subject had been announced as 'The Fundamental Unity of Religious Thought'. Opening his sermon with the assertion that fundamentally all religion was intended to bring about human advancement he proceeded to show that basically all religions were alike since their fundamental purposes were the same. If they are the same on this fundamental foundation, he argued, there should be universal religion, a faith marked throughout the world by peace instead of dissension.

Christ had recognized Moses as a prophet, said the preacher, and had declared for the validity of the Mosaic law. Mohammed had done the same, so had the civilized world, said Abdul Baha. Why, then, he asked, should religion divide the world into factions, rife with dissension and hatred?

'Is it not better,' he queried, waving his hands in forceful gesture, 'to enjoy living together and unite in the love of God? Then can we observe how this world would grow to a Paradise.'

Abdul Baha said that religion ever helped humanity toward progress and was the cause of everlasting honor among men. As substantial proof to the services done humanity by religion, the Persian preacher told of how Moses had given religion to the Israelites at a time when they were most oppressed and were held in bondage. Religion, he declared, had been responsible for the growth of the Jewish people as a nation after they had been rescued from bondage and had caused their intellectual and moral advancement to a remarkable degree.

All religions, he said, could be divided into two classes. First, that class which concerned moral and ethical teachings, that fundamental basis of the whole belief which makes for human progress. The other division is a matter of rites and customs. He said, changed with the times, and is only incidental.

'The essentials which have to do with development of men are the foundations of all religions, and they are the same,' said the preacher.[59]

Describing 'Abdu'l-Bahá's message as modern, the *Chronicle* carried on 13 October the following account:

PERSIAN HEARD AT TEMPLE EMANU-EL

ABDUL BAHA ABBAS GIVES HIS MESSAGE OF THE UNITY OF RELIGIONS

Abdul Baha Abbas, prophet of universal religion, the eradication of prejudice and dogma, and the establishment of universal peace and the fellowship of humanity, spoke at the regular service in Temple Emanu-El yesterday morning.

Speaking through an interpreter, and standing by the curtains of Ark of the Torah, the aged Persian in his patriarchal robes, white turban and with his white beard appeared as a figure from the distant past of religion inspiration. His message was as modern as his appearance was as from the past.

He said that all religions are divided into two parts, the fundamental truth and the ephemeral dogma, and that the fundamental truth was one. Taking the illustration of how 'His Holiness Moses' is venerated alike by the Jews, the Christians and the Mohammedans, he appealed for a universal recognition of the holiness of all great religious leaders.

His theme was that, while the fundamental truth of religion had ever been the inspiration of progress and the enlightenment of mankind, the dogma and prejudice had been evil in their effect.

'This is the century,' he said in conclusion, 'for the recognition of the oneness of God, for the attainment of the fellowship of humanity, for the eradication of prejudice and for the realization of universal peace.'

Dr. Meyer in introducing the visiting teacher said that he welcomed one who came from the East, where the first religious message was given, and from the land where the teaching of the fatherhood of God was first promulgated.[60]

The report in the *Examiner* read:

ABDUL BAHA DEVOTES TALK TO UNIVERSAL PEACE

PERSIAN PROPHET SAYS TIME HAS COME TO ABOLISH RELIGIOUS AND RACIAL PREJUDICE

Abdul Baha, the Persian philosopher and Bahai leader, expounded the fundamental unity of religions yesterday from the pulpit of Temple Emanu-El and declared that the time had come for religious and racial prejudices to cease and world peace to become an established fact.

Abdul Baha spoke in Persian, and his remarks were translated to the audience by an interpreter. He was introduced to the congregation by Rabbi Martin A. Meyer. The philosopher wore a tan garment and a white turban.

'Is it not better to enjoy living together and unite in the love of God?' the aged apostle queried. He pointed out that Christ and Mohammed had both recognized the validity of the laws of Moses, and that the civilized world had accepted both. Why, then, should there be factions in religion?

All religions, the venerable Persian said, could be divided into two classes – those dealing with moral and ethical teachings, and those concerned with rites and customs.[61]

On 1 November the *Palo Altan* published the full text of Bijou Straun's notes of the talk. The newspaper also reproduced the introductory remarks made by Meyer:

Brethren of the Congregation Emmanu-El: It is our privilege and a very high privilege indeed to welcome in our midst this morning Abdu'l Baha, a great teacher of our age and generation.

The heart of the Orient seems to be essentially religious, whatever else it might be or might not be, and now and again, out of the heart of the Orient the fundamental religious message of the world is stated and restated.

Abdul Baha is the representative of one of the religious systems of life, and it appeals to us Jews because we Jews feel that we have fathered that ideal throughout the centuries of men.

This morning he will speak in his native tongue through his interpreter Dr. Fareed, on 'The Fundamental Unity of Religious Thought', and I know that what he will say will be of significance to us. We thank him in advance for the message and for consenting to address us at this service this morning.[62]

In many addresses and personal interviews given later 'Abdu'l-Bahá made reference to the importance of the talk He delivered at Temple Emanu-El. He also directed that the text of the talk, which according to Ella Cooper was corrected by Faríd, Sohrab and 'Abdu'l-Bahá Himself,[63] be published in other journals and even translated into other languages to be shared with the press.

In America, for instance, 'Abdu'l-Bahá encouraged the editor of the *Palo Altan* to publish it. In England *The Christian Commonwealth* also printed the talk in a special issue about the Bahá'í Faith published on 1 January 1913.[64] Weeks before, in a note to the editor of *The Christian Commonwealth*, the Master stated that 'When this address, delivered in the synagogue, is read, the reader will be most pleased and most enlightened.'[65] He also mentioned this talk in Liverpool,[66] London[67] and Budapest.[68] In Vienna he encouraged a local Bahá'í to translate and publish it in the press.[69]

Interviews with John D. Barry

One of San Francisco's most renowned journalists was John D. Barry (1866–1942).[70] He was granted two consecutive interviews with 'Abdu'l-Bahá which were published in his column 'Ways of the World'. Barry gave a detailed account of his visits to the Master in two articles, the first of which was published on 12 October:

WAYS OF THE WORLD

ABDUL BAHA. A CALL ON THE PERSIAN PROPHET WHO HAS BEEN MAKING A VISIT TO SAN FRANCISCO, CARRYING THE MESSAGE OF UNIVERSAL HARMONY

When I entered the comfortable house at 1815 California Street, where the prophet was staying, I saw a great many people. They were sitting about in the wide hall and in the rooms that radiated into the distance. While I waited for my turn to be received I asked one of the prophet's followers, a very pleasant woman, what those people were doing.

'They have come to see the Abdul Baha about their own affairs,' she replied. 'He is willing to receive everyone.'

'Do most of them come for advice?' I said.

'O, yes. The Abdul Baha spends his life in helping others. His religion is essentially practical. It is not enough for one to have faith. One must work all the time.'

'But he must be overrun.'

My remark was received with a charming smile. 'Can one spend one's time to better advantage than in helping?'

Our talk turned to the spread of the new religion. 'There are many of us in this country now,' said the disciple.

'Do you have a ceremonial?'

'No. But we have meetings. And then we have lectures. I, myself, often lecture on the faith. You see, we have nothing really new to promulgate. We recognize the good in all religions. What we wish to do is to reconcile human beings, to make them see that they belong to one family. But good deeds are the most important expression of the faith.'

This reiteration interested me. It sounded like practical Christianity. 'Are you devoting yourself to the new religion?' I ventured to ask.

The reply came quite frankly, 'Yes.'

'And you help all who apply to you?'

'I do what I can.'

The words seemed almost too good to be true. 'People often apply to me for help,' I went on, 'because I write for a newspaper. It is hard to know what to do. Only the other day a man came to ask me to help him get out of the clutches of a money-lender.'

'Send him to Abdul Baha. Or send him to me.' The reply was quiet, serene.

'And the day before a woman came in great distress. Her case was most difficult.'

Again came that serene reply: 'Send her to me.'

As I sat there scarcely able to believe my ears I wondered if indeed the spirit of Christianity has returned to earth, this time by way of Persia. I also speculated on what would happen if it were generally known in San Francisco that the new religion was not merely a philosophical cult, appealing to the fashionable, but a broad, practical religion, reaching out to all mankind with special tenderness for those in distress. At the people sitting about I looked with new interest. I had to admit that they all seemed to be prosperous. Whatever their troubles tonight have been, they were probably not the result of immediate need.

Someone came forward and asked if the Abdul Baha was visiting friends here. A young woman who had been swiftly and noiselessly passing and repassing and consulting in a low voice, replied: 'No. He has rented this house for himself and for his suite for one month. We were very lucky to be able to secure it for him. He prefers a house to a hotel.'

Dark-faced men, with black silky hair were moving about. A smooth-faced young fellow, who looked like an American, kept opening the door to admit visitors. Someone near me said he was a recent college graduate who intended to devote his life to the new faith.

Presently one of those dark men approached. 'The Abdul Baha will see you now,' he said.

I walked up the wide, thickly carpeted stairs, and passed through the upper hall. From one of the rooms in the rear came a loud voice, speaking a foreign language, different from any language I knew the sound of. I entered a sunny bedroom, where I was met by two dark-faced men, one young, in a conventional gray suit, with a pointed black beard and large luminous eyes, his silky hair partly covered with a black fez; and the other old, yet vigorous, with a flowing gray beard and with long gray hair under a white turban, dressed in a loose, flowing brown robe, reaching to his feet.

The young man held out his hand and said:

'Welcome.'

The prophet spoke with a marked accent: 'Welcome, very welcome.' He sank on the couch in Turkish fashion. He looked much older than his sixty-eight years; but he spoke like a man endowed with tremendous vitality. As soon as he stopped his companion interpreted, in a low, even voice.

The Abdul Baha explained that he was glad to be in this country. He brought a message from his friends in Persia. No matter what differences there might be between human beings, of race, or of nationality, or of climate, they all belonged to the same family. He spoke in rather prolonged intervals. His words had a kind of exaltation. They sounded like quotations from a book. The manner, however, was simple and direct.

There was one question that I wished particularly to ask this prophet of the new faith that embraced all humanity, that excluded no one. What message did it have for the disinherited millions?

When I asked the question and it was repeated in Persian, there was a brief silence before the answer began:

'Society is like the army. There must be degrees. There must be officers and there must be soldiers. Thus far there has not been a just distribution of rewards. The few have had more than their share. The soldiers have been neglected. Their rights must be safeguarded. The reform will have to start with the land, the source of all wealth. I should like to develop an agrarian community, founded on perfect justice. The government must be concerned for the resources of nature. Those who make great discoveries, like the discovery of a rich mine, should receive a large portion for their enterprise. The rest should go to the government, for all the people. The weak and the poor must be cared for.'

Then, in response to questions, Abdul Baha outlined in detail his idea of taxation, founded on the old system of tithes. He made it plain that he looked forward to the day when men should learn to live in harmony, co-operating for the advantage of the mass and for their own welfare and happiness. As he spoke, his words would be deftly turned into English by his companion.

Meanwhile, at the door, one of the faithful was busily writing. Then I recalled that nearly everything he said was recorded. Presently, faces appeared at the door. Visitors were eager to be received. Already I had taken more than a fair allowance of time. But when I rose to leave it was arranged that I should come for further talk the next day.[71]

The second article included a summary of the origins of the Bahá'í Faith attributed to 'Abdu'l-Bahá Himself:

WAYS OF THE WORLD

ABDUL BAHA: THE PROPHET TELLS OF THE SPIRITUAL GROWTH OF THE MOVEMENT WHICH CALLS UPON HUMANITY TO PUT ASIDE DIFFERENCES AND TO ACHIEVE UNITY

When I called to see Abdul Baha for the second time I again found the house in California Street filled with people. In a few moments I was told that the master was ready to talk. He was sitting in the same place, on the couch near the window, a gray robe flowing down from his shoulders over his thick-set figure, his thin gray hair falling behind his neck, his gray beard partly hiding his aged face. He explained that he had not been feeling very well. He had not as yet become adjusted to the California climate. But he spoke with his characteristic vigor and authority.

Our talk turned to the spiritual development of the Bahai movement. As Abdul Baha spoke, his words would be translated by that quiet and courteous interpreter.

'Our movement goes back to the young leader who called himself The Gate or The Door, in our language, The Bab. He said: "I have the feeling that I am the gate to an Invisible personage. Whosoever desires to communicate with that personage must need go through this gate." Bab had an inner effulgence. He began his career as prophet at twenty-five. He worked for seven years. Then he was put to death. It was claimed by the ecclesiastical authorities of Persia that his teachings were harmful. They anathematized him on account of his books. They said: "This person is a source of misguidance to the nation. His existence will destroy the reigning monarchy." Though his followers were bitterly persecuted they rapidly multiplied. In all his books His Holiness, The Bab, proclaimed the glories of the person who was coming. He was like John the Baptist. He said: "That which you have inflicted upon me I forgive. But beware lest you disobey Him whom God will manifest. Beware lest my books be used as pretexts of denying him." At the time prophesied the Baha Ullah appeared. He was then forty years old.'

Abdul Baha spoke with reverence. He said nothing with regard to his being the son of Baha Ullah. When I asked him to give me some details of his father's early life he seemed to hesitate. He evidently regarded my question as unimportant. But I was curious to know what the forces were in the life of Baha Ullah that made him believe he was the prophet foretold of Bab. 'Long before he revealed himself Baha Ullah knew that he was the destined one. But he kept silent. He was a man of great wealth and of wonderful natural gifts. As a boy he went to no school. But his power was such that he was recognized as a great figure.'

'Did he have any personal relations with the Bab?' I asked.

'The two never met. But at the age of thirty-two Baha Ullah received a tablet from him, saying that he was the one prophesied.

Of the two Baha Ullah was by far the greater. Some of the teachings of Bab he discarded. For example, Bab said: "War is good." Yes, he advocated war. He praised conquest. Baha Ullah declared that war was contrary to the oneness of humanity. Bab considered that all scientific books should be burned. But Abdul Baha had no such belief.'

'What did Baha Ullah do after he revealed himself?'

'The first thing he did was to write an epistle to all the kings of the earth and to the pope and to your president, then U. S. Grant, proclaiming the brotherhood of man and the importance of international peace. Soon the followers of the Bab, who had been dwindling away, came and others joined the movement. The government then strove against Baha Ullah; they banished him to Bagdad, and then to Constantinople and then to Romania. In spite of all this tyranny the apostles went abroad and spread the word. At last the authorities imprisoned Baha Ullah in the Fortress of Akka, in Syria. Even in prison while under surveillance, he was able to promulgate his teachings and to write his messages to the world.'

I should have been glad to hear from Abdul Baha of his own early experience in taking up the work left by his father. But the interpreter explained that he disliked talking about himself. Perhaps, too, it would have been a painful history to discuss. For, as I knew, it included long years of imprisonment for the sake of the faith. But it was plain that this experience instead of harming, had given the teacher a greater spirituality.

During our talk figures had been hovering about the door, one of them busily writing. Word came that the house was crowded with visitors, all anxious to secure an interview. The Abdul Baha announced that he would go down and speak. They should all be invited into one room. In a few moments the drawing room on the ground floor was crowded. Abdul Baha entered, walking vigorously. At once he began to speak of the message of the new faith. It came not to destroy or to disrupt, but to create in mankind universal harmony. In Persia the members of the faith had suffered great trials; but they were strong in their devotion. From far away they send loving remembrances, inviting the East and the West to shake hands. It was folly for mankind to contend on account of thoughts and feelings. Such things were in the hands of God. Mankind must

> learn to control nature and to become identified with the spirit. As the speaker went on he grew more and more metaphysical and rhapsodic. His words, repeated by the interpreter, assumed quaint English form. When he had finished he turned and strode into the hall and up the stairs.[72]

A further interview with 'Abdu'l-Bahá in San Francisco was published in the *Call*. It was presumably granted on the morning of 13 October, just before 'Abdu'l-Bahá left San Francisco to be the guest of Phoebe Hearst at Pleasanton. The article read in part:

> 'We have not come to establish a new religion. It is not a new religion. We seek no converts from other churches, but we do seek to unify all churches of all creeds and all denominations.'
>
> His temporary home at 1815 California Street, which is the beautiful F.W. Dohrman residence, gave evidence yesterday of the success of his appeal. It was thronged all day with visitors, not converts, but 'believers' or 'friends' as they are called, of all types and nationalities. Several San Francisco society women were present, also many who are not in the social register, while scattered about were many Hindoos, Japanese, Chinese, and men and women of other races.
>
> Upstairs in a sunny apartment sat Abdul Baha – 'Servant of God' – surrounded by roses. He wore a fawn colored cloak drawn on at the waist with a loose belt, and on his head a spotless white turban. His face is seamed and yellow, but full of expression. When a visitor was presented to him he would smile benignly and begin to talk of Bahaism. At the close of his discourse he would present the visitor with a rose.
>
> Roses to Abdul Baha Abbas are symbolical.
>
> 'Every rose has its thorn,' he is fond of saying, 'but like the rose we should learn to live above the thorn.'
>
> His followers reverence the aged man. Many of them have been Bahaists for a dozen years or more. Others have adopted the belief since the teacher came to San Francisco two weeks ago.
>
> 'A beautiful soul came into our faith yesterday, or last week, or last month,' is the way they describe the conversion of a new 'friend'.[73]

A social note in the *Call* reported on 13 October that among the people who visited 'Abdu'l-Bahá in San Francisco were Dr and Mrs C. S. Gunther Nagel of Palo Alto who 'went to San Francisco Sunday to hear an address by Abdul Baha'.[74]

During the stay of 'Abdu'l-Bahá in San Francisco, news reached North America about the increasing hostilities between the Ottoman Empire, the Balkans and Greece. The Greek colony in San Francisco organized a demonstration against Turkey that was supported by some three thousand people. This prompted the publication of an editorial by William Rader[75] of the *San Jose Mercury and Herald*, a Republican newspaper with a circulation of 11,100 copies, condemning the position of Turkey. In the last paragraph of the editorial the author declared that 'while guns are booming in the Balkan country, Abdul Baha, the venerable apostle of universal peace, is speaking to the people of the United States, and he comes from the adjoining country of Persia. Could the gospel of Abdul Baha be put into practice, the guns in the forest of Serbia would be silenced. Not until the Eastern world grasps and applies the new gospel of light and love will our Eastern friends reach a conclusion which will forever put to silence the rifles of contending armies.'[76]

Outside California, the *Coos Bay Times* (Marshfield, OR), a Republican newspaper with a circulation 1,500 copies daily, published an article apropos the sojourn of 'Abdu'l-Bahá in San Francisco which also quoted from the recently published collection of His addresses, *Paris Talks*.[77]

Visit to Los Angeles

On 18 October 'Abdu'l-Bahá left San Francisco bound for Los Angeles, where He arrived in the evening of the same day. He spent a total of four nights in the city, staying at the Hotel Lankershim.

On the first morning after His arrival 'Abdu'l-Bahá visited the Inglewood cemetery to pay tribute to Thornton Chase (1847–1912), one of the first western believers and an outstanding figure in the early history of the Bahá'í Faith in America. His passing, occurring on the same day that 'Abdu'l-Bahá arrived in California, prompted an article in the *Morning Oregonian*:

> PERSIAN MYSTIC LANDS
>
> THORNTON CHASE, ADMIRER, DIES DAY OF ARRIVAL AFTER LONG WAIT
>
> After looking forward for some months to the arrival of the Persian prophet and mystic, Abdul Baha, in San Francisco, Thornton Chase, the general Western manager of the Union Mutual Life Insurance Company of New York, died last Wednesday, the very day the prophet arrived.
>
> For some time Mr. Chase had made periodical visits to Portland, his most recent one being in the month just past. On that occasion he spoke at Eilers' Hall on the forthcoming visit to be paid by the prophet Baha to Portland and of the growth of the Bahai faction.
>
> Of this movement Mr. Chase had written much and studied deeply. He had paid a visit to the prophet when the latter was in prison in Syria, and was a leader in the movement on the Coast.[78]

'Abdu'l-Bahá instructed that the grave of Thorton Chase be visited by the Bahá'ís. More than a year after His visit to the Inglewood cemetery, the Sunday edition of the *Los Angeles Times* published an interview with Emily Chase, the widow of Thornton Chase, offering some interesting information on the way in which Bahá'ís obeyed 'Abdu'l-Bahá's wish:

> SHRINE OF BAHAISM DRAWING MANY HERE
>
> The grave of the late Thornton Chase, the first American convert to the Persian religion of Bahaism, in Inglewood Park Cemetery, has been designated as a sacred shrine by Abdul Baha, head of the religious order that numbers its converts in the millions.
>
> Baha was in America and was on the way to Los Angeles to visit Chase when the latter died October 1, 1912. When the leader reached San Francisco he sent a telegram to Chase announcing that he would soon be here. Mrs. Chase read the message to her husband an hour before his death.
>
> The Persian was overcome with grief when he arrived and learned that Chase had passed away. He visited the grave.
>
> Mrs. Chase said yesterday at her home in the Young apartments that she estimated that more than 1000 of the followers of Baha have made a pilgrimage to her husband's grave in the past year.
>
> Baha recently issued a proclamation in Persian expressing the

wish that all Bahais who visit America kneel at the grave of Chase.

The Persian Minister to the United States, Ali Kuli Khan, made a secret visit to Los Angeles recently and talked with Mrs. Chase in regards to rearing a permanent memorial to her husband.

Charles Mason Remy of Washington, son of Rear-Admiral Remy, has charge of the erection of the memorial. Remy is one of the prominent leaders of Bahaism in America and is devoting his wealth and energy to spreading the religion.

Chase was a native of Massachusetts. He was superintendent of a life insurance company in Portland, Me., for twenty-six years. He was in the insurance business in Los Angeles two years before his death. Chase was a graduate of Brown University. He had made a comparative study of the great religions of the world before he accepted the teachings of Baha.

'The Persian Minister and Mr. Remy inform me that arrangements have been made to place the body of my husband in an indestructible stone casket and erect a monument with an inscription in Persian,' Mrs. Chase said. 'I believe that it is the plan to erect some sort of a chapel or temple in the future.'[79]

When 'Abdu'l-Bahá returned to Hotel Lankershim from the cemetery, He received reporters who had requested to interview Him. The *Herald*, a Democratic evening newspaper with a circulation of 20,600 copies, was the first local newspaper to publish information about the arrival of 'Abdu'l-Bahá in the city. Through this publication the Master conveyed a message to the citizens of Los Angeles:

NOTED PERSIAN IS HERE TO PLEAD FOR PEACE

Abdul Baha Abbas of Teheran, Persia, head of the great Bahai movement, a leader in the campaign for universal peace and a man whose teachings are read in every land, arrived in the city today to preach the gospel of universal peace and to address the local followers of the Bahai faith.

With him are Dr. Ameer N. Fareed, Mirza Ali Akbar, Mirza Ahmed Sohrab and Mirza Hahmood of Persia, who act as his interpreters. Upon his arrival he immediately took quarters at the Hotel Lankershim. He had hardly become seated when the telephone began ringing and his followers came flocking in to see him.

This morning Abdul Baha announced that one of the causes for his visit here was to conduct a memorial service for Thornton Chase of 227 Rampart Boulevard, who up to the time of his death two weeks ago was one of the strongest followers of the Bahai movement on the Pacific coast. The ceremony took place this morning in Inglewood cemetery in the presence of several friends of the deceased.

'Will you take a message to the people of Los Angeles?' he asked the Evening Herald through his interpreter. And then he spoke the following:

'Praise be to God. The United States has made wonderful progress. Its prosperity is daily on the increase. Educational facilities are unsurpassed, science is marching on, industrialism is expanding and agriculture is thoroughly scientific.

'America's success is due to the fact that she is a commercial, not a fighting nation. She is not contemplating war with other nations.

'International peace is the greatest issue of today. The time will come when all races and creeds will be united into one race and religion.'[80]

A short notice about the arrival of the Master was also published in the recently launched *Los Angeles Tribune*.[81] To the reporter with the *Los Angeles Times*, a Republican newspaper issuing 54,900 copies daily, 'Abdu'l-Bahá said:

'In the world's existence,' said Abdul Baha yesterday, 'there are two civilizations, the one material, the other spiritual or divine. Philosophers founded the material civilization. The divine prophets were the founders of the spiritual. The Greek philosophers were founders of the material. Christ was one of the founders of civilization, but that of divine character.

'Material civilization serves the world of bodies. Divine civilization serves the world of morality. The first is the cause for happiness in this world. The other is the cause for eternal happiness. If the divine civilization exists, it will include all that is necessary for the material. Where intellect and its virtues obtain, the physical attributes are presupposed. The physical virtues are not productive of the intellectual virtue. Nevertheless, it is strange that the people of the world have forgotten divine civilization and are steeped in material civilization. This is the reason for the restlessness in the world, for the wars, the bloodshed, the destruction and sinfulness of every character.'[82]

The following day, a public meeting was held at the Hotel Lankershim. A brief report of it appeared in the *Los Angeles Times* stating that 'Abdu'l-Bahá 'held a reception yesterday afternoon at his rooms in the Hotel Lankershim, giving advice and comfort to several hundred followers, mostly women, who crowded the parlors listening to his words with intense interest. The gray bearded patriarch delivered his lectures and private interviews through an interpreter.'[83]

Visit to Sacramento

'Abdu'l-Bahá left Los Angeles on 21 October and returned to San Francisco. On 25 October He traveled to Sacramento where He stayed for two nights in the Hotel Sacramento before leaving California.

Two public meetings were held at His hotel. The first address was delivered on the evening of Friday, 25 October, soon after His arrival in the city. Frederick R. Hinkle, a reporter with the *Sacramento Union*, which at the time had a daily circulation of 10,000 copies, interviewed the Master:

> PERSIAN PROPHET, LEADER OF BAHAI MOVEMENT, LECTURES ON DOCTRINES
>
> Abdul Baha Abbas, the Persian prophet and world leader of the Bahai movement, last night at the Hotel Sacramento expounded the doctrine and principles of his cause to an audience of mixed nationalities. Universal brotherhood, international peace, religious unity and the establishment of an ultimate world tribunal of arbitration make up the chief foundations for the movement which already has 12,000,000 followers in the world.
>
> The venerable prophet, with his long gray beard, cloak and turban, spoke in Persian. His remarks were translated by Dr. Ameen Fareed, a graduate of University of Illinois, and also of Johns Hopkins University. In appearance he represented a true incarnation of the far Eastern patriarchs and prophets of old.

ON TOUR OF UNITED STATES

Abdul Baha's home is in Mount Carmel, Syria. He arrived in New York April 7, 1912, and is touring the United States. This is his first visit to this country. To a Union reporter, in his apartment at the Hotel Sacramento yesterday afternoon following his arrival from San Francisco, he gave a brief synopsis of what the Bahai movement really stands for.

Universal peace is possible, he claims, only through the harmonizing of religious differences among races and nations. Jews, Christians, Mohammedans, Hindus and believers of all Divine religions, he declares, if they go back to the fundamental principles of their respective religions, will find a common meeting ground. All religions, he asserts, after a lapse of centuries have been corrupted by dogmas.

EXPOUNDS PRINCIPLES

Summarizing the Bahai idea he dictated the following statement, declaring its purpose to be: To investigate reality or truth; the declaration concerning the oneness or solidity of human kind, meaning God is one and humanity is one; international peace among races, among nations and among religions; the comparison of religion with science with a view of conforming the two; the general spread of education; international language as a means of international communication; the adoption of the Bahai formula for a definitive regime of economics, which although it conserves the social degrees, makes it possible for each individual to enjoy fully the resources of the Creator; the equality of rights, spiritual solidity, and heavenly fraternity; the establishment of an international parliamentary tribunal to which all nations shall send authorized representatives to settle by arbitration international disputes.

Abdul Baha's party is composed of four other Persians and a Japanese fugitive. In the party are Dr. Ameen Fareed, Mirza Ahmad Sohrab, Mirza Mahmood, and Mirza Ali Akbar . . .

BARS AMERICAN POLITICS

With regard to the Balkan war, Abdul Baha merely pronounced it the result of a ferocious state of affairs. He did not care to discuss American politics, although he declared himself interested in the outcome of the coming election.

A few days ago Abdul Baha spoke to the students of Stanford University. He is now on his way to Salt Lake. On his return trip across the continent he will speak in Salt Lake, Denver, Omaha, Chicago, Des Moines, and other larger cities in the middle West and East. He will repeat his lecture at the hotel this morning at 9 o'clock. He will leave Sacramento today to continue his journey East.[84]

As announced in the *Union*, the second public meeting was held on Saturday, 26 October, at nine in the morning. William A. Lawson, associate editor of the evening *Sacramento Bee*, which at the time had a circulation of 22,500 copies, was present during the address and wrote the following account:

NOTED PERSIAN TEACHER HERE PLEADS FOR WORLD PEACE

HEAD OF BAHAI RELIGION SAYS OLD TEACHINGS MUST BE REFORMED

Speaking through his interpreter, Dr. Ameen Fareed, this morning in Hotel Sacramento, Abdul-Baha Abbas, the Persian prophet and head of the Bahai religion, whose profound thoughts and learning have impressed the whole world, preached universal brotherhood and love, international peace, universal unity of religion and universal education. The respectful attention of an audience composed of persons interested in the doctrines and those interested in the prophet was given as the prophet communicated his message through his interpreter.

The soft flowing words in the Persian language as they dropped from the lips of the venerable prophet seemed to carry one back across many centuries to the time that others of his character traveled about preaching to the world. Clothed in Persian robes, with a turban covering his white locks, he seemed to have stepped directly from the age of the patriarchs.

PLEADS FOR WORLD PEACE

Speaking of universal peace, he said,

'The greatest affair of the world is universal peace. It is time to stop the shedding of blood and time for the East to meet the West.'

Many men of affairs, he said, have come to uphold the doctrine of peace and altruism.

The people, of California are particularly fitted for peace, he declared, and hoped the first flag of universal peace may be raised, in this State.

No limit can be set on the power of achievement, he said, because no matter how humanity advances, there are always achievements further on. He then declared that nothing is subject to termination and that the bounties of the Divine have no limitation. The reality of the sun and the reality of the Divine are akin. Were the sun's rays to cease, it would mean the ending of the sun. Were the Divinity's bounties to cease so would the Divinity.

WOULD REFORM RELIGION

The speaker declared that the teaching of religion must be developed and reformed. Past teachings, he said, are not good for the present. The laws of the past must be reformed. The world has so advanced that we need things suited to us now.

Love must be introduced into religion, said the speaker, and the oneness of humanity recognized. Class and National feeling must be done away with. One must not say 'I am a Frenchman', or 'an Englishman', 'a Jew', or 'Turk', but 'I am a member of humanity'.

The time of ferocity has passed – the medieval age of ignorance also, he said. An age of understanding has arrived and it is behooving that all of us should cast aside ignorance and race feeling . . .

Abdul Baha Abbas gave a lecture similar to the one of this morning at Hotel Sacramento last night, having as an audience persons interested in the doctrines and those interested in the prophet.

After his address this morning Abdul Baha, an adopted Persian name, which means 'Servant of God', talked for a time, through an interpreter, with a Bee representative and answered numerous questions. He speaks no English, but Persian very fluently and without hesitation. His style is highly poetic and he uses much Oriental imagery in his conversation, as in his lectures. To make his meaning clear to the general reader, it is needful to paraphrase his words as translate.

Abdul Baha explained that he does not call himself a prophet, nor does he claim divine inspiration. He wishes it understood that his mission is that of a teacher; to spread the gospel of enlightenment and peace; that the aim of Bahaism is not to destroy any religion or creed, but to associate all religious sects and denominations in a world-wide movement to do away with war and link all mankind in a spirit of brotherhood and good fellowship. One may be a Christian, he says, or a Mohammedan, as well as a Bahaist.

So it would appear from all his metaphorical exposition that Bahaism is not properly spoken of as a religion, but is best described as a 'movement', whose purpose is much like that of Matthew Arnold's aim of spreading 'sweetness and light'.

The word 'Bahai', in fact, is Persian for 'glorious', 'enlightened', or 'radiant'.

WHAT HE THINKS OF AMERICA

Asked as to his impressions of America, after six months travel and lecturing in many large cities, Abdul Baha said that, materially speaking the progress of this country is marvelous and leaves nothing to be desired, and that her future is very, bright.

'But,' he added, 'you are in need of what I would term divine civilization; civilization with morality and aesthetics. Material civilization is like a glass chimney; divine civilization is like the light within the chimney.'

NO CONFLICT WITH CREEDS

This Persian apostle of the gospel of peace and humanity regards all religions as having a common divine foundation, and for this 'heresy' he is said to have endured forty years of imprisonment under the old Turkish rule in Persia, his teaching having been regarded as in conflict with Mohammedanism. But he explains that he has no quarrel with any creed, although dogmatic theology must keep step with the advance of science.

A PLEASING OLD MAN

Abdul Baha is 68 years of age of benign and patriarchal appearance. His hair and full beard are white and he wears a flowing robe of unbleached linen. He sat as he talked to his audience this morning, and was most simple and unassuming in manner. His style of delivery is entirely unaffected and purely conversational, and he is sparing of gesture. Both in voice and expression of countenance he is pleasant, and he gives one the impression of being entirely sincere.

> SON OF THE FOUNDER OF BAHAISM
>
> Members of his traveling party of Persians say he is the son of the founder of Bahaism, who was one of the leading men of Persia, and that the family was one of large wealth and distinction. His lectures are free to all, and it is said that he refuses to receive compensation from any source, his own private income being more than ample for all his needs and expenses. In fact, he is said to dispense alms with liberal hand to the poor and needy.
>
> The apostle departed at noon today, with his party, for the East.[85]

The *Sacramento Star*, at the time publishing 5,900 copies daily, published a short article based on the article in the *Bee*.[86]

The *Sacramento Union* published an account of the farewell dedicated to 'Abdu'l-Bahá and also mentioned details of His last public address in the city:

> Abdul Baha Abbas Effendi, Persian world leader and apostle of the Behai movement, in an address on universal peace and religious unity yesterday morning in the Hotel Sacramento, so played upon the emotions of an audience composed mainly of women that when he walked through the hotel lobby later in the day to enter a taxicab for the depot, many Sacramento women stirred to frenzy fought to reach the Persian. Others salaamed and bowed in true Oriental style and kept their faces to the floor until the apostle passed.
>
> The novelty of seeing American women prostrate themselves before the Bahai leader, clad in long flowing robe and turban, was a sensation for the patrons at the hotel. They stood in open-mouthed amazement at the proceeding.[87]

The *Palo Altan*

On 1 November 1912, the *Palo Altan*, a weekly newspaper appearing on Fridays, published a special issue about the visit of 'Abdu'l-Bahá to California.

This newspaper was founded in 1901 as the *Palo Alto Press* and in 1903 it changed its name to *Palo Altan*, merging in 1910 with the *Palo Alto Tribune*. By 1912 the newspaper had a very modest circulation of 350 copies.

The *Palo Altan* was owned and co-edited by Henry Walter Simkins and William H. Kelly. Simkins was among the guests at the dinner in honor of 'Abdu'l-Bahá hosted by Mrs Merriman at Palo Alto the day of 'Abdu'l-Bahá's address at Stanford University and at the First Unitarian Church. It is probable that he also attended one of the two addresses.

According to Ella Cooper, once other guests left the dinner, Simkins had the chance of having a long conversation with 'Abdu'l-Bahá during which he expressed his wish to publish a special issue on the Bahá'í Faith. According to notes by Bijou Straun of their conversation, 'Abdu'l-Bahá said to Simkins as he was leaving, 'I praise God that there is unity between us, and I will never forget this meeting and this association. You will be always in my memory as long as I live, and I will beg of God confirmation and assistance for you. It is my hope that the highest desire of your heart may be fulfilled. I wish you many years of happiness and prosperity.'[88]

In its issue of 11 October, the *Palo Altan* published 'Abdu'l-Bahá's address at Stanford. 'Abdu'l-Bahá wrote afterwards a Tablet for Simkins which was also published in that newspaper together with a facsimile of the original Persian:

> To his honor Mr. H. W. Simkins
> Upon him be Baha Ullah El Abha
>
> At the time I met you and felt the susceptibilities of your conscience my heart and soul became greatly attached to that dear friend (i. e. yourself) and the utmost love was produced, and the spiritual emotions were obtained. Your visit gave me the utmost happiness.
>
> The address delivered in Stanford University and published completely in your paper was observed today and on account of it I became both pleased and grateful. In order to express my pleasure and appreciation for this service of yours I am writing you this epistle.
>
> I shall never forget your cordiality, and as long as life lasts I shall remember you. I beg of God, that that dear friend (yourself) may become like unto a shining star in the horizon of Reality, and become the cause of bestowing spiritual life upon the world of humanity.
>
> The address delivered at the Jewish temple establishing the validity of His Holiness Jesus Christ and inviting the Jews to believe in

Him is enclosed herein. From its powerful contents you will realize that though there were many conservative Jews in the audience, yet in the most dauntless manner the validity of Christ was proven. After reading its contents should you think it best you may print it fully without abbreviation in the columns of your paper that others of the Jews may read it. Perchance this may prove an impetus for their respect for, and belief in Christ, that this strife and contention that has lasted between the two nations for two thousand years may disappear, and the oneness of the world of humanity be unveiled.

Upon thee be greeting and praise!

Abdul Baha Abbas[89]

The special issue on 'Abdu'l-Bahá had four pages. The front page included the account of the visit to Stanford University and an introductory article on 'Abdu'l-Bahá and the Bahá'í Faith. It also included a portrait of 'Abdu'l-Bahá, a photograph of Him with Rev. Clarence Reed, and a portrait of Dr Starr Jordan. The second page carried the text of the talk at Stanford as well as Simkins's editorial on the Bahá'í Faith. The third page included the text of the address at the Emanu-El Synagogue, and the fourth page reproduced the talk at the Palo Alto First Unitarian Church and the tablet to the editor.

Simkins's editorial on the Bahá'í Faith will best describe his attitude towards the movement:

THE NEW EVANGEL

Wednesday morning at the university assembly and in the evening at the Unitarian Church in Palo Alto appeared and spoke the leader in a world movement for unity in religion, international peace and universal brotherhood. This is Abdul Baha, a native of Persia who has devoted his life to the mission handed down to him by his father. This mantle of inspired evangelism was consecrated by the persecution of forty years of imprisonment imposed by the sultan of Turkey upon Baha'u'llah, the elder.

As the stone that was rejected may become the head of the corner, or like the prophet's dream expand until it fills up the whole world, so may be the mantle of the wise man of the east, who rediscovers a glorified star shining over the birth of a world movement toward idealism.

This idealism is the further perfection of the ideals of all the great religions of the world. In the science of photography there is a process by which any number of images of different faces may be composited together to produce the dominant type. What is truly representative leaves its impress upon the final result. What is vague and non-intrinsic surpluses into the shadow and disappears. Such a scientific process to arrive at the true composite of religious truth may be likened to the aim of the Bahai movement. It seeks the true common denominator of all religions, rejecting nothing which is good and afraid of nothing which is true.

The spiritual kingdom is full of clashes and contradictions, just as the political and industrial worlds are full of contention and strife. And just as in the latter fields volunteers are spending their lives to pave a better way, so in the spiritual kingdom we have the dawning of a more perfect light. This light will shed its peaceful rays over all contentious factious and will show them the form and substance of truth, which may have been obscured by the dust of strife.

To build a structure by taking a plank from here and a plank from there and a stone from hither and a stone from yonder, as some vague fancy might dictate, would result in an architectural monstrosity that would violate all the rules of unity and proportion. In no such way is the temple of true light to be founded. It is to be brought together in one focus of rays forming an image of all the elements which stand the searching test. This temple may be surrounded on all sides by the images of those beautiful non-essentials which have not gained entrance to the inner structure, but which the true spirit within may yet see as outer landscapes unfolding before the temple windows.

This is the task of the Bahai. It is a true ideal. Truly catholic and universal, it provides a meeting ground for Christian, Jew, Moslem and Buddhist. There is one God who is the God of all religions. His will is the law of all harmony and good. He stands revealed in the last analysis of universal truth. His truth is a gospel of love which surrounds and comprehends all things. In this there is no room for strife and discord, no place for darkness or deceit, and no beginning for bitterness and woe.

Whenever science discovers any great truth, that truth is not the property of science, but it is the heritage of the whole world. We do not refer all the marvels of electricity to Edison nor worship his laboratory at Menlo Park. We use the blessing and pass it along. It

> matters little, in the long run, who made the discovery. If the founders of Bahai arose from the ancient plains of Persia and sent out the true message it matters little whether Persia is of the east or of the west. From the cradle of the human race and the oldest nation of the world comes a voice reaching down the centuries, to bring a message of peace to the strong young giant of the west, bidding America to usher in the dawn.
>
> H. W. SIMKINS[90]

The newspaper ceased publication in 1915. While a modest local with a small circulation in a town with a population at the time of scarcely 4,500 people, its connection with 'Abdu'l-Bahá has made this journal an important one in Bahá'í history. It is interesting to note that 'Abdu'l-Bahá mentioned this newspaper in at least one of his Tablets.[91]

23

RETURN TO THE EAST COAST

'Abdu'l-Bahá returned to the East Coast, visiting several cities on the way. In some of them He gave public talks and granted interviews to the press.

His first stop on His return journey was Denver, where He arrived at one o'clock in the morning on 29 October. 'Abdu'l-Bahá stayed for two nights at the Oxford Hotel. Despite the fatigue of the journey and the fact that He was to spend only one day in the city, He gave two talks, one at the home of a local Bahá'í and another at the Universalist Church.

According to Maḥmúd, local newspapermen interviewed 'Abdu'l-Bahá just after His arrival.[1] One of them was a reporter for the *Denver Post* who asked 'Abdu'l-Bahá questions about His activities in California and about the situation in Europe. It can be inferred from the words attributed to 'Abdu'l-Bahá that He again spoke about an upcoming war in Europe:

> BAHIAN PROPHET RETURNS AFTER A TRIP TO COAST
>
> Abdul Baha Abbas, apostle of the Bahaian faith, who, with his five faithful followers and disciples, was in Denver a month ago on his way west, returned this morning after a trip to the Pacific coast.
>
> 'We were treated everywhere with kindness and courtesy,' said the Persian, 'and we know that our journey was not made in vain.'
>
> The expounder of Bahai addressed crowds at San Francisco and at various of the suburbs. He addressed the students of Leland Stanford University at the special instance of David Starr Jordan, the president of that institution.
>
> 'Europe will render our work of spreading the gospel of universal peace and brotherhood more difficult,' said Abdul Baha, 'but it will by no means discourage us. No, I do not think Persia will be actively

drawn into the trouble, but the war will, of course, have its usual and far-spreading evil influence. But I never discuss political questions. As for war, we have nothing to do with it. We are for peace.'[2]

Chicago

After two nights' travel by train, 'Abdu'l-Bahá reached Chicago from Denver on Thursday, 31 October. His arrival was announced in various newspapers. *The Day Book*, for instance, briefly reported that 'Abdul Baha Abbas, head of Bahai movement toward universal peace, is here',[3] while the *Inter-Ocean* reported that 'He will be given a reception Saturday night at Frederick Douglass Center, 3032 South Wabash Avenue. Sunday he will speak in the morning at Pilgrim Congregational Church and in the afternoon at 4 o'clock in the Plymouth Congregational Church, his subject on the latter occasion being "Universal Peace".'[4]

Cincinnati

From Chicago 'Abdu'l-Bahá proceeded to Cincinnati where He arrived on the evening of Monday, 4 November. Despite spending only one day in the city, the attention paid by the local press to His visit was considerable. The *Cincinnati Times-Star*, a Republican newspaper with a circulation of 148,000 copies, which was owned and edited by Charles H. Taft, brother of President Taft, announced the arrival of the Master and His public talk in the city in an article appearing on 4 November.[5] A similar article was published on the same day in the *Cincinnati Post*.[6]

Just two hours after His arrival, 'Abdu'l-Bahá addressed a public meeting at the Grand Hotel, located at the southwest corner of 4th and Central Streets, where He was staying. According to the local press, over three hundred people attended the meeting at which 'Abdu'l-Bahá spoke on the role of America in the establishment of universal peace and mentioned President Taft, who was born near Cincinnati.[7] Two brief accounts about the meeting were published in the *Cincinnati Post*,[8] which had a circulation of 151,800 copies, and the *Enquirer*, with a circulation of 60,000 copies. The latter also reported that 'A banquet, at which 40 or more of the local followers and officers, with Abdul Baha and his six native Persians, were present, [was offered] following the cult leader's address.'[9]

The Republican *Commercial Tribune*, Cincinnati's oldest daily newspaper with a circulation of 41,600 copies, offered its readers the following account of the meeting:

> WORLD PEACE DREAM MANTLES LECTURER
>
> ABDUL BAHA, PERSIAN, DEVOTES HIS LIFE TO SUFFERING AND UNSEEING HUMANITY
>
> Abdul Baha told the interesting story of his life and work last evening to a gathering of 300 people at the Grand Hotel. When 9 years old Abdul' Baha accompanied his father, Baha'o'llah, in his exile from Bagdad to Constantinople, thence to Adrianople and at last to Akka, where the party of Persians lived from 1868 to 1908. When Baha'o'llah died his son was the acknowledged head of the Bahai movement. In 1908, when Abdul Hamid was imprisoned, Abdul Baha was freed. Since that time he has traveled in all the countries of the world advocating international peace.
>
> In his speech last evening he said: 'His holiness, Baha'o'llah, like unto the sun, appeared in the East and guided the people of religion. He summoned all to the oneness of the world of humanity and called them for international peace. We have no religious prejudices; we have no political prejudices: our purpose is to serve humanity, and we are striving so that the dark world may become enlightened, the East and the West may embrace each other and all humanity become as one family. We are the soldiers of one general, subjects of one king, servants of one God.'
>
> Abdul Baha said that America is in a fair way to make peace with all nations. He said: 'I am exceedingly pleased with America because she is well built. Her people are kind and her government is just . . .'[10]

The *Times-Star* published on 6 November the text of the talk given at the Grand Hotel.[11]

Washington

At noon on Tuesday, 5 November, 'Abdu'l-Bahá left Cincinnati for Washington. His third visit to the American capital renewed the interest of the local press in the Bahá'í Faith and the figure of the Master. The *Herald* announced on 2 November that 'Abdu'l-Bahá 'who is now in Chicago, is expected in Washington the first of next week'.[12] The day after 'Abdu'l-Bahá's return, the *Washington Times* reported in a general article about His visit that 'He will deliver an address to which the general public is invited this evening at 8 o'clock, at the Church of Our Father, Universalist, of which the Rev. John Van Schaick, Jr., is pastor.'[13]

In His talk at the church of John Van Schaick, which He had already visited on 21 April, 'Abdu'l-Bahá spoke on progressive revelation and the unity of religions and also expounded some of the Bahá'í principles.[14] Some local newspapers published accounts of the meeting. The *Washington Times* published on 7 November the following report:

> HEAD OF BAHAISTS WILL SPEAK AGAIN
>
> Abdul Baha, the head of the Bahaist movement, will speak again on universal peace at the Eighth Street Temple this evening.
>
> Last evening he addressed an audience at the Church of Our Father, Universalist, of which the Rev. John Van Schaick, Jr., is pastor. Abdul Baha was a picturesque figure as he stood on the rostrum at Dr. Van Schaick's church. He was clad in flowing cream-colored robes, and he wore a white turban on his head.
>
> Abdul Baha reiterated his thesis of the need for universal love, which he preached here last spring, and told his audience that Americans ought to study all religions, saying that 'if we dare not investigate others, it shows we have not the fullest confidence in our own creed'.[15]

On 7 November, the *Herald* published the following account:

> ABDUL BAHA TALKS OF UNIVERSAL PEACE
>
> HEAD OF MOVEMENT WELCOMED IN UNIVERSALIST CHURCH BY REV. DR. VAN SCHAICK
>
> Abdul Baha, head of the Bahai movement, spoke last night at the Church of Our Father, Universalist.
>
> In extending his welcome in behalf of the officers and members of the church to Abdul Baha, Rev. Dr. John Van Schaick, the pastor of the church, answered certain criticisms directed against Abdul Baha and those who accord him the right to tell his message.
>
> 'What we in America need,' said Rev. Dr. Van Schaick, 'is the study of all religions. We need to learn what other nations have

> discovered; what all great prophets have proclaimed. If we dare not investigate others, it proves we have no real confidence in our own. The men who have the greatest faith in their own religion are the men most willing to hear what others have to say. Those who will not listen to others are cowards. As we send missionaries to your country (addressing Abdul Baha), we ought to welcome the missionaries you send. Only by a free interchange of thought; only by sitting down and talking it over together; only by listening to all honest teachers, can world unity come. We listen to you with reverence because we believe you have a vision of the truth, because we believe you are an honest and fearless man, because you believe in liberty, because you oppose the butchery of Christians by Mohammedans, because you oppose the butchery of Mohammedans by Christians, because in substance, you believe in human brotherhood.'
>
> The venerable Persian teacher, with flowing white beard, and cream-colored long gown, and turban-like headcovering, presented a picturesque figure as he paced to and fro on the platform and delivered in low voice his message which was translated by Dr. Fareed, one of his assistants. Abdul Baha reiterated his admonition of universal love, kindness and brotherhood, and condemned superstition, saying that the Balkan war had been brought about by religious prejudice and superstition.
>
> 'If religion brings about enmity and rancor,' said the speaker, 'it would be much better not to have any religion.' He advocated a religion which could stand the test of science and reason, declaring that all others were superstition. Abdul Baha made an earnest plea for the equality of the sexes, saying that if woman had the same educational facilities as man, she would be his equal in every respect.
>
> Abdul Baha will speak at the Eighth Street Temple at to-morrow night's services.[16]

In a similar account, the *Evening Star* reported that 'Abdul Baha, speaking through an interpreter, Dr. Fareed, advocated universal love, kindness, and brotherhood. He condemned superstition and said that the Balkan war was brought on by religious prejudices and superstition. Any religion is better, he asserted, than one that brings on enmity and rancor. He also urged the equality of sexes, saying that with equal educational advantages woman is equal to man. Abdul Baha will speak this afternoon and tomorrow afternoon at the residence of Mrs. A. J. Parsons, 18th and R Streets Northwest, and tomorrow night at the Eighth Street Temple.'[17]

Some time after 'Abdu'l-Bahá's second visit to the Church of Our Father, Van Schaick gave a sermon in which he mentioned some of the Bahá'í teachings. When 'Abdu'l-Bahá learned about this He wrote a tablet to Van Schaick encouraging him.[18]

On Friday, 8 November, 'Abdu'l-Bahá spoke to the Jewish community of Washington.[19] The same day the *Herald* announced that 'Abdul Baha, leader of the Bahai movement, will speak again on universal peace at Eighth Street Temple this evening. Rev. Dr. Abram Simon will conduct regular services.'[20] In a brief account published on 9 November the same newspaper stated that 'Abdul Baha, founder of the Bahai movement, spoke at Eighth Street Temple last night on universal brotherhood, love, and peace.'[21] The *Washington Post* also published a brief account of the meeting, reporting that Simon introduced the Master 'as the messenger of peace and unity of the world'.[22]

On 10 November, the *Herald*, a newspaper which during the first visit of 'Abdu'l-Bahá to Washington acted as the voice of the local Christian churches opposing 'Abdu'l-Bahá (see chapter 36, vol. 2), published a sympathetic article about 'Abdu'l-Bahá and the Bahá'í Faith, outlining its basic teachings and summarizing some of the Master's activities during His travels. Regarding His relationship with churches, the article highlighted the fact that He delivered addresses in churches representing ten denominations.'[23] On the same day, the *Washington Times* published an article about Agnes Parsons, 'Abdu'l-Bahá's hostess during His stay in the city, mentioning that local Bahá'ís 'meet every night at Mrs. Parsons' residence to hear the teachings of the religion expounded by Abdul Baha, who is the guest of Mrs. Parsons while in the city'.[24]

Baltimore

'Abdu'l-Bahá left Washington for Baltimore on 11 November, staying there one day. The visit of the Master to Baltimore had been long expected. From the announcements published in the local press even before the arrival of 'Abdu'l-Bahá in America it is apparent that it was originally expected that He would visit the city after His first visit to Washington in April. Baltimore's *Sun*, an independent newspaper with a circulation of over 79,200 copies, published on 6 April the news that 'Abdu'l-Bahá would arrive in the city on 21 April, and went as far as announcing that 'Abdu'l-Bahá 'will speak at the First Independent Christ's Church (Unitarian), Mulberry and Charles Streets. Rev. Alfred R. Hussey is pastor of the church. He will also address the Bahai assembly in this city.'[25] In an article published shortly afterwards, the same newspaper reported that 'Abdu'l-Bahá 'is expected to arrive in Baltimore within the next week' and added that 'Mr. Edward D. Struven, one of his followers, who resided on the Rolling Road, Catonsville, stated yesterday that several invitations to lecture had been extended Abdul Abbas during his stay in this city, but so far he had not accepted any on account of his limited time in this city and no further arrangements for addresses will be made until his arrival here.'[26]

On 20 April, one day before the date originally announced for the arrival of 'Abdu'l-Bahá, *The Sun* further reported that 'It is uncertain whether or not Abdul Baha the Persian philosopher and leader of the movement for the unification of religions and the establishment of universal peace, will come to this city. He had been invited to come here tomorrow and speak, but the engagement had to be canceled.[27] The Baltimore *Star*, however, published on the same day another article announcing the imminent visit of 'Abdu'l-Bahá to the First Independent Christ's Church.[28]

Months later, it was finally confirmed that 'Abdu'l-Bahá would visit Baltimore after His visit to Washington en route to New York and would arrive on Monday, 11 November. *The Sun* reported that 'Abdul Baha, Persian philosopher, linguist and exponent of the "brotherhood of man", will deliver a lecture at noon tomorrow in First Unitarian Church, Charles and Franklin Streets', and added that 'He will arrive in Baltimore shortly before the time set for the lecture and will probably leave for New York soon after the lecture is concluded. He may, however, be entertained for a short time at the home of the pastor of the church, Rev. Alfred R. Hussey, or at the home of Mr. Edward Struven.'[29]

An account of 'Abdu'l-Bahá's talk at Rev. Alfred R. Hussey's[30] Unitarian Church of Baltimore was published in *The Sun*:

WOMEN KISS HIS HAND

PERSIAN ADVOCATE OF HUMAN BROTHERHOOD IS VENERATED.

FOLLOWERS SURROUND HIM

LECTURES IN UNITARIAN CHAPELS EXPOUNDING DOCTRINES WHICH MADE HIM FAMOUS

Hailed as prophet by his followers in this city, Abdul Baha Abbas, Persian teacher, came to Baltimore yesterday and at noon addressed a large audience in the chapel of the First Unitarian Church, Charles and Franklin Streets.

That he is held in veneration by those who have accepted his doctrine of the unity of the human race and the oneness of all religions was evidenced by the attention that was bestowed upon him after the lecture. Escorted to a waiting automobile by his companions, six in number, he was surrounded by a crowd of well dressed women who pressed forward eagerly in their desire to meet him.

With condescension, he greeted his followers as they were presented by the interpreter, Dr. Ameen U. Fareed, a Persian and a graduate in medicine of Johns Hopkins University. 'Oh, I am so glad to see you,' was uttered in tones of reverence by the women as they bowed before him and kissed his wrinkled hand.

ROBED IN BLACK

In appearance the Persian teacher is a striking looking man of about 70 years. He is of the average height, with a strong, rugged face covered with a short white beard. His cheekbones are high, his eyes bright and flashing.

At the lecture he wore a robe of black, with a triangular insert of light tan in front reaching from the hem to the neck. The long sleeves of the garment were turned back from the strong hands. Distinguishing him from his escort was a white turban which he wore, from beneath which gleamed locks of iron gray. Members of his escort wore black turbans.

THE LECTURE INTERPRETED

The lecture was delivered in Persian and was translated by Dr. Fareed. While his words were, of course, unintelligible to his audience, his manner of deliverance was impressive. His voice, except at rare intervals, was pitched low. At times, however, it increased in volume and he would speak for several minutes before pausing to let the interpreter translate. He used frequent gestures, the favorite one being an inclusive swing of both arms to show the universality of the doctrine he propounded. He also frequently leaned over the reading desk and looked at his hearers.

ONENESS OF THE HUMAN RACE

'God is one, we are His children, submerged in the sea of his kindness,' was his theme. He said all divine religions had two parts, the essentials, which dealt with morality and ethical standards, and the non-essentials, which changed with time and place.

In proof of this he compared the teachings of Moses and Christ. Both of whom he styled 'His Holiness'. He declared that the penal code announced by Moses was necessary for the Israelites traveling through the wilderness, but was repealed by Christ. Theological dogmas, which, he said, had crept into religions, he declared were useless and should be forsaken. These minor differences, he declared were the cause of the world's bitterness and strife and their elimination would bring about universal peace and love.

FORTY YEARS IN PRISON IN SERVIA

. . . After the lecture he declared that the nations of the world looked to America as the leader in the worldwide peace movement, and declared the situation of this country, not being the rival of any other power and not considering colonization or conquests, made it an ideal country to lead in the movement.

The lecturer arrived in Baltimore yesterday morning from Washington. While here he was the guest of H. J. Struven, 180 Bentalou Street, who entertained him and his escort at the Rennert and later at his home.

The followers of the Persian number almost 600 in this country, it is said. There are a dozen or so believers in his doctrine in Baltimore. He left for New York at 3 o'clock in the afternoon.[31]

24

DEPARTURE FROM AMERICA

After seven months traveling across North America, 'Abdu'l-Bahá returned to New York as His final stop before leaving for Europe. On His last visit to the City of the Covenant new accounts published in the press described some of His activities.

One little known episode during the last days of the Master in America was His visit to the library of the famous financier and businessman John Pierpont Morgan (1867–1913).

On 18 November the Master, was invited by the Consul General of Persia to have lunch at the National Democratic Club in New York (617 Fifth Avenue). Afterwards they visited the personal library of J. P. Morgan where 'Abdu'l-Bahá was invited to see some of the art pieces and manuscripts kept in his private collection.[1] Before leaving He wrote a prayer in Morgan's guest book. An account of the whole episode was published in the *New York Herald*:

> After viewing many of the pictures, manuscripts and art treasures in the library of J. Pierpoint Morgan in East Thirty-sixth Street yesterday afternoon, Abdul Baha Abbas, the Persian prophet, wrote his autograph, together with his blessing, in an album which Mr. Morgan keeps in his private room. The blessing upon Mr. Morgan, which was written in Persia, was translated by Dr. Ameen Fareed, a member of the party. The writing translated reads:
>
> O Thou Generous Lord, verily this famous personage has done considerable philanthropy, render him great and dear in Thy Kingdom, make him happy and joyous in both worlds, and confirm him in serving the Oneness, the world of humanity, and submerge him in the sea of Thy Favors. ABDUL BAHA ABBAS.
>
> Abdul Baha, accompanied by five other distinguished Persians, upon invitation saw the Morgan library yesterday afternoon. They

> were introduced by Hagizonne H. Topakyan, the Persian Consul General. They remained in the library from one to four o'clock in the afternoon looking over the rare art treasures, especially the old Persian manuscripts and documents. So well pleased was Abdul Baha with what he saw that he insisted on leaving some token of appreciation for Mr. Morgan, and it was then that he suggested the autograph and blessing. Mr. Morgan did not arrive at his home until the Persian party had gone.[2]

On the same day *The Sun* (New York) published a similar report in which it was stated that the party stayed at Morgan's private library for two hours and that it was Morgan who had 'asked Abdul Baha to write his autograph in the Morgan album'.[3] The report in *The Sun* was the basis of an article released through press agencies and published in several newspapers,[4] including one in Chile.[5]

On Saturday, 23 November, a banquet in honor of 'Abdu'l-Bahá and in commemoration of the day of the Covenant was held in the Great Northern Hotel, West Fifty-seventh Street, New York. *The Sun* published on 24 November a detailed account of the meeting and quoted from the words of 'Abdu'l-Bahá:

> SENDOFF FOR ABDUL BAHA
>
> WHEN SPIRIT MOVES HIM HE SPEAKS FOR SOLIDARITY OF MAN
>
> The Bahai Assembly of New York City gave a farewell reception to Abdul Baha at the Great Northern Hotel last night. Three hundred members of the assembly sat down to dinner at 9 o'clock and Abdul Baha, with his Persian retinue, arrived at the hotel about 10 o'clock and was ushered into the dining room by Miss Nellie H. Lloyd, who was in charge of the dinner.
>
> Ali Kuhli Khan, Persian Charge d'Affaires at Washington, and H. H. Topakyan, Persian Consul in New York, were among those present. As is the custom at all meetings of the Bahai Assembly, Abdul Baha did not speak before 'the spirit' moved him and was translated by Ameen U. Fareed and Dr. Zia M. Bagdadi of his staff of interpreters.
>
> W. H. Hoar, member of the Board of Council of the Bahai Assembly, introduced the speaker as a man 'who devoted his life to the enlightenment of his fellow men and for the universal love and

brotherhood of all mankind' and the man 'who opened the Eastern world to us'.

It was some time after Mr. Hoar's remarks that the spirit moved Abdul Baha to speak. He said in part:

'This meeting of yours is a universal one – a heavenly one. It serves the oneness of the earth. It serves international peace, the equality between man and woman, morality and morals. It serves and proclaims the oneness of humanity, international peace among the religions and lastly peace among races.

'We are met for love and good fellowship. With us there is a bond to unite East with West. We hold aloft the banner of the solidarity of man, for it purifies the world of religion, and we know the foundation of the law of God is oneness.

'All religion should be kind to one another. The causes of disruption among them is envy, rancor and sedition, but these will pass away. Every limited and self-centered movement is human nature, but every universal movement is inspired by divine nature.

'Your purposes are great and sincere, your intentions lofty and blessed. Therefore I leave you with this: Entertain no intention except for the good of all mankind.'[6]

A further account was published on the same day in the *Tribune*:

ABDUL BAHA GOING AWAY

PERSIAN PROPHET SAILS SHORTLY – DINNER FOR HIM LAST NIGHT

Abdul Baha Abbas Effendi, the Persian prophet and center of the Bahai movement, received assurances of unswerving loyalty last night from members of the Bahai Assembly of New York City, who gathered at a farewell dinner in his honor at the Great Northern Hotel. The Oriental savant is to leave this country this week, presumably on the steamship Mauritania, though none of his followers would venture to make a definite date, as Abdul Baha, they said, made his plans from day to day.

The hour of the farewell dinner was unusually late. At precisely 9:40 o'clock Abdul Baha appeared, a venerable figure, with a long gray beard and a Persian cloak and white turban, walking slowly to his place of honor.

He was accompanied by Ali Kuhli Khan, the Persian chargé

> d'Affaires at Washington; H. H. Topakayan, Persian Consul General; Dr. Ameen Fareed, a graduate of an American university and the prophet's interpreter, and Dr. Zia M. Bagdadi. He was received with a silent greeting by the three hundred members of the assembly, who rose at his approach,
>
> W. H. Hoar, who presided, said that the dinner was a spiritual banquet of love, and this although the followers of the Bahai movement here felt sorrow at the prophet's departure, they took consolation in the thought at the happiness that awaited their brothers in the Orient through Abdul Baha's return there. Abdul Baha was the center of the Bahai movement, which meant universal humanity, and which has done more for women than any other spiritual effort to free them from the bondage of ages and do away with the distinction of sex.
>
> He then pledged the assembly to absolute obedience to Abdul Baha, who, he said, was the God-appointed prophet to interpret the works of Baha-u-llah.[7]

The *New York Press*, in turn, published a short note reporting the banquet.[8]

On 5 December, the day of the departure of 'Abdu'l-Bahá from New York, the *Evening Post* published an account of His last moments in America:

> ABDUL BAHA'S BLESSING ON PIER
>
> PERSIAN PHILOSOPHER SAILS BIDING HIS FOLLOWERS FAREWELL
>
> With his followers crowding the pier to bid him farewell, Abdul Baha Abbas, the Persian philosopher and advocate of universal peace, stretched out his hands and gave his blessing from the deck of the Celtic, just as the White Star liner swung free of her dock to-day. During the last moments of farewell, his followers had been almost fanatical in their signs of devotion.
>
> Abdul Baha is going to return to Persia where he has spent forty years of his life in prison because of his religious beliefs and his defiance of the sheiks. He has been in this country since last April and said on departing that he had made thousands of converts, who would carry on his work among the churches. Through an interpreter he said he had visited all the big cities here and that

> everywhere he had been received first with curiosity, then with credulity, and then with devotion to the cause. Abdul Baha wore a long black robe and red fez and as he moved among his people he chanted words of encouragement to them.[9]

A further account was published in the *New York Times* on 6 December:

> ABDUL BAHA SAILS AWAY
>
> PERSIAN PROPHET BIDS FOLLOWERS HERE A FAREWELL FOR LIFE
>
> Abdul Baha, the Bahai prophet and peace advocate, sailed yesterday for Liverpool on the Celtic, after spending seven months in this country preaching to his followers and bidding them farewell on this earth. The prophet, who wore his white turban, was accompanied by his secretary, interpreter, and body servant.
>
> About 100 members of the New York Bahai Society, 80 per cent of whom are women, went to the pier to see Abdul Baha off and were deeply moved as he delivered his final address to them in the lounge. He said that during his tour of the United States he had converted thousands of men and women and that they would work among their churches after he had gone for the furtherance of the movement for universal peace.
>
> A large bunch of American Beauty roses was handed to him and the prophet then distributed the flowers with a parting benediction among his followers.[10]

Other newspapers also gave the news of the departure of 'Abdu'l-Bahá.[11] A large picture of the Master was sent though press agencies with the following caption: 'Abdul Baha, the venerable Persian who has been touring the United States expounding his new doctrine of world peace and unity of religion, has departed for London, where he will continue his work. During his stay in this country he won over to his beliefs thousands of converts, including many women prominent in social circles. Abdul Baha was imprisoned for twenty years in a Turkish dungeon because of the unpopularity of his doctrines in that country, but his faith in the universal religion is unshaken, and it is said that his following now numbers over 10,000,000.'[12]

Albert R. Vail (1880–1966) was the Unitarian pastor at the University of Illinois when he met 'Abdu'l-Bahá. This meeting and his study of the Bahá'í teachings deeply affected Vail, who in later years would become a Bahá'í. Long before his conversion, Vail wrote an article for the *Unitarian Advance* in which he described the figure of 'Abdu'l-Bahá as the embodiment of Unitarian ideals:

> There sailed from New York a few weeks ago a man who incarnated in his daily living the open mind, good-will, and the unity of spirit which we liberals have made our central gospel for the past hundred years. Abdul Baha recalls the picture of our saints – our Emerson, James Freeman Clarke, Edward Everett Hale. The more we saw of him the deeper sank the impression of his pure spirituality.
>
> Once more we realize the power of the life made flesh. A thousand words though they fall from the tongues of angels are not equal in their spiritual effect to one glimpse of the life itself incarnate in a living personality. Then there flashes on us the wealth of the meaning of the life of which we talk and dream . . .

'Is there a greater service Unitarianism can render than to become a living witness of this power of the spirit to unite modern individualists into one spiritual army and finally bind all sects and religions into a world unity? ' concluded Vail. 'Such is the reflection started by the visit of this Persian prophet.'[13]

25

GENERAL ARTICLES ABOUT 'ABDU'L-BAHÁ

Besides the many interviews and articles describing specific episodes of the visit of 'Abdu'l-Bahá to Europe and North America, His visit also prompted the publication of a large number of general articles introducing the public to the Bahá'í Faith and the figure of 'Abdu'l-Bahá. In some cases these articles were written by Bahá'ís and in others they were distributed by press agencies.

While it would be impossible to reproduce all of these articles here, a survey of them is useful to gain an insight into the admiration that 'Abdu'l-Bahá attracted from the public.

Between May and July 1912 several journals published a syndicated column that carried an article about 'Abdu'l-Bahá and His portrait. 'Never before in recorded history', stated the article, 'has one of the founders of an Oriental religious movement – since become world-wide – visited America. The personality and life history of one who has spent sixty years of his life in banishment, imprisonment and exile from his native land, makes a story of fascinating interest, vividly impressing upon the mind of the investigator the fact that the days of religious persecution are not ended, and that even in this modern age a drama has been enacted which for human interest equals or surpasses Biblical history.' The text then offered some biographical information about 'Abdu'l-Bahá.[1]

In Baltimore, the *Sun*, which at the time had a circulation of 79,300 copies, published in its 13 April edition a portrait of 'Abdu'l-Bahá with a long caption containing biographical information.[2] In Philadelphia, the *Star* dedicated its column 'By the Way' to the Bahá'í Faith, offering information about its genesis and history.[3] On 20 April the *Loraine Herald* (Ohio), a Republican newspaper with a circulation of 4,100 copies, published an article about 'Abdu'l-Bahá and a portrait of Him, distributed by Underwood & Underwood, together with two caricatures depicting Him in the desert. The tone of the article, which apparently was sent from New York, was however moderate and respectful.[4] The *Detroit Free Press*, with a circulation of 58,000 copies, published on 21 April an editorial dedicated to 'Abdu'l-Bahá which, after describing some of the teachings of the Bahá'í Faith and summarizing its history, stated that 'Abbas Effendi is in many ways a remarkable man. He has wide learning and such of his sayings as are available are considerably superior to the later portions of the Koran. He writes as Mohammed might have written in the light of modern science, except that unlike Mohammed he has a weakness for metaphysics . . . It is not necessary to accept Abbas Effendi as a veritable prophet, or to fall at his feet in adoration, in order to recognize in him one of the great religious thinkers and teachers of the time.'[5] This editorial was the basis of an article published on 4 May in the *Literary Digest* (New York).[6] On 22 April, the Cleveland *Leader*, with a circulation of 55,000 copies, published another account about the Bahá'í Faith and the arrival of the Master which also included the portrait distributed by Underwood & Underwood.[7] On 25 April the Indianapolis *Sun*, with a daily circulation of 31,900 copies, published a further article containing biographical notes about 'Abdu'l-Bahá.[8]

The monthly *The Survey* (New York), a magazine edited by Paul U. Kellogg (1879–1958), focused on social and charitable work and had a circulation of 16,000 copies. On 27 April it published an article signed by the New York Bahá'í Irene Earl which, after introducing the Bahá'í Faith, summed up some of the social work done by the Bahá'ís of the time and mentioned the Bahá'í schools in Persia.[9]

On 12 May the *Fort Wayne Journal-Gazette* (Indiana), a Democratic newspaper with a circulation of 19,100 copies, published another article about 'Abdu'l-Bahá which also included a portrait. The text quoted some of the Hidden Words of Bahá'u'lláh and also reproduced excerpts from various writings of 'Abdu'l-Bahá. 'By sacrifice and noble deeds,' stated the article, 'he has for years taught the people to love each other, whatever their race, environment, or religion. The story of his captivity, persecution and ultimate freedom is one of the most impressive romances of the world.'[10]

The *Kansas City Star*, a newspaper with a circulation of 171,000 copies, published on 13 May a lengthy article with biographical information about 'Abdu'l-Bahá together with a drawing made from one of

His portraits.[11] In Ithaca, New York, the *Daily News*, with a circulation of 3,500 copies daily, published on 24 May an article about the Bahá'í Faith in which the author stated that 'much interest has been aroused throughout the entire country by the coming of Abdul Baha' and added the He 'takes no money for his lectures or his expenses. He has a wonderful personality and speaks as one inspired.'[12] The *Youngstown Telegram* (Ohio), a Republican newspaper with a circulation of 14,000 copies, published on 25 May another lengthy article about the Faith and 'Abdu'l-Bahá, including a portrait. 'Wherever there is misery,' stated the article, 'he has always been ready to take the part of a good Samaritan.'[13] On 16 June, J. D. Flenner[14] wrote for the *Statesman* of Idaho, a Republican newspaper issuing 9,300 copies daily, a sympathetic article presenting the Bahá'í Faith.[15]

Current Literature (New York), a literary monthly published nationally with a circulation of 101,000 copies, published in its June edition an article summarizing some of the comments in the press about the presence of 'Abdu'l-Bahá in America. 'Those who have met him bear witness to his loving kindness, to his spiritual breadth, and to his physical frailty,' stated the article. It also quoted the Boston *Congregationalist* as having stated that 'The religion of the Bahaists has nothing of the eccentricity or faddism of so many modern religions and none of their shallow philosophy. It is simply a synthesis of the noblest ethics of the world around one common center – love and good-will to all men.'[16]

Also in June the *North American Review* (New York), a monthly literary journal issuing 15,000 copies, published an article entitled 'What is Behaism' by the Unitarian minister Rev. James T. Bixby (1842–1921)[17] who had met 'Abdu'l-Bahá in New York soon after His arrival. While Bixby echoed some of the accusations against the Bahá'í Faith made by a few missionaries (see chapter 36, vol. 2) his article was nevertheless sympathetic in its conclusions about 'Abdu'l-Bahá.

> In the brief personal acquaintance with the head of the new faith, with which I have been honored, Abbas has impressed me as a man of great mental ability, tact, and persuasive power; friendly in disposition, affable in his manners, and amiable and progressive in his spirit. He is wisely putting the emphasis in the Behai community more and more on those great principles of international fellowship and friendly relations between diverse faiths and races that best

realize the essence of the Christian spirit. Moreover, he has practically exemplified these principles in his own pacific conduct and charitable activities. The descriptions that visitors to Akka have given of his daily personal benefactions is, indeed, beautiful and impressive.[18]

Also in June 1912 the literary monthly *Twentieth Century Magazine* (Boston), with a circulation of 18,000 copies, carried a three-page article about the Bahá'í Faith by the socialist, pacifist and suffragist writer Louise Adams Grout. While some priests in America repeatedly expressed the view that the Bahá'í teachings are essentially Christian and thus unoriginal (see chapter 36, vol. 2), Grout openly expressed her view that the major Christian denominations in the United States had failed to bring social equality to the nation and wrote of her hopes in the Bahá'í Faith:

THE COMING OF ABDUL BAHA

Has Father Time a sense of humor? It is to be hoped that some such solace is granted this patient watcher of the centuries, lest he grow discouraged by the ever-recurring contradictions and vagaries of the race of man. The failure of the great majority to view questions of their own time with any degree of historic perspective is nowhere so clearly shown as in the work of spreading the gospel. In the short period since the appearance of European races upon American soil, at least three exclusive versions of the Word of God have been relayed over seas and continents.

The first message of the East to the West came with the Jesuit priest who penetrated our virgin woods and waters and told to the wondering Indian the story of Jesus Christ according to the infallible doctrine of the Holy Roman Catholic Church. Not so long afterward, from Father Time's point of view, the Only True Gospel was again sped on its mission towards the setting sun, and the 'Morning Star' set sail to carry back to the East from the West the remodeled Protestant dogma of the same Risen Lord. Again, after a lapse of a short half-century, the Ark of the Covenant made its reappearance on our Atlantic horizon. This third version took the form of the Holy Scripture of the Indian Vedas, and was borne by a yellow-turbaned Swami. He expressed, though far more delicately, the same solicitude for the spiritual good of the American people that the Jesuit priest had first felt for the Red Indian, and that had later inspired the earnest missionaries on board the 'Morning Star' to seek out the contented Celestial in his own flowery land. Surely Father Time must wearily wonder if little man is never to wake up to the significance of this jest!

While there may have been some slight increase of tolerance toward varying points of view, keeping step with the advance of man's knowledge of man, there has always been the implication, at least, of the mental attitude on the part of the teacher, 'I am holier than thou' . . . This is the characteristic attitude of the evangelist, though it is not always so naively expressed. He really feels 'The language of the Lord is my language, and the will of the Lord is what I interpret it to be.'

In the year 1912, however, the hope of a more universal platform comes to us when we learn of the arrival in this country of one who, bearing the title of Abdul Baha (Servant of God), gives us this unique message:

'I come to bring you no new religion, but to rekindle the fading lamps of your own faith, whatever its name may be. For the light behind each faith is one light.'

'The cause of unity is the cause of life itself.'

'The East has ever been the home of meditation and the source of inspiration, but the West is the sphere of action, and should find its special duty in the practical application of spiritual truth. East and West should be one in sympathy.'

Whatever of occultism may lurk in the heart of this teaching, the outsider finds only simple, human, universal doctrines. So familiar, indeed, that we wonder how it has come about that even in modern America many thousands reverence the name of this Persian prophet and feel that they owe to his teaching the deepest inspiration of their lives.

We can well see how the Bahai message has come as a great revelation to Persia, where the Brahmin scorns the Mohammedan, and the Mohammedan feels that the casual presence of a Christian inside his house of worship is so unclean a thing that the building is forever polluted and must be razed to the ground. To proclaim to such a people that all men are brothers and that all religions are of the same essence is a direct attack upon the established custom and teaching of the orthodox Persian. Persecution and exile for such a prophet are but the natural results to be expected from those who still hold the power in so effete a nation.

But to announce on American soil that men of all colors – black, yellow, or white – are not only equal in the sight of God but should be treated as such by one another, would seem an unnecessary platitude, for is not this the land where thousands of white men died to free the negro slaves in the name of brotherhood? Surely we have been graduated from this text!

Let us take care, however, that the searching eyes of the prophet do not chance to fall upon a copy of some morning paper which nonchalantly reports – so much a matter of course is it – that a few more negroes have been shot or burned on suspicion of crime by an angry mob of white citizens, or upon the next day's issue, which is quite likely to mention in an equally casual manner that the identity of the actual criminal was discovered when the excitement died down, but that he had made his escape. Let us also keep from this expounder of the obvious, who calls every man brother, any close acquaintance with the many rural pulpits from which warnings still come against a belief in this modern doctrine of the Brotherhood of Man, lest that of Universal Salvation might follow in its track. These are the people who are still attempting to measure the complex problems of modern life with the inelastic yardstick found in grandmother's garret – or perhaps it is fairer to say that they are as yet unconscious of the fact that any new problems have arisen. They are still worrying over the possibility that Heaven may be overcrowded, and the necessity of securing front seats early for themselves and families . . .

Can we establish convincingly to an astute and far-seeing Persian inquirer our national claim that we are at peace with all mankind, when within our boundaries, from Los Angeles to the factories of New England, the feeling between employer and employed grows ever more bitter, and the methods of combat employed in their differences more desperate? The heathen in our laundries and factories, upsetting our industrial world and displaying an increasing facility in making trouble for respectable people of hitherto irreproachable and orderly lives, present a far more puzzling problem than when they placidly bowed before their native gods in their own far-away countries.

And here the once satisfying standard of Christian charity has to be taken down from the old-fashioned pulpit, carefully dusted, and held up to present needs. Rarely does it show any signs of fitness, for a new civilization demands new ethics, and the modern conception of the sphere of individual duty has widened its field from that of the purely personal to the national. Before we dare claim that we have nothing to learn from the Bahai teacher, it behooves us to consider one fact.

We have contented ourselves with the presence of the laws of love and humanity upon our religious statute books, and have made only a feeble beginning toward their enforcement. It is no longer enough to bank the flame of brotherly love in our hearts; the draughts must be thrown open until our whole national house shall become heated with the most scientific apparatus which can be procured. Certain locked chambers and cold cellars must be explored and aired – a worthy task for our idle maids. When we have squarely faced the surprises which await us there, and are still willing to pray, 'Give peace in our time, O Lord' – having discovered how very large a share of the cost of such peace we must ourselves bear – then only may we meet with entire frankness Abdul Baha of Akka.

He comes to us after an imprisonment of forty years for the double offense of declaring God to be a Father rather than a Shah, and of making a logical effort to put his belief into practice. What heroic examples of justice and mercy may he not reasonably expect of us, if we are to uphold, with a sincerity equal to his own, our avowed American ideals![19]

In the same month the *American Review of Reviews* (New York), with a circulation of 200,000 copies, printed a review of the articles about the Bahá'í Faith published in London in the *Contemporary Review* and the *Fortnightly Review* (see chapter 6).[20] Another literary journal, *The Outlook* (New York), a popular magazine of which Theodore Roosevelt was associate editor and which had a circulation of 125,000 copies, published on 15 June, an editorial under the title 'The Bahai Movement' which expressed the following views about the Bahá'í Faith:

> Thus Bahaism is one phase of a great worldwide movement toward a religious faith at once more spiritual and more practical than the religions of creed and ceremonial; a religion which agrees with the mystics of all ages in believing that the relation between the Spirit of God and the spirit of man is immediate and direct, so that converse between the two is possible; and with humanitarians of all ages, that the fruit of religion is in works of justice, mercy, and love, and whether a religion is true or false is to be known by its works . . .[21]

On 15 June, *The World's Work* (New York), with a circulation of 119,000 copies, also included an article dedicated to 'Abdu'l-Bahá, which was later reproduced in other newspapers, and which concluded with the following comments:

> There is something arresting – as there is in every effort to draw men together – in the visit to the West of this wise man of the East, this lover of his race who seeks to promote better understanding among men by persuading them that their religions are really all one. If there is any fact of contemporaneous history evident, it is the fact that the nations and races are drawing together; civilization is breaking down the barriers; knowledge is showing how vitally the interests of all people of all lands are connected. But religion can scarcely be said to have been in the past a unifying force; it has rather estranged than united. Abdul Baha says: 'If a religion be the cause of hatred and disharmony, it would be better for it not to exist than to exist.' Yet it is a question how far a religion can surrender its distinctive character without ceasing to exist.[22]

Charles Johnston, a regular contributor to *Harper's Weekly* (New York), a national literary journal with a circulation of 80,000 copies, devoted an article entitled 'A Ray from the East' to the figure of 'Abdu'l-Bahá and the teachings of the Bahá'í Faith. The article carried a well-informed description of some of the salient features of the history of the Bahá'í Faith and the lives of its founders and quoted parts of the address of 'Abdu'l-Bahá at the All Souls' Church in Chicago. Replying to the accusation of unoriginality made by some Christian pastors against the Bahá'í teachings, Johnston stated: 'Does it follow, then, because these two Persian teachers are repeating, in slightly varied phrase, the world-old and age-worn truths that their mission is the less real and valuable? By no means. The very fact that these men of strange race and alien tongue come to us and tell us, out of the depth of their hearts, what we have heard from the beginning, does much to bring the sense of unity that is the very center of their thought. It is a great and compelling thing to find a deeply religious man not of one's own faith and civilization. Such a one cannot fail to deepen our sense of religion. And these men have this in addition, that, holding the universal truths, they have honestly and in the face of dire persecution striven to carry them out. They live their religion, as well as teach it. This is their power.'[23] Portions of this article were later reproduced in other newspapers.[24]

On 20 July an article about 'Abdu'l-Bahá appeared in the *Tennessean* (Nashville) stating, among other things, that 'New York suffragettes will doubtless welcome the new prophet, for one of the first tenets he set forth was that men and women are created equal and will stand on an equal footing and live without strife as soon as woman has the same education as man'.[25]

In Boston, H. Clinton Hay, editor of the *New-Church Review* – the organ of the followers of the Swedenborgian organization 'Boston Society of the New Jerusalem' – published a long article about the Bahá'í Faith based on articles previously published in other American magazines in which the author compared the Bahá'í teachings with those of the New Church and expressed his view that 'Divine Providence is in the raising up of these leaders of a great reformation of the Mohammedan religion,' and that 'the introduction of the Bahai religion in the Orient is doing a work connected, in some hidden ways of the Lord, with that of the New-Christian Church in the Occident. For while Mohammed came with the literal sword bathed in blood to compel belief, the Bahais come with the sword of reason bathed in love to win it.'[26]

On 22 July the *Hearst's Magazine* (formerly *World To-day*), a newspaper acquired in 1912 by the Hearst group with a circulation of 80,000 copies, published an article entitled 'A Modern Prophet' written by the famous author and philosopher Elbert Hubbard (1856–1915)[27] who months before had written 'Abdu'l-Bahá in Alexandria to invite Him to East Aurora, New York.[28]

The article was actually a shortened version of an essay by the same title that Hubbard devoted to 'Abdu'l-Bahá and included in his work *Hollyhocks and Goldenglow* (1912). In his article Hubbard described the

Master in glowing terms, stating that 'no man of recent times has shown such a magnificent affirmative spirit as this man Abdul Baha'. While sympathetic, the article was, however, inaccurate on some points, such as the statements about a visit to the White House, which most probably never took place, or the comments attributed to 'Abdu'l-Bahá about Christian Science. From the contents it can be inferred that Hubbard personally met the Master.

What follows is the text of the essay as published in *Hollyhocks and Goldenglow*. The parts not included in the version published in *Hearst's Magazine* are reproduced between brackets and a few paragraphs with no direct relevance have been omitted:

> A VERY extraordinary man has recently visited America. He came from Persia. He is Abdul Baha, who calls himself 'The Servant of God'.
>
> His followers are known as 'Bahais'.
>
> This man has diverted one-third of the population of Persia from Mohammedanism. Throughout all Asia, Europe and the United States, there are constantly growing bodies of adherents to the faith of Abdul Baha.
>
> [This man is the modern Messiah.] This man comes to the Western world on a distinct mission, and no one who meets him can doubt his sincerity. He is no mere eccentric.
>
> The message he brings is the unification of the East and West in the bonds of brotherly love, mutual aid, reciprocity and an understanding which means peace on earth and good will toward men.
>
> It presages a world-wide up-springing of vital religion.
>
> According to Abdul Baha, we are now living in a period of time that marks the beginning of the millennium – a thousand years of peace, happiness and prosperity. [After that, Abdul Baha does not say what will happen, but he does not preach disaster.]
>
> [He thinks that after the thousand years, still better things are in store for us. He has the world-vision and sees clearly this new time upon which we are now reaching. He beholds the dawn of the Great Peace upon the horizon of the world. His business is to proclaim it.]
>
> [The refrain of his message is always and forever: 'The day of the Lord is at hand. God's kingdom of peace and love shall be established upon the earth, and the dreams of all the prophets and poets are to become true.']

[Literally, poetically and symbolically, the desert shall blossom like the rose, and the waste places shall be made green, and sorrow and sighing shall flee away.]

One distinguishable and peculiar thing about Abdul Baha is that he does not make war upon, or even criticize, any other religious faith.

Every faith fits a certain attitude of mind and has a peculiar province to fulfill. [It is all a part of the work of the Creator, and it is good in its time and place; and at the right time it will be sloughed and left behind and the imprisoned soul will burst its bonds, and the captive shall be made free.]

Abdul Baha is now sixty-eight years of age. He began his public work when eighteen. For just fifty years he has proclaimed his faith.

But from his forty-second year to his sixty-sixth – twenty-four years – he was in prison. But even his jailers dared not forbid him sending out his messages of faith.

Even in prison he was treated with a reverence and awe that is not very difficult to understand when you meet the man.

Abdul Baha is a most remarkable individual. He has magnetism, plus. His zeal, enthusiasm, animation, hope and faith run over and inundate everything.

No man can argue with him. No man can dispute with him. Everyone has to agree with him – and everyone does. He is what he is. He was born to this work, and for this work, and considers himself divinely appointed.

His father was Baha'ullah. His birth was in answer to prayer. His father was a prophet of God, and proclaimed, to the best of his ability, the new time.

But Baha'ullah knew that he would pass away before the world was ready to accept the new tidings of great joy. And so he prayed for this son who should come, and carry on this work. And so the son was born on May 23, 1844 . . .

And now comes Abdul Baha and leads a revolt from Islam and takes with him as followers, today, the intellectual pick of Mohammedanism. He is to Persia what Emerson was to America – only more so.

It is believed to be but a question of time when the Bahais will be supreme and orthodox Mohammedanism will take its place in that museum of theological things that were.

This revolt against the literal interpretations of the words of Mohammed and the Koran is very similar, indeed, to the revolt that has gone on throughout Christendom against a literal interpretation of the Bible.

America has never produced a religious leader with the zeal and health and insight and patience and intellectual reach of this man Abdul Baha – save with one exception, and that was a woman.

Abdul Baha; has recently spoken before the Peace Conference at Lake Mohonk, in New York City, in Boston, Chicago and elsewhere.

He does not give his message to the lowly and the ignorant.

The man is regal in his way of living and in his mental attitude. He travels with a retinue of servants, secretaries and followers, all caftan robed. Evidently, he is well supplied with money. He has everything he needs and wants. Wherever he goes he rides in automobiles and stops at the best hotels.

He is in touch with big people, and meets all classes and kinds of people on an equality.

[Let him visit any bank, factory, office building, church, and everything is laid aside and eyes bulge and ears listen until he takes his departure.

[When he went to Washington and swept through the capitol, even the Supreme Court of the United States saw fit to adjourn; the House the same; and the Senate – for a while, at least – forgot matters of investigation.

[When Abdul Baha went to the White House, one might have thought that he was going with the intent to take possession of it.

[But his is not a kingdom of this world, so far as a desire to rule is concerned. Governments are mere matters of detail, matters of business, and they do not much interest this servant of God.

[Yet, for the business genius of the West, Abdul Baha has a great regard.

[He says we must teach the people of the East how to plant and sow and reap.

[And when Abdul Baha made a little journey to the International Harvester Company offices in Chicago, he was told that already his prophecy was coming true; and on a map of his own country there was pictured to him just what Chicago is doing in the way of supplying agricultural implements to his people. Brass tacks showed agencies throughout the Orient.

[Abdul Baha listened with wide-open tear-filled eyes. Everything he sees proves to him the truth of his own message. The fact that we are supplying Persia automobiles, plows, reapers, threshing-machines, traction engines, locomotives, trolley-cars, proves, for him, his case.

[And so he, in degree, repays us by bringing to us the message of love and good-will . . .

[War, he says, is to be done away with absolutely. The governments of the world are merely to be business institutions. In fact, mankind no longer needs government. We are learning what is best, and what is best is righteous and right. Sin is merely the wrong thing, and sin brings bad results. That is why we should avoid sin.

[There is no greater wickedness than that men should kill one another, destroy one another, seek to thwart and embarrass one another. National lines are silly and absurd. Let every man live his life and do his work the best he can. We must love humanity so much that we will be kind to all people, even to those who do wrong, having full faith that they, in time, will see that error brings pain, and love and unselfishness bring happiness and every good thing.]

Abdul Baha is a non-resistant. He says we must be silent concerning the beliefs of others; we must pray for them and help them through kindness to correct their faults. Also, at the same time we would do well to consult the mirror and correct a few of our own limitations. We must look always at the good and not at the bad.

Christian Science interests Abdul Baha greatly. It is a somewhat humiliating thing for us when we think that this new American religion was never heard of by Abdul Baha until very recently. Now he has practically embraced it. He says it represents one arc of the great circle of truth, and that if he had learned nothing else from his trip to America but the truths of Christian Science, he would be amply repaid.

[He says he comes to us as a learner more than as a teacher. Nevertheless, he is obliged to give out the light that has been given to him. He keeps the good by giving it away.

[He quotes Ralph Waldo Emerson freely, delights in Walt Whitman, and loves the memory of Tolstoy, and is on terms of great tenderness toward every good and noble thing that makes for human betterment.]

No man of recent times has shown such a magnificent affirmative spirit as this man Abdul Baha.

The man is of medium size, very strong in form, muscularly built, active, with great good common sense. He has a large and impressive head, well-developed features, eyes set wide apart, big and luminous.

He listens with much appreciation and sympathy and when he speaks it is slowly, distinctly, and most impressively. He knows what he is saying. His heart is full and his emotions are brimming, although kept well under control.

Genius is akin to madness. But this man's poise, power, unselfishness and worldwide vision mark him as something more than a religious enthusiast.

Those twenty-four years in jail, when he was separated from the practical world of work, made him take on the habits of the scholar. Prison to him was merely a place to study, an opportunity for learning.

He speaks many languages and certainly speaks English better than most Americans do.

Thousands of his followers were shot, beheaded and banished during his imprisonment. But the recent revolution in Persia and Turkey gave him his liberty.

So he comes, seemingly out of college, fresh, uncontaminated by the world of work and worry.

[He has the ambition, the faith, and the heart of youth. He looks at things with the innocence of a man who sees them absolutely for the first time.]

He is reverential, respectful, filled with a great and holy zeal. And this zeal takes the form of a message of unification to the world.

There is no doubt among thinking people that this man represents, in great degree, the growing and evolving spirit of our times.

[Aside from his religious zeal, the fact still remains that the nations are getting together in a way that they never have before in history. Of course, there are physical factors that make this possible.

[We can call up the Mikado of Japan by telegraph, and get his reply in two hours.

[If the Czar of Russia wishes to talk with the President of the World's Panama Exposition, he can be accommodated and his questions answered the same day.

[Quick transportation, the telegraph, the telephone, and the manifold uses of electricity are bringing men together in a way that was never possible before.]

Abdul Baha is certainly one of the great modern prophets. We do not doubt his divinity any more than we doubt our own.

[Ernst Haeckel believes in Monism, and Monism is the One. There is only one thing in the world and this is Divine Energy, and this Divine Energy takes a million myriad forms.

[When Abdul Baha was asked what he thought of Ernst Haeckel, he bowed his head in reverence, and said that Ernst Haeckel was one of God's anointed.

[This is the mental attitude of Abdul Baha, to give everybody due credit, and he sees the hand of God in everything, everywhere.]

The influence of this man for the next ten years will be great and profound.

Evidently, his twenty-four years in prison were a benefit and an advantage.

Horace Greeley was once locked up in a prison in Paris, and from his prison cell he wrote, 'Thank God, at last, for once I am free from intrusion.'

Abdul Baha has had a wonderful experience and that he has been born again in his old age is certainly true. Time will check his enthusiasm and diminish his divine ardor, but before this happens he is bound to make the world his debtor.

And Abdul Baha, in degree, not only cleanses Persia from the taint of superstition, but comes across the sea and proclaims to all the world a Universal Peace through the acceptance of Commonsense, poetized, as a counselor and guide.

[Religions grow by the budding process. They are grafted on to a parent stem . . .]

Abdul Baha is a rebel from orthodox Mohammedanism. He has modernized the religion of Islam. [Mohammed Ali tried the same thing, and was shot in the public square of Shiraz, the day being set apart as a Feast or Holy Day.

[But you cannot get rid of a strong man by killing him. If he is of the right fiber he is never so much alive as when he is dead.

[Baha'u'llah took up the work of Mohammed Ali and was banished.

[Abdul Baha gathers around him a band of followers, and the ambitions and aspirations of Mohammed Ali and Baha'u'llah, refined and spiritualized, are now carried to successful victory.]

It is not for us to accept Abdul Baha's messages literally. In the world of economics, we in America are infinitely beyond anything that can come to us from the Orient. But the divine fire of this man's spirituality is bound to illuminate the dark corners of our imaginations and open up to us a spiritual realm which we would do well to go in and possess.

So here is health and happiness and long life to Abdul Baha, the servant of God. We cannot but echo back to him the love, the good will, and the high and holy faith which he brings to us.[29]

This article was published on several occasions in different newspapers in the United States.[30] Spanish translations also appeared in the Dominican Republic,[31] Mexico[32] and El Salvador.[33]

Hubbard continued to mention 'Abdu'l-Bahá in some of his writings. In a syndicated article distributed by the International News Service about the historical background of beggary and its elimination in some European countries, Hubbard quoted 'Abdu'l-Bahá as saying 'Man must be conciliated to man – not God to man.'[34] This article was later published in his monthly magazine, *The Philistine*, which had a circulation of 100,000 copies.[35]

In September the *West Coast Magazine* (Los Angeles), an illustrated monthly periodical with a circulation of 12,300 copies, published a lengthy article on the origins of the Bahá'í Faith penned by the Bahá'í aristocrat of Hungarian background Aurelia Bethlen. The poet and writer John S. McGroarty (1862–1944), editor of the magazine, added to the information presented by Bethlen one page and a half of passages from 'Abdu'l-Bahá's writings and utterances.[36] Two months later the artist Elizabeth Naker Bohan (1849–1930) published in the same magazine an article in which she listed the names of figures she considered 'the best types of the real Christian' and included 'Abdu'l-Bahá, describing Him as 'a very embodiment of love'.[37]

On 23 September, the *Seattle Times* published a transcript of a sermon delivered by Rev. Jesse D. O. Powers, pastor of the First

Unitarian Church, suffragist, president of the Washington State Peace Society, and perhaps among those who saw the Master at the Unitarian Convention held in Boston. The sermon was devoted to a description of 'Abdu'l-Bahá and the Bahá'í teachings and quoted from information published in the press. It was a remarkable defense of the Bahá'í Faith and can be interpreted as an answer to the attacks on 'Abdu'l-Bahá made by some American Christian ministers (see chapter 36, vol. 2):

UNITARIANS HEAR OF MERITS OF BAHAISM

REV. J. D. O. POWERS GIVES AUDITORS MASTERLY RESUME OF UNIVERSAL RELIGION WHICH INCLUDES ALL OTHERS

FOUNDERS SUFFER MANY TORMENTS IN PRISON

TELLS OF WIDESPREAD APPROVAL GIVEN UNIVERSAL BELIEF BY PRESS OF THE WORLD – MEANS TRUE BROTHERHOOD

'Bahaism, the Birth of a "Universal Religion" was the subject' taken yesterday by Rev. J. D. O. Powers at the Boylston Avenue Unitarian Church. He said in part:

The presence of Abdul Baha, the venerable and revered head of Bahaism, in this country has called attention anew to one of the most remarkable religious movements of modern times, exceeding even Christian Science in the rapidity of its growth and the undying loyalty of its adherents and the universality of its appeal to thinking men and women . . .

So powerful has been the appeal and the message of these modern prophets that the membership of Bahaism is now more than 3,000,000, including one-third of the population of Persia, thousands in America and other countries, including some of the most notable minds of the modern world.

So remarkable is its message to the world that Prof. E. G. Browne wrote of it twenty years ago in its infancy as a 'faith which may possibly win a place amidst the great religions of the world'.

PRESS GIVES APPROVAL

'No religious movement of modern times,' in the judgment of The Portland Oregonian, 'is nearly so significant as that of Bahaism.'

The Boston Congregationalist declares: 'The religion of the Bahaists has nothing of the eccentricity or faddism of so many modern religions and none of their shallow philosophy. It is simply a synthesis of the noblest ethics of the world around one common center – love and good will to all men.'

Francis H. Skrine, a deep student of it, writes that the new cult is suited to the present American mood of revolt against materialism and predatory wealth. 'Bahaism,' he says, 'may come in the great republic with a rush which nothing can resist.'

His first appeal is to the heart-hunger of the world, the unity, the spiritual oneness of humanity. Many years ago the great reformer of Italy, Mazzini, said that the question which agitates the world is a religious question; and he pathetically asked what the world appears to be asking today with a poignant insistence, 'Shall we never more possess a bond of common brotherhood, or religion, or conception of universal, providential law, that all may take and believe?' A writer in The Contemporary Review says that 'Bahaism appears to me to be calculated, as nothing else is I know of, to inspire and promote modern religious movements and developments in the direction of a truly Catholic religion adequate to meet the needs of the modern world.'

Abdul Baha himself says: 'The time has arrived for the world of humanity to hoist the standard of the oneness of the human world, so that solidarity and unity may connect all the nations of the world, so that dogmatic formulas and superstitions may end, so that the essential reality underlying all religions founded by all the prophets may be revealed. That reality is one. It is the love of God. It is the progress of the world. It is the oneness of humanity. It is the bond which can unite all the human race.'

The ultimate aim of Bahaism, then, is the spiritual unification of mankind. Its mission is not to supply the world with a new ethic, for a lofty ethic is already furnished us in the world's religious literature, but to unite all the faiths of the World and all the peoples of the world into one. 'The gift of God to this enlightened age is the knowledge of the oneness of mankind and the fundamental oneness of religion.' The great word of Bahaism is therefore unity.

RECOGNIZE ALL LEADERS

The distinguishing feature is that it sets out to demonstrate the fundamental unity of all religions and to trace them back to a single divine source. It recognizes not only all the bibles of the world but also all the saviours, prophets, mediators, manifestations, teachers, Jesus, Mohammed, Buddha, Zoroaster, Confucius – all were necessary in their time and place – each one was a part of the divine revelation to mankind.

It is not a sect or a new religion so much as it is a spirit and a new life embodied in a new dispensation, or great reconciling order, intent on achieving unity through diversity by means of a deeper outpouring of spirit through all forms. It has implicit faith that spirit cannot fail to act through all forms when once it has secured due embodiment.

It would not have us leave any of our loyalties. On the contrary, it bids us cleave to our particular church or faith and to work there to purify, ennoble, enlarge, spiritualize, and merge in a larger unity the expression of our particular expression of faith. It would, however, lift us out of the merely local and temporary and the particular into the omnipresent, the eternal and the universal. It would have us remain Christian or Buddhist or Mohammedan or Unitarian, but all these in the deepest sense these words convey, and embodying the finest insight modern times may find in them.

Abdul Baha is the pioneer of an eclectic gospel which teaches the fundamental unity of all religions, which would seek to sum up and preserve the best that the world has had of thought and deed and moral and spiritual insight. This is quite different from a doctrine of universal tolerance. I quite agree with The Chicago Advance that 'universal tolerance as a civil creed is sound, but that as an ethical creed it is rotten'. This is why we need critics and criticism. Some things in civic and ethical and spiritual creeds are partial; some are damnable, and the sooner we are rid of them the better. But in doing this we should not cast away that which is omnipresent, permanent and universal.

With countless others he sees the necessity of universal peace before man shall achieve other and higher things. And so he teaches the substitution of international tribunals of arbitration for the hideous arbitrament of war and enjoins his followers not to join the army. If this could only be made the command of modern Christianity we never again would see a war and vast resources would be freed for the uplift of mankind now worse than destroyed.

Universal education he believes in profoundly. He teaches the equality of man and woman, and directs that girls shall be educated not less efficiently than the boys. Along with this he believes in and pleads for a universal language as a medium of bringing the different races into closer communion with each other and now that commerce has belted the world this is not so much a dream.

The last fact to be noted is the spiritual quality of his message. In the Bahai scripture we are reminded again and again of that indescribable quality which flashes forth from the sublimest passages of the Psalms and the gospels and epistles of the new. They are simple and direct in utterance and are communicated as insight and revelation, and not as rationalism and intellect. Flashes of immediate intuition they are and yet frequently of marvelous ethical penetration as regards some of the most complicated problems of the twentieth century. Baha'u'llah's 'Hidden Words' can be unhesitatingly compared to many classics of devotion, with this added advantage that they have about them nothing of the ascetic spirit, and are therefore more fitted for the wayfaring man. The appeal is always, as in Quakerism, to the Inner Light, and there are no priests and no ritual observances.

Its dominant note is joy, faith, hope, love. It teaches what our own Unitarian leader has recently said: 'Sin, sorrow, renunciation, the cross, are pessimistic, characteristic words of Christianity, while, the dominant note of true religion is joy.'[38]

On the following Sunday, Powers again briefly mentioned 'Abdu'l-Bahá. His sermon dealt with the need for religious regeneration and the abandonment of superstitions and old religious practices like asceticism. At a certain point in his sermon, Powers declared that the character of the individual is of more importance than his religious beliefs and stated that 'no one doubts of the importance of a character like that of Washington or Lincoln, or Jesus or Abdul Baha.'[39]

BIBLIOGRAPHY

Books

'Abdu'l-Bahá. *Khatábát-i-Hadrat-i-'Abdu'l-Bahá.* vol. 1: Cairo: Faraju'lláh Zaki al-Kurdí, 1921; vols. 2 and 3: Tehran: Bahá'í Publishing Trust, 1970–1.

— *Paris Talks.* London: Bahá'í Publishing Trust, 1967.

— *The Promulgation of Universal Peace.* Wilmette, IL: Bahá'í Publishing Trust, 1982.

— *Selections from the Writings of 'Abdu'l-Bahá.* Haifa: Bahá'í World Centre, 1978.

— *Some Answered Questions.* Haifa: Bahá'í World Centre, 2015.

— *A Traveller's Narrative.* Cambridge: Cambridge University Press, 1891.

'Abdu'l-Bahá in Canada. Thornhill: Bahá'í Canada Publications, rev. ed. 1987.

Abdul Baha on Divine Philosophy. Boston: The Tudor Press, 1918.

'Abdu'l-Bahá in London. London: Bahá'í Publishing Trust, 1982.

Afnan, Elham. 'Abdu'l-Bahá and Ezra Pound's Circle', *Journal of Bahá'í Studies* 6:2 (June–Sept. 1994).

Afroukhteh, Youness. *Memories of Nine Years in 'Akká.* Oxford: George Ronald, 2003.

Aikins, J.A.M. *Report on the Second International Moral Education Congress.* Ottawa: C.H. Parmelee, 1913.

Alkan, Necati. *Dissent and Heterodoxy in the Late Ottoman Empire.* Piscataway, NJ: Gorgias Press & The Isis Press, 2010.

American Annual and Newspaper Directory. 3 vols. Philadelphia: N.W. Ayer and Son, 1912.

Atherton, Gertrude. *Julia France and Her Times: A Novel.* New York: Macmillan, 1912.

Atkinson, Anne G., et al. *Green Acre on the Piscataqua.* Eliot, ME: Green Acre Bahá'í School Council, 1991.

Atwood, Thomas. *My Work in the Spirit World: An address delivered to the members and associates of the London Spiritualist Alliance, in the French Drawing Room, St. James's Hall, Piccadilly*, 1902.

Bahai News/Star of the West/The Bahai Magazine, vols. 1–25 (1910–35). Digital reproduction in CD. Talisman Education Software, 2001.

The Bahá'í World. vols. 1–12, 1925–54. Wilmette, IL: Bahá'í Publishing Trust, rpt. 1980.

Balyuzi, H. M. *'Abdu'l-Bahá: The Centre of the Covenant of Bahá'u'lláh*. Oxford: George Ronald, 2nd ed. with minor corr. 1987.

Bellanger, Claude. *Histoire générale de la presse française*, vol. III. Paris: Ed. Universitaires de France, 1972.

Blomfield, Lady [Sitárih Khánum; Sara Louise]. *The Chosen Highway*. Oxford: George Ronald, rpt. 2007.

Bluysen, Paul. *Annuaire de la Presse Française*. Paris, 1911 and 1913.

Brown, Ramona Allen. *Memories of 'Abdu'l-Bahá*. Wilmette, IL: Bahá'í Publishing Trust, 1980.

Bryan, William Jennings. *The Old World and Its Ways*. New York: Thompson, 1907.

Buckton, A. M. [Alice Mary]. *Eager Heart: A Christmas Mystery Play.* New York: Chappell, 1910.

Campbell, R. J. [Reginald John]. *The New Theology*. London: Chapman and Hall, 1907.

— *A Spiritual Pilgrimage*. London: Williams and Norgate, 1916.

Caton, Peggy. 'The Sacramento Bahá'í Community, 1912–1987', in Richard Hollinger (ed.). *Community Histories*, pp. 241–80.

Cheyne, Thomas K. *The Reconciliation of Races and Religions*. London: Adam and Charles Black, 1914.

Clark, Deb. 'The Bahá'ís of Baltimore, 1898–1990', in Richard Hollinger (ed.). *Community Histories*, pp. 111–52.

Cobb, Stanwood. *My Memories of 'Abdu'l-Bahá*. Washington DC: Avalon Press, 1962.

Cooper, Ella. Collection of notes of talks and conversations of 'Abdu'l-Bahá in California. US National Bahá'í Archives.

Curtis, William Eleroy. *To-day in Syria and Palestine*. Chicago: F. H. Revell, 1903.

Curtiss, Samuel Ives. *Primitive Semitic Religion Today: A record of researches, discoveries and studies in Syria, Palestine and the Sinaitic peninsula*. London: Hodder and Stoughton, 1902.

Dahl, Roger. 'A History of the Kenosha Bahá'í Community', in Richard Hollinger (ed.). *Community Histories*, pp. 1–66.

Dreyfus, Hippolyte. *Essai sur le Béhaïsme*. Paris: Ernest Leroux, 1909.

Duff, Mountstuart E. Grant. *Notes from a Diary, 1886–1888*, vol. 1. London: John Murray, 1900.

Dyserinck, Attie G. (ed.). *Mémoires sur L'Éducation Morale*. La Haye: Martinus Nijhoff, 1912.

Fenge, Gerry. *The Two Worlds of Wellesley Tudor Pole*. Everett, WA: Lorian Press, 2010.

Ford, Mary Hanford. *The Oriental Rose*. New York: Broadway Publishing, 1910.

Forty-Second Annual Report of the Women's Presbyterian Board of Missions of the Northwest. Chicago, April 1913.

Frazer, Sir James George. *Lectures on the Early History of the Kingship*. London: Macmillan, 1905.

Gail, Marzieh. "Abdu'l-Bahá in America', *World Order* 10:4 (July 1944), pp. 110–19.
— "Abdu'l-Bahá: Portrayals East and West', *World Order* 6:1 (Fall 1971), pp. 29–46.
— *Arches of the Years*. Oxford: George Ronald, 1991.
— *Dawn over Mount Hira*. Oxford: George Ronald, 1976.
— *Summon Up Remembrance*. Oxford: George Ronald, 1987.

Ganachari, Aravind Gururao. *Nationalism and Social Reform in a Colonial Situation*. New Delhi: Kalpaz, 2005.

Griffiths, Dennis (ed.). *The Encyclopedia of the British Press*. London: Macmillan, 1992.

Grundy, Julia M. *Ten Days in the Light of Akka*. Chicago: Bahai Publishing Society, 1907.

Hartmann, Martin. *The Arabic Press of Egypt*. London: Luzac, 1899.

Herrick, Elizabeth. *Unity Triumphant*. London: Kegan Paul, Trench, Trubner & Co., 1923.

Hogenson, Kathryn Jewett. *Lighting the Western Sky: The Hearst Pilgrimage and the Establishment of the Bahá'í Faith in the West*. Oxford: George Ronald, 2010.

Holley, Horace. *Bahai: The Spirit of the Age*. New York: Brentano's, 1921.
— *The Modern Social Religion*. London: Sidgwick & Jackson, 1913.

Hollinger, Richard, (ed.). *'Abdu'l-Bahá in America: Agnes Parsons' Diary*. Los Angeles: Kalimát Press, 1996.
— *Community Histories: Studies in the Bábí and Bahá'í Religions*, vol. 6. Los Angeles, CA: Kalimát Press, 1992.

The Holy Bible. Authorised King James Version. London: The Gideons, International, 1957.

Honnold, Annamarie. *Vignettes from the Life of 'Abdu'l-Bahá*. Oxford: George Ronald, 1982.

van den Hoonard, Will C. *The Origins of the Bahá'í Community of Canada, 1898–1948*. Waterloo, ON: Wilfrid Laurier University Press, 1996.

Huart, Clément Imbault-. 'Bahá Alláh'. *Encyclopaedia of Islam*, vol. 1 (A–D). Th. Houtsma, T.W. Arnold, R. Bassett (eds.). Leiden: E.J. Brill, 1913. (Fascicle 9 or 10, in which this article appeared, was published separately in 1911).

Hubbard, Elbert. *Hollyhocks and Goldenglow*. East Aurora, NY: Roycrofters, 1912.
— 'A Modern Prophet', *Hearst's Magazine*, July 1912.

Inchbold, A. C. *Under the Syrian Sun*, vol. 2. Philadelphia: Hutchinson, 1907.

Ives, Howard Colby. *Portals to Freedom*. Oxford: George Ronald, 1973.

Jessup, Henry Harris. *Fifty-Three Years in Syria*. New York: Fleming H. Revell, 1910.

Jordan, David Starr. *The Days of a Man: Being Memories of a Naturalist, Teacher and Minor Prophet of Democracy*, vol. 2. New York: World Book Co., 1922 .

Jung, Eugène. *Les Puissances devant la Révolte Arabe*. Paris: Hachette, 1906.

Khursheed, Anjam. *The Seven Candles of Unity*. London: Bahá'í Publishing Trust, 1991.

Lacroix-Hopson (Eliane A.). *'Abdu'l-Bahá in New York: The City of the Covenant*. New York: Newvistadesign, 1999.

de Lorey, Eustache, and Douglas Sladen. *Queers Things about Persia*. Philadelphia, PA: J.B. Lippincott, 1907.

Lucas, Mary L. *A Brief Account of My Visit to Acca*. Chicago: Bahai Publishing Society, 1905.

Margoliouth, D.S. *Mohammedanism*. London: Williams and Norgate, 1911.

Maud, Constance. *Sparks Among the Stubble*. London: Allan, 1924.

McEwen, John M. 'The National Press during the First World War', *Journal of Contemporary History*, July 1982 (17:3).

Metelmann, Velda Piff. *Lua Getsinger: Herald of the Covenant*. Oxford: George Ronald, 1997.

Minutes and Proceedings of London Yearly Meeting of Friends, 1911. London: Library of the Religious Society of Friends. London, 1912, p. 207.

Momen, Moojan. *The Bábí and Bahá'í Religions, 1844–1944. Some Contemporary Western Accounts.* Oxford: George Ronald, 1981.

Morrison, Gayle. *To Move the World: Louis G. Gregory and the Advancement of Racial Unity in America*. Wilmette, IL: Bahá'í Publishing Trust, 1982.

Nakhjavani, Violette. *The Maxwells of Montreal.* Oxford: George Ronald, 2011.

Newspaper Press Directory. London: C. Mitchell and Co., 1911 and 1913.

Oliphant, Laurence. *Haifa or Life in the Holy Land.* Jerusalem: Canaan Publishing House, 1887, 2nd ed. 1916.

Parsons, Agnes (ed. Richard Hollinger). *'Abdu'l-Bahá in America: Agnes Parsons' Diary.* Los Angeles: Kalimát Press, 1996.

The Passing of 'Abdu'l-Bahá: A Compilation. Los Angeles: Kalimát Press, 1991.

Perkins, Mary. *Servant of the Glory: The Life of 'Abdu'l-Bahá.* Oxford: George Ronald, 1999.

Phelps, Myron H. *Life and Teachings of Abbas Effendi*. New York: Knickerbocker Press, 1903.

Philip, Percy J. *France in Defeat*. London: Frederick Muller, 1905.

Proceedings of the Forty-Fifth Annual Meeting. Free Religious Association: Boston, 1912.

Randall-Winckler, Bahíyyih. *William Henry Randall*. Oxford: Oneworld, 1996.

Report of the Eighteenth Annual Lake Mohonk Conference on International Arbitration. Brandow: Albany: Brandow, 1912.

Report of the Seventeenth Annual Lake Mohonk Conference on International Arbitration. Albany: Brandow, 1911.

Rideout, Anise. *Early History of Bahá'í Community, Boston, Mass*. n.d., n.p. Unpublished manuscript.

Robbins, Keith. *History, Religion and Identity in Modern Britain*. London: Bloomsbury, 1993.

Russell, George W.E. *Basil Wilberforce: A Memoir*. London: John Murray, 1917.

Rutstein, Nathan. *Corinne True: Faithful Handmaid of 'Abdu'l-Bahá*. Oxford: George Ronald, 1987.

Shoghi Effendi. *God Passes By*. Wilmette, IL: Bahá'í Publishing Trust, rev. ed. 1995.

Skrine, Francis H. *Bahaism: The Religion of Brotherhood*. London: Longmans, Green and Co., 1912.

Sohrab, Ahmad. *'Abdu'l-Bahá in Egypt*. New York: New History Foundation, 1929.
— Correspondence with Harriet Magee from 5 December 1912 to 12 June 1913. US National Bahá'í Archives.

Le Soudier, H. *Annuaire des Journaux*. Paris: Librairie H. Le Soudier, 1911 and 1913.

Speer, Robert E. *Missions and Modern History*. New York: Fleming H. Revell, 1904.

Spiller, Gustav. *The Mind of Man: A Text-Book of Psychology*. London: Swan Sonnenchien, 1902.

Stanford University. *Twenty-Second Annual Register 1912–1913*.

Star of the West. rpt. Oxford: George Ronald, 1984.

Stevens, E. S. *The Mountain of God*. London: Mills and Boon, 1911.

Stockman, Robert H. *The Bahá'í Faith in America: Early Expansion, 1900–1912*, vol. 2. Oxford: George Ronald, 1995.

Tamadun ul Molk. *Report of an Address on the Bahai Movement, given at the City Temple on Sunday Afternoon, Oct. 16th, 1910 by Tamadun ul Molk*. East Sheen, England: Bahai Press, 1910.

Thompson, Juliet. *'Abdu'l-Bahá the Center of the Covenant*. Wilmette, IL: Bahá'í Publishing Committee, 1948.
— *Abdul Baha's First Days in America*. East Aurora, NY: The Roycrofters, n.d.
— *The Diary of Juliet Thompson*. Los Angeles: Kalimát Press, 1995.

Townshend, George. *'Abdu'l-Bahá: The Master*. Oxford: George Ronald, 1987.

Tudor Pole, Wellesley. *The Silent Road*. London: C. W. Daniel, 1960.

— *Writing on the Ground*. London: Neville Spearman, 1968.

Tussing, Phillip E. 'Finishing the Work: 'Abdu'l-Bahá in Dublin, New Hampshire, 1912'. http://bahai-library.com/tussing_abdul-baha_dublin

Universal Principles of the Bahai Movement: Social, Economic, Governmental. Washington DC: Persian-American Bulletin, 1912.

Ward, Allan L. *239 Days: 'Abdu'l-Bahá's Journey in America*. Wilmette, IL: Bahá'í Publishing Trust, 1979.

— *An Historical Study of the North American Speaking Tour of 'Abdu'l-Bahá and a Rhetorical Analysis of His Addresses*. PhD thesis. Ohio University, 1960.

Weinberg, Robert. *Ethel Jenner Rosenberg: The Life and Times of England's Outstanding Bahá'í Pioneer Worker*. Oxford: George Ronald, 1995.

Whitehead, O. Z. *Portraits of Some Bahá'í Women*. Oxford: George Ronald, 1996.

— *Some Bahá'ís to Remember*. Oxford: George Ronald, 1983.

— *Some Early Bahá'ís in the West*. Oxford: George Ronald, 1976.

William, David Rhys. *World Religions and the Hope for Peace*. Boston: Beacon Press, 1951.

Woods, C.E. *Archdeacon Wilberforce: His Ideals and Teaching*. London: Elliot Stock, 1917.

Zarqání, Maḥmúd-i-. *Maḥmúd's Diary*. Oxford: George Ronald, 1998.

Newspapers, Journals and Periodicals

ABC (Geneva, Switzerland)
Aberdeen Daily News (SD)
Aberdeen Weekly News (SD)
Aberdeen World (WA)
Ada Evening News (OK)
Adams County Free Press (Corning, IA)
Advent News and Sabbath Herald (Washington DC)
The Advertiser (Adelaide, Australia)
The Advertiser (Montgomery, AL)
The Advocate of Peace (Washington DC)
African Times and Orient Review (London)
The Age (Melbourne, Australia)
The Age (New York)
Agitator (Wellsboro, PA)
al-Ahram (Cairo, Egypt)
Alameda Times (CA)
Albany Evening Journal (NY)
Albany Press (New York)
America (New York)
American (Baltimore, MD)
American (Fort Smith, AR)
American (New York)
American Friend (Philadelphia, PA)
The American Journal of Religious Psychology and Education (Worcester, MA)
American Review of Reviews (New York)
Amerika Esperantisto (Washington DC)
Amsterdam Evening Recorder (Amsterdam, NY)
Anaconda Standard (Anaconda, MT)
Annales Théosophiques (Paris)

The Appeal (St Paul, MN)
The Arena (Boston)
Argus (Middletown, NY)
Armenia (Boston)
The Atlanta Constitution (GA)
The Atlanta Georgian (GA)
Augusta Chronicle (GA)
Australasian (Melbourne, Australia)

Bahai News (Chicago)
Baltimore Star (MD)
Baltimore Sun (MD)
The Baptist Missionary Magazine (Boston)
La Bastille (Paris)
Bataviaasch Nieuwsblad (Jakarta, Indonesia)
Bath Chronicle and Weekly Gazette (Bath, England)
Bedford Daily Mail (IN)
Bee (Omaha, NE)
Belfast News Letter (Belfast, Northern Ireland)
Bellman (Minneapolis, MN)
Berkeley Daily Gazette (CA)
Berkeley Gazette (CA)
Berkeley Independent (CA)
Bible Review (Applegate, CA)
Bible Society Record (New York)
The Biblical World (Chicago)
Biddeford Weekly Journal (ME)
Bill Barlow's Budget (Douglas, WY)
Binghamton Press (Binghamton, NY)
Blessed be Egypt (London)
Blue Glass Blade (Lexington, KY)
Bombay Courier (India)
The Bombay Times and Journal of Commerce (India)
The Bookman (New York)
Boston Advertiser (MA)
Boston American (MA)
Boston Daily Globe (MA)
Boston Evening Transcript (MA)
Boston Herald (MA)
Boston Journal (MA)
Boston Post (MA)
The Boston Sunday Globe (MA)
Boston Transcript (MA)
Boston Traveler (MA)
La Bourse Egyptienne (Cairo, Egypt)
Brooklyn Daily Eagle (NY)
Brotherhood (Letchworth, England)
Brownsburg Record (IN)
Buffalo Commercial (NY)
Buffalo Courier (NY)
Buffalo Enquirer (NY)
Buffalo Evening News (NY)
Buffalo Evening Times (NY)
Buffalo Examiner (NY)
Buffalo Express (NY)
Bunbury Herald (Bunbury, Australia)

Le Canada (Montreal)
Canton Repository (OH)
El Católico (Madrid)
Cayley Hustler (Cayley, Alberta)
Charlotte Daily Observer (NC)
Chicago Advance (IL)
Chicago Daily Tribune (*Chicago Tribune*) (IL)
Chicago Daily World (IL)
The Chicago Defender (IL)
Chicago Examiner (IL)
The Chicago Journal (IL)
Chicago Live Stock World (IL)
Chicago Post (IL)
Chicago Record-Herald (IL)
Chicago Sunday Tribune (IL)
Chihrih-Nimá (Cairo)
The Christian Commonwealth (London)
The Christian Endeavour World (Boston)
The Christian Globe (London)
Christian Herald (New York)
The Christian Life (London)
Christian Register (Boston)
Christian Register (New York)
Christian Science Monitor (Boston)
Christian Workers Magazine (Chicago)
The Christian World (London)
Le Christianisme au XXe Siècle (Paris)
Chronicle (Houston, TX)
Churchman (New York)
Church's Officers Gazette (Washington DC)

The Cincinnati Enquirer (OH)
Cincinnati Post (OH)
Cincinnati Times-Star (OH)
Cincinnati Tribune (OH)
City Herald (Dakota City, NE)
Clark College Monthly (WA)
Cleveland News (OH)
Cleveland Press (OH)
Clifton Chronicle and Directory (Clifton, Bristol, England)
Clinton Mirror (Clinton, IA)
Cloverdale Reveille (CA)
Columbia Republican (Hudson, NY)
Columbia Spectator (New York)
Commercial Tribune (Cincinnati, OH)
The Commoner (Lincoln, NE)
Concord Monitor (NH)
Congregationalist and Christian World (Boston)
The Contemporary Review (London)
The Continent (Chicago)
La Convicción (Barcelona, Spain)
Coos Bay Times (Marshfield, OR)
Cranbury Press (Cranbury, NJ)
The Critic (New York)
Current Literature (New York)

Daily Argus (Mt Vernon, NY)
Daily Bulletin (Van Wert, OH)
The Daily Chronicle (Bristol)
Daily Chronicle (London)
Daily Express (London)
Daily Gazette (Janeswille, WI)
The Daily Graphic (London)
Daily Journal (Chicago)
Daily Journal (Stevens Point, WI)
Daily Mail (London)
Daily Mirror (London)
Daily News (Chicago)
Daily News (Elkhart, IN)
Daily News (Greensboro, NC)
Daily News (Ithaca, NY)
The Daily News (London)
Daily News (Perth, Australia)
Daily News (Springfield, MA)
Daily News and Leader (London)
Daily Northwestern (Oshkosh, WI)
Daily Observer (Charlotte, NC)
Daily Palo Alto (CA)
Daily People (New York)
The Daily Picayune (New Orleans, LA)
Daily Press (Bristol, England)
Daily Press (Utica, NY)
Daily Reporter (Waterloo, IA)
Daily Sketch (London)
Daily Sun (Brandon, Manitoba)
The Daily Telegraph (London)
Daily Times (Seattle, WA)
Daily Times News (Ann Arbor, MI)
The Dallas Morning News (TX)
Davenport Times (IA)
Day Book (Chicago)
Democrat (Nashville, TN)
Democrat and Chronicle (Rochester, NY)
Denver Express (CO)
Denver Post (CO)
The Des Moines News (IA)
Detroit Free Press (MI)
Detroit Tribune (MI)
Le Devoir (Montreal)
The Dial (Chicago)
Diario de la Marina (Havana, Cuba)
Diario del Salvador (San Salvador, El Salvador)
Duluth Herald (MN)

Eau Claire Leader (Eau Claire, WI)
L'Echo du Merveilleux (Paris)
L'Écho de Paris (Paris)
Eclectic Magazine (London)
Edwardsville Intelligencer (Edwardsville, IL)
The Egyptian Gazette (Alexandria, Egypt)
El Paso Herald (TX)
Emerson College Magazine (Boston)
English Illustrated Magazine (London)
La España Moderna (Madrid, Spain)
La Estrella (Las Cruces, NM)
Evening American (Chicago)
Evening Bulletin (Philadelphia, PA)
Evening Call (New York)
Evening News (London)
Evening News (San Jose, CA)
Evening News (Sault Ste. Marie, MI)

Evening Observer (Dunkirk, NY)
Evening Post (Chicago)
Evening Post (Frederick, MD)
The Evening Post (New York)
Evening Press (Grand Rapids, MI)
Evening Recorder (Amsterdam, NY)
Evening Standard (Odgen, UT)
The Evening Standard and St. James Gazette (London)
Evening Star (Washington DC)
Evening Sun (Baltimore, MD)
Evening Telegram (New York)
Evening Telegram (Salt Lake City, UT)
Evening Times (New York)
Evening Times (Pawtucket, RI)
Evening Times (Trenton, NJ)
Evening Transcript (Boston, MA)
Evening Tribune (San Diego, CA)
Evening Union (Springfield, MA)
The Evening World (New York)
Everybody's Magazine (New York)
Excelsior (Paris)
Expositor and Current Anecdotes (Cleveland, OH)
Express and Telegraph (Adelaide, Australia)

Family Herald and Weekly Star (Montreal)
Le Figaro (Paris)
Fort Wayne Journal-Gazette (IN)
Fort Wayne News (Fort Wayne, IN)
Fort Wayne Sentinel (IN)
Fort Worth Star-Telegram (TX)
The Fortnightly Review (London)
Forum (Boston)
Forward (Philadephia, PA)
Le Foyer Protestant (Nîmes, France)
The Fra (East Aurora, NY)
La France (Paris)
Frederick News (MD)
Free Press (Burlington, VT)
The Friend (London)
Friends' Intelligencer (Philadelphia, PA)
Friends' Review (Philadelphia, PA)
Friends' Witness to Scriptural Truth (London)

al-Garida al-Misrija (Cairo, Egypt)
Gazette (Cleveland, OH)
Gazette Times (Pittsburgh, PA)
Gettysburg Times (PA)
Gil Blas (Paris)
Glasgow Herald (Scotland)
Glen Falls Daily Times (New York)
Globe-Democrat (St Louis, MO)
Gloucester Citizen (England)
Gran Valley Times (Moab, UT)
Grand Forks Daily Herald (ND)
Grand Rapids Press (MI)
Grey River Argus (Greymouth, New Zealand)

Harper's Weekly (New York)
Hartford Courant (CT)
Hawaiian Gazette (Honolulu, HI)
Hearst's Magazine (New York)
Heimir (Winnipeg, MB)
Herald (El Paso, TX)
Herald (Washington DC)
Herald of Gospel Liberty (Dayton, OH)
Heraldo de Madrid (Madrid, Spain)
al-Hoda (New York)
Houston Chronicle (TX)

Idaho Sunday Statesman (Boise, ID)
Illustrated Buffalo Express (NY)
Illustrated Companion (New York)
Illustrated London News (London)
El Imparcial (Madrid, Spain)
The Independent (New York)
Indianapolis Star (IN)
Indianapolis Sunday Star (IN)
International Psychic Gazette (London)
Inter-Ocean (Chicago, IL)
Investment (New York)
Iowa Recorder (Greener, IA)
Item (New Orleans, LA)
Jamestown Evening Journal (NY)
Jersey Journal (NJ)
Journal (Columbus, OH)
Le Journal (Paris, France)
Journal de Constantinople (Turkey)
Journal of Contemporary History (England)

Journal-Gazette (Fort Wayne, IN)
Journal de Genève (Switzerland)

Kansas City Star (KS)
Kansas City Times (KS)
Keene Evening Sentinel (NH)
Kenosha Evening News (WI)
Knox Starke County Democrat (IN)

Leader (Cleveland, OH)
Leicester Daily Mercury (Leicester, England)
Lewiston Evening Journal (ME)
The Lexington Herald (KY)
La Liberté (Paris, France)
Light (London)
Lima News (OH)
Lincoln Daily News (NE)
Lincoln Daily Star (NE)
Listín Diario (Santo Domingo, Dominican Republic)
The Literary Digest (New York)
The Literary Gazette (London)
Literary World (Boston)
Liverpool Mercury (England)
Logansport Times (IN)
Loraine Herald (OH)
Los Angeles Herald (CA)
Los Angeles Sunday Times (CA)
Los Angeles Times (CA)
Los Angeles Tribune (CA)
Lowell Sun (MA)

M.A.P. (London)
Malden Mail (MA)
Malden Mirror (MA)
Malden News (MA)
The Manchester Guardian (England)
Manitoba Free Press (Winnipeg, Canada)
The Manti Messenger (UT)
Marble Rock Journal (IA)
Marion Daily Star (OH)
Maryborough Chronicle, Wide Bay and Burnett Advertiser (Australia)
Maysville Public Ledger (KY)
Medicine Hat Daily News (Alberta, Canada)
Mercure de France (Paris)
El Mercurio (Santiago, Chile)
Mercury (Hobart, Australia)
Miami Herald (FL)
Miles City Star (MT)
Milford Dispatch (PA)
Milwaukee Journal (WI)
The Minneapolis Journal (MN)
Minneapolis Morning Tribune (MN)
Minneapolis Tribune (MN)
Missions (Boston)
Modesto News (CA)
The Monitor and the New Era (London)
Montclair Times (NJ)
Montgomery Advertiser (AL)
Montreal Daily Herald (Canada)
Montreal Daily Star (Canada)
Montreal Daily Witness (Canada)
Montreal Gazette (Canada)
Mooresville Times (IN)
Morning Herald (London)
Morning News (Dallas, TX)
Morning Oregonian (Portland, OR)
The Morning Post (London)
Morning Star (Rockford, IL)
Moving Picture World (New York)
al-Mu'ayyad (Cairo, Egypt)
al-Muqattam (Egypt)

La Nación (Buenos Aires, Argentina)
Nation (New York)
National Democrat (Des Moines, IA)
National Labor Tribune (Pittsburgh, PA)
Le Nationaliste (Montreal)
The Near East (London)
Neue Metaphysische Rundschau (Berlin, Germany)
Nevada State Journal (Reno, NV)
The New Age (London)
New Age Magazine (New York)
New-Church Review (Boston)
New Era (Humeston, IA)
New Orleans Daily Picayune (LA)
New Orleans Item (LA)
New York Age (NY)
New York Herald (NY)
New York Press (NY)

The New York Times (NY)
New-York Tribune (NY)
Newcastle Morning Herald and Miner's Advocate (Australia)
News (Fort Wayne, IN)
News (New Castle, PA)
News Chronicle (Muskegon, MI)
Newton Register (New York)
Niagara Falls Gazette (NY)
Nieuwe Rotterdamsche Courant (Rotterdam, Netherlands)
Nineteenth Century (London)
North American (Philadelphia, PA)
North American Review (New York)
The Northern Star (Lismore, Australia)
Northwestern Christian Advocate (Chicago)
Les Nouvelles (Algiers, Algeria)

Oakland Inquirer (CA)
Oakland Tribune (CA)
The Observer (London)
Observer (New York)
Occult Review (London)
Odgen Evening Standard (UT)
Oelwein Daily Register (IA)
The Ohio State Journal (OH)
Omaha Daily News (NE)
Omaha News (NE)
L'Opinion (Paris)
Oregonian (Portland, OR)
Oriental Review (New York)
Oswego Palladium (NY)
Outlook (New York)

Pacific Unitarian (San Francisco, CA)
El País (Madrid, Spain)
Palo Altan (CA)
Palo Alto Times (CA)
Palo Alto Tribune (CA)
Paris-Journal (Paris)
Paterson Evening News (NJ)
Paterson Morning Call (NJ)
La Patria (Mexico City, Mexico)
La Patrie (Montreal)
Pawtucket Evening Times (RI)
The Peacemaker and Court of Arbitration (Philadelphia, PA)
Peterborough Transcript (NH)
Petersburg Pike County Democrat (IN)
Le Petit Marseillais (France)
Philadelphia Inquirer (PA)
The Philadelphia Press (PA)
Philadelphia Record (PA)
Philadelphia Star (PA)
Philistine (East Aurora, NY)
Phoenix Republican (AZ)
Pike County Press (Milford, PA)
Pioneer Press (St Paul, MN)
Pittsburg Times (Pittsburgh, PA)
Pittsburgh Chronicle-Telegraph (PA)
Pittsburgh Dispatch (PA)
Pittsburgh Gazette Times (PA)
Pittsburgh Post (PA)
The Pittsburgh Press (PA)
Pittsburgh Sun (PA)
The Plain Dealer (Cleveland, OH)
Port Jervis Gazette (NY)
Portland Telegram (OR)
The Portsmouth Herald (NH)
Post Express (NY)
Poverty Bay Herald (Gisborne, New Zealand)
Presbyterian (Philadelphia, PA)
La Presse (Montreal)
La Presse (Paris)
Le Progrés Spirite (Paris)
Public Ledger (Philadelphia, PA)
Public Opinion (New York)
Putman County Republican (Carmel, NY)

A Quarterly Record of Higher Thought Work (London)

Racine Journal-News (WI)
Reality (New York)
Record of Christian Work (Northfield, MA)
Record-Herald (Chicago)
Red Cloud Chief (NE)
Redcliff Review (Redcliff, Alberta)
Reform Advocate (Chicago)
The Register (Adelaide)
Reporter (Fond du Lac, WI)

Reporter (Le Grand, IA)
Repository (Canton, OH)
Republican (Cedar Rapids, IA)
Republican (Denver, CO)
Republican (Springfield, MA)
Reseignements Utiles, Supplément d'Aesculape (Paris)
Review of Reviews (London)
Revue Anti-Maçonnique (Paris)
Revue Bleue (Paris)
Revue d'histoire diplomatique (Paris)
Revue de Métaphysique et Morale (Paris)
Revue de l'Orient, d'Algérie et des Colonies (Paris)
Riverside Daily Press (CA)
Riverside Enterprise (CA)
Rochester Democrat (New York)
Rochester Post-Express (New York)
Rocky Mountains News (Denver, CO)

Sacramento Bee (CA)
Sacramento Star (CA)
Sacramento Union (CA)
Saginaw Daily News (MI)
Saginaw News (MI)
Al-Saih (New York)
St. Hilaire Spectator (MN)
St. Paul Dispatch (MN)
St. Paul Pioneer Press (St Paul, MN)
Salt Lake City News (UT)
Salt Lake Evening Telegram (UT)
Salt Lake Herald (UT)
Salt Lake Tribune (UT)
San Francisco Bulletin (CA)
San Francisco Call (CA)
San Francisco Chronicle (CA)
San Francisco Examiner (CA)
San Francisco News Daily (CA)
San Francisco Post (CA)
San Jose Herald (CA)
San Jose Mercury (CA)
Sandusky Register (OH)
Savannah News (GA)
Schenectady Gazette (NY)
The Scotsman (Edinburgh, Scotland)
Seattle Daily Times (WA)
Seattle Times (WA)
Semiweekly Journal (Auburn, NY)
Sheboygan Press (WI)
Shoreditch Observer (Hackney, England)
Sidney Morning Herald (Australia)
Sophia (Madrid, Spain)
South Bend Tribune (IN)
Southern Argus and Wagin-Arthur Express (Perth, Australia)
Spartanburg Herald (SC)
The Spokane-Review (WA)
Springfield Daily Republican (MA)
Springfield News (MA)
The Springfield Republican (MA)
The Standard (London)
Standard (Montreal)
Standard Union (Brooklyn, NY)
The Star (Baltimore, MD)
Star (London)
Star (Wilmington, DE)
Star Weekly (Toronto)
Star of the West (Chicago)
Stenographer (Philadelphia, PA)
Le Stéphanois (Saint Etienne, France)
Süddeutsche Warte (Stuttgart, Germany)
Sullivan Daily Times (IN)
The Sun (Baltimore)
The Sun (Indianapolis, IN)
The Sun (New York)
Sunbeam (MN)
Sunday News Tribune (Duluth, MN)
Sunday Oregonian (Portland, OR)
Sunday Times (Sidney, Australia)
Superior News Tribune (WI)
Survey (NY)
Syracuse Herald (NY)
Syracuse Journal (NY)
Syracuse Post Standard (NY)
Syracuse Telegram (NY)

T.P.'s Weekly (London)
Telegraph (Brisbane, Australia)
Telegraph (Philadelphia, PA)
Le Temps (Paris)
Tennessean (Nashville, TN)
Theosophic Messenger (Chicago)
The Theosophic Messenger (Los Angeles)
The Theosophical Forum (New York)

Theosophical Quarterly (New York)
Theosophy in Scotland (Edinburgh)
De Tid (Amsterdam, Netherlands)
The Times (London)
The Times (Tacoma, WA)
The Times of India (Bombay)
Times-Press (Middletown, NY)
Times-Tribune (Waterloo, IA)
The Transcript (Toodle, UT)
A Travers le Monde (Paris)
La Tribune de Genève (Geneva, Swtizerland)
Tri-States Union (Port Jervis, NY)
Troy Press (NY)
Twentieth Century Magazine (Boston)
Twenty-Second Annual Register 1912–1913 (Stanford University, CA)

Unitarian Advance (New York)
Unitarian Word and Work (Boston)
Unity (Chicago)
L'Univers Israélite (Paris)
El Universal (Mexico City, Mexico)
University of Tennessee Record (Knoxville, TN)
Utica Daily Press (Utica, NY)
Van Nuys News (CA)
La Vie Nouvelle (Paris)
Wádí al-Níl (*Wadinnil*) (Alexandria)
The Washington Bee (Washington DC)
Washington County Post (Cambridge, NY)
Washington Herald (Washington DC)
The Washington Post (Washington DC)
Washington Star (Washington DC)
Washington Times (Washington DC)
The Watchman (Sidney, Australia)
Waterloo Reporter (IA)
The West London Gazette (Westminster, London)
Weekly Budget (London)
Weekly Sun (Singapore)
West Australian (Perth, Australia)
West Coast Magazine (Los Angeles)
Wet Mountain Times (Westcliffe, CO)
Whim (Newark, NJ)
The Whittier News (CA)
Worcester Evening Gazette (MA)
Worcester Post (MA)
Worcester Telegram (MA)
World (New York)
The World's Work (New York)

Youngstown Telegram (OH)
Youth's Instructor (Washington DC)

NOTES AND REFERENCES

Introduction and A Note from the Publisher

1. Numbers 23:23.
2. *Bombay Times and Journal of Commerce*, 12 Apr. 1845, p. 246, col. 2; 'Epitome of News – Foreign and Domestic', *Illustrated London News*, 19 Apr. 1845.
3. *Bombay Courier*, 19 Sept. 1845. The first known journal in the West to publish this news was 'Persia', *Times* (London), 1 Nov. 1845, p. 5, col. 4.
4. See *Journal de Constantinople*, 24 June 1848, p. 1, col. 5.
5. See, for instance, *Journal de Constantinople*, 29 Mar. 1849, p. 1, col. 2, n. t.; 'Persia', *Daily News* (London), 23 Apr. 1849, p. 5, col. 4; *Revue de l'Orient, d'Algérie et des Colonies* (Paris), Apr. 1849, vol. 5, p. 264.
6. See, for instance, *Morning Herald* (London), 2 July 1850, p. 5, col. 2; *El Católico* (Madrid), 24 Oct. 1850, p. 171, col. 2; *La Presse* (Paris), 18 Oct. 1850, p. 2, col. 4.
7. The Persian–American Educational Society hired the services of Henry Romeike's clipping bureau and collected many of the references to the Master published in the American press during His visit to the United States. This collection comprises some three hundred items and is now preserved in the US Bahá'í National Archives.
8. *Star of the West*, 23 Nov. 1914 (5:14), p. 213.
9. 'Epitome of News – Foreign and Domestic', *Illustrated London News*, 19 Apr. 1845.
10. 'Persia', *Times* (London), 1 Nov. 1845, p. 5, col. 4.

1. Exile and Imprisonment

1. See the introduction to *A Traveller's Narrative* (1891), pp. xxxix–xl.
2. See Momen, *Bábí and Bahá'í Religions*, pp. 237–8.
3. 'The Babs of Persia', *Times* (London), 5 Oct. 1871, p. 8, col. 3. For the whole text of the letter see Momen, *Bábí and Bahá'í Religions*, pp. 210–12.
4. 'The Babs of Persia', *Liverpool Mercury*, 7 Oct. 1871, p. 7, col. 7; 'A New Christian Sect', *Belfast News Letter*, 10 Oct. 1871, p. 2, col. 8.
5. 'Religious Intelligence', *Nevada State Journal* (Reno), 23 Dec. 1871, p. 1, col. 6; 'Missions', *Independent* (New York), 1 Aug. 1872, p. 4, col. 6; 'The Babs of Persia', *Friends' Review* (Philadelphia), 26 Jan. 1878, pp. 382–3.
6. *La Convicción* (Barcelona), 14 Oct. 1871, pp. 6357–8.
7. *Süddeutsche Warte* (Stuttgart), 20 July 1871, pp. 113–14, mentioned in Momen, *Bábí and Bahá'í Religions*, p. 237.
8. 'Colportage in Egypt', *Bible Society Record* (New York), 15 Apr. 1874 (19:4), p. 51.

9. 'The Babs of Persia', *Sun* (New York), 10 Dec. 1883, p. 4, col. 5. Also published in Oliphant, *Haifa or Life in the Holy Land* (1887), p. 131.
10. 'The Sea of Galilee', *English Illustrated Magazine* (London), Dec. 1887, p. 162.
11. 'The Sea of Galilee', *Eclectic Magazine* (London), Feb. 1888, p. 162.
12. 'A Winter in Syria', *Contemporary Review* (London), Oct. 1888, p. 525. See also Duff, *Notes from a Diary, 1886–1888*, vol. 1 (1900), p. 251, in which the author stated that 'He ['Abbás Effendi] promised some day to come to see me at Haifa and to give me an account of their history, which is most imperfectly known in Europe.' For other references to the Bahá'í Faith in the same work see Momen, *Bábí and Bahá'í Religions*, pp. 214–15.
13. Emin Arslan, 'Une Visite au chef du Babisme', *Revue Bleue* (Paris), 5 Sept. 1896, pp. 314–16. See also Momen, *Bábí and Bahá'í Religions*, pp. 224–5.
14. 'Sect of the Babites', *Evening Star* (Washington), 14 May 1902, p. 6, col. 3. Text reproduced from the *Chicago Record-Herald*. Portions were published in Curtis's book *To-day in Syria and Palestine* (1903), pp. 219–22.
15. 'Deified Men', *Biblical World* (Chicago), May 1902 (19:5), p. 352; minor references also on pp. 345, 347, 351, 358. Reprinted in *Primitive Semitic Religion Today* (1902). Curtiss's comments were later mentioned in Frazer, *Lectures on the Early History of the Kingship* (1905), p. 139. Curtiss visited 'Abdu'l-Bahá in August 1901.
16. 'The Babites', *Outlook* (New York), 22 June 1901 (68:8), pp. 451–6. The article in *Literary Digest* (New York) mentioned by Jessup contained an account of the pilgrimage of Phoebe Hearst and was published as 'The Religious World', 20 Oct. 1900, p. 466. Portions of Jessup's article were later included in his book *Fifty-Three Years in Syria* (1910), vol. 2, pp. 688–9. Jessup visited 'Abdu'l-Bahá in November 1900. His knowledge of the Bahá'í Faith was not based on first-hand information but on Browne's works. In later years he maintained direct or indirect contact with some of the Covenant-breakers and their relatives and from them learned of the divisions caused by the brothers of 'Abdu'l-Bahá and of the disaffection and character of Ibrahim Kheiralla. This circumstance, mixed with his indignation at the progress that the Bahá'í Faith was making among Christians in the West, greatly biased his opinion of the new religion. Jessup's article was also reproduced in *Baptist Missionary Magazine* (Boston), Nov. 1902 (82:11), p. 700; and Speer, *Missions and Modern History* (1904), pp. 118–82.
17. The titles of these pamphlets were 'Bahaism and its Claims' and 'Is Baha More Generous than Christ?'. For announcements see 'Missionary Work', *The Continent* (Chicago), 9 Jan. 1913, p. 52, col. 2 and *Forty-Second Annual Report of the Woman's Presbyterian Board of Missions of the Northwest* (Chicago), Apr. 1913, p. 15.
18. Sébastien Voirol, 'Chez les Babis', *Mercure de France* (Paris), 1 Nov. 1905, pp. 5–23.
19. G.H., 'Les Réformes en Perse et l'Influence du Bâbisme', *A Travers le Monde* (Paris), 19 Jan. 1907 (3:3), pp. 17–20.
20. Sébastien Voirol, 'Livres et Idées', *Revue d'histoire diplomatique* (Paris), 25 Apr. 1909, p. 12, col. 1. Review of Dreyfus's 'Essai sur le Béhaïsme'.
21. 'Bryan sees the Sultan at worship and attends a weird meeting of the howling dervishes', *Minneapolis Journal*, 26 Aug. 1906, p. 8, col. 5. This article, also

mentioning 'Abdu'l-Bahá, was published two days earlier; see 'When the Sultan Prays', ibid. 24 Aug. 1906, p. 14, col. 7.

22. ibid. 26 Aug. 1906, col. 7. No doubt the book was *Life and Teachings of Abbas Effendi* (1903), see below.
23. See, for instance, 'Queer Customs of the Land of the Moslem are Described by William Jennings Bryan', *Atlanta Constitution*, 26 Aug. 1906, p. 4; 'Turkish Censor Seized Bryan's Books', *Boston Sunday Globe*, 26 Aug. 1906, p. 4; 'The Turks and their Despot', *Dallas Morning News*, 26 Aug. 1906, p. 3; 'Queer Customs in the Land of the Turk', *Plain Dealer* (Cleveland), 26 Aug. 1906, p. 5; 'Queer Customs in the Land of the Turk', *Salt Lake Herald* (UT), 26 Aug. 1906, p. 2b; 'William Jennings Bryan in Unspeakable Turkey', *Sun* (Baltimore), 26 Aug. 1906, p. 12; 'Islam and its Chief', *Sun* (New York), 26 Aug. 1906, p. 4; *Commoner* (Lincoln, NE), 31 Aug. 1906, p. 2; 'Around the World with William Jennings Bryan', *Daily Picayune* (New Orleans), 26 Aug. 1906, p. 4; 'The Government of the Sultan', *Armenia* (Boston), Oct. 1906 (2:12) , pp. 19–28.
24. Inchbold, *Under the Syrian Sun*, vol. 2 (1907), pp. 356–7, 361.
25. See Weinberg, *Ethel Jenner Rosenberg*, pp. 66–8.
26. Phelps, *Life and Teachings of Abbas Effendi* (1903), p. xl. It is interesting to note that Phelps entertained Vivekananda at his home in New York in 1895; see Ganachari, *Nationalism and Social Reform in a Colonial Situation* (2005), p. 157.
27. For an account by one of 'Abdu'l-Bahá's secretaries about these interviews and anecdotes related to Canavarro, see Afroukhteh, *Memories of Nine Years in 'Akká* (2003), pp. 144–8.
28. 'The Babs of Persia', *New York Times*, 15 Aug. 1903, p. 567, col. 3.
29. See 'G. P. Putman's and Sons', *New-York Tribune*, 21 Nov. 1903, p. 7, col. 6; and 'Books of the Week', 28 Nov. 1903, p. 11, col. 1. See also *New York Times*, 21 Nov. 1903, p. 835.
30. 'New Persian Religion is Taking Hold', *Brooklyn Daily Eagle*, 21 Dec. 1903, p. 8, col. 6.
31. 'Why Don't You Try Babism?', *New York Herald*, 16 Jan. 1904, p. 14, col. 2.
32. 'Babism', *New York Times*, 26 Dec. 1903, p. 978, col. 3.
33. 'News of the Book World', *Minneapolis Journal*, 29 Feb. 1904, p. 4, col. 6.
34. 'Christian Past and Future', *Springfield Daily Republican* (MA), 30 Dec. 1903, p. 11, col. 5.
35. 'New Books at the City Library', *Springfield Daily Republican* (MA), 5 Dec. 1904, p. 5, col. 3.
36. 'Life and Teachings of Abbas Effendi', *Record of Christian Work* (Northfield, MA), June 1904, p. 456.
37. 'Whimsies', *Whim* (Newark), Aug. 1904, pp. 11–18.
38. See, for instance, 'Babism and its Founder', *Chicago Daily Tribune*, 23 Jan. 1904, p. 7, col. 4; 'Religious', *Los Angeles Times*, 30 Jan. 1904, p. 4, col. 2; 'NT', *New-York Tribune*, 19 Mar. 1904, p. 10, col. 4; 'A New Religion', *Blue Glass Blade* (Lexington, KY), 19 June 1904, following *Cincinnati Enquirer*; 'Religious', *Sun* (Baltimore), 26 May 1904, p. 8, col. 3, review by J. W. Moncrief, professor of theology at the University of Chicago; 'From the Golden Books', *Springfield Daily Republican* (MA), 8 Aug. 1908, p. 13, col. 7. See also the following magazines: 'History and Biography', *Literary World* (Boston), Oct. 1903,

p. 276; 'Books of the Week', *Outlook* (New York), 12 Dec. 1903, p. 912; 'List of New Books', *Dial* (Chicago), 16 Dec. 1903, p. 482; 'Life and Teachings of Abbas Effendi', *Record of Christian Work* (East Northfield, MA), Dec. 1903, p. 456; 'Abbas Effendi His Life and Teachings', *Bookman* (New York), Jan. 1904, p. 564;'Life and Teachings of Abbas Effendi', *Literary World* (Boston), Jan. 1904, p. 7; 'The Bookman Advertiser', *Bookman* (New York), Feb. 1904, p. 741; 'A Persian Religious Reformer', *Churchman* (New York), 6 Feb. 1904, p. 181; 'Life and Teachings of Abbas Effendi', *Congregationalist and Christian World* (Boston), 2 Apr. 1904, p. 485; 'Life and Teachings of Abbas Effendi', *Nation* (New York), 7 Apr. 1904, pp. 277–8; 'Life and Teachings of Abbas Effendi', *Christian Register* (Boston), 14 Apr. 1904, pp. 407–8; 'Literature', *American Journal of Religious Psychology and Education* (Worcester, MA), May 1904, p. 104; 'Phelps – Life and Teachings of Abbas Effendi', *Critic* (New York), May 1904, p. 475; 'Abbas Effendi', *Christian Register* (Boston), 30 June 1904, p. 714 (an answer by Sidney Sprague to the review appeared on 14 Apr.); 'Books of the Day', *Arena* (Boston), Nov. 1904, pp. 556–8.

39. 'Books of the week', *Manchester Guardian*, 26 Apr. 1904, p. 5, col. 4.
40. 'Der Meister von Akka', *Neue Metaphysische Rundschau* (Berlin), Jan, 1905, pp. 22–8.
41. See, for instance, 'Babist Propaganda Making Headway Here', *New York Times*, 18 Dec. 1904; 'Strange Religion of Babists Who Follow Abbas Effendi', *Washington Post*, 18 Dec. 1904; 'New Religious Propaganda that is Making Headway in America', *Appeal* (St Paul, MN), 21 Jan. 1905, p. 1, col. 3; 'New Religious Propaganda that is Making Much Headway in America', *Manti Messenger* (UT), 16 Feb. 1905, p. 4.
42. See 'The One Religion', *Theosophical Forum* (New York), Aug. 1904, pp. 69–80; 'The One Religion', Feb. 1905, pp. 187–92. See also *Theosophical Quarterly* (New York) 1905–1906, pp. 224–33, 302–10 and 391–7.
43. He was invited, for instance, to speak at a meeting arranged by the Quakers in Philadelphia. See 'Notes', *Friends' Intelligencer* (Philadelphia), 13 Feb. 1904, p. 105.
44. For a historical analysis of this revolution see Jung, *Les Puissances devant la Révolte Arabe* (1906).
45. This is clearly shown in Necati Alkan's *Dissent and Heterodoxy in the Late Ottoman Empire* (2010), pp. 166–9. See also pp. 160–5 for documents, testimonies and background information on the commissions of inquiry sent to 'Abdu'l-Bahá. For British diplomatic correspondence on the episode see also Momen, *Bábí and Bahá'í Religions*, pp. 320–2.
46. That this was an actual order and not just a menace is clear from a document quoted in Alkan, *Dissent and Heterodoxy*, p. 162.
47. 'Exploits d'une Commission de Pachas', *L'Écho de Paris*, 18 Aug. 1905, p. 3, col. 5.
48. 'The Arab Revolt', *Times* (London), 19 Aug. 1905, p. 3, col. 6. Similar information was later published in *Les Puissances devant la Révolte Arabe* (1906), pp. 20–1.
49. 'Religious Leader Exiled', *Egyptian Gazette* (Alexandria), 26 Aug. 1905, p. 4, col. 4.
50. 'La Révolte Arabe', *Le Journal* (Paris), 21 Sep. 1905, p. 2, col. 1. The dismissal of some local officials is confirmed in Momen, *Bábí and Bahá'í Religions*, pp. 320–2.

51. 'Visit to Head of Bahais', *Evening Post* (New York), 13 Apr. 1912, p. 2, col. 4. Excerpts were also published in the *Utica Daily Press* (Utica, NY), 'A Visit to Abdul Baha Abbas', 17 Apr. 1912.

2. Western Pilgrims

1. For the history of the first pilgrimage by western Bahá'ís see Hogenson, *Lighting the Western Sky* (2010).
2. 'These Believe that Christ has Returned to Earth', *New York Herald*, 12 Aug. 1900, p. 1f. This article includes a facsimile of writings by 'Abdu'l-Bahá and a drawing made from His passport portrait.
3. 'Babism in the United States', *Springfield Daily Republican* (MA), 9 Sept. 1900, p. 12, col. 6. Based on an article in the *Chicago Advance*.
4. 'Prophet of Abbas Has Sailed Away', *New York Herald*, 3 Aug. 1900, p. 5, col. 6.
5. On Kheiralla see Stockman, *Bahá'í Faith in America: Origins 1892–1900* and Hogenson, *Lighting the Western Sky*.
6. 'A Weird Sect', *Egyptian Gazette*, 9 Nov. 1911, p. 5, col. 4. Many newspapers in the United States published news about the crisis created by Kheiralla and the efforts of the early Bahá'ís, assisted by teachers sent by 'Abdu'l-Bahá, to maintain their unity and to clarify some misconceptions that were circulating as a result of Kheiralla's lessons. See for instance, 'Babists are Divided', *Sun* (New York), 20 Jan. 1901, p. 3, col. 5.
7. 'Sarah Farmer and the Green Acre Cult', *Saginaw News* (MI), 22 June 1901.
8. 'Prophet of Abbas Has Sailed Away', *New York Herald*, 3 Aug. 1900, p. 5, col. 6. See also 'Followers of Beha Ullah', *Evening Times* (New York), 15 Dec. 1900, p. 2, col. 4; 'Missionaries are sent to Chicago', *Denver Post* (Denver, CO), 17 Dec. 1900, p. 6, col. 3; 'Hearing Babist Gospel', *Sun* (New York), 4 Feb. 1901, p. 5, col. 3; 'The introduction of Babism into the United States', *Public Opinion* (New York), 21 Feb. 1901, p. 243.
9. 'Visit to the Babist Chief's', *Sun* (New York), 24 Nov. 1901, p. 6, col. 1.
10. See, for example, 'Woman Leader of Bahaists', *Sun* (New York), 23 July 1905, p. 8, col. 1. Portions were also published in 'Woman Their Leader', *Washington Post*, 23 July 1905, p. 4, col. 3; 'Woman Leader of Bahaists', *Illustrated Buffalo Express*, 23 July 1905, p. 28, col. 4; 'Leads Sect that Needs no Money', *Washington Times*, 6 Aug. 1905, p. 6, col. 1; 'Woman Leader of Bahaists', *Syracuse Telegram*, 23 Aug. 1905; 'The Costumes of Mrs. Getsinger, Bahaist', *Hartford Courant* (CT), 2 Sept. 1905, p. 8, col. 5; 'Costumes of Mrs. Getsinger, Bahaist', *Dallas Morning News*, 2 Oct. 1905.
11. *New York Herald*, 30 Oct. 1904, pp. 1–2 (magazine section), 'America the Garden of New Religions'.
12. 'Miss Barney and Babism', *Sun* (New York), 28 Sept. 1902, p. 3, col. 1.
13. 'A Washington Society Girl's Romantic Pilgrimage to Syria to Rescue the Beha', *Washington Times*, 30 Oct. 1904.
14. 'Strange New Cult in Fashionable Washington', *Washington Times*, 30 Dec. 1906.
15. 'Calls Him Messiah', *Morning Oregonian* (Portland), 9 Mar. 1906, p. 5, col. 3.
16. 'Sees Abdul Baha in Akka Prison', *Morning Oregonian* (Portland), 26 Apr. 1907, p. 13, col. 1.

3. Visitors in Haifa

1. 'Abbas Effendi: His Personality, Work and Followers', *Fortnightly Review* (London), June 1911 (89:534), pp. 1067–84.
2. An announcement of this article was included in the *Review of Reviews* (London), June 1911 (43:258), p. 60, 'Abbas Effendi and the Bahaists'. Portions were quoted as 'The Phenomenal Spread of Bahaism', in *Current Literature* (New York), Sept. 1911, pp. 298–300. A review appeared in 'Reviews and Magazines', *Times* (London), 1 June 1911, p. 4, col. 2. See also 'The Fortnightly Review', *Scotsman* (Edinburgh), 29 May 1911; 'Personal and Social', *Egyptian Gazette* (Alexandria), 28 June 1911, p. 3, col. 6; 'Abbas Effendi', *Sidney Morning Herald* (Australia), 8 July 1911; 'Missions in the Magazines', *Missions* (Boston), Aug. 1911, p. 560; *Theosophic Messenger* (Chicago), Aug. 1911, p. 697; 'Fortnightly Review', *Times of India* (Bombay), 21 June 1911, p. 9.
3. 'The Mountain of God', *Christian Commonwealth* (London), 30 Aug. 1911, p. 820, col. 2. See also the reviews 'The Mountain of God', *Scotsman* (Edinburgh), 2 Jan. 1911, p. 2, col. 3; 'New Novels', *Manchester Guardian*, 18 Jan. 1911, p. 4, col. 1; 'New Novels', *Australasian* (Melbourne), 25 Mar. 1911, p. 53, col. 5; 'One of the Sails of the World', *Mercury* (Hobart), 18 Apr. 1911, p. 2, col. 5.
4. The copyrights were held by the Pictorial News Co.
5. 'The Light in the Lantern', *Everybody's Magazine* (New York), Dec.1911 (25:6), pp. 775–86.
6. 'A Visit with Abdul Baha at Haifa', *Buffalo Examiner* (Buffalo), 19 Sept. 1912.
7. 'Editorial', *Bible Review* (Applegate, CA), July 1909 (7:10), pp. 565–8.

4. First Visit to Egypt

1. From an undated letter printed in *Bahai News* (Chicago), 12 Dec. 1910 (1:15), pp. 2–3.
2. Yazdi, 'A Call to the American Bahais', *Bahai News* (Chicago), 19 Jan. 1911 (1:17), p. 5.
3. 'Mirza Abbas Effendi', *al-Mu'ayyad* (Cairo), 16 Oct. 1910, p. 5, col. 1. Translated by Anneliese Garvie. For alternative translations of portions of this article see *Bahai News* (Chicago), 23 Nov. 1910 (1:14), p. 2; and *'Abdu'l-Bahá in London*, p. 136.
4. *Bahai News* (Chicago), 23 Nov. 1910 (1:14), p. 2.
5. ibid. p. 3. Balyuzi gives the name of the editor and states that the periodicity of the newspaper was weekly. See *'Abdu'l-Bahá in London*, p. 137.
6. *al-Muqattam*, a daily newspaper, was founded in Beirut and later transferred to Egypt. Its founders and editors were Christians.
7. Yazdi, 'A call to the American Bahais', *Bahai News* (Chicago), 19 Jan. 1911 (1:17), p. 5.
8. The daily *al-Ahram* was founded in 1876 in Alexandria by Lebanese Maronites. At the turn of the 20th century the publication was transferred to Cairo. Its orientation was conservative and anti-British. At the time of 'Abdu'l-Bahá's visit it had one of the largest circulations in Egypt.
9. *al-Ahram* (Cairo), 19 Jan. 1911. Translation published in *Bahai News* (Chicago), 2 Mar. 1911 (1:19), p. 4.

10. *Star of the West*, 28 Apr. 1911 (2:3), p. 5. The *Wádí al-Níl* was founded in 1863 with the support of the Khedive.
11. *al-Garida al-Misrija*, see Hartmann, *Arabic Press of Egypt* (1899), p. 83.
12. 'The Acre Deity', *Egyptian Gazette* (Alexandria), 20 Sept. 1910, p. 3.
13. 'Personal and Social', *Egyptian Gazette* (Alexandria), 27 Sept. 1910, p. 3, col. 2.
14. 'A Persian Philosopher in Egypt', *Egyptian Gazette* (Alexandria), 18 Jan. 1911, p. 3, col. 2.
15. 'Mr Hall Caine', *Egyptian Gazette* (Alexandria), 18 Oct. 1911, p. 5, col. 1.
16. 'Abbas Effendi', *Egyptian Gazette* (Alexandria), 27 Mar. 1911, p. 3, col. 3.
17. 'Universal Races Congress', *Egyptian Gazette* (Alexandria), 1 Apr. 1911, p. 4, col. 4.
18. 'Personal and Social', *Egyptian Gazette* (Alexandria), 28 June 1911, p. 3, col. 6.
19. 'Personal and Social', *Egyptian Gazette* (Alexandria), 12 July 1911, p. 3, col. 1.
20. *Bahai News* (Chicago), 19 Jan. 1911 (1:17), p. 9. Sohrab also mentions several meetings between 'Abdu'l-Bahá and Atwood in 1913; see *Abdul Baha in Egypt* (1929), pp. 143, 148 and 283. The British Library holds a booklet by Atwood, *My Work in the Spirit World.*
21. 'Letters to the Editor. Christian Missionaries and Islam', *Egyptian Gazette* (Alexandria), 29 Aug. 1911, p. 3, col. 5. Letter dated Aug. 27 and sent from Schutz, Ramleh.
22. Some of the newspapers that reproduced this article were: *The Advertiser* (Montgomery, AL), 7 May 1911; 'The Awakening of Older Nations', *The Atlanta Georgian*, 18 May 1911, p. 1; *Daily Journal* (Stevens Point, WI), 28 Oct. 1911, p. 14, col. 2; *Adams County Free Press* (Corning, IA), 4 Nov. 1911; *Clinton Mirror* (Clinton, IA), 4 Nov. 1911, p. 6, col. 1; *Reporter* (Le Grand, IA), 4 Nov. 1911; *Transcript* (Toodle, UT), 10 Nov. 1911, p. 7, col. 2; *City Herald* (Dakota, NE), 3 Nov. 1911, p. 2, col. 5. Parts of the interview were included in another article by Ellis published in *The Continent* on 30 May 1912, p. 760. The article was also commented upon in 'Bahaism', *Christian Workers Magazine* (Chicago), Aug. 1912, p. 814.
23. *Star of the West*, 19 Jan. 1911(1:17), p. 8.
24. For a biography of Wellesley Tudor Pole see Gerry Fenge's *The Two Worlds of Wellesley Tudor Pole* (2010). See pp. 53–8 for details about his first meeting with 'Abdu'l-Bahá.
25. Tammadun'ul Mulk was almost blind owing to a badly treated eye disease that doctors diagnosed as irreversible. When he arrived in Egypt, however, 'Abdu'l-Bahá cured him. Both Tudor Pole and Tammadun'ul Mulk met soon after in England during 'Abdu'l-Bahá's travels in the West. For these and other anecdotes see Tudor Pole's *The Silent Road* (1960), pp. 145–52.
26. 'Table Talk', *Christian Commonwealth* (London), 7 Dec. 1910, p. 182, col. 1.
27. 'Table Talk', *Christian Commonwealth* (London), 21 Dec. 1910, p. 221, col. 4.
28. *Christian Commonwealth* (London), 28 Dec. 1910, p. 231.
29. ibid. The whole article was reprinted in *Bahai News*, 7 Feb. 1911 (1:18), pp.1–5.
30. 'The World Uprising', *Christian Commonwealth* (London), 4 Jan. 1911, p. 246, col. 4.
31. 'A Coming Awakening', *Light* (London), 7 Jan. 1911, p. 5, col. 2. Tudor Pole later presented the Bahá'í Faith at the Union Conference of Advanced Metaphysics on

7 May 1911. See 'The Thunder of the Waters', *Light* (London), 13 May 1911, p. 228.

32. 'Bath Theosophical Society', *Bath Chronicle and Weekly Gazette*, 12 Jan. 1911, p. 7, col. 5.
33. 'The Bible of the Bahais', *Christian Commonwealth* (London), 29 Mar. 1911, p. 456, col. 1.
34. Instead of the meeting, a lengthy article about the Bahá'í Faith was published in *Theosophy in Scotland* (Edinburgh), May 1911, p. 4. See also chapter 34, vol. 2.
35. 'Lecture at Lincoln Temple', *Washington Herald*, 10 June 1912, p. 5, col. 7.
36. *Appeal* (St Paul, MN), 17 June 1911, p. 2, col. 5.
37. Samuel F. Hurnard, in 'Modern Errors: The Bahai Revelation', *Friends' Witness to Scriptural Truth* (London), May 1911, p. 66. This was stated by Campbell during a meeting held at the City Temple on 16 October 1910, in which Tammaddun'ul Mulk lectured on the Bahá'í Faith. See also the Bahá'í booklet *Report of an Address on the Bahai Movement* (1910).
38. Library of the Religious Society of Friends (London), Box no. 190. The message 'To a Worker in a Crowded City' was afterwards quoted by Harrold Johnson in his article on the Bahá'í Faith which appeared in *The Christian Commonwealth* on 6 September 1911 (see chapter 6).
39. 'Persian Mystic and Friends' Quarterly Meeting', *Friend* (London), 5 May 1911, pp. 284–5.
40. ibid. Translated into English by Y. Dawud in April 1911.
41. 'The Bahai Movement in Persia', *Friend* (London), 10 Mar. 1911, p. 152.
42. *Extracts from Minutes and Proceedings of London Yearly Meeting of Friends*, 1911, p. 207. Library of the Religious Society of Friends (London).
43. ibid. p. 208. The commission was confirmed in a further meeting held on 5 May 1911.
44. 'Bahaism', *American Friend* (Philadelphia), July 1911, pp. 439–40.
45. ibid.
46. *Extracts from Minutes and Proceedings of London Yearly Meeting of Friends*, 1911, pp. 217–18. Library of the Religious Society of Friends (London).
47. Samuel F. Hurnard, in 'Modern Errors: The Bahai Revelation', *Friends' Witness to Scriptural Truth* (London), May 1911, p. 66.
48. 'Bahaism', *American Friend* (Philadelphia), July 1911, pp. 439–40.
49. Hubert W. Peet (1886–1951) became a Quaker in 1910. Professionally he was journalist who had worked for various London publications such as *The Bystander*, *The Daily News* and *The Daily Sketch*. During the First World War he was imprisoned owing to his pacifist position and his refusal to be enlisted. In 1932 he was appointed editor of *The Friend*.
50. R.E.M., 'Bahaism: A New Moral Force in Persia', *T.P.'s Weekly* (London), 21 July 1911, p. 75.
51. 'T.P.'s Letter Box: Bahaism', *T.P.'s Weekly* (London), 4 Aug. 1911, p. 150.

5. Arrival in Europe

1. 'Personal and Social', *Near East* (London), 28 June 1911 (4:44), p. 174, col. 3.
2. 'Personal and Social', *Egyptian Gazette* (Alexandria), 12 July 1911, p. 3, col. 1. *La Bourse Egyptienne* (Cairo) of 4 August published the news of the departure of

'Abdu'l-Bahá from Egypt; see 'Départ du Chef D'une Religion Nouvelle'. The present author has been unable to consult this article.

3. 'Table Talk', *Christian Commonwealth* (London), 10 May 1911, p. 562, col. 1.
4. 'Table Talk', *Christian Commonwealth* (London), 28 June 1911, p. 681, col. 4.
5. 'Table Talk', *Christian Commonwealth* (London), 23 August 1911, p. 810, col. 2.
6. A reference to an article about E. S. Stevens's *The Mountain of God* published on p. 820 of the same issue.
7. 'Table Talk', *Christian Commonwealth* (London), 30 August 1911, p. 826, col. 1.
8. 'Chronique Locale', *Journal de Genève*, 4 September 1911, p. 2, col. 3.
9. 'Chronique Locale', *La Tribune de Genève*, 5 October 1911, p. 9.
10. 'Nos Hôtes', *ABC* (Geneva), 5 October 1911, p. 4, col. 2.

6. First Visit to England

1. 'Bahaism and its Prophet', *Daily Mail* (London), 2 Sept. 1911, p. 2, col. 6.
2. 'Current Comments', *Near East* (London), 6 Sept. 1911 (4:54), p. 418, col. 1 See chapter 5 for the reference made to 'Abdu'l-Bahá in the issue of 28 June 1911. The letter mentioned was published on pp. 416–17 and was one of the letters by Francis Henry Skrine published under the title 'Bahaism: A Universal Religion'.
3. 'The Churches', *Daily News* (Perth), 11 Nov. 1911, p. 4, col. 8; 'A New Religion from the East', *Bunbury Herald*, 11 Nov. 1911, p. 3, col. 3.
4. 'Persian Mystic Comes to London', *Daily Sun* (Brandon, Manitoba), 21 Sept. 1911, p. 1.
5. 'Personal and Social', *Egyptian Gazette* (Alexandria), 12 July 1911, p. 3, col. 1.
6. See *Poverty Bay Herald* (Gisborne, New Zealand), 21 Oct. 1911, p. 1b, col. 5; and *Grey River Argus* (Greymouth, New Zealand), 6 Nov. 1911, p. 1, col. 4.
7. 'Prophet of Bahai Faith', *Weekly Sun* (Singapore), 25 Nov. 1911, p. 7, col. 1. I thank Jan Jasion for kindly sharing this document with me.
8. See for instance 'Persian Prophet in London', *Boston Transcript*, 9 Sept. 1912, p. 15, col. 4; 'Persian Prophet to Visit England', *Repository* (Canton, OH), 24 Sept. 1911; 'Abbas Effendi A World Prophet', *Kansas City Times*, 5 Oct. 1911, p. 8, col. 5; *Indianapolis Sunday Star*, 26 Sept. 1911, p. 8, col. 4.
9. 'London Correspondence', *Glasgow Herald*, 4 Sept. 1911, p. 9, col. 1.
10. Henry Harrold Johnson (1869–1940) studied at Cambridge, Sorbonne and Leipzig universities and served as a Unitarian minister from 1897 to 1939. He was minister at the Waverley Road Church in Birmingham (1897–9) and at the Cross Street Chapel in Manchester (1919–28), among other churches. He was a member of the Moral Instruction League and was its secretary from 1903 to 1913. He was also one of the organizers of the Universal Congress on Moral Education that was held in The Hague in 1912 and to which 'Abdu'l-Bahá was invited (see chapter 8). Johnson was author of several works including various volumes of poetry such as *The Road-makers and Other Poems* (1903), *The Bridge-builders and Other Poems* (1908) and the eight-volume series *The Voice of One* (1933–8). One of his poems was included in *'Abdu'l-Bahá in London*. He certainly met 'Abdu'l-Bahá during His first visit to London but the date is not clear. In 1913 he was invited to have dinner with Him on 19 January. Johnson gave the following particulars about how he was acquainted for the first time with the new religion:

> It has been my privilege during the past few weeks to come into close personal contact with representatives of a religious movement destined, I believe, to have a large influence in the world. I had read, and been deeply impressed by, shortly after its appearance two years ago, a volume in John Murray's 'Wisdom of the East' series entitled 'The Splendour of God', by Mr. Eric Hammond, being an account of the origin and development of the Bahai religion, together with a considerable body of extracts (translated from the Arabic and the Persian) of its Sacred Writings. But I had not met an adherent of this religion until the First Universal Races Congress, held during the closing days of July in the University of London, furnished me with the befitting occasion. Since that congress closed several meetings of sympathisers with the Bahai movement have been held in London, and to these and to the scanty literature at present accessible in translation I owe the following particulars . . .

Apart from the article in *The Christian Commonwealth* he wrote at least one more article about the Bahá'í Faith which was published in the *Contemporary Review* (London) and is quoted in this chapter.

11. 'A world religion', *Christian Commonwealth* (London), 6 Sept. 1911, p. 843, col. 1. The same issue contained, also on page 843, a notice on the meetings organized by the London Bahá'í community and an advertisement related to the Bahá'í Faith.
12. 'Table Talk', *Christian Commonwealth* (London), 6 Sept. 1911, p. 841, col. 4.
13. 'Bahai Leader in London', *Times* (London), 6 Sept. 1911, p. 7, col. 4.
14. Information regarding the circulation of this and other British newspapers is based on John M. McEwen, 'The National Press during the First World War', *Journal of Contemporary History*, July 1982 (17:3), pp. 459–86. Unless otherwise stated, the data relates to the year 1910.
15. Wellesley Tudor Pole, 'Abdul-Baha in London', in *Star of the West*, 27 Sept. 1911 (2:11), p. 3.
16. 'Table Talk', *Christian Commonwealth* (London), 6 Sept. 1911, p. 841, col. 4.
17. This is an excerpt from Phelps, *Life and Teachings of Abbas Effendi* (1903).
18. 'Towards Spiritual Unity', *Christian Commonwealth* (London), 13 Sept. 1911, p. 849.
19. 'Persian Prophet', *Evening News* (London), 6 Sept. 1911, p. 3, col. 4.
20. Percy J. Philip (1886–1956) was a Scottish-born journalist who began his career as a reporter with the London *Daily News*. During the First World War the *Daily News* sent him to Belgium and later to France, where he also acted as correspondent for other British newspapers. In 1920 he entered the Paris bureau of the *New York Times* and in 1932 was appointed its head. During the Second World War he left France and in 1941 became the *New York Times* correspondent in Canada until his retirement in 1954. He was author of *France in Defeat* (1941).
21. Gustav Spiller (1864–1940) was a psychologist of German origin and Jewish background. He was the author of several books, among them *The Mind of Man* (1902). He was the Secretary General of the first Universal Races Congress (1911), one of the organizers of the second International Moral Education

Congress (1912) and editor of the proceedings of both events. 'Abdu'l-Bahá was invited to speak at both congresses and His Tablets to these meetings were published in their respective proceedings.

22. 'Abdul Baha', *Daily News* (London), 8 Sept. 1911, p. 4, col. 6.
23. 'Prophet of Bahaism', *Daily Mail* (London), 7 Sept. 1911, p. 3, col. 3. The words quoted from 'Abdu'l-Bahá can also be found in a report by Arthur Cuthbert published in *Star of the West*, 16 Oct. 1911 (2:12), p. 3. The satirical magazine *M.A.P.* (London) made a brief reference to this article. See Vaughan Dryden, 'In Passing', 16 Sept. 1911, p. 18.
24. 'Abdul Baha', *Christian Globe* (London), 14 Sept. 1911, p. 19, col. 1.
25. 'Abbas Effendi in London', *Egyptian Gazette* (Alexandria), 25 Sept. 1911, p. 5, col. 6.
26. 'Religious Records', *Telegraph* (Brisbane), 14 Oct. 1911, p. 24, col. 5; 'New Religion from Persia', *Sunday Times* (Sidney), 15 Oct. 1911, p. 9, col. 1; 'New Religion from Persia', *Newcastle Morning Herald and Miner's Advocate*, 21 Oct. 1911, p. 3, col. 6; 'New Religion from Persia', *Southern Argus and Wagin-Arthur Express* (Perth), 18 Nov. 1911, p. 5, col. 2.
27. 'The Bahai Leader', *Evening Standard and St. James Gazette* (London), 7 Sept. 1911, p. 11, col. 2. See also 'Mysterious Eastern Prophet', *Leicester Daily Mercury* (Leicester), 8 Sept. 1911, p. 2, col. 5; 'Mysterious Eastern Prophet', *Daily Press* (Bristol), 8 Sept. 1911, p. 5, col. 2.
28. 'The Prophet's Motor-Car', *Evening News* (London), 7 Sept. 1911, p. 3, col. 3.
29. *Daily Mirror* (London), 8 Sept. 1911, p. 8, col. 4. According to Cuthbert, 'On the Wednesday following Abdul-Baha's arrival in London, Mrs. Thornburgh-Cropper gave an "At Home" to the believers and between fifty and sixty were present to meet him.' See the account 'Abdul Baha in London' by Mason Remey in *Star of the West*, 16 Oct. 1911 (2:12), p. 3.
30. 'Eastern Prophet in London', *Daily Graphic* (London), 8 Sept. 1911, p. 11, col. 2.
31. Data for 1914.
32. 'Wise Man from the East', *Daily Sketch* (London), 8 Sept. 1911, p. 7, col. 4.
33. 'Abdul Baha Abbas', *Evening Standard and St. James Gazette* (London), 8 Sept. 1911, p. 4, col. 2.
34. Data for 1914.
35. 'Bahaism', *Observer* (London), 10 Sept. 1911, p. 8, col. 5.
36. *Near East* (London), 13 Sept. 1911 (4:55), p. 434, col. 1. On p. 445 of the same issue the following note was published: 'Abdul Baha Effendi, leader of the Bahaists, arrived in England last week and is staying at Lady Blomfield's flat in Cadogan Gardens, Lady Blomfield being one of his followers. He has already been visited by many clergymen of all denominations, and on Sunday evening he visited the City Temple and addressed the congregation for about eight minutes, speaking in Persian.' In the issue of 20 September the following clarification was made: 'The Lady Blomfield, with whom, as announced in our issue of last week, Abdul Baha Effendi is staying, is not to be confused with Lady Massic Blomfield, who was so well known and popular in Egypt' (p. 472, col. 2).
37. The original church was destroyed during World War II.
38. Campbell, *New Theology*, 1907.

39. For a biography see Robbins, *History, Religion and Identity in Modern Britain*, pp. 133–48. For an autobiography see Campbell, *A Spiritual Pilgrimage*.
40. 'Meeting Between Abdul Baha and Mr. Campbell', *Christian Commonwealth* (London), 13 Sept. 1911, p. 850, col. 1.
41. For English notes of this talk see *'Abdu'l-Bahá in London*, pp. 19–20. For Persian notes see *Star of the West*, 4 Nov. 1911, p. 4 (Persian section) and 'Abdu'l-Bahá, *Majmu'ih-i-Khatábát-i-Hadrat-i-'Abdu'l-Bahá*, vol. 1, pp. 19–21. There are considerable differences between the Persian and the English versions.
42. According to Tudor Pole, 'Abdul-Baha in London', p. 3, despite the visit being kept secret 'the congregation was as usual very large, probably well over 2,000'. Mason Remey, however, estimates the number to be three thousand. See *Star of the West*, 16 Oct. 1911 (2:12), p. 10.
43. Text from 'The New Religion', *Morning Post* (London), 11 Sept. 1911, p. 8, col. 2. Other periodicals that published this note or versions of it include 'Abdul Baha at the City Temple', *Daily Chronicle* (London), 11 Sept. 1911, p. 5, col. 3; 'Abdul Baha', *Daily News* (London), 11 Sept. 1911, p. 1, col. 3; 'Eastern Prophet in City Temple', *Daily Mirror*, 11 Sept. 1911, p. 4, col. 2; 'Bahaism at the City Temple', *Daily Telegraph* (London), 11 Sept. 1911, p. 13, col. 1; 'Occasional Notes', *Evening News* (London), 11 Sept. 1911, p. 2, col. 4; 'Bahaism', *Evening Standard and St. James Gazette* (London), 11 Sept. 1911, p. 7, col. 4; 'Baha Leader in London Pulpit', *Standard* (London), 11 Sept. 1911, p. 7, col. 6; 'Abdul Baha at City Temple', *Star* (London), 11 Sept. 1911, p. 1, col. 7 (the article was introduced by a note stating that an article about 'Abdu'l-Bahá had been published previously in the same newspaper, but the present author has been unable to locate it); 'Notes of the Week', *Christian Life* (London), 16 Sept. 1911, p. 1, col. 1; 'Bahaism at the City Temple', *Shoreditch Observer* (Hackney), 16 Sept. 1911, p. 7, col. 4. *The Morning Post* had a circulation of 60,000 copies, *The Daily Telegraph* 230,000, *The Standard* 80,000 and *The Star* 330,000. This note was also published in some Australian journals, see 'Bahaism at the City Temple', *Sunday Times* (Sidney), 22 Oct. 1911, p. 19, col. 3; 'Bahaism at the City Temple', *Northern Star* (Lismore), 7 Nov. 1911, p. 7, col. 6.
44. 'Prophet at the City Temple', *Daily Express* (London), 11 Sept. 1911, p. 5, col. 2.
45. *Observer* (London), 17 Sept. 1911, p. 5, col. 6.
46. He was at the time Deacon of the City Temple.
47. 'Abdul Baha at the City Temple', *Christian Commonwealth* (London), 13 Sept. 1911, p. 850. The article finishes with a reference to Laura Dreyfus-Barney's drama *God's Heroes*.
48. 'Abdul Baha at the City Temple', *Christian World* (London), 14 Sept. 1911, p. 5, col. 2.
49. *The Monitor and the New Era* (London), 16 Sept. 1911, p. 3, col. 4, n.t.
50. 'Persian Prophet Society Cult', *Los Angeles Times*, 1 Oct. 1911, p. 21, col. 3.
51. 'Abdul Baha the Prophet', *Buffalo Express*, 8 Oct. 1911, p. 5, col. 4. This article was mentioned in the following issues: 4 Oct., p. 10, col. 3; 5 Oct., p. 12, col. 1; 6 Oct., p. 14, col. 1; 7 Oct., p. 6, col. 7.
52. 'London Bows at the Feet of a New Prophet', *American* (Baltimore), 8 Oct. 1911, p. 16, col. 2.
53. 'De Bahai-Profeet to London', *Nieuwe Rotterdamsche Courant* (Rotterdam), 27

Sept. 1911, p. 2, col. 4. For another Dutch newspaper carrying an article on the Bahá'í Faith apropos of the visit to Europe of 'Abdu'l-Bahá see 'Het Bahaisme', *De Tid* (Amsterdam), 16 Oct. 1911, p. 5, col. 4.

54. 'De Bahai-Profeet to London', *Bataviaasch Nieuwsblad* (Jakarta, Indonesia), 25 Oct. 1911, p. 13, col. 2.
55. 'El Behaismo', *Sophia* (Madrid), Mar. 1912, pp. 156–63. The cover of the issue included a one-page portrait of 'Abdu'l-Bahá.
56. For an account of this episode see Lady Blomfield, *Chosen Highway*, p. 164.
57. *Los Angeles Times*, 1 Oct. 1911, p. 21, col. 3. Also published as 'Persian Prophet Supplies England with New Religion', *Medicine Hat Daily News* (Alberta, Canada), 4 Oct. 1911; and 'Persian Stirs London with His Eloquence', *Indianapolis Star*, 3 Dec. 1911, p. 15, col. 1.
58. 'Eastern Prophet in London', *Daily Mirror*, 12 Sept. 1911, p. 4, col. 3; 'Abdul Baha Photographed', *Daily News*, 12 Sept. 1911, p. 10; 'Persian Seer's First Photograph', *Daily Sketch*, 12 Sept. 1911. *The Daily Chronicle* wrote: 'Abdul Baha, the leader of the Bahai Movement, who is now in London on his way through Europe. The religion, which was founded in Persia, now claims three million adherents. The above photograph is the latest to be taken of the prophet who is paying his first visit to this country.' The caption in the *Daily News* read: 'Abdul Baha, who has hitherto refused to sit for his portrait, has yielded to the requests of his English followers, and permitted the photograph reproduced above to be taken.' And the *Daily Sketch* commented that 'Abdul Baha Abbas, the mysterious Persian prophet of the Bahai faith, is now in London on his first visit to the Western people. The above photograph is understood to be the first ever taken of the aged seer, he having a rooted objection, said to be on religious grounds, to the camera.'
59. *New York Times*, 24 Sept. 1911, p. 2c. The caption of the photograph contained a summary of information that later appeared in the *Los Angeles Times*, see note 57 above.
60. The London branch of Lafayette studios was located at 179 New Bond Street. The photographer's number for one of 'Abdu'l-Bahá's images was 50.885a.
61. *Christian Commonwealth* (London), 13 Sept. 1911, p. 857, col. 4.
62. ibid. 20 Sept. 1911, p. 871, col. 3.
63. 'London Correspondence', *Glasgow Herald*, 11 Sept. 1911, p. 9, col. 1.
64. 'Bahaism', *Daily Mail* (London), 14 Sept. 1911, p. 4, col. 4.
65. See for instance *New York Times*, 24 Sept. 1911, p. 2c.
66. 'The Social Hound', *Gloucester Citizen*, 12 Sep. 1911, p. 4. Also published in *West London Gazette* (Westminster, London), 16 Sept. 1911, p. 3, col. 5.
67. 'To Abdul Baha', *M.A.P.* (London), 16 Sept. 1911, p. 16.
68. 'Interview With Abdul Baha', *Weekly Budget*, 24 Sept. 1911, p. 3, col. 3. The same account was later reprinted as 'The Prison Experiences of Abdul Baha', *Christian Commonwealth* (London), 13 Aug. 1913, p. 792, col. 1; 'The Prison Experiences of Abdul Baha', 20 Aug. 1913, p. 804, col. 4; 'The Prison Experiences of Abdul Baha', 27 Aug. 1913, p. 824, col. 1.
69. See also Fraser's *Abdul Baha on Divine Philosophy* (1918), pp. 16–24.
70. 'Bahaism and its Prophet', *Daily Chronicle* (London), 22 Sept. 1911.
71. See 'Abbas Effendi A World Prophet', *Kansas City Times*, 5 Oct. 1911, p. 8, col. 5.
72. Text from 'The Traveller', *Watchman* (Sidney), 16 Nov. 1911, p. 3, col. 5.

73. 'Leader of Bahaism Talks about its Ethics', *Christian Science Monitor* (Boston) 21 Oct. 1911, p. 6.
74. Promotho Loll Sen (1866–?) was a Calcutta-born representative of the Brahmos in England. He lectured at Manchester College (1896–8) and wrote a book about the founder of the Brahmo Samaj of India, *Keshub Chunder Sen: A Study* (1902). In 1913 'Abdu'l-Bahá sent through him a Tablet to Mararaj Couch Baha; see *Abdul Baha in Egypt*, pp. 149–50.
75. A reference to the public lectures that Keshub Chandra Sen used to give yearly, especially on the anniversaries of the foundation of his movement.
76. Probably Laura Dreyfus-Barney.
77. 'Keshub Niketon', *Christian Commonwealth* (London), 20 Sept. 1911, p. 871.
78. Letter from Arthur Cuthbert to Albert Windust, 25 Sept. 1911. Windust papers, box 13, US National Bahá'í Archives.
79. Basil Wilberforce (1841–1916) was the second son of Samuel Wilberforce. He graduated from Exeter College in 1865 and was ordained in 1866. After holding positions in the Anglican church as curate, rector and honorary canon, he was appointed Canon of Westminster Abbey in 1894 and Archdeacon of Westminster in 1900. He was author of several works and articles. His liberal ideas in the field of religion and politics made him a respected and followed leader among social workers and Christian reformists. For his life and ideas see Woods, *Archdeacon Wilberforce* (1917) and Russell, *Basil Wilberforce* (1917).
80. *Star of the West*, 2 Mar. 1916 (6:19), p. 166.
81. *Star of the West*, 9 Apr. 1911 (2:2), p. 2.
82. This is, in fact, St John the Evangelist. It may be that is has been confused with the cathedral of St John the Divine in New York.
83. Blomfield, *Chosen Highway*, p. 153.
84. From a letter of Dorothy Hodgson, quoted in *Star of the West*, 16 Oct. 1911 (2:12), p. 12.
85. For English notes of this talk see *'Abdu'l-Bahá in London*, pp. 22–5. For Persian notes of this talk see *Star of the West*, 4 Nov. 1911, p. 10 (Persian section) and 'Abdu'l-Bahá, *Majmu'ih-i-Khatábát-i-Hadrat-i-'Abdu'l-Bahá*, vol. 1 (1921), pp. 26–9. There are considerable differences between the Persian and the English versions.
86. 'The Vanishing of the Veil', *Christian Commonwealth* (London), 20 Sept. 1911, p. 1; see also *Star of the West*, 16 Oct. 1911 (2:12), pp. 2, 12. The prayer was also published in the magazine *Light* (London), 20 July 1912, p. 338.
87. Constantino Román Salamero (1868–1935) was a journalist, writer and literary critic. He worked for *El Imparcial* (Madrid), *El País* (Madrid) and other journals. He is best known for his translation into Spanish of Montaigne's works.
88. *El Imparcial* (Madrid), 11 Dec. 1911, p. 1 (literary supplement), col. 5. The article also included some brief comments about 'Abdu'l-Bahá's stay in Paris.
89. *Wádí al-Níl* (Alexandria), 23 Dec. 1911, p. 1, col. 4.
90. Constance Elisabeth Maud (1860–1929) was a prolific novelist and noted suffragist writer. She was a member of the Women's Social and Political Union and a contributor for *Votes for Women*. Her many works include *No Surrender* (1911) and *Sparks among the Stubble* (1924).
91. Text quoted in 'Archdeacon Wilberforce: A Tribute', *Review of Reviews* (London),

May 1917 (55:329), p. 483. For other articles by Maud about 'Abdu'l-Bahá and the Bahá'í Faith see below.

92. 'Brotherhood', *Christian Commonwealth* (London), 20 Sept. 1911, p. 872, col. 3.
93. ibid.
94. 'Second Day's Conference', ibid. p. 884, col. 3.
95. 'A Message From Abdul Baha', *Christian Commonwealth* (London), 20 Sept. 1911, p. 871. The same page carried a story from E. S. Stevens's *The Mountain of God* published with the title 'A Bahai Parable'.
96. See 'Autógrafos de Abdul Baha', *Sophia* (Madrid), Mar. 1912, pp. 162–3.
97. 'Hojas del Blok', *Diario del Salvador* (San Salvador), 7 May 1912, p. 2, col. 5.
98. 'The Bahai Message', *Christian Commonwealth* (London), 20 Sept. 1911, p. 875.
99. 'Abdu'l-Bahá at the Pioneer Preacher's Hostel', *Christian Commonwealth* (London), 27 Sept. 1911, p. 896, col. 3.
100. For details about this visit see Tudor-Pole, 'Abdul-Baha at Bristol, Eng.' in *Star of the West*, 16 Oct. 1911 (2:11), p. 7.
101. Prospectus of the Clifton Guest House. Albert Windust Papers, B12, US National Bahá'í Archives.
102. 'Abbas Effendi', *Daily Chronicle*, 25 Sept. 1911.
103. 'Abdul Baha at Bristol', *Christian Commonwealth* (London), 27 Sept. 1911, p. 898, col. 3.
104. *Clifton Chronicle and Directory* (Clifton, Bristol), 27 Sept. 1911, p. 8, col. 4. 'THE CLIFTON GUEST HOUSE, 15 and 17, ROYAL YORK CRESCENT. – His Excellency Abdul Baha Abbas, and suite (Persia), Lady Blomfield (London), Mrs. Thornburgh Cropper (London), Lady Agnew (Kensington), the Misses Blomfield (London), Miss Louise Heron (California), Mr. and Mrs. Thos. Pole (Letchworth), Miss L. Starling (London), Miss Maxwell Harrison (London), Mrs. and Miss Buckton (Lympsfield), Miss Platt (London), Colonel Seymour, Mrs. S. Dudley, Mr. T. Murray Sowerby (London), Tammadou ul Molk and Khorassimi (Persia), and Mr. A. T. Pole.'
105. Alice Buckton (1867–1944) was a Froebelian educator and a noted author. Her best-known work is the play *Eager Heart*. She probably came into contact with the Bahá'í Faith through Wellesley Tudor Pole, although she was also closely associated with Lady Blomfield. During the visits of the Master to England she was instrumental in arranging some of the public and private meetings where He participated and she also met 'Abdu'l-Bahá in America. *The Hartford Courant* called her 'an ardent advocate of Bahaism' (31 May 1912, p. 8, col. 7).
106. Claude Joseph Goldsmid Montefiore (1858–1938) was an Oxford-educated scholar and writer. He was the founder of British Liberal Judaism, president of the Anglo-Jewish Association as well as a member of the School Board for London. His interest in child education was also from the viewpoint of Froebelianism.
107. Sir Michael Ernest Sadler (1861–1943), a renowned educationalist, was the vice chancellor of the University of Leeds and had been a lecturer of History of Education at Manchester University. He later became Master of University College, Oxford.
108. Sir Richard Stapley (1843–1920) was a businessman and philanthropist. In 1919 he founded the Sir Richard Stapley Educational Trust. He met 'Abdu'l-Bahá several times during His two visits to England.

109. 'Farewell to Abdul Baha', *Christian Commonwealth* (London), 4 Oct. 1911. Also published in *'Abdu'l-Bahá in London*, pp. 33–9.
110. 'Abdul Baha Departs', *Christian World* (London), 5 Oct. 1911, p. 3, col. 4.
111. 'Personal and Social', *Near East* (London), 27 Sept. 1911 (4:57), p. 504, col. 1.
112. One of the members of the Higher Thought Centre, J. Bruce Wallace, editor of the *Brotherhood* magazine, was a brother-in-law of Tudor Pole.
113. Reports in *A Quarterly Record of Higher Thought Work* show that Wellesley Tudor Pole represented the Bahá'í Faith in a Conference on Advanced Metaphysics held in May 1911 and convened by the Higher Thought Centre (Aug. 1911, p. 1). Another Bahá'í who had close ties with the HTC was William Patchin (1882–1910), a worker at the Indo-European Telegraph who died in Persia just after sending a letter to a member of the HTC with 'an account of the Behai teaching' (*A Quarterly Record of Higher Thought Work*, May 1911, p. 3); see also *Star of the West*, 7 Feb. 1911 (1:18), p. 6 for a note on his passing. Lady Blomfield and Eric Hammond were invited to speak on the Bahá'í Faith at one of the sessions of the Conferences on Reconciliation and Reconstruction convened by the HTC and the Alpha Union in September 1915 (*A Quarterly Record of Higher Thought Work*, Nov. 1915, p. 7).
114. *A Quarterly Record of Higher Thought Work* (London), Nov. 1911, pp. 2–3. Parts of this account were used in *'Abdu'l-Bahá in London*, pp. 40–1.
115. *A Quarterly Record of Higher Thought Work* (London), Nov. 1911, p. 1. This text is part of a Tablet by 'Abdu'l-Baha sent 'to a worker in a crowded city' and published as a pamphlet in 1910.
116. 'Current Comments', *Near East* (London), 27 Sept. 1911, p. 503, col. 1.
117. 'The Teaching of Mohammed', *Near East* (London), 2 Aug. 1911, p. 292, col. 2.
118. The letters appeared under the title 'Bahaism: A Universal Religion' and were published on the following dates: 16 Aug. 1911, p. 344; 6 Sept. 1911, pp. 416–17; 13 Sept. 1911, pp. 442–3; 20 Sept. 1911, pp. 468–9. A further letter under the title 'Bahaism and the State' was published on 18 Oct. 1911, p. 555. These articles eventually became the nucleus of Skrine's book *Bahaism: The Religion of Brotherhood and Its Place in the Evolution of Creeds* (1912).
119. 'Bahaism', *Near East* (London), 27 Sep. 1911, p. 498.
120. 'Bahaism', ibid. p. 555.
121. John Bruce Wallace (1853–?) was a Congregational minister who in 1891 founded in London the Brotherhood Church. His movement was heavily influenced by Tolstoy's writings and was basically created as an anarchist Christian church advocating the formation of socialist cooperative communities. The *Brotherhood* magazine was founded in 1887. Wallace also formed the 'Alpha Union', which regularly held summer schools at the Cloisters building (Letchworth).
122. The family of Wellesley Tudor Pole had strong ties with Wallace. Both Wallace and Pole's parents lived at Letchworth. Thomas Pole, father of Wellesley, was, like Wallace, a member of the Garden City Association of Letchworth and other of the various movements that had the Cloisters building as their headquarters. Wallace married Tudor Pole's eldest sister, Mary, in 1912.
123. 'The Bahai Movement', *Brotherhood* (Letchworth), Oct. 1911, pp. 421–2.
124. 'The Universal Movement Towards Unity', *Christian Commonwealth* (London), 6 Dec. 1911, p. 154.

125. 'The Star in the East', ibid. p. 169.
126. 'The Bahai Movement', *Christian Commonwealth* (London), 3 Jan. 1912, p. 230, col. 4.
127. 'Until Seventy Times Seven', *Christian Commonwealth* (London), 31 Jan. 1912, p. 295, col. 5.
128. 'A Harmony of Religions', *Christian Commonwealth* (London), 3 Apr. 1912, p. 435, col. 3.
129. 'Table Talk', *Christian Commonwealth* (London), 28 Aug. 1912, p. 782, col. 2.
130. 'Bahaism: The Birth of a World Religion', *Contemporary Review* (London), Mar. 1912, pp. 401–2. For a review of this article see 'Periodical Literature', *Occult Review* (London), Apr. 1912, pp. 235–6.
131. 'Table Talk', *Christian Commonwealth* (London), 27 Mar. 1912, p. 393, col. 4.
132. 'Bahaism: The Birth of a World Religion', *Christian Register* (Boston), 9 May 1912, pp. 441–2.
133. Muriel Jean Eliot Chase (1880–1936) was a journalist who from 1903 was in charge of the social section of the *West Australian*. She was, however, better known for her philanthropic work for children, women and aged people and for her support to various social organizations.
134. 'Bahaism: A Remarkable Religious Movement', *West Australian* (Perth), 11 May 1912, p. 7, col. 3.
135. Constance Maud, 'Abdul Baha', in *Fortnightly Review* (London), Apr. 1912 (91:544), pp. 707–15.
136. 'Will Bahaism Unite All Religious Faiths?' *American Review of Reviews* (New York), June 1912 (45:6), pp. 748–9.
137. 'Universal Brotherhood', *The Register* (Adelaide), 20 May 1912, p. 6, col. 3.
138. 'The Reviews Reviewed', *Review of Reviews* (London), Apr. 1912, p. 397.
139. The Bookman, 'A Reader's Note', *Manitoba Free Press* (Winnipeg), 9 May 1912, p. 4, col. 3.
140. Eric Hammond, 'The Bahai Movement', *African Times and Orient Review* (London), Aug. 1912 (no. 2), pp. 42–4. An announcement mentioning this article appeared in *The New Age* (London), 8 Aug. 1912, p. 360.
141. 'The New Religion', *Express and Telegraph* (Adelaide), 11 Oct. 1912, p. 2, col. 2. Also published in 'The New Religion', *Advertiser* (Adelaide), 15 Oct. 1912, p. 11, col. 1. The present author has been unable to locate the original article in the *Daily News and Leader*.
142. See, for instance: 'The Phenomenal Spread of Bahaism', *Current Literature* (New York), Sept. 1911, p. 298–300. This article is a potpourri of portions of the following texts: Stevens's article 'Abbas Effendi: His Personality, Work and Followers' in the *Fortnightly Review* (London), June 1911; and 'Bahaism, Founded in Martyrdom, Taking Root Here' appeared in the *New York Times*, 2 July 1911, p. 8; 'The Bahai Prophet', *Chicago Sunday Tribune*, 24 Sept. 1911, p. 4a, cols. 3–4; *New York Times*, 24 Sept. 1911, p. 2c; 'London Bows at the Feet of a New Prophet'. This article was published at least in *Los Angeles Times*, 1 Oct. 1911; *The American* (Baltimore) 8 Oct. 1911; and the *Buffalo Express*, 8 Oct. 1911. The *Buffalo Express* announced the publication of the article on the four previous days. *American* published with the article a drawing based on one of pictures taken from the Master in London. See also: 'Another Religion Born', *Daily*

People (New York), 21 Oct. 1911, p. 2, col. 5; 'Persia produces another noble religion', *Spokane-Review* (Spokane, WA), 5 Nov. 1911; 'Bahaism at the City Temple', *Northern Star* (Lismore, Australia), 7 Nov. 1911, p. 7, col. 6; 'Things Worth Knowing', *Brooklyn Daily Eagle*, 11 Nov. 1911, p. 14, col. 4.

143. 'Abdu'l-Bahá had breakfast with the Lord Mayor of London on October 2. Letter from Arthur Cuthbert to Albert Windust (Windust papers, box 13, US National Bahá'í Archives).
144. George William Kitchin (1827–1912), Dean of Durham Cathedral (1894–1912) and noted scholar.
145. 'Hopes to Convert U.S.' *Washington Post*, 7 Jan. 1912, p. 2, col. 1. The article referred to by Buckton is 'The Coming of Abbas Effendi Messiah of 6,000,000 Souls' appeared on 31 Dec. 1911 (see chapter 9, p. 194 above).
146. 'The Call of the Hour', *Emerson College Magazine* (Boston), Feb. 1912 (19:4).
147. 'Abdul Baha, Head of New Religion, Coming Here', *Sun*, 17 Mar. 1912, p. 2, part 4. This article was also published as 'A Gentle Oriental Here', *Kansas City Star*, 27 Mar. 1912, p. 8b, col. 1 (includes a portrait of 'Abdu'l-Bahá taken in Paris).

7. First Visit to France

1. Data extracted from Bellanger, *Histoire générale de la presse française*, vol. 3, p. 296. Unless stated otherwise, the circulation numbers in this chapter correspond to the month of November 1910.
2. Guy Darés, 'Abdou'l-Baha', *Le Figaro* (Paris), 6 Oct. 1911, p. 4, col. 4 (translated by Elham Simmons).
3. Guy Darés, 'Une Religion Nouvelle', *Le Figaro* (Paris), 10 Apr. 1909, p. 2, col. 1.
4. *L'Opinion* (Paris), 7 Oct. 1911, p. 452, col. 2, n.t. The magazine was edited by Henri Massis (1886–1970), a Catholic conservative journalist who was also an art critic and the author of several novels. During the Second World War Massis supported French collaboration with Nazi Germany and entered Vichy's 'Conseil National'. Baron d'Estournelles de Constant de Rebecque, Paul Henri Benjamin Balluet (1852–1924), was not a Bahá'í. He had received in 1909 the Peace Nobel Prize for his work at various Hague Peace Conferences and on various committees of arbitration.
5. Data for 1914.
6. 'Bahaïsme', *Le Petit Marseillais*, 10 Oct. 1911, p. 1, col. 5.
7. 'Bahaism', *La Liberté* (Paris), 13 Oct. 1911, p. 2, col. 2.
8. 'Échos', *L'Echo du Merveilleux* (Paris), 15 Oct. 1911, pp. 361–2.
9. Jean Lefranc, 'Le bahaïsme et son prophète', *Le Temps* (Paris), 3 Nov. 1911, p. 4, col. 2 (translated by Elham Simmons). On 9 Oct. the same newspaper carried an article stating that a British woman of Hungarian background, Cornelia Buckley, was a Bahá'í. She was famous at the time for having left her husband and children for another man, Sir Coleridge Kennard, attaché at the British Legation in Persia. See p. 1, col. 6.
10. E. Th., 'Behaïsme', *Le Petit Marseillais*, 5 Nov. 1911.
11. 'Le Bahaïsme', *Le Stéphanois* (Saint Etienne), 13 Nov. 1911, p. 2, col. 2.
12. See note 19 below.
13. 'El profeta Baha', *Heraldo de Madrid* (Madrid), 4 Nov. 1911, p. 1, col. 3.

14. Fernando Araujo, 'Revista de revistas', *La España Moderna* (Madrid), Oct. 1912 (24:286), pp. 207–8.
15. 'El Profeta Baha', *El Universal* (Mexico City), 4 Dec. 1911, p. 4, col. 5.
16. Rubén Darío,'Un profeta en Paris' [A prophet in Paris], *La Nación* (Buenos Aires), 30 Nov. 1911, p. 7.
17. 'Bahaism', *La France* (Paris), 21 Oct. 1911, p. 1, col. 4 (translated by Elham Simmons).
18. 'Informations', *Gil Blas* (Paris), 23 Oct. 1911, p. 2, col. 5.
19. 'Les Journaux', *Mercure de France* (Paris), 16 Nov. 1911 (94:346), pp. 402–6. At the time of the visit of the Master to Paris, Remy de Gourmont was a close friend of Natalie Clifford Barney who inspired his *Lettres intimes à l'Amazone.*
20. Camille de Sainte-Croix began his career as a journalist working for the left-wing newspaper *Le Réveil* (Paris) and later for *Le Gaulois* (Paris). He also worked for *La Bataille* (Paris), *Revue d'Aujourd'hui* (Paris) and *L'Echo de Paris*, and was art critic for *Le Petite Republique* (Paris), *Gil Blas* (Paris) and *Petit Journal* (Paris), among other periodicals. He was also the author of several novels and works of poetry.
21. 'Abdoul-Béha', *Paris-Journal* (Paris), 8 Nov. 1911, p. 1, col. 1. The article also included a photograph of the Master. *Le Progrés Spirite* (Paris), an organ of the Société d'Études Psychiques (Society of Psychic Studies) of Geneva, reproduced the text in its issue of Dec. 1911 (17:12), pp. 169–72.
22. 'Le Bahaïsme, fera-t-il la conquête de Paris?' *Excelsior* (Paris), 7 Nov. 1911, p. 2, col. 6 (translated by Elham Simmons).
23. Lorey had been assigned to the French legation in Persia for two years. In 1922 he was appointed director of the Institut Français d'Archéologie et d'Art Musulmans (Damascus). In a book on Persia written with Douglas Sladen, *Queer Things about Persia* (1907), he dedicated one chapter to the Bahá'í Faith, see pp. 307–17. He also intermediated for Francis Henry Skrine in the submission of the manuscript of *Bahaism: The Religion of Brotherhood and its Place in the Evolution of Creeds* (1912) to 'Abdu'l-Bahá, see p. 12.
24. 'Mondanités', *Excelsior* (Paris), 12 Nov. 1911, p. 1, col. 3.
25. *Le Figaro* (Paris), 22 Nov. 1911, p. 1, col. 6, n.t.
26. 'The New Religions in America III. Babism and Bahaism', *Forum* (Boston), July 1925, pp. 1–13.
27. Charles Wagner was ordained as a Lutheran minister in 1877. He held various posts until 1892 when he was given his own church. He was author of more than 20 works, among them *La Vie Simple* (1895). Its English translation was a great success in America, and President Theodore Roosevelt invited Wagner to tour the United States in 1904. With funds collected in France and America, Wagner inaugurated in 1907 the church Foyer de l'Âme (Home of the Soul), located at rue Daval, today 7 Rue du Pasteur Wagner.
28. 'Informations Diverses', *Le Temps* (Paris), 25 Nov. 1911, p. 4, col. 6.
29. Benjamin Couve, was a reformist priest and a religious journalist who from 1880 was director of *Le Christianisme au XXe Siècle* (Paris). He also took the pulpit of the Pentemont Reformed Church (Paris).
30. This account appears to be borrowed from the monthly revue *La Vie Nouvelle* (Paris). Bernard Le Gouis, a teacher by profession, was a contributor to *Le*

Christianisme au XXe Siècle and other religious periodicals. He was also president of the Ligue de Moralité Publique, author of several works on morality and leader of various campaigns against public immorality.

31. 'Le Behaïsme', *Le Christianisme au XXe Siècle* (Paris), 5 Jan. 1912, p. 2 (translated by Elham Simmons). A second article containing further attacks was published in the same newspaper on 19 January.
32. 'Une Religion d'Amour: Le Béhaisme', *Reseignements Utiles, Supplément d'Aesculape* (Paris), Jan. 1912, pp. 22–4. I thank Jan Jasion for kindly sharing this document.
33. *Le Foyer Protestant* (Nimes), 16 Dec. 1911.
34. *El Imparcial* (Madrid), 11 Dec. 1911, p. 1 (literary supplement), col. 5.
35. See Sohrab, Letter to Harriet Magee, 11 Feb. 1913, p. 11.
36. 'Le Pasteur Charles Wagner', *L'Univers Israélite* (Paris), 24 May 1918, p. 250.
37. *Revue Anti-Maçonnique* (Paris), Feb. 1912 (2:2–3–4), pp. 108–10.
38. Louis Dasté, 'Le Bahaïsme', *La Bastille* (Paris), 30 July 1910 (9:401), p. 4, col. 2.
39. 'Le Modernisme Mussulman I', *Les Nouvelles* (Alger), 29 Jan. 1912, p. 1, col. 1. The talk mentioned in the article is 'Abdu'l-Bahá's address delivered on 26 October at the headquarters of the Theosophical Society. Notes of it were published on Dec. 1911 in *Annales Théosophiques* (Paris) (see chapter 34, vol. 2).
40. *Washington Post*, 19 Nov. 1911, p. 21, col. 1. The same article was published as 'Bahaian Priest is Given Home by an American', *Buffalo Courier*, 19 Nov. 1911, p. 40, col. 1; 'Gray Persian Prophet Reveals Strange Faith', *Oakland Tribune* (CA), 19 Nov. 1911, p. 3, col. 3; 'Says Bahaism is Universal Love', *Plain Dealer* (Cleveland), 19 Nov. 1911, p. 10d, col. 8.
41. *Christian Commonwealth* (London), 1 Nov. 1911, p. 71, col. 2. It is not certain that 'Abdu'l-Bahá visited the Académie Française or the Sorbonne.
42. *Washington Post*, 19 Nov. 1911, p. 21, col. 1. The same article was published as 'Bahaian Priest is Given Home by an American', *Buffalo Courier*, 19 Nov. 1911, p. 40, col. 1; 'Gray Persian Prophet Reveals Strange Faith', *Oakland Tribune* (CA), 19 Nov. 1911, p. 3, col. 3; 'Says Bahaism is Universal Love', *Plain Dealer* (Cleveland), 19 Nov. 1911, p. 10d, col. 8.
43. 'Abdul Baha, Head of New Religion, Coming Here', *Sun* (New York), 17 Mar. 1912, p. 2, part 4.

8. Second Visit to Egypt

1. 'Personal and Social', *Egyptian Gazette* (Alexandria), 11 Sept. 1911, p. 3, col. 1. This note was actually a copy of 'Current Comments', *Near East* (London), 6 Sept. 1911 (4:54), p. 418, col. 1.
2. 'Abdul Baha in London', *Egyptian Gazette* (Alexandria), 22 Sept. 1911, p. 3, col. 6.
3. 'Personal and Social', *Egyptian Gazette* (Alexandria), 27 Sept. 1911, p. 3, col. 1.
4. 'Letters to the Editor', *Egyptian Gazette* (Alexandria), 5 Dec. 1911, p. 5, col. 3.
5. 'Mr. Atwood and the Missionaries', ibid. p. 2, col. 5.
6. 'Abbas Effendi in London', *Egyptian Gazette* (Alexandria), 25 Sept. 1911, p. 5, col. 6.
7. 'Personal and Social', *Egyptian Gazette* (Alexandria), 27 Sept. 1911, p. 3, col. 1.
8. 'Personal and Social', *Egyptian Gazette* (Alexandria), 2 Oct. 1911, p. 3, col. 1.
9. 'Current Comments', *Near East* (London), 27 Sept. 1911, p. 503, col. 1.

10. 'The Bahai Leader. A Notable Appreciation', *Egyptian Gazette* (Alexandria), 4 Oct. 1911, p. 5, col. 5.
11. 'The Bahai Leader', ibid. p. 4, col. 1. Letter signed on 25 September.
12. 'The Bahai Leader', *Egyptian Gazette* (Alexandria), 29 Sept. 1911, p. 5, col. 2. Letter signed on 28 September.
13. 'The Bahai Leader', *Egyptian Gazette* (Alexandria), 3 Oct. 1911, p. 5, col. 4. Letter signed on 30 September.
14. ibid. p. 5, col. 4. Letter signed on 29 September.
15. 'The Bahai Leader', *Egyptian Gazette* (Alexandria), 5 Oct. 1911, p. 3, col. 5. Letter signed on 4 October. For the letter mentioned by Atwood, see chapter 4, p. 68.
16. 'Personal and Social', *Egyptian Gazette* (Alexandria), 6 Oct. 1911, p. 3, col. 1.
17. 'The Bahai Movement', *Egyptian Gazette* (Alexandria), 11 Oct. 1911, p. 3, col. 3.
18. 'Letters to the Editor. The Bahai Movement', *Egyptian Gazette* (Alexandria), 16 Nov. 1911, p. 5, col. 4. For the full text of this article see also *Star of the West*, 12 Dec. 1911 (2:15), pp. 8–10.
19. 'The Return of Abbas Effendi', *Egyptian Gazette* (Alexandria), 16 Nov. 1911, p. 2, col. 6.
20. 'Personal and Social', *Egyptian Gazette* (Alexandria), 16 Dec. 1911, p. 3, col. 1.
21. 'Personal and Social', *Egyptian Gazette* (Alexandria), 15 Feb. 1912, p. 3, col. 1.
22. 'Personal and Social', *Egyptian Gazette* (Alexandria), 1 Mar. 1912, p. 3, col. 1.
23. *Wádí al Níl* (Alexandria), 23 Dec. 1911, p. 1, col. 4.
24. 'Annual Meeting', *Blessed be Egypt* (London), July 1912 (12:51), p. 98.
25. ibid. p. 99.
26. 'Quarterly Report of Work Done', *Blessed be Egypt* (London), Oct. 1912 (12:52), p. 147. A similar report was published in July 1913, p. 93.
27. 'List of Mission Press Publications', *Blessed be Egypt* (London), Jan. 1913 (12:53), p. 147.
28. See chapter 6, p. 92.
29. Aikins, *Report* (1913).
30. 'Le Congrès International d'Éducation Morale', *Revue de Métaphysique et Morale* (Paris), Nov. 1912 (20:6), p. 897.
31. ibid. pp. 901–2.
32. Dyserinck, *Mémoires sur L'Éducation Morale*, pp. 218–19 (Harrold Johnson's lecture can be found on p. 93 of the same volume). A few paragraphs were included in Isabella Fraser's compilation *Abdul Baha on Divine Philosophy* (1918). The Persian text can be found in 'Abdu'l-Bahá, *Majmu'ih-i-Khatábát-i-Hadrat-i-'Abdu'l-Bahá*, vol. 3, pp. 35–7.
33. 'A Wise Man from the East', *International Psychic Gazette* (London), Jan. 1913 (6:1), pp. 158–9.
34. These where previously published in *Star of the West*, 11 Dec. 1911 (2:16), p. 6.
35. See for instance: 'After Forty Years in Prison, Bahai Leader Plans to Visit Followers in United States', *Evening News* (Sault Ste. Marie, MI), 5 Feb. 1912, p. 6, col. 1; 'After Forty Years in Prison, Bahai Leader Plans to Visit Followers in United States', *News Chronicle* (Muskegon, MI), 6 Feb. 1912, p. 3, col. 4; 'After Forty Years in Prison, Bahai Leader Plans to Visit U.S.', *Times* (Tacoma, WA), 13 Feb. 1912, p. 3, col. 2; 'After Forty Years in Prison, Bahai Leader Plans to Visit Followers in United States', *Des Moines News* (IA), 15 Feb. 1915, p. 4, col. 3;

'Coming to America', *Evening Press* (Grand Rapids, MI), 16 Feb. 1912, p. 9, col. 1; 'After Forty Years in Prison, Bahai Leader Plans to Visit Followers in United States', *Pittsburgh Press*, 18 Feb. 1912, p. 8c.

9. 'Abdu'l-Bahá Expected in America

1. 'Still Another Expected One', *Los Angeles Times*, 1 Nov. 1910, p. 8, col. 1.
2. 'Persian Prophet Fails to Appear,' *New York Herald*, 6 Nov. 1910, p. 9, col. 5.
3. 'Coming to Convert Us', *Sandusky Register* (OH), 24 Dec. 1911, p. 1b, col. 5. Also published in the *Daily News* (Greensboro, NC), 24 Dec. 1911; *Herald* (El Paso, TX), 19 Jan. 1912, p. 11, col. 5.
4. 'The Coming of Abbas Effendi Messiah of 6,000,000 Souls', *New York Herald*, 31 Dec. 1911, p. 4, magazine section; *Washington Post*, 31 Dec. 1911, p. 1c; *Morning Star* (Rockford, IL), 21 Jan. 1912, p. 14. The original article in the *Herald* was announced in the issues of 25 Dec., p. 11, col. 7; 27 Dec., p. 13, col. 2 and p. 16, col. 2; 28 Dec. 1912, p. 11, col. 4; and 29 Dec. 1912, p. 7, col. 4.
5. 'Earnest Pleas Made for World Peace', *Brooklyn Daily Eagle*, 8 Jan. 1912, p. 5, col. 3.
6. 'Head of Bahai Religion Plans to Visit America', *Brooklyn Daily Eagle*, 21 Jan. 1912, p. 4b, col. 5.
7. 'Roosevelt Among Sylphs', *New-York Tribune*, 20 Jan, 1911, p. 7, col. 5. Theodore Roosevelt and his family were close acquaintances of the Washington Bahá'í Agnes Parsons and had even visited her home on different occasions before Roosevelt's election as president. In a letter of 27 November 1911 Parsons told Ahmad Sohrab that she had sent to Roosevelt a number of documents on the Bahá'í Faith and informed him of the upcoming visit to America of 'Abdu'l-Bahá (Parsons to Sohrab, Ahmad Sohrab papers, B12, US Bahá'í National Archives).
8. 'Editorial', *Christian Register* (Boston), 25 Jan. 1912, pp. 1–2. The editor was Bradley Gilman (1857–1932), who held this position from 1903 to 1917.
9. See 'The teachings of Abdul Baha', *Hartford Courant* (CT), 15 Feb. 1912, p. 14, col. 5; 'The Coming of Abdul Baha Abbas', *Boston Evening Transcript*, 27 Jan. 1912, p. 7, col. 2.
10. Rev. Thomas Van Ness, 'The Bahai Movement', *Christian Register* (Boston), 8 Feb. 1912, p. 138, col. 1. On 7 Mar., p. 222, the same newspaper published: 'In May 1844, a world peace movement originated in Shiraz, Persia. Abdul Baha, who is to visit America this spring, brings its message. In London and Paris he has spoken to many great gatherings.'
11. *al-Hoda* (New York), 28 Jan. 1911, p. 4. This newspaper, founded in 1898, was edited and published by the Syrian Naoum A. Mokarzel. In a letter from Mokarzel to Ahmad Sohrab, the editor states that 'I had written regarding the gentleman ['Abdu'l-Bahá] and produced his picture two or three times, and my friends have written articles about him.' (27 Feb. 1912, Ahmad Sohrab papers, B12, US Bahá'í National Archives). Thus *al-Hoda* published other references to the Master in the months previous to His arrival which have not been located. It is probable that it also published some references to Him after His arrival. This is one of the many instances of ethnic periodicals printed in America into which more research needs to be conducted.
12. Text from 'Bahais and Abbas Effendi', *Springfield Daily Republican* (MA), 7 Feb.

1912, p. 4, col. 6. Also published as 'Bahais and Abbas Effendi', in the *Charlotte Daily Observer* (NC), 21 Feb. 1912, p. 4, col. 6.

13. 'New Impetus for World Peace', *Advocate of Peace* (Washington), Feb. 1912 (74:2), pp. 49–50.
14. 'Abdul Baha', *Peacemaker and Court of Arbitration* (Philadelphia), Apr.–June 1912 (31:4–5–6), pp. 113–15; and 'Bahais and the New Woman Movement', pp. 115–16.
15. 'Abdul Baha, Head of New Religion, Coming Here', *Sun* (New York), 17 Mar. 1912, p. 2, part 4. For Ford's comments about 'Abdu'l-Bahá's visit to London and Paris see chapters 6 and 7.
16. 'The News in a Nut Shell', *Washington Bee* (Washington DC), 27 Jan. 1912, p. 8, col. 2.
17. 'Abdul Baha to visit Rochester', *Democrat and Chronicle* (Rochester, NY), 2 Mar. 1912, p. 4, col. 2.
18. 'Persian Teacher of Peace Coming', *New York Herald*, 3 Mar. 1912, p. 6, col. 1.
19. 'Persian Proselyte Working for Peace', *Seattle Daily Times*, 15 Mar. 1912, p. 16, col. 3.
20. 'Interesting People', *Brooklyn Daily Eagle*, 19 Mar. 1912, p. 6, col. 8. Martha Ewing, one of the owners of the Harris & Ewing agency, was a close acquaintance of Isabel Fraser. It was through her that Ewing contacted Ahmad Sohrab, who gave her a picture of the Master which was afterwards distributed to over one hundred newspapers and published in some of them (letter from Isabel Fraser to Ahmad Sohrab, 19 Jan. 1912, from Ewing to Sohrab, 7 Feb. 1912, and from Sohrab to Fraser, 12 Mar. 1912, Ahmad Sohrab Papers, B11, US National Bahá'í Archives). In Washington a Harris & Ewing photographer took a picture of 'Abdu'l-Bahá that was published in *The Washington Post* on 26 April 1912.
21. 'Servant of God Visiting America', *Brooklyn Daily Eagle*, 7 Apr. 1912, p. 8, col. 7. The article was part of the Sunday special edition and was therefore advertized in earlier issues of the same periodical, see 6 Apr., p. 8, col. 7.
22. *Detroit Tribune* (Detroit, MI), 7 Apr. 1912.
23. 'Bahai Revelation', *Washington Bee*, 11 Nov. 1911, p. 1, col. 1.
24. 'The Bahai Movement', *Independent* (New York), 11 Apr. 1912 (72:3306), pp. 770–2.
25. 'Abdul Baha Abbas Coming', *Chicago Defender*, 12 Apr. 1912, p. 1, col. 6.
26. 'Abdul Baha in America', *Oriental Review* (New York), Apr. 1912, pp. 360–3.
27. *Unitarian Advance* (New York), Apr. 1912, p. 253.
28. These were John Haynes Holmes, Charles Wesley Casson, Edgar Swan Wiers and Frederick R. Griffin.

10. Arrival in America

1. For published accounts and sources about 'Abdu'l-Bahá's arrival in New York, see 'Abdu'l-Bahá, *Promulgation*, pp. 3–34; Zarqání, *Maḥmúd's Diary*, pp. 34–48; Bagdadi, 'Abdul Baha in America', *Star of the West*, May 1928 (19:5), pp. 52–7; *Diary of Juliet Thompson*, pp. 231–67; Ward, *239 Days*, pp. 13–36.
2. 'Abdul-Baha's Arrival in America', *Star of the West*, 28 Apr. 1912 (3:3), p. 2.
3. Some of the newspapers that published parts of Dodge's article or reproduced the AP telegram were: 'World Religionist in U.S.', *Chicago Journal*, 11 Apr.

1912; 'Bahai Leader Arrives', *Evening Star* (Washington), 11 Apr. 1912, p. 8, col. 5; 'Brings Cult From Persia', *Kansas City Star*, 11 Apr. 1912, p. 5A, col. 1; 'Famous Persian Reaches America', *Oakland Tribune*, 11 Apr. 1912, p. 5, cols. 2–3 (includes picture); 'Bahaism Leader Here to Expound Creed', *Portland Telegram*, 11 Apr. 1912; 'Favors World Wide Religious Unity', *Salt Lake Evening Telegram* (UT), 11 Apr. 1912, p. 9, col. 3; 'Abdul Baha Abbas, Bahai Leader, Arrives', *Salt Lake City News* (UT), 11 Apr. 1912; 'Apostle of Religious Unity Comes to U.S.', *San Francisco Bulletin*, 11 Apr. 1912; 'Bahai Movement Head Lands in New York', *San Francisco Post*, 11 Apr. 1912; 'Persian Comes to Unify all Religion', *Los Angeles Herald*, 12 Apr. 1912; 'Urges Religious Unity', *Los Angeles Times*, 12 Apr. 1912, p. 5; 'Great Persian Here', *Baltimore Sun*, 12 Apr. 1912; 'Philosopher on Board Big Quarantined Liner', *Buffalo Courier*, 12 Apr. 1912, p. 3, col. 7; 'Wants Religion United', *Grand Forks Daily Herald* (ND), 12 Apr. 1912, p. 3, col. 3; 'Persian Philosopher and Leader of Bahai Arrives', *New York Press*, 12 Apr. 1912, p. 5, col. 5; 'In Exile for 50 Years', *Washington Post*, 12 Apr. 1912, p. 4, col. 4; 'Abdul Baha to Preach Peace to Americans', *Springfield News* (MA), 12 Apr. 1912, p. 4, col. 2; 'Warm Reception for Baha', *Sullivan Daily Times* (IN), 13 Apr. 1912, p. 3, col. 4; 'Abbas Effendi, Apostle of World Peace, Arrives', *Record-Herald* (Chicago), 14 Apr. 1912 (includes portrait); 'Abdul Baha Decries Symbol of Liberty', *Davenport Times* (IA), 16 Apr. 1912; 'America Most Hospitable', *Baltimore Star*, 17 Apr. 1912; *Buffalo Commercial*, 17 Apr. 1912, n.t.; 'Persian Philosopher on a Peace Mission', *Cleveland News*, 17 Apr. 1912 (includes picture); 'Says Service of Men Proves Love of God', *Duluth Herald* (MN), 24 Apr. 1912 (includes picture); 'Our New York Letters', *Houston Chronicle*, 24 Apr. 1912; 'Abdul Baha Abbas', *Phoenix Republican*, 25 Apr. 1912 (includes picture). All these newspapers had a combined circulation of some 1,110,750 copies.

4. 'Abdul Baha is Here to Preach Brotherly Love', *Evening World* (New York), 11 Apr. 1912, p. 3, col. 4.
5. 'Persian Prophet Here', *New-York Tribune*, 12 Apr. 1912, p. 13, col. 3.
6. 'Persian Quits Prison, Here to Fight for Peace', *Evening Telegram* (New York), 11 Apr. 1912, p. 4, col. 3.
7. 'Abdul Baha Comes for Peace', *Evening Post* (New York), 11 Apr. 1912, p. 6, col. 4.
8. 'Abas Effendi Arrives', *New York Herald*, 11 Apr. 1912, p. 1, col. 5.
9. 'Abdul Baha Here to Convert America to his Peace Doctrine', *New York Herald*, 12 Apr. 1912, p. 8, col. 2.
10. 'Prophet of Bahais Here', *Sun* (New York), 11 Apr. 1912, p. 1, col. 2.
11. 'Abdul Baha Here', *New York Times*, 11 Apr. 1912, p. 9b, col. 3. 'On the pier a thousand people, most of them followers of Abdul Baha, were there to greet him and the welcome pleased him immensely. Fellow-passengers of Abdul Baha were Senator Pasquale Fiore of the Italian Senate in Rome; Mr. and Mrs. B. C. Barber; the Rev. Dr. and Mrs. Francis E. Clark; Tomaso D'Armato, Chancellor of Italian Embassy in Washington; Dr. J. M. Knott; Dr. and Mrs. Stanley Millar, who have been on a tour of the Nile country; Mr. and Mrs. John Paret, and Mr. and Mrs. C. B. Tyler.'
12. Nixola Greeley-Smith (1880–1919) started her career as a journalist working for

Joseph Pulitzer on the *St. Louis Post-Dispatch* and later on the New York *World* and the *Evening World*. Her work centered on personal interviews and on sections dedicated to women.

13. 'Abdul Baha Abbas, Head of Newest Religion, Believes in Woman Suffrage and Divorce', *Evening World* (New York), 12 Apr. 1912, p. 3, col. 2. Also published in 'Aged Head of New Religion Gives Views', *Pittsburg Press*, 15 July 1912, p. 9, col. 5.
14. 'Persian Teacher of World-Peace is Here', *World* (New York), 12 Apr. 1912.
15. For the talk at the home of the Kinney's see 'Abdu'l-Bahá, *Promulgation*, pp. 3–4, and *Star of the West*, 8 Sept. 1912 (3:10), p. 4.
16. 'Disciples Here Hail Abdul Baha', *Sun* (New York), 12 Apr. 1912, p. 5, col. 1. The article includes a portrait of the Master in Paris.
17. 'Persian Teacher to Preach Unity', *Evening Call* (New York), 12 Apr. 1912, p. 3, col. 2.
18. 'Servant of God Speaks', *New York Tribune*, 13 Apr. 1912, p. 2c, col. 3.
19. See 'Abdu'l-Bahá, *Promulgation*, pp. 4–7.
20. See 'Abdu'l-Bahá, *Promulgation*, pp. 7–9 and *Star of the West*, 1 Aug. 1912 (3:8), pp. 3–4.
21. 'Listen to Abdul Baha', *Sun* (New York), 13 Apr. 1912, p. 2b, col. 1.
22. 'Abdul Baha, Dazed by City's Rush, Calls New York a Beehive', *New York Herald*, 13 Apr. 1912, p. 6, col. 6.
23. 'Bahaist Leader Here in Interest of World Peace', *American* (New York), 14 Apr. 1912.
24. The only references to this episode known to this author are a short mention in *Star of the West*, 8 Sept. 1912 (3:10), p. 3, and the entry for 13 April in *Maḥmúd's Diary* where he mentions that 'a photographer with a movie camera received permission to photograph Him, together with His companions', see Zarqání, *Maḥmúd's Diary*, p. 42.
25. 'Independent', *Moving Picture World* (New York), 11 May 1912, p. 529, col. 1.
26. Data extracted from advertisements of the company.
27. See 'Taking of the Moving Picture of Abdul Baha', *Star of the West*, 8 Sept. 1912 (3:10), p. 3.
28. *Diary of Juliet Thompson*, p. 239. The ship carrying 'Abdu'l-Bahá had to pass through Gibraltar.
29. ibid. For English notes of the talk see 'Abdu'l-Bahá, *Promulgation*, pp. 11–13 and *Star of the West*, 21 Mar. 1913 (4:1), pp. 7–8. For Persian notes see 'Abdu'l-Bahá, *Majmu'ih-i-Khatábát-i-Hadrat-i-'Abdu'l-Bahá*, vol. 2, pp. 16–20.
30. 'Church Services Tomorrow', *New York Times*, 13 Apr. 1912, p. 14, col. 6.
31. 'Abdul Baha in Ascension Church', *Sun* (New York), 14 Apr. 1912, p. 11, col. 5. For an account of the visit to the house of Marjorie Morten, see *Diary of Juliet Thompson*, pp. 241–2; for the talk there, see 'Abdu'l-Bahá, *Promulgation*, pp. 9–11.
32. Text in *Star of the West*, 28 Apr. 1912 (3:3), pp. 5–6. Some excerpts were published in 'Leader Expounds Bahia Movement', *American* (New York), 15 Apr. 1912; 'Finds America Helping', *Boston Daily Globe*, 15 Apr. 1912, p. 5, col. 2; 'For Religious Unity', *Boston Transcript*, 15 Apr. 1912, p. 11, col. 7; 'Western World Behind in Spiritual Civilization', *Buffalo Courier*, 15 Apr. 1912, p. 1, col. 4; 'Abdul Baha Preaches', *New York Tribune*, 15 Apr. 1912; 'Abdul Baha Makes

His First Speech', *Philadelphia Inquirer*, 15 Apr. 1912, p. 16, col. 1; 'America Lags in Spiritual Things', *Philadelphia Press*, 15 Apr. 1912; 'Peace Messenger from the East', *Pittsburgh Gazette Times*, 15 Apr. 1912, p. 13, col. 2; 'Abdul Baha Abbas Talks', *Pittsburgh Post*, 15 Apr. 1912; 'Persian Explains Plan to Unite All Religions', *Albany Press*, 15 Apr. 1912; 'Persian Philosopher in New York', *Utica Press*, 15 Apr. 1912; 'Abdul Baha Preaches the Unity of Mankind', *Sun* (New York), 15 Apr. 1912, p. 10b, col. 1; 'Bahai Leader in Pulpit', *Washington Post*, 15 Apr. 1912, p. 4, col. 4. The combined number of copies circulated by these newspapers was 1,120,600.

33. 'Abdul Baha Prays in Ascension Church', *New York Times*, 15 Apr. 1912, p. 9, col. 5.
34. 'Abdul Baha Preaches in Ascension Church', *Daily News* (Springfield, MA), 15 Apr. 1912, p. 12, col. 3.
35. 'Abdul Baha in Episcopal Pulpit', *New York Herald* (New York), 15 Apr. 1912, p. 6, col. 1. *The Sun* (New York), 15 Apr. 1912, reproduced the article under the title 'Baha in Pulpit'. The text was partially reproduced in the *Evening Sun* (Baltimore), 21 Apr. 1912.
36. 'News in Nutshells', *New York Herald*, 15 Apr. 1912, p. 8, col. 2.
37. 'New York Notes and News', *Observer* (New York), 18 Apr. 1912, p. 508.
38. 'Bahaism in the Pulpit', *Churchman* (New York), 27 Apr. 1912, p. 550. This editorial was quoted in 'The Universal Gospel that Abdul Baha Brings Us', *Current Literature* (New York), June 1912 (52:6), pp. 676–8.
39. *Independent* (New York), 20 June 1912, p. 1392.
40. 'The Coming of a Prophet', *Congregationalist and Christian World* (Boston), 4 May 1912, p. 620. The article included a portrait.
41. 'The Unity of Mankind', *New York Age*, 9 May 1912, p. 2, col. 4.
42. *New Age Magazine* (New York) July 1912 (17:1), pp. 18–23.
43. ibid. p. 59.
44. 'From the East', *Los Angeles Times*, 19 June 1912.
45. For the text of this talk see 'Abdu'l-Bahá, *Promulgation*, pp. 14–16. For Persian notes see 'Abdu'l-Bahá, *Majmu'ih-i-Khatábát-i-Hadrat-i-'Abdu'l-Bahá*, vol. 2, pp. 21–4.
46. 'Abdul Baha Preaches the Unity of Mankind', *Sun* (New York), 15 Apr. 1912, p. 20, col. 1.
47. 'Persian Preaches on Unity of the World', *Evening Call* (New York), 15 Apr. 1912, p. 1, col. 3.
48. See 'Abdu'l-Bahá, *Promulgation*, pp. 29–32, and *Star of the West*, 1 Aug. 1912 (3:8), pp. 8–10.
49. 'Baha Leader Here Today', *Columbia Spectator* (New York), 19 Apr. 1912.
50. 'Abbas Effendi to Speak', *New York Herald*, 19 Apr. 1912, p. 12, col. 6.
51. 'Abbas Effendi at Columbia', *New York Herald*, 20 Apr. 1912, p. 16, col. 1.
52. Abraham Valentine William Jackson (1862–1937) was a specialist in Indo-Iranian languages and author of several essays and manuals in this field.
53. For Jackson's words at this occasion see *Star of the West*, 1 Aug. 1912 (3:8), p. 13.
54. *Star of the West*, 28 Apr. 1919 (10:3), p. 37.
55. 'Abdul Baha Talks to Kate Carew of Things Spiritual and Mundane', *New York Tribune*, 5 May 1912, 1b.

56. *Diary of Juliet Thompson*, pp. 254–61.
57. See 'Abdu'l-Bahá, *Promulgation*, pp. 32–4.
58. *New York Tribune*, 20 Apr. 1912, p. 16, col. 4.
59. Excerpts were also published in *Star* (Baltimore, MD), 20 Apr. 1912; 'Free Silver on Bowery', *Herald* (Washington), 22 Apr. 1912, p. 4, col. 7; 'Gave Away Silver', *Sun* (New York), 26 Apr. 1912; 'Free Silver on Bowery', *Sun* (Baltimore, MD), 21 May 1912; *Milwaukee Journal*, 27 May 1912, p. 6, col. 1.
60. 'Derelicts Pay Honor to Persian Preacher', *New York Press*, 5 May 1913, p. 6, col. 8.
61. Text from the *Bee* (Omaha, NE), 22 Apr. 1912. Also published in the *El Paso Herald* (El Paso, TX), 22 Apr. 1912, p. 13, col. 4; *New Orleans Item*, 24 Apr. 1912, p. 9, col. 5.
62. *Star of the West*, 19 Jan. 1919 (9:17), p. 198.
63. Published in *Reality* (New York), Apr. 1921, pp. 35–6.
64. 'A Message from Abdul Baha, Head of the Bahais', *New York Times*, 21 Apr. 1912, p. 14.
65. See Bahoum Angat, 'Abdul Baha', *Star* (Wilmington, DE), 30 June 1912.
66. 'Woman Suffrage', *Schenectady Gazette* (Schenectady, NY), 23 Apr. 1912, p. 4, col. 4.
67. 'Church Services To-Morrow', *New York Times*, 27 Apr. 1912, p. 20, col. 3; 'Services for the Titanic Dead', *New York Herald*, 27 Apr. 1912, p. 15, col. 5.
68. As appeared in 'Head of New Cult', *Pittsburg Times* (Pittsburg, PA), 17 Apr. 1912.
69. 'Bahaism', *Fort Wayne News* (Fort Wayne, IN), 20 Apr. 1912, pp. 11, col. 3.
70. 'Abdul Baha', *New York Tribune*, 18 Apr. 1912, p. 6, col. 5.
71. Dr Franck Crane (1861–1928) was born in Urbana, Illinois. He was educated as a Methodist minister at the Illinois Wesleyan University where he graduated in 1883 and years later obtained his doctorate in divinity from the Nebraska Wesleyan University. From 1896 to 1903 he was pastor of the Trinity and Hyde Park Methodist Church in Chicago. From 1904 to 1909 he served as pastor of the Union Congregational Church of Worchester, Massachusetts. He introduced into his services the reading before his sermon of editorials on general topics and for this he gained some notoriety. In 1909 he entered the field of journalism as an editorialist and over the years his editorials gained a wide popularity. At the end of his life more than 50 newspapers subscribed to his syndicated articles. He was also the author of over ten books and published several compilations of his editorials.
72. Text from the *Daily News* (Springfield, MA), 18 Apr. 1912, p. 11, col. 6, n.t.
73. *Evening Telegram* (New York), 13 Apr. 1912, p. 6, col. 4. The text was reproduced in the *Globe-Democrat* (St. Louis, MO), 21 Apr. 1912.
74. 'Wise and otherwise', *Binghamton Press* (Binghamton, NY), 13 Apr. 1912, p. 6, col. 3.
75. *Springfield News* (Springfield, MA), 12 Apr. 1912, p. 2, col. 1, n.t.
76. *Brooklyn Daily Eagle* (Brooklyn, NY), 14 Apr. 1912, p. 4b, col. 1, n.t.
77. 'Elucidations', *Illustrated Companion* (New York), Apr. 1912, p. 4.
78. 'The Ideal Unity', *Oakland Inquirer* (CA), 12 Apr. 1912.
79. 'Greeting is sent by Abdul-Baha', *Glen Falls Daily Times*, 17 Apr. 1912, p. 3, col. 1. This Republican newspaper had a circulation of 5,000 copies.

11. Washington

1. *Washington Post,* 10 Mar. 1912, p. 2, col. 5 (includes a portrait). *The Lexington Herald* (KY) published similar information in 'Servant of God is Headed for America', on 14 Apr. 1912, p. 4, col. 1.
2. See 'Abdul Baha to Speak', *Evening Star* (Washington), 5 Apr. 1912, p. 24, col. 3; and 'Leader of Bahai Movement Coming to Capital Soon', *Washington Times,* 5 Apr. 1912, p. 8, col. 1.
3. Some of the newspapers that announced the visit of 'Abdu'l-Bahá to Washington in the context of the annual convention of the Persian–American Educational Society were: 'Orient–Occident Unity to Aid Persian Youth', *Washington Times,* 3 Mar. 1912, p. 14, col. 4; 'Day's News Condensed', *Chicago Live Stock World,* 4 Mar. 1912, p. 4, col. 4; 'Bahai Leader Due Here', *New York Times,* 4 Mar. 1912, p. 8, col. 4; 'Noted Persian to Speak', *New Era* (Humeston, IA), 6 Mar. 1912; 'Personal', *Iowa Recorder* (Greener), 6 Mar. 1912, p. 2, col. 2. A lengthy article was also published as 'Brings Gospel of Love' in the *Kansas City Star,* 6 Mar. 1912, p. 5, col. 1. A shorter note including a portrait of 'Abdu'l-Bahá was published a few days later in the following newspapers: 'Brings Gospel of Brotherhood', *Kansas City Star,* 17 Mar. 1912, p. 12, col. 4; 'Bahai Cult Chief Seeking Converts', *Augusta Chronicle* (GA), 20 Mar. 1912, p. 2, col. 6; 'Head of Religious Cult', *Times-Tribune* (Waterloo, IA), 20 Mar. 1912, p. 4, col. 5; 'Plans for Persian Conference Here', *Washington Herald,* 21 Mar. 1912, p. 2, col. 4; 'Head of Religious Cult', *Eau Claire Leader* (Eau Claire, WI), 22 Mar. 1912, p. 10, col. 5; 'Head of Religious Cult', *Morning Star* (Rockford, IL), 31 Mar. 1913, p. 16, col. 4; 'Bahai Leader May Address Bethel Literary', *Washington Bee,* 30 Mar. 1912. See also the following articles which include references to 'Abdu'l-Bahá: 'Persian Conference Called to Urge Cooperation', *Christian Science Monitor* (Boston), 16 Mar. 1912, p. 5; *Saginaw Daily News* (MI), 16 Mar. 1912, p. 5, col. 5, n.t.; 'Friends of Persia Meet in Washington', *Brooklyn Daily Eagle* on 17 Mar. 1912, p. 1b, col. 4; 'Seeks Trade of Asia', *Washington Post,* 17 Mar. 1912, p. 11, col. 8; *Washington Herald,* 7 Apr. 1912, p. 7, col. 3; 'Persian Confab Plans Complete'; 'Persian–American Education Meet Begins Tomorrow', *Washington Times,* 17 Apr. 1912, p. 11, col. 1; 'Bahaism and its Leader', *Springfield Daily Republican* (MA), 13 Apr. 1912, p. 19, col. 4. The program of the convention of the Persian–American Educational Society included a reception and a musical performance in honor of 'Abdu'l-Bahá. On Apr. 14, the *Washington Star* offered interesting details about the musical program: 'The Persian–American Educational Society have sent out invitations for a musical and reception to take place Saturday afternoon at Rauscher's in honor of Abdul Baha Abbas, who is expected to arrive in Washington during the week. The musical program will be given by Miss Marian McFall, soprano, who will sing "Chanson Provencal" by Del Acqua and "A Toy" by Bemberg; Miss Ruby Stanford, violinist, who will play "Adagio" by Ries; Miss Katharine McNeal, pianist, who will give "Impromptu" by Chopin, and "In Autumn" by Moszkowski, and Richard P. Backing, tenor, who will be heard in "Spirit Flower" by Campbell-Tipton: "I Know of Two Bright Eyes" by Clutsam, and a duet, "Vieni il mio sen" by Millard, with Miss McFad. Miss Mildred Harrison will assist as accompanist.' 'Musical Mention', *Evening Star* (Washington), 14 Apr. 1912. For an account of this musical program see

'Music and musicians', *Washington Herald*, 28 Apr. 1912, p. 3, col. 4.

4. 'Current Comments', *Near East* (London), 19 Apr. 1912, p. 792, col. 3.
5. Text from *Evening News* (San Jose, CA), 18 Apr. 1912, p. 5, col. 2. The note was also published in at least the following newspapers: 'Advocates of Bahia Movement', *Argus* (Middletown, NY), 18 Apr. 1912; 'Advocates of Bahai', *Daily Reporter* (Waterloo, IA), 18 Apr. 1912, p. 4, col. 6; 'Advocates of Bahai Movement Meet', *Evening Post* (Frederick, MD), 18 Apr. 1912, p. 5, col. 3; 'Bahai Movement Followers Meet', *Star* (Baltimore), 18 Apr. 1912; 'Advocates of Bahai Movement Meet', *Miami Herald*, 19 Apr. 1912, p. 7, col. 5.
6. 'Bahai Head Due Today', *Washington Post*, 19 Apr. 1912, p. 14, col. 4. 'Abdul Baha Coming', *Evening Star* (Washington), 19 Apr. 1912, p. 22, col. 2; 'Orient–Occident Conference Meets', *Washington Herald*, 19 Apr. 1912, p. 5, col. 4; 'Disaster shows need of unity', *Washington Herald*, 20 Apr. 1912, p. 9, col. 4; 'Orient–Occident Unity Launched at Meeting Today', *Washington Times*, 20 Apr. 1912, p. 7, col. 1.
7. For examples of published accounts and sources about the first visit of 'Abdu'l-Bahá to Washington see 'Abdu'l-Bahá, *Promulgation*, pp. 35–64; Bagdadi, 'Abdul Baha in America', *Star of the West*, June 1928 (19:6), pp. 87–92; Hannen, 'Abdul-Baha in Washington, D.C.' in *Star of the West*, 28 Apr. 1912 (3:3), pp. 6–8; Zarqání, *Maḥmúd's Diary*, pp. 48–65; Ward, *239 Days*, pp. 37–46; *Diary of Agnes Parsons*, pp. 1–68; *Diary of Juliet Thompson*, pp. 267–82.
8. 'Bahai Head Arrives', *Washington Star*, 20 Apr. 1912.
9. For the English text of this talk see 'Abdu'l-Bahá, *Promulgation*, pp. 35–6; *Star of the West*, 28 Apr. 1912 (3:3), pp. 8–9. For the Persian text of this talk see 'Abdu'l-Bahá, *Majmu'ih-i-Khatábát-i-Hadrat-i-'Abdu'l-Bahá*, vol. 2, pp. 30–3.
10. John Barrett (1866–1938) was an American diplomat who acted as minister to Siam, Argentina, Colombia and Panama. In 1907 he was appointed Director General of the Pan-American Union (at the time known as the Bureau of American Republics) and held this position for 14 years.
11. Samuel Gompers (1850–1924) was a prominent labor leader and the founder of the American Federation of Labor.
12. Herman Schoenfeld (d. 1926) was professor of German at Georgetown University where he worked for 32 years. He was also a pacifist and the author of several works, among them *Essays on Universal Peace and German Armaments* (1913).
13. 'Orient–Occident Unity Launched at Meeting Today', *Washington Times*, 20 Apr. 1912, p. 7, col. 1.
14. 'Due to Speed Mania', *Evening Star*, 21 Apr. 1912. The article also offered abundant details about the business sessions of the convention held that day.
15. 'Women and Men Join in Worship of Abdul Baha', *Washington Herald*, 21 Apr. 1912, p. 2, col. 1.
16. 'Bow to Bahai Leader', *Washington Post*, 21 Apr. 1912.
17. 'Leader of Cult Urges the Unity of Nations', *Washington Times*, 22 Apr. 1912 (includes a large portrait of 'Abdu'l-Bahá).
18. 'A Message from Abdul Baha', *Amerika Esperantisto* (Washington), June 1912 (11:5), p. 19.
19. 'Abdul Baha in America', *Oriental Review* (New York), May 1912, p. 427. Brief reference also on p. 391.

20. 'Evening Services in the Churches', *Washington Times*, 21 Apr. 1912, p. 10, col. 4; also mentioned in 'Services Last Night', *Washington Post*, 22 Apr. 1912, p. 2, col. 4.
21. See Hannen, 'Abdul-Baha in Washington, D.C.', in *Star of the West*, 28 Apr. 1912 (3:3), pp. 6–8.
22. John Van Schaick (1873–1949) was ordained pastor at the Church of Our Father in 1901 and held that position until 1918 when he left for Europe to work for various relief organizations assisting Belgium during the World War. His humanitarian work was awarded by the Belgian government with the Order of Leopold. In 1920 he returned to the Church of Our Father until 1922 when he was appointed as the editor of the *Universalist Leader*, a position he held until 1945. He was also author of four books.
23. For English notes of the talk see 'Abdu'l-Bahá, *Promulgation*, pp. 39–42, and *Star of the West*, 28 Apr. 1912 (3:3), pp. 10–12. For Persian notes see 'Abdu'l-Bahá, *Majmu'ih-i-Khatábát-i-Hadrat-i-'Abdu'l-Bahá*, vol. 2, pp. 33–9.
24. 'Abdul Baha to Remain in City Most of Week', *Evening Star*, 22 Apr. 1912.
25. *Washington Herald*, 22 Apr. 1912, p. 2, col. 5.
26. *Washington Times*, 22 Apr. 1912, p. 6, col. 6.
27. Hannen, 'Abdul-Baha in Washington, D.C.', in *Star of the West*, 28 Apr. 1912 (3:3), pp. 6–8.
28. Alice Lee Roosevelt Longworth (1884–1980), the eldest daughter of President Theodore Roosevelt, was the wife of the Republican member of the House of Representatives Nicholas Longworth (1869–1931). She lived a very controversial life and was a well-known figure in social circles. Interestingly, she campaigned against the entry of the United States into the League of Nations. She was an acquaintance of Agnes Parsons (see chapter 9).
29. 'Persian Priest Attracts Society Women to the Cult of Bahaism', *Washington Post*, 26 Apr. 1912, p. 12, col. 3. The article included a picture of the Master taken by the Harris and Ewing agency.
30. Hannen states in that 'It had not been contemplated to have such a large meeting that evening, but the interest became so intense that it was deemed necessary.' Hannen, 'Abdul-Baha in Washington, D.C.', in *Star of the West*, 28 Apr. 1912 (3:3), pp. 6–8.
31. The minister of the All Souls Unitarian Church at the time was Rev. Ulysses G. B. Pierce (1865–1943), who during the presidency of William Taft also held the position of Chaplain of the Senate and who counted Taft as the most prominent member of his congregation. Contact with him regarding the visit of 'Abdu'l-Bahá to his church was established as early as November 1911; see letter of Henrietta Brittingham to Ahmad Sohrab, 18 Nov. 1911 (Ahmad Sohrab papers, Persian–American Educational Society files, box 10, US Bahá'í National Archives).
32. 'Abdul Baha Abbas Leaves City on Saturday', *Washington Times*, 24 Apr. 1912, p. 16, col. 1.
33. 'Persian Savant to Give Last Lecture', *Washington Times*, 26 Apr. 1912, p. 14, col. 2.
34. 'Abdul's Farewell To-morrow', *Washington Herald*, 25 Apr. 1912, p. 2, col. 6.
35. 'Tells of Bahai Ideals', *Evening Star*, 27 Apr. 1912.

36. 'Abdul Baha a Suffragist', *Washington Post*, 27 Apr. 1912, p. 6, col. 8.
37. 'Flays Baha's Teachings', *Washington Herald*, 25 Apr. 1912.
38. 'In Washington Society', *New York Tribune*, 28 Apr. 1912, p. 8, col. 6.
39. *Washington Times*, 28 Apr. 1912, p. 9, col. 2.
40. ibid. p. 10, col. 5.
41. Milton Earl Kern (1875–1961) was at the time the dean of the Foreign Missionary Seminary and secretary of the Young People's Department. Before this appointment he had launched the Young People's Society of Christian Service (1893). In 1934 he was appointed dean of the Seventh Day Adventist Theological Seminary.
42. M. E. Kern, 'For Such a Time as This', in *Youth's Instructor* (Washington DC), 14 May 1912, p. 1.
43. See M. E. Kern, 'For Such a Time as This', *Church's Officers Gazette* (Washington DC), Jan. 1922 (9:1), p. 10.

12. Chicago

1. 'Abdul Baha in Chicago', *Chicago Post*, 13 Apr. 1912, p. 1, col. 6.
2. 'Leader of Bahaian Movement is Coming', *Chicago Examiner*, 14 Apr. 1912, p. 11, col. 3; 'Head of Bahaists Coming', *Chicago Examiner*, 28 Apr. 1912, p. 9, col. 1; 'Organizer of Baha Coming', *Record-Herald* (Chicago), 30 Apr. 1912. See also 'Ancient Sect to Meet in Chicago', *Whittier News* (CA), 29 Apr. 1912, p. 4, col. 2. This newspaper had a circulation of 2,000 copies.
3. O. Terence, 'The Human Procession', *Evening Times* (Trenton, NJ), 26 Apr. 1912. Also published as 'Notable Folk Sketches' in the *Democrat* (Nashville, TN), 25 Apr. 1912. Fragments were also published as 'People Worth While' in the *Chronicle* (Houston), 24 Apr. 1912. Other announcements made outside Chicago regarding the visit of 'Abdu'l-Bahá were published as 'Abdul Baha Addresses Congress of Followers', in the *Philadelphia Star*, 27 Apr. 1912, and as 'Abdul Baha Arrives in United States', in the *Miles City Star* (MT), 26 Apr. 1912.
4. For published accounts and sources about the first visit of 'Abdu'l-Bahá to Chicago see 'Abdu'l-Bahá, *Promulgation*, pp. 65–100; *Wisdom Talks of Abdul-Baha (Abbas Effendi) at Chicago, Illinois* (supplement of *Star of the West*, 17 May 1912); Zarqání, *Maḥmúd's Diary*, pp. 65–81; Bagdadi, 'Abdul Baha in America', *Star of the West*, July 1928 (19:7), pp. 111–15; Jaxon, 'Dedication of the Mashrak-el-Azkar Site' and 'A Stroll With Abdul Baha' in *Star of the West*, 17 May 1912 (3:4), pp. 5–7, 27–29; Ward, *239 Days*, pp. 47–58.
5. 'Bahaist Leader Opens Oriental Court Here', *Record-Herald* (Chicago), 30 Apr. 1912.
6. 'Baha is Peace Herald', *Daily News* (Chicago), 30 Apr. 1912.
7. 'Baha Brings Word to City', *Evening Post* (Chicago), 30 Apr. 1912.
8. 'Bahaist Chief for Suffrage', *Evening American* (Chicago), 30 Apr. 1912.
9. 'Throng Hotel to Greet Leader of Bahaists', *Daily Journal* (Chicago), 30 Apr. 1912.
10. 'The Leader of Bahaist Movement is in Town', *Day Book* (Chicago), 30 Apr. 1912, p. 10.
11. 'Prophet Abdul Baha Here', *Chicago Examiner*, 1 May 1912.
12. 'Open Pulpits to Abdul Baha', *Evening American* (Chicago), 1 May 1912.

13. 'World Harmony is Aim of Abdul Baha', *Inter-Ocean* (Chicago), 1 May 1912.
14. *Inter-Ocean* (Chicago), 2 May 1912.
15. 'Believe Abdul Baha May be Second Dowie', *Chicago Examiner*, 2 May 1912, p. 2, col. 4.
16. For accounts of the Convention see Hannen, 'The Public Meetings of the Fourth Annual Convention of Bahai Temple Unity', *Star of the West*, 17 May 1912 (3:4), pp. 3–5; 'Record of the Fourth Annual Convention of Bahai Temple Unity', *Star of the West*, 5 June 1912 (3:5), pp. 2–7.
17. 'Bahaist Chief Missing', *Daily News* (Chicago), 29 Apr. 1912.
18. See 'Abdu'l-Bahá, *Promulgation*, pp. 65–7.
19. 'Wants City Bahaist Center', *Chicago Tribune*, 1 May 1912, p. 3, col. 5.
20. 'The Balm of Abdul', ibid. p. 8, col. 1.
21. 'For Baha Temple', *Record-Herald* (Chicago), 1 May 1912.
22. 'Baha to Dedicate New Site', *Daily Journal* (Chicago), 1 May 1912.
23. 'Bahaist Site Dedicated', *Evening Post* (Chicago), 1 May 1912.
24. 'Baha Will Talk on Suffrage', *Record-Herald*, 2 May 1912.
25. 'Waits Vainly for Baha', *Daily News* (Chicago), 1 May 1912.
26. *Christian Commonwealth* (London), 26 June 1912, p. 631.
27. *Sophia* (Madrid), Aug. 1912, pp. 492–3.
28. 'Baha Will Talk on Suffrage', *Record-Herald*, 2 May 1912.
29. See notes 14 and 15 above. Maḥmúd wrongly dates the visit as having taken place the day before.
30. Charles Johnston, 'A Ray From the East', *Harper's Weekly* (New York), p. 9.
31. 'New Universalism', *Unity* (Chicago), 16 May 1912, pp. 165–7.
32. In 1883 Jenkin Lloyd Jones (1843–1918) founded the All Souls' Unitarian Church in Chicago after extensive missionary work across the United States. He acted as general secretary for the organization of the World Parliament of Religions.
33. The sermon was opened with the following account of how Jones heard firsthand about the Bahá'í Faith: 'At the Parliament of Religion the Rev. Henry H. Jessup, a Presbyterian missionary from off in Pennsylvania, but who at that time was president of a missionary college at Beirut, Syria, read a paper before the conference of religious missions of the English speaking nations. The paper was commonplace enough, familiar enough until he came to the last paragraph which was one more of the many surprises that breaks upon a would be intelligent audience . . .

    'Here was a good Presbyterian engaged in missionary work seeking to convert the pagan world. His particular portion of it being the pagan known as Mohammed, closing his appeal for Christian missions with this message of a man who, as he said, a few months before had succumbed to a lifelong hardship of imprisonment of forty years paying the penalty with death. That was the first news that most of the Christian world, certainly in the American world and the English world, had of the existence of anything answering to a reform movement in the supposed stolid and brutal Mohammedan world.' The sermon consisted of 24 pages. I am grateful to Eric Biddy, Library of Assistant of the Meadville Lombard Theological School, for kindly sharing with me this and other documents related to Jenkin Lloyd Jones. The sermon was also published in 'The Pulpit', *Unity* (Chicago), 28 Feb. 1918, p. 410–14.

34. Caroline Kirkland (1870?–1930), granddaughter of the writer Caroline Kirkland (1801–64) and daughter of Joseph Kirkland (1830–94), a novelist and the literary editor and book reviewer of the *Chicago Tribune*. Caroline was the permanent social chronicler of the *Tribune*. Among other works she wrote *Some African Highways: A Journey of Two American women to Uganda and the Transvaal* (1908), an account of her travels in Africa.

13. Cleveland

1. For some published accounts and sources about the first visit of 'Abdu'l-Bahá to Cleveland, see 'Abdu'l-Bahá, *Promulgation*, pp. 101–4; Zarqání, *Maḥmúd's Diary*, pp. 81–3; Bagdadi, 'Abdul Baha in America', *Star of the West*, Aug. 1928 (19:8), p. 140; Ward, *239 Days*, pp. 59–63.
2. 'Head of Big Cult was Often Jailed', *Plain Dealer* (Cleveland), 15 Apr. 1912, p. 4, col. 2.
3. 'Persian, Hailed as New "Messiah", Comes to Teach Unity of the World', *Leader* (Cleveland), 22 Apr. 1912, p. 11, col. 1.
4. 'Prophet May Come Here', *Leader* (Cleveland), 30 Apr. 1912, p. 6, col. 4.
5. 'Persian Sage is Coming', *Leader* (Cleveland), 4 May 1912, p. 14, col. 6.
6. 'Give New Creed Talk', *Plain Dealer* (Cleveland), 5 May 1912.
7. *Plain Dealer* (Cleveland), 6 May 1912, p. 5, col. 4.
8. 'Abdul Abbas Here Today', *Leader* (Cleveland), 6 May 1912.
9. 'Bahaist Leader Coming', *Cleveland News*, 6 May 1912, p. 4, col. 2.
10. For the text of this talk see 'Abdu'l-Bahá, *Promulgation*, pp. 101–3, and *Star of the West*, 17 May 1912 (3:5), p. 29 and 31.
11. 'Shows Thoughts in Picture Form', *Plain Dealer* (Cleveland), 6 May 1912, p. 2.
12. 'Bahaist to Hear Venerable Leader', *Plain Dealer* (Cleveland), 6 May 1912, p. 2, col. 4.
13. 'Wed races? Sure says woman here', *Cleveland News*, 7 May 1912, p. 2, col. 3.
14. 'Prophet of Persian Peace Cult Shies at Camera on Arrival with His Aides', *Leader* (Cleveland), 7 May 1912, p. 4.
15. 'Bahaist Approves Union of Races', *Plain Dealer* (Cleveland), 7 May 1912, p. 1, col. 3, and p. 3, col. 3. The caption to the photographs reads 'Camera Reveals World Teacher of Bahaism'.
16. 'Leader of Bahaists Indorses Suffrage', *Cleveland Press*, 7 May 1912, p. 6, col. 1.
17. See note 13 above. The article included a picture of Mrs Swingle.
18. Zarqání, *Maḥmúd's Diary*, p. 83.
19. *Gazette* (Cleveland), 11 May 1912, p. 2, col. 1, n.t.
20. 'The Bahai Movement', *Plain Dealer* (Cleveland), 12 May 1912, p. 4, col. 2.

14. Pittsburgh

1. For some published accounts and sources about the first visit of 'Abdu'l-Bahá to Cleveland see 'Abdu'l-Bahá, *Promulgation*, pp. 105–10; Zarqání, *Maḥmúd's Diary*, pp. 81–3; Bagdadi, 'Abdul Baha in America', *Star of the West*, Aug. 1928 (19:8), p. 140; Ward, *239 Days*, 63–4.
2. 'Leader of Bahaism is Coming to Pittsburgh', *Gazette Times* (Pittsburgh), 4 Apr. 1912, p. 7b, col. 2 (includes a portrait of the Master). The article reviewed the

document distributed by the Persian–American Educational Society, *The Universal Principles of the Bahai Movement.*

3. 'Abdul Baha', *Pittsburgh Dispatch*, 6 May 1912 (includes a portrait of 'Abdu'l-Bahá).
4. 'Abdul Baha to Speak', *Pittsburgh Post*, 6 May 1912.
5. 'Abdul Baha to Speak at Hotel Schenley', *Pittsburgh Chronicle-Telegraph*, 7 May 1912, p. 8, col. 7.
6. Maḥmúd mentions that among the many people who visited 'Abdu'l-Bahá in Pittsburgh were a number of Jews (Zarqání, *Maḥmúd's Diary*, p. 83). Leonard Levy (1865–1917) was the rabbi of the Rodeph Sholom Congregation. Arthur M. Dahl, a Bahá'í, suggested that Levy, despite not knowing him personally, invite 'Abdu'l-Bahá to his synagogue. On 18 March Levy wrote to the Persian–American Educational Society to extend a formal invitation. (Dahl to Joseph Hannen, 20 Mar. 1912, and Sohrab to Levy, 22 Mar. 1912, Hannen-Knobloch family papers, Persian–American Educational Society, B21 and B22, US Bahá'í National Archives).
7. 'Abdul Baha Will Speak in Schenley', *Pittsburgh Sun*, 7 May 1912, p. 13, col. 3.
8. 'Abdu'l-Bahá, *Promulgation*, pp. 105–9, *Star of the West*, 24 June 1912 (3:6), pp. 2–4, 8.
9. 'Picturesque Persian Prophet Lectures Here', *Pittsburgh Dispatch*, 8 May 1912, p. 22, col. 2.
10. Marion Brunot Haymaker (1884–1941) worked at the *Chronicle-Telegraph* from the age of 18. She was also the president of the Women's Press Club of Pittsburgh.
11. 'Baha Expounds His Religion', *Chronicle-Telegraph*, 8 May 1912, p. 11, col. 2.
12. 'Abdul Baha Lectures on the Religion and Peace', *Pittsburgh Press*, 8 May 1912, p. 15, col. 4.
13. 'War Will be Eliminated by Women Says Apostle', *Pittsburgh Post*, 8 May 1912, p. 7, col. 6.
14. 'Preaches Doctrine of Oneness of Humanity', *Pittsburgh Sun*, 8 May 1912, p. 13, col. 1.
15. Sohrab, Letter to Harriet Magee, 8 May 1913, p. 13.
16. Sohrab, Letter to Harriet Magee, 10 May 1913, p. 1. The present author has been unable to locate this newspaper in any library holdings.

15. Second Visit to New York

1. See 'Abdu'l-Bahá, *Promulgation*, pp. 113–16, and *Star of the West*, 13 July 1912 (3:7), pp. 12–14.
2. 'Persian prophet in town', *Montclair Times* (Montclair, NJ), 18 May 1912. The article was reprinted on 8 June 1912. For another an announcement see *Unitarian Advance* (New York), May 1912, p. 269. For a brief mention of the meeting by Wiers himself see *Unitarian Advance* (New York), June 1912, p. 315 and July 1912, p. 351.
3. Ahmad Sohrab to Agnes Parsons, 13 May 1913 (Agnes Parsons papers, B14, US National Bahá'í Archives).
4. Maḥmúd notes that the night before the Master also made a similar comment. See Zarqání, *Maḥmúd's Diary*, pp. 88–9.

5. 'Baha Likes All Right', *New York Times*, 13 May 1912, p. 18, col. 3. Other newspapers that published similar information were: 'U. S. Optimistic, Says Persian', *New York Press*, 13 May 1912, p. 10, col. 6; 'All Right key optimism of America, Says Abdul Baha', *News Chronicle* (Muskegon, MI), 13 May 1912, p. 1 col. 1; 'All Right Secret of our Optimism', *Denver Post*, 13 May 1912, p. 1, col. 7; 'Prophet Puts His O.K. on All Right', *Oakland Tribune*, 13 May 1912; 'We are All Right', *Chicago Live Stock World*, 14 May 1912, p. 2, col. 2; 'All Right, Nation's Slogans', *Record-Herald* (Chicago), 14 May 1912; 'Everything All Right', *The Repository* (Canton, OH), 14 May 1912, p. 2, col. 2; 'All Right Keynote Expressing Optimism of American People', *Riverside Enterprise* (CA), 14 May 1912, p. 8, col. 4; *Daily Press* (Utica, NY), 17 May 1912, p. 8, col. 4; 'All Right is American Slogan', *Daily News* (Elkhart, IN), 17 May 1912, p. 5, col. 5; *Buffalo Express*, 18 May 1912, p. 6, col. 4; *Evening Union* (Springfield, MA), 18 May 1912; *Omaha News*, 18 May 1912; *Sunday News Tribune* (Duluth, MN), 19 May 1912, p. 4, col. 2; 'All Right', *Lima News*, 20 May 1912, p. 4, col. 1; 'All Right is Keynote', *Morning Oregonian* (Portland), 20 May 1912, p. 3, col. 3, and 21 May 1912, p. 8, col 2; *Unity* (Chicago), 23 May 1912, p. 1; *Semiweekly Journal* (Auburn, NY), 24 May 1912, p. 4, col. 4; 'Contemporary Comment', *New Orleans Daily Picayune*, 25 May 1912, p. 6, col. 4; 'The All Right Nation', *Brooklyn Daily Eagle*, 31 May 1912, p. 4, col. 5; 'The All Right Nation', *Grand Rapids Press*, 26 July 1912, p. 6, col. 4. Also published in Cuba, 'El All Right Americano', *Diario de la Marina* (Havana), 18 May 1912, p. 1, col. 4.
6. For the text of the talk in English see 'Abdu'l-Bahá, *Promulgation*, pp. 116–22. For the Persian notes of the same talk see 'Abdu'l-Bahá, *Majmu'ih-i-Khatábát-i-Hadrat-i-'Abdu'l-Bahá*, vol. 2, pp. 60–71.
7. 'Church and Religious News-Notes', *New York Tribune*, 11 May 1912, p. 10, col. 7.
8. 'Church Services To-Morrow', *New York Times*, 11 May 1912, p. 20, col. 2. The Grace Methodist Church was located at West 104th Street, between Columbus and Amsterdam Avenues.
9. *Report of the Eighteenth Annual Lake Mohonk Conference on International Arbitration*, Brandow: Albany, 1912.
10. See *Star of the West*, 12 Dec. 1911 (2:15), p. 5.
11. ibid. pp. 3–4.
12. 'New Impetus for World Peace', *Advocate of Peace* (Washington), February 1912 (74:2), pp. 49–50. This correspondence was started after Mason Remey and other Bahá'ís established contact with both Smiley and Phillips at the Third National Peace Congress held in Baltimore in May 1911 where Remey presented a paper on the Bahá'í Faith. See letter of 'Abdu'l-Bahá to Mason Remey translated 4 Aug. 1911. See also 'Records of the Lake Mohonk Conference on International Arbitration', Box 148, in Swarthmore College Peace Collection. At least two Bahá'ís attended the 1911 Lake Mohonk Peace Conference: Ali Kuli Khan, *Chargé d'Affaires* of the Persian Legation in the United States, gave a presentation in one of the plenary sessions on the subject of 'The Conditions of Universal Peace'; Ahmad Sohrab attended as representative of the Persian–American Educational Society. See *Report of the Seventeenth Annual Lake Mohonk Conference on International Arbitration* (1911).

13. Letter from H. C. Phillips to 'Abdu'l-Bahá, 10 Nov. 1911, 'Records of the Lake Mohonk Conference on International Arbitration', Box 116, in Swarthmore College Peace Collection.
14. He shared the Nobel Peace Prize with Jane Addams who, when he was in Chicago, invited 'Abdu'l-Bahá to speak at Hull House.
15. See for instance *New York Times*, 28 Apr. 1912, p. 4c, col. 1. Similar notes were published in the 'Mohonk Conference', *Evening Recorder* (Amsterdam, NY), 25 Apr. 1912, p. 7, col. 2; 'Mohonk Conference', *New York Tribune*, 29 Apr. 1912, p. 6, col. 6; 'Lake Mohonk Conference', *Glen Falls Daily Times*, 1 May 1912, p. 3, col. 5; 'Lake Mohonk Conference', *Northwestern Christian Advocate* (Chicago), 1 May 1912, p. 556; 'Lake Mohonk Conference', *Reform Advocate* (Chicago), 4 May 1912, p. 466; 'Lake Mohonk Conference', *Herald of Gospel Liberty* (Dayton, OH), 9 May 1912, p. 605; 'Lake Mohonk Conference', *Aberdeen Daily News* (SD), 11 May 1912, p. 4, col. 3; 'Plans for the Lake Mohonk Arbitration Conference', *Congregationalist and Christian World* (Boston), 11 May 1912, p. 657; 'Lake Mohonk Conference', *Friend's Intelligencer* (Philadelphia), 11 May 1912, p. 290; 'Ready for Approaching Third Hague Conference', *Marion Daily Star* (OH), 11 May 1912, p. 7, col. 3; 'Third Hague Conferences', *Lima News*, 12 May 1912, p. 13, col. 1; 'Third Hague Conferences', *Oakland Tribune*, 12 May 1912, p. 30, col. 4; 'Peace Conference', *Syracuse Herald*, 12 May 1912, p. 5d, col. 2; 'News at Home', *Expositor and Current Anecdotes* (Cleveland), 1 June 1912, p. 555. The magazine *The Outlook* (New York) also announced the participation of the Master in a brief note published in its issue of 27 Apr. 1912, p. 988. For a list of participants see the appendixes of *Report of the Eighteenth Annual Lake Mohonk Conference on International Arbitration* (1912).
16. Among the newspapers that published it were: 'Arbitration is the Topic', *Edwardsville Intelligencer* (IL), 15 May 1912, p. 2, col. 2; 'Lake Mohonk Conference to Discuss Arbitral Court', *Evening Post* (Frederick, MA), 15 May 1912, p. 5, col. 1; 'Scolds Nations in a Peace Talk for Going to War', *Evening World* (New York), 15 May 1912; 'To Discuss Arbitral Court', *Jamestown Evening Journal* (NY), 15 May 1912, p. 6, col. 3; 'To Discuss Arbitration at Lake Mohonk Meeting', *Riverside Daily Press* (CA), 15 May 1912, p. 2, col. 4; 'Peace Advocates at Lake Mohonk', *Standard Union* (Brooklyn), 15 May 1912, p. 8, col. 6; 'Arbitration will be Chief Topic in Meet', *Waterloo Reporter* (IA), 15 May 1912, p. 4, col. 6; 'To Discuss Arbitral Court', *Ada Evening News* (OK), 16 May 1912, p. 4, col. 5; 'Arbitral Court is Discussed', *Aberdeen Weekly News* (SD), 16 May 1912, p. 1, col. 3; 'Discuss Arbitral Court', *Grand Forks Daily Herald* (ND), 16 May 1912, p. 4, col. 6; 'Mohonk Conference Opens at Lake Mohonk', *Miami Herald*, 17 May 1912; 'Discussing Arbitration', *St. Hilaire Spectator* (MN), 18 May 1912, p. 1, col. 3. A different note was published as 'Mohonk Conference May 15' in the *Boston Transcript*, 22 Apr. 1912.
17. Newspapers that published this picture included *Binghamton Press* (NY), 17 May 1912, p. 1; *Paterson Morning Call* (NJ), 20 May 1912, p. 9; *Boston Traveler*, 23 May 1912; *Idaho Sunday Statesman* (Boise), 26 May 1912, p. 4; *Niagara Falls Gazette* (NY), 28 May 1912, p. 14; *Sunday Oregonian* (Portland), 2 June 1912, p. 4; 'The Mohonk Peace Conference', *Christian Herald* (New York), 5 June 1912.
18. The newspapers that published this picture included 'Picturesque Figure',

Binghamton Press (NY), 17 May 1912, p. 2, col. 4; 'Head of New Religion Prominent at Lake Mohonk Conference', *Lowell Sun* (MA), 18 May 1912, p. 6, col. 3; 'Head of New Religion', *Pawtucket Evening Times* (RI), 18 May 1912, p. 11, col. 1; 'Head of New Religion of Peace', *Atlanta Constitution*, 20 May 1912; 'Head of New Religion of Peace is Picturesque Figure at Lake Mohonk', *Canton Repository* (OH), 20 May 1912, p. 5, col. 2; *Gettysburg Times*, 20 May 1912, n.t.; 'Head of New Religion of Peace Picturesque Figure Lake Mohonk', *Augusta Chronicle* (GA), 22 May 1912, p. 2, col. 4; 'Many Countries Were Represented at the Eighteenth Annual Session of the Lake Mohonk Conference', *Chicago Daily World*, 22 May 1912; 'Head of New Religion of Peace Prominent at Lake Mohonk Conference', *Evening Tribune* (San Diego, CA), 22 May 1912, p. 1, col. 5; 'Head of New Religion of Peace is Picturesque Figure at Lake Mohonk Arbitration Conference', *Frederick News* (MD), 22 May 1912, p. 7, col. 3; 'Figure at Lake Mohonk Arbitration Conference', *Savannah News* (GA), 22 May 1912; 'Peace Preacher is Picturesque Figure', *Aberdeen World* (WA), 23 May 1912; 'Head of New Religion of Peace is Picturesque Figure at Lake Mohonk Arbitration Conference', *Odgen Evening Standard* (UT), 23 May 1912, p. 8, col. 6; *Albany Evening Journal* (NY), 24 May 1912, p. 14, col. 3; 'Head of New Religion at Arbitration Conference', *Berkeley Gazette*, 24 May 1912; 'Head of New Religion Picturesque Figure', *South Bend Tribune* (IN), 31 May 1912; 'Head of New Religion of Peace is Picturesque Figure', *Superior News Tribune* (WI), 7 June 1912, p. 1, col. 4; 'Abdul Baha', *Racine Journal-News* (WI), 17 Aug. 1912, p. 12, col. 3. These newspapers had a combined circulation of over 302,000 copies daily.

19. According to a telegram from 'Abdu'l-Bahá to H.C. Phillips dated 4 May, He chose the title of the talk Himself. See 'Records of the Lake Mohonk Conference on International Arbitration', Box 116, in Swarthmore College Peace Collection.
20. *Report of the Eighteenth Annual Lake Mohonk Conference on International Arbitration*, pp. 42–5. The text of the talk was sent from Egypt in early 1912 and was translated by Ahmad Sohrab. See, for instance, letter from H. C. Phillips to Ahmad Sohrab of 13 April which requests a translation of 'Abdu'l-Bahá's address to be used with the press and to be read after His presentation in Persian ('he having first spoken a few paragraphs in his native tongue and remaining standing during the reading'). Each participant was given a 20-minute session. See 'Records of the Lake Mohonk Conference on International Arbitration', Box 116, in Swarthmore College Peace Collection.
21. 'Peace Conference Enlarges Circle', *Washington Herald*, 20 May 1912, p. 2, col. 4.
22. 'Ultimate Triumph of Peace Predicted at Mohonk Conference', *Christian Science Monitor* (Boston), 16 May 1912, p.1, col. 1.
23. 'Ball Returns from Lake Mohonk Well Pleased', *Montgomery Advertiser* (Montgomery, AL), 21 May 1912, p. 3, col. 2. The newspaper in which an article announcing the participation of Ball at Lake Mohonk appeared, also mentioned 'Abdu'l-Bahá, see 29 Apr. 1912.
24. Bradley Gilman, 'The Conference at Lake Mohonk', *Christian Register* (Boston), 23 May 1912, p. 498, col. 2.
25. 'The Chicago Office and Field Secretaryship', *Advocate of Peace* (Washington), June 1912 (74:6), p. 149.

26. 'The Lake Mohonk Arbitration Conference', ibid. p. 130.
27. 'The Ethics of Democracy', *University of Tennessee Record* (Knoxville), Aug. 1912 (15:6), p. 22.
28. For the notes of their meeting see *Star of the West*, 13 July 1912 (3:7), pp. 4–5.
29. The original idea of arranging such a meeting for 'Abdu'l-Bahá was suggested by Nicholas Butler, President of Columbia University, and winner of the Peace Nobel Prize in 1931. For details, see correspondence involving himself, James Scott – secretary of the Carnegie Endowment for International Peace – and Ahmad Sohrab in Columbia University, Carnegie Endowment for International Peace Records, Subseries III.A. Division of Intercourse and Education – General, vol. 36 (1912), pp. 398–404.
30. For the text of the talk see 'Abdu'l-Bahá, *Promulgation*, pp. 123–6 and *Star of the West*, 1 Aug. 1912 (3:8), pp. 10–15.
31. Maḥmúd wrongly identified Wise as the president of the New York Peace Society. He certainly presided at the meeting but the president of the Society was Andrew Carnegie.
32. 'Reception to Abdul Baha', *New York Times*, 12 May 1912, p. 8, col. 2. The same issue carried another announcement on p. 4-X, col. 5.
33. 'Carnegie Peace Reception', *Brooklyn Daily Eagle*, 12 May 1912, p. 6, col. 6.
34. 'Announcements', *Evening Call* (New York), 13 Apr. 1912, p. 6, col. 5.
35. 'The Week in Town', *Evening Post* (New York), 6 May 1912, p. 6, col. 3; 'The Week in Town', 7 May 1912, p. 6, col. 2; 'The Week in Town', 10 May 1912, p. 4, col. 5; 'The Week in Town', 13 May 1912.
36. 'News of Women's Clubs', *Evening Telegram* (New York), 10 May 1912.
37. 'Plan Reception to Peace Advocate', *New York Press*, 12 May 1912, p. 5, col. 3.
38. 'What is going on today', *New York Tribune*, 13 May 1912, p. 7, col. 4.
39. 'Baha Talks on Peace', *New York Tribune*, 14 May 1912, p. 3, col. 3.
40. 'Baha Denounces Warfare', *New York Times*, 14 May 1912, p. 6, col. 6.
41. 'Abdul Bahai's Peace Plea', *Sun* (New York), 14 May 1912, p. 5, col. 6.
42. 'Persian Prophet Speaks for Peace', *New York Herald*, 14 May 1912, p. 22, col. 3.
43. 'Urges Americans to End War', *New York Press*, 14 May 1912, p. 7, col. 5.
44. 'What the Peace Organizations are Doing', *Advocate of Peace* (Washington DC), June 1912 (74:6), p. 133.
45. 'The New York Peace Society', *Advocate of Peace* (Washington DC), June 1912 (74:6), p. 150.
46. 'Elaborate Reception for Abdul Baha', *Oakland Tribune* (Oakland, CA), 19 May 1912, p. 7, col. 4.
47. 'America Foremost Champion of Universal Brotherhood of Man', *Evening News* (San Jose, CA), 15 June 1912, p. 5, col. 3; 'America Foremost Champion of Universal Brotherhood of Man', *Reporter* (Fond du Lac, WI), 6 June 1912; 'America Foremost Champion of Universal Brotherhood of Man', *Jersey Journal* (NJ), 13 June 1913, p. 12, col. 5.
48. 'Apóstol de la Paz', *Diario de la Marina* (Havana), 21 May 1912, p. 1, col. 5.
49. 'Visiting Pastors in City Pulpits', *New York Herald*, 18 May 1912, p. 14, col. 2.
50. For the text of the talk see 'Abdu'l-Bahá, *Promulgation*, pp. 126–9, and *Star of the West*, 20 Aug. 1912 (3:9), pp. 9–12. Maḥmúd wrongly states that the address took place on Saturday, 18 May.

51. 'Abdul Baha Heard', *Sun* (New York), 20 May 1912, p. 8, col. 7.
52. Ives states in his biography, *Portals to Freedom* (1937), that the article he read was published in October 1911. There is, however, no article in that issue mentioning the Faith. *Everybody's Magazine* did publish an article on the Bahá'í Faith in December 1911. It was authored by Ethel S. Stevens (1879–1972) and described at considerable length her impressions of a visit to 'Abdu'l-Bahá in 'Akká. It is thus probable that Ives was actually referring to this article. See chapter 3 above for this article and other writings by Stevens on 'Abdu'l-Bahá.
53. 'The Bahai Movement', *Jersey Journal*, 5 Feb. 1912, p. 2, col. 2.
54. 'Philosopher from Persia to Speak Here', *Jersey Journal*, 18 May 1912, p. 3, col. 1. For another announcement see *Unitarian Advance* (New York), May 1912, p. 269.
55. For the text of this talk see 'Abdu'l-Bahá, *Promulgation*, pp. 129–32, and *Star of the West*, 20 Aug. 1912 (3:9), pp. 5–7, 9.
56. *Jersey Journal* (Jersey City, NJ), 20 May 1912, p. 3, col. 4.
57. 'Jersey City', *Christian Register* (Boston), 23 May 1912, p. 502.

16. Boston

1. According to Anise Rideout in her unpublished *Early History of Bahá'í Community, Boston, Mass* (n.d.) 'Abdu'l-Bahá first stayed at Hotel Victoria but then changed to Hotel Charesgate to comply with the wishes of one local believer who had paid for a suite for Him in that hotel. 'Abdu'l-Bahá nevertheless kept the room in the Victoria and there he would hold many of His public and private meetings with visitors. I thank Peter J. Andrews for kindly sharing with me this document. For published accounts and sources for the visit of 'Abdu'l-Bahá to Boston see 'Abdu'l-Bahá, *Promulgation*, pp. 138–46; Zarqání, *Maḥmúd's Diary*, pp. 71–3; Bagdadi, 'Abdul Baha in America', *Star of the West*, July 1928 (19:6), pp. 183–4; Ward, *239 Days*, pp. 47–58.
2. 'Bahaist Leader to Seek Converts Here', *Boston Journal*, Dec. 18, 1911, p. 7, col. 4.
3. Cable from Matthew Hale to Ahmad Sohrab, 10 Nov. 1911 (Sohrab papers, B11, US National Bahá'í Archives). Besides contacting the Persian–American Educational Society, Fitzgerald wrote to 'Abdu'l-Bahá in Paris extending a formal invitation. Matthew Hale was a member of the Boston City Council from 1910 to 1912 and a prominent member of the Progressive Party in Massachusetts. The Persian–American Educational Society approached him by letter, probably on 7 Nov. 1911, to inform him about the upcoming visit to America of 'Abdu'l-Bahá.
4. 'Bahai New Year Celebrated by Followers of Persian Prophet', *Lowell Sun* (MA), 22 Mar. 1912.
5. It was the Bahá'í Stanwood Cobb who suggested to Rev. Thomas Van Ness that 'Abdu'l-Bahá be invited to this conference (Stanwood Cobb to Joseph Hannen, 11 Mar. 1912, Hannen-Knobloch family papers, B21, US National Bahá'í Archives).
6. William, *World Religions*.
7. *Christian Register* (Boston), 16 May 1912, pp. 475, 477.
8. 'Persian to Explain His Cult', *Boston Transcript*, 18 May 1912, p. 5, col. 5. On 20 January 1912 Rev. Thomas Van Ness of the Second Church of Boston wrote to the Persian–American Educational Society extending an invitation to 'Abdu'l-Bahá to speak at his church. His letter was translated and sent to 'Abdu'l-Bahá

in Alexandria (Sohrab to Thomas Van Ness, Sohrab papers, B13, US National Bahá'í Archives).

9. 'Persian Prophet at Unitarian Festival', *Boston Post*, 20 May 1912. The article included a portrait distributed by Curtis Brown News Bureau. The same article was published as 'Unitarian Anniversary' in the *Brooklyn Daily Eagle*, 20 May 1912, p. 3, col. 5. Other announcements were published as 'Social and Personal Notes', in the *Boston Herald*, 22 May 1912, p. 7, col. 4.
10. For the English text of this talk, see 'Abdu'l-Bahá, *Promulgation*, pp. 140–3. This talk is wrongly identified as 'Talk at Free Religious Association, or Unitarian Conference' and wrongly dated as having taken place on 24 May, whereas as we shall see that the Festival of the Free Religious Association and the Unitarian Conference were actually two different events. See below in this chapter for the talk at the Free Religious Association which was held on 24 May. For the Persian text of the talk at Tremont Temple see 'Abdu'l-Bahá, *Majmu'ih-i-Khatábát-i-Hadrat-i-'Abdu'l-Bahá*, vol. 2, pp. 71–6.
11. 'Persian Prophet at Unitarian Festival', *Boston Post*, 23 May 1912, p. 4, col. 3. The article also carried the portrait of the Master taken at the Lafayette studios in London with the caption 'Abdul Baha Abbas Effendi, the founder of the new universal religion, who was one of the principal speakers at the Unitarian congress last night.'
12. 'Hear Prophet from Orient', *Boston Transcript*, 23 May 1912, p. 14, col. 5.
13. 'Busy Day for Unitarians', *Springfield Daily Republican* (MA), 24 May 1912, p. 2, col. 3.
14. 'Tuckerman School Graduation Starts Day for Unitarians', *Christian Science Monitor* (Boston, MA), 23 May 1912, p. 5, col. 4.
15. 'Noted Persian Gives Address', *Boston Journal*, 23 May 1912, p. 2, col. 6. Also published as 'Noted Persian Gives Address' in the *Daily News* (Springfield, MA), 23 May 1912, p. 7, col. 5.
16. 'Abdul Baha Effendi Talks to Unitarians', *Boston Advertiser*, 23 May 1912, p. 2, col. 1.
17. 'Unitarians Rise to Greet Persian Speaker at Tremont Temple', *Boston Herald*, 23 May 1912, p. 5, col. 3.
18. 'Women Clash Over the Vote', *Boston Daily Globe*, 23 May 1912.
19. 'The Unitarian Festival', *Christian Register* (Boston), 30 May 1912, p. 515. Brief reference also on p. 513.
20. 'Editorial', *Unitarian Word and Work* (Boston), June 1912, p. 2, col. 2.
21. Ellen M. Mitchell (1838–1920) was one of the early American women philosophers. In 1888 she received a faculty position at the University of Denver, becoming one of the first American women to lecture in a university. She was author of *A Study of Greek Philosophy* (1891), *The Hidden Sound of Harmony* (1900) and *The Paradise of Dante* (1898), as well as several articles on philosophy, some of them published in the *Journal of Speculative Philosophy*, the first American journal on philosophy.
22. 'Tidings from Boston', *Syracuse Post Standard*, 28 May 1912, p. 4, col. 4.
23. 'Ameriska Únítarafélagio', *Heimir* (Winnipeg, MB), July 1912 (8:7), p. 154.
24. 'A Persian Shorthand', *Stenographer* (Philadelphia), Jan. 1913, pp. 718–20.
25. For Persian notes of this talk see 'Abdu'l-Bahá, *Majmu'ih-i-Khatábát-i-Hadrat-*

i-'Abdu'l-Bahá, vol. 2, pp. 77–82.

26. 'Abbas Effendi Coming to Give Talk at Clark', *Worcester Evening Gazette*, 21 May 1912, p. 2, col. 1; 'Abdul Baha to Speak', *Worcester Telegram*, 22 May 1912. I thank Eugenio Marcano for kindly sharing with me the Worcester articles in this section, which were found in Clark University's Archives and Special Collections Department, Robert H. Goddard Library and in the Worcester Public Library.
27. 'Bab Religion's Leader Talk to Clark Students', *Worcester Evening Gazette*, 24 May 1912, p. 8, col. 3.
28. 'Head of New Religion Clark College Speaker', *Worcester Post*, 24 May 1912.
29. 'Abdul Baha's Address', *Clark College Monthly*, June 1912 (1:10), p. 544.
30. 'New Faith Head Heard', *Worcester Telegram*, 24 May 1912.
31. See Zarqání, *Maḥmúd's Diary*, p. 108.
32. 'Abdul Baha has Creed He Declares will Finally Eliminate Criminal', *Boston Traveler*, 24 May 1912.
33. 'The Free Religious Association', *Christian Register* (Boston), 16 May 1912, p. 476, col. 1, p. 477, col. 1, and p. 479, col. 3.
34. 'Abdul Baha to Speak', *Boston Journal*, 20 May 1912.
35. 'Suffrage Motion is Protested', *Boston Post*, 24 May 1912, p. 13, col. 3.
36. For Persian notes of this talk see 'Abdu'l-Bahá, *Majmu'ih-i-Khatábát-i-Hadrat-i-'Abdu'l-Bahá*, vol. 2, pp. 86–91. For the English notes see below.
37. 'Church vs. State', *Boston Transcript*, 25 May 1912, p. 6, col. 1.
38. 'Urges Unity of Religions', *Boston Herald*, 25 May 1912.
39. 'Catholics Lauded by Minister', *Boston Post*, 25 May 1912, p. 2, col. 5. 'Replies to Defence of Catholic Church', *Springfield Daily News* (MA), 25 May 1912, p. 7, col. 4.
40. 'Free Religious Association', *Christian Register* (Boston), 4 July 1912, p. 651, col. 1. See also *Proceedings of the Forty-Fifth Annual Meeting* (1912).
41. *Proceedings of the Forty-Fifth Annual Meeting* (1912).
42. ibid. p. 84.
43. ibid. pp. 86–90.
44. ibid. p. 94.
45. 'A Honest Man', *America* (New York), 31 Aug. 1912, pp. 194–5.
46. 'Abdul Baha is Birthday Guest', *Boston Herald*, 26 May 1912, p. 5, col. 3.
47. 'In the Public Eye', *Boston Advertiser*, 27 May 1912, p. 4, col. 5.
48. The Twentieth Century Club was founded in 1894 by Edwin Mead, who was its first president. The club's main interest was social progress. Its main activities were the Saturday luncheons at which speakers were invited to address the club's members. The invitation to 'Abdu'l-Bahá to speak at the Twentieth Century Club arrived as early as January 1912 through Edwin H. Chandler (letter from Ahmad Sohrab to Edward H. Chandler, 23 Jan. 1912, Ahmad Sohrab papers, Persian–American Educational Society papers, box 11).
49. 'Favors one Religion', *Boston Sunday Globe*, 26 May 1912, p. 24, col. 7. Similar information was also published as 'Explains Bahaism' in the *Boston Herald*, 26 May 1912. An announcement of this meeting was published as 'In the Public Eye' in the *Boston Advertiser*, 24 May 1912, p. 4, col. 5.
50. 'Described Bahaism', *Boston American*, 26 May 1912, p. 7, col. 3.

51. See 'Abdul Baha Abbas to Speak', *Boston Daily Globe*, 25 May 1912, p. 2, col. 7; 'Abdul Baha to Speak', *Christian Science Monitor*, Boston, 25 May 1912, p. 26, col. 3; 'Abdul Baha to Speak in Huntington Hall', *Boston Herald*, 25 May 1912, p. 7, col. 8.
52. See 'Abdu'l-Bahá, *Promulgation*, pp. 143–6.
53. 'Baha Speaks in Evening', *Boston Herald*, 26 May 1912.
54. 'Farewell Message of Abdul Baha', *Boston Post*, 26 May 1912, p. 5, col. 1.
55. 'Abdul Baha Gives His Last Talk to Boston Audience', *Christian Science Monitor*, 27 May 1912, p. 4, col. 6.
56. 'Finds Land Full of Taken for Granted Divorces', *Boston Herald*, 27 May 1912, p. 2, col. 4. The article also included portions of an interview that was granted to Sophie I. Loeb a few days before in New York; see next chapter.

17. New York, New Jersey and Pennsylvania

1. Sophie Irene Loeb (1876–1929), was born in Russia and moved with her family to the United States when she was six years old. In 1910, after divorcing her husband Anselm Loeb, she moved to New York and started working for *The Evening World*. Her work as reporter focused on social issues and she was especially interested in the widows and children of the working class. She dedicated her life as a social activist to campaigning for public support and funding for destitute children. In 1915 she was appointed to New York City's Child Welfare Board. In 1924 she became the first president of the Child Welfare Committee of America, an institution she helped to create. She is author of several books and articles, among them *Epigrams of Eve* (1913); *Everyman's Child* (1920) and *Palestine Awake* (1926).
2. 'Nothing Else is So Free in this Country as Marriage, Says Abdul Baha', *Evening World* (New York), 24 May 1912, p. 20, col. 1.
3. See for instance 'Finds Land Full of Taken for Granted Divorces', *Boston Herald*, 27 May 1912, p. 2, col. 4; 'Telegraphic Tabloids', *Daily News* (Springfield, MA), 27 May 1912, p. 2, col. 3; 'June Roses and Wedding Bells', *Syracuse Herald*, 3 June 1912, p. 5, col. 1; 'June Roses and Wedding Bells', *Pittsburgh Press*, 17 June 1912.
4. See *Brooklyn Daily Eagle*, 26 May 1912, p. 6, col. 2. A similar announcement was published under 'To-day in New York' in the *New York Herald*, 28 May 1912, p. 8, col. 6.
5. For the text of this talk see 'Abdu'l-Bahá, *Promulgation*, pp. 150–3, and *Star of the West*, 13 July 1912 (3:7), pp. 14–15, 19–21. *Star of the West* also includes the addresses of other guests at the reception.
6. 'Baha Points Toward Peace', *New York Times*, 29 May 1912, p. 10, col. 6; also published in 'The last of June', *Columbia Republican* (Hudson, NY), 4 June 1912, p.1, col. 6.
7. 'City Jottings', *New York Herald*, 29 May 1912, p. 7, col. 4.
8. *Rochester Post-Express*, 3 June 1912, n.t.
9. 'Religion and World Amity', *Democrat and Chronicle* (Rochester, NY), 1 June 1912, p. 8, col. 1.
10. *Evening Telegram* (Salt Lake City), 30 May 1912, p. 4, col. 2, n.t. The reference in the *Brooklyn Times* is also reproduced in the same note. The present author has been unable to locate the original.

11. For this talk see 'Abdu'l-Bahá, *Promulgation*, pp. 161–3.
12. Newspaper clipping held at US Bahá'í National Archives and dated 31 May. No publication title. In 'Abdu'l-Bahá, *Promulgation* this talk is dated 31 May. The announcement stated that the talk was to be held on the next day, that is, 1 June. The account of the talk published in the same newspaper stated that the talk was given 'Saturday evening'; again, the date could only be 1 June. Thus, both the date given in Zarqání, *Maḥmúd's Diary* and the date in 'Abdu'l-Bahá, *Promulgation* are mistaken.
13. Text in *Star of the West*, 27 Sept. 1914 (5:11), pp. 169–70. Hoar gives the date of this article as 1 June.
14. *Evening Post* (New York), 1 June 1912, p. 11, col. 7, n.t.
15. *New York Times*, 1 June 1912, p. 17, col. 2, n.t.
16. *New-York Tribune*, 1 June 1912, p. 10, cols. 5–6, n.t.
17. For the text of this talk and 'Abdu'l-Bahá's answers to questions from the public see 'Abdu'l-Bahá, *Promulgation*, 8 Sept. 1912 (3:10), pp. 163–71, and *Star of the West*, pp. 24–9.
18. 'Questions', *Theosophic Messenger* (Los Angeles), Dec. 1912, p. 193. See also 'Abdu'l-Bahá, *Promulgation*, p. 167.
19. 'One Sunday School Division Paraded for Admiral Peary', *Standard Union* (Brooklyn), 7 June 1912, p. 8, col. 2.
20. Gifford Pinchot (1865–1946), served as governor of Pennsylvania for two terms (1923–7 and 1931–5). He is, however, best known for being the first American forest conservationist and the first chief of the Forest Service of the United States, founder of the Society of American Foresters and for many years president of the National Conservation Association. Pinchot was probably acquainted with Agnes Parsons, as can inferred from a letter from Joseph Hannen to Gifford Pinchot in which the latter is invited to participate at the 1912 annual conference of the Persian–American Educational Convention (Hannen to Pinchot, 18 Mar. 1912, Hannen-Knobloch family papers, B23, US Bahá'i National Archives).
21. For Persian notes of some of 'Abdu'l-Bahá's comments in Milford see 'Abdu'l-Bahá, *Majmu'ih-i-Khatábát-i-Hadrat-i-'Abdu'l-Bahá*, vol. 2, pp. 110–27.
22. Zia Bagdadi, 'Abdul Baha Speaks on Divine Politics and Other Subjects'. See *Star of the West*, 20 Aug. 1916 (7:9), pp. 77–9. For the Persian text see 'Abdu'l-Bahá, *Majmu'ih-i-Khatábát-i-Hadrat-i-'Abdu'l-Bahá*, vol. 2, pp. 110–27.
23. 'Did you see Abdul Baha?' *Port Jervis Gazette* (Port Jervis, NY), 5 June 1912. This newspaper had a circulation of 1,800 copies. Mahmud gives the date of arrival as 3 June, see Zarqání, *Maḥmúd's Diary*, p. 120. That the correct date is 4 June is confirmed by Bagdadi, see note 22 above.
24. 'Noted Persian Here', *Milford Dispatch*, 6 June 1912, p. 2, col. 2.
25. *Pike County Press* (Milford), 7 June 1912, p. 2, col. 2, n.t.
26. 'Abdul Baha Noted Persian Visited Pinchots at Milford', *Tri-States Union* (Port Jervis, NY), 6 June 1912, p. 3, col. 5.
27. 'Leader of Bahia Cult Here', *Philadelphia Record*, 9 June 1912.
28. 'Abdul Baha Here for Full Suffrage', *Philadelphia Press*, 9 June 1912.
29. 'Persian Baha Urges Vote for all Women', *North American* (Philadelphia), 9 June 1912.
30. *Age* (New York), 20 June 1912, p. 4, col. 4, n.t.

31. The minister of this church was Dr Kenneth E. Evans. He called on the Master on the same day at 9 a.m. and had a long interview with Him.
32. 'Week's Religious News', *Philadelphia Inquirer*, 8 June 1912, p. 9, col. 7.
33. See 'Abdu'l-Bahá, *Promulgation*, pp. 172–6, and *Star of the West*, 13 July 1914 (5:7), pp. 99–102. For the Persian notes see 'Abdu'l-Bahá, *Majmu'ih-i-Khatábát-i-Hadrat-i-'Abdu'l-Bahá*, vol. 2, pp. 129–38.
34. 'Old Persian Mystic Stirs by Teachings', *Evening Bulletin* (Philadelphia), 10 June 1912.
35. 'Abdul Baha Asks for World Peace', *Philadelphia Inquirer*, 10 June 1912, p. 6, col. 6.
36. 'Persian Priest Tells Belief', *Philadelphia Press*, 10 June 1912.
37. 'Persian Sage Pays Visit to this City', *Public Ledger* (Philadelphia), 10 June 1912.
38. Dr Russell H. Conwell (1843–1925) was ordained a Baptist minister in 1880. In 1888 he founded the Temple University and in 1891 the new Baptist Temple in Philadelphia, the one visited by 'Abdu'l-Bahá. He was the author of over 15 works, including *Acres of Diamonds* (1890) which became the most popular of his books. His invitation to 'Abdu'l-Bahá was extended on 31 January 1912 after he corresponded with Elizabeth B. Nourse, a Bahá'í from Atlantic City (letter from the secretary of the Baptist Temple to the Persian–American Educational Society, Ahmad Sohrab papers B10, US Bahá'í National Archives).
39. Letter from Ahmad Sohrab to Joseph Hannen, 11 June 1912 (Hannen-Knobloch family papers, B9, US National Bahá'í Archives).
40. See 'Abdu'l-Bahá, *Promulgation*, pp. 176–82, *Star of the West*, 13 July 1914 (5:7), pp. 102–3 and 105–6. For the Persian notes of the talk see 'Abdu'l-Bahá, *Majmu'ih-i-Khatábát-i-Hadrat-i-'Abdu'l-Bahá*, vol. 2, pp. 138–51.
41. 'Persian for Suffrage', *Philadelphia Record*, 10 June 1912.
42. *Telegraph* (Philadelphia). No date available.
43. *Evening Post* (New York), 15 June 1912, p. 7, col. 5.
44. 'Pulpit and Pew', *Standard Union* (Brooklyn), 8 June 1912, p. 4, col. 2; and 'Pulpit and Pew', 15 June 1912, p. 3, col. 2.
45. 'Events To-morrow', *Standard Union* (Brooklyn), 15 June 1912, p. 7, col. 6.
46. 'Abdu'l-Bahá, *Promulgation*, pp. 197–203, and *Star of the West*, 8 September 1912 (3:10), pp. 19–23.
47. 'Abdul Baha Abbas in Dr Cadman's Pulpit', *Brooklyn Daily Eagle*, 17 June 1912. Also published as 'Universal Peace' in the *Washington County Post* (Cambridge, NY), 28 June 1912, p. 1, col. 4. This newspaper had a circulation of 1,800 copies.
48. 'Baha to Live in Montclair', *New York Times*, 2 June 1912, p. 11, col. 2; 'Jersey's New Resident', *Times-Press* (Middletown, NY), 3 June 1912, p. 6, col. 2; the article included a portrait. Similar news was published in 'General News Events' in the *Newton Register* (New York), 4 June 1912, p. 1, col. 1; 'Baha to Live in Montclair', *Daily Argus* (Mt Vernon, NY), 6 June 1912, p. 8, col. 1; 'Baha to Live in Montclair', *Paterson Evening News* (NJ), 6 June 1912, p. 1, col. 2 and p. 11, col. 3; 'Personal', *Putman County Republican* (Carmel, NY), 8 June 1912, p. 1, col. 5; *Cranbury Press* (Cranbury, NJ), 14 June 1912, p. 2, col. 1, n. t.; and the 'Gossip of the Metropolis', *Anaconda Standard* (Anaconda, MT), 16 June 1912, p. 4, col. 5.

49. Some of the newspapers that published this picture were *Evening Observer* (Dunkirk, NY), 1 July 1912, p. 2, col. 6; *News* (Fort Wayne, IN), 1 July 1912, p. 11, col. 1; *Syracuse Journal* (Syracuse, NY), 1 July 1912; *Republican* (Cedar Rapids, IA), 2 July 1912, p. 4, col. 4; *Daily Gazette* (Janeswille, WI), 2 July 1912, p. 3, col. 5; *Reporter* (Waterloo, IA), 2 July 1912, p. 4, col. 5; 'Persian Prophet to Remain in U.S.', *Janesville Gazette* (WI), 2 July 1912, p. 3, col. 5; *Riverside Enterprise* (CA), 5 July 1912, p. 4, col. 4; *News* (New Castle, PA), 5 July 1912, p. 5, col. 2; *Agitator* (Wellsboro, PA), 5 July 1912, p. 2, col. 3.
50. *Star of the West*, 20 Aug. 1916 (7:9), p. 77. Also published as 'Hearts are the Real Country', in *Christian Commonwealth* (London), 8 Nov. 1916, p. 72, col. 1.
51. 'General Notes', *Agitator* (Wellsboro, PA), 3 July 1912, p. 2, col. 3.
52. 'Prophets Dash for Train', *Sun* (New York), 30 June 1912. A shorter version of this article was published the same day as 'Prophets Dash for Train' in the *New York Times*, 30 June 1912, p. 6, col. 4.
53. *Sun* (New York), 28 June 1912, p. 11, col. 3, n.t.
54. 'New Yorkers Enjoy a Persian Barbecue', *Sun* (New York), 1 July 1912, p. 9, col. 3.
55. 'Barbecue for Abdul Baha', *New York Herald*, 1 July 1912, p. 16, col. 5.
56. Gertrude Käsebier (1852–1934) studied photography in France and Germany and became a professional photographer around 1895. Her work was soon recognized by critics and was included in different publications. By the turn of the century her studio in New York was a well-known photography center and a number of exhibitions were dedicated to her work. She was a founder of the Women's Professional Photographers Association of America.
57. *Sun* (New York), 7 July 1912, p. 8.
58. *Brooklyn Daily Eagle*, 13 July 1912, p. 9; *New-York Tribune*, 13 July 1912, p. 12; *Evening Post* (New York), 13 July 1912, p. 4; 'Events To-day', *Standard Union* (Brooklyn), 14 July 1912, p. 8, col. 6.
59. 'Notes and News of the Churches', *World* (New York), 13 July 1912, p. 5.
60. See 'Abdu'l-Bahá, *Promulgation*, pp. 228–35, and *Star of the West*, 27 Sept. 1912 (3:11), pp. 12–16.
61. 'Persian Prophet Favors Equal Rights for Women', *New York Press*, 15 July 1912, p. 5, col. 4.
62. *New York Times*, 15 July 1912, p. 2, col. 3. A short note sent via agencies was also published as 'Urges Universal Religion' in the *Public Ledger* (Philadelphia), 15 July 1912.
63. 'Persian Prophet Preaches', *New York Herald*, 15 July 1912, p. 8, col. 6.
64. *Unitarian Advance* (New York), Sept. 1912 (3:1), p. 30.
65. 'New York Letter', *Christian Register* (Boston), 15 Aug. 1912, p. 793.
66. 'Abdu'l-Bahá, *Promulgation*, p. 232.
67. *Daily Observer* (Charlotte, NC), 14 July 1912, p. 11, col. 1.
68. Text from 'Pointed Points', *Daily Bulletin* (Van Wert, OH), 15 July 1912, p. 1, col. 5. Also published as 'Universal Religion' in the *Journal* (Columbus, OH), 2 July 1912; and as 'With the Press', in the *Spartanburg Herald* (Spartanburgh, SC), 10 July 1912.
69. 'The Persian Prophet', *Independent* (New York), 18 July 1912 (73:3320), p. 159.
70. 'America and World Peace', *Independent* (New York), 12 Sept. 1912, pp. 606–9.
71. 'Memorial Services for General Khan', *New York Herald*, 20 July 1912, p. 9, col. 3.

72. *New-York Tribune*, 22 July 1912, p. 12, col. 4.
73. 'Abdul Baha', *New York Press*, 21 Aug. 1912, p. 5, col. 1.

18. Boston, Dublin, Green Acre, Malden

1. See 'Abdu'l-Bahá, *Promulgation*, pp. 238–9; *Star of the West*, 13 July 1913 (5:7), p. 122.
2. 'Abdul Baha Abbas Comes Again', *Boston Evening Transcript*, 24 July 1912, p. 15, col. 7.
3. 'Bahaist Leader has Reception', *Boston Herald*, 24 July 1912, 5, col. 2.
4. 'The Observant Citizen', *Boston Post*, 25 July 1912, p. 11, col. 3.
5. The secretary of the Golden Links Society, Elias G. Sabbag, formally invited 'Abdu'l-Bahá in a letter dated 24 January 1912 and addressed to the Persian–American Educational Society. 'Our Society would very much like to hear Abdul Baha when he is in Boston', stated the letter, 'as we have been looking forward to this opportunity for some time.' Ahmad Sohrab papers, B11, US Bahá'í National Archives. For a reference to this event see the Arabic periodical *Al-Saih* (New York), 31 May 1912.
6. 'Syrian Meal for Persian Prophet', *Boston Herald*, 26 July 1912. For a report of 'Abdu'l-Bahá's first address to this society, see the Arabic journal *Al-Saih*, 30 May 1912.
7. *Concord Monitor* (NH), 26 July 1912, n. t.
8. The minister of this church was Josiah Lafayette Seward (1845–1917). He is reported as having opened the service with the following prayer dedicated to 'Abdu'l-Bahá: 'We thank Thee, O God, that Thou didst appear in Persia. The radiance of Thy Divine Love became manifest in that far off land. Bless this chosen one who has received the fore dreams of Thy Love. O God! He has come to us from the distant land with the message of Thy peace and brotherhood. He has suffered years of persecutions and trials in Thy Path! May Thy blessing rest upon him! And we shall hear from his lips those doctrines of love and peace for which he has suffered.' Quoted in a letter from Ahmad Sohrab to Joseph Hannen, 14 Aug. 1912 (Hannen-Knobloch family papers, B9, US National Bahá'í Archives).
9. Articles mentioned by Phillip Tussing in *Finishing the Work: 'Abdu'l-Bahá in Dublin, 1912* available at http://bahai-library.com/tussing_abdul-baha_dublin#notes (last accessed 5 May 2011).
10. Letter from Ahmad Sohrab to Joseph Hannen, 16 Aug. 1912 (Hannen-Knobloch family papers, B9, US National Bahá'í Archives).
11. 'Our Weekly Boston Letter', *Springfield Daily Republican* (MA), 27 July 1912, p. 17, col. 2. The same was published as 'The Green Acre Conferences', 1 Aug. 1912, p. 12, col. 7. The letter was dated 25 July.
12. 'Abdul Baha at Green Acre', *Portsmouth Herald* (NH), 14 Aug. 1912, p. 8, col. 4.
13. Letter from Ahmad Sohrab to Joseph Hannen, 17 Aug. 1912 (Hannen-Knobloch family papers, B9, US National Bahá'í Archives).
14. 'Our Weekly Boston Letter', *Springfield Daily Republican* (MA), 24 Aug. 1912, p. 17, col. 2. On 15 Aug., the *Springfield Daily Republican* had published a further reference to 'Abdu'l-Bahá in a literary article by a Boston correspondent – perhaps the same one who attended Green Acre – who wrote about ancient Persia. The article was introduced with the following words: 'The new attention excited by

Persia in the religious world since the Koranic reformer, Abbas Effendi or Abdul Baha, has appeared in person among English and American Christians speaking in Persian, writing in Arabic, and preaching a doctrine of peace and good-will, very unlike the violent texts of the Arabs, give a new interest to the share that Persia had of old in the religions and philosophies of Jews and Gentiles.' 'Our Boston Literary Letter', *Springfield Daily Republican* (MA), 15 Aug. 1912, p. 3, col. 5.

15. 'Abdul Baha at Green Acre Conferences', *Biddeford Weekly Journal* (ME), 6 Sept. 1912.
16. *Lewiston Evening Journal* (ME), 26 Aug. 1912, n.t.
17. 'Persian to Plead for World Peace', *Boston Post*, 23 Aug. 1912. The article included a large portrait of 'Abdu'l-Bahá, the caption of which read: 'Abdul Baha, who is to make several addresses in Boston for Universal Peace'. Another announcement was also published as 'In the Public Eye', in the *Boston Advertiser*, 27 Aug. 1912, p. 4, col. 5.
18. 'Abdul Baha Coming Here', *Malden Mail* (MA), 22 Aug. 1912, p. 1, col. 5. According to this newspaper, Miss Wilson moved to '127 Main Street while 'Abdu'l-Bahá and His party stayed at her house. See also 'Abdul Baha Here', *Malden Mail* (MA), 24 Aug. 1912, p. 1, col. 7; 'Wealthy Woman Gives Up Her Home', *Malden News* (MA), 24 Aug. 1912, p. 4, col. 4. This newspaper had a circulation of 6,700 copies.
19. See 'Abdu'l-Bahá, *Promulgation*, pp. 276–80.
20. 'Abdul Baha Returns', *Evening Transcript* (Boston), 26 Aug. 1912, p. 4, col. 6.
21. See 'Abdu'l-Bahá, *Promulgation*, pp. 280–4.
22. 'Baha Talks on Sex Equality', *Boston Post*, 27 Aug. 1912, p. 7, col. 2.
23. See ibid. and 'Personal and Social News', *Boston Herald*, 26 Aug. 1912, p. 5, col. 5; 'Personal and Social News', 27 Aug. 1912, p. 5, col. 4.
24. Abby Ellen Beale Morey was a former Rosicrucian. She studied piano, organ and vocal music in Germany, Italy and England. Once back in America she combined her work directing a chorus and an orchestra she herself created through her music teaching.
25. For the text of this talk see 'Abdu'l-Bahá, *Promulgation*, pp. 200–96.
26. 'Abdul Beha Abbas a Guest', *Boston Transcript*, 31 Aug. 1912, p. 4, col. 2.
27. 'Boudoir Chat', *Malden Mirror* (MA), 7 Sept. 1912, p. 1, col. 5.
28. 'Johnson Breed', *Boston Evening Transcript*, 29 Aug. 1912. For an account of the wedding see Gail, *Arches of the Years*, p. 90.
29. 'Abdul Baha Leaves Malden', *Malden Mail* (MA), 30 Aug. 1912, p. 1, col. 3.

19. Canada

1. For the list of participants at the Lake Mohonk Conference see *Report of the Eighteenth Annual Lake Mohonk Conference on International Arbitration*, pp. 206–10.
2. Nakhjavani, *Maxwells of Montreal*, vol. 1, p. 279.
3. 'Persian Teacher to Preach Peace', *Montreal Gazette*, 29 Aug. 1912; 'Visite d'un Pacificateur Persan', *La Presse* (Montreal), p. 7, col. 4; 'Abdul Baha, Prophet of Peace to Visit Canada', *Family Herald and Weekly Star* (Montreal), 1 Sept. 1912.
4. *Free Press* (Burlington, VT), 31 Aug. 1912.
5. See Balyuzi, *'Abdu'l-Bahá*, p. 257. For the press coverage of 'Abdu'l-Bahá's visit to

Montreal see also van den Hoonard, *Origins of the Bahá'í Community*, pp. 43–70, 300–1.

6. 'Apostle of Peace Here Predicts an Appalling War in the Old World', *Montreal Daily Star*, 31 Aug. 1912, p. 1, col. 1.
7. *Standard* (Montreal), 31 Aug. 1912, p. 13, col. 1. The article includes a portrait. The article was reprinted on 7 Sept. 1912, p. 13, col. 1.
8. 'News of the Churches', *Montreal Gazette*, 31 Aug. 1912, p. 11, col. 1.
9. See 'Abdu'l-Bahá, *Promulgation*, pp. 297–302. For Persian notes of this talk see 'Abdu'l-Bahá, *Majmu'ih-i-Khatábát-i-Hadrat-i-'Abdu'l-Bahá*, vol. 2, pp. 224–32.
10. 'Persian Preacher in Flowing Robes Calls for Unity', *Montreal Daily Star*, 2 Sept. 1912, p. 2, col. 1.
11. 'Racialism Wrong, Says Eastern Sage', *Montreal Gazette* (Montreal), 2 Sept. 1912, p. 6, col. 1.
12. 'Abdul Baha's Doctrine', *Montreal Daily Witness*, 3 Sept. 1912, p. 4, col. 4.
13. 'Un Prophète Persan', *La Patrie* (Montreal), 4 Sept. 1912, p. 9, col. 3.
14. 'Abdul Baha's Word to Canada', *Star Weekly* (Toronto), 11 Sept. 1912.
15. 'Abdul Baha in Canada', *Cayley Hustler* (Cayley, Alberta), 18 Dec. 1912, p. 4, col. 6.
16. 'Abdul Baha in Canada', *Redcliff Review* (Redcliff, Alberta), 13 Dec. 1912, p. 4, col. 6.
17. See 'Abdu'l-Bahá, *Promulgation*, pp. 308–12. For Persian notes see 'Abdu'l-Bahá, *Majmu'ih-i-Khatábát-i-Hadrat-i-'Abdu'l-Bahá*, vol. 2, pp. 233–9.
18. 'Materialism no Philosophy, Says Oriental Seer', *Montreal Daily Star*, 3 Sept. 1912, p. 9, col. 5.
19. 'Materialists Like Animals', *Montreal Gazette*, 3 Sept. 1912, p. 16, col. 1.
20. For English notes of this talk see *'Abdu'l-Bahá in Canada*, pp. 10–13.
21. 'Earth Should be Paradise, Says Seer Abdul Baha', *Montreal Daily Star*, 4 Sept. 1912, p. 2, col. 1.
22. *Le Nationaliste* (Montreal), 8 Sept. 1912, p. 1, col. 4.
23. 'Apostle of Peace Meets Socialists', *Montreal Gazette*, 4 Sept. 1912, p. 2, col. 3.
24. 'Man's Dependence', *Montreal Daily Witness*, 4 Sept. 1912, p. 8, col. 4.
25. *Le Canada* (Montreal), 4 Sept. 1912, p. 8, col. 3. A similar but shorter article was published the same day as 'Une Conferénce de Abdul Baha', in *Le Devoir*, p. 3.
26. 'Une Conferénce de Abdul Baha, le sage Turc', *La Presse* (Montreal), 4 Sept. 1912, p. 5.
27. 'Socialism Not Cure for Evils of Present Day', *Montreal Daily Star*, 5 Sept. 1912, p. 2, col. 1.
28. 'Socialism Must Be Met', *Montreal Gazette*, 5 Sept. 1912, p. 4, col. 4.
29. 'Abdul Baha's Views', *Montreal Daily Witness*, 5 Sept. 1912, 11, col. 6.
30. See 'Abdu'l Bahá, *Promulgation*, pp. 312–19.
31. 'World Peace Urged by Abdul Baha in Closing Message', *Montreal Daily Star*, 5 Sept. 1912, p. 6, col. 4.
32. 'Apostle of Peace Said Farewell', *Montreal Gazette*, 6 Sept. 1912, p. 4, col. 2.
33. 'Investigate the Realities', *Montreal Daily Witness*, 6 Sept. 1912, p. 11, col. 2.
34. 'Départ d'Abdul Baha', *La Presse* (Montreal), 6 Sept. 1912, p. 14.
35. 'Le Prophète Abdul Baha', *Le Devoir* (Montreal), 6 Sept. 1912, p. 5.
36. 'Le Prestige de l'Exotisme', *La Patrie* (Montreal), 6 Sept. 1912, p. 9.

37. *Montreal Daily Star*, 11 Sept. 1912, p. 2.
38. 'War Must Precede Universal Peace', *Montreal Daily Star*, 11 Sept. 1912, p. 12, col. 1.
39. 'Church and Bench Give a Farewell Tribute to Sage', *Montreal Daily Herald*, 6 Sept. 1912, p. 5.
40. 'Message of the Great Persian Reformer', *Manitoba Free Press* (Winnipeg), 19 Sept. 1912, p. 9, col. 3.
41. 'Abdul Baha in Canada', *Christian Commonwealth* (London), 2 Oct. 1912, p. 13.

20. Buffalo

1. 'Advocate of Universal Religion Coming Here', *Buffalo Express*, 28 Apr. 1912, p. 25, col. 5.
2. 'Abdul Baha, Priest of Akka Comes to Buffalo on Wednesday', *Buffalo Express*, 5 May 1912, p. 6, col. 7.
3. 'Bahaist Leader Does Not Arrive', *Buffalo Express*, 9 May 1912.
4. 'Abdul Baha in Washington', *Buffalo Express*, 11 May 1912, p. 5, col. 5.
5. 'Abdul Baha on the Way', *Illustrated Buffalo Express*, 1 Sept. 1912, p. 1, col. 5.
6. 'Abdul Baba Abbas Comes to Buffalo', *Buffalo Commercial*, 10 Sept. 1912, p. 9, col. 6.
7. 'Prophet of Peace Comes to Buffalo', *Buffalo Evening Times*, 10 Sept. 1912, p. 4, col. 3. Portrait included.
8. 'Prophet and Prince of Royal Persian Blood in Buffalo', *Buffalo Enquirer*, 10 Sept. 1912, p. 1, col. 3 (continued on p. 5, col. 4).
9. 'Persian Leader on Visit to Converts', *Buffalo Evening News*, 10 Sept. 1912, p. 9, col. 2.
10. 'Persian Teacher Abdul Baha Abbas, Scents Great War', *Buffalo Evening Times*, 11 Sept. 1912, p. 1, col. 4.
11. 'Persian Peace Apostle Predicts War in Europe', *Buffalo Courier*, 11 Sept. 1912, p. 7, col. 2.
12. 'Message of Love Conveyed by Baha', *Buffalo Enquirer*, 11 Sept. 1912, p. 5, col. 3.
13. 'Urges America to Spread Peace', *Buffalo Commercial*, 11 Sept. 1912, p. 14, col. 3.
14. See Zarqání, *Maḥmúd's Diary*, p. 254.
15. 'Abdul Baha an Optimist', *Buffalo Express*, 11 Sept. 1912, p. 1, col. 1.
16. 'Abdul Baha Leaves Today', *Buffalo Express*, 12 Sept. 1912, p. 5, col. 4.
17. 'Abdul Baha Abbas Leaves for Chicago', *Buffalo Commercial*, 12 Sept. 1912, p. 5, col. 4.
18. 'Abdul Baha Has Gone to Chicago', *Buffalo Enquirer*, 12 Sept. 1912, p. 6, col. 1. A very similar article was published as 'Equality and Peace Abdul Baha's Topic', in *Buffalo Evening News*, 12 Sept. 1912, p. 8, col. 1.
19. 'Persian Peace Apostle Would Prevent War', *Buffalo Courier*, 12 Sept. 1912, p. 7, col. 3.
20. 'A Visit With Abdul Baha at Haifa', *Buffalo Examiner*, 19 Sept. 1912. See chapter 3 above.

21. En Route to California

1. *Day Book* (Chicago), 13 Sept. 1912, p. 13, n. t.
2. 'Abdul Baha Visiting Here', *Chicago Examiner*, 13 Sept. 1912, p. 9, col. 4. In New Jersey the Trenton *Evening Times* briefly mentioned in an article about the Bahá'í House of Worship that 'Baha will return to Boston soon from a Canadian tour. He will then consider plans for establishing a temple, it is said.' See 'Will Give Toward Bahaist Temple', *Evening Times* (Trenton, NJ), 4 Sept. 1912, p. 14, col. 5.
3. See 'Abdu'l-Bahá, *Promulgation*, pp. 320–4.
4. 'Rich Chicagoans Pay Homage to Abdul Baha', *Chicago Examiner*, 14 Sept. 1912, p. 11, col. 1.
5. For Persian notes of this talk see 'Abdu'l-Bahá, *Majmu'ih-i-Khatábát-i-Hadrat-i-'Abdu'l-Bahá*, vol. 2, pp. 240–4.
6. 'Abdul Baha Coming', *Kenosha Evening News*, 14 Sept. 1912, p. 1, col. 7.
7. 'Hear Great Leader', *Kenosha Evening News*, 15 Sept. 1912, p. 1, col. 1.
8. 'Plans for Abdul Baha', *St. Paul Pioneer Press* (St Paul, MN), 5 June 1912.
9. *Appeal* (St Paul, MN), 8 June 1912, p. 2, col. 4. Also published on 22 June 1912, p. 2, col. 4 and 29 June 1912, p. 2, col. 4.
10. 'Head of Bahaists Arrives Tonight', *Minneapolis Journal*, 18 Sept. 1912, p. 7, col. 4. 'Persian Teacher a Visitor', *Minneapolis Tribune*, 18 Sept. 1913, p. 12, col. 6 (includes portrait). See also 'Servant of Glory Comes to City From Far East', *Minneapolis Tribune*, 19 Sept. 1912, p. 12, col. 5.
11. 'Bahaist Leader, in Minneapolis, Tells of Mission', *Minneapolis Journal*, 19 Sept. 1912, p. 1, col. 1 (continued on p. 3, col. 5).
12. 'Head of Bahaists is in Twin City', *St. Paul Dispatch* (MN), 19 Sept. 1912, p. 4, col. 2.
13. 'Prophet of Glory Visits Minneapolis', *Minneapolis Morning Tribune*, 20 Sept. 1912, p. 7, col. 1. The article included a picture of 'Abdu'l-Bahá taken in Minneapolis with a group of Bahá'ís.
14. Zarqání, *Maḥmúd's Diary*, p. 272.
15. For Persian notes of this talk see 'Abdu'l-Bahá, *Majmu'ih-i-Khatábát-i-Hadrat-i-'Abdu'l-Bahá*, vol. 2, pp. 245–54.
16. 'Temple Shaari Tov', *Minneapolis Morning Tribune*, 23 Sept. 1912, p. 10, col. 3.
17. 'Preaches Doctrine of Universal Love', *Pioneer Press* (St Paul, MN), 20 Sept. 1912, p. 12, col. 1.
18. 'Abdul Baha in Awe Contemplates Styles', *Minneapolis Morning Tribune*, 21 Sept. 1912, p. 18, col. 1.
19. 'Head of Bahaists is in Twin City', *St. Paul Dispatch*, 20 Sept. 1912, p. 7, col. 5.
20. *The Appeal* (St Paul, MN), 21 Sept. 1912, p. 2, col. 2, n. t.
21. 'Urges All Races to Single Faith', *Pioneer Press* (St Paul), 21 Sept. 1912, p. 9, col. 1 (includes portrait).
22. 'Educators Meet Abdul Baha Abbas', *Minneapolis Journal*, 20 Sept. 1912, p. 10, col. 1. The Walker Art Gallery was located at the time at 803 Hennepin Avenue at the residence of the successful businessman Thomas Barlow Walker (1840–1928).
23. 'The Northwestern Bellman', *Bellman* (Minneapolis), 28 Sep. 1912, p. 406.
24. 'Persian, With Title of Prophet, in Omaha', *Omaha Daily News*, 23 Sept. 1912.
25. Translated by Faríd. A digital image of the prayer is available at http://www.

nebraskahistory.org/lib-arch/research/treasures/bahai_bryan.htm (last accessed 12 Oct. 2011).

26. 'Persian Peace Advocate Pays Visit to Lincoln', *Lincoln Daily News*, 23 Sept. 1912, p. 1, col. 5.
27. 'Abbas Brings New Creed to Lincoln', *Lincoln Daily Star*, 23 Sept. 1912, p. 4.
28. The fact that the accounts of the arrival of 'Abdu'l-Bahá were published one day after the date given by Maḥmud indicates that the actual date of the arrival of 'Abdu'l-Bahá in the city was Tuesday 24th and not Monday 23rd.
29. See 'Abdul Baha, Head of Bahaism to Visit Believers in Denver', *Denver Post*, 22 Sept. 1912, p. 6, col 4; and 'Abdul Baha Coming, Persian Prophet Teaches New Faith', *Rocky Mountains News* (Denver, CO), 22 Sept. 1912. The author of this last article was probably Kate Russell.
30. Alice Rohe (1876–1957) was a graduate of Kansas University. She started her career as a journalist in the Kansas *City World* and the *City Star*. In Denver she had worked for the *Rocky Mountain News*, where she had a permanent column, the *Denver Times* and the *Denver Post*. Later she moved to New York and worked for the *Evening World*. From 1914 she worked for United Press, becoming the first woman to work for an international press association. She was sent as correspondent to Rome and was also the first woman to interview Benito Mussolini.
31. 'New John the Baptist Preaching Universal Brotherhood', *Rocky Mountains News* (Denver, CO), 25 Sept. 1912.
32. The caption wrongly identified Na<u>kh</u>javání as 'Mirza Asadullah'.
33. This is the picture mentioned by Maḥmúd (see Zarqání, *Maḥmúd's Diary*, p. 284). Maḥmúd dated wrongly the visit to Denver by one day.
34. Frances Wayne (1871–1951) was the daughter of the Colorado member of the House of Representatives James Beldford. She started her career as a journalist in 1906 working for the *Rocky Mountains News*. Soon after, she was hired by the *Denver Post* where she worked as one of its senior journalists for nearly 40 years.
35. 'Abdul Baha Abbas, Persian Teacher, to Convert Denver', *Denver Post*, 25 Sept. 1912, p. 3, col. 2.
36. 'Message of Universal Religion is Brought by Persian', *Denver Express*, 25 Sept. 1912.
37. See 'Abdu'l-Bahá, *Promulgation*, pp. 234–7, and *Star of the West*, 4 Nov. 1913, pp. 219–20, 226.
38. 'Persian Prophet Pleads for Union of All Religions', *Republican* (Denver, CO), 26 Sept. 1912.
39. Probably Rev. Charles Edgar Prather. It should be noted that at the time Denver was the headquarters of Divine Science.
40. See 'Abdu'l-Bahá, *Promulgation*, pp. 337–42.
41. 'Women Back Abdul Ba-ha, Few Men Attend Service', *Denver Post*, 26 Sept. 1912, p. 7, col. 1.
42. 'Universal Peace and Religion Theme of Persian Nobleman, Guest of Denver', *Rocky Mountains News* (Denver, CO), 26 Sept. 1912.
43. 'Leader of Religious Cult Tours Country', *News* (New Castle, PA), 8 Oct. 1912, p. 12, col. 5.
44. 'Abdul Baha', *Wet Mountain Times* (Westcliffe, CO), 4 Oct. 1912, p.8, col. 1.
45. In *Maḥmúd's Diary* it is stated that 'Abdu'l-Bahá left Denver at 9:00 a.m.,

reaching Glenwood Springs at 2:00 a.m (see pp. 291–2). However, the distance between the two places is only 157 miles. It is very improbable, therefore, that the train would take 17 hours to cover that distance. It would be more plausible that 'Abdu'l-Bahá left on the evening of 26 September, as stated in the *Republican*.

46. *Salt Lake Tribune* (UT), 30 Sept. 1912, p. 14, col. 6; also published as 'Comes to Lecture on Bahai Religion', *Evening Standard* (Odgen, UT), 30 Sept. 1912, p. 5, col. 4. A summary was also published in the *Salt Lake Telegram* (UT), 30 Sept. 1912, p. 12, col. 4. 'To speak on Religion' and in 'City Brevities', *Salt Lake Herald* (Salt Lake, UT), 1 Oct. 1912, p. 12, col. 3.
47. Cable from Sohrab to Helen Goodall, 30 Sept. 1912 (Helen Goodall papers, B10, US National Bahá'í Archives). Sohrab states that 10,000 people were present but the building had a capacity of only 7,000.
48. Joseph H. Hannen, 'With Abdul Baha in America', *Christian Commonwealth* (London), 6 Nov. 1912, p. 100.

22. California

1. 'Famous Persian Reaches America', *Oakland Tribune*, 11 Apr. 1912, p. 5, col. 2–3 (includes picture).
2. '40 Years in Jail Brings Wisdom', *San Francisco Examiner*, 25 Sept. 1912.
3. 'Persian Teacher Coming Here to Preach Bahaism', *San Francisco Chronicle*, 29 Sept. 1912, p. 30, col. 3.
4. 'Abdu'l-Bahá left Salt Lake City on the Southern Pacific train no. 5, which made a brief stop in Montello, Nevada. Cable from Sohrab to Helen Goodall, 1 Oct. 1912 (Helen Goodall papers, B10, US National Bahá'í Archives).
5. For published accounts and sources about the first visit of 'Abdu'l-Bahá to San Francisco see 'Abdu'l-Bahá, *Promulgation*, pp. 343–80; Zarqání, *Maḥmúd's Diary*, pp. 299–353; Frances O. Allen, 'Abdul Baha in San Francisco,' *Star of the West*, 16 Oct. 1912 (3:12), pp. 9–10, and 4 Nov. 1912 (3:13), pp. 11–13; Ward, *239 Days*, pp. 165–72.
6. 'Venerable Persian Arrives', *San Francisco Bulletin*, 2 Oct. 1912. See also 'Baha', *San Francisco News Daily*, 2 Oct. 1912, p. 1, col. 3.
7. 'Abdul Baha Abbas, Noted Persian Teacher Arrives', *San Francisco Chronicle*, 4 Oct. 1912, p. 9, col. 2.
8. 'Suffrage Advocate Sex Equality Need for Progress', *San Francisco Examiner*, 4 Oct. 1912.
9. 'Aged Persian, a Prisoner for Half a Century, Comes to America to Preach the Gospel of Universal Peace', *American* (Fort Smith, AR), 13 Oct. 1912. This Democratic newspaper had a circulation of 6,800 copies.
10. 'Aged Persian Prisoner for Half a Century Comes to America to Preach Gospel of Universal Religion', *Fort Wayne Sentinel* (IN), 8 Nov. 1912, p. 2, col. 1.
11. See *Star of the West*, 16 Oct. 1913 (4:12), pp. 206–7.
12. 'Abdul Baha, Persian Savant, Discusses on Esperanto', *Alameda Times* (CA), 4 Oct. 1912.
13. 'Persian Prophet to Lecture Here', *Oakland Tribune* (CA), 4 Oct. 1912, p. 3, col. 1.
14. 'Leader of Bahaists Makes Lecture Dates', *San Francisco Bulletin*, 7 Oct. 1912. A similar but shorter announcement had been published in the same journal two

days before under the title 'Abdul Baha to Speak from Unitarian Pulpit'.

15. Braford Leavitt (b. 1868) was a Harvard-educated minister. He served as pastor of the First Unitarian Church of San Francisco from 1900 to 1913. He had previously been minister at the All Souls Church in Washington (1897–1900).
16. 'First Unitarian Church', Ella Cooper Papers, US National Bahá'í Archives, p. 10; notes by Bijou Straun. For Persian notes of this talk see 'Abdu'l-Bahá, *Majmu'ih-i-Khatábát-i-Hadrat-i-'Abdu'l-Bahá*, vol. 2, pp. 255–66.
17. 'Abdul Baba Brings Gospel of Peace', *San Francisco Examiner*, 7 Oct. 1912.
18. 'Peace is Topic of Abdul Baha', *San Francisco Bulletin*, 7 Oct. 1912.
19. 'Abdul Baha Preaches Peace and Brotherhood', *San Francisco Post*, 7 Oct. 1912.
20. 'Abdul Baha Abbas Says Object of Mission is to Unify All Creeds', *San Francisco Chronicle*, 8 Oct. 1912.
21. 'Abdul Baha Speaks', *Sacramento Bee*, 7 Oct. 1912.
22. *Pacific Unitarian* (San Francisco), Dec. 1912, p. 37.
23. 'Abdul Baha to Give Lecture in Oakland', *San Francisco Bulletin*, 4 Oct. 1912.
24. 'Persian to Lecture on Universal Peace', *San Francisco Call*, 4 Oct. 1912.
25. 'Abdul Baha Will Speak', *San Francisco Examiner*, 5 Oct. 1912.
26. 'New Church to be Dedicated', *Oakland Tribune*, 5 Oct. 1912, p. 9, col. 1.
27. 'Abdul Baha to Speak', *Berkeley Gazette*, 5 Oct. 1912. This note also reported that 'Baha is arranging for a meeting in Berkeley'.
28. David Starr Jordan (1851–1931) was a naturalist trained at Cornell University. He held various teaching positions and in 1885 was appointed president of Indiana University, where he had been teaching since 1879. In 1891 he was appointed president of Stanford University, a position he held until 1913. He was a member and officer of several scientific societies and author of many scientific works and articles. Starr Jordan was also a nationally known and respected pacifist and from 1900 to 1914 presided over the World Peace Foundation. He was also author of various essays on international politics and peace.
29. Letter of Ahmad Sohrab to David Starr Jordan, 14 Feb. 1912, Ahmad Sohrab Papers B11, US National Bahá'í Archives. Jordan's sent the invitation to 'Abdu'l-Bahá through the Persian–American Educational Society.
30. See for instance 'Abdul Baha to talk at Stanford', *San Jose Herald*, 3 Oct. 1912.
31. 'Jordan not Ready to Abandon Reins', *San Francisco Call*, 2 Oct. 1912, p. 5, col. 3.
32. 'Doctor Jordan Denies Report', *Palo Altan*, 4 Oct. 1912.
33. 'Venerable Persian Will Talk Peace in Assembly Tomorrow', *Daily Palo Alto*, 7 Oct. 1912, p. 1, col. 2.
34. Ella Cooper Papers, US National Bahá'í Archives.
35. For English notes of the talk see 'Abdu'l-Bahá, *Promulgation*, pp. 348–55, and *Star of the West*, 16 Oct. 1912 (3:12), pp. 10–14. For Persian notes see 'Abdu'l-Bahá, *Majmu'ih-i-Khatábát-i-Hadrat-i-'Abdu'l-Bahá*, vol. 2, pp. 267–79.
36. 'Persian Indicts the Futility of War', *Daily Palo Alto*, 8 Oct. 1912, pp. 1 and 3.
37. 'Palo Alto Hears Abbas Effendi', *Palo Alto Times*, 9 Oct. 1912, p. 1, col. 3.
38. 'Palo Alto Hears Abbas Effendi', *Palo Altan*, 11 Oct. 1912, p. 7, col. 1.
39. 'Abdul Baha Speaks at Stanford University', *Palo Alto Times*, 11 Oct. 1912, p. 7; 'Abdul Baha Speaks at Stanford University', *Palo Altan*, 18 Oct. 1912, p. 6.
40. ibid.
41. ibid.

42. 'Persian Apostle of Peace Makes Plea', *San Francisco Chronicle*, 10 Oct. 1912, p. 9, col. 6. Similar information was published on the same day as 'Plea for Peace Made by Persian Apostle', in the *Oakland Tribune*, p. 9, col. 3.
43. 'Leland Stanford', *New York Times*, 10 Nov. 1912, p. 13, col. 7.
44. See 'Lectures, Recitals, Literary Contests, Honors and Clubs', *Twenty-Second Annual Register 1912–1913*, p. 206.
45. Jordan, *Days of a Man*, vol. 2 (1922).
46. Rev. Clarence Reed was the longest serving minister at the church, from 1909 to 1915. He was also the author of two pamphlets: *The Fine Art of Living* and *The Worth of Friendship*.
47. 'Message to the Church', *Palo Altan*, 1 Nov. 1912, p. 3, col. 1. For Persian notes of this talk see 'Abdu'l-Bahá, *Majmu'ih-i-Khatábát-i-Hadrat-i-'Abdu'l-Bahá*, vol. 2, pp. 280–8.
48. Ella Cooper Papers, US National Bahá'í Archives.
49. 'Mrs. Isabelle Merriman of Palo Alto May Go to Far East in Aid of Charitable Work', *Evening News* (San Jose, CA), 12 Oct. 1912, p. 5, col. 2.
50. ibid.
51. 'Persian Prophet's Call Heeded by Woman of Palo Alto', *Oakland Tribune*, 12 Oct. 1912, p. 12, col. 1. Similar articles were published as 'Charitable Woman may Aid Bahaism' in the *San Francisco Call*, 12 Oct. 1912, p. 1, col. 3; as 'Woman Heeds Call of Persian Prophet', in the *San Francisco Examiner*, 12 Oct. 1912; as 'Palo Alto Woman is Convert of Abdul Baha' in the *Modesto News*, 14 Oct. 1912; and as 'Beginning Charity at Home', in the *Seattle Daily Times*, 18 Oct. 1912, p. 2, col. 2.
52. See Zarqání, *Maḥmúd's Diary*, pp. 309–10.
53. 'Abdul Baha to Speak at Berkeley', *Berkeley Independent*, 3 Oct. 1912. A similar article was published the same day in the *Berkeley Daily Gazette*, p. 1, col. 5.
54. 'Abdul-Baha Here Tomorrow Night', *Berkeley Daily Gazette*, 8 Oct. 1912, p. 1, col. 4. This journal also published announcements on 3 Oct. 1912, p. 1, col. 5 ('Abdul Baha to Speak in Berkeley') and 5 Oct. 1912, p. 5, col. 1 ('Abdul Baha to Speak').
55. 'Abdul Baha to be Speaker at Berkeley', *Oakland Tribune*, 9 Oct. 1912, p. 12, col. 5 and 'Abdul Baha to Speak on Faith', *Oakland Enquirer*, 9 Oct. 1912.
56. 'Persian Philosopher to Speak at the Open Forum', *San Francisco Bulletin*, 5 Oct. 1912. The *Bulletin* published a further announcement on 5 Oct.: 'Abdul Baha to Speak Tonight'. For the English notes of this talk see 'Abdu'l-Bahá, *Promulgation*, pp. 355–61. For the Persian notes see 'Abdu'l-Bahá, *Majmu'ih-i-Khatábát-i-Hadrat-i-'Abdu'l-Bahá*, vol. 2, pp. 298–307.
57. Martin Abraham Meyer (1879–1923) was a renowned Jewish scholar who served as a reform rabbi at Temple Emanu El from 1910 till his death. He was also a lecturer in Semitics at the University of California. The meeting was briefly announced under the title "City News' in the weekly *Emanu-El* (San Francisco), 11 Oct. 1912, p. 5, col. 1.
58. See 'Abdu'l-Bahá, *Promulgation*, pp. 361–70, and 'Message to the Jews', *Star of the West*, 4 Nov. 1912 (3:13), pp. 3–8. For Persian notes of this talk see 'Abdu'l-Bahá, *Majmu'ih-i-Khatábát-i-Hadrat-i-'Abdu'l-Bahá*, vol. 2, 307–19.
59. 'Bahaist Leader in Jewish Pulpit Pleads Unity', *San Francisco Post*, 12 Oct. 1912.

60. 'Persian Heard at Temple Emanu-El', *San Francisco Chronicle*, 13 Oct. 1912, p. 48, col. 5.
61. 'Abdul Baha Devotes Talk to Universal Peace', *San Francisco Examiner*, 13 Oct. 1912.
62. 'Message to the Jews', *Palo Altan* (Palo Alto, CA), 1 Nov. 1912, p. 3, col. 1.
63. Ella Cooper papers, US National Bahá'í Archives.
64. 'The Fundamental Unity of All Religions', *Christian Commonwealth*, 1 Jan. 1913, pp. 263–4, col. 2.
65. *Christian Commonwealth*, 11 Dec. 1912, p. 206.
66. See the talk at Pembroke Chapel (chapter 26, vol. 2).
67. See the talk at the Westminster Palace Hotel (chapter 26, vol. 2).
68. Sohrab, Letter to Harriet Magee, 14 Apr. 1913, p. 8.
69. Sohrab, Letter to Harriet Magee, 20 April 1913, p. 5. The Bahá'í was Mr Herrigel.
70. John Daniel Barry graduated from Harvard University in 1888 and moved to San Francisco in 1910 where he worked as a columnist for the *San Francisco Bulletin* and soon became a noted chronicler of San Francisco life. He was also author of novels and essays dealing with contemporary San Francisco.
71. 'Ways of the World', *San Francisco Bulletin*, 12 Oct. 1912, editorial page.
72. 'Ways of the World', *San Francisco Bulletin*, 13 Oct. 1912, editorial page.
73. 'Bahai Leader a Stoic', *San Francisco Call*, 14 Oct. 1912, pp. 1–2.
74. 'Palo Alto Society', *San Francisco Call*, 20 Oct. 1912, p. 54, col. 5.
75. Probably Rev Dr William Rader (1863–1930), who for 36 years served as Congregationalist minister. At the time of the publication of this article he was pastor at the Calvary Church in San Francisco.
76. 'Cross Vs. Crescent', *San Jose Mercury* (CA), 14 Oct. 1912, p. 14, col. 1.
77. 'Persian Teacher Who is Now Preaching Bahaism in 'Frisco', *Coos Bay Times* (Marshfield, OR), 17 Oct. 1912, p. 3, col. 5.
78. 'Persian Mystic Lands', *Morning Oregonian* (Portland), 4 Oct. 1912, p. 26, col. 3.
79. 'Shrine of Bahaism Drawing Many Here', *Los Angeles Sunday Times*, 28 Dec. 1912, p. 1b, col. 6.
80. 'Noted Persian is Here to Plead for Peace', *Los Angeles Herald*, 19 Oct. 1912.
81. 'Abdul Baha Abbas is in Los Angeles', *Los Angeles Tribune*, 20 Oct. 1912.
82. 'Twenty Million Followers', *Los Angeles Times*, 20 Oct. 1912, p. 14, col. 1. (The passage quoted here is preceded by a short introduction to the Bahá'í Faith). This seems to be the same statement that Maḥmúd reproduces in Zarqání, *Maḥmúd's Diary*, pp. 337–8.
83. 'Foreign Tongue Soothes', *Los Angeles Times*, 21 Oct. 1912, p. 10, col. 1.
84. 'Persian Prophet, Leader of Baha Movement, Lectures on Doctrines', *Sacramento Union*, 26 Oct. 1912.
85. 'Noted Persian Teacher Here Pleads for Universal Peace', *Sacramento Bee*, 26 Oct. 1912, p. 1, col. 1.
86. 'Persia Priest Lectures Here', *Sacramento Star*, 26 Oct. 1912.
87. 'Women Grovel to Persian Prophet', *Sacramento Union*, 27 Oct. 1912, p. 1, col. 2.
88. Ella Cooper papers, US National Bahá'í Archives. Ahmad Sohrab acted as translator.

89. *Palo Altan*, 1 Nov. 1912, p. 4, col. 5, n.t. This Tablet was translated by Ahmad Sohrab on 17 Oct.
90. 'Abdul Baha, Abbas Effendi', *Palo Altan*, 11 Oct. 1912, and 'The New Evangel', *Palo Altan*, 1 Nov. 1912, p. 2, col. 1.
91. See Preface.

23. Return to the East Coast

1. See Zarqání, *Maḥmúd's Diary*, p. 356.
2. 'Bahian Prophet Returns After a Trip to Coast', *Denver Post*, 29 Oct. 1912, p. 7, col. 1.
3. *Day Book* (Chicago), 1 Nov. 1912, p. 6, n.t.
4. 'Peace Advocate in Chicago', *Inter-Ocean* (Chicago), 1 Nov. 1912.
5. 'Abdul Baha, Advocate of Universal Religion, Will Greet Local Believers', *Cincinnati Times-Star*, 4 Nov. 1912, p. 8, col. 1.
6. 'Cult Members to Hail Their Prophet', *Cincinnati Post*, 4 Nov. 1912, p. 8, col. 1.
7. See 'Abdu'l-Bahá, *Promulgation*, pp. 388–9, and *Star of the West*, 27 Sept. 1915 (6:11), pp. 81–2. For Persian notes of this talk see 'Abdu'l-Bahá, *Majmu'ih-i-Khatábát-i-Hadrat-i-'Abdu'l-Bahá*, vol. 2, pp. 321–5.
8. 'Explains Bahaism', *Cincinnati Post*, 5 Nov. 1912, p. 3.
9. 'Explains Bahaism', *Cincinnati Enquirer*, 5 Nov. 1912, p. 14.
10. 'World Peace Dream Mantles Lecturer', *Commercial Tribune*, 5 Nov. 1912.
11. 'Baha-Allah's Message to People of America', *Cincinnati Times-Star*, 6 Nov. 1912, p. 18.
12. 'Lectures on Bahaism', *Washington Herald*, 2 Nov. 1912, p. 2, col. 5.
13. 'Abdul Baha Back on Capital Visit', *Washington Times*, 6 Nov. 1912, p. 7, col. 1.
14. See 'Abdu'l-Bahá, *Promulgation*, pp. 390–7, and *Star of the West*, 4 Nov. 1914 (5:13), pp. 195–9.
15. 'Head of Bahaists Will Speak Again', *Washington Times*, 7 Nov. 1912, p. 6, col. 6.
16. 'Abdul Baha Talks of Universal Peace', *Washington Herald*, 7 Nov. 1912, p. 5, col. 5.
17. 'Dr. Van Schaik Urges Study of All Cults', *Evening Star*, 7 Nov. 1912.
18. The English translation is dated 19 Nov. 1912. Ahmad Sohrab to Joseph Hannen (Hannen-Knobloch family papers, B9, US National Bahá'í Archives).
19. Rev. Dr. Abram Simon was acquainted with Joseph Hannen and Hannen suggested to Simon in a letter dated 29 March 1911 that he invite 'Abdu'l-Bahá to speak to his congregation (Hannen to Simon, Hannen-Knobloch family papers, B23, US National Bahá'í Archives).
20. 'Abdul Baha to Speak', *Washington Herald*, 8 Nov. 1912, p. 2, col. 3.
21. 'Speaks on Universal Peace', *Washington Herald*, 9 Nov. 1912, p. 7, col. 5.
22. 'Appeals to the Jews', *Washington Post*, 9 Nov. 1912, p. 3, col. 2.
23. 'Abdul Baha Attracts Attention on U.S. Tour', *Washington Herald*, 10 Nov. 1912, p. 8, col. 2.
24. 'Capital Woman Leader of Bahaism in United States', *Washington Times*, 10 Nov. 1912, p. 6, col. 1.
25. 'Abdul Baha Coming', *Sun* (Baltimore), 6 Apr. 1912, p. 8, col. 4.
26. 'Abdul Baha Within Week', *Sun* (Baltimore), 15 Apr. 1912, p. 6, col. 4.

27. 'Persian May Yet Speak', *Sun* (Baltimore), 20 Apr. 1912.
28. 'Abdul Baha Expected', *Star* (Baltimore), 20 Apr. 1912.
29. 'Abdul Baha Here Tomorrow', *Sun* (Baltimore), 10 Nov. 1912, p. 12, col. 3. This article included five caricatures of 'Abdu'l-Bahá.
30. Alfred Rodman Hussey (1869–1947) served as minister of Baltimore's First Unitarian Church from 1902 to 1916 and was a collaborator with the *Christian Register* (Boston). He had invited 'Abdu'l-Bahá to visit his church as early as March 1912. (Reply to Alfred Hussey, 8 March 1912, Ahmad Sohrab papers, Persian–American Educational Society, B11, US National Bahá'í Archives).
31. 'Women Kiss His Hand', *Sun* (Baltimore), 12 Nov. 1912, p. 9, col. 7. The article was accompanied by a series of drawings of 'Abdu'l-Bahá.

24. Departure from America

1. Ahmad Sohrab to Ella Cooper, 18 Nov. 1912, Ella Cooper papers, B9, US National Bahá'í Archives. After visiting the library of J. P. Morgan 'Abdu'l-Bahá visited the businessman and former senator William A. Clark (1839–1925).
2. 'Abdul Baha Views Morgan Library', *New York Herald*, 19 Nov. 1912, p. 8, col. 7. In a different section of the same issue, 'News in Nutshells', the following was published: 'Abdul Baha, the Persian prophet views the Morgan art treasures and writes his blessing in Mr. Morgan's album'. See p. 10, col. 2.
3. 'Blessing for Mr. Morgan', *Sun* (New York), 19 Nov. 1912, p. 1, col. 6.
4. See, for instance: 'Miss Morgan Blessed by Persian Prophet', *Buffalo Commercial*, 19 Nov. 1912; 'Prophet Blesses Morgan', *Daily News* (Springfield, MA), 19 Nov. 1912, p. 12, col. 3; 'Blessing for Morgan', *Evening Times* (Pawtucket, RI), 19 Nov. 1912, p. 11, col. 6; 'Prophet Blesses Morgan', *New York Times*, 19 Nov. 1912, p. 1, col. 6; 'Prophet Blesses Morgan', *Daily Times News* (Ann Arbor, MI), 4 Dec. 1912, p. 4, col. 4; 'Prophet Blesses Morgan', *Hawaiian Gazette*, 6 Dec. 1912, p. 2, col. 3; *Investment* (New York), Dec. 1912, p. 244.
5. 'Estados Unidos', *El Mercurio* (Santiago de Chile), 21 Nov. 1912, p. 6, col. 1.
6. 'Sendoff for Abdul Baha', *Sun* (New York), 24 Nov. 1912, p. 13b, col. 2.
7. 'Abdul Baha Going Away', *New York Tribune*, 24 Nov. 1912, p. 11, col. 4.
8. 'Dinner for Abdul Baha', *New York Press*, 24 Nov. 1912, p. 4, col. 7.
9. 'Abdul Baha's Blessing on Pier', *Evening Post* (New York), 5 Dec. 1912, p. 2, col. 6.
10. 'Abdul Baha Sails Away', *New York Times*, 6 Dec. 1912, p. 4, col. 3.
11. See for instance 'Personal', *Putman County Republican* (Carmel, NY), 14 Dec. 1912, p. 1, col. 3; 'Religious Intelligence', *Daily News* (Springfield, MA), 14 Dec. 1912, p. 19, col. 2; 'News and Miscellany', *Advent News and Sabbath Herald* (Washington), p. 20, col. 2.
12. *Amsterdam Evening Recorder* (Amsterdam, NY), 14 Dec. 1912, p. 5; 'New Religious Cult Head Has Many Followers', *Journal-Gazette* (Fort Wayne, IN), 15 Dec. 1912; 'Head of New Religious Cult has Thousands of Followers', *Troy Press* (NY), 16 Dec. 1912; 'Head of New Religious Cult has Thousands of Followers', *Whittier News*, 23 Dec. 1912, p. 1, col. 5.
13. 'Abdul Baha and his Gospel of Unity', *Unitarian Advance* (New York), Jan. 1913, pp. 134–5.

25. General Articles about 'Abdu'l-Bahá

1. The article was part of a column entitled 'In the Limelight', which also included biographical articles about the British politician David Lloyd-George (1863–1945), philanthropist Henry Phipps Jr. (1839–1930) and member of the House of Representatives William Brown McKinley (1856–1926). It was published in a number of newspapers, including: *Bill Barlow's Budget* (Douglas, WY), 1 May 1912, p. 3, col. 5; *Knox Starke County Democrat* (IN), 1 May 1912, p. 7, col. 1; *Maysville Public Ledger* (Maysville, KY), 1 May 1912, p. 1, col. 4; *National Democrat* (Des Moines, IA), 2 May 1912; *Red Cloud Chief* (NE), 2 May 1912, p. 3, col. 1; *Brownsburg Record* (IN), 3 May 1912, p. 3, col. 1; *Logansport Times* (IN), 3 May 1912, p. 3, col. 1; *Mooresville Times* (IN), 3 May 1912, p. 3, col. 1; *Sunbean* (MN), 3 May 1912, p. 1, col. 3; *La Estrella* (Las Cruces, NM), 4 May 1912; *Putman County Republican* (Carmel, NY), 4 May 1912, p. 1, col. 1; *Palo Alto Tribune* (CA), 8 May 1912; *Marble Rock Journal* (IA), 9 May 1912; *Gran Valley Times* (Moab, UT), 10 May 1912; *Oelwein Daily Register* (IA), 10 May 1912, p. 5, col. 2; *Petersburg Pike County Democrat* (IN), 10 May 1912, p. 6, col. 2; *Bedford Daily Mail* (IN), 11 May 1912, p. 3, *Oswego Palladium* (NY), 11 May 1912, p. 11, col. 3; *Sheboygan Press* (WI), 15 May 1912; *Cloverdale Reveille* (CA), 15 June 1912; *Van Nuys News* (CA), 5 July 1912; *Agitator* (Wellsboro, PA), 5 July 1912. The combined daily circulation of twelve of these journals was 20,100 copies.
2. 'Leader of New Cult', *Sun* (Baltimore,), 13 Apr. 1912.
3. The Bystander, 'By the Way', *Philadelphia Star*, 17 Apr. 1912.
4. 'Abdul Baha Abbas, Founder of New Oriental Religion, Visits America: Venerable Persian has Many Followers', *Loraine Herald* (OH), 20 Apr. 1912.
5. 'Abbas Effendi, Prophet of Bahaism', *Detroit Free Press*, 21 Apr. 1912.
6. 'Personal Glimpses', *Literary Digest* (NY), 4 May 1912, pp. 955–7. This was a national magazine with a circulation of 230,500 copies.
7. 'Persian, Hailed as New "Messiah", Comes to Teach Unity of the World', *Leader* (Cleveland), 22 Apr. 1912.
8. 'Servant of God Head for America', *Sun* (Indianapolis), 26 Apr. 1912.
9. *Survey* (NY), 27 Apr. 1912 (28:4), pp. 178–9, n.t. Portrait of 'Abdu'l-Bahá included.
10. 'Abdul Baha, Leader of a World Movement in Religion Comes to This Country', *Fort Wayne Journal-Gazette* (IN), 12 May 1912, p. 9, cols. 1–7.
11. 'Abou Ben Adhem Among Us', *Kansas City Star* (MS), 13 May 1912, p. 18, col. 3. The drawing is signed 'Zack'.
12. 'The Bahai Movement', *Daily News* (Ithaca, NY), 24 May 1912, p. 4, col. 3.
13. 'Teaches Harmony of All Religions', *Youngstown Telegram* (OH), 25 May 1912.
14. John D. Flenner (1850?–1916), had been pastor of the Methodist Episcopal Church in Boise and also served as judge, writer, journalist and lecturer. He contributed regularly to *The Statesman*, a newspaper of which his son, Guy Flenner, was editor.
15. 'Highways and Byways of Comment', *Idaho Sunday Statesman* (Boise), 16 June 1912.
16. 'The Universal Gospel that Abdul Baha Brings Us', *Current Literature* (NY), June 1912 (52:6), pp. 676–8. Other publications quoted were the *New York Times*,

the *Oregonian* (Portland), the *Churchman* (NY), the *Presbyterian* (Philadelphia), *Advance* (Chicago) and the *Christian Register* (Boston). Included a page-size portrait of the Master by Underwood & Underwood. For a reference to this article see *Unity* (Chicago), 13 June 1912, p. 229.

17. James Thompson Bixby (1842–1921) graduated from Harvard in 1864 and was ordained as a Unitarian minister in 1870. For four years he served as pastor of the Unitarian Church of Watertown, Massachusetts, and afterwards served in Meadville, Pennsylvania. For an account of the visit of Bixby to 'Abdu'l-Bahá see Ives, *Portals to Freedom*, pp. 47–9.
18. 'What is Behaism?' *North American Review* (New York), June 1912 (195:6), pp. 833–46.
19. *Twentieth Century Magazine* (Boston), June 1912 (6:2), pp. 82–4.
20. 'Will Bahaism Unite All Religious Faiths?' *American Review of Reviews* (New York), June 1912 (45:6), pp. 748–9.
21. *Outlook* (New York), 15 June 1912 (101:7), pp. 326–7. Partly reproduced in 'The Bahai Movement', *Age* (Melbourne), 10 Aug. 1912, p. 22, col. 5; 'The Bahai Movement', *Maryborough Chronicle, Wide Bay and Burnett Advertiser*, 22 Aug. 1912, p. 2, col. 3.
22. *World's Work* (New York), July 1912 (24:3), p. 273. Some newspapers later reproduced the article. See *Item* (New Orleans), 7 July 1912, p. 6, col. 3; 'Bahaism', *Morning News* (Dallas, TX), 1 Sept. 1912, p. 11, col. 5.
23. Charles Johnston, 'A Ray from the East', *Harper's Weekly* (New York), 20 July 1912, p. 9.
24. One newspaper that reproduced parts of this article was 'A Prophet from the East', the *San Francisco Chronicle*, 29 July 1912, p. 6, col. 5. It was reviewed in 'An Apostle from Persia', *Times-Press* (Middletown, NY), 30 July 1912, p. 4, col. 4, and in 'An Apostle from Persia', *Standard Union* (Brooklyn), 27 Aug. 1912, p. 11, 6. It was reported in *The Daily Northwestern* (Oshkosh, WI), 27 July 1912, p. 6, col. 6, n.t. Fragments were also reproduced in 'A Prophet from the East', *Rochester Democrat* (New York), 1 Sept. 1912.
25. 'Abdul Baha Abbas', *Tennessean* (Nashville), 20 July 1912.
26. 'Bahaism and Islam's Messiah', *New-Church Review* (Boston), July 1912 (19:3), pp. 438–45. The article quotes from the following magazines: 'The Bahai Movement', *Outlook* (New York), 15 June 1912 (101:7), p. 326; 'The Bahai Movement', *Independent* (New York), 11 Apr. 1912 (72:3306), pp. 770–2, and *Christian Register* (New York).
27. 'A Modern Prophet', *Hearst's Magazine* (New York), 22 July 1912, pp. 49–51. The article was later published in the New York *American* on 1 Mar. 1915.
28. Hubbard founded in East Aurora the Roycroft colony, a meeting place and residence for artists and craft workers. The invitation to 'Abdu'l-Bahá was sent in January 1912. See Ahmad Sohrab to Elbert Hubbard, 24 January 1912, Ahmad Sohrab papers, B11, US National Bahá'í Archives.
29. Elbert Hubbard, 'A Modern Prophet', *Hearst's Magazine*, July 1912.
30. 'Abdul Baha Comes as a Prophet of Peace', *Chicago Examiner* (Chicago), 3 Mar. 1915, p. 16; 'Abdul Baha Comes as a Prophet of Peace', *National Labor Tribune* (Pittsburgh), 9 Nov. 1916; 'Abdul Baha Comes as a Prophet of Peace', *Fort Worth Star-Telegram* (TX), 15 Mar. 1915, p. 4, col. 4.

31. 'Un Profeta Moderno', *Listín Diario* (Santo Domingo, Dominican Republic), 2 Sept. 1912, p. 2, col. 3. Interestingly, the same newspaper had stated some days before that Hubbard's 'teachings are borrowed from the apostle of religion, Abdul Baha'. 'La Fe Salva', 27 Aug. 1912, p. 2, col. 1.
32. 'Un Profeta Moderno', *La Patria* (Mexico City), 14 Aug. 1912, p. 2, col. 1.
33. 'Desde Nueva York. Un Profeta Moderno Ilega de Persia', *Diario del Salvador* (San Salvador, El Salvador), 4 Nov. 1912, p. 3, col. 3.
34. Published as 'Elimination of the Beggar', *Daily Times* (Seattle), 12 Aug. 1912, p. 6; 'Spain Harks to the Voice of Francisco Ferrer', *Plain Dealer* (Cleveland, OH), 25 Aug. 1912, p. 7.
35. *Philistine* (East Aurora, NY), Dec. 1912, p. 22. Another of the magazines edited by Hubbard, *The Fra* (East Aurora, NY), published on Nov. 1912 a list of questions to be used as topics for discussion at the meetings of the different branches of the Roycroft fraternity. One of these questions was 'Who is Abdul Baha and what is his message?' (p. xxxviii).
36. 'The Origin of the Bahai Movement', *West Coast Magazine* (Los Angeles), Sept. 1912, pp. 749–50.
37. 'Woman's Angle of Vision', *West Coast Magazine* (Los Angeles), Sept. 1912, pp. 217–19.
38. 'Unitarians Hear of Merits of Bahaism', *Seattle Times*, 23 Sept. 1912, p. 10, col. 5.
39. 'Says Superstition Must Be Eliminated', *Seattle Times*, 30 Sept. 1912, p. 10, col. 1.

INDEX

This index is alphabetized word for word; thus 'Free Religious Association' precedes 'Freemasonry'. Hyphenated names are considered as two separate words. The words 'a', 'an', 'and', 'de', 'for', 'in', 'is' 'of', 'on', 'the', 'to' and 'with' in entries are ignored.

Proper names are indexed according to the spelling most often found in the book, e.g. 'Mohammed', rather than the transliteration 'Muhammad'. The exceptions to this are the 'Báb', 'Bahá'u'lláh' and "Abdu'l-Bahá', the 'Bábí Faith' and the 'Bahá'í Faith'.

Owing to the length and nature of the book, the index has been restricted to individuals, organizations and a few Bahá'í concepts and principles mentioned by 'Abdu'l-Bahá and reported in the press. As 'Abdu'l-Bahá discussed the same concepts in many places, it was not possible to list them all in the index. Thus foundational Bahá'í principles such as the oneness of humanity, the brotherhood of man, unity, peace, education, progressive revelation, the Manifestation of God and God Himself are not indexed, as they appear in most of 'Abdu'l-Bahá's talks and newspaper interviews. However, principles which 'Abdu'l-Bahá expanded upon and developed during His western travels and which were in some way new to the discourses about religion, for example, women's suffrage, gender quality, the harmony of science and religion, and the rights of workers and economics, have been indexed.

As the whole book is about 'Abdu'l-Bahá, only a few highlights about His life are indexed. Similarly, references to the Bahá'í Faith are limited.

Only those newspapers and journals that published a number of articles about 'Abdu'l-Bahá and the Bahá'í Faith, such as *The Christian Commonwealth*, have been indexed but a list of all the print media cited can be found in the Bibliography, in the section 'Newspapers, Journals and Periodicals', starting on p. 592.